JSP Tag Libraries

GAL SHACHOR

ADAM CHACE

MAGNUS RYDIN

MANNING

Greenwich
(74° w. long.)

For electronic information and ordering of this and other Manning books, go to www.manning.com. The publisher offers discounts on this book when ordered in quantity. For more information, please contact:

Special Sales Department
Manning Publications Co.
32 Lafayette Place   Fax: (203) 661-9018
Greenwich, CT 06830   email: orders@manning.com

Library of Congress Cataloging-in-Publication Data
Shachor, Gal.
    JSP tag libraries / Gal Shachor, Adam Chace, Magnus Rydin.
      p. cm.
    Includes bibliographical references and index.
    ISBN 1-930110-09-X
      1. Java (Computer program language) 2. JavaServer Pages. I. Chace,
Adam. II. Rydin, Magnus. III. Title.

QA76.73.J38.S44 2001
005.2'762--dc21

                                2001030933

 Manning Publications Co.   Copyeditors: Elizabeth Martin, Sharon Mullins
32 Lafayette Place   Typesetter: Tony Roberts
Greenwich, CT 06830   Cover designer: Leslie Haimes

Printed in the United States of America

1 2 3 4 5 6 7 8 9 10 – VHG – 05 04 03 02 01

JSP Tag Libraries

brief contents

contents

8 Using JavaBeans with Tags 235

preface

Six years ago, Java burst onto the computing scene and dramatically changed the way programmers develop applications. Misunderstood initially, Java was typecast as a client-side language suitable only for building simple browser applications (i.e., applets). Though some patient developers built entire applications with Java, many dismissed it as an experimental language with little enterprise potential. As Java matured, bolstered by a firm focus on server-side functionality, it began to turn the heads of enterprise and web developers.

Servlet technology, the first server-side Java offering, was introduced in 1996. Web developers could now create Java components that extended the web server to provide dynamic content to their users. Servlets were followed by other technologies, such as JavaServer Pages and, more recently, by custom JSP tag libraries which aim to give nonprogrammers and web designers all the power of Java with a simple, tag-based syntax.

When servlets first appeared, we used them in real-world projects and saw how useful Java was for creating dynamic, data-driven sites. However, servlets and JSP were still too difficult for nonprogrammers to use, requiring them to learn at least some Java to accomplish most tasks. With the arrival of JSP tags, developing dynamic content with JSP became easier than ever. For the first time, it was possible for the HTML developer to perform complex operations like querying databases, iterating results, and performing other server-side activities without needing to understand any high-level programming language. The Java community has been quick to see the merits of this new technology, with dozens of companies and organizations already offering custom JSP tag libraries that perform everything from database access to translation of content for wireless devices.

The amazing experience we had working with custom JSP tags is what drove us to write this book. Its goal is to share our hard-earned knowledge with you, our readers, so you can begin building tags that suit the needs of your applications. We hope that you will share our excitement.

acknowledgments

The efforts, support, and understanding of many people made this book possible. We acknowledge:

Our publisher, Marjan Bace, for assembling our team of three authors from around the world and giving us the opportunity to write this book.

Our developmental editor, Lianna Wlasiuk, who offered exceptional guidance and patience in helping this book take shape.

Our editors, Elizabeth Martin and Sharon Mullins, for their work in making our prose more readable and succinct. Their insights and advice were invaluable.

Our review editor, Ted Kennedy, and the following expert reviewers he assembled, whose comments greatly improved our manuscript in its various stages of development: Ram Anantha, Michael Andreano, Pierre Delisle, Vimal Kansal, Dave Miller, and Bob Rudis. Also Matthew Hansbury who reviewed all the code listings in the book before it went to press.

Our production team at Manning Publications, including Mary Piergies who managed the project; Tony Roberts who typeset the book; and Syd Brown, the design editor.

Our friends, families, and coworkers for their support, assistance, and understanding throughout the writing process. Without them this book would not have been possible.

Gal Shachor   My thanks and gratitude to Shlomit and Bar for enriching my life and making it complete.

Adam Chace   I would like to thank my wife and best friend Heather for her patience and encouragement throughout this project. I would also like to thank my family, friends, and my business partner Dennis for his support and comic relief.

Magnus Rydin   My sincere thanks to my family, my colleagues at Cypoint, and the Orion team.

about this book

JSP custom tags is a new technology that has one main objective: defining a component model for JavaServer Pages (JSP). JSP tags let programmers develop JSP-aware components that can later be used by others in the development process, starting with peer developers and ending with nonprogrammer HTML coders who are part of the team.

Using custom tags in web projects is a great productivity boost. By building a tag-based application you can assemble your project, using existing tags that are available from third parties (either as open-source or for purchase) and, more importantly, develop your own JSP tags to meet your specific needs. Developing custom tags is the focus of this book.

Who should read it?

We assume that our readers know their way around Java, are familiar with HTML, and have some background working with JSP, although the latter is not necessary.

JSP custom tags are related to JSP, and JSP in turn relates to the Web and to Java; however, we are not going to devote much space to those three subjects. There are many good Java books in print and we did not see a reason to write yet another one. Nor is this book intended to be an HTML reference or a JSP primer; again, each of these subjects deserves (and has) books of its own. This book does include two chapters that introduce the Web and JSP so that you can dive right in, even without prior JSP knowledge.

How is it organized?

The book has 15 chapters organized into 5 parts, plus 3 appendices, as follows:

Part I The language of tags   Chapter 1 introduces the ABCs of the Web. It is intended for readers with modest knowledge of web technologies, such as HTTP and web servers, and will bring them up to speed on these topics. The chapter answers questions such as: How are web clients and servers able to communicate? Why is there a need to extend the web server? This chapter also presents traditional non-Java server extension methods that are common practice today. The chapter ends with a discussion of the cellular device and the new complexity it adds to the Web.

Chapter 2 presents Java methods used to extend the web server: servlets and JSP. Servlets are the foundation for JSP, and, in order to develop JSP tags you need to know something about JSP. The chapter presents these technologies in enough detail to enable you to follow the examples in later chapters.

Chapter 3 is the first to deal entirely with tags. It presents a set of "hello world" tags that covers the two basic tag types (tags with and without body) and shows how to compile and test them. By the end of this chapter not only will you know what tags look like, you will also know the mechanics related to compiling and testing tags within the Tomcat container.

Chapters 4 and 5 present the rules for writing JSP tags. These rules are the tag API set and life cycle as defined in the JSP specification and the chapters will show how the tags reflect their needs and integrate them into the JSP runtime. The JSP specification defines which API the tags can use, which API the tag needs to implement, as well as the life cycle for the tag (i.e., when it gets created, when it executes, etc.) but it falls short in fully explaining them. Explaining the "dry" specification is what these two chapters aim to do. After reading them, you will know when and why the methods in your tags are being called and who is calling them. Chapter 5 marks the end of part I whose role was to introduce the basics of tags and their environment. The next chapters will deal directly with tag development.

Part II Basic techniques   Chapter 6 presents several elements of tag programming and code snippets that are the cornerstone of tag development. For example, many tags need to print information back to the user, yet the Tag API does not contain a print method—so how do you print? Many tags need to access their body content and manipulate it—but how do you do that? These questions and others are posed, answered, and explained in chapter 6, accompanied by sample code that shows you how to take advantage of various techniques. Later chapters take the issues discussed here and integrate them into the full-fledged tag libraries developed throughout the book.

Chapter 7 presents the development of a mail-sending tag library. The key issue here is not sending mail but rather doing it in a user-friendly manner. First, the chapter presents the API that a Java component can use to send email, and then shows the development of several mail-sender tags. The chapter starts with a naïve implementation that is hard for the nonprogrammer to use and ends with a small mail-sender library that is powerful enough to send complex email, yet simple enough to be used by nonprogrammers. At the end of the chapter we show how parameters can be validated using assertion tags.

Chapter 8 deals with JavaBeans and JSP tag integration. JavaBeans are Java components; JSP tags are another type of Java component, geared toward the Web and the nonprogrammer. It is obvious that one day these two component models will come together. Indeed, this chapter explains how JSP tags can take advantage of JavaBeans and use them. Making your tags JavaBeans-aware can help you in reusing all the logic already implemented in the beans. This chapter shows you how. Chapter 8 ends part II of the book, which covered programming techniques. Part III will discuss developing tags whose goals are more ambitious; for example, controlling the flow of a JSP file or accessing the application back end.

Part III Advanced techniques   Chapter 9 discusses posing conditions with tags, or, to be more precise, tags with conditional body execution. Posing conditions on a tag's body is the equivalent of having an `if` clause in a programming language; it is important when you want to generate conditional content (e.g., for Internet Explorer, generate this content; for Netscape, generate another content). This chapter presents techniques for creating tags whose semantics closely resemble those of the `if` and `switch` statements in Java.

Chapter 10 is devoted to performing loops with tags. Tags can repeat their body execution, which means that tags can loop over their body much like the `for` statement can do in Java. Implementing loops with JSP tags can be tricky, especially if you want to take advantage of some of the new JSP1.2 features and still have the same code run with JSP1.1. Chapter 10 solves all of these problems for you. Essentially this framework lets you iterate on anything with iteration semantics (e.g., arrays, vectors, hashtables, etc.) and exposes the iterator object to the JSP file (to be used by other tags or scriptlets) across all JSP versions.

Chapter 11 is geared toward developers who wish to develop database-driven sites with JSP tags. Databases are one of the most common tools on the Web and there is a need to bring them to the nonprogrammer in a pervasive way. This chapter presents the development of a tag library whose role is to integrate data queried from a database into the content returned to the user. The library is developed with several goals in mind, such as integration with servlets (to assist Model-2 architectures), application configuration, and ease of use.

Chapter 12 explains how tags can be integrated into a J2EE web application. J2EE is an emerging standard for server-side Java applications; it builds around Enterprise Java Beans (EJBs) to access distributed and transactional business logic and around servlets and JSP to provide web interface. This chapter explains the basics of J2EE and then shows how J2EE can easily be accessed from within tags. For this purpose, chapter 12 presents tags which use EJBs, access J2EE resources using JNDI, and so forth.

Part IV Case studies   This part deals with practical issues related to tag development and deployment. Chapters 13 and 14 present two full-fledged case studies which demonstrate how tags can be used. First, a database-driven web store is developed where users can buy goods (cosmetic products in our case). In the second case study, the cosmetics web store is converted into an EJB-based application that is accessed through WAP devices. By following these two cases, you should experience hands-on what tags can do for you.

Part V Design   Chapter 15 rounds out the book by presenting a set of recommendations for designing, developing, and testing tag libraries. It is very easy to write a tag or two that executes well in a single container–it is harder to develop libraries that run on all containers and perform a significant task. In chapter 15 we provide tips for developing complex tag libraries.

Appendices   The last section of the book consists of three appendices that introduce the reader to the Extensible Markup Language (XML) which is used throughout the book in the deployment descriptors, describe the exact syntax of the tag library descriptor, and provide guidelines for using the listings.

Source code

The book is loaded with code listings, some of which were snipped in order to focus on the new ideas presented in them. All source code for the listings presented in *JSP Tag Libraries* is available to purchasers of the book from the Manning web site. The url http://www.manning.com/shachor includes a link to the source code files.

In the two case study chapters (13 and 14), you will come across tags that were not discussed in other parts of the book. We recommend that you download the source code from the publisher's site before reading these two chapters.

Typographical conventions

The following typographical conventions are used throughout the book:

- New terms when introduced are set in an *italic* typeface.
- Code examples and fragments (Java, JSP, HTML, XML) are set in `Courier`, which is a fixed-width font.
- Elements and attributes, method names, classes, interfaces, and other identifiers are also set in `Courier`.

- As code listings are modified from one step to the next, the changes are highlighted in **`Courier bold`**.
- Code annotations accompany many segments of code. Annotated code is marked with chronologically ordered bullets, such as ❶. The annotations themselves follow the code and are marked with the corresponding bullets for identification purposes.
- Code line continuations are indented.

Which version of JSP?

This book covers JSP1.2 and JSP1.1. During the development of the book, JSP1.1 was in use and JSP1.2 was still under development. After using the public review mechanism for the JSP1.2 specification, we can report that there are not many substantial changes between the two versions.

The tags in this book should run on both JSP1.2 and JSP1.1, which is significant since both versions will continue to be used in the future. However, whenever JSP1.2 diverges from JSP1.1 and presents an improved functionality (such as improved iteration and clean up), we call the reader's attention to this fact.

How to use the book

The most obvious approach to the book is to read it chapter by chapter. However, you will then lose many of the book's hidden benefits. A better approach would be to download the source code for the examples and to walk through them, testing the code while reading the corresponding chapters. Appendix C explains how to obtain the code and build it; chapter 3 explains how you can set up a testing environment using the various tags.

If you find yourself confused with the tag life cycle (the various methods, their return codes, and when they get called), it might be a good idea to deploy the samples and use them from within an IDE, such as VisualAge Java, Forte, or Jbuilder. These IDEs are known for their ability to run Tomcat from within. All you have to do is to place a break point in the tags, execute the JSP file, and step through the various breakpoints that you set. This way, you will gain the in-depth understanding that you are looking for.

If you still need help or have questions for the authors, please read about the unique Author Online support that is offered from the publisher's web site.

author online

Purchase of *JSP Tag Libraries* includes free access to a private web forum run by Manning Publications where you can make comments about the book, ask technical questions, and receive help from the authors and from other users. To access the forum and subscribe to it, point your web browser to http://www.manning.com/shachor. This page provides information on how to get on the forum once you are registered, what kind of help is available, and the rules of conduct on the forum.

Manning's commitment to readers is to provide a venue where a meaningful dialog between individual readers and between readers and the authors can take place. It is not a commitment to any specific amount of participation on the part of the authors, whose contribution to the AO remains voluntary (and unpaid). We suggest you try asking the authors some challenging questions, lest their interest stray!

The Author Online forum and the archives of previous discussions will be accessible from the publisher's web site as long as the book is in print.

about the cover illustration

The figure on the cover of *JSP Tag Libraries* is a "Gran General," a high-ranking military officer from Abyssinia, today called Ethiopia. While the exact meaning of his title and military rank is for us lost in historical fog, there is no doubt that we are facing a man of power and ambition. The illustration is taken from a Spanish compendium of regional dress customs first published in Madrid in 1799. The book's title page informs us:

> *Coleccion general de los Trages que usan actualmente todas las Nacionas del Mundo desubierto, dibujados y grabados con la mayor exactitud por R.M.V.A.R. Obra muy util y en special para los que tienen la del viajero universal*

Which we loosely translate as:

> *General Collection of Costumes currently used in the Nations of the Known World, designed and printed with great exactitude by R.M.V.A.R. This work is very useful especially for those who hold themselves to be universal travelers*

Although nothing is known of the designers, engravers and artists who colored this illustration by hand, the "exactitude" of their execution is evident in this drawing. The Gran General is just one of a colorful variety of figures in this collection which reminds us vividly of how distant and isolated from each other the world's towns and regions were just 200 years ago. Dress codes have changed since then and the diversity by region, so rich at the time, has faded away. It is now often hard to tell the inhabitant of one continent from another. Perhaps we have traded a cultural and visual diversity for a more varied personal life—certainly a more varied and interesting world of technology. At a time when it can be hard to tell one computer book from another, Manning celebrates the inventiveness and initiative of the computer business with book covers based on the rich diversity of regional life of two centuries ago—brought back to life by the pictures from this collection.

Part I

The language of tags

Chapters 1 through 5 set the stage for tag development with an introduction to JSP tags, the world in which they exist, and a look at the rules by which they are developed and used. In this section, you'll learn what tags are, why they are needed, and the basic ground rules for building custom JSP tags. This introduction prepares you for part II, which will teach you to enhance your skills by learning common tag building techniques.

The big picture

1.1   *The JSP custom tags solution*

Building data-driven, dynamic web sites is a problem as old as the Internet. Developers have progressed from Common Gateway Interface (CGI), server-side Java-Script, and web server plug-ins to Java servlets to build sites. As with any technology, something newer and greater, bigger and better is always just around the corner. Today's newer and greater, bigger and better technology is JavaServer Pages (JSP) custom tags.

Although custom tags (and the servlet technology from which custom tags are derived) are much easier to develop and learn than some of their predecessors, they still require a solid understanding of the environment in which they run, namely, the Internet.

Since JSP custom tags represent a way to serve dynamic content in a web site, you'll need a strong working knowledge of basic web concepts before you begin. Before exploring JSP custom tags, familiarity with the Web and developing dynamic web sites is strongly recommended. If you are thoroughly versed in this, you may skip to the next chapter where we discuss the basics of servlets and JSPs. If you are new to web development we suggest you read this chapter to obtain an overview of fundamental topics that will prove useful later in this book:

- Basic Internet programming concepts such as HTTP
- Existing techniques to extend a web server to serve dynamic content
- How tag-based techniques like custom JSP tags work.

This chapter is not meant to replace a book dedicated to any of these topics. It will, however, explain the fundamentals of Internet development and discuss existing web development platforms that explain the basis for using JSP custom tags and the environment in which they function.

We finish this chapter with a brief discussion of alternative web clients, such as WAP phones/devices, and we cover the growing trend to extend web development to nontraditional devices, such as phones and pagers, and how this has created an even greater demand for custom tags.

Before learning JSP custom tags, you may be asking yourself "Why should I?" There is, after all, no shortage of technologies available to anyone who wishes to build a dynamic web application. The question is best answered by reading through this chapter and learning about web development techniques, their shortcomings, and how JSP custom tags compare to these techniques. You'll learn how JSP custom tags offer a way to create flexible web solutions that fit several bills: they are built on industry standards, they enjoy Java's cross-platform feature, and they solve one of the most troubling problems of web development—cleanly separating business logic from presentation logic. We'll discuss this separation in detail in section 1.3.4. We present a discussion of the benefits of using JSP custom tags in chapter 15.

1.2   HTTP review

We begin this chapter with a brief discussion of Internet fundamentals and basic web development that provides a grounding for exploring the complexities of JSP custom tag development.

The Web is a client/server application on a huge scale. The client (a browser) connects to the server (also known as a web server or an HTTPserver) using a protocol called HyperText Transfer Protocol (HTTP). The server then returns content to the browser which presents this content (for example, as a GIF image or an HTML page) to the user.

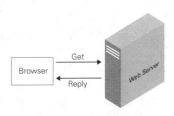

Figure 1.1   An HTTP client and server

Each client/server connection is initiated by the browser and the browser alone. This procedure begins by opening a TCP/IP connection to the server and sending an HTTP request. The server then processes the incoming request and returns an HTTP response. These requests and responses follow a very specific, yet simple, syntax as specified by the HTTP protocol.

1.2.1   HTTP protocol

Since HTTP is a *pull* technology, meaning that a connection starts when a client requests a document, we start our discussion with the request.

The HTTP request

An HTTP request begins with a request line whose structure is http-method request uri http-version, and is terminated with the carriage return-line feed characters. The http-method portion of the request line should be one of the methods defined in the HTTP protocol specification:

- GET—This asks the server to serve a resource as referenced in the request-uri. Request parameters should be coded in the request-uri. This is the method your web browser uses when you type in a URL for it to retrieve.

- POST—Similar to GET, except that POST contains a body wherein the request parameters are encoded. A web browser most often uses this method to submit HTML forms, such as those you fill out when making an online purchase.

- HEAD—Similar to GET, but the server only returns the response line and response headers. By using this information, the browser maintains a cache and reloads files only when needed.

Following the HTTP request method, the browser should specify a request URI, which references the resource serviced by the server. In many cases[1] the request URI starts with a "/" and references a static file resource located relative to the web server's root directory, but the request URI can reference more than just static HTML files. It can also reference Java servlets, CGI scripts, and other dynamic entities, as we will soon see. The versions of the HTTP protocol used by the client come after the request URI. The current supported versions of the protocol are HTTP/1.0 and HTTP/1.1, and thus the server expects to see one of these in the request line.

After sending the request line, the browser may send a few headers which provide information about the request, its content, the browser which sent the request, and so forth. The headers appear in consecutive lines of the form header-name: header-value. Each header line is terminated with the carriage return-line feed characters, and the entire set of request headers is terminated with a line containing only carriage return-line feed. Some important request headers are presented in table 1.1.

Table 1.1   Important HTTP request headers and their roles

Header name	Role	Sample value
User-Agent	Informs the server of the type of browser that sent the request (i.e., Navigator, Explorer, etc.).	`Mozilla/4.7 [en] (WinNT; I)`
Content-Type	Indicates the media type of the request body (if available).	`text/html`
Content-Length	Indicates the length of the request body (if available).	`10`
Authorization	Contains the values of user credentials (if sent by the user).	`Basic QWxhZGRpbjpvcGVuIHNlc2FtZQ==`
Cookie	Echoes a cookie from the browser to the server.	`Name=value`
Accept	Specifies certain media types which are acceptable for the response.	`text/*, text/html`

---

[1] When the browser connects to the server through a proxy, the request URI received by the proxy does not start with a "/", but we will not be discussing proxies in this book.

Table 1.1 Important HTTP request headers and their roles (continued)

Header name	Role	Sample value
Host	Specifies the Internet host and port number of the resource being requested, as obtained from the original URI given by the user. This header is extremely important for virtual hosting.	www.site.com

After sending the headers, the browser may send content (also known as request body). The content is an arbitrary set of bytes as defined by the request headers. Note that in most cases the browser does not send any content to the server in this way.

The HTTP response

The HTTP response has a status line (similar to the request line) and response headers, as well as an optional response body. Nonetheless, there are differences in the headers used and in the status line.

The response starts with a status line that informs the browser of (1) the HTTP version used to send this response and (2) the status for this service request. The syntax for the response line is http-version status-code reason-phrase and, as is typical in HTTP, the line is terminated with the carriage return-line feed sequence. The http-version in the status line is the same as in the request line; the other two portions of the status line are new. The *status code* is a number whose value can be one of a set of codes as defined in the HTTP specification. For example, the HTTP specification defines the value 200 as representing a successful service. Following the response code, the server can send an optional reason phrase for the code: 200 will usually mean "OK," but 400 can indicate "Bad Request." Exact reason phrase values are not defined in the HTTP specification, and servers can append their own values.

After returning the status line, the server can add response headers. The response headers' syntax is identical to that used by the request headers, yet the actual headers used through the response may differ from those used in the request. For example, the User-Agent header does not have a place in the response, but there is a Server header that the server can use to identify its version. Table 1.2 lists important response headers and, as you can see, it contains a few that can only be part of the response.

The server can then position the response body after the response headers. This body is the content the browser will show to the user. Be aware that, unlike the

Table 1.2   Important HTTP response headers and their roles

Header name	Role	Sample value
Content-Type	Indicates the media type of the response body (if available).	`text/html`
Content-Length	Indicates the length of the response body (if available).	`10`
Set-Cookie	Sets a cookie into the browser. A server can set cookies into the browsers and, as a result, the browser saves these cookies and later echoes them back to the server using the (request) Cookie header. This way the server can keep track of the clients visiting it and save per-client data.	`Part ="Rocket_Launcher";` `Path="/acme"`
Server	Identifies the server version returning the response (i.e., Apache, Netscape, IIS, etc.).	`Apache/1.3.9 (UNIX)`
WWW-Authenticate	Specifies to the browser how to authenticate its user to the server.	`Basic realm="MyWorld"`
Location	Instructs the browser to redirect itself to the location indicated by the header value.	`http://some.other.host/` `index.html`

HTTP request, the response usually has some body text. Responses to the HEAD method should not include any content.

> **NOTE**   Once the browser receives the response from the server, the TCP/IP connection between the browser and the server can be closed. A user may connect from the same browser to the same server and have the request served each time on a different TCP/IP socket. This HTTP feature is one of the reasons that HTTP is considered a stateless protocol.

A sample HTTP session

Let's take a look at a hypothetical request-response pair. Assume that a user directs the browser to http://www.name.com:8080/some/file.html. What will happen, and what will the request and response look like? In our example we will be using Netscape Navigator 4.7 (HTTP/1.1) to submit the request to an Apache web server.

First we open a TCP/IP connection from the browser to the server. The browser will analyze the URL entered by the user and see that the user is asking for information located on the host www.name.com and on port 8080. The browser subsequently opens a TCP/IP connection (socket) to this host and port.

The next step is to send an HTTP request to the server, which may look something like:

```
GET /some/file.html HTTP/1.1
Host: www.name.com:8080
User-Agent: Mozilla/4.7 [en] (WinNT; I)
Accept: text/*, text/html
```

Note that the request URI was extracted from the URL specified by the user.

The server will return the requested content to the browser. The response sent by the server should look something like the following (assuming that the response is OK and that the server returns 100 bytes of type text/html):

```
HTTP/1.1 200 OK
Server: Apache/1.3.9 (UNIX)
Content-Type: text/html
Content-Length: 100

<html> And now some 100 bytes of text/html…
```

Now both server and browser can close their sockets and we have finished serving this request. Although we presented only a small portion[2] of HTTP in this section, it was enough to serve a file.

As demonstrated in the sample, all we need to do to serve an HTML file is parse incoming requests that follow the HTTP protocol, read the file, and return its content to the browser using HTTP. In general, the core web server only knows how to use HTTP to return static content.

Serving static content was fine in the old days when all you wanted from the Web was to read information, but now that ecommerce is a mantra, many sites cannot get along with static content alone. If your web server only knows how to serve static files, how will you save form data in a database or search a catalogue for a specific product? You just can't.

To solve this problem, all web servers come with an extension mechanism. The next section explores the most common of these.

1.3 *Dynamic web servers*

There are many methods for executing code on a web server, each with its own merits. Why should you concern yourself with these other mechanisms if you're

---

[2] HTTP/1.1 is more complex than the simplified protocol we have just presented, and includes complex content negotiation as well as many performance-related options.

only trying to find out about custom JSP tags? The answer is two-fold. First, since custom JSP tags function in the same environment (the Web) as these technologies, learning other approaches is helpful for understanding how tags work. Second, discussing the shortcomings of these earlier technologies and how they could be improved helps us understand Sun's reasons for introducing JSP custom tags.

We will present the extension methods more or less in the order of their births, starting with CGI followed by Server API, Server pages, and ColdFusion.

1.3.1 *Common Gateway Interface*

CGI was the earliest extension mechanism that web servers had and, even today, it serves as the workhorse of many sites. Figure 1.2 shows how CGI operates. It is a very simple mechanism that spawns background processes in the same manner as a UNIX command-line interpreter (not surprising, as CGI was invented by UNIX folks).

In a CGI-served request:

1 A user sends a request to the web server.

2 The web server analyzes the request and determines (based on some part of the request URI) that it should execute an external program to handle it.

3 The web server spawns a child process which executes the external program.

4 The external program reads the parameters sent by the user as well as the request parameters via its command-line arguments, environment variables, and standard input. The program processes these parameters and generates output to be seen by the user.

5 The web server grabs the output from the child process and sends it to the user.

6 The child process dies.

Implementing CGI as part of your web server is relatively simple, as is developing external programs that work with your web server. You can code your external programs in the desired language, generate an executable program, and the web server will take its output and send it over to the client. Its ease of use and support for known languages helped CGI become the technology of choice for creating dynamic web sites. CGI, in fact, still powers a sizable number of dynamic sites, though that percentage is declining as newer, faster solutions become available.

CGI drawbacks

If CGI is so great, why have other extension techniques been introduced? One of the major disappointments with CGI is that it requires a process per request. This

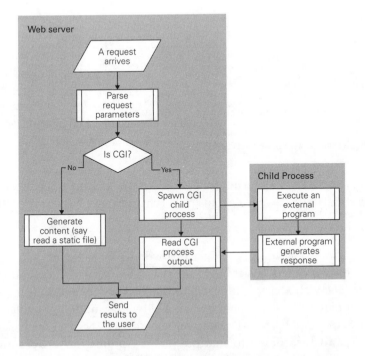

Figure 1.2 **Executing a CGI program from within the web server**

means that the per-request burden on the hosting computer can be quite taxing. A lot of memory and processor overhead is involved in creating, executing, and cleaning up after a new process. With CGI, this overhead is incurred for each and every request to the web server, and naturally affects performance as the number of requests increases. When a busy site meant a few thousand requests per day, the performance challenge associated with CGI was acceptable. Today, busy sites serve thousands of concurrent requests and the degradation in performance associated with CGI cannot be overlooked.

The process-per-request policy of CGI hurts performance in other ways as well. These processes often end up performing the same processing (i.e., opening a database connection) over and over again with no way to share or cache results from one request to another. This is hardly acceptable for applications that rely on database access or other time-consuming operations that may need to repeat themselves.

There are other disincentives to using CGI, but the two we've mentioned were probably the most pressing catalysts for the web community's development of new approaches to serving dynamic content. As we'll see in chapter 2, custom tags don't suffer from these drawbacks. But even before custom tags were introduced (or the

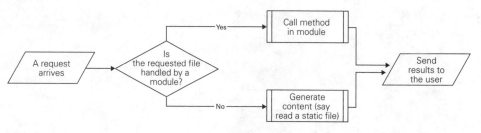

Figure 1.3   Executing a module with a web server API

servlets or JSPs they're based on), the industry addressed the performance shortcomings of CGI by introducing a new web extension mechanism, the web server API.

1.3.2   *Web server APIs*

In a web server API, the application developer first writes a loadable module (a DLL in Microsoft Windows, a shared object in UNIX) that follows the API definition for the specific server. The web server loads this module on startup, and calls it whenever a user makes a request which should be handled by that module. Popular APIs include Netscape Server Application Programming Interface (NSAPI) for Netscape Enterprise Server, and Internet Information Server Application Programming Interface (ISAPI), though all popular servers have one. Most web servers use a configuration file which contains directives specifying which modules to load and the requests a particular module should handle.

By loading the extension module directly into the web server, we gain unmatched performance since invoking our extension is merely a function call. Unlike CGI, the function calls take place within a single process that is already running; namely, the web server process itself. We can also save state inside the web server address space. This allows us to save the results of expensive processing (such as objects that are slow to initialize) in a central location so that they can be shared by requests instead of being created over and over again. These two features alone address both of the major shortcomings we saw with CGI.

Server API drawbacks

Oddly enough, the unmatched performance available by writing to the web server API did not win this extension method the popularity of CGI or other extension techniques that we will discuss. It failed to catch on for several reasons:

- Each server has a different API. This means there is no standard that can be learned once and applied across servers.

■ The extensions need to be developed in a low-level language such as C or C++. This places the extension development knowledge bar at a fairly high level.

■ A bug in an extension can often bring an entire web server down. This means extensions must be tested thoroughly and the extension developer must be an experienced developer.

The overall result is that developing a server API extension is very expensive (in terms of salaries and development time), rendering server API inapplicable for many tasks. Some other extension technique was needed. We'll see in chapter 2 how JSP and its custom tags can be developed with far more ease than a server API extension; namely because they are written in the well known, standard Java language. This fact alone addresses all the weaknesses of an API approach since the Java is fairly high-level, strictly standard, and robust enough that a simple bug won't blow up an entire web server, and JSP greatly simplifies the generation of dynamic content.

NOTE   We are not saying that the server API is useless. In fact, many interesting problems (e.g., content filtering and redirection in the native web server) can only be solved within the context of the server API. Moreover, most of the extension techniques that we are about to see use the server API to link to the web server. This API is, however, more suited for low-level tasks and too cumbersome and costly to use in developing full-scale web applications.

1.3.3   *Server pages techniques*

The goal of the server pages approach to web development is to support dynamic content without the performance problems of CGI, or the difficulty of using a server API. The most popular server page approaches today are Microsoft Active Server Pages (ASP), JSP from Sun Microsystems Inc., and an open-source approach called PHP. Server pages development simplifies dynamic web development by allowing programmers to embed bits of program logic directly into their HTML pages. This embedded program logic is written in a simple scripting language (which, depending on what your server supports, could be VBScript, JavaScript, Java, or something else). At runtime, the server interprets this script and returns the results of the script's execution to the client. Let's look at an example of ASP in listing 1.1.

Listing 1.1   Sample ASP fragment that generates dynamic content

```
<% @Language = "VBScript" %>
<HTML>
    <BODY>

<% If Request.ServerVariables("SERVER_NAME") = "localhost" then %>
    You asked for the server located on your local machine.
<% else %>
    You asked for the server <%= Request.ServerVariables("SERVER_NAME") %>
<% end if %>

    </BODY>
</HTML>
```

This fragment obviously contains standard HTML, with the exception of special text found between the `<%` and `%>` characters. That special text is the script the server executes when this page is requested. In this case (and in most ASPs), the script is written in Microsoft VBScript language. This particular ASP fragment creates dynamic content which is affected by the value of a server variable, SERVER_NAME. You should be able to make out the conditional logic in this fragment, which dictates that if the value pointed to by SERVER_NAME is the string "localhost", a message is returned to the user stating they are on their local machine. Otherwise, a different message is returned, including the value of the variable SERVER_NAME. This logic is pretty easy to identify, even if you've never before seen ASP. The scripting languages for server page technologies have been designed to keep the entry barrier low, so that both beginning programmers and ambitious HTML developers can readily grasp the syntax.

To further simplify the generation of dynamic content, server pages technologies provide a means of extending the core scripting syntax with objects that enable low-level functionality, such as database access and email support. Most server pages environments ship with built-in support for popular databases, which greatly simplifies the task of generating data-driven web applications. This simplicity, coupled with the fact that the server does not have to repeatedly open (and initialize) new processes, makes server pages technologies the foundation of many web applications. Yet, as you may imagine, this simplicity comes at a price.

Server pages drawbacks

A number of issues must be admitted in any complete discussion of server pages. To begin, there is the matter of speed. Server pages-based applications are slow relative to the server API counterpart. Yes, the programmer's productivity is enhanced, but the performance decline makes it obvious there is room for improvement.

Another issue is the proprietary nature of the server pages. Aside from PHP (an open-source software freely available to most web servers), server pages technologies are only available on a single server (e.g., server side JavaScript on Netscape servers) and sometimes even only on a single operating system (ASP, which relies heavily on COM and is, largely, Microsoft-only). This means that you usually cannot leverage your ASP experience on Netscape and UNIX. Furthermore, the API used to extend the scripting language with low-level services is very different among the various systems; thus, porting complex projects requiring custom language extensions is very difficult. Simply put, when using server pages you lock yourself in with a vendor, which is often an unpleasant arrangement. These disadvantages are insignificant compared to the most egregious shortcoming of server page technologies: the lack of separation between your application's business logic and the presentation logic that displays it. This unfortunate weakness isn't the problem of server page mechanisms alone, in fact all the mechanisms we've explored thus far have suffered from it. Before we discuss the way to overcome this hurdle we should define the need for separation.

1.3.4 *Separating business and presentation logic*

One of the greatest challenges in web development is in cleanly separating presentation and business logic. All of the web server extension methods we've looked at so far have suffered from this obstacle. What does it mean to separate these layers? To start with, we can partition any application into two parts:

- Business logic—The portion of the application that solves the business need (e.g., the logic to look into the user's account, draw money, and invest it in a certain stock). Implementing the business logic often requires a great deal of coding and debugging, and is the task of the programmer.
- Presentation layer—Takes the results from the business logic execution and displays them to the user. The goal of the presentation layer is to create dynamic content and return it to the user's browser, which means that those responsible for the presentation layer are graphics designers and HTML developers.

If applications are composed of a presentation layer and a business logic layer, what separates them, and why would we want to keep them apart?

Clearly there needs to be interaction between the presentation layer and the business logic, since the presentation layer presents the business logic's results. But how much interaction should there be, and where do we place the various parts? At one extreme, the presentation and the business logic are implemented in the same set of files in a tightly coupled manner, so there is no separation between the two.

At the other extreme, the presentation resides in a module totally separate from the one implementing the business logic, and the interaction between the two is defined by a set of well-known interfaces. This type of application provides the necessary separation between the presentation and the business logic.

Why is this separation so crucial? In most cases the developers of the presentation layer and the business logic are different people with different sets of skills. Usually the developers of the presentation layer are graphics designers and HTML developers who are not necessarily skilled programmers. Their main goal is to create an easy-to-use, attractive web page. The goal of programmers who develop the business logic is to create a stable and scalable application that can feed the presentation layer with data. These two developers differ in the tools they use, their skill sets, their training, and their knowledge. When the layers aren't separated, the HTML and program code reside in the same place. Think back to our previous discussions of CGI and web server API extension techniques. Many sites built with those techniques have code (either in a module or a CGI script) that executes during a page request and returns HTML. Imagine how difficult it is to modify the User Interface if the presentation logic, HTML in our example, is embedded directly in a script or compiled code. Though developers can overcome this difficulty by building template frameworks that break the presentation away from the code, this requires extra work for the developer since the extension mechanisms don't natively support such templating.

Server pages technologies are not any more helpful with this problem. Many developers simply place Java, VBScript, or other scripting code directly into the same page as the HTML content. Obviously, this implies maintenance challenges as the server pages now contain content requiring the skills of both content developers and programmers. They must check that each updating of content to a specific server goes through without breaking the scripts inside the server page. This check is necessary because the server page is cluttered with code that only the business developer understands. This leaves the presentation developer walking on eggshells out of concern for preserving the work of the business logic developer. Worse, this arrangement can often cause situations in which both developers need to modify a single file, leaving them the tedious task of managing file ownership. This scenario can make maintaining a server pages-based application an expensive effort (which undermines many of the achievements related to server pages).

Listing 1.2   A tightly coupled page

```
<html>
<body>
<h1>Welcome to my dot-com
(some program code)
```

```
<table>
(more program code)
</table>
</html>
```

Separating these two layers is a problem in the other extension mechanisms we've mentioned, but the page-centric nature associated with server pages applications makes the problem much more pronounced. Whereas a CGI developer can come up with his or her own page-generation template system to separate presentation and business logic, server pages technologies dictate a specific template system into which the developer is locked. In addition, the powerful scripting language that can be used within the pages makes it possible to implement quick and dirty applications that place the majority of the business logic directly inside the server page. The result is that many server pages-based applications lack an adequate separation of layers.

1.4   *Tag-based programming*

Thus far we've covered a number of different approaches to dynamic web development. We've seen how CGI scripts allow the building of dynamic sites, but suffer from some significant performance problems. We've seen how server API solutions may overcome CGI's speed issues, but add a lot of complexity to development and tie you very closely to a particular server vendor. We've looked at server page approaches which are acceptably quick at execution time and much easier to implement than API solutions, but encourage poor separation between presentation and business logic layers. What is the next step in the evolution of dynamic web development? It is none other than the subject of this book: tag-based development.

JSP custom tags are not the first tag-based approach. ColdFusion, a product from Allaire Corp., is a well-known implementation of this tag-based concept and was introduced before custom JSP tags. ColdFusion still enjoys a solid market share for web development, but is less attractive to many developers because it is a proprietary solution while custom tags are defined in the open JSP specification. Being a purely Java solution, custom tags also enjoy all the normal benefits such as being cross platform, widely supported, and written in a fully functional language. ColdFusion does not boast this same cross platform ability, nor is it an open standard that is available to multiple vendors. As we'll see in future chapters, engines that run custom JSP tags within a web server can be built by any company willing to adhere to certain open standards. At least a dozen vendors have built these solutions today, Allaire being one of them.

What is a tag-based solution like? We'll defer specifics about custom JSP tags until chapter 3, but will mention some of the basics of this extension mechanism to afford a glimpse at its benefits.

Developing with tags resembles the server pages development model with one crucial difference—the development language is not a script, but is rather based on sequences of characters (usually starting with a "<" and ending with a ">") known as tags.

A tagged server page includes the page's content (usually HTML) plus tags that can be used to add logic to the content. When the user asks for a tagged page, the server interprets the page, finds all the logic tags, and executes them along with the page content.

To see an example of tag-based programming, let's look at a ColdFusion fragment (listing 1.3) which mimics the ASP code in listing 1.1.

Listing 1.3   Sample ColdFusion fragment that generates dynamic content

```
<HTML>
    <BODY>

    <CFIf (CGI.SERVER_NAME eq 'localhost') >
    You asked for the server located on your local machine.
<CFELSE>
    You asked for the server #CGI.SERVER_NAME#
</CFIf>

    </BODY>
</HTML>
```

As you can see, instead of using VBScript (the language of choice in listing 1.1) we are now using special ColdFusion tags (prefixed with CF). Using these tags, the developer can easily implement simple logic. ColdFusion started up with a limited tag set geared toward database manipulation and presentation. They soon added tags to perform programming tasks, including iteration over arrays with tags such as CFLOOP; catching exceptions with tags such as <CFTRY> and <CFCATCH>; and performing various utility operations with tags such as <CFLDAP>, and <CFREGISTRY>.

1.4.1   *Benefits of a tag-based approach*

How is using tags any different from embedding script in a server page? After all, this may look like yet another case of server pages with just a different scripting syntax (tag-based, instead of the more common programming syntax). In a way, this is correct; however, tag-based technologies offer advantages. Using tags is much more comfortable for many HTML developers who are very familiar with the use of tags from their HTML development. Since coding with tags is usually simpler then using a full-fledged language and, since most content creation tools already accept tags, two benefits are:

- There is a single, consistent, and easy-to-follow style in the page. This makes tagged pages a breeze to work with for many content creators (and their tools).
- Many HTML developers can program *simple* tagged pages such as the one presented in listing 1.3.

This introduction of the tag-based approach continues in chapters 2 and 3, where we talk at length about JSPs, servlets, and custom tags themselves.

1.5 WAP, voice, and other alternative web clients

Up to now our discussions have assumed a classic web programming model, with an HTML browser and HTML content being generated by the server. Today, however, there is a great deal of buzz surrounding the concept of wireless and nontraditional access to the Web. At the forefront of this new wave of web clients is the Wireless Application Protocol (WAP*)* device.

WAP is a set of specifications which enables users to browse online content and services using a wireless device. WAP devices range from cellular phones to pagers and Personal Digital assistants (PDA), such as PalmPilots. WAP preserves the architecture used through the Web, in which servers are holding the information and clients are accessing it through requests to the servers. The creators of WAP (the WAP Forum) took great pains to ensure that this model was very close to the traditional HTML web model, in order to keep the barrier to entry for this new technology as low as possible.

How can a WAP device access a traditional web server? To access a web server, the WAP device should communicate using HTTP and TCP/IP; isn't that too complex for a cellular phone? To expect that level of software support from a mobile phone today is still a bit ambitious (although it is being anticipated), but WAP architecture obviates the need for HTTP and TCP/IP support on the phone by using gateways.

WAP architecture
As figure 1.4 shows, the telephone network is connected to the Web through a transcoding gateway. This gateway takes WAP requests and passes them to the Web as if they were HTTP requests; it then takes the HTTP responses and transforms them to WAP and returns them to the WAP device. Using these gateways, WAP devices can interoperate with the Web and fetch content without changing too much of the web infrastructure. In fact, any standard web server can receive

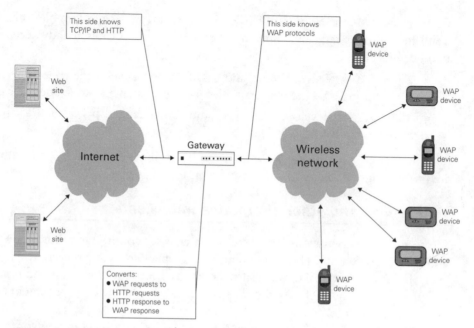

Figure 1.4 Connecting the WAP device to the Web

requests from a WAP device with this model; it simply needs to format the responses to conform to the capabilities of the device.

Today, the resources available for the WAP device are very limited:

- The display is extremely small and its drawing capabilities range from basic to nonexistent. While HTML applications are normally designed for clients running at least 800 x 600 in 256 or more colors, WAP applications are normally designed to show only a few characters in a row, and only a small number of rows on the same display.

- Compared to the Internet, the network connection is slow but improving, especially in Europe and Asia, which means that the application utilizes the fewest connections possible during a user's session.

- Processing power and memory are minimal.

Based on these limitations, it is easy to imagine why WAP devices cannot support full-fledged HTML. What they do support is an XML dialect known as Wireless Markup Language (WML) and WMLScript, JavaScript's counterpart that supports a limited JavaScript subset feasible for weak phone processors. Thus, any content we return to a WAP request must be in WML, instead of in standard HTML.

Brief WML overview

Each WML file contains a "deck" of "cards," each card being a presentation view and a possible point of interaction.[3] WAP interaction is accomplished in much the same way as in HTML applications, through links or options that take the user to other cards within the same deck (similar to anchors in HTML), or to resources outside the current deck. One of the major differences between WML and HTML applications is that WML is based upon XML, while HTML is based upon SGML. This means that stricter rules apply to WML than to HTML, and that there is a document type definition (DTD) that tells the parser of the WML the order in which certain elements may appear. The following fragment constructs a WML deck of cards and, as you can see, although WML resembles HTML's look and feel, they are not the same.

```
<?xml version="1.0"?>
<!DOCTYPE wml PUBLIC "-//WAPFORUM//DTD WML 1.1//EN"
"http://www.wapforum.org/DTD/wml_1.1.xml">
<wml>
  <card id="image"
        ontimer="#login"
        title="Cosmetix">
    <timer value="100"/>
    <p>
      <img src="images/logo.wbmp"
           alt="Cosmetix"/>
    </p>
  </card>
  <card id="login"
        title="Cosmetix">
   <do type="Login">
        <go href="somewhere.wml"/>
    </do>
    <p align="left">
     <input type="text"
            name="username"
            format="32A"
            title="Username:"/>
      <input maxlength="32"
             type="password"
             size="7"
             name="passwd"
             title="Password"/>
   </p>
  </card>
</wml>
```

---

[3] It is possible for the deck to contain just one card.

Why are we discussing WAP in a book concerned with custom JSP tags? Because WAP and the pervasive cellular devices are much more than another client type. There are many more mobile phones than computers in use today and, although most of those phones cannot yet access the Internet, most market research suggests it won't be long before there are more wireless than standard wired clients. Other technologies, such as VoiceXML, extend the web paradigm even further by enabling users to browse web sites using only their voice from any standard telephone. Imagine how large your potential user base becomes when anyone in the world with access to a phone can visit your site. This increase in nontraditional web clients is likely to continue to grow, making the Internet as ubiquitous and accessible as one can imagine. As a result of these growing trends, it is important to keep in mind that application designs will be targeting a multitude of presentation types.

Figure 1.5   WML in action

Using custom JSP tags with a well-designed Java component layer can help your web application accommodate these different device types. The advantages tags offer in this arena are their content-agnostic behavior, that is, custom JSP tags don't have any predisposition to HTML, and can seamlessly support returning HTML, WML VoiceXML, or any other markup language you choose. Also, since alternative client types work (at some level) with Internet cornerstones such as HTTP, any tags that you write to handle cookies, request parameters, and the like can be reused for different client types. Moreover, with JSP custom tag libraries defined in the widely accepted and popular J2EE standard, it is very likely that third-party tag libraries will become prevalent. These third-party libraries might take care of some of the tedious tasks associated with alternative clients, such as identifying devices, their attributes (screen size, color, etc.), and general content formatting for a particular device.

1.6   Summary

You should now be able to see how previous extension mechanisms have fallen short of providing a fast, easy-to-use, and well-designed approach to building dynamic web applications. These goals are especially important in light of the growing trend toward alternative web clients (such as WAP, PDA, and Voice) and the likely additional development efforts and complexity required for their support.

After our cursory look at extension techniques, we will focus more closely on the extension techniques that relate to this book, namely, those offered by Java. In our quest to learn about JSP custom tags, we'll take one more crucial side trip to learn the basics of the technologies on which custom tags are built: Java servlets and JavaServer Pages. These technologies are the focus of our next chapter.

Web development
with Java

2

To learn more about the present, we must take a look at the past. In this case, we will study Java's evolution as a web development leader—servlets to JSP to JSP custom tags—which stands on the shoulders of the previous two technologies. The servlet API outlined here is used heavily by both JSP and custom tags. Equally important are the deployment techniques which are identical for any of the Java extension techniques. A working knowledge of the servlet API and JSP basics will be crucial to understanding the rest of this book.

If you have extensive servlet or JSP experience, this chapter will be review. If you are less experienced with either of these technologies (or the deployment techniques associated with them), you'll be well served by taking a look at it.

2.1   Java and dynamic web content

None of the server extension techniques discussed in chapter 1 are Java-based. Although you could write CGI scripts with Java, or extend the scripting languages in server pages with Java classes, such techniques are not natively based on Java as most of them were created when it was in its infancy. Today, however, it has matured into a stable, high performance, and scalable server platform. As a result, there has been an explosion in Java's usage on the server.

Extending a server with Java

Developers can use Java to extend the web server by using servlets and JSPs, both of which allow you to specify some Java code to be executed when a specific HTTP request is made (figure 2.1). The Java code you embed in a servlet or JSP can do everything normally associated with dynamic web programming such as looking at cookies, headers, or form parameters, and returning dynamic content based on that information. While servlets are Java classes that you can write to handle HTTP requests (somewhat like CGI, seen in chapter 1), JSPs are a server page technology based on Java (more like ASP, also seen in chapter 1). The two technologies are very similar; however, before receiving a request, a JSP is translated into a functionally

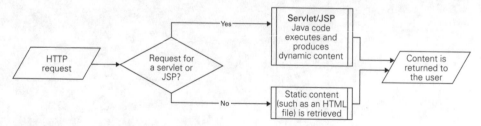

Figure 2.1   Extending the server with JSP

identical servlet which takes HTTP requests on its behalf. Since JSP custom tags are actually part of JSP technology, we'll place more emphasis on JSP topics. JSP is, however, based on the servlet infrastructure and, as such, requires some understanding of servlets as well.

2.2 Introduction to Java servlets

Servlets are Java components whose role is to extend web servers, enabling them to return dynamic content, instead of just static files. A common comparison describes servlets as the server-side version of applets. Whereas applets are small bits of Java code that execute on a web client, servlets are bits of Java code (not necessarily small) that execute on a web server. These servlets are handed an incoming HTTP request (including any parameters, headers, cookies, etc.) which they then process and, ultimately, return a response to the user. Servlets started out as the extension API of JavaWebServer, a Java-based web server product from JavaSoft. The only remains of JavaWebServer are servlets, which became the first successful and widespread server-side Java API.

There are many reasons for the success of servlets: ease of use, ease of development, and the maturity of the Java language. The most important feature is that servlets can extend practically any web server on virtually all operating systems. This means that using a servlet does not tie you into a specific vendor, unlike many of the techniques we saw in chapter 1. Servlet-based applications developed on IIS and NT can later be deployed on Linux and Apache, and vice versa.

The next few sections will present the servlet API and programming model, and will also discuss how servlets and web servers interact.

2.2.1 The servlet API and programming model

Extending the web server with a Java servlet consists of four steps:

- The developer provides a servlet class that obeys the servlet API (presented later in this section).
- The server administrator deploys the servlet in a web container (a web server that knows how to handle servlets) and informs the container which requests should be handled by the servlet (e.g., any request URI suffixed with .jsp should be forwarded to the JSP servlet).
- When a request arrives, the web container checks the request URI against the servlet mappings and invokes a servlet, if needed.
- The servlet takes over the request and serves it.

NOTE   The term *web container* evolved out of an attempt to harmonize the terms
used in Java 2 Enterprise Edition (J2EE). A web container is the runtime
environment in which servlets operate; the container is responsible for the
instantiation, initialization, execution, and termination of the servlets.
There are other names for the servlet runtime environment; the most common of which is servlet engine. Think of a web container as a web server
with servlet support.

As developers, we will concentrate on how the servlet API and the servlets themselves look. Later sections will present a way to configure the web container in a cross-server fashion.

The servlet API defines:

1 How the servlet appears to the web container and its life cycle
2 What services the web container renders on the servlet's behalf
3 Container-neutral application bundling

To understand the servlet API, keep in mind that servlets are essentially Java classes whose job is to receive the parameters of the HTTP request and return an HTTP response. To facilitate this, the servlet API defines a set of Java interfaces (table 2.1[1]) that define what a servlet can do for a container, and what the container offers to a servlet.

Table 2.1   Important interfaces in the servlet API

Interface	Role	Useful methods/services
javax.servlet.Servlet	Defines the look of a servlet. Any servlet class must implement this interface.	The Servlet interface contains three important methods: (1) init()—initializes the servlet instance. init() has a single parameter which is the ServletConfig for this servlet; using the ServletConfig the servlet can initialize itself. (2) service()—serves a single user request. This method has two parameters, request and response objects, which let the servlet read the request information and write a response back to the user. (3) destroy()—cleans up the servlet instance prior to destroying it.

[1] For specific information, such as method names and their parameters, please take a look into the servlet API javadocs available from http://www.javasoft.com/products/servlet/index.html.

Table 2.1 Important interfaces in the servlet API (continued)

Interface	Role	Useful methods/services
`javax.servlet.Servlet Request &` `javax.servlet.http. HttpServletRequest`	These two interfaces represent the HTTP request sent by the user as well as adding request related services such as, sharing of attributes among the entities serving the request.	We are talking about a set of useful services rendered by the request object. Some of these services are: (1) Obtaining a `Reader/InputStream` object to let the servlet read from the user. (2) Reading parameters as sent by the user (say, HTML form parameters). (3) Looking up the values of the request headers and various request information (for example, the request URI). (4) Sharing the request attribute among the various entities that serve the user request.
`javax.servlet.Servlet Response &` `javax.servlet.http. HttpServletResponse`	These two interfaces let the servlet construct an HTTP response and send it over to the user.	Using the servlet response, the servlet can obtain a `Writer` that can later write the content of the response back to the user. Additionally, the servlet can use the response to add headers and set the HTTP status code for the response.
`javax.servlet.Servlet Config`	Lets the servlet read per-servlet configuration parameters as well as retrieve the `ServletContext`.	The servlet can read per-servlet configuration parameters using methods such as `getInitParameter()`. It can also reference its `ServletContext` using the method `getServletContext()`.
`javax.servlet.Servlet Context`	A context is a group of servlets and other web entities grouped together to form a web application. The `ServletContext` is shared by all the servlets belonging to the context and provides services such as attribute sharing, logging, and application-based configuration, and referencing various entities that are part of the context through `RequestDispatchers`.	The `ServletContext` provides: (1) Application-scoped object sharing through methods such as `getAttribute()` and `setAttribute()`. (2) Application-scoped configuration through methods such as `getInitParameter()`. (3) Access to other entities (JSP and Servlets) in the application through the use of `RequestDispatchers`. (4) Miscellaneous utility methods to perform chores such as logging and resource reading.

Table 2.1   Important interfaces in the servlet API (continued)

Interface	Role	Useful methods/services
`javax.servlet.http.HttpSession`	A session is a sequence of requests from a browser to a certain site on behalf of a certain user. The `HttpSession` is a placeholder that the servlet can use to place data it collects in the course of a certain user session. Each session has an `HttpSession` of its own and the servlet container is responsible for handing over the current `HttpSession` to the servlet on demand.	The job of the session object is to let the servlets store user-related objects through its visit in the site. The `HttpSession` provides the methods `getAttribute()`, `getAttributeNames()`, `setAttribute()`, and `removeAttribute()` that let the servlet save objects inside the session state. Additionally, the `HttpSession` provides methods to fetch metainformation on the session such as maximum inactivity time, etc.
`javax.servlet.RequestDispatcher`	A `RequestDispatcher` wraps a resource and lets the servlet execute this resource and have the results of this execution written into the response flowing to the user. Using the `RequestDispatcher`, a servlet can delegate the request handling to other entities in the server such as JSP pages and other servlets.	The `RequestDispatcher` lets a servlet reference other entities in its application (`ServletContext`). Usually these entities are other servlets and/or JSP files. To obtain a `RequestDispatcher`, the servlet approaches the `ServletContext` and uses one of its `getRequestDispatcher()`/`getNamedDispatcher()` methods. The servlet can then call one of the `include()` or `forward()` methods on the `RequestDispatcher` and, in this way, execute the referenced entity and include its output in the response flowing to the user.

The interfaces presented in table 2.1 form the backbone of the servlet API. Additional interfaces such as `Filter` were added in servlet API version 2.3, but these interfaces are less crucial for understanding servlets, JSP, and eventually JSP tags.

Table 2.2 lists important classes in the servlet API. Some are exceptions that the servlet may throw; others are basic implementations of the interfaces defined by the servlet API (geared toward easing the work performed by the servlet writer).

Table 2.2   Important classes in the servlet API

Class	Use
`javax.servlet.GenericServlet`	Provides abstract implementation for the servlet interface to define a generic, protocol-independent servlet. `GenericServlet` does not implement the `service()` method (left to the user). This is purely a keystroke saver class.
`javax.servlet.http.HttPServlet`	`HttPServlet` extends `GenericServlet` to provide an abstract implementation for an HTTP aware servlet. `HttpServlet` implements the method `service()` which handles requests by dispatching them to the handler methods for each HTTP request type. For example, a request that uses the HTTP `GET` method will be dispatched to a method named `doGet()`.
`javax.servlet.ServletException`	An exception that a servlet can throw to signal some error. Generally the servlet will throw a `ServletException` when it hits an unexpected problem prohibiting it from serving some request.
`javax.servlet.UnavailableException`	An exception that a servlet can throw to signal that it hit some unexpected problem, prohibiting it from serving requests permanently or temporarily.

The technical content of tables 2.1 and 2.2 can be distilled into the following guidelines:

1   Your servlet should extend `HttpServlet`.

2   You should implement the `service()` method or `doGet()`, `doPost()`, and so forth (depending on the HTTP methods that you want your servlet to support).

3   In the service phase, take parameters from the `HttpServletRequest` object and use them to produce a response that you write using the `HttpServlet-Response` object.

4   You can perform servlet initialization in the `init()` method.

5   You can perform servlet cleanup in the `destroy()` method.

To illustrate these guidelines, let's look at a servlet example. The servlet in listing 2.1 generates a response to the user that identifies the name of the server requested.

Listing 2.1   Sample servlet that generates dynamic content

```
import java.io.IOException;
import java.io.PrintWriter;
import javax.servlet.*;
import javax.servlet.http.*;

public class SampleServlet
    extends HttpServlet {

    // init is already implemented in HttpServlet
    // and GenericServlet as an empty method.
    // ditto for destroy.

    public void doGet(HttpServletRequest request,
                      HttpServletResponse response)
                      throws ServletException, IOException
    {
        PrintWriter out = response.getWriter();

        out.println("<HTML>\r\n<BODY>\r\n");
        if(request.getServerName().equals("localhost")) {
            out.println("You asked for the server " +
                        "located on your local machine.");
        } else {
            out.println("You asked for the server " +
                        request.getServerName());
        }
        out.println("</BODY>\r\n</HTML>\r\n");
    }
}
```

The servlet created in listing 2.1 extends `HttpServlet` so the methods `init()` and `destroy()` are already implemented as empty methods. All we have left to do is to implement the service logic, which we do in `doGet()`. Note in `doGet()` how the servlet uses the request object to read request parameters and generate the response using the response object (or, more precisely, the `PrintWriter` available from the response). The practice of getting parameters and using them in some logic to produce a response represents a common occurrence in servlet development. A good grasp of this example will provide solid footing in the basics of servlet development.

2.2.2   *Servlets and non-Java web servers*

How can so many different web servers work with servlets? It is obvious that Java-based web servers can work with servlets since both are written in Java, but how does a web server written in a native language such as C or C++ interact with

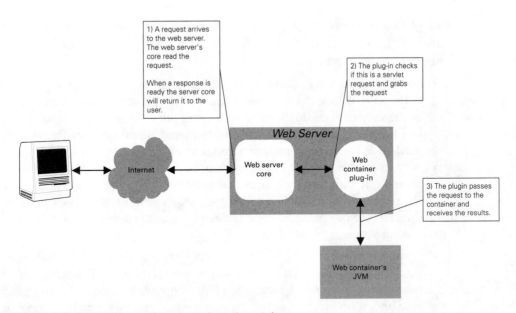

Figure 2.2 **Integrating a web server and a web container**

servlets? Servlet support is added to these servers by "plugging" a web container into them.

Plugging servlet support into the web server is accomplished in the following way. The container vendor takes advantage of the web server-specific API exported by the web server and writes a plug-in to connect the web server and the web container. The plug-in filters the requests and, whenever it sees one that should be executed by a servlet, grabs the request from the server and has the container serve it. Some of the popular servlet plug-ins available include the open-source TomCat for Apache, Allaire Corporation's JRun, and New Atlanta's ServletExec.

A schematic description of a web server extended to include servlet support is presented in figure 2.2, in which a user request arrives at the core web server, is accepted, grabbed by the container redirector plug-in, and handed over to the web container JVM.

As illustrated in figure 2.2, we can now execute a servlet from within a legacy web server that was written in a native language.

2.2.3 *Servlet shortcomings*

Once we understand how servlets work, life should be much simpler, right? After all, servlets offer a usable web server extension method that performs well and is cross-platform. Unfortunately, we aren't out of the woods yet. Even with their many benefits, servlets still possess shortcomings that make them less than ideal for dynamic web development.

- Servlets do not encourage a separation of presentation and logic. To start with, servlets (such as the one in listing 2.1) present an enormous challenge in the now familiar dilemma of separating presentation from logic. As we saw in listing 2.1, the servlet often contains the actual content (the HTML) as hard-coded text. Imagine how tedious a task it is to cut and paste HTML content from the presentation developers directly into servlets. This can be avoided by building templates that your servlets parse, modify, and write to the response; but this still places a great deal of knowledge about presentation directly into our business logic and requires us to come up with our own templating syntax.

- Servlets require mastery of Java. Another obvious drawback is that creating a servlet is much more difficult than creating a server page. The servlet developer must master a complex language (Java), compile source code, and generally take on far too great a burden, especially when merely rendering simple pages.

For Java to become a viable dynamic page technology, it needed to improve the servlet technology to:

- Adapt it to a wider audience (one that does not know Java).
- Make it easy to separate presentation and business logic.

The outcome of these requirements was a technology known as JSP.

2.3 Introduction to JavaServer Pages

Servlets offer several improvements over other server extension methods, but still suffer from a lack of presentation and business logic separation. In response, developers created servlet-based environments that provided the sought-after separation, and some of them (e.g., FreeMarker and WebMacro) gained considerable acceptance in the marketplace. Parallel to the efforts of these individual developers, the Java community worked to define a standard for a servlet-based server pages environment. The outcome was what we now know as JSP.

In a nutshell, JSP is a server page technology based on servlets that let its users embed Java code and special tags within a page's content.

JSP developers were able to accept the good and reject the bad in the popular server extension products that came before it. JSP, for example, allows you to embed logic in a page using tags (as in ColdFusion) or scriptlets (as in ASP). A considerable amount of work went into making sure that content developers and business logic coders can now cooperate in ways that minimize the interactions between them, either by using standard JavaBeans and scriptlets or by using special JSP tags. The business logic can thus produce data and the content developer can seamlessly embed this data in dynamic content.

2.3.1 Basic JSP syntax elements

A JSP page contains HTML (or other text-based format such as XML) mixed with elements of the JSP syntax. Table 2.3 shows the most commonly used JSP elements:

Table 2.3   JSP Syntax elements

Element	Description
scriptlets	Snippets of Java code that let the developer add things like flow-control (and other logic they choose) into the server pages.
JSP implicit variables	A number of objects that are available in any JSP file and provide access to the servlet API services.
Page translation directives	Directives to the JSP translator.
JSP tags	Standard tags that are included in any implementation of the JSP specification. These tags let the developer add functionality to the JSP file without writing any code. The number of these tags (and the extent of their functionality) is limited.
Custom JSP tags	The JSP specification explains how to extend the page functionality with custom made tags that allow the JSP developer to expose complex Java code in a simple tag. Developing these custom tags is the subject of this book.

We'll look at each of these syntax elements later in this chapter, but let's first look at an actual JSP file to see its syntax.

2.3.2 A JSP example

A sample JSP file is in listing 2.2 which, again, implements a simple dynamic content generation task. The syntax uses scriptlets to perform conditional HTML and is easier to follow than the servlet. All we've done is embed standard Java syntax directly in an HTML file, and embedded it between <% and %> characters.

Listing 2.2   Sample JSP file

```
<HTML>
<BODY>
<% if(request.getServerName().equals("localhost")) { %>
You asked for the server located on your local machine.
```

```
<% } else { %>
You asked for the server <%= request.getServerName() %>
<% } %>
</BODY>
</HTML>
```

It is very obvious by the title that JSP is central to this book. It is mandatory that you know how to create the simple JSP files in which your custom tags will be contained. To this end, we will discuss its syntax elements, how to use them, and how the JSP runtime executes the generated pages.

2.3.3 *Scriptlets*

Scriptlets are probably the most common JSP syntax element. In essence, a scriptlet is a portion of regular Java code embedded in the JSP content within `<% ... %>` tags. The Java code in scriptlets is executed when the user asks for the page. Scriptlets can be used to do absolutely anything the Java language supports, but some of their more common tasks are:

- Executing logic on the server side; for example, accessing a database.
- Implementing conditional HTML by posing a condition on the execution of portions of the page.
- Looping over JSP fragments, enabling operations such as populating a table with dynamic content.

The bits of code we saw in listing 2.2 were scriptlets that performed some conditional logic. To see another scriptlet in action, take a look at listing 2.3.

Listing 2.3   Sample JSP file that uses scriptlets

```
<html>
<body>
<%
    double num = Math.random();
    boolean bigger = num > 0.5;         ❶
    int cap = (int)(num * 10);
%>
    <p>
    Is <% out.print(num); %> bigger then 0.5? <br>    ❶
<% if(bigger) { %>     ❷
    Yes!
<% } else { %>
    No!
<% } %>
    </p>
```

```
    <p>
    Now, let's loop randomly ... <br>
<% for(int i = 0 ; i < cap ; i++) { %>
    This is iteration number <% out.print(i); %>. <br>
<% } %>
    </p>
</body>
</html>
```

❶ Our very simple business rules and output scriptlets The first scriptlet is embedding java code that represents the business logic, in this case just some simple math. Once our math logic is complete, we print the response to the user with the `out.print.()` statement.

❷ Some conditional control based on the value of bigger The second set of scriptlets is performing conditional HTML; the condition is posed over the results of the "business logic," namely, the variable `bigger`.

❸ Looping more output The last set of scriptlets is performing a simple iteration using a `for` loop.

As you can see, listing 2.3 uses scriptlets for all the tasks we mentioned in our bulleted list.

You probably recognize the syntax of these scriptlets immediately since, again, it is standard Java.

The special Writer object

In listing 2.3 we are using a scriptlet that looks like `<% out.print(expression); %>`. This code is used to print the value of an expression to the output that is returned to the user. The `out` object we're referring to is a special `Writer` object that is available at all times in any JSP, known by the simple name "out." Anything written to this special `Writer` will be returned within the page to the user. This is exactly the same `Writer` we write to in a servlet (which we retrieve by calling `response.getWriter()`). JSP also offers a simpler syntax defined for writing to the response. The syntax defined for JSP expression printing is of the form `<%= java-expression %>`, where "java-expression" is simply Java code that evaluates to a result. The Java expression is converted into a string and then placed into the response flowing to the user. It is important to make sure the expression you are trying to use has a meaningful string conversion, since whatever the expression evaluates to will be converted to a string and then sent in the response. Listing 2.4 shows what the JSP in listing 2.3 would look like using this simpler JSP printing syntax:

Listing 2.4   Improved JSP file that uses scriptlets and expression printing

```
<html>
<body>
<%
    double num = Math.random();
    boolean bigger = num > 0.5;
    int cap = (int)(num * 10);
%>
    <p>
    Is <%= num %> bigger then 0.5? <br>
<% if(bigger) { %>
    Yes!
<% } else { %>
    No!
<% } %>
    </p>

    <p>
    Now, let's loop randomly ... <br>
<% for(int i = 0 ; i < cap ; i++) { %>
    This is iteration number <%= i %>. <br>
<% } %>
    </p>
</body>
</html>
```

As you can see, using the expression printing syntax made the code cleaner and more readable.

NOTE   Many see scriptlets as a necessary evil since using too many scriptlets in code breaks the separation of presentation and business logic. Scriptlets are a powerful weapon; after all, they are written in Java—a full-blown programming language. Yet, like most powerful weapons, consider carefully before using them. For example, implementing business logic or some reusable code by using a scriptlet in your page is dangerous and could harm your content developers. As we will see in this book, custom JSP tags are an excellent tool to avoid the scriptlet overflow.

Having seen a simple scriptlet example, let's look at how scriptlets interact with the rich JSP environment on which they depend for web functionality. We saw an example of this in listing 2.2 where we used an object called `request` to fetch the server name.

2.3.4 *Implicit variables*

To gain access to crucial objects like the HTTP parameters, sessions, cookies, and the response, JSPs and servlets need to interact with the container environment in which they run. These objects, in the JSP world, can be accessed any time in any JSP file using a simple one-word name (like the "out" and "request" objects we've just seen). These ever present objects are known as the JSP *implicit variables*. Implicit variables enable the JSP environment to expose itself to the JSP developer. A summary of all of the implicit objects is presented in table 2.4.

Table 2.4 **Implicit JSP objects and their use**

JSP implicit object	Type	Typical use by the scriptlet writer
pageContext	javax.servlet.jsp.PageContext	Barely in use. This is more of a backbone object used by the servlet that was auto-generated from the servlet code. We will discuss the autogenerated servlet later in this chapter.
request	javax.servlet.http.HttpServletRequest	Queries request information; for example, queries form parameters, inbound cookies, request headers, etc.
response	javax.servlet.http.HttpServletResponse	Manipulates the response; for example, add cookies, redirect, etc.
session	javax.servlet.http.HttpSession	Accesses the session state information associated with the request. For example, get/set session attributes or invalidate the session.
config	javax.servlet.ServletConfig	Obtains configuration parameters for this page.
application	javax.servlet.ServletContext	Obtains configuration parameters for this application and uses its utility method (for example, log()).
out	javax.servlet.jsp.JspWriter	Writes data into the page and manipulates the output buffer used by JSP.
page	java.lang.Object	Represents the Java this variable for the current page invocation.
exception	java.lang.Exception	In error pages only (see more on error pages in the upcoming sections), represents the exception that triggered the error page.

The implicit objects are the same ones used by a servlet through the servlet API, with the addition of one object, `pageContext`, which is unique to JSP (and seldom used by scriptlet developers). Using the implicit objects, the scriptlet writer can accomplish the same tasks as a servlet developer, such as reading user submitted form variables (as demonstrated in listing 2.5) and checking for configuration variables.

Listing 2.5   A JSP file that presents the submitted form variables using implicit objects

```
<html>
<body>
    <p>
<%
    java.util.Enumeration e = request.getParameterNames();
    if(e.hasMoreElements()) {
%>
    Your form variables are:
    <table>
        <tr><th>name</th><th>value</th></tr>
    <% while(e.hasMoreElements()) {
        String name  = (String)e.nextElement();
        String value = request.getParameter(name);          ❶
    %>
        <tr><td><%= name %></td><td><%= value %></td></tr>
    <% } %>
    </table>
<% } else { %>
    No parameters are available!
<% } %>
    </p>
</body>
</html>
```

❶ **Use of the "request" implicit variable to get user posted parameters.**

As listing 2.5 shows, using the implicit variables is powerful; however, their use renders the JSP relatively difficult to follow for the nonprogrammer (and has very limited support in most content developer's tools).

2.3.5   *Directives*

JSP directives are instructions to the JSP runtime (similar to what `#pragma` is to C and C++). A directive does not produce output visible to the user, but tells the JSP runtime how to execute the page. The general syntax of a directive is `<%@ directive attribute="…" %>`. Directives are:

- `include`—Instructs the JSP environment to statically include the content of a specific file in the generation of the servlet. The file to include is specified using an attribute called `file`. For example, the following directive instructs the JSP environment to include the content of header.html in the page: `<%@ include file="header.html" %>`

- `taglib`—Instructs the JSP environment to import a certain tag library. We will look into this directive in the next chapters.
- `page`—Specifies page-related parameters to the JSP environment. For example, the parameters can be the length of the buffer used by the page, any Java imports to perform, whether the page uses session state, and so forth. A partial list of the more useful `page` directive attributes is in table 2.5.

Table 2.5 Useful attributes for the page directives

Page attribute	Sample syntax	Use
`import`	`<%@ page import="class" %>`	Specifies which Java classes and packages to import into the servlet generated from the JSP file.
`session`	`<%@ page session="false" %>`	Specifies whether the page is using session state. The value of the session attribute can be `true` or `false` (default is `true`).
`contentType`	`<%@ page contentType="text/html" %>`	Defines the MIME type for the response. The default is "text/html;charset=ISO-8859-1".
`buffer`	`<%@ page buffer="12KB" %>`	Specifies the buffer length used for the "out" writer. Can take the value none (in which case buffering will not take place) or some numeric value (the default is 8KB).
`errorPage`	`<%@ page errorPage="/pathto-page" %>`	Each page can have an error handler page. The error handler will be invoked by the JSP runtime upon an exception in the page. The JSP developer specifies the error handler using the `errorPage` attribute.

Table 2.5   Useful attributes for the page directives (continued)

Page attribute	Sample syntax	Use
isErrorPage	`<%@ page isErrorPage="true" %>`	Identifies the page as an error handler. The JSP runtime will let error handlers (and only error handlers) access the exception implicit variable, and this variable will hold the value of the exception that caused this errorPage to be invoked.

Listing 2.6 uses the JSP directives to perform simple daily tasks.

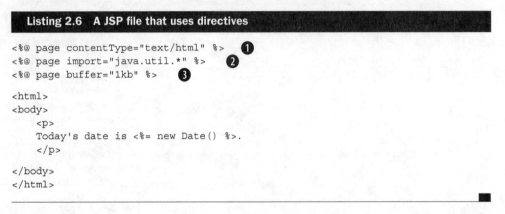

Listing 2.6   A JSP file that uses directives

```
<%@ page contentType="text/html" %>    ❶
<%@ page import="java.util.*" %>    ❷
<%@ page buffer="1kb" %>    ❸

<html>
<body>
    <p>
    Today's date is <%= new Date() %>.
    </p>
</body>
</html>
```

❶ **Sets the content type of this HTTP response for HTML content.**

❷ **Performs an import of the classes in java.util. Works just like "import" in any Java file.**

❸ **Sets the buffer for this page to 1KB.**

As listing 2.6 shows, the JSP page attribute is extremely useful for configuring your page. Many JSP files use directives to define error handling, package import, and the like.

2.3.6   *Tags*

The last element of JSP syntax to discuss is the group of JSP tags defined in the JSP specification. These are basic JSP tags that perform a few simple duties and are included in every product that fully implements the JSP 1.1 specification. They can be placed into roughly two groups:

- Tags that make JSP services available by simple means, accessible to the non-programmer, such as the `<jsp:forward/>` tag that allows a JSP developer to forward a request to another page.

- Tags that allow the JSP developer to manipulate a JavaBean component, without knowing Java.

The first group of tags performs basic page-level functionality such as forwarding the page, including other files' content in the page, or downloading a plug-in (typically an applet) to a browser. These tags are listed in table 2.6.

Table 2.6 The standard JSP tags that perform functions other than bean manipulation.

Tag	Duty
`<jsp:forward>`	Forwards a client request to another URL.
`<jsp:include>`	Includes the text of a particular file (or JSP/servlet, etc.) in a page.
`<jsp:plugin>`	Downloads a Java plug-in (applet or Bean) to a client browser).

The second group of tags is discussed in the next section.

2.3.7 *Tags for JavaBean manipulation*

The standard JSP tags that permit you to interact with JavaBeans are used quite regularly in JSP development, and require a bit of know-how. We'll explore their usage now.

NOTE   We will discuss the JavaBean component model at length in chapter 8. For the time being, think of JavaBean components as regular Java objects.

The goal of the JavaBean-related tags is to minimize the amount of hand-coding needed to work with JavaBeans. The tags let the JSP developer instantiate Java-Beans, place/fetch them from the session state, and get and set their attribute values. This goes some distance toward realizing the goal of separating content from logic, since the business logic developer can build JavaBeans with which a content developer can interact using only simple tags. To unleash these capabilities, the JSP specification defines three tags:

<jsp:useBean>   Introduces a bean reference into the page. This is a rather complex tag that makes the bean instance accessible to the other bean-related tags as well as the scriptlets in the page. If the bean instance already exists, `<jsp:useBean>` will only reference the instance; but, if the instance is not available, `<jsp:useBean>`

will create it. This tag's attributes include: (1) The `scope` used by the bean; for example, a session-scoped bean should be available through the user's session state object and, if `<jsp:useBean>` needs to instantiate it, the new instance is placed into the session object. (2) The bean's `type` and `class`. These attributes instruct the JSP environment which class to instantiate to create the bean, and what type to be used by the JSP environment for the Java variable to reference it. (You can get by with specifying either `type` or `class`.) (3) The bean ID. The ID will be the name of the bean.

<jsp:getProperty/> Gets the value of a named bean property and prints it to the response (the bean must be previously introduced by `<jsp:useBean>`).

<jsp:setProperty/> Sets the value of the bean's properties (again, the bean must be introduced by `<jsp:useBean>` before calling `<jsp:setProperty/>`). This is a very useful tag that can even take the values sent by an HTML form and set them into the bean.

Tag example

To see these concepts in action, listings 2.7 and 2.8 present a Java bean component and a JSP file that handles this component through tags.

Listing 2.7   The session counter JavaBean component

```java
public class SessionCounterBean
{
    int visitCount = 0;
    public int getCount()
    {
        return visitCount;
    }
    public void incCount()
    {
        visitCount++;
    }
}
```

`SessionCounterBean` can be used to track the number of visits that a certain user has made to the site. By keeping `SessionCounterBean` in the user's session and incrementing the visit count each time the user comes to the site, you may retrieve the exact number of visits by calling `getCount()` (listing 2.8).

Listing 2.8   A JSP file that uses JavaBean tags

```
<%@ page import="SessionCounterBean" %>

<jsp:useBean id="counter"                              ❶
            scope="session"
            class="SessionCounterBean"/>
<%
  counter.incCount();
%>

<BODY>
<h1> JSP Session Counter using JavaBeans </h1>
You visited this page <b> <jsp:getProperty name="counter"   ❷
                                   property="count"/></b>
times.
</BODY>
```

❶ **Defines an instance of SessionCounterBean, called counter in the session scope.**

❷ **Gets the count property of this bean (by calling getCount).**

Listing 2.8 demonstrates the aspects associated with using the JSP tags. First, the JSP code uses `<jsp:useBean>` to reference the bean, and possibly even creates it if the bean is not available in the session. Later on, a scriptlet is used to increment the visit count. Note how the value of the `id` property from `<jsp:useBean>` is used to name the variable that holds a reference to the bean. Lastly, the JSP fragment uses `<jsp:getProperty/>` to show how many times the user visits this site. As you can see, using the JavaBean tags relieved us from writing long (and messy) scriptlet code, and kept listing 2.8 concise and tidy.

2.3.8   *Executing a JSP page*

JSP syntax clearly allows you to embed Java scriptlets or tags directly in a page in order to produce dynamic content. But how does the JSP runtime execute these JSP pages? You probably have a few questions about what happens to the JSP file after you've written it. Are the pages interpreted or compiled? Does JSP parsing happen at runtime or beforehand?

In answer to the first question, JSPs are not interpreted;[2] they are instead compiled into servlets which ultimately handle requests for the JSP file. As depicted in figure 2.3, when a user asks for a JSP file, the JSP runtime intercepts the request and

---

[2] Some might make the academic argument here that the JVM interprets bytecode, and therefore JSPs *are* interpreted. We understand this perspective, but our point is that JSPs themselves are compiled into bytecode, not interpreted on the fly as are ASPs and the like.

checks if the JSP file already has a servlet representation. If it does, the runtime will execute the servlet. If there is no servlet representation, or the file was modified, the JSP runtime will:

1 Read the JSP file into the memory.

2 Translate the JSP file into a Java source file containing a servlet representing this page.

3 Compile the translated servlet into a class.

4 Load the autogenerated servlet.

5 Execute the autogenerated servlet.

How a JSP becomes a servlet

You can probably guess that the most trying is the translation step that takes an ordinary JSP file and produces a servlet representing it. The JSP specification provides some guidelines for the generation of the Java code, but normally the emitted servlet is vendor specific. Although the translation may be vendor specific, we can create a set of general guidelines regarding the translation from JSP to Java. For example, a section of static HTML (or other content) in a JSP is translated to multiple `write()` calls on the response's `PrintWriter` in the servlet. Scriptlets in a JSP are simply embedded verbatim into the servlet source code. While translating the page, the JSP translator also consults the page translation directives to better understand how to generate the servlet (i.e., what Java code to emit into the servlet). For example, a `<%@ page import="…" %>` directive gets mapped into an import statement in the emitted Java code and a `<%@ include … %>` directive causes the translator to include verbatim the content from a specific file into the resulting servlet.

To help illustrate this translation phase, look at listing 2.9, which shows the servlet produced by the translator for the JSP in listing 2.2. It is clear that the method `jspService()` (where the service logic of the JSP page is implemented) merely initializes the implicit variables and then executes the page. This execution produces the static HTML via calls to `out.write()` and executes the scriptlet logic. The scriptlets were added to the file "as is."

Web server

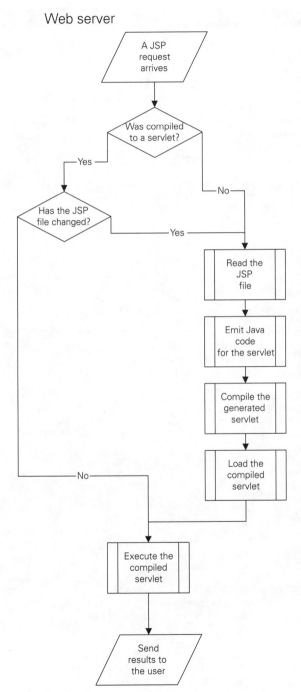

Figure 2.3   Executing a JSP file

Listing 2.9   Sample JSP autogenerated servlet

```
import javax.servlet.*;
import javax.servlet.http.*;
import javax.servlet.jsp.*;
import javax.servlet.jsp.tagext.*;
import java.io.PrintWriter;
import java.io.IOException;
import java.io.FileInputStream;
import java.io.ObjectInputStream;
import java.util.Vector;
import org.apache.jasper.runtime.*;
import java.beans.*;
import org.apache.jasper.JasperException;

public class jspsample1 extends HttpJspBase {

    static {
    }
    public jspsample1( ) {
    }

    private static boolean _jspx_inited = false;

    public final void _jspx_init() throws JasperException {
    }

    public void _jspService(HttpServletRequest request,
                            HttpServletResponse  response)
        throws IOException, ServletException {

        JspFactory jspxFactory = null;
        PageContext pageContext = null;
        HttpSession session = null;
        ServletContext application = null;
        ServletConfig config = null;
        JspWriter out = null;
        Object page = this;
        String  value = null;
        try {

            if(_jspx_inited == false) {
                _jspx_init();
                _jspx_inited = true;
            }
            jspxFactory = JspFactory.getDefaultFactory();
            response.setContentType("text/html;charset=8859_1");
            pageContext = _jspxFactory.getPageContext(this,
                                                      request,
                                                      response,
                                                      "",
                                                      true,
                                                      8192,
                                                      true);
```

```
        application = pageContext.getServletContext();     ❶
        config = pageContext.getServletConfig();
        session = pageContext.getSession();
        out = pageContext.getOut();

        out.write("<HTML>\r\n<BODY>\r\n");      ❷

        if(request.getServerName().equals("localhost")) {        ❸
            out.write("\r\nYou asked for the server located on your
                local machine.\r\n");
        } else {
            out.write("\r\nYou asked for the server ");        ❷
            out.print( request.getServerName() );
            out.write("\r\n");

        }
        out.write("\r\n</BODY>\r\n</HTML>\r\n");
    } catch(Exception ex) {
        if(out.getBufferSize() != 0)
            out.clearBuffer();
        pageContext.handlePageException(ex);
    } finally {
        out.flush();
        _jspxFactory.releasePageContext(pageContext);
    }
  }
}
```

❶ **Initialization of the JSP implicit objects. We see here why they are always available to a JSP by name.**

❷ **Static content written to the out object.**

❸ **Scriptlet content is copied verbatim into our servlet file.**

NOTE   In JSP1.2, the translation from JSP to Java is not direct but involves an intermediate step whereby the JSP code is translated into an XML representation. This representation is important for reasons such as page validation. Once the page validation is complete, the XML representation is transformed into the Java source.

Note from listing 2.9 that the servlet emitted by the JSP runtime does not add any real overhead to a hand-coded counterpart. As a result, other than the initial overhead associated with the servlet generation, JSP files share the performance advantages attributed to servlets because the just-in-time (JIT) compiler available with the Java virtual machine (JVM) will compile them into native code. JIT compilers compile Java on the fly, allowing interpreted Java to execute at speeds comparable to native C++.

2.4   *Access models for business/presentation de-coupling*

Concurrent with the JSP specification's release, two JSP "access models" (architectures) were introduced in order to further the crusade to separate presentation from business logic (commonly called decoupling). These access models were mentioned first in version 0.92 of the JSP specification and are known in the industry as Model-1 and Model-2. The JSP access models specify an overall architecture for servlet/JSP web applications, defining how servlets, JSP files, JavaBean components, and back-end systems should cooperate. The architecture enforced by these models provides rules of thumb that ease the conflict between Java business code and HTML (or other) presentations. These models help provide structure to JSP web development, which can occasionally be so flexible that it inadvertently encourages poor programming practices (such as overusing scriptlets). Both models are gaining popularity as architectures for the building of JSP applications, and therefore warrant some discussion of them here. We will first talk about the Model-1 access model, and then explore Model-2.

2.4.1   *Model-1*

To understand the Model-1 architecture, look at figure 2.4. This figure sketches a simple system that adheres to the Model-1 architecture. As it shows, a request arriving at the server is served in the following manner:

- The container assigns the request to some JSP file.
- The JSP file accesses the business logic using JavaBeans (and scriptlets or bean tags).
- The JavaBeans access the enterprise information systems and return dynamic data to the JSP file.

Altogether, a single JSP file and a collection of beans serve the user. Separating presentation and business logic is achievable in Model-1 by restricting all the business logic into JavaBeans and confining the JSP file to generating the response.

Model-1 has a distinct advantage over unstructured JSP development, since all of the complex, bulky Java code that is central to our application is hidden from the content developer inside the JavaBean. This results in JSP files that are relatively free of scriptlets and easy to understand. We have, in fact, already seen a tiny Model-1 example in listings 2.7 and 2.8. There is, however, a problem with Model-1: any

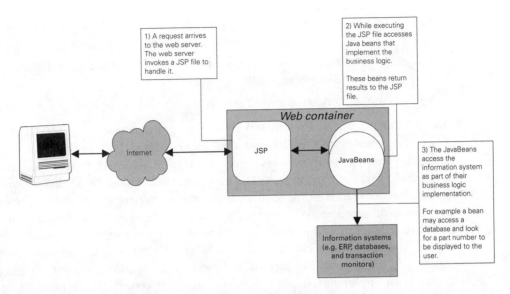

Figure 2.4   Serving a request using the Model-1 architecture

processing before or after accessing the JavaBean still must be done with scriptlets. The need for processing at these times is quite normal for validating user parameters, getting session variables, setting cookies, and so forth. Introducing scriptlets in these cases undoes some of the abstraction we achieved with this model. As a result, Model-1 is suitable for simpler applications, and requires careful attention to prevent scriptlet overuse. The pitfalls of Model-1 were remedied in Model-2, at the expense of simplicity.

2.4.2   *Model-2*

A schematic description of Model-2[3] is in figure 2.5. When a request arrives to a web application built on the Model-2 architecture:

- The container assigns the request to some *Controller* servlet.
- The servlet manipulates the request if needed. For example, it can verify the input parameters.
- The servlet selects a Model object. This object is responsible for executing the business logic that should be performed for this request.

---

[3] Model-2 is also known as model view controller (MVC) because it is a special case of this well-known design pattern.

- The results of the business logic execution are wrapped within a set of Java-Beans and forwarded from the controller servlet to a presentation (View) JSP.

- The JSP file accesses the results of the Model execution and generates a response based on those results.

- The content generated by the JSP file is included in the result to the user.

Under Model-2, the request is served using a controller servlet, Model objects, beans to encapsulate the results, and a JSP file to format the returned content. Separating presentation and business logic can easily be achieved in Model-2, since all of the code is written by the Java (business logic) developer. Recall that in Model-1 the separation of layers breaks down when we need to perform processing before or after using the JavaBean(s). Model-2 overcomes this flaw by adding a controller servlet to handle any special processing needed prior to or after the execution of the model. This controller servlet also acts as the error handler. The business logic is, of course, still implemented in Java (in the model objects). With the model and controller both implemented as Java classes (and not scriptlets) we insure that any meaningful logic is executed outside the JSP file. Achieving separation between Java and content developers is not without its price however; the controller servlet in Model-2 introduces complexity that was not part of Model-1.

To better understand Model-2, we'll look at a short sample that implements the Model-2 counterpart in listing 2.8. If you recall, listing 2.8 counted and presented the number of hits to our site for a specific user. We will now implement the same logic in Model-2 using a servlet and a JSP file. Listing 2.10 shows the new presentation JSP file in the Model-2-based implementation. The scriptlet in listing 2.8 was dropped, and now all we have is presentation logic that is easily accomplished with the JavaBean tags.

Listing 2.10   The Model-2 presentation JSP

```
<%@ page import="SessionCounterBean" %>
<jsp:useBean id="counter"
            scope="session"
            class="SessionCounterBean"/>
<BODY>
<h1> JSP Session Counter using JavaBeans and a Controller
Servlet </h1>
You visited this page <b> <jsp:getProperty name="counter"
                                property="count"/></b>
times.
</BODY>
```

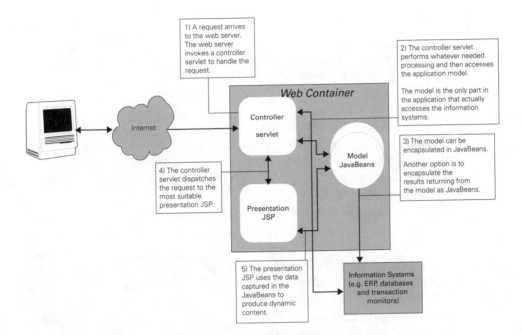

Figure 2.5   Serving a request using the Model-2 architecture

The controller servlet is available in listing 2.11 and the action of incrementing the visit count is implemented in it.

Listing 2.11   The Model-2 controller servlet

```
import java.io.IOException;
import javax.servlet.*;
import javax.servlet.http.*;

public class ControllerServlet
    extends HttpServlet
{
    public void doGet(HttpServletRequest request,
                      HttpServletResponse response)
                throws ServletException, IOException
    {
        HttpSession s = request.getSession(true);
        SessionCounterBean b =
            (SessionCounterBean)s.getAttribute("counter");
        if(null == b) {
            b = new SessionCounterBean();
            s.setAttribute("counter", b);
        }
```

```
        b.incCount();

        RequestDispatcher rd =
            request.getRequestDispatcher("/show_count.jsp");
        rd.forward(request, response);
    }
}
```

In addition to the manipulation of the counter bean, the controller servlet selects the JSP presentation to be used and forwards the request to its destination. This dispatch operation can be implemented using the `RequestDispatcher` object available in the servlet API.

Each architecture presented in this section has its pitfalls, beginning with the rather weak presentation and logic separation in Model-1 and ending with the relative complexity of Model-2. In spite of their weaknesses, both models offer vast improvements over undisciplined use of scriptlets and Beans in JSPs. Using the standard JSP tags in our JSP files dramatically reduces the amount of Java code needed inside the files. In fact, the Model-2 implementation of our counter was able to forgo any scriptlets by using JSP tags instead. Don't let these simple scriptlet-free examples lull you into believing that standard JSP tags alone can eliminate scriptlets entirely from your JSPs. In real-world applications one often needs more than the minimal JavaBean manipulation offered by canned JSP tags. Luckily, there is a solution that offers the promise of scriptlet-free JSPs. This is where custom tags libraries finally come into the picture.

2.5   *Servlets, JSP, and application configuration*

For some time, the cross server capabilities of servlets and JSP were overshadowed by the challenges of configuring them to work with web containers. Each of the ten or so servlet/JSP containers used in the industry operated differently and required different configurations for servlets to work. Why should developers and server administrators learn the specifics of their server merely to deploy Java components? Why couldn't the server be responsible only for knowing how to deploy the application by itself? Since the application developers knew exactly what initialization variables were needed and what URIs to use, why shouldn't the developers provide all this information in a standard document that all servers understood and could deploy? Java-based web applications could then be distributed using this standard format and be easily deployed.

For these reasons, the servlet API specification was developed to define a standard web archive (WAR) for distributing web applications. This archive includes a predefined directory structure that facilitates finding application components and a *web application deployment descriptor* (web.xml). A web application deployment descriptor is an XML[4] file with specific tags that make it possible for the developer to define—in a server-neutral manner—servlets, initialization parameters, and servlet-to-URI mappings. The benefits of using a WAR for distribution are obvious to anyone who has ever muddled through the configuring of a web application on their server—or, worse yet—ported a Java web application from one server vendor to the next. In the following sections we introduce WARs, starting with the archive structure and followed by a description of the WAR deployment descriptor.

2.5.1 *The WAR file and its structure*

A web application is distributed in a WAR file, which is largely a jar file with a specific structure and a fancy suffix (.war). The structure of a web archive file includes a root directory that serves as the application document root for serving application files, and a special directory named WEB-INF where you place application metadata, class files, and jar files.

The root directory includes files that are to be served to the client. The files in this directory may be simple flat files (HTML, audio, and video), class and jar files that implement a certain Applet, or certain files processed by servlets to produce output to the user (JSP, SSI, and other types of files). Files placed under the root directory will appear to the user as if they were under the URI where the application is rooted. For example, if an application is rooted under the URI "/shop" and the application root directory includes the following files:

```
/index.jsp
/file_with_applet.html
/images/next.gif
/images/ok.gif
/classes/MyApplet.class
/effects/ping.au
```

the user will see these files as if they were accessible by issuing requests for:

```
http://www.host.com/shop/index.jsp
http://www.host.com/shop/file_with_applet.html
http://www.host.com/shop/images/next.gif
http://www.host.com/shop/images/ok.gif
http://www.host.com/shop/classes/MyApplet.class
http://www.host.com/shop/effects/ping.au
```

---

[4] For more XML information, see appendix A.

SECURITY   Since the root directory will become the application root, users will be able to access all its content (with the exception of the WEB-INF directory). Be careful about placing sensitive information there.

The WEB-INF directory is the repository for the application's configuration as well as its building blocks such as servlets, beans, utility classes, and so forth. Since the content of the directory is very sensitive, this directory is not a part of the public document tree and its files should not be served to users. The content of the WEB-INF directory includes three entities:

- The deployment descriptor file named web.xml.
- A Classes directory in which you can place the servlets and utility classes that comprise your application.
- A Lib directory in which you can place jar files that comprise your application.

Let's look at a sample WAR directory structure:

```
/index.jsp
/file_with_applet.html
/images/next.gif
/images/ok.gif
/classes/MyApplet.class
/effects/ping.au
/WEB-INF/web.xml
/WEB-INF/lib/myean.jar
/WEB-INF/lib/myotherean.jar
/WEB-INF/lib/utility.jar
/WEB-INF/classes/com/seomecompany/Aservlet.class
/WEB-INF/classes/com/seomecompany/Anotherservlet.class
/WEB-INF/classes/com/seomecompany/Utility.class
/WEB-INF/classes/com/seomecompany/localstrings.properties
```

This WAR file contains an application whose implementation comprises three jar files and four classes as located in the Lib and Classes directories, exposing a lot of files to the user.

Sharing a common structure makes it possible to automatically deploy an application from its WAR file since the container knows what to do with each file (e.g., add the content of the Lib and Classes to the classpath, present the files under the root directory to the users, etc.). It should be clear where you need to put the different components of your application. Now we look at the deployment descriptor used by the container to configure the app.

2.5.2 *The application deployment descriptor*

Each application has a deployment descriptor, a simple XML file containing the application configuration. The goal of the deployment descriptor is to provide a common file format developers can use to specify application configuration information. By enforcing a universal XML format (via a DTD), developers know that all containers will support and understand the descriptor.

Some of the configuration information associated with an application (and thus detailed in a deployment descriptor) includes:

- Global initialization parameters
- Associations between servlet names and their implementing class, as well as any private initialization parameters for that servlet
- Mappings of servlets to URIs
- Session state for the application
- MIME type mappings
- The welcome file list
- Error pages
- Security constraints
- J2EE environment information.

Rather than try to showcase all these configuration options, we will select two configuration tasks—defining an application configuration parameter and defining a servlet. This introduction will provide a grounding in the deployment descriptor's nature so that other configuration tasks will be easy to pick up.

Initialization parameters in the deployment descriptor

The first task we'll look at is defining context (or application-based) initialization parameters. These are parameters that specify initialization information for an entire application, such as what database to connect to, or the name of the email server to use. Application-scoped initialization parameters are supplied using three tags, `<context-param>`, `<param-name>`, and `<param-value>`. As an example, the following descriptor includes two application-scoped initialization parameters:

```
<?xml version="2.0" encoding="ISO-8859-1"?>
<!DOCTYPE web-app
    PUBLIC "-//Sun Microsystems, Inc.//DTD Web Application 2.2//EN"
    "http://java.sun.com/j2ee/dtds/web-app_2.2.dtd">

<web-app>
  <context-param>
    <param-name>adminemail</param-name>
```

```
    <param-value>admin@site.com</param-value>
  </context-param>
  <context-param>
    <param-name>adminpager</param-name>
    <param-value >12345678</param-value>
  </context-param>
</web-app>
```

Each initialization parameter is encapsulated within a `<context-param>` tag that holds the `<param-name>` and `<param-value>` tags, encapsulating the values of the parameter name and the parameter's value. In this example, we specify an admin email address and pager number that, hypothetically, would be used by all the error pages in our application to send notification of a problem to the administrator. Specifying these parameters in this way lets us add and modify parameters in a central location, accessible by our entire Java web application.

Configuring servlets in the deployment descriptor

Our next configuration task is defining a servlet to the container. Defining a servlet involves the usage of a fair number of tags. A servlet may include an optional icon, display name, and description, but these are of less interest to us. More important elements in a servlet configuration include:

- The name you selected for the servlet, encapsulated within a `<servlet-name>` tag.

- The class implementing the servlet, encapsulated within a `<servlet-class>` tag.

- Optional servlet initialization parameters, encapsulated within `<init-param>`, `<param-name>`, and `<param-value>` tags (similar in usage to the manner in which application initializations are provided).

- Optional startup loading indicator that causes the container to load the servlet in its boot time. You can specify such requirements using the `<load-on-startup>` tag. The content encapsulated within the `<load-on-startup>` tag should be an integer, and the container will use it to determine the servlet loading order. Servlets with more negative `<load-on-startup>` values are initialized first.

The following example shows a descriptor defining a servlet. The servlet loads on startup and accepts two initialization variables.

```
<?xml version="2.0" encoding="ISO-8859-1"?>
<!DOCTYPE web-app
    PUBLIC "-//Sun Microsystems, Inc.//DTD Web Application 2.2//EN"
    "http://java.sun.com/j2ee/dtds/web-app_2.2.dtd">

<web-app>
  <servlet>
```

```
    <servlet-name>aservletname</servlet-name>
    <servlet-class>com.corp.servlet.Aservlet</servlet-class>
    <load-on-startup>-1</load-on-startup>
    <init-param>
      <param-name>param-name1</param-name>
      <param-value>some value </param-value>
    </init-param>
    <init-param>
     <param-name>param-name2</param-name>
     <param-value>some other value </param-value>
    </init-param>
  </servlet>
</web-app>
```

And, as you can see, configuring a servlet through the deployment descriptor is a fairly simple task requiring only a few intuitive tags.

This section presented how to configure and distribute a Java-based web application in a server-neutral manner. This solves one of the more acute problems in the servlet and JSP world, making it possible for developers to distribute preconfigured applications in a standard way. Any server touting Java servlet and JSP support should support the WAR standard. This means any WAR file you create should be readily deployable on such a server with no modifications needed whatsoever. Combine this with Java's inherent cross-platform support and you can see why WAR files are the Visa cards of web application development—accepted just about anywhere.

2.6   *Summary*

We've devoted a lot of time to learning about servlets and JSPs because they have so much in common, a point we made in this chapter's introduction. JSP custom tags are intimately tied to these two predecessor technologies in both API and deployment. We will soon learn how custom tags use the servlet API extensively (in the same way a JSP does) to interact with the web server, the client, HTTP parameters, cookies, and more. We'll also see that tags cannot exist by themselves, and must be embedded in a JSP file in order to function. Thus, knowledge of how to write and deploy a JSP is a critical prerequisite for learning JSP custom tags.

With our knowledge of servlets, JSPs, and the motivation for tag-based development in hand, we are finally ready to introduce ourselves to custom JSP tags.

Developing your first tags

Thus far we have seen how servlets and JSPs can be used to build a web application. These technologies go some distance toward making web development easier, but do not yet facilitate the separation of Java from HTML in a reusable way. Custom tags make this possible by bundling Java code into concise, HTML-like fragments recognizable by presentation developers. Custom tags are therefore an attractive choice for Java-based web applications and in this chapter, we'll introduce custom tags and walk through examples of their development and use. We'll also look at how to set up a development environment and deploy, test, and troubleshoot tags.

This chapter takes a mountain-top view of custom JSP tags in order to provide a clear, high-level look at the subject's landscape. Later chapters will dive deeper and home in on each of the topics touched upon here. So don't be concerned if the finer details are left for later explanation. The goal now is to jumpstart your tag development and ensure that you're sufficiently comfortable with the basics so that you may start building tags on your own.

3.1 What are JSP custom tags?

At its most fundamental level, a *tag* is a group of characters read by a program for the purpose of instructing the program to perform an action. In the case of HTML tags, the program reading the tags is a Web browser, and the actions range from painting words or objects on the screen to creating forms for data collection. Custom JSP tags are also interpreted by a program; but, unlike HTML, JSP tags are interpreted on the server side—not client side. The program that interprets custom JSP tags is the runtime engine in your application server (TomCat, JRun, WebLogic, etc.). When the JSP engine encounters a custom tag, it executes Java code that has been specified to go with that tag. Common tasks performed by tag codes include retrieving database values, formatting text, and returning HTML to a browser. Since a tag references some Java code to run when it's encountered, one way to think of a tag is simply as a shorthand notation for a block of code.

Notice in figure 3.1 that when the JSP runtime encounters the tag, it causes a block of Java code to execute and return a message to the client's browser.

3.1.1 Anatomy of a tag

Tags are often structured with a body and/or attributes which are the places where a page author (the user of the tag) can include more information about how the tag should do its job. The following snippet shows the general structure of a tag.

```
<tagname attributename="attributevalue"
        otherattributename="otherattributevalue">
Tag's body... can contain about anything.
</tagname>
```

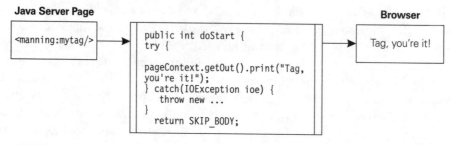

Figure 3.1   A tag in action

This syntax should look familiar, since we see it so often in HTML tags, such as:

```
<font face="Tahoma" size=3">
Tag, you're it!
</font>
```

Tags can also appear without a body, meaning that the start tag does not have a matching end tag. These "bodyless" tags look like this:

```
<bodylesstagname attributename="attributevalue"
                 otherattributename="otherattributevalue"/>
```

You've probably seen examples of bodyless tags in HTML, such as:

```
<input type="input" name="body">
```

Bodyless tags usually represent a certain function, as in the printing of the value of a database field onto the page. Tags often have bodies in order to perform an operation on the content in the body, such as formatting, translating, or processing it in some way.

JSP custom tags are merely Java classes that implement one of two special interfaces. Since tags are standard Java classes, they can interact with, delegate to, or integrate with any other Java code in order to make that functionality available through a tag. For instance, we might have a library of utility classes we've written for composing and sending email, or for accessing a particular database that we'd like to make available to HTML developers. We need build only a few tags that collect the necessary information through attributes and pass this information to our utility classes.

3.1.2   Using a tag in JSP

JSP code that uses email and database tags such as those just mentioned might look something like this:

```
<html>
I am sending you an email with your account information
<jspx:sendmail server="mail.corp.com"
               from="john.doe@corp.com"
               to="foo@bar.com"
               subject="mail from a tag">
Look at how easy it is to send an email from a tag... here is
your status.

<jspx:dbaccess>
    <jspx:wdbcon id="con1"/>

    <jspx:wjitdbquery>
        select reserves from account where id='<%= userid %>'
    </jspx:wjitdbquery>

You have <jspx:wdbshow field="reserves "/>$ in your saving account.
</jspx:dbaccess>

</jspx:sendmail>
</html>
```

Among the JSP and HTML fragments are special tags prefixed with jspx. Even to the untrained eye, these tags appear to query a database, present the information in the content of an email, and send the message. Notice how the attributes help gather information such as the email sender and subject and the field in the database to display. Also, note how the <jspx:wjitdbquery> tag contains a Structured Query Language (SQL) statement within its body that it uses for the database query. This is a good example of what a JSP using custom tags might look like. Consider how much messier this JSP would look if we had to include all the Java code necessary for creating classes, setting properties, catching exceptions, and so forth.

3.1.3   *The tag library descriptor*

An important step in creating tags is specifying how they will be used by the JSP runtime that executes them. To properly work with a tag, the runtime must know several things about it, such as what (if any) attributes it has, and whether or not it has a body. This information is used by the runtime to verify that the tag is properly employed by a JSP author and to correctly execute the tag during a request. This crucial information is made available to the runtime engine via a standard XML file called a tag library descriptor (TLD), a key component of the JSP Specification and standard across all products that implement it. How to create a TLD is discussed in section 3.2.4, and covered in greater detail in chapter 5 and appendix B.

3.2 Why tags?

JSP already makes it possible to embed *scriptlets* (bits of Java code) and JavaBeans in line with HTML content, so why do we need JSP tags? We need them because tags were never intended to offer more functionality than scriptlets, just better packaging. JSP tags were created to improve the separation of program logic and presentation logic; specifically, to abstract Java syntax from HTML.

Scriptlets are not a suitable solution for all web development because most content developers (art designers, HTML developers, and the like) don't know Java and, perhaps, don't care to. Though much Java code can be encapsulated in beans, their usage in a JSP still requires the presentation developer to have a basic knowledge of Java syntax and datatypes in order to be productive. JSP tags form a new "scriptlet-free" and even a completely "Java-free" component model that is adapted perfectly to the JSP environment with its different developer types. If custom tags are properly constructed, they can be of enormous use to HTML developers, even those who have no working knowledge of Java—they won't even have to know they're using it. Tags can reduce or eliminate the number of scriptlets in a JSP application in four ways:

- A tag is nothing more than a Java component that takes its arguments from attribute and body. Since tags can have attributes and body, any necessary parameters to the tag can be passed within the tag's body or as one of its attributes. No Java code is needed to initialize or set properties on the component.

- JSP requires a considerable quantity of scriptlets for tasks such as iteration, setting of initial values, and performing conditional HTML. All of these tasks can be cleanly abstracted in a few simple tags.

- In many cases, a JavaBean component is configured and activated using scriptlets. One can develop a set of JSP tags to perform this configuration and activation without any Java.

- Tags can implement many utility operations, such as sending email and connecting to a database, and in this way reduce the number of utility scriptlets needed inside JSP.

The benefits of custom tags also include the creation of a neat abstraction layer between logic and presentation. This abstraction creates an interface that allows Java developers to fix bugs, add features, and change implementation without requiring any changes to the JSPs that include those tags. In short, JSP tags help bring you one step closer to the Holy Grail of web development—true abstraction of presentation and control. For more on the benefits of custom tags, see chapter 15.

3.2.1 *Comparisons of scriptlets and custom tags*

The differences between scriptlets and custom tags are fairly concrete:

1. Custom tags have simpler syntax. Scriptlets are written in Java and require the author to be familiar with Java syntax, whereas tags are HTML-like in syntax and require no Java knowledge.

2. Custom tags are easier to debug and are less error prone than scriptlets, since omitting a curly bracket, a semicolon, or some other minute character in a scriptlet can produce errors that are not easy to understand. Custom tag syntax is extraordinarily simple and, with most JSP runtime products, even the occasional typo in custom tag usage will produce meaningful error messages.

3. Custom tags are easy to integrate in development environments. Since tags are a common component of many web technologies, HTML editors have support for adding tags into the development environment. This allows JSP authors to continue using their favorite integrated development environment (IDE) to build tag-based JSPs. Support for JSP scriptlets syntax in development environments exists, but is only useful to JSP authors well versed in Java.

4. Custom tags can eliminate the need for Java in your JSPs. By containing most of your logic within objects in your scriptlets, you can vastly reduce the amount of Java code in a JSP; however, custom tags still carry the advantage of imposing absolutely no Java syntax, something scriptlets cannot achieve.

For small projects in which all your JSPs will be authored by developers knowledgeable in Java, scriptlets are a fine solution. For larger projects, where content developers unfamiliar with Java will be handling most of the presentation, JSP custom tags provide a real advantage and are a logical choice.

3.3 *Setting up a development environment*

Before we can build our first tag, we need to configure our development environment. This development environment should at least make it possible to:

- Compile the tags with the servlet, JSP, and JSP custom tags API[1]
- Test the developed tags
- Browse the JSP custom tags API documentation.

---

[1] We will take a look at the JSP custom tag API in chapter 4.

There are several Java IDEs in today's market, some of which provide fine support for servlet and JSP development; however, we are not going to work with any particular IDE because it is highly unlikely that you would have the same one that we select. Also, IDEs are notorious for lagging behind the leading edge of the Servlet and JSP API. Instead we explain how to fetch all the ingredients for a minimal development environment and how to set them up so that you may start developing tags immediately. This development environment will be concentrated around Tomcat,[2] the reference implementation of the servlet API, and the JDK1.2.2 or above (as available to most operating systems).

3.3.1 Installing the JDK

The first step in setting up the development environment is to install JDK1.2.2 (or higher) on your development system. More than two years since its first appearance, JDK1.2 can be found in a matured state on most operating systems, and this book uses many of its new classes and interfaces, such as `java.util.Iterator`. Although JDK1.2 is recommended for tag development, a JDK1.1.x version should suffice. Installing the JDK is an operating system-dependent task and will not be covered here, so we'll assume that you have a JDK installed and that you point into the installation directory with an environment variable named `JAVA_HOME`.

3.3.2 Installing Tomcat

Tomcat is the reference implementation of the Servlet and JSP API. It is easy to use and install, has a very small footprint (both on the hard drive and in memory), and is Open Source—all of which makes it a perfect learning tool. Installing Tomcat with the basic functionality of a stand-alone servlet and JSP container is really a cinch:

1 Extract the Tomcat binary distribution archive[3] (available as either .zip or tar.gz archives).

2 Define an environment variable named `TOMCAT_HOME` to point to Tomcat's installation root directory.

3 Make sure that the environment variable `JAVA_HOME` is defined and points to the directory wherein you installed your JDK.

---

[2] Tomcat's home on the web is at http://www/jakarta.apache.org

[3] You can download the binary distribution directly from Tomcat's web site. The installation directives supplied in this book apply to Tomcat versions 3.1 and 3.2.

3.3.3 *Testing your Tomcat installation*

To test-drive Tomcat, change the directory to TOMCAT_HOME and execute the startup script in Tomcat's bin directory. Tomcat should start running in the background and you can test it by issuing an HTTP request (i.e., http://your.machine.name:8080/). Once Tomcat is running, the installation of the development environment is complete and you may start immediately to develop tags; but first, let's look at the Tomcat distribution.

servlet.jar

The .jar file is where you find the interfaces and classes constituting the Servlet and JSP API. This file is named servlet.jar and is located in Tomcat's Lib directory. When compiling a servlet or JSP custom tag, you should make sure that this file is in your compilation CLASSPATH definition.

webapps directory

Where to place your web applications for Tomcat is the next consideration. Tomcat can generally be configured to take applications from any place you choose, but why bother configuring individual applications when you can simply drop your application into a single directory for deployment? The one directory approach will prove much simpler for your first applications. Under TOMCAT_HOME there is a subdirectory named webapps; and whenever Tomcat starts to run, it inspects this subdirectory, searches for web-application archive files (.war), and automatically deploys them. Moreover, if Tomcat finds subdirectories under webapps, it will assume that these directories contain web applications. Deployment to this directory is thus a simple task.

Javadoc documentation

One last thing to consider with Tomcat is the location of the Javadoc documents for the Servlet and JSP API. These documents are located in an application bundled with the Tomcat samples. In the webapps directory, there's a directory named ROOT, the home of Tomcat default root application. The root application has a subdirectory path named docs/api where you can find the Javadoc documents for the Servlet and JSP API (start with the file index.html).[4]

With the environment configured and a basic understanding of the deployment picture, it's time to build our first custom tag.

---

[4] You can also browse these documents by starting Tomcat and referring to http://your.machine.name:8080/docs/api/index.html.

3.4   Hello World example

Our goal in this section is to create a simple tag that may not be particularly reusable, but it will introduce most of the concepts needed for building useful tags. This simplicity is necessary now, as the myriad details involved with constructing even a Hello World tag can be daunting at first. Later sections in this chapter will present tags that have more real-world relevance.

Our Hello World tag is merely going to print "Hello JSP tag World" out to an HTML page. Listing 3.1 presents the source code for the Hello World implementation.

Listing 3.1   Source code for the HelloWorldTag handler class

```
package book.simpletasks;

import java.io.IOException;

import javax.servlet.jsp.PageContext;
import javax.servlet.jsp.JspException;
import javax.servlet.jsp.JspTagException;
import javax.servlet.jsp.tagext.TagSupport;

public class HelloWorldTag
     extends TagSupport {                      ❶

   public int doStartTag()
             throws JspException               ❷
   {
       try {
           pageContext.getOut().print("Hello JSP tag World");   ❸
       } catch(IOException ioe) {              ❹
           throw new JspTagException("Error:
   IOException while writing to the user");
       }
       return SKIP_BODY;
   }
}
```

❶ **TagSupport is an abstract class which is part of the JSP tag APIs**   Listing 3.1 presents a Java class that implements a tag handler, but it also contains methods and objects that are new to you unless you already have a very solid background in servlets and JSPs. We mentioned earlier that tags are Java classes that implement one of two special interfaces. These interfaces define all the methods the JSP runtime uses to get at the tag's functionality. As with many Java interfaces, some utility-only classes that provide basic implementations of these interfaces are available, making development easier. In the case of our HelloWorldTag, we extend one such utility class called TagSupport. TagSupport and the interface it implements, Tag, are both part of the custom JSP tag API. Don't worry too much over the specifics of this interface. For now it's important to know only that we need to implement `Tag` to create a tag, and we've done so by extending `TagSupport`.

❷ **JSP runtime calls `doStartTag()` to execute the tag** Here we note that there is no explicit constructor for this tag, nor is there a `main()` method for invoking the class. This is because a tag handler is not a stand-alone class, but is instantiated by the JSP runtime that invokes its methods. The JSP custom tags API defines a set of methods for custom tags (which are included in the two special interfaces previously mentioned) that the JSP runtime calls throughout a tag's life cycle. One of these methods, `doStartTag()`, can be seen in our example and is called by the JSP runtime when it starts executing a tag (more about the `Tag` methods in chapter 4). The `doStartTag()` method is a repository for code that we wish to have executed whenever the JSP runtime encounters our tag within the page.[5]

❸ **Tag echoes the `hello` message to the user** In our implementation of `doStartTag()`, we perform three operations. We print the `hello` message using an `out` object that we got from the `PageContext` (in chapter 2).

❹ **Aborts the execution upon errors** We watch out for `IOExceptions` that may be thrown by the response `Writer`, catch them, and abort the tag's execution by throwing a `JspTagException`. Finally, as required by the method, we return an integer value which tells the JSP runtime how to proceed after encountering our tag. A value of `SKIP_BODY` tells the runtime engine to simply ignore the tag's body, if there is one, and go on evaluating the rest of the page. There are, of course, other valid return values for `doStartTag()`, which we'll explore in future chapters.

As listing 3.1 shows, the tag is only a few lines long and, indeed, all it does is write out to the page, but a few details that will reappear in other tags are already evident.

Now that we have the Java source of our tag, it is time to compile it.

3.4.1 *Compiling the tag*

Compiling Java source into its class (without an IDE) requires careful setting of the compilation `CLASSPATH` (a list of all directories and .jar files that hold the classes referenced in our source code). Basically, the `CLASSPATH` for a tag handler must include the Servlet and JSP APIs; you should also include any additional classes or libraries that you are using within the tag handler (such as JavaMail and JNDI). In

---

[5] Though this would seem to imply that the runtime evaluates a JSP each time a page is requested, we know from JSP development that the page is only interpreted and compiled into a servlet once. Tags are no exception; this is just a convenient way to think about how the tag will behave at runtime.

the case of `HelloWorldTag`, we are not using any additional libraries, and can settle with the following Javac command line (assuming that `JAVA_HOME` and `TOMCAT_HOME` are both defined and we are compiling the source file into a directory named classes):

For UNIX:

```
$JAVA_HOME/bin/javac -d ../classes -classpath $TOMCAT_HOME/lib/servlet.jar
    book/simpletasks/HelloWorldTag.java
```

For Windows:

```
%JAVA_HOME%\bin\javac -d ..\classes -classpath %TOMCAT_HOME%\lib\servlet.jar
    book\simpletasks\HelloWorldTag.java
```

Both command lines use the `TOMCAT_HOME` environment variable to add the Servlet and JSP API into the `CLASSPATH`, and this is actually the only JSP-`Tags`-specific portion in the compilation command. When the compilation ends, we have our compiled tag handler in the classes directory and we are ready to continue to the next step—creating the tag library descriptor (TLD).

3.4.2 *Creating a tag library descriptor (TLD)*

The JSP runtime requires your assistance if it is to understand how to use your custom tag. For example, it has to know what you want to name your tag and any tag attributes. To do this you need to create a file called a tag library descriptor for your tag. An in-depth explanation of the exact use of a TLD will be covered in chapter 5, and its syntax is explained in appendix B, so we needn't go into great detail on these now. Instead, if we look at our example for the `HelloWorldTag`, the ways to use a TLD will emerge.

The TLD is nothing more than a simple extended markup language (XML[6]) file, a text file including a cluster of tags with some predefined syntax. Since the TLD is just a text file, you can create it with your preferred editor (Emacs, VI, notepad, etc.) as long as you keep to some rudimentary guidelines as explained in appendix B. The TLD created for the `HelloWorld` tag is presented in listing 3.2.

Listing 3.2 Tag library descriptor for the HelloWorldTag

```
<?xml version="1.0" encoding="ISO-8859-1" ?>
<!DOCTYPE taglib
    PUBLIC "-//Sun Microsystems, Inc.//DTD JSP Tag Library 1.1//EN"
    "http://java.sun.com/j2ee/dtds/web-jsptaglibrary_1_1.dtd">

<taglib>
```

---

[6] XML is briefly described in appendix A.

```
<tlibversion>1.0</tlibversion>
<jspversion>1.1</jspversion>
<shortname>simp</shortname>
<uri> http://www.manning.com/jsptagsbook/simple-taglib </uri>
<info>
    A simple sample tag library
</info>

<tag>
    <name>hello</name>
    <tagclass>book.simpletasks.HelloWorldTag</tagclass>
    <bodycontent>empty</bodycontent>
    <info>
        Say hello.
    </info>
</tag>
</taglib>
```

Listing 3.2 defines a tag whose name is "hello," and whose implementing class is `HelloWorldTag`, which we just developed. This means that whenever the JSP runtime sees the tag `<hello/>` it should actually execute the methods contained in our `HelloWorldTag`.

The portion of listing 3.2 unique to this tag is in bold face and, as it demonstrates, creating a tag library involves many "overhead lines" that specify such information as the desired version of JSP and the like. Normally you can just grab (and update) these overhead lines from a pre-existing library descriptor and add your own tags below them.

Let's assume that we saved the TLD in a file named simpletags.tld. We now have our tag handler class and the TLD to help the JSP runtime use it. These two files are all we need to deploy our `HelloWorldTag` and begin using it in a JSP.

3.4.3 *Testing HelloWorldTag*

Testing `HelloWorldTag` involves deploying it to a JSP container and writing a JSP file to use the tag. To do this:

1 Create a web application for your tags (in our case, `HelloWorldTag`).

2 Deploy your tags in the application.

3 Write a JSP file that will use `HelloWorldTag`.

4 Execute the JSP file created in step 3 and look at the results.

Creating a web application

What must be done to create a new web application in Tomcat? This can be accomplished either by deploying a web application archive or creating an application directory that follows the WAR structure. We are going to create an application directory, as follows:

1 Make a directory named testapp in Tomcat's webapps directory.

2 Under the testapp directory make another directory named WEB-INF, and inside this create directories named lib and classes.

Create a file named web.xml in the WEB-INF directory and add the content of listing 3.3 into it; web.xml is going to be your web application deployment descriptor; and listing 3.3 contains an "empty" deployment descriptor content.

> **Listing 3.3   An empty web application deployment descriptor**

```
<?xml version="1.0" encoding="ISO-8859-1"?>
<!DOCTYPE web-app
    PUBLIC "-//Sun Microsystems, Inc.//DTD Web Application 2.2//EN"
    "http://java.sun.com/j2ee/dtds/web-app_2.2.dtd">

<web-app>
</web-app>
```

Deploying a tag

You now have an application structure under the testapp directory into which you may deploy your tags. Tag deployment takes the following steps:

1 Copy your tag implementation classes or jar files into the application directory; .jar files should go into the newly created lib directory, .class files should go into the classes directory. In the present case, we will copy the compiled class into the classes directory (while preserving the package directory structure).

2 Copy the TLD into a location in the application's directory structure (WEB-INF is a good location). In our example we will copy our TLD from listing 3.2 (simpletags.tld) into the WEB-INF directory.

3 Add a tag library reference into the web application deployment descriptor. In our case, edit web.xml and add the content of listing 3.4 into the `<web-app>` section (these last two steps set up a reference to the TLD as will be explained in chapter 5).

Listing 3.4   A TLD reference entry for the tags described in simpletags.tld

```
<taglib>
    <taglib-uri>
        http://www.manning.com/jsptagsbook/simple-taglib
    </taglib-uri>
    <taglib-location>
        /WEB-INF/simpletags.tld
    </taglib-location>
</taglib>
```

The tag was deployed into the web application; all we need to do now is to create a JSP that uses the tag and verify whether it works.

Creating a JSP file to test HelloWorldTag

Developing a JSP file to test `HelloWorldTag` is a relatively simple task. All we need to do is craft a JSP file similar to the one presented in listing 3.5.

Listing 3.5   A JSP file to drive HelloWorldTag

```
<%@ taglib
    uri="http://www.manning.com/jsptagsbook/simple-taglib"          ❶
    prefix="jspx" %>
<html>
<title><jspx:hello/></title>          ❷
<body>
Executing your first custom tag... <b><jspx:hello/></b>          ❷
</body>
</html>
```

❶ **Declares that the JSP file uses the library referenced by the URI and that the library's tags are referenced by jspx**   Listing 3.5 is elementary, yet it illustrates a few important points about tags. The first is the `taglib` directive at the beginning of the JSP file. The `taglib` directive is further discussed in chapter 5, but for now we need to note that it indicates to the JSP runtime where the tag library lives and the prefix by which we'll refer to tags in this library. With this directive in place, the JSP runtime will recognize any usage of our tag throughout the JSP, as long as we precede our tag name with the prefix "jspx."

❷ **Uses the `hello` tag through the JSP file**   We also see how the custom tag can be used through the JSP file. We use the `HelloWorldTag` twice, and we could, of course, have used it as much as we wanted. All that's needed is to add it to the JSP content. Note that our tag is bodyless, necessitating the use of the trailing backslash.

Figure 3.2 Output generated using the `hello` tag driver JSP

Figure 3.2 shows the results achieved by executing the JSP file in listing 3.5. Observe that wherever we had the `<hello>` tag, we now have the content generated by it.

Executing HelloWorldTag

Once we've created a web application, deployed the tag, and created and deployed a JSP to use it, all that's left is to view the page in a browser.

3.4.4 Did it work?

If your tag didn't work properly there is always some recourse. The error messages you see will vary, depending on which JSP runtime engine you've chosen. If, however, the messages you're seeing aren't helpful, here are a couple of suggestions:

- Make sure there are no spelling errors in the URL that you specified for the browser when asking for the JSP file (it should look like http://www.host.name/appname/jspfile.jsp).

- Make sure there are no spelling errors in your TLD file and that you've specified the fully qualified class name for your tag—package names and all.

- Verify that your TLD file is in a location where the JSP engine will be seeking it, such as the WEB-INF directory in your web application.

- Make sure the `taglib` directive has been properly placed at the top of the JSP. Without this, the engine doesn't know where to find the code for your tags and will just ignore them. When that happens, you'll actually see the tag in the HTML source.

3.4.5 A tag with attributes

Our `HelloWorldTag` is predictable; in fact, it always does exactly the same thing. In the dynamic world of web development, that is seldom the case, so let's look at a tag that behaves realistically, based on some user-specified attributes.

A web page might, for instance, need to display the value stored in a cookie such as a user name. Rather than forcing the page author to learn Java to access that value, we'll build a simple tag that does this for him. The tag should be flexible enough to be used in retrieving the value of any accessible cookie, so we'll create a tag attribute called cookieName to allow this. The first step in supporting this new attribute is to modify our tag handler class to receive and make use of this new attribute(listing 3.6):

Listing 3.6   Source code for the CookieValueTag handler class

```
package book.simpletasks;

import java.io.IOException;

import javax.servlet.jsp.PageContext;
import javax.servlet.jsp.JspException;
import javax.servlet.jsp.JspTagException;
import javax.servlet.jsp.tagext.TagSupport;
import javax.servlet.http.*;

public class CookieValueTag extends TagSupport {

    String cookieName;       ❶
     public int doStartTag()
                throws JspException
    {
      try {
        Cookie[] cookies =
         ((HttpServletRequest)pageContext.getRequest()).getCookies();
        if ( cookies != null ) {
          for ( int i=0; i < cookies.length; i++ ) {
            if ( cookies[i].getName().equalsIgnoreCase( cookieName ) ) {
              pageContext.getOut().print( cookies[i].getValue() );   ❷
              break;
            }
          }
        }
      } catch(IOException ioe) {
throw new JspTagException("Error: IOException while writing to the user");
      }
      return SKIP_BODY;     ❸
    }

    public void setCookiename( String value ) {        ❹
    cookieName = value;
    }
}
```

❶ **The field that will get set by the attribute.**

② Prints the value of the cookie to the response.

③ Returns SKIP_BODY to tell the JSP runtime to skip the body if one exists.

④ Invokes the set method when the JSP runtime encounters this attribute.

All we needed to do was add a set method called setCookieName() and assign a variable within it. The value of that variable is examined within our tag handler's doStartTag() to decide which cookie value to return. Now we need to inform the JSP runtime of this new tag and its attribute. Recall that the TLD is where we specify this kind of information, so we need to modify our previous TLD to support CookieValueTag. The tag declaration in our TLD file (listing 3.7) now looks like the following:

Listing 3.7 The new TLD file with our CookieValueTag

```xml
<?xml version="1.0" encoding="ISO-8859-1" ?>
<!DOCTYPE taglib
    PUBLIC "-//Sun Microsystems, Inc.//DTD JSP Tag Library 1.1//EN"
    "http://java.sun.com/j2ee/dtds/web-jsptaglibrary_1_1.dtd">

<taglib>
    <tlibversion>1.0</tlibversion>
    <jspversion>1.1</jspversion>
    <shortname>simp</shortname>
    <uri> http://www.manning.com/jsptagsbook/simple-taglib </uri>
    <info>
        A simple sample tag library
    </info>

    <tag>
        <name>hello</name>
        <tagclass>book.simpletasks.HelloWorldTag</tagclass>
        <bodycontent>empty</bodycontent>
        <info>
            Say hello.
        </info>
    </tag>
    <tag>
      <name>cookievalue</name>
      <tagclass>book.simpletasks.CookieValueTag</tagclass>
      <bodycontent>empty</bodycontent>
      <info>
          Get a cookie's value.
      </info>
      <attribute>                              ①
        <name>cookiename</name>
        <required>true</required>              ②
      </attribute>
    </tag>
</taglib>
```

❶ This tag will have an attribute called `cookiename`.

❷ Specifies that this attribute is always required for this tag.

The tag definition itself should look familiar, since it is very similar to our `Hello-WorldTag`. The important difference is, of course, the attribute we've included. Note that the name of an attribute, in our case `cookiename`, is used by the JSP runtime to find `setCookieName()` to use in the tag handler; therefore, these need to match exactly for the tag to function.

To use this attribute within a JSP, syntax such as in listing 3.8 works well:

Listing 3.8   A JSP file to drive HelloWorldTag

```
<%@ taglib
    uri="http://www.manning.com/jsptagsbook/simple-taglib"      ❶
    prefix="jspx" %>
<html>
<title>C is for Cookie</title>
<body>
Welcome back, <jspx:cookievalue cookiename="username">        ❷
</body>
</html>
```

❶ Declares that the JSP file uses the library referenced by the URI and that the library's tags are referenced by jspx.

❷ Uses the `cookieivalue` tag to retrieve a cookie called "username".

Assuming we've used this tag in a case where a cookie named "username" will be accessible, we'll see a message like that shown in figure 3.3.

Adding attributes to your tags makes them much more flexible and useful to the web pages where they are used. We explore the use of tag attributes in further detail in chapters 4 and 6.

3.4.6   *Packaging tags for shipment*

Once the tags have been tested to your satisfaction, it's time to package them in a standard deployable manner. Packaging

Figure 3.3   CookieValueTag in action.

tags means putting the implementation classes along with the library descriptor in a .jar file following a convention that further instructs you to:

- Put your tag class files inside the .jar archive while maintaining their package structure.
- Put your TLD in the .jar file in a directory called META-INF.

For example, packaging our lone `HelloWorldTag` will require the following .jar file structure:

```
/book/simpletasks/HelloWorldTag.class
/META-INF/simpletags.tld
```

This .jar packaging need not be complicated; all that's required is to create the desired directory structure on your file system and use the `jar` command (bundled with the JDK) to archive this structure into the .jar file. The command to place our class and TLD in a jar called hello.jar looks like this:

```
jar cf hello.jar META-INF book
```

Now you can distribute your tag.

3.5   A tag with a body

Remember that tags can have a body or be bodyless. Our `HelloWorldTag` was an example of a tag without a body, so let's see an example of a tag with one. We create them whenever we want to take a block of content (typically HTML) and modify it or include it in the server's response. Think back to the HTML `<font>` tag. The body of the `<font>` is where you put text to which you wish to apply a particular font. Tags with bodies are great for translating content (from, say, HTML to WML), applying formatting, or indicating that a grouping of content should be treated in a special way, as is the case with the HTML `<form>` tag.

Here is an extremely simplified example that illustrates how a tag with a body works. Suppose we need to create a tag that will change a block of text from capital letters to lower case. We'll be creative and call this tag `LowerCaseTag`. Our new tag will have a lot in common with `HelloWorldTag`, but there are a few differences. The first is that `LowerCaseTag` doesn't extend from `TagSupport`, rather from `BodyTag-Support`. The formula is elementary: if your custom tag doesn't have a body or will include just its body verbatim, it should either implement the `Tag` interface or extend its utility class, `TagSupport`. If, however, your tag will modify or control its body, it needs to implement `BodyTag` or extend its utility class called `BodyTagSupport`. We'll cover several additional examples of both types in the next chapters.

3.5.1 LowerCaseTag handler

Here is the code for our LowerCaseTag handler class:

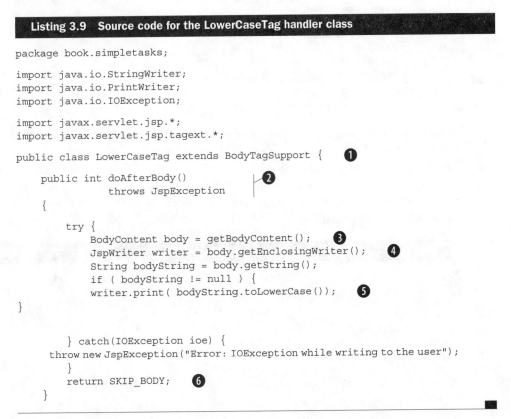

Listing 3.9 Source code for the LowerCaseTag handler class

```
package book.simpletasks;

import java.io.StringWriter;
import java.io.PrintWriter;
import java.io.IOException;

import javax.servlet.jsp.*;
import javax.servlet.jsp.tagext.*;

public class LowerCaseTag extends BodyTagSupport {      ❶

    public int doAfterBody()            ❷
              throws JspException
    {
        try {
            BodyContent body = getBodyContent();        ❸
            JspWriter writer = body.getEnclosingWriter();   ❹
            String bodyString = body.getString();
            if ( bodyString != null ) {
            writer.print( bodyString.toLowerCase());    ❺
}

        } catch(IOException ioe) {
    throw new JspException("Error: IOException while writing to the user");
        }
        return SKIP_BODY;       ❻
    }
```

❶ **BodyTagSupport is an abstract class which is part of the JSP tag APIs.**
❷ **The method doAfterBody() is executed by the JSP runtime, once it has read in the tag's body.**
❸ **Retrieves the body that was just read in by the JSP runtime.**
❹ **Gets JspWriter to output the lowercase content.**
❺ **Writes the body out to the user in lowercase.**
❻ **Returns SKIP_BODY is returned to tell the JSP runtime to continue processing the rest of the page.**

With the tag handler class written, the next step is, once again, to create a TLD. This time our tag entry looks like this:

Listing 3.10   Tag entry for LowerCaseTag

```
<tag>
    <name>lowercase</name>
    <tagclass>book.simpletasks.LowerCaseTag</tagclass>
    <bodycontent>JSP</bodycontent>
    <info>
        Put body in lowercase.
    </info>
</tag>
```

The only difference in this listing is that the `<bodycontent>` field is no longer empty but now must be JSP. This is the way to indicate to the runtime that `Lower-CaseTag` will have a body, unlike our `HelloWorldTag` that did not. There will be much more about bodycontent and other TLD fields in chapters 5 and 6.

We have returned to the stage where we need to use this new tag in a JSP file. Our JSP looks like this:

Listing 3.11   A JSP file to drive the LowerCaseTag

```
<%@ taglib
    uri="http://www.manning.com/jsptagsbook/simple-taglib"
    prefix="jspx" %>
<html>
<title>LowerCaseTag </title>
<body>
<jspx:lowercase>

I've got friends in low places.</jspx:lowercase>
</body>
</html>
```

❶

❷

❶ Declares that the JSP file uses the library referenced by the URI and that the library's tags are referenced by jspx.

❷ Uses the lowercase tag to change its body to lowercase.

Now we add our tag to our deployment directory, pull up the JSP in our browser (figure 3.4), and voila!

This tag doesn't do anything especially useful, however it is always possible to modify it to do something worthwhile with the body. Some examples might include the body as the message of an email, translating the body from one markup language to another, or parsing the body of XML and outputting certain nodes or attributes. In the next chapters, we'll see how the body of a custom tag can include other custom tags to allow cooperation with very powerful results.

3.6   *Summary*

What are custom tags? Why use them? Custom tags are unique JSP components that make it easy to integrate portions of Java logic into a JSP file in an easy-to-use, well-recognized format. Custom tags also answer to well-known API and life cycle definitions (to be discussed in chapter 4) that make it clear how tags behave in any development or runtime environment.

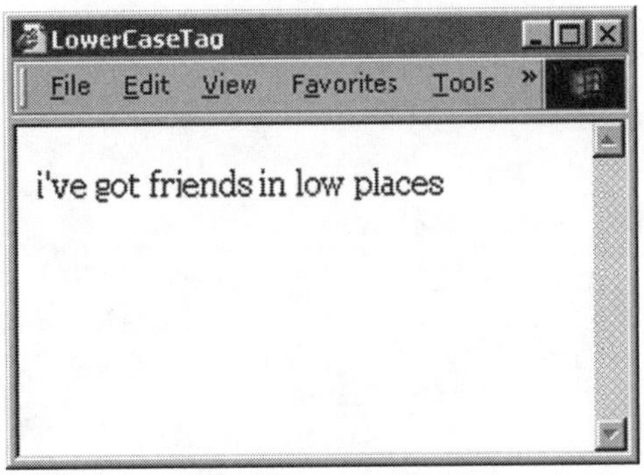

Why use custom tags? Custom tags represent a great way to separate the business logic and presentation, thus

Figure 3.4   Output generated using the lowercase tag driver JSP

enhancing manageability and reducing overall maintenance costs. Another benefit is their ease of use. By using tag syntax, many of the scriptlets and other portions of Java code associated with the classic JSP programming are no longer needed, and the JSP development can be opened to content (commonly, HTML) developers.

We also discussed the mechanics related to tag development, and saw that it is not so difficult to develop simple, but useful, tags.

This chapter provided a solid foundation for you to start developing custom JSP tags. It presented four important tools that you will use in your daily tag development:

- How to configure a simple (and free) development environment with which you can compile and test your tags.
- How to develop, compile, and test simple tags using this development environment.
- How to write a TLD file to describe your tag's runtime behavior and attributes.
- How to package your tag library in a distributable .jar file.

If you have a lot of questions at this point, that's good. We've only lightly touched on many of the nuances of tag development in order to help you get started right away. In the next chapters, we will dive in and explore more fully each of the topics presented here.

Custom JSP tag API and life cycle

4

While an aerial view is all encompassing, there is nothing like a walking tour to get a clear sense of the landscape, to learn the environment close at hand. In the previous chapter, in our aerial view, we used doStartTag() throughout our examples, but didn't discuss what it does or why we chose to use it. In the narrower scope of this chapter we discuss all the methods in custom JSP tag handlers, how they are called, the processes that call them, and when.

This chapter concentrates on two important topics in tag development: the JSP custom tag API and the life cycle of a tag. These topics can be thought of as sets of rules that answer the all important what, when, why, and how of creating custom tags. We saw in chapter 3 that building your own tags requires the use of special interfaces, classes, and methods that exist specifically for tag building. These classes, interfaces, and methods make up what is known as the JSP custom tag API, which we will call custom tag API. Similarly, the developers of your JSP runtime engine also need a set of rules specifying how their product is to run your custom tags. The rules dictating a tag's role, once it's deployed to a JSP engine, constitute the custom tag life cycle. A working knowledge of both sets of rules (the custom tag API and tag life cycle) is crucial for building reliable, predictable web applications that contain custom tags.

This chapter strives to make the rules come alive for you. To do so, we walk through the methods classes and interfaces that comprise the custom tag API and examine the tag life cycle in detail. By the end of this chapter you will have a solid, working knowledge of all the building blocks you need to confidently construct custom tags.

NOTE The concepts discussed here are formally presented in Sun's JSP specification.[1] Though most of this chapter focuses on version 1.1 of the specification, at the time of our publication version 1.2 was nearing its final draft. Therefore, we'll finish the chapter by discussing the changes this new version proposes and how they affect tag development.

We'll begin our discussion by talking about the goals of custom tags.

4.1 Requirements of custom tags

To understand what the custom tag API and life cycle are, it is helpful to know the requirements they were designed to support. The needs of tag developers who use

---

[1] This specification can be found online at http://java.sun.com/products/jsp/. For JSP 1.1, custom tags are described in chapter 5, "Tag Extensions."

custom tags are actually pretty straightforward—we want to be able to write code, create a tag that uses that code, and then embed those tags in logical places throughout our web pages. The latter part of this statement makes an obvious but important point, which is that these tags will be used in web applications. Hence, tags must be able to perform all the tasks we'd expect in a web application, such as reading post and query string parameters, redirecting a client browser, using cookies, and so forth. Tags also need to be able to cooperate with one another in order to create single-purpose tags that can be combined to produce complex solutions. The ability of tags to interact with the JSP content in which they are embedded is also a necessity in order for them to read state from and write results to their environment. Let's reiterate for clarity:

- Tags should make it possible to reference complex code via simple tag syntax.
- Tags should allow us to perform tasks associated with web applications (such as reading parameters, cookies, redirecting, etc.) in a simple way.
- Tags should be able to cooperate with one another and share information.
- Tags should be able to read information from and write information to the JSP content in which they are embedded.

Perhaps the ultimate goal of custom tags is to have all the power and flexibility that free-standing Java code has in a JSP, but without the messiness of mixing Java and HTML. In order to accomplish these goals, the authors of the JSP specification needed to answer several questions:

- How does the JSP environment know the identity of the tags and the handler classes implementing them?
- How does the JSP environment know the attributes allowed for a specific tag?
- How does a tag handler interact with a JSP page?
- How does a JSP page interact with a tag handler?
- How do tag handlers interact with each other?

Solutions to these and other questions were agreed upon and made available in version 1.1 of the JSP specification. There are four elements of the JSP specification in particular that address the use of custom tags. They are:

1   A special JSP custom tag API that all tags must obey (e.g., all tags must implement the `Tag` interface)
2   A strict life cycle and programming model for the tags
3   The Tag Library Descriptor (TLD), which maps tag names to handler classes and provides tag-based syntactic information

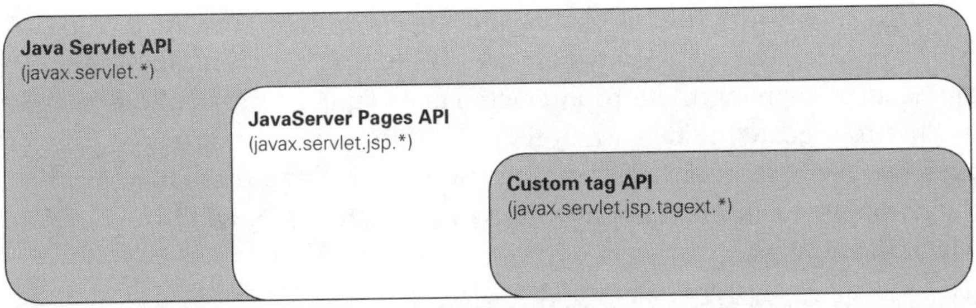

Figure 4.1 The Servlet, JSP, and Custom tag APIs

4   An extension to the web application deployment descriptor making it possible to point to the tag libraries used within the web application

In this chapter we'll discuss the custom tag API and life cycle (elements 1 and 2). Elements 3 and 4, the TLD and web deployment descriptor, are covered in chapter 5.

4.2   *Overview of the tag API*

The first stop on our walking tour is the custom tag API. The API is actually a small collection of Java classes and interfaces that allows developers to build their own custom tag libraries. The key definitions made by the API include:

1   How a tag should look to the JSP environment.
     In other words, the methods a tag exposes to the JSP runtime.

2   What the JSP environment looks like to a tag.
     In other words, the methods and objects the JSP runtime makes available to tags.

Judging from its role, you might expect the custom tag API to be huge, but it is not. The number of classes and interfaces directly related to custom tags is surprisingly small. In JSP1.1 there are only two interfaces and nine classes in the Java package containing the custom tag API (`javax.servlet.jsp.tagext`). These classes and interfaces are listed in tables 4.1 and 4.2. We can accomplish so much with so few classes because many of the classes and interfaces we use during our development actually belong to the much broader JavaServer Pages API, which is itself a part of the broader-yet Java Servlet API (see figure 4.1). Tasks commonly performed by tags, such as reading HTTP parameters, modifying cookies, using the `Session`, and writing content to a response are actually supported by classes and interfaces in these higher level APIs.

What then is the role of classes and interfaces that are part of the custom tag API? The interfaces we'll study here act as contracts between the JSP engine and the tag handler, enabling them to interact. They define all the methods the JSP engine will use to execute the tags when they are found within a particular page. The nine classes in the custom tag API serve a variety of purposes that range from describing the components in a tag library to providing interaction with the environment in which the tags live.

Table 4.1   The interfaces in the Custom tag API (Package `javax.servlet.jsp.tagext`)

Interface Name	Description
Tag	The interface all tags must implement. Defines all the methods the JSP runtime engine calls to execute a tag.
BodyTag	Extends the `tag` interface and defines additional methods that enable a tag handler to inspect and change its body.

Table 4.2   The classes in the Custom tag API (Package `javax.servlet.jsp.tagext`)

Class	Description
BodyContent	A `JspWriter` subclass that provides the tag handler with methods to read and manipulate its body.
BodyTagSupport	A convenience class that provides default implementations of the methods in the `BodyTag` interface.
TagAttributeInfo	Contains information about attributes for a tag. Based on information in the TLD.
TagData	Contains the values for tag attributes.
TagExtraInfo	Specifies extra information about a tag such as the scripting variables it introduces, or how attributes are validated.
TagInfo	Information about a specific tag within a library. Based on information in the TLD.
TagLibraryInfo	Represents the information in a particular tag library's TLD.
TagSupport	A convenience class that provides default implementations of the methods in the `Tag` interface.
VariableInfo	Contains information about the type and scope of scripting variables that are created and/or modified by a tag handler.

At the heart of this API is an interface called `Tag`. All tag handlers must implement this interface. The `Tag` interface contains several methods used by the JSP runtime engine to initialize, activate, and prompt the tag handler to do its work. Table 4.3

shows these methods and a brief description of each. We'll explore each of these methods in detail in the following sections.

Table 4.3   The `Tag` interface and its methods

Method name	Description
setPageContext(PageContext pc)	Called by the JSP runtime to set the PageContext for this tag. This gives the tag handler a reference to all the objects associated with the page it is in.
setParent(Tag t)	Called by the JSP runtime to pass a tag handler a reference to its parent tag (if it has one).
getParent()	Returns a Tag instance that is the parent of this tag.
doStartTag()	Called by the JSP runtime to prompt the tag handler to do its work and indicate (via return value) what the engine runtime should do next.
doEndTag()	Called by the JSP runtime when it reaches the end mark of a tag to allow it to do additional work and indicate (via return value) what to do next.
release()	Called by the JSP runtime to prompt the tag handler to perform any cleanup necessary before it is reused.

Some tags need to be able to inspect their bodies and make changes to them before they're included in the JSP's response to the user. These tags implement an interface called `BodyTag` (which itself extends from `Tag`), and offer extra methods to facilitate body manipulation. In addition to the methods in table 4.3, `BodyTag` includes those in table 4.4.

Table 4.4   `BodyTag`'s additional methods

Method name	Description
setBodyContent(BodyContent bc)	Called by the JSP runtime to set a BodyContent object for this tag. This gives the tag handler access to its processed body.
doInitBody()	Called by the JSP runtime to prompt the tag handler to perform any needed initialization before processing its body.
doAfterBody()	Called by the JSP runtime after it reads in and processes a tag's body to prompt the tag handler to perform any inspection or modification of the processed body.

Both the `Tag` and the `BodyTag` interface have convenience classes that are also part of the custom tag API. These convenience classes, `TagSupport` and `BodyTagSupport`, offer default implementations of `Tag` and `BodyTag` interfaces (respectively) and facilitate the writing of a tag handler. Most tag handlers we'll develop extend from one of these convenience classes, rather than implementing all their interface methods explicitly. We've seen examples of these tag handlers in chapter 3, and will see many more in the coming chapters.

Seven more classes round out the custom tag API (table 4.2). At least one of them, `BodyContent`, will be recognizable from chapter 3. `BodyContent` is a class that represents the processed body of a tag and offers methods for reading this body and writing back to it. The complete method list for `BodyContent` can be found in table 4.5.

Table 4.5   The key methods in `BodyContent`

Method name	Description
`clearBody()`	Wipes out the current contents in this instance.
`getReader()`	Gets a `Reader` for the contents of this instance.
`getString()`	Gets the contents of this instance as a String.
`writeOut(Writer writer)`	Writes the contents of this instance to a `Writer` object.
`getEnclosingWriter()`	Returns the `JspWriter` that encloses this instance. This is the writer we use to write back to the tag's body.

The `TagLibraryInfo`, `TagInfo`, and `TagAttributeInfo` classes are of little importance to you as a tag developer, and you will rarely have to interact with them. They are mostly used by the JSP runtime engine and serve to represent the information contained in a library's TLD file. Thus, the `TagLibraryInfo` class represents and offers access methods for the high-level information in an entire tag library. `TagInfo` represents and allows access to the information in the TLD regarding a particular tag, while the `TagAttributeInfo` class represents individual tag attributes.

The three remaining classes in the custom tag API, `TagExtraInfo`, `VariableInfo`, and `TagData` will be discussed along with more advanced tag development in later chapters. For now, it's enough to know that we'll need to use these classes if our tag is to introduce new scripting variables into a JSP, or if we want to provide some precise validation of a tag's attributes. Both of these features are very useful and come in handy in any significant custom tag library and are, therefore, covered in great detail in chapters 6 and 8.

The single most important component of the custom tag API is the `Tag` interface. This interface is so vital because every tag handler you create must implement it. In addition to learning the methods of this interface (and what they do), you need to know when and how the JSP runtime will call them. These topics comprise the next two sections.

4.2.1 *Tag interface*

The `Tag` interface defines several methods that are called by the JSP runtime during a page request. The tags you develop will implement, sometimes indirectly, all of these methods in order to perform their various functions (sending email, querying a database, etc.) when the runtime engine calls upon them. To start, let's look at the `Tag` interface in detail. Listing 4.1 shows the full source code for the `Tag` interface.

> **Listing 4.1   The Tag interface**

```
package javax.servlet.jsp.tagext;
import javax.servlet.jsp.*;

public interface Tag {

    public final static int SKIP_BODY = 0;
    public final static int EVAL_BODY_INCLUDE = 1;
    public final static int SKIP_PAGE = 5;
    public final static int EVAL_PAGE = 6;

    void setPageContext(PageContext pc);

    void setParent(Tag t);

    Tag getParent();

    int doStartTag() throws JspException;

    int doEndTag() throws JspException;

    void release();
}
```

Understanding the `Tag` interface is extremely important, so we will walk through each method in it.

setPageContext() method

The first method in the `Tag` interface is `setPageContext()`. This method takes, as its single parameter, an instance of the `PageContext` class. `PageContext` primarily provides the tag developer with access to the JSP runtime in which it is executing. You may recall that in chapter 3 we called `pageContext.getOut()` to get a reference to the JSP's `JspWriter` with which we wrote HTML to client. There are several other methods in this class which perform functions such as retrieving the servlet response or request object, or setting variables into the JSP scope. The `PageContext` was originally introduced to promote portability among JSP environments. In chapter 6, `PageContext` is covered in detail; for now it is sufficient to understand that each and every executing JSP has its own `PageContext` instance which provides custom tags with a regulated interface into the current page. The `setPageContext()` method, therefore, is used by the runtime to pass the current `PageContext` into a tag so that the tag may reference it later.

setParent() and getParent() methods

The next two methods in the `Tag` interface are `setParent()` and `getParent()`. First, we'll need to provide background by looking at the important issue of tags that contain other tags (commonly called nesting). Consider the following JSP code fragment:

```
<jspx:dbaccess>
    <jspx:wdbcon id="con1"/>

    <jspx:wjitdbquery>
        select reserves from account where id='<%= userid %>'
    </jspx:wjitdbquery>

You have <jspx:wdbshow field=" reserves "/>$ in your saving account.
</jspx:dbaccess>
```

As you can see, some of the tags are enclosed (nested) within the bodies of other tags. For example, in the above fragment `<jspx:wdbcon>` is enclosed within `<jspx:dbaccess>`. Tags are nested in this way so that they may cooperate with one another. An outer tag will often contain state information and variables that will be accessed and/or modified by an inner tag. In such inclusion relationships, the outer tag is considered the *parent* of the inner tag. The example above provides a scenario in which a parent tag holds all the information about a particular database query while child tags create the database connection, specify the structured query language (SQL) query, and extract a particular field from the query's results. The nested tags cooperate by storing and reading values (such as the database connection, the query results, etc.) in their common parent. This type of cooperation is very useful in tag development, as we'll see in several examples in later chapters. To facilitate nested tags, the JSP runtime passes each tag a reference to its parent via the tag's `setParent()` method. For tags that are not nested, and therefore don't have a parent, their parent is just set to `null`. The `getParent()` method can later be used to retrieve the value passed to `setParent()`.

doStartTag() method

One of the key methods is `doStartTag()`, in which the tag performs its unique logic. When the JSP runtime engine calls this method, it is a cue to the tag handler that the engine has reached the custom tag within a JSP and the tag should now do its work. It isn't the first method that's called on the tag (as we'll learn in our discussion of the tag life cycle), but if we think of a tag as an alias for a block code, then `doStartTag()` begins execution of that code block. In chapter 3 we saw this method in action with several examples that wrote some contents back to the user within it. Those examples, however, merely scratched the surface of what can be done in `doStartTag()`. When called, the tag handler is given an opportunity to run any Java code we wish and to respond to the user with any content we choose (or, perhaps, none at all). This method also offers an opportunity to control what the JSP runtime does after reading the tag. We exercise this control by specifying different return values from the method.

To illustrate, consider a typical case in which the JSP page execution path brings it to a custom tag. The runtime first calls `setPageContext()` and `setParent()` and then calls `doStartTag()`. When `doStartTag()` is called, the tag is notified that its moment has arrived and it can now perform its work. Most often, the tag executes some business logic and writes the outcome of that logic back to the user. Once this business logic is complete, the tag has the ability to control what happens next. Its options are:

- Tell the JSP runtime to ignore the tag's body and therefore not return it to the user. This is done by returning `SKIP_BODY` from the method. Tags that don't have a body at all, such as `HelloWorldTag` from chapter 3, always return `SKIP_BODY`. Tags containing a body may also want to return `SKIP_BODY` based on the result of some business logic. An example might be a tag that includes text about special offers for repeat customers. In this case, the tag could determine through a query if the user requesting the page has placed a previous order and, if not, return `SKIP_BODY` so that they don't see the offer.

- Tell the JSP runtime to evaluate the tag's body as standard JSP and then return it to the user. This is accomplished by returning `EVAL_BODY_INCLUDE` from the method. In the example of the special offer tag, `doStartTag()` would return `EVAL_BODY_INCLUDE` for customers who had placed a previous order. Remember here that the body is processed by the JSP engine, so we could include any standard JSP syntax in the body (including other tags) and it would be evaluated before returning to the user.

- Tell the JSP runtime that it is going to inspect the body and possibly modify it. We will discuss this option later.

Our discussion of a tag's life cycle will illustrate these control flow options again with a helpful diagram to clarify these concepts.

doEndTag() method

The `doEndTag()` method, like `doStartTag()`, is one of the methods of a tag in which it performs its unique logic. As with `doStartTag()`, its name indicates when it will be called; in this case, when the end of a tag is reached. For tags without a body (`<jspx:wdbshow field="reserves"/>`), this means it is called when the trailing backslash ("/") is reached. For tags with a body, this method is called when the close tag is encountered (i.e., `</jspx:dbaccess>`). By calling `doEndTag()`, the JSP runtime is notifying the tag that its processing is complete, and that the runtime is about to continue processing the rest of the page. However, it may be that at this point the tag would prefer to have the page terminate instead of continuing its execution. For example, a tag implementing an abort semantic, or a tag whose job it is to redirect the user to another URL, would not want the page to continue its execution when the tag's execution is complete. Like `doStartTag()`, `doEndTag()` indicates to the runtime what to do next, based on its return value. Its options are:

- Tell the JSP runtime to continue evaluating the rest of the page as usual. To do so, `doEndTag()` returns a value of `EVAL_PAGE`.
- Tell the JSP runtime to abort the processing of the rest of the page. To do so, `doEndTag()` returns a value of `SKIP_PAGE`.

Again, we will look at `doEndTag()` and its role in tag processing when we discuss tag life cycle.

release() method

The role of `release()` will become clearer after we discuss the tag's life cycle; for now, note that the JSP runtime will call `release()` to allow your tag handler to clean up.

4.2.2 Tag life cycle

After having discussed the `Tag` interface, you should have a better grasp of the rules to follow as a developer in creating a custom tag. Now we look at the rules that dictate what happens to our tag when it is executed. The steps during the tag's execution time from creation to cleanup are collectively known as the life cycle.

The tag's life cycle determines:

- When and how it is created
- When and how it is initialized
- When and how it will perform cleanup
- Its reuse options.

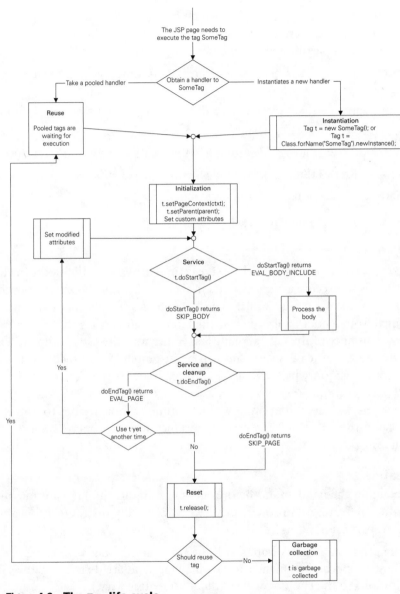

Figure 4.2   The Tag life cycle

In the case of the BodyTag, to be discussed later, it also determines how a tag can take a look at its body.

Figure 4.2 shows a tag's life cycle, which may look a little daunting at first, but after we explain each part in detail it will be much more comprehensible. As you can see, the life cycle is partitioned into phases:

- Instantiation—Takes place when the JSP runtime needs a fresh copy of the tag handler.
- Initialization—Takes place before the tag can be used by the JSP runtime.
- Service—Performs its unique logic.
- Cleanup—Lets the tag clean itself from the state generated during the service.
- Reuse—Reuses the tag handler for further tag executions.
- Garbage Collection—Lets the tag handler go.

Now to examine each phase in detail.

Instantiation

The life cycle story begins with the JSP runtime arriving at the point in the page where it needs to execute a tag (`SomeTag` in figure 4.2). For this execution, the page needs an instance of the tag handler. The JSP specification allows the tag handler to be obtained from a pool of already instantiated tag handlers, or the page can instantiate a fresh instance of the tag handler class. Either way, the JSP runtime will need to instantiate the tag at least once. Tags can be instantiated by executing the default constructor: an action which may happen directly (`Tag foo = new FooTag()`) or indirectly using `Class.forName()` (`Tag foo = (Tag)Class.forName("FooTag").newInstance()`), depending on how the runtime author decides to implement it. In both cases, the final result is a new tag instance whose properties are set to some initial values.

Initialization

After obtaining the handler and before actually using it, the JSP runtime initializes the handler by setting its properties. We can generally distinguish between two types of properties:

- The `pageContext` associated with the page and the tag's `parent`.
  These properties are mandatory with all tags and are dictated by the JSP specification (so the runtime will set them no matter what).
- Custom tag attributes that the JSP runtime set into the handler.
  We saw an example of a custom tag attribute with our `CookieValueTag` in chapter 3. The values of these attributes are specified in the JSP file.

The JSP runtime will set the properties in the following order: pageContext, parent, and last, the tag's custom attributes. When the JSP runtime has finished setting the attributes, the tag instance is considered initialized.

Service

Once the properties are set, the runtime will start executing the tag and will first call the doStartTag() method. As previously stated, doStartTag() grants the tag author an opportunity to execute business logic, print output to the user, save intermediate results in its instance variables, or perform any other useful action the tag author chooses.

When doStartTag() returns, it must specify to the JSP runtime how to proceed. Again, the values it could return are SKIP_BODY (which instructs the page to skip the tag's body) or an EVAL_BODY_INCLUDE (which forces the page to process the tag's body and include it in the content returned to the user). The page will process the body, if so instructed, and eventually it will call the method doEndTag(). Here, after executing any additional business logic, a value of SKIP_PAGE will abort processing and EVAL_PAGE will continue.

Cleanup, reuse, and garbage collection

Upon the return of doEndTag(), the tag should be left in a state such that its reuse is possible. We recommend, in doEndTag(), making sure any instance variables such as database connections, Vectors, and so forth, be reinitialized to the state they were in when the tag was first encountered. This cleanup is needed because one of the rules of the JSP specification is that custom tag instances can be pooled and reused. If we didn't reset all these variables, we would run the risk of our tag producing unexpected results by executing with some leftover state from a past execution. If you're wondering why such a requirement exists for custom tags, look at the following JSP fragment:

```
<jspx:wdbenum>
    <jspx:wdbshow field="NAME"/> ,
    <jspx:wdbshow field="PRICE"/> ,
    <jspx:wdbshow field="TYPE"/> ,
    <jspx:wdbshow field="SERIAL"/>
    <br>
</jspx:wdbenum>
```

With so many tags of the same type in close proximity, it would beneficial for performance reasons if the JSP runtime could decide to reuse the same tag instance for all four <jspx:wdbshow> incidents. In this case, the JSP runtime grabs the allocated tag, initializes it once, and then uses it over and over again. Before each reuse, the JSP runtime must set the modified attributes; therefore, in the JSP fragment in the example, the runtime will need to set the `field` attribute for each of the tag executions (the `pageContext` and `page` attributes remain unmodified).

When the JSP runtime has finished with the tag, it should have the tag clear its properties by calling `release()`. This call signals the tag that the JSP runtime has finished with it (at least for now), and that its internal state should be restored to its original, prior to setting its properties (prior to the call to `setPageContext()` and `setParent()`). When `release()` returns, the JSP runtime assumes that the tag handler state is identical to its state after the execution of the empty constructor, meaning that the JSP runtime has yet another option for reuse optimizations. If the handler is in the same state as it was after the empty constructor, then the next time the JSP environment needs a handler it can use this instance instead of creating one. The JSP runtime can decide to keep the handler in a pool of free tag handles and reuse this tag from the pool the next time one is needed.

You are probably wondering, justifiably, about what to do in `release()` versus what should be done before `doEndTag()` returns. It should be noted that we are looking at two types of tag reuse here, though the differences are subtle. One option is to reuse the tags in their closest proximity by setting only the modified attributes and calling them again. The second option is to pool tags and reuse them over and over again, without releasing them to the garbage collector. Both of these reuse techniques are optional to the JSP runtime vendor, but always program your tags with the assumption that your JSP runtime will reuse your tag aggressively. What this means for most tags is having two cleanup methods: one that is called by `doEndTag()` to clear the tag's private per-invocation state and one that is called by `release()` to return the tag to the state it was in after creation.

4.3   The BodyTag interface and its life cycle

For many tags (such as those which implement iteration), it is important to get a hold of their bodies and manipulate them. We saw an example of this in chapter 3 with the `LowerCaseTag`, which converted any text in its body to lowercase. This section covers the second of our two tag interfaces, `BodyTag`, which offers methods to support these body-changing tags.

4.3.1   BodyTag interface

To fully grasp the `BodyTag` interface, you need to know its goals, which are:

- To provide a tag the ability to obtain its processed body; meaning, to get its JSP body after it is processed by the JSP runtime. A tag often requires access to its body because that content is used to process the tag's logic. An example is a database query tag whose body contains an SQL statement that it must retrieve and use.

- To make it possible for the tag to instruct the JSP runtime to process its body repeatedly until a particular condition is met. An example is a tag that implements looping.

- To support the practice of nesting tags within the bodies of other tags.

Based on the goals of the interface, the solution provided in the JSP specification is rather simple, and it includes the extended BodyTag interface and its extended body life cycle.

The BodyTag interface is presented in listing 4.2.

Listing 4.2   The BodyTag interface

```
import javax.servlet.jsp.tagext.*;
public interface BodyTag extends Tag {

    public final static int EVAL_BODY_TAG = 2;

    void setBodyContent(BodyContent b);
    void doInitBody() throws JspException;
    int doAfterBody() throws JspException;
}
```

A tag that needs to process its body will implement the interface BodyTag, which extends the Tag interface. So, although only some tags implement BodyTag, all tags implement Tag in one way or another. This means that tags implementing BodyTag still have all the same methods we saw in Tag (setParent(), getParent()*set-PageContext(), doStartTag(), and doEndTag()), except that BodyTag introduces a new static return code and three new methods to support body modification. Let's look at these additions in detail.

EVAL_BODY_TAG return code
The BodyTag interface presents a new value to the return code protocol we saw in the Tag interface called EVAL_BODY_TAG. For tags implementing BodyTag, the doStartTag() method should return EVAL_BODY_TAG instead of EVAL_BODY_INCLUDE whenever it needs to process its body (SKIP_BODY can still be returned to skip the body altogether). Returning EVAL_BODY_TAG instructs the JSP runtime that the tag wants to inspect and possibly modify its body. As a result, the JSP runtime will evaluate the tag's body as JSP[2] and hand it over to the tag.

setBodyContent() method

This method is used to pass the tag a reference to its body so it can inspect and possibly modify it. The method takes a single argument of type `BodyContent`, a class that encapsulates all the information we need to know about the body of our tag. `BodyContent` exposes methods that allow reading the tag's body and then writing any changes back to the user. In section 6.6 we cover this more thoroughly.

We should note here that `setBodyContent()` is called only if our tag is going to look at its body; that is, if `doStartTag()` returns `EVAL_BODY_TAG`. If `doStart-Tag()` returns `SKIP_BODY`, there is no reason for the runtime to bother passing the tag its body, since it's simply going to be skipped.

doInitBody() method

This method is called by the JSP runtime to give the tag an opportunity to perform any initialization it requires before the body is evaluated and passed to the tag. This method is a good place to create any necessary objects or set variables to be used during the tag's evaluation and/or modification of its body.

An example will make things clearer. Imagine a tag that takes XML as its body and parses that XML for a few important values to return to the user as HTML. This tag could use `doInitBody()` to create an instance of the XML parser of its choice, as well as initialize any other variables set during parsing. Why not just perform this initialization during `doStartTag()`? The reason we choose `doInitBody()` is because we know it is only called if the body is going to be evaluated; that is, if `doStart-Tag()` has returned `EVAL_BODY_TAG`. So, by placing initialization in `doInitBody()`, we can be assured of incurring only the performance costs of initialization when it is necessary.

doAfterBody() method

With the `doAfterBody()` method, you finally get the chance to look at the tag's body and change it. All of our `BodyTag` initialization and setup led up to this method.

As its name implies, `doAfterBody()` is called after the JSP runtime has read and evaluated a tag's body. What a tag does most often during this method is inspect its body and make changes to it, based on what it sees. As discussed in chapter 3, this process involves getting a reference to the `BodyContent` object, calling `get-String()` on it, and using that string to produce output to the user. Once `doAf-terBody()` has completed its work, it too must indicate to the JSP runtime its next step. It shares the same options for this return value as `doStartTag()`; that is, it can

---

[2] The body of the tag can contain any legal JSP syntax you want (not just text or HTML), which will be interpreted by the JSP runtime. The result of this interpretation will be given to the tag as its body.

return either SKIP_BODY or EVAL_BODY_TAG. If the tag needs to evaluate the body again, it returns EVAL_BODY_TAG, causing the JSP runtime to call doAfterBody() again. This is used most often when a tag wants to repeat its body until a certain condition is satisfied. While the condition evaluates to false, doAfterBody() returns EVAL_BODY_TAG, forcing another processing of the body and a call to itself. Once the condition is satisfied (or if the tag doesn't want to repeat in the first place), doAfterBody() simply returns SKIP_BODY. This instructs the JSP runtime that body processing is complete and to proceed to doEndTag(). We'll provide examples of using the EVAL_BODY_TAG return value for the purpose of iterating with a tag in future chapters, but you can probably think of some useful scenarios already, such as repeating a tag's body for each row in the result set of a query.

To illustrate the order in which the JSP runtime calls the methods in BodyTag, we'll examine the tag life cycle it follows.

4.3.2 *BodyTag life cycle*

The BodyTag life cycle (figure 4.3) is a slightly modified version of the Tag life cycle in which the body-handling portion of the life cycle is extended.

Figure 4.3 provides a visual representation of the body handling steps we've just discussed. All of the additions to the Tag life cycle occur in a new phase we call Body Handling (in gray). This new phase takes place within the previously discussed Service phase. That phase begins when doStartTag() returns EVAL_BODY_TAG, at which point the JSP runtime initializes the tag for body handling by calling setBodyContent() (to pass the body to the tag) and doInitBody() (giving the tag a chance to initialize its state). Once the body handling initialization is complete, the body is processed by the JSP runtime and doAfterBody() is called, allowing the tag to manipulate its body and decide how to proceed. If the tag needs to repeat its body processing phase, it returns EVAL_BODY_TAG and goes another round. If the tag has finished inspecting and/or changing its body, it returns SKIP_BODY to bail out. Once SKIP_BODY is returned, the tag exits from this phase and returns to the last step of the Service phase, calling doEndTag().

4.4 *Tag API classes*

Up to now, we have only discussed the Tag and BodyTag interfaces. This section will cover the classes included in the custom tag API.

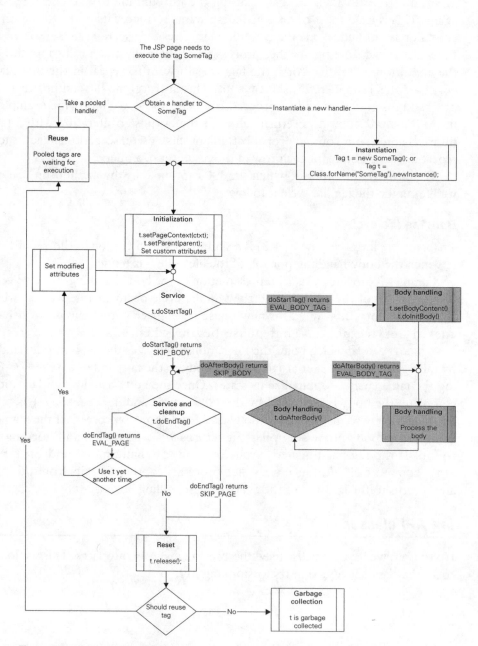

Figure 4.3 The BodyTag **life cycle**

4.4.1 *TagSupport and BodyTagSupport*

All tags must implement the `Tag` interface, and those that want to process their body should implement `BodyTag`. Implementing these interfaces, however, requires a good bit of coding. You will not usually be interested in implementing all of the methods in either interface; for example, consider a tag that returns some content to the user. Such a tag can get by with implementing only `doStartTag()`; none of the other methods of the `Tag` interface are needed, and are therefore something of a nuisance to code. As a result, the custom tag API includes standard basic implementation classes for the `Tag` and `BodyTag` interfaces. `TagSupport` and `BodyTagSupport` classes provide full implementation for all the mandatory tag properties (such as `parent`, `pageContext`, and `bodyContent`) as well as an implementation for a property named `id`, to be discussed later. `TagSupport` and `BodyTagSupport` even provide default implementations for the life cycle methods according to the following rationale:

- Most tags do not need a body, so the default `doStartTag()` implementation returns `SKIP_BODY`.
- Most tags want the page execution to continue, so the default `doEndTag()` implementation returns `EVAL_PAGE`.
- `release()` just clears the mandatory tag properties.
- Empty `doInitBody()`.
- Most body tags do not need to repeat their body execution, so the default `doAfterBody()` implementation returns `SKIP_BODY`.

In our discussion of the `Tag` and `BodyTag` interfaces, we saw many methods new to us, even though we'd already written several tags in chapter 3. We didn't have to worry about those methods because our examples extended these helper classes and inherited their default implementations. Though extending `TagSupport` or `BodyTagSupport` in your tags can save you work, these classes are not mandatory. They have been included in the custom tag API for your convenience, but you may choose not to extend them and to use your own base classes instead, or none at all.

4.4.2 *PageContext class*

The `PageContext` class can best be seen as an interface to all the information associated with a particular page execution. Through it we can access the `Request`, `Response`, and `Session` objects for a request, as well as a `Writer` object with which we can write results back to the user (see chapter 3). `PageContext` also provides access to the `ServletContext` and `ServletConfig` objects associated with a JSP, as well as an `Exception` object if one has been passed to it. If you have written JavaServer Pages before, you'll probably recognize these objects as the implicit objects always available in any JSP (such as request, response, etc.). In addition to providing access to these implicit objects, PageContext offers methods for dispatching page requests and interacting with attributes. Most of our interaction with this class will focus on the accessor methods for implicit JSP objects (table 4.6). Information about additional methods in PageContext can be found in the Java Servlet API documentation at http://www.javasoft.com.

> **NOTE** Technically, PageContext is not a member of the custom tag API. It belongs to the javax.servlet.jsp package, and is used in standard JSP development as well. Its recurring role in our tag development makes it an unofficial member of the custom tag API, however.

Table 4.6 **PageContext's accessor methods for the implicit JSP objects**

Method	Description
getException()	Returns the Exception object passed to this page (for use in error pages).
getOut()	Returns the output Writer for the current page.
getRequest()	Returns the ServletRequest object that initiated this page's processing.
getResponse()	Returns the ServletResponse object associated with this page.
getServletConfig()	Returns the ServletConfig object for this JSP.
getServletContext()	Returns the ServletContext for this JSP.
getSession()	Returns the Session object associated with the current page request.

4.4.3 *BodyContent class*

The BodyContent class serves as a placeholder for the results of the processed tag body. While processing the body of a BodyTag, the JSP runtime writes the results of the processed body into an instance of the BodyContent class. Later on, the tag can use its BodyContent to read the results of the processed body and possibly change them. Once again, we look back to chapter 3 where we saw this class used in our LowerCaseTag example. That example contained code similar to listing 4.3.

Listing 4.3   Using BodyContent

```
BodyContent body = getBodyContent();
String bodyString = body.getString();
JspWriter writer = body.getEnclosingWriter();
writer.write( bodyString.toLowerCase() );
```

This code snippet illustrates two of the most common methods used with Body-
Content:

- getString() simply returns a string containing the tag's body.

- getEnclosingWriter() returns a special instance of the now familiar Jsp-
  Writer class, which we use to write content back to the user.

BodyContent also offers the following methods for use by the tag author:

- getReader() lets the tag read its body using a Reader instead of a string.

- writeOut(Writer out) writes the results held in the BodyContent into some
  Writer object. This method could be used to write the body out to a file, a
  stream, a URL, and so forth.

The methods in BodyContent are fairly intuitive and essentially grant options to the
tag author for reading and writing the tag's body.

4.5   *Tag-related features of JSP 1.2*

Thus far we have discussed the JSP1.1 view of the custom tag API and life cycle,
but JSP1.2 has a few enhancements:

- Adding a new tag interface called TryCatchFinally. This interface provides
  the tag developer with better exception-handling capabilities.

- Adding a new tag interface called IterationTag. This is a cross between Tag
  and BodyTag, in the sense that it lets the developer repeat the evaluation of
  the tag's body over and over again, but does not require the setting of a
  BodyContent object into the tag (and the associated overhead).

- Adding new API protocol return codes (EVAL_BODY_AGAIN and EVAL_-
  BODY_BUFFERED) and deprecating one (EVAL_BODY_TAG) to improve clarity
  and promote tighter control over the body evaluation.

4.5.1   *TryCatchFinally interface*

The tag life cycle as defined in JSP1.1 pays no attention to exceptions. Nowhere will
you see a description of the actions that must be taken in the face of an exception

that is thrown out of the tag handler. However, exception handling is important. When the tags need to clean up and free resources, the interface `TryCatchFinally` provides the much needed exception-handling assistance.

A tag implementing the interface `TryCatchFinally` exposes two methods used by the JSP runtime when the tag's methods or its body throw exceptions:

- `doCatch()` allows the JSP runtime to inform the tag that an exception was thrown while executing it. The tag can then respond to the exceptional condition based on the exception parameter and the general state of the tag.

- The method `doFinally()` is called by the JSP runtime whenever the tag finishes its service phase. This way the tag can free the state it accumulated when serving the request.

We will take a closer look into the `TryCatchFinally` interface when we will deal with the issue of tag cleanup.

4.5.2 *IterationTag interface*

As you will see in chapter 10 when we discuss tag-based iteration, the `Iteration-Tag` interface is an important addition to the `Tag` and `BodyTag`, since it lets the tag developer iterate efficiently on the tag's JSP body.

A tag implementing the `IterationTag` interface provides extended body control via the method `doAfterBody()`. In JSP 1.1, this method was only included in the `BodyTag` interface. To implement iteration, the tag uses this method's return code protocol. You may question why this tag is associated with so much hoopla since it is a mere subset of the `BodyTag` interface (which was already a part of JSP1.1) with some restricted functionality. The answer is simple: the new tag provides a significant gain when performing iterations because, unlike `BodyTags`, the `IterationTag` does not requires double buffering. In chapter 10, we will look at how to achieve this improved performance.

4.5.3 *EVAL_BODY_BUFFERED, EVAL_BODY_AGAIN return codes*

JSP 1.2 introduces new names to the return codes whose role is largely to improve code readability.

NOTE The changes to the return codes were made in a backward compatible manner. Changes were made only to the names of the return codes (such as EVAL_BODY_TAG), and not to the values themselves, meaning that legal JSP1.1 tags should also run in JSP1.2.

JSP 1.2 deprecates the return code `EVAL_BODY_TAG`. In JSP1.1, `EVAL_BODY_TAG` is used in two methods, and in neither is it explicit enough to explain how the tag's body is evaluated. A JSP1.1 tag developer should return `EVAL_BODY_TAG` in the following cases:

- From `doStartTag()` in `BodyTag`, to indicate that the tag's body must be evaluated into a new `BodyContent` that was created for this `BodyTag` execution.
- From `doAfterBody()` in `BodyTag`, to indicate that the JSP runtime should again execute the tag's body.

In both cases, the name `EVAL_BODY_TAG` was found to be confusing; thus JSP1.2 compliant tags should use other named constants as the return codes of the tag's methods.

The problem associated with returning `EVAL_BODY_TAG` from `doStartTag()` is that the variable name (`EVAL_BODY_TAG`) provides no indication that the evaluation will go into a buffer. `EVAL_BODY_INCLUDE`, on the other hand, does indicate that the body is included in the JSP output without buffering, possibly creating confusion for the tag developer. To solve this, JSP1.2 introduced a new member to `BodyTag`, named `EVAL_BODY_BUFFERED`, to replace `EVAL_BODY_TAG` in `doStartTag()`. In order to ensure that tags developed according to JSP1.1 will remain compatible with JSP1.2, `EVAL_BODY_BUFFERED` preserved the value of the old `EVAL_BODY_TAG` (2), allowing tags built according to JSP1.1 to run in a JSP1.2 environment.

The problem with returning `EVAL_BODY_TAG` from `doAfterBody()` is that, again, the name `EVAL_BODY_TAG` is confusing, as it does not indicate explicitly that the JSP runtime will re-evaluate the tag's body. Also, with the introduction of `Iteration-Tag` in JSP1.2, tags can ask the JSP environment to re-evaluate their body, even if these tags are not `BodyTag`s. JSP1.2 solves these problems by introducing a new constant member named `EVAL_BODY_AGAIN` into the interface `IterationTag`. JSP1.2-compliant tags return this value from `doAfterBody()` to ask the JSP runtime to re-evaluate their body. Again, to provide backward compatibility with JSP1.1, `EVAL_BODY_AGAIN` preserves the values of the old `EVAL_BODY_TAG` and, in this way, JSP1.1 tags should be able to run in a JSP1.2 environment.

The addition of the `IterationTag` renders a slight change in the tag life cycle. We will take a look at this change in the next section.

4.5.4 *Updated Tag life cycle*

The JSP1.2 tag's life cycle is almost identical to the JSP1.1 version, except for a few changes attributed to the new return codes and new `IterationTag` interface. This section will address these differences by presenting the life cycle diagrams of the tags, emphasizing the changes made to the life cycle.

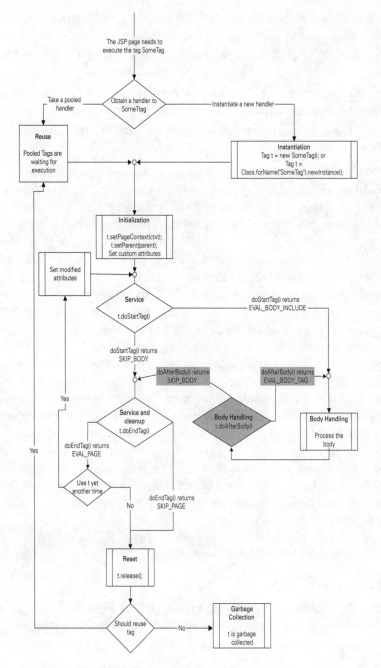

Figure 4.4 The JSP1.2 `IterationTag` life cycle

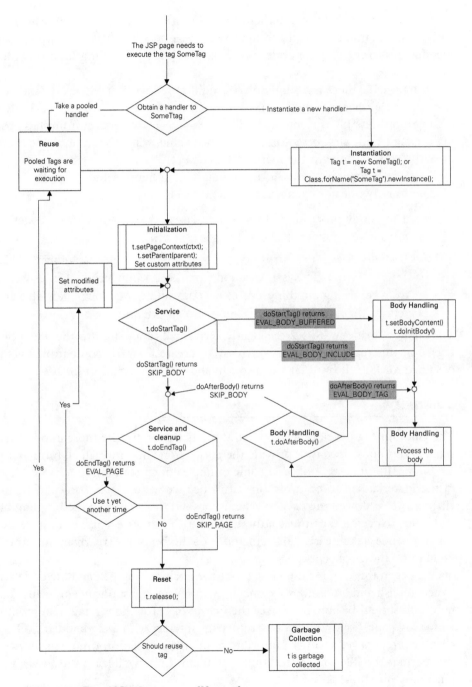

Figure 4.5 The JSP1.2 BodyTag life cycle

Because JSP 1.2 does not include substantial changes to the basic `Tag` life cycle, we'll examine instead the new `IterationTag` life cycle. Figure 4.4 shows the changes to the `Tag` life cycle, as well as the body processing loop provided by the `IterationTag`.

In figure 4.4 there is a single place (highlighted with gray background) where `IterationTag` diverts from the JSP1.1 `Tag` life cycle with a brand new body-processing loop. The JSP runtime will call `doAfterBody()` whenever it finishes processing the tag's body and, based on the returned value, will either re-evaluate the body or skip it and continue to the method `doEndTag()`.

life cycle changes in `BodyTag`, are highlighted in figure 4.5.

There are two major changes to the `BodyTag` life cycle:

1   The body-processing loop now uses the new return codes (i.e., `EVAL_BODY_BUFFERED` and `EVAL_BODY_AGAIN`).

2   If `doStartTag()` returns `EVAL_BODY_INCLUDE`, `BodyTag` behaves like an `IterationTag`. This is a deviation from JSP1.1 in which `BodyTags` were kept from returning anything but `SKIP_BODY` and `EVAL_BODY_TAG`. This change reflects the fact that the `BodyTag` is also an extension of `IterationTag`.

The changes made in JSP1.2 are clearly very small (compared to the life cycle of a tag). For this reason, it is relatively easy to create forward-compatible tags (tags designed for JSP1.1, but that will also run and take advantage of JSP1.2).

4.6   *Summary*

The rules for tag development and runtime behavior are the most important concepts in this book since they provide the cornerstone upon which all future chapters are built. Although we looked at some examples of custom tags in chapter 3, much of the material had to be taken on faith since we were moving so quickly. In this chapter, we've slowed the pace to establish a solid foundation in the building blocks and rules to which tags must adhere. If you're not sure you've mastered every single nuance, take heart. The remainder of the book will reaffirm and gradually build upon these concepts.

We began this chapter thinking about the goals the tag API and life cycle set out to accomplish and, in doing so, came up with several questions needing answers. By now, you should be able to answer the first two, "How does a tag handler interact with a JSP page?" and "How does a JSP page interact with a tag handler?" Our next chapter presents yet another important issue, the translation time behavior of tags that permits the JSP runtime to bond with them. In it, we'll learn the answers to the remaining questions posed here.

Integrating custom tags with the JSP runtime

In this chapter
- Custom tags and the JSP runtime
- The deployment descriptor
- How the JSP runtime works
- Translating a JSP with tags into a servlet

The API and life cycle to which custom tags must adhere are essential guidelines that will serve us every time we build a tag. However, missing from our discussions have been the details of what happens to a JSP after we've written some custom tags and embedded them in that JSP.

As you may recall, before taking requests, a JSP file is actually translated into a servlet, which then serves any HTTP requests made to the JSP file. The time at which the JSP is looked at by the runtime engine, verified for correctness, and output as a servlet, is called *translation* time. The particulars of this translation, and the information we developers must provide the JSP runtime, are the foci of this chapter.

Initially, it may seem that this issue should be of no consequence. After all, both custom tags and servlets are simple Java classes, so wouldn't the translation process simply write a servlet that creates and runs the tags within `service()`? Actually, this is exactly what occurs during translation, but there are a few questions the runtime needs answers to in order to translate the file correctly:

- What are all of the valid custom tags for a page (as opposed to the invalid tags it must reject)?
- What tag handler class is used for a particular tag?
- How is the custom tag syntax validated (for example, which tag attributes are allowed for a particular tag)?

Only after answering these questions will the JSP runtime be able to generate the Java code for the translated servlet.

How then do we provide the runtime with the answers it needs? We've already seen, in chapters 2 and 3, the instrument, the tag library descriptor (TLD) file, that provides these answers. In it, we supply all the necessary information about our tags so that the JSP runtime engine can translate each page in our application flawlessly. This chapter focuses entirely on the translation time semantics and syntax associated with the TLD.

5.1 *Tag library descriptor in a nutshell*

In essence, the TLD (see appendix B) is a simple XML (see appendix A) file containing information regarding JSP tags. The information in a TLD specifies many details regarding a tag or tag library, such as the names of the tags, the handler classes associated with them, and any of their attributes. The best way to start talking about this file is to look at an example. listing 5.1 shows a sample of the structure of the TLD.

Listing 5.1   Sample tag library descriptor

```
<?xml version="1.0" encoding="ISO-8859-1" ?>
<!DOCTYPE taglib
    PUBLIC "-//Sun Microsystems, Inc.//DTD JSP Tag Library 1.1//EN"
    "http://java.sun.com/j2ee/dtds/web-jsptaglibrary_1_1.dtd">

<taglib>
    <tlibversion>1.0</tlibversion>                                          ❶
    <jspversion>1.1</jspversion>
    <shortname>simpletags</shortname>
    <uri> http://www.manning.com/jsptagsbook/simple-taglib </uri>
    <info> A simple sample tag library </info>

    <tag>
        <name>viewError</name>                                             ❷
        <tagclass>book.simpletasks.ExceptionWriterTag</tagclass>
        <bodycontent>empty</bodycontent>
        <info>
            Prints the stack trace of the exception object
        </info>
    </tag>

    <tag>
        <name>formparam</name>
        <tagclass>book.simpletasks.ShowFormParamTag</tagclass>
        <bodycontent>empty</bodycontent>        ❸
        <info>
            Shows a single named FORM parameter
        </info>
        <attribute>                                    ❹
            <name>name</name>
            <required>true</required>
            <rtexprvalue>true</rtexprvalue>
        </attribute>
    </tag>

    <tag>
        <name>log</name>
        <tagclass>book.simpletasks.LogWriterTag</tagclass>
        <bodycontent>JSP</bodycontent>        ❺
        <info>
            Logs information based on the enclosed body content.
        </info>
    </tag>
</taglib>
```

1 **General TLD material, the version of the library, the required version of the JSP specification, and information that can be used by tools such as a short name and informative string**   Each TLD contains the definition of a single tag library. This definition should contain basic tag library information (such as the name of the library and a description for it), as well as one or more tag definitions. The general tag library information contains data that will be of use to library management and JSP development tools, such as short name, informative string, and the like. It also contains the JSP version required for this tag library (e.g., we require JSP1.1 for our sample TLD, but one may require JSP1.2).

2 **Simple tag definition, enclosed within a body of a <tag> and should contain the name of the tag and the handler class**   Following the general tag library information, we can find the tag definitions. Each tag definition must contain at least the tag's name and its implementing handler class. All other tag related data is not mandatory and, when not specified, is given reasonable default values.

3 **Body specification. This particular tag must have an empty body** **4** **Attribute definition, enclosed within the body of an <attribute> and should contain the name of the attribute** **5** **Body specification. This particular tag body contains JSP compliant text**   Other than the obvious name and handler, the tag definition may also contain a declaration regarding the type of body it is willing to accept. For example, in our case we see tags declaring their body as empty, and others declaring that they can have body and that the JSP runtime should consider this body to be JSP (we saw some examples of this in chapter 3). This is also where we specify any of the tag's attributes, and whether or not those attributes will be mandatory or optional.

Since the TLD is an XML file, it begins with a standard XML header specifying the DTD for this document. You needn't understand everything this header is doing; just make sure it's included (verbatim) at the top of every TLD you write. Immediately following this header is the open tag for our tag library definition, `<taglib>`.

5.1.1   *The role of the TLD*

An important lesson from this discussion is that the TLD serves two purposes: (1) It contains information to assist JSP authoring tools which in turn analyze, use, and display this information. (2) It contains all the syntactic data required by the runtime engine during JSP translation. How does the JSP runtime engine use this? In a nutshell, when the runtime translates a JSP file into a Java servlet, it first loads the TLD for each of the tag libraries associated with the page. Next, it parses the TLD and populates a few helper classes with the information contained within the file. Finally, when the runtime encounters a custom tag in the JSP, it consults the data stored in these helper classes, validating the tag's syntax, and creates the Java stubs for the tags.

In figure 5.1 each arrow is numbered according to its order in the process. The steps in that process are:

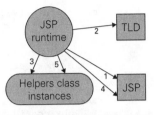

Figure 5.1   JSP runtime use of the TLD

1   The JSP runtime reads a `taglib` directive at the top of the JSP, indicating that this page uses tags and where to find the TLD file for the tag library or libraries it uses.

2   The JSP runtime next locates the TLD and reads all the information about the library from it.

3   The TLD's information is placed in instances of the helper classes.

4   The runtime returns to reading the JSP. When it encounters a tag, it needs to validate its usage, meaning: (1) checking if it is indeed a tag defined in the TLD and (2) whether or not it is used properly (i.e., the tag has valid attributes and proper body type). The TLD also informs it of the tag handler class that implements this tag, in order for it to use that class in the servlet being produced.

5   To validate the tag against the TLD, the runtime can make calls to the in-memory helper objects, instead of referring to the TLD.

NOTE   The JSP specification defines a standard set of helper classes to hold the information extracted from the TLD. These are classes such as: (1) `TagLibraryInfo`, that gives the JSP runtime access to all the information in the TLD (including the library and JSP versions, as well as an array of tags); (2) `TagInfo`, that contains per-tag information (such as the attribute list and the implementing handler class); and (3) `TagAttributeInfo`, that contains per-attribute information. The JSP runtime will instantiate these classes based on the TLD and use them later in the context of the JSP file translation

---

For additional information, such as exact tags that can be used within a TLD and their semantics, see appendix B. There is still one question: how does the JSP runtime know which tag libraries a given JSP uses, and where do you find the TLDs for those libraries? Let's look at a typical JSP fragment to illustrate this question. The example fragment uses two different tag libraries (differentiated by their tag prefix): one for sending email and the other for database access.

```
<html>
I am sending you an email with your account information
```

```
<mail:send server="mail.corp.com"
           from="john.doe@corp.com"
           to="foo@bar.com"
           subject="mail from a tag">
Look at how easy it is to send an email from a tag... here is
your status.

<dbx:access>
    <dbx:con id="con1"/>
    <dbx:query>
        select reserves from account where id='<%= userid %>'
    </dbx:query>
    You have <dbx:show field=" reserves "/>$ in your saving account.
</dbx:access>

</mail:send>
</html>
```

Notice the use of tags like send and access, preceded by the prefixes dbx and mail (respectively). As discussed in our chapter 3 examples, these prefixes are used before the name of a tag as a nickname for the library to which they belong. How do we assign a prefix to a tag library within a JSP? How do we refer to a tag library from a JSP in the first place? The answers to these questions are the topic of the next section.

5.2 *Referencing a tag library from a JSP*

We already know that a JSP must let the runtime know which tag libraries it will be using, but how does it do this? JSP files use a JSP directive called <@ taglib> to indicate which tag libraries they intend to make use of. The syntax for the taglib directive is:

```
<@ taglib uri="unique uri referencing the library"
          prefix="someprefix" %>
```

The taglib directive serves the following goals:

- Declares that the JSP file uses a specified tag library.
- Identifies the TLD for this tag library by referencing it with a unique uri (the uri can either point to the TLD directly or to a tag library section in web.xml that references it).
- Assigns a prefix to all the tags that are part of the library. This provides a namespace for your tags, not unlike Java package names, to prevent name collisions (two or more tags having the same name in different libraries). Thus, when naming your tag, you needn't worry that it will have the same name as a tag in another library, existing HTML tag, XML tag, or any other tagged language's tag.

By using the `taglib` directive we can reference one or more tag libraries from a single JSP. Let's see, in listing 5.2, what the JSP fragment from the previous section might look like when we add the proper `taglib` directives.

Listing 5.2 Sample JSP files with tag library references

```
<%@ taglib
    uri="http://www.manning.com/jsptagsbook/mail-taglib"            ❶
    prefix="mail" %>
<%@ taglib
    uri="http://www.manning.com/jsptagsbook/db-taglib"              ❷
    prefix="dbx" %>

<html>

I am sending you an email with your account information
<mail:send server="mail.corp.com"                ❸
          from="john.doe@corp.com"
          to="foo@bar.com"
          subject="mail from a tag">
Look at how easy it is to send an email from a tag... here is your status.

<dbx:access>            ❹
    <dbx:con id="con1"/>
    <dbx:query>
        select reserves from account where id='<%= userid %>'
    </dbx:query>
    You have <dbx:show field=" reserves "/>$ in your saving account.
</dbx:access>

</mail:send>
</html>
```

❶ Declaring that we are using some tag library referenced by the uri http://www.manning.com/jsptagsbook/mail-taglib and that all tags associated with this library are prefixed with mail.

❷ Declaring that we are using some tag library referenced by the uri http://www.manning.com/jsptagsbook/db-taglib and that all tags associated with this library are prefixed with dbx.

❸ This tag is associated with the mail library by the mail prefix.

❹ These tags are associated with the database library by the dbx prefix.

5.2.1 *The Taglib's uri attribute*

In our discussion of the `taglib` directive we glossed over an important issue: how to know what the `uri` attribute of the directive should be in any given JSP. Earlier, we mentioned that the `uri` usually points to a tag library section in the web application deployment descriptor, but what did we mean by this? To answer, we first need to note that there are two ways we can point to a TLD within the `taglib` directive:

- Directly
  The `uri` attribute must be a relative URI and point directly at the TLD. A relative URI does not begin with a protocol scheme or authority (such as http://), and is relative either to the root directory of the web application (if the `uri` attribute begins with "/" as in /WEB-INF/taglib.tld) or to the current JSP file location (if the `uri` attribute does not begin with a "/" as in tlds/taglib.tld).

- Indirectly
  The `uri` attribute refers to a special `taglib` section in the web application deployment descriptor that in turn points to the TLD. This is the approach we mentioned in the last section. Refer to chapter 2 if you are unsure how a web application deployment descriptor works.

Indirectly referencing a TLD

The direct approach is quite straightforward, since referring to files by their relative URIs is commonplace in web development. The indirect approach is more typical and more involved, warranting a look at it in some depth. To reference the tag library indirectly one must use the `taglib` section in the web application deployment descriptor (the file web.xml) that is structured as follows:

```
<taglib>
    <taglib-uri>
        The uri defined in the <%@ taglib %> directive in
        the JSP file
    </taglib-uri>
    <taglib-location>
        The location of the TLD in the web application.
    </taglib-location>
</taglib>
```

Using the `taglib` section you reference the tag library's TLD.

To see an example of this indirect reference, we will create a web.xml file for a web application that contains the JSP file in listing 5.2. For this example, assume that the TLDs for the mail and database tag libraries are located under the web application root in the /WEB-INF/mail.tld and /WEB-INF/database.tld files, respectively. Based on that directory structure, the web application descriptor should contain the `taglib` sections we see in listing 5.3.

Listing 5.3   Employing two taglib entries that point to two tag library descriptors

```
<?xml version="1.0" encoding="ISO-8859-1"?>

<!DOCTYPE web-app
    PUBLIC "-//Sun Microsystems, Inc.//DTD Web Application 2.2//EN"
    "http://java.sun.com/j2ee/dtds/web-app_2.2.dtd">

<web-app>

    <!-Note: All portions of the deployment descriptor that are
        not a strict part of the taglib sections where removed.
    -->

    <taglib>      ❶
        <taglib-uri>
            http://www.manning.com/jsptagsbook/mail-taglib
        </taglib-uri>
        <taglib-location>
            /WEB-INF/mail.tld
        </taglib-location>
    </taglib>
    <taglib>      ❷
        <taglib-uri>
            http://www.manning.com/jsptagsbook/db-taglib
        </taglib-uri>
        <taglib-location>
            /WEB-INF/database.tld
        </taglib-location>
    </taglib>
</web-app>
```

❶ **First taglib entry, points to the exact location of the mail library tld.**

❷ **Second taglib entry, points to the exact location of the database library tld.**

A sketch of this indirect referencing is shown in figure 5.2. In it, the JSP `taglib` directives reference the appropriate `taglib` sections in web.xml, which in turn point to the precise location of the TLDs.

NOTE   Although it is possible to point directly at the location of the TLD, it is not recommended and this (as well as its simplicity) is partially the reason we did not refer to it at length. Normally, you will have more than one JSP file referencing your tag library in a given web application. With all these JSP files pointing directly to the TLD, if the TLD changes name or location you will have to modify all JSP files instead of a single web.xml file. Referencing the TLD indirectly adds some inconvenience to a quick-and-dirty development, but it makes better sense in the long run.

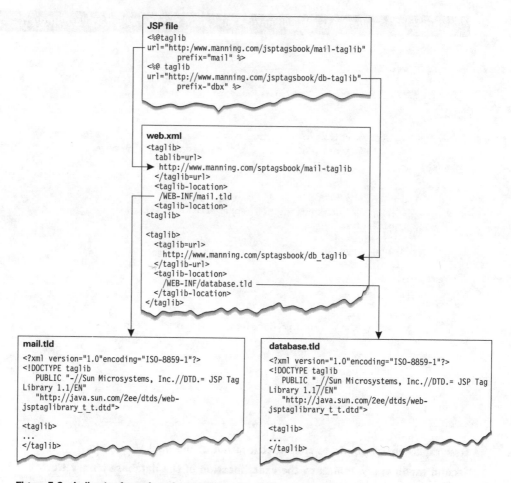

Figure 5.2   Indirect referencing of a tag library descriptor

By now it should be clear how the JSP runtime and the custom tags work together. However, all you have seen so far are small details piling up; that is, how the JSP runtime locates the TLDs, what the methods call sequence is in the tags life cycle, and so forth. You have yet to see a complete case in which the JSP runtime processes a file containing custom tags and eventually executes it. The next section provides such an example.

5.3   *How the JSP runtime works*

We'll now look at each stage in the life of a JSP containing custom tags, from creation through translation and, finally, execution. To present this case, we will use a custom tag that provides email functionality. For a more solid understanding of what the JSP translation process involves, we'll also take a look at the servlet generated by the JSP runtime when it translates our page.

5.3.1   *Send tag example*

The JSP file in listing 5.4 has a very simple goal: to provide users with web-based email-sending service. In our application, the user will be able to write an email using a simple HTML form, as seen in figure 5.3. The contents of this form will be submitted to a JSP page which sends the email to the specified address via a custom JSP tag.

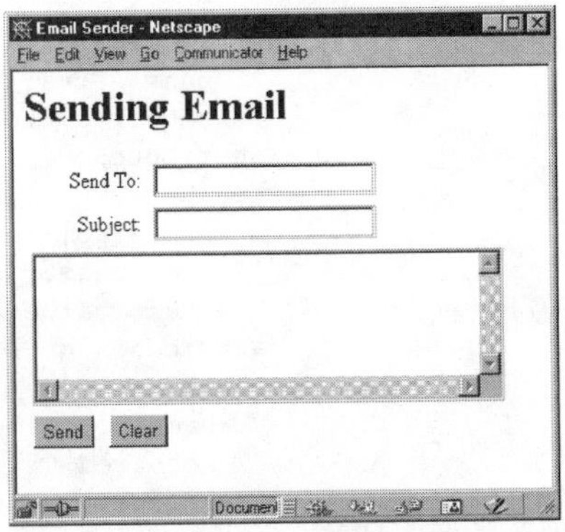

Since it is not the goal of this example to fully develop the email-sending (send) tag, we will take only a cursory look at the attributes associated with this tag and discuss their uses. We will develop and discuss this tag and other, more sophisticated email tags in chapter 7.

Figure 5.3   Form-based interface for the email sender JSP

Understanding the send tag

The send tag is a simple custom tag that supports sending standard email. Everything we need to know about it is provided in its TLD, as presented in listing 5.4:

Listing 5.4   Tag library descriptor for our mail sender tag

```
<?xml version="1.0" encoding="ISO-8859-1" ?>
<!DOCTYPE taglib
        PUBLIC "-//Sun Microsystems, Inc.//DTD JSP Tag Library 1.1//EN"
        "http://java.sun.com/j2ee/dtds/web-jsptaglibrary_1_1.dtd">

<!-- A tag library descriptor for the simple mail tag -->

<taglib>

        <tlibversion>1.0</tlibversion>
        <jspversion>1.1</jspversion>
        <shortname>simplemail</shortname>
        <uri> http://www.manning.com/jsptagsbook/mail-taglib </uri>
```

```
<info>
    A tag library that describes the simple mail tag
</info>

<tag>
    <!-- This tag sends emails. -->
    <name>send</name>
    <tagclass>book.mail.SimpleJavaMailTag</tagclass>
    <bodycontent>empty</bodycontent>
    <info>
        Sends an email based on the provided attributes.
    </info>

    <attribute>
        <name>server</name>
        <required>true</required>
    </attribute>
    <attribute>
        <name>from</name>
        <required>true</required>
        <rtexprvalue>true</rtexprvalue>
    </attribute>
    <attribute>
        <name>to</name>
        <required>true</required>
        <rtexprvalue>true</rtexprvalue>
    </attribute>
    <attribute>
        <name>subject</name>
        <required>false</required>
        <rtexprvalue>true</rtexprvalue>
    </attribute>
    <attribute>
        <name>body</name>
        <required>true</required>
        <rtexprvalue>true</rtexprvalue>
    </attribute>
</tag>
</taglib>
```

You can see from the TLD that the tag is controlled by several attributes which specify the parameters to use when sending the email. These tag attributes are described in table 5.1.

Table 5.1   The mail sender tag attributes

Attribute name	Use	Comments
server	Provides the DNS of the outgoing SMTP server that is used by the tag.	Mandatory attribute, the tag cannot survive without an SMTP server.
from	Provides the email address of the sending entity.	Mandatory. Can be a runtime expression and should be set from the session state (based on some authentication).
to	The destiny of the email.	Mandatory. Should be a runtime expression that flows from the FORM filled by the user.
subject	The mail subject.	Optional. Should be a runtime expression that flows from the FORM filled by the user.
body	The mail body content.	Mandatory. Should be a runtime expression that flows from the FORM filled by the user.

Note in table 5.1 that many of the `send` tag's attributes can be the result of a runtime expression. Instead of hard-coding an attribute's value directly in the JSP file, we can specify a scriptlet. When the JSP is executed, the scriptlet is evaluated (as with any other Java code in the JSP) and the result is passed as the attribute. Specifying attributes in this way offers a great deal of flexibility and is especially useful for this type of application in which the attribute values differ from user to user.

> **NOTE**   All input to our mail program comes from tag attributes, but that this approach isn't always optimal. For example, attributes don't support multi-line values (ones with a carriage return) or those containing characters that ought to be escaped (such as """"). To support more complex values, it is better to pass the information using the tag's body.

Creating the JSP that uses the Send tag

We aren't going to be looking at the code for the `send` tag's tag handler class here, since it is largely irrelevant to our discussion. We will see this code in all its splendor in chapter 7. For now, we'll assume we've written the tag handler as required, and jump right to writing our JSP and the HTML form that will POST to it.

The HTML form should submit three variables to the JSP page:

- the recipient of the email (named as the form parameter `"to"`)
- the subject of the email (named as the form parameter `"subject"`)
- the body of the email (named as the form parameter `"content"`)

These variables will arrive at the JSP file and will be fed into the `send` tag's attributes using runtime expressions (meaning, using scriptlets).

To prevent the user from specifying an arbitrary "from" address for the email, we'll retrieve the user's email address from the session state object (where we assume it is placed when the user logs into our site). Under this design we create the JSP file presented in listing 5.5.

Listing 5.5   JSP file employing the mail sender tag

```
<%@ page session="true" %>        ❶
<%@ taglib        ❷
    uri="http://www.manning.com/jsptagsbook/simplemail-taglib"
    prefix="mail" %>
<html>
<body>

<p>
    Dear <%= session.getAttribute("sender") %> we are now
    sending your email.
</p>

<mail:send        ❸
    server="mail.corp.com"
    from='<%= (String)session.getAttribute("sender") %>'
    to='<%= request.getParameter("to") %>'
    subject='<%= request.getParameter("subject") %>'
    body='<%= request.getParameter("content") %>' />

<p>
    Mail was sent to: <tt><%= request.getParameter("to") %></tt>
    <br>
    Subject was: <tt><%= request.getParameter("subject") %></tt>
    <br>

    Content was: <br>
    <pre>
    <%= request.getParameter("content") %>
    </pre>
</p>
</body>
</html>
```

---

❶ Informs the JSP runtime that we are going to use session state in this page.

❷ References the simple mail library. This is clearly an indirect reference.

❸ Uses the `send` tag. Note how all the information is provided via the attributes.

Deploying the JSP

Now it is time to deploy the JSP file. As in chapter 3, deploying the JSP file includes the following tasks:

- Copying the JSP file to the appropriate location in the web application.
- Copying the tag to a place where it is accessible to the web application class loader. For example, if the tag is wrapped inside some jar file, copy the jar file to the WEB-INF/lib directory of the web application.
- Copying the TLD so that it will be accessible in the context. For example, copy the TLD file to the WEB-INF directory.
- Updating the deployment descriptor (web.xml) to include a reference to the TLD associated with the tag library.
- Restarting the application so that changes in the deployment descriptor will take effect.

5.3.2 Translating the JSP into a servlet

After deploying the JSP file, we can actually access it by submitting an email from the form. The JSP runtime will translate our JSP into a new servlet and then compile it. This occurs when the JSP is requested for the very first time, which means the first time we submit the HTML form.[1]

Translation of static content

When a JSP is translated, the runtime engine opens a new file to which it will write the servlet source code. The first things it writes to this new servlet source include all the Java import statements the servlet will need, the first line of the servlet class definition, and a few lines of code to initialize the JSP implicit objects (see chapter 2). With this information in place, the runtime engine begins reading the JSP and translating its contents into Java code in the servlet. For static JSP content, the conversion between JSP syntax and Java servlet code is straightforward and intuitive. Static content within a JSP, whether it is HTML, WML, or another language, is simply translated into a familiar `out.write("")` statement within the servlet (see figure 5.4).

---

[1] Some JSP runtime engine vendors offer the ability to precompile your JSPs, but in most cases the JSP is not compiled until the server receives its first request for it.

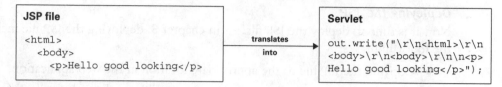

Figure 5.4   Static content translated from a JSP to servlet code

Translation of scriptlets

For scriptlets that appear in a JSP, the translation process is even simpler. The runtime engine takes the Java code within the scriptlet tags (`<%` and `%>`) and copies it verbatim into the servlet. See figure 5.5 for an example.

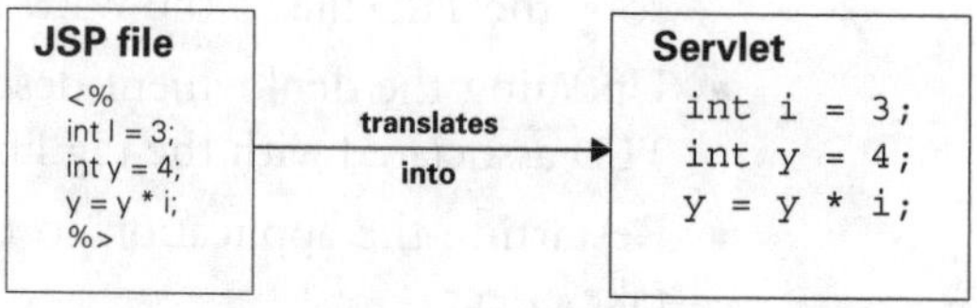

Figure 5.5   Scriptlets translated from JSP to servlet code

Translation of custom tags

Both scriptlets and static content offer fairly obvious syntax translations from a JSP to a servlet, but are custom tag translations so simple? Translating a custom tag from its JSP syntax to servlet code is trickier, but it makes perfect sense when looked at closely. What then are the steps that take place when the runtime engine translates a tag-bearing JSP? When translating the file to a servlet, the JSP runtime will first inspect the `taglib` directive at the beginning of the file and determine from its `uri` attribute which tag library to use. It then looks for a matching `taglib` entry inside web.xml, finds it, and extracts the location of the actual TLD. Once the TLD is known, the JSP runtime reads its content and uses it to create the appropriate helper classes (merely Java objects that represent the information in the TLD). For each custom tag that the runtime finds within the JSP, it refers to the helper classes to determine whether a particular tag name is valid for this library, what handler class implements the tag, and what attributes the tag allows. The runtime engine uses this information to decide which handler class to create within the servlet it is producing, and which methods to call on the handler. Perhaps the best way to understand what happens to a tag when it is translated is to look line by line at an example, such as the one in listing 5.6.

Listing 5.6   JSP file employing the send tag

```
import javax.servlet.*;
import javax.servlet.http.*;
import javax.servlet.jsp.*;
```

```
import javax.servlet.jsp.tagext.*;
import java.io.PrintWriter;
import java.io.IOException;
import java.io.FileInputStream;
import java.io.ObjectInputStream;
import java.util.Vector;
import org.apache.jasper.runtime.*;
import java.beans.*;
import org.apache.jasper.JasperException;

public class mailsender
    extends HttpJspBase {

    private static boolean _jspx_inited = false;

    public final void _jspx_init() throws JasperException {
    }

    public void _jspService(HttpServletRequest request,
                            HttpServletResponse  response)
        throws IOException, ServletException {

        JspFactory _jspxFactory = null;
        PageContext pageContext = null;
        HttpSession session = null;
        ServletContext application = null;
        ServletConfig config = null;
        JspWriter out = null;
        Object page = this;
        String _value = null;
        try {
            if(_jspx_inited == false) {
                _jspx_init();
                _jspx_inited = true;
            }
            _jspxFactory = JspFactory.getDefaultFactory();
            response.setContentType("text/html;charset=8859_1");
            pageContext = _jspxFactory.getPageContext(this, request, response,
                                                "", true, 8192, true);

            application = pageContext.getServletContext();
            config = pageContext.getServletConfig();
            session = pageContext.getSession();
            out = pageContext.getOut();

            out.write("\r\n");
            out.write("\r\n<html>\r\n<body>\r\n\r\n<p>\r\n     Dear ");
            out.print( session.getAttribute("sender") );
        out.write(" we are now \r\n     sending your email.\r\n</p>\r\n\r\n\r\n");
                        /* ----  mail:send ---- */
            book.mail.SimpleJavaMailTag _jspx_th_mail_send_0 =
                new book.mail.SimpleJavaMailTag();
            _jspx_th_mail_send_0.setPageContext(pageContext);
            _jspx_th_mail_send_0.setParent(null);
```

❶

❷

❸
```
      _jspx_th_mail_send_0.setServer("mail.corp.com");
      _jspx_th_mail_send_0.setFrom( (String)session.getAttribute("sender") );
      _jspx_th_mail_send_0.setTo( request.getParameter("to") );
      _jspx_th_mail_send_0.setSubject( request.getParameter("subject") );
      _jspx_th_mail_send_0.setBody( request.getParameter("content") );

    try {
```
❹
```
      int _jspx_eval_mail_send_0 = _jspx_th_mail_send_0.doStartTag();
      if(_jspx_eval_mail_send_0 == BodyTag.EVAL_BODY_TAG)
          throw new JspTagException("Since tag handler class " +
                                    "book.mail.SimpleJavaMailTag does" +
                                    " not implement BodyTag, it can't "+
                                    "return BodyTag.EVAL_BODY_TAG");
      if(_jspx_eval_mail_send_0 != Tag.SKIP_BODY) {
          do {
              // This is where the tag's body should be.
          } while(false);
      }
      if(_jspx_th_mail_send_0.doEndTag() == Tag.SKIP_PAGE)
          return;
    } finally {
      _jspx_th_mail_send_0.release();
    }

    out.write("\r\n\r\n<p> \r\n    Mail was sent to: <tt>");
    out.print( request.getParameter("to") );
    out.write("</tt>\r\n    <br>\r\n    Subject was: <tt>");
    out.print( request.getParameter("subject") );
    out.write("</tt>\r\n    <br>\r\n    \r\n    Content was: <br>\r\n
<pre>\r\n    ");
    out.print( request.getParameter("content") );
    out.write("\r\n    </pre>\r\n</p>\r\n</body>\r\n</html>\r\n");

  } catch(Exception ex) {
      if(out.getBufferSize() != 0)
          out.clearBuffer();
      pageContext.handlePageException(ex);
  } finally {
      out.flush();
      _jspxFactory.releasePageContext(pageContext);
  }
 }
}
```

❶ Allocates a new tag instance The first segment is allocating a fresh tag instance for the current tag. You probably remember from our previous chapter that the JSP runtime can decide to reuse tags. In this case, however, the JSP runtime (the one bundled with Tomcat 3.2) is not reusing this tag but is creating one.

❷ **Sets the standard tag attributes into the tag** ❸ **Sets the custom tag attributes into the tag** After obtaining a fresh instance of our tag, the JSP runtime is setting the tag's property values. First, the page will set the mandatory `pageContext` and `parent` properties (whose roles were discussed in chapter 4). Later, it will set the tag's custom properties, including the server, from, to, and so forth, using the values specified in the TLD. Note that in runtime expression values, the JSP runtime is setting the current values of expressions and not the string containing them.

❹ **Executes the tag method call protocol according to the life cycle diagram** The last code segment that handles the tag executes the tag's method call protocol. It is interesting to note how the codes returned by the `doStartTag()`/`doEndTag()` pair are scanned for the special protocol return codes, and how the JSP runtime includes/excludes the tag's body and aborts the execution of the JSP page based on these codes. This is where we get to see the API and life cycle in action. It is also interesting to note that since this is not a `BodyTag`, the page will not try to call methods that are associated with the body protocol (such as `doAfterBody()`).

Understanding the servlet source code

Listing 5.6 presents the somewhat beautified source for the servlet generated by Tomcat for the JSP fragment in listing 5.5 (it was autogenerated by the JSP runtime and its coding style required some polishing to make it readable). The area marked in bold is where the JSP runtime placed the code fragment that handles the `send` tag and, as you can see, we've partitioned it into four segments. We will now take a closer look at these segments.

Finally, we see in this example what happens to the tag when the JSP runtime finishes executing it. At this point the tag is recycled to its initial state via a call to `release()`, after which the page is free to pool the tag for further reuse or let it be garbage collected.

If you followed chapter 4 closely, you should be experiencing a real sense of aha! We've dispelled some of the mystery of the JSP runtime by looking under the hood to see the code used to run custom tags. The rather abstract concepts of tag life cycles and the custom tag API become very concrete in this example when we see, in no uncertain terms, the exact order and nature of each method call on a tag handler. This approach, looking at the source code for a JSP-translated servlet, can be very helpful in becoming more comfortable with the runtime behavior of a tag-bearing JSP.

The rest of the autogenerated servlet is not that important to us. The page will simply finish its execution and the resulting content will be written to the requesting user.

5.4 *Summary*

By now you should have a solid grounding in how the TLD helps the JSP runtime validate tag usage, and how you, as a developer, can author a TLD. You also know how the JSP runtime uses the various bits of information in the TLD to translate a JSP into a servlet. We hope our page translation and execution samples have aided you in understanding how custom tags and JSPs are wrapped into a servlet that ends up handling the page requests.

Having covered the guidelines for tag development (API and life cycle) and the ins and outs of the TLD, we have a firm grasp of the ground rules for writing and deploying custom tags. What we've seen so far can be thought of as the language of JSP custom tags; but we have yet to put this language to good use, to learn how we'll speak it in our daily tag development. These topics are the focus of the next part of the book, where we explore some of the common techniques you'll use in your day-to-day tag development, and we build our first real-world tag library.

Part II

Basic techniques

With the foundations for a basic understanding of tag development in hand, it is time to focus on honing these skills to take advantage of all the functionality custom tags can offer. In chapters 6 through 8 you'll learn several common coding techniques that are needed to build a successful tag library, from sending content back to the client browser to writing tags that make use of their body content. In part IV we will showcase these techniques by building two full-fledged tag libraries; one for sending email within a JSP and a second that integrates with JavaBeans.

Tag development techniques

129

Just when you thought you might be able to settle in and start using all your new-found knowledge about writing tags, the custom tag API, and life cycles, you discover that there needs to be something more. Mastering the details of a TLD's anatomy and its role in making tags known to the JSP runtime engine may mean the ability to build and deploy simple tags; unfortunately, as with any technology, knowing the basics will only get you so far. To build tags that can actually make a difference in your projects, you need a few key programming techniques that will prove highly beneficial for most of the tags you build. You can think of these techniques as tools in the toolbox that holds all your tag development knowledge. The tools we discuss in this chapter will be the mainstays in your daily tag construction.

6.1   Reusable tag programming techniques

Once you've tried out the examples in the previous chapters and built some basic tags, you're likely to find yourself in need of additional techniques pertaining to tag behavior, initialization, configuration, and cleanup. It's vital that you know how to reliably write content to the user, pass parameters to tags, and share information between tags. You may also benefit from knowing how to configure an entire tag library via a single application variable, and how to create tags that inspect and modify their body. Of course, after adding all this functionality, you'll have to be able to write your tags in a way that they can be properly cleaned up after the runtime has finished with them. Though these techniques vary greatly, the common theme is that each is a typical component in the construction of a production tag library.

6.1.1   The techniques you'll use most

What kinds of applications will benefit from the techniques in this chapter? Most of them! This chapter covers the programming techniques most commonly used when building a tag-based application. They are:

- Writing content back to the user
- Logging and messaging
- Using tag attributes
- Using the Servlet API
- Configuring tags
- Writing tags that modify or use their body
- Properly cleaning up state after your tag has executed.

Let's discuss these techniques and how they fit into a typical web application.

Writing content back to the user

Almost any web application you build with tags is likely to have at least one tag that performs the task of getting a value and returning it to the user. This value may come from a database, a cookie, another web server, or perhaps an Enterprise JavaBean (EJB). This kind of tag can be used to echo a username, as in "Welcome back, Cole," report a bank balance, or present some other piece of data stored in the database.

Using tag attributes

Sometimes a tag will take a parameter from the JSP author so that it may behave differently under different circumstances. The ability of tags to take parameters (typically made possible by tag attributes) is what makes your tags flexible enough to be reused across projects.

Logging and Messaging

Like any programming project, writing tags will require the ability to log error messages as they occur and propagate them to the developer/administrator.

Using the servlet API

Since JSP custom tags run in the same environment as servlets and JSPs, namely the Web, it is also to be expected that your tags need to interact with the same kinds of web-related information that most servlets and JSPs use. This includes reading from and writing to cookies, looking at HTTP headers, redirecting requests, and so forth. Almost any web application has a need for some of these functions, and web applications built on custom tags are no different.

Configuring tags

When building a web application that uses tags, you might like to configure some aspects of a tag (or group of tags) in a central place, rather than in each and every JSP that uses those tags. We may, for example, wish to build a suite of tags that send email and use a particular mail server to do so. It would, in such a case, be ideal to indicate that server name once in a central place, and allow any JSP that has our email tags to pick up and use that property. This type of configuration, though optional, can often clean up your design and make implementing changes fairly painless. Not all tag libraries will require this kind of configuration, but even most small libraries will have at least one or two settings that would benefit from being configured in a central place.

Writing tags that modify/use their body

For many (if not most) tags, looking at or changing their bodies is not necessary. This tactic is useful for tags that need to take parameters too complex to be passed as attributes, or for tags that want to operate on a block of HTML or text.

Cleaning up

Of all the techniques, learning how to properly clean up after your tags is the most important we'll discuss, since any and all applications should have tags that leave resources and state clean after they've run.

Now that we know what these techniques can do for us, let's look at each technique in detail.

6.2 Writing content back to the user

Returning content from your tags is probably the most widely known technique. Generally, custom tags write a bit of content to the page for the user to see. Though some tags may run without creating any user-visible output, such as a tag that iterates through a set of parameters or exports new beans into the page, the majority of tags will ultimately write text into the response flowing back to the user. We saw three such tags in chapter 3.

To facilitate this requirement, the JSP infrastructure provides tags with a special `Writer` class called `JspWriter`. With this class, a tag can include any text you choose in the web server's response to a user. The advantage of including text in this way is that it appears in the proper place on the page in the user's browser.[1] The methods that are of greatest interest to us in the `JspWriter` are in table 6.1.

Table 6.1 Important methods in the `JspWriter` class

Methods use for printing to the user	Methods used for buffer manipulation
abstract public void newLine()	abstract public void clear()
abstract public void print(boolean b)	abstract public void clearBuffer()
abstract public void print(Object obj)	
abstract public void println()	abstract public void flush()
abstract public void println(Object x)	public int getBufferSize()

---

[1] Much of our discussion in this chapter assumes a classic web application model with a standard HTML browser for a client. It should be mentioned that, like any servlet or JSP, custom tags can return data to anything that issues an HTTP request. This includes WAP browsers, Internet spiders, or any other process that asks the web server for a page.

Table 6.1 Important methods in the `JspWriter` class (continued)

Methods use for printing to the user	Methods used for buffer manipulation
	public boolean isAutoFlush()

As you can see, the `JspWriter` offers the following facilities in addition to those available in the simple `Writer` we already know:

- Print—The original Java `Writer` only supports writing chunks of data from an array. `JspWriter`, on the other hand, adds those methods that usually exist in the `PrintWriter` class. This way you can easily print data (such as `String`, primitive types, and Objects) to the response.

- Buffer manipulation—The output returned by a servlet or JSP typically is buffered. This buffering is implemented by the Servlet/JSP container. The `JspWriter` class provides methods to query the buffer's internal state and to clear its contents.

A tag may obtain a reference to the `JspWriter` to use for output in the current page by calling the method `PageContext.getOut()`.

NOTE   The `JspWriter` returned by `PageContext.getOut()` is not always connected directly to the user. The JSP runtime can use multiple `JspWriters` to collect the output of certain page fragments. For this reason, the returned `JspWriter` may change from call to call; in fact, the JSP engine is holding a stack of `JspWriters` that correspond to the file structure of an individual JSP. The contents of all these individual `JspWriters` are concatenated after the processing and it's that concatenated content that is sent to the user. This is explained in greater detail later in this chapter.

Now, we look at how to use the `JspWriter` to manipulate the response.

6.2.1 *Adding data to the output*

Listing 6.1 shows a code fragment taken from `ShowFormParamTag` which demonstrates writing data to the user.

Listing 6.1 Printing output to the user

```
public class ShowFormParamTag extends TagSupport {

    // Some other code was omitted here.

    public int doStartTag()
```

```
                throws JspException
{
    try {
        HttpServletRequest req =
            (HttpServletRequest)pageContext.getRequest();
        String value = req.getParameter(name);
        if(null != value) {
            writeHtml(pageContext.getOut(), value);          ❶
        }
        return SKIP_BODY;
    } catch(java.io.IOException ioe) {                        ❷
        // User probably disconnected ...
        //log an error and throw a JSPTagException
        //...
    }
}
// Some other code was omitted here too.
}
```

❶ **Performs HTML special tags filtering and writes the output back to the user** Show-
FormParamTag prints the value of a particular form parameter sent by the user, but
for this discussion we've tried to omit all the code that is not directly related to the
actual printing. From this code fragment you can see that the JspWriter is
obtained through a call to pageContext.getOut().

❷ **Handles the ever annoying IOException. Logs the exception and interrupts the JSP
execution by throwing a JSPTagException.**

Writing HTML properly with writeHtml()

You'll note that we are not using the JspWriter directly, as we did in chapter 3.
Instead of calling pageContext.getOut().print(value) we are calling a method
we've written called writeHtml() to print the parameter value to the response.
Why take this extra step? If you look at writeHtml() (listing 6.2) you'll see that it
simply applies the proper escape sequences for special HTML characters such as "<",
">", and "&". The incidents in which we'll need to pass our output through write-
Html() will be those when we aren't sure if the String we are writing to the user
contains any of these special characters. We want to make sure the user reads the
String as it was intended to be; and not allow it to be accidentally interpreted by the
browser as HTML. Consider, for example, a case where our ShowFormParamTag is
being used to echo an individual's username that was just submitted on a previous
form. A malicious user could enter the username as the following:

```
<script>
    alert("this is a big bad virus, the site is not protected!!!")
</script>
```

If we write this username back to the response unescaped, the browser will interpret it as standard Javascript and the user's evil alert message will pop up. By passing the parameter through `writeHTML()` instead, we convert all of the "<" and ">" characters to their escaped equivalents. The user then sees the text they've typed echoed back to them verbatim, instead of the ill-intentioned JavaScript message.

Listing 6.2 The writeHtml() method defined.

```
protected void writeHtml(JspWriter out,
                         String html)
    throws IOException
{
    if((html.indexOf('<') == -1) &&
       (html.indexOf('>') == -1) &&
       (html.indexOf('&') == -1)) {
        out.print(html);
    } else {
        int len = html.length();
        for(int i = 0 ; i < len ; i++) {
            char c = html.charAt(i);
            if('<' == c) {
                out.print("&lt;");
            } else if('>' == c) {
                out.print("&gt;");
            } else if('&' == c) {
                out.print("&amp;");
            } else {
                out.print(c);
            }
        }
    }
}
```

Defining base classes for our tags

Since `writeHtml()` is a useful method to have in any tag that returns content to a user, we'll want to use it in most of the tags we develop. Now is a good time to define a base class for our tags where we can place fuctionality like this. We'll call this class `ExTagSupport` and it will serve as the base for most of our tag examples for the remainder of the book. Throughout the upcoming chapters, we'll add to `ExTagSupport` as we encounter logic that we want inherited by all our tags. For now, `ExTagSupport` will define only one method, `writeHtml()`, and, of course, extend the `TagSupport` utility class. We'll need a base class for our BodyTags which will extend `BodyTagSupport`. We'll call that class `ExBodyTagSupport`. You'll see references to both these classes throughout examples in the remainder of this book.

NOTE We don't need to list `ExBodyTagSupport` separately here because, for now, it is identical in listing 6.3, except for the class name and the fact that it extends `BodyTagSupport` instead of `TagSupport`.

Listing 6.3   Our base class for future tag development: ExTagSupport

```java
package book.util;

import java.util.Enumeration;
import java.io.Exception;

import javax.servlet.ServletContext;
import javax.servlet.ServletConfig;
import javax.servlet.jsp.PageContext;
import javax.servlet.jsp.JspException;
import javax.servlet.jsp.JspWriter;
import javax.servlet.jsp.tagext.TagSupport;

public class ExTagSupport extends TagSupport {

    protected void writeHtml(JspWriter out,
                             String html)
    throws IOException
    {
      if((html.indexOf('<') == -1) &&
         (html.indexOf('>') == -1) &&
         (html.indexOf('&') == -1)) {
        out.print(html);
      } else {
          int len = html.length();

          for(int i = 0 ; i < len ; i++) {
            char c = html.charAt(i);
            if('<' == c) {
                out.print("<");
            } else if('>' == c) {
                out.print(">");
            } else if('&' == c) {
                out.print("&");
            } else {
                out.print(c);
            }
          }
      }
    }
}
```

6.2.2   *Exceptions and writing to the user*

Note that the `print` methods in the `JspWriter` may throw `IOExceptions`. This is nothing new. IO-related methods throw `IOExceptions` all the time, but if you understand what is going on you can react accordingly. In the context of custom tags, why should there be an `IOException`? There are several reasons, some of which have to do with problems in connection with the user. For example, an `IOException` would be thrown if the user's browser crashed or the user pressed Reload while we were writing back to them. Other reasons stem from the implementation of JSPs. For example, if the JSP output buffer overflows and the autoFlush directive is set to `false`, the JSP runtime will generate an `IOException`.

No matter what the reason for the exception, we handle it properly and in a way consistent with the policy acceptable for our web server. To begin with, you'll definitely want to abort the page execution. To do so, throw a `JspException` (or, even better, a `JspTagException`) from your tag and the JSP runtime will do the rest. Unfortunately, aborting the page is typically not enough. `JspExceptions` can be a symptom of several problems, such as poor design (buffer overflow), slow site (a reason why the user pressed Reload), or denial of service attacks. To help identify any of these potential problems, we should also log this exception to the servlet container's log file for later analysis.

6.2.3   *Flushing the JspWriter's internal buffer*

The `JspWriter` is heavily buffered, as that allows the servlet container and the JSP runtime to provide services such as error pages and improved performance. Also, when an error occurs, the JSP runtime can erase the content of the buffer and forward the request to the error page. Despite its benefits, buffering also has the drawback of delaying the receipt of the user's response. Imagine that you are writing a JSP file that will access several databases, and that each database query provides enough information to build a portion of the output. Since JSP uses buffering, the user may need to wait a long time until the page preparation is completed (many database queries). In the meantime, the waiting user could become bored and switch to another site.

To keep this from happening, most developers flush the response buffer whenever a significant portion of the page is ready. Flushing the buffer causes its current contents to be sent immediately to the user. The `JspWriter` facilitates this by exposing a method named `flush()`, which allows an override of the normal buffering behavior of a JSP and assures that the user receives the buffered content immediately.

NOTE   The `flush()` method does not work when tags are executed within the body of other tags. Body-modifying tags like to collect the contents of their bodies and manipulate them. The JSP runtime implements that behavior by creating an instance of `BodyContent` (a special derivative of `JspWriter`) in which to hold the processed body. Since `BodyContent` is created only for the purpose of collecting the content of the tag's body, it doesn't really represent the stream of content flowing back to the user. It is, rather, a holding tank for the content in a tag's body. It makes sense then that flushing a `BodyContent` has no meaning and, therefore, any call to `BodyContent.flush()` will result in an `IOException`. It is therefore important that, before flushing the `JspWriter`, you verify that it is not actually an instance of `BodyContent`.

FlushWriterTag example

The next tag we'll look at is called `FlushWriterTag`, whose job is to flush the `JspWriter` to the user. With this tag, a JSP author can specify places in the page where the output of the processing (up to that point) will be flushed to the user. Since we are placing all of the necessary logic for a flush within this custom tag, a page author can use its functionality without knowing anything about Java, the internals of the `JspWriter`, or the exact type of `JspWriter` currently in use. `FlushWriterTag`'s source code appears in listing 6.4.

Listing 6.4   Source code for FlushWriterTag's handler class

```
package book.simpletasks;

import book.util.LocalStrings;
import book.util.ExTagSupport;
import javax.servlet.jsp.JspWriter;
import javax.servlet.jsp.JspException;
import javax.servlet.jsp.tagext.BodyContent;

public class FlushWriterTag extends ExTagSupport {

    //some code was omitted for clarity

    public int doStartTag()
            throws JspException
    {
        try {
            JspWriter out = pageContext.getOut();
            if(!(out instanceof BodyContent)) {          ❶
                out.flush();
            }
        } catch(java.io.IOException ioe) {               ❷
            // User probably disconnected ...
```

```
            // log an error and throw a JspTagException
            // …
        }
        return SKIP_BODY;
    }
}
```

❶ **Check if the `JspWriter` can be flushed and flush it to the user (if applicable)**   We first check if the `JspWriter` in use is actually an instance of `BodyContent`. If so, flushing it would throw an exception since the method is not implemented. But in cases in which the `JspWriter` is not a `BodyContent`, it will trigger a flush call that will immediately write the buffer contents to the user.

❷ **Handle the `IOException`. Log the exception and abort the JSP execution by throwing a `JSPTagException`**   As always, methods executing on the `JspWriter` can throw `IOExceptions`. We handle them here by throwing a `JspTagException` that causes the JSP runtime engine to abort the processing of the page.

6.3   *Setting tag attributes*

The second technique is one you will use in most of the tags you develop. In order to make tags more flexible and reusable it is often necessary to let JSP authors pass parameters to them. One way to do this is through tag attributes. As noted in chapter 3, attributes are very common in HTML tags. One example is the HTML `<font>` tag, in which we see usage like the following:

```
<font face="verdana" size="3">Manning Press</font>
```

In this case, `face` and `size` are attributes that allow the page author to specify how the tag should format the text in its body. Imagine how useless the `<font>` tag would be if it always formatted text in the same size, style, and face.

The custom tags we build likely need attributes as well. We saw the use of attributes in chapter 3 with our `CookieValueTag`, but we did not, up until now, conduct a serious discussion on how attributes are implemented, nor did we discuss the different options available with the custom tags attributes mechanism. Now is a good time to start, because almost any tag (including most of our future samples) requires a great deal of configuration, and attributes are the prime tool for that.

Before describing the JSP runtime behavior when it tackles a tag attribute, let's think of the possible requirements associated with custom attributes for custom tags:

1   We need to specify, for a given tag, all of the attributes valid for it and indicate which are mandatory and which are not. This information must be

available at translation time to the JSP engine so that it can make decisions about whether a particular tag is being used properly.

2   Some criteria have to be specified for validating the values an author sets for a particular attribute. For example, if we are writing a custom version of the HTML `<font>` tag, we want to specify logic that checks if the `size` attribute is a positive integer.

3   In some pages and tags you may want to pass dynamic value, such as the results of a JSP scriptlet, as attribute values. Functionality is required to support this.

4   We need a standard way to define methods in our tag handler class that can be called to set an attribute's value. The JSP specification could mandate a special method with the signature of `void setAttribute(String name, Object value)` in all tags, and pass the values this way. But this is a brute force technique requiring additional work by the tag developer (something that specification writers prefer to avoid).

All of these requirements are met through the following conventions described by the JSP specification:

- Special entries in the TLD indicate the valid attributes (by name) for a particular tag, as well as whether or not each attribute is mandatory. The entry can also specify whether a particular attribute is the result of evaluating Java code embedded in the JSP. Recall the case in which we are writing our own version of the HTML `<font>` tag. We might want our `size` attribute to equal the result of some arithmetic we perform on local variables within the page.

- A special helper class that lets the tag writer code attribute validity checks being performed by the JSP runtime during translation time.

- JavaBeans coding conventions for defining methods in the tag handler to be used in setting methods.

We will review each of these in detail.

6.3.1   *Specifying tag attributes in the TLD*

In addition to the tag name and implementing class, each tag entry in the TLD file can contain attribute information (if nothing is specified, the tag cannot have any attributes). For each attribute the tag supports, a name must be specified, whether or not the attribute is mandatory (defaults to no), and whether the attribute's value is the result of runtime expression (again, the default is no). For example, assume that we have a tag called `Greeting` that will greet a returning user to our site.

`Greeting` will be implemented by a class called `book.simpletasks.GreetingTag`. Its TLD entry should look something like this:

```
<tag>
    <name>Greeting</name>
    <tagclass>book.simpletasks.GreetingTag</tagclass>
<tag>
```

Assume that `Greeting` has the following set of attributes:

- user
  The person to greet. This is a mandatory attribute whose value can be the outcome of a runtime expression.

- type
  The type of greeting. This is a mandatory attribute whose value must be hard-coded into the JSP file. Some possible values for this might be `tip` (to show a helpful tip with this greeting), `promotion` (to include a link to the current promotion on the site), `standard` (to output the standard greeting), and so forth.

- tip
  A tip to include with the greeting (used only if its type attribute equals `tip`). This might be a tip about how to navigate the site or help for the current page the user is on. This is an optional attribute whose value must be hard-coded into the JSP file.

In order to support these tag attributes, our TLD entry should have three attribute entries and will look like:

```
<tag>
    <name>Greeting</name>
    <tagclass>book.simpletasks.GreetingTag</tagclass>
    <attribute>
        <name>user</name>
        <required>true</required>
        <rtexprvalue>true</rtexprvalue>
    </attribute>
    <attribute>
        <name>tip</name>
    </attribute>
    <attribute>
        <name>type</name>
        <required>true</required>
    </attribute>
<tag>
```

As you can see, each definition is enclosed within an `<attribute>` tag that wraps the following three subtags: `<name>` to specify a name, `<required>` to specify whether an attribute is mandatory (`true`) or optional (`false`, the default), and `<rtexprvalue>` specifying whether the value can result from a runtime expression (`true`) or is a hard-coded value (`false`, the default).

NOTE   The runtime expression assigned to an attribute value must be a JSP language expression of the form `<%= expression %>`. If you want to provide dynamic input whose complexity exceeds a scriptlet, you will need to employ another way such as using the tag's body to provide the complex dynamic input. Future sections in this chapter will deal with body processing and custom tags.

Now that each possible attribute for the tag is specified, the JSP runtime can perform syntactic checks when translating the JSP file to a servlet. These checks determine whether any required attributes are missing or if a certain attribute is not legal for a tag (meaning it's not listed in the TLD). The JSP runtime also determines whether a certain attribute is allowed to contain the results of a runtime expression and handles it accordingly.

Introducing the attribute information into the TLD solved many of the translation time syntax problems associated with custom tag attributes. This affords us a basic level of control, but what if we desire some specific conditions with which to validate our attributes? For example, in our `Greeting` tag, we might want to be sure that when the greeting includes a tip, that the page author provides its text. Recall that specifying a value of `tip` for the `type` attribute in our tag will indicate that this greeting should include some helpful text along with our standard "Good afternoon, so and so" message. We could make our `tip` attribute mandatory, but then page authors using the `Greeting` tag would be required by the JSP runtime to include a tip even when it won't be used. What is optimal is to make the `tip` attribute required in some cases (namely, when `type` equals `tip`) and optional in others (when `type` is anything besides `tip`). This type of conditional check is commonly needed for tags and, luckily, the authors of the JSP specification made provisions for it. For such a complex check, the JSP specification allows tag developers to define a `TagExtraInfo` object which specifies the logic for our condition.

6.3.2   *Providing validity checks at translation time*

You say you want to provide extra syntax checks on your attribute data? No problem. The way we accomplish this is by coding the checks in Java and injecting that code into the JSP runtime by overriding a method in a class called `TagExtraInfo`. But first, let's take a look at `TagExtraInfo` and how the JSP runtime uses it.

TagExtraInfo

The JSP runtime associates each custom tag with a set of metadata objects derived from the information stored in the TLD. These metadata objects contain all the information specified about a tag such as its name, implementing class, valid attributes, and so forth. During the translation phase, the JSP translator consults the data stored in these objects and, based on that, determines how to invoke a tag handler and whether or not a tag is being used properly. One of these metadata objects is `TagExtraInfo` but, unlike all other metadata objects the translator uses, `TagExtraInfo` does not simply echo data that is in the TLD. Instead, it is written explicitly by the tag developer and then registered with the JSP runtime for a particular tag. This `TagExtraInfo` object provides extra attribute checks and scripting variables information to the JSP runtime.

NOTE   `TagExtraInfo` is not mandatory and most tags manage without it. But if you want your tag to perform special syntax checks or export scripting variables (a feature we'll talk about in the next chapter), you need it.

Table 6.2 shows the methods in `TagExtraInfo`.

Table 6.2   `TagExtraInfo`'s methods

Method name	Description
public VariableInfo[] getVariableInfo(TagData data)	Used to expose new scripting variables into the JSP. This method will be discussed in the next chapter.
public boolean isValid(TagData data)	The method we'll override to check conditions on our tag attributes. We return `true` if the attributes are valid or `false` otherwise.
public final void setTagInfo(TagInfo tagInfo)	Setter method for the TagInfo object (discussed later in the book).

The only method we'll need to use for now is `isValid()`. This is where we will place the code for the JSP runtime to use in evaluating our attributes.

Here are the steps to follow if we want our tag to have its own attribute checks:

1   Create a class that extends `javax.servlet.jsp.tagext.TagExtraInfo`. This class will serve the JSP runtime during the translation phase of the page and provide it with the extra tag-related information.

2   In the new class, override the method `boolean isValid(TagData data)`. The JSP runtime will call this method with the attribute information inside

the `data` parameter, and you will need to check these attributes and return `true` if you approve them (`false` if not).

3 Inform the JSP runtime that the custom tag has a `TagExtraInfo` associated with it. You will need to add a `<teiclass>` entry for your tag description in the TLD.

Attribute validation in GreetingTag

To clarify, let's relate this to our `Greeting` tag. Remember, the rule is that if the `Greeting` tag's `type` attribute is `tip`, then the tag user must specify a value for the `tip` attribute. This new requirement forces us to implement a `TagExtraInfo` for `Greeting` tag (let's name it `GreetingTagInfo`). We associate the `GreetingTagInfo` class with the `Greeting` tag in the TLD file:

```
<tag>
    <name>Greeting</name>
    <tagclass>book.simpletasks.GreetingTag</tagclass>
    <teiclass>book.simpletasks.GreetingTagInfo</teiclass>
    <attribute>
        <name>user</name>
        <required>true</required>
        <rtexprvalue>true</rtexprvalue>
    </attribute>
    <attribute>
        <name>tip</name>
    </attribute>
    <attribute>
        <name>type</name>
        <required>true</required>
    </attribute>
<tag>
```

And the implementation of `GreetingTagInfo` will be:

```
import javax.servlet.jsp.tagext.TagData;
import javax.servlet.jsp.tagext.TagExtraInfo;

public class GreetingTagInfo extends TagExtraInfo {

    public boolean isValid(TagData data)
    {
        String greetType = data.getAttributeString("type");    ❶
        if(greetType.equals("tip")) {
            String tip = data.getAttributeString("tip");        ❷
            if(null == tip || 0 == tip.length()) {
                return false;
            }
        }

        return true;
    }
}
```

❶ **Gets the String value of type** isValid() uses TagData.getAttributeString() to collect the values of the attributes. Once collected, we determine whether the values satisfy our condition and return either true or false. Normally, the values stored in the TagData are instances of String, with runtime expression attributes as the exception. These attributes, by their very nature, have no value until runtime, whereas the TagExtraInfo is used for checks at translation time. Because of this, runtime expressions are assigned a value for a plain Java Object[2] to represent them in TagData.

❷ **Performs the syntactic check on type and tip.**

With our GreetingTagInfo class in place we are now assured that our JSP runtime engine will enforce proper usage of our tag. If a JSP author attempts to set the attribute type to the value tip and not set a value to the tip attribute, the compiler will produce an error when it tries to translate the JSP that this tag is in. The error will produce output that varies slightly from vendor to vendor, but will ultimately inform the developer via some message in his or her web browser that the attributes are invalid for this tag.

Specifying attributes and their associated syntax and content constraints should be clear by now. The last piece left in the puzzle is how we write our tag handler to accept and use these attributes.

NOTE   In JSP1.2, the JSP file is translated into an XML document, then the JSP runtime translates this XML document into a servlet. A JSP1.2-compliant library can provide a validator class to work on the intermediate XML document representing the JSP file, and in this way perform a more rigorous validation spanning a whole document instead of one tag at a time. However, the majority of tags do not require the power, nor the complexity, of this validator.

6.3.3 *Using the JavaBeans coding conventions*

Setting the attributes of Java objects is not a new problem, so the designers of the JSP specification selected a tried-and-true solution—having the tag attribute setters follow the JavaBeans coding conventions. JavaBeans, as you know, is the Java

---

[2] To facilitate working with non-String attributes, TagData also has a method named getAttribute() that returns an Object value. If your attribute is the result of a runtime expression, this is the method to use.

component model, and its specification defines the way to set a property into an object based on the property's name. JavaBeans uses a simple coding convention that implies that a Bean with a writable property named foo should have a setter method named setFoo(). Using this convention, a JavaBean's environment can discern the method to call for every property value it needs to set.

Instructing the tags to expose attribute properties as JavaBeans properties solves the problem in a very pleasant way, since the names of the attributes are known in advance. Let's look at what the attribute setters of the Greeting tag should look like:

```
public class GreetingTag extends TagSupport {

// Omitted code
    String user;
    String type;
    String tip;

    public void setUser(String user) {
        this.user = user;
    }

    public void setType(String type) {
        this.type = type;
    }

    public void setTip(String tip) {
        this.tip = tip;
    }

// Some more omitted code
}
```

Nice and intuitive. After we've defined our setter methods, we need only refer to those local variables in any of the tag methods where attributes are required. As you might guess by their usefulness, the majority of the custom tags you build will include attributes. This is also true for most of the custom tags we build in the remainder of this book, and you'll see plenty of examples of this in the coming chapters.

6.4   Logging and messaging

Another important practice in any tag development project is logging error and informational messages and handling errors. It is important for debugging and troubleshooting, especially with web applications, to be able to review log files or inspect error pages to determine where things went wrong. Virtually all the tags we write in this book will need to have this ability. Here is an approach that will prove useful in future tag development.

6.4.1 Logging

Logging messages to a file is a very common practice in software development and, as such, is already integrated into the language or runtime environment. A JSP runtime container is no exception, with built-in logging facilities at your disposal. The actual location of the log file (as well as other, more advanced features, such as whether or not they can be rolling logs) typically varies depending on the runtime container vendor. The method for logging, however, is the same for any web container and is done via `log()` of the `ServletContext` object. This method allows either the logging of a simple `String` message or a `String` message and a `Throwable` in which case the stack trace for the `Throwable` is printed to the log.

It would be best not to have to write the logging code in every tag we develop, so we'll add two simple methods to our tag base classes (`ExTagSupport` and `ExBodyTagSupport`). These methods are:

```
protected void log(String msg)
{
    getServletContext().log(msg);
}

protected void log(String msg,
                   Throwable t)
{
    getServletContext().log(msg, t);
}

protected ServletContext getServletContext()
{
    return pageContext.getServletContext();
}
```

These methods are basically delegates to the log methods in the `ServletContext`. They remove the step of having to explicitly get the `ServletContext` in each tag and provide a place where we can enhance our logging, for example, by adding logging levels or checking debug flags.

6.4.2 Handling and throwing exceptions

Now that we have logging functionality, we can log any exceptions caught within our tags, but merely logging an error typically isn't enough. Many times, an exception will mean that the action the user was trying to process in the JSP, such as saving registration information or performing a search, has failed. In these cases, we want to log the problem and handle the exception properly so that the user is aware that the intended action failed and can contact technical support or otherwise correct the situation.

Once again, we find that the functionality for handling errors this way is built into any JSP/Servlet container. For any JSP we write we can indicate easily where the users's browser should be redirected should an error occur. We do this through the `errorPage` attribute of the `page` directive. For example:

```
<%@ page errorPage="errorpage.jsp" %>
```

indicates that if an uncaught exception is thrown during the JSP's execution, the user should be redirected to `errorpage.jsp`, which can either show a default message to warn the user that there is a problem and/or inspect the exception that was thrown and display information about it.[3] By specifying an error page in our JSP's in this way, we only need to throw a `JspTagException` when an error occurs (such as the following).

```
public int doStartTag()
    throws JspException
{
    try {
        JspWriter out = pageContext.getOut();
        //some code that could create an exception
        out.println("Look Ma, no errors!");
    } catch(Exception e) {
        // Log the error and throw a JspTagException
        log("An error occurred");
        throw new JspTagException("Yikes!");
    }
    return SKIP_BODY;
}
```

If a problem is encountered, we log the error and throw a `JspTagException` which, assuming the JSP has the `errorPage` defined, will cause the user to be redirected to the proper error page.

6.4.3 *Improving logging*

The logging and error handling code we've written thus far is pretty straightforward. It satisfies our needs but we could improve it slightly by getting our messages from a resource file to gain flexibility for changing our messages and retrieving support internationalization in our tags. This ability is achieved with the addition of two simple helper classes: `LocalStrings`, which will read the properties file with our messages and make them available to the tags and `Constants`, which will provide tag-specific keys with which to refer to messages in `LocalStrings`.

---

[3] For more information on how to write an error page, see the Sun tutorial at http://developer.java.sun.com/developer/onlineTraining/JSPIntro/exercises/ErrorHandling/.

LocalStrings

Essentially, all our `LocalStrings` class will do is read the LocalStrings.properties file from the classpath which will hold name-value pairs of keys and messages. The format for the LocalStrings.properties file is:

Key=message or, for example:

```
IO_ERROR=Error: IOException while writing back to the user
```

Defining error messages in this way lets us create LocalStrings.properties files for every locale in which our application is deployed and lets us quickly change, add, or delete messages. As the implementation of this class is not specifically relevant to tag development as a whole, we will forgo an in-depth look here. You can, however, download the source for this class from the book's web site.

Constants

The keys to the messages in the LocalStrings.properties files will be stored in tag-specific classes that we'll call `Constants` (one `Constants` class for each package, since each package is likely to have different error or information message needs). For the previous `IO_ERROR` example, this key would be stored in a `Constants` class, such as:

```
public class Constants {

    public static final String IO_ERROR = "IO_ERROR";
    //other keys follow
}
```

Putting it together

How does our revised error handling look with the addition of our two new classes? See listing listing 6.5.

Listing 6.5   Improved error handling in ShowFormParamTag

```
public class ShowFormParamTag extends TagSupport {
    // Some other code was omitted here.
    static LocalStrings ls =
        LocalStrings.getLocalStrings(ShowFormParamTag.class);        ❶

    public int doStartTag()
        throws JspException
    {
        try {
            HttpServletRequest req =
                (HttpServletRequest)pageContext.getRequest();
            String value = req.getParameter(name);
            if(null != value) {
```

```
            writeHtml(pageContext.getOut(), value);
        }
        return SKIP_BODY;
    } catch(java.io.IOException ioe) {
        // User probably disconnected ...
        log(ls.getString(Constants.IO_ERROR), ioe);       ❷
        throw new
            JspTagException(ls.getStr(Constants.IO_ERROR));    ❸
    }
  }
}
```

❶ Loads the key-value pairs in the **LocalStrings.properties** file in which this class is deployed.

❷ Gets the proper message string for an `IO_ERROR`.

❸ Gets the proper message string for an `IO_ERROR` and throws a `JspTagException` with it.

We now have a simple and clean logging and messaging interface that lets us handle errors in our tags and send those errors to the client (with built-in internationalization). This approach is used in the examples throughout the book.

6.5   *Using the Servlet API*

Another technique central to custom tag development is interacting with the Servlet API. If you've had any experience with JSP or servlet development (or you have read through chapters 1 and 2), you are familiar with the classes and interfaces in the Servlet API that enable web development. These are the objects that make web programming possible by allowing access to request parameters, session variables, the HTTP response, the user session, and so forth. To be of any use in a web environment, custom tags must be able to access these same objects to do their work. Since we know that custom tags and JSPs are ultimately compiled into servlets, it is no wonder that all Java web technologies (serlvets, JSPs, or tags) eventually interact with the same classes to do their jobs. The only difference is the way in which each technology gains access to the objects.

In servlets, these objects are retrieved via method parameters and local variables. In JSPs, the objects are always available (in scope) and can be referred to by name anywhere in the file (i.e., request, response, etc.). For JSPs, these ever present objects are referred to as the implicit JSP objects. Since tags actually sit within JSPs, we refer to this group of objects as the implicit JSP objects in the context of tags as well. This simple naming convention mustn't distract you from the fact that we're talking about a few key classes that reside in the Servlet API and in which all three technologies share an interest.

What then are the implicit JSP objects and what are they used for? They are:

- The `request` object—To obtain request parameters and other information.
- The `response` object—To add headers and redirect the request.
- The `session` object—If we want the tag to manipulate the session directly (e.g., when we want to perform metaactions on the session, such as invalidation).
- The `application (ServletContext)` and `ServletConfig` objects To obtain context and page-level initialization variables.
- All of the JSP attribute objects in the four scopes used by a JSP (application/ session/request/page)—This way the tag can interact with other portions of the web application. For example, one tag may open a JDBC connection and place it as an attribute in the page scope; later on another tag can take this connection and use it to query a database.

If servlets have variables and methods to access these objects and JSPs can refer to them by name, how do custom tags obtain them? The solution is straightforward: all of these variables are made available to custom tags via the `PageContext`.

Each tag has two mandatory attributes: its parent and the `PageContext`assigned to the current JSP execution. The `PageContext` has many roles, but as far as JSP tags are concerned, the most important ones are to connect the tag to the JSP environment and to provide access to this environment's services and the implicit objects. Let's look at how tags can use the `PageContext` to get a reference to the different objects in the environment.

6.5.1 *Accessing the implicit JSP objects*

A JSP implicit object represents a key object in the Servlet API and it is always available. Table 6.3 shows the available JSP implicit objects and how a tag can attain reference to each:

Table 6.3   Implicit JSP objects and their tag counterpart

JSP implicit objects	Custom tags counterpart	Typical use by the tags
pageContext	The pageContext attribute of the tag. This attribute is set on tag initialization by the page implementation.	Obtains other implicit variables. Obtains JSP attribute. Accesses `RequestDispatcher` type services.
request	Calling pageContext.getRequest()	Queries request information; for example, query form parameters or in-bound cookies.

Table 6.3 Implicit JSP objects and their tag counterpart (continued)

JSP implicit objects	Custom tags counterpart	Typical use by the tags
response	Calling pageContext.getResponse()	Manipulates the response; for example, add cookies, redirect, etc.
session	Calling pageContext.getSession()	Manipulates the session directly; for example, invalidate the session or set a different inactivity timeout.
config	Calling pageContext.getServletConfig()	Obtains configuration parameters for this page.
application	Calling pageContext.getServletContext()	Obtains configuration parameters for this application and uses its utility method (for example, log()).
out	Calling pageContext.getOut()	Writes data into the page.
page	Calling pageContext.getPage()	Usually not in use. Unless coded specifically for a certain page, the tag cannot know the services exposed by the page class.
exception	Calling pageContext.getException()	Analyzes and displays in the response.

All the implicit JSP objects are accessible for the custom tags and the key to all of them is the tag's pageContext attribute. We'll now show how to use these variables through a few examples.

ShowFormParam tag example

In web development, we know that the only way to pass information from the browser to the server (other than a cookie) is through the use of POST variables or query string parameters. Accessing these parameters is, therefore, one of the most important tasks we need to perform in a JSP. Regular JSPs can access the form parameters through the implicit request object (usually by means of the method String req.getParameter(String name)). How does a tag do this?

The answer recalls the workings of a JSP or servlet except, in custom tags we don't have the request object at our fingertips, so we must first get a reference to it. Looking back at the ShowFormParamTag, we remember that it prints the value of a named form parameter into the response that is returning to the user. Since we need to print a named value, ShowFormParamTag has an attribute that specifies the name of the parameter to print. And, of course, we will need to have the implementation of this tag's unique logic actually fetch the form parameter and print its value to the user. The resulting tag source is in listing 6.6:

Listing 6.6   Source code for ShowFormParamTag's handler class

```
package book.simpletasks;

import book.util.LocalStrings;
import book.util.ExTagSupport;

import javax.servlet.http.HttpServletRequest;
import javax.servlet.jsp.JspException;
import javax.servlet.jsp.JspTagException;

public class ShowFormParamTag extends ExTagSupport {

    static LocalStrings ls =
        LocalStrings.getLocalStrings(ShowFormParamTag.class);

    protected String name = null;                          ❶

    public void setName(String name)
    {
        this.name = name;
    }

    public int doStartTag()
            throws JspException
    {
        try {
            HttpServletRequest req =                        ❷
                (HttpServletRequest)pageContext.getRequest();
            String value = req.getParameter(name);
            if(null != value) {
                writeHtml(pageContext.getOut(), value);
            }
            return SKIP_BODY;
        } catch(java.io.IOException ioe) {
            // User probably disconnected ...
            log(ls.getStr(Constants.IO_ERROR), ioe);
            throw new
                JspTagException(ls.getStr(Constants.IO_ERROR));
        }
    }

    protected void clearProperties()
    {
        name = null;
        super.clearProperties();
    }
}
```

❶ **Implements the tag's name attribute**   The tag starts by defining a setter for the name attribute (setName()), and continues by implementing the doStartTag()

method that simply fetches the `request` object from the `pageContext` and queries it for the named parameter. The tag ends with an odd-looking method named `clearProperties()` that we will discuss in the section dealing with tag cleanup.

❷ **Fetches the request object from the `pageContext` and obtains the needed form parameter.**

After creating this tag, the next step is to put together a TLD for it and test drive it using a JSP file. Listing 6.7 is the result.

Listing 6.7   Tag library descriptor for ShowFormParamTag

```xml
<?xml version="1.0" encoding="ISO-8859-1" ?>
<!DOCTYPE taglib
        PUBLIC "-//Sun Microsystems, Inc.//DTD JSP Tag Library 1.1//EN"
            "http://java.sun.com/j2ee/dtds/web-jsptaglibrary_1_1.dtd">

<taglib>
            <tlibversion>1.0</tlibversion>
            <jspversion>1.1</jspversion>
            <shortname>simp</shortname>
            <uri> http://www.manning.com/jsptagsbook/simple-taglib </uri>
            <info>
            A simple sample tag library
            </info>

    <tag>
        <name>formparam</name>
        <tagclass>book.simpletasks.ShowFormParamTag</tagclass>
        <bodycontent>empty</bodycontent>
            <info> Show a single named form parameter</info>
            <attribute>
                    <name>name</name>                       ❶
                    <required>true</required>
                    <rtexprvalue>true</rtexprvalue>
            </attribute>
        </tag>
</taglib>
```
---

❶ **The `name` attribute is required and can be the result of a runtime expression, providing of flexibility in listing the parameters.**

The JSP can be found in listing 6.8.

Listing 6.8   Sample page employing ShowFormParamTag

```jsp
<%@ page errorPage="error.jsp" %>       ❶
<%@ taglib
```

```
        uri="http://www.manning.com/jsptagsbook/simple-taglib"
        prefix="simp" %>
```
❷

```
<html>
<body>

Here are your FORM request parameters:

<table>
<tr><th>Name</th> <th>Value</th> </tr>
<% java.util.Enumeration e = request.getParameterNames();
    while(e.hasMoreElements()) {
        String paramname = (String)e.nextElement();
%>
    <tr>
        <td> <%= paramname %></td>
        <td><simp:formparam name='<%= paramname %>'/> </td>
    </tr>
<% } %>
</table>
That's all for now.
</body>
</html>
```
❸

❹

❶ **Uses the error page that we developed in our first hello chapter.**

❷ **Instructs the page to use the simple tags library.**

❸ **Walks through all the request parameters** ❹ **Prints a named request parameter based on its runtime value** The test JSP simply gets the list of FORM parameters and iterates on them, printing the different values for each. This is also a demonstration of how runtime expressions in attributes can come in handy. Since we'd like this JSP to work with any HTML form, each with any number of parameters, we couldn't possibly hard-code a value for the tag's `name` attribute. Because we specified in the TLD that the `name` attribute can be the result of a runtime expression, the JSP engine evaluates `<%= paramname %>` first and then passes the results of this evaluation to our tag handler (by calling `setName()` with the result).

Figure 6.1 shows the results of accessing showform.jsp with a few parameters. The output of our JSP is a table displaying the names and values of the FORM parameters.

RedirectTag example

Once you know how to manipulate values in the `request`, it is time to look at the response. To do so, we'll look at a tag we'll call `RedirectTag` which redirects the user's browser to another location. Since we'll want the JSP author to specify which URL to redirect to, the tag will have an attribute called `location`.

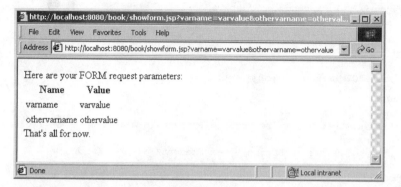

Figure 6.1 The results of accessing showform.jsp

To ensure that our redirect tag works reliably, we need to build it with one key nuance of HTTP in mind. An HTTP redirect response includes a standard HTTP redirect response code as well as unique redirection headers. Once a response to the user begins, it is too late to modify the headers and response code (and thus, too late to send a redirect). The `RedirectTag` must watch closely to make sure it is not too late to modify the HTTP header. If it is, we should inform the executing JSP by throwing an exception.

Fortunately, the JSP infrastructure is buffering the response, which makes it possible to ask for a redirection at any time, as long as the buffer hasn't already been flushed. The buffer can be flushed explicitly by calling `pageContext.getOut().flush()`, or automatically when it becomes full. Once the response is flushed to the user it is considered committed, and you will be unable to modify the headers. listing 6.9 presents the source code for the `RedirectTag`.

Listing 6.9 Source code for RedirectTag's handler class

```
package book.simpletasks;

import book.util.LocalStrings;
import book.util.ExTagSupport;

import javax.servlet.http.HttpServletResponse;
import javax.servlet.jsp.JspException;

public class RedirectTag extends ExTagSupport {

    static LocalStrings ls =
        LocalStrings.getLocalStrings(RedirectTag.class);

    protected String location = null;

    public void setLocation(String location)                ❶
    {
```

```
            this.location = location;        ⬆❶
        }
    public int doStartTag()
            throws JspException
        {
        HttpServletResponse res =                                   ❷
            (HttpServletResponse)pageContext.getResponse();
        if(res.isCommitted()) {
            throw new JspException(ls.getStr(Constants.COMMITTED));
        }
        try {                                                       ❸
            res.sendRedirect(res.encodeRedirectURL(location));
            return SKIP_BODY;
        } catch(java.io.IOException ioe) {
            // User probably disconnected ...
            // log an error and throw a JspTagException
            // …
        }
    }
    public int doEndTag()
            throws JspException              ❹
        {
        super.doEndTag();
        return SKIP_PAGE;
    }
    protected void clearProperties()
        {
        location = null;
        super.clearProperties();
    }
}
```

❶ **Implements the tag's location attribute. This is the location to which we redirect the browser.**

❷ **Fetches the response object from `pageContext` and checks to see if it is commited (which is an error).**

❸ **Uses the response object to redirect the browser (keeps URL-based rewrite session state in place)** Since Servlet/JSP-based applications have two methods to keep session state, namely cookies and URL encoding, one must support URL encoding when redirecting the user from one page to another. To facilitate this, the request object exposes a method (`encodeRedirectURL()`) whose job is to rewrite the redirected URL according to the URL encoding specifications. Calling this method is exactly what we are doing prior to calling the utility redirect method. Remember also to call `encodeURL()` any time you print a URL or FORM action field into the output sent to the user.

> **NOTE** URL encoding is a method wherein session tracking is accomplished by encoding the user's session `id` inside all the JSP file's URLs (each user therefore receives a slightly different set of URLs in his content). In most web servers, this approach is a backup to the preferred method of placing session information in a cookie. Some users choose not to use cookies, or their firewalls prevent it, so embedding the session `id` in a URL is a fallback approach. For more information about URL encoding, refer to the Servlet API specification of any servlet book.

❹ **Terminates the execution of the page by returning `SKIP_PAGE` from `doEndTag`** This is the first time any of our tags has implemented `doEndTag()`. We can usually leave `doEndTag()` out of our tag handlers since it is implemented by our `ExTagSupport` base class; however, in this tag we must alter the value returned from `doEndTag()` to tell the JSP runtime engine to stop page execution after the redirection. The default implementation of `doEndTag` returns `EVAL_PAGE`, a constant value that instructs the JSP runtime to continue executing the remainder of the JSP page. This default behavior is not appropriate for our redirect tag, because a redirection means that we do not want to continue with this JSP file execution. We would like to instruct the JSP runtime to stop the execution and return immediately. As you recall from chapter 3, this can be accomplished by overriding the default `doEndTag()` method and returning `SKIP_PAGE`.

Testing RedirectTag

It is useful to test the `RedirectTag` in cases in which the output is already committed (to see how the tag works in case of an error), and fortunately we can accomplish that by using a tag-only approach. Earlier we developed `FlushWriterTag` whose job was to flush the output to the user, so combining these two tags serves as a good test case for both of them.

Listing 6.10 presents the TLD we are using which includes two tags. We define the two tags, redirect and flush, their respective attributes (flush does not have any), and we're through.

Listing 6.10 Tag library descriptor for the redirect tag

```
<?xml version="1.0" encoding="ISO-8859-1" ?>
<!DOCTYPE taglib
    PUBLIC "-//Sun Microsystems, Inc.//DTD JSP Tag Library 1.1//EN"
           "http://java.sun.com/j2ee/dtds/web-jsptaglibrary_1_1.dtd">
<taglib>
    <tlibversion>1.0</tlibversion>
    <jspversion>1.1</jspversion>
```

```
<shortname>simp</shortname>
<uri> http://www.manning.com/jsptagsbook/simple-taglib </uri>
<info>
   A simple sample tag library
</info>

<tag>      ❶
    <name>redirect</name>
    <tagclass>book.simpletasks.RedirectTag</tagclass>
    <bodycontent>empty</bodycontent>
    <info>
       Redirect the browser to another site. Stop the response.
    </info>
    <attribute>
        <name>location</name>
        <required>true</required>
        <rtexprvalue>true</rtexprvalue>
    </attribute>
</tag>
<tag>      ❷
<name>flush</name>
<tagclass>book.simpletasks.FlushWriterTag</tagclass>
<bodycontent>empty</bodycontent>
<info> Flush the JSP output stream. </info>
</tag>
</taglib>
```

❶ Defining the `redirect` tag.

❷ Defining the `flush` tag.

After naming each of the tags, we can also write the JSP driver (flushredirect.jsp) as presented in listing 6.11:

Listing 6.11 Sample page employing RedirectTag and causing an exception

```
<%@ page errorPage="error.jsp" %>      ❶
<%@ taglib
    uri="http://www.manning.com/jsptagsbook/simple-taglib"
    prefix="simp" %>
<html>
<body>

Here is some text before the redirection. <br>
<simp:flush/>                               ❷
<simp:redirect location="/"/>
Here is some text after the redirection. <br>
</body>
</html>
```

❶ Assigns an error page

❷ Flushes the output before trying to rediret. This should cause an exception   Note that we force the committing of the response prior to the redirect via our `<simp:flush/>` tag. The redirect tag is forced to throw an exception because the response will already have been committed by the time it is executed. With the response committed, the user's browser has received our server's response and it is too late to perform a redirect.

Note that we set a standard JSP error page in the very first line of listing 6.11. In most cases, doing so will cause the user's browser to be directed to the specified error page whenever an exception is thrown within the JSP. In this case, will the exception that is thrown by the redirect tag cause this type of error handling? The answer is, of course, no. Since we can't redirect with our tag because the response is already committed, it would only make sense that we cannot redirect to an error page either. What we will see instead is a notification from the container that something went awry (figure 6.2).

6.5.2 *Accessing the JSP attributes*

JSPs are executed in the context of a Java web application, as defined in the Servlet API specification. This specification defines a set of scopes wherein the entities taking part in the application (i.e., servlets, JSPs, custom tags, etc.) can store Java objects. We store objects in this way in order to share them between entities and from request to request. These Java objects are called attributes, but should not be confused with the tag attributes we discussed earlier in this chapter. The scopes defined for attributes are request, session, application, and page. Let's look at each scope in detail.

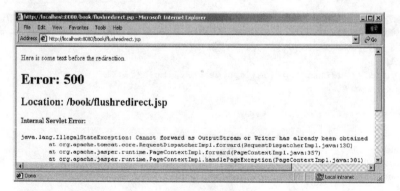

Figure 6.2   The results of accessing flushredirect.jsp

Request scope

Web application entities can store objects within the `ServletRequest` object. This scope makes an attribute available to all the entities taking part in the service of a particular request. For example, a servlet can retrieve data from the database, embed that data in a JavaBean, set the Bean as an attribute in the `request` object and, finally, forward the user to a JSP. A custom tag in the JSP can then retrieve the bean from the request and format its data for presentation to the user as HTML.[4] In this case, the servlet and the custom tag are functioning within the same HTTP request and, therefore, the `request` scope is the proper choice for their data sharing.

Session scope

When web application entities are associating attributes with a particular user, they can store objects within the `HttpSession` object. This scope allows all the entities taking part in the service of a user session (typically more than one page request) to exchange information. For example, in an ecommerce application, a certain request may put the shopping cart as a session attribute, and the next request may perform the checkout operation based on the previously stored cart session attribute. This scope differs from the `request` scope in that it renders stored attributes available for the life of a user's visit (their session) instead of a single page request.

Application scope

Web application entities can store objects within the `ServletContext`. Associating objects in this way makes them available to any entity, no matter what session or request it is serving. Setting attributes in the application scope means that all entities taking part in the application can exchange information. For example, a certain servlet can initialize a database connection pool and store it inside the `ServletContext`; later on, other parts of the application can fetch the initialized connection pool attribute and use it to query values from the database.

Page scope

The scripting elements within a certain JSP file may need to share information between themselves. For example, we may want a custom tag to produce information and a JSP scriptlet in the same page to display it. How can these elements share this informa-

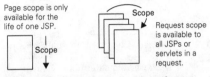

Figure 6.3   Page scope vs. request scope

tion? Of the scopes we've covered, the most appropriate one for such a need is the

---

4 This facilitates the popular Model-2 approach described in chapter 2.

request. Using the request scope means, however, that the shared information will be available through all the different stages of the request. Though a single JSP will often handle the entire life of a client request, there are times when the request will be forwarded to or included by another JSP or servlet. In such a case, storing attributes in the request scope may pollute our request scope and attributes of the same name from different pages may clash. To avoid this rare but possible case, the JSP specification adds a new page scope that is implemented by the PageContext instance. The PageContext instance for a given page holds a table with attribute names and their values and, whenever a page's scoped attribute is required, the PageContext is used to fetch/store it.

Accessing attributes through PageContext

We've now discussed four different scopes, each with its own job, and our custom tags need to access objects in all of them. How will the tags do that? One simple way is to fetch the needed JSP implicit object (the request, session, application, or pageContext) and ask that object for the attribute. The problem with this approach is that it forces tight coupling between the tags and the different implicit objects and their methods which (from a design and reusability perspective) is not a good idea. Since the access methods for getting and setting attributes on each object are so similar, a better way to handle attribute interaction might be to have uniform access to all the different scopes. This design goal was considered in the implementation of the JSP specification and, as was realized in several methods, exposed by PageContext. The role of these methods is to provide a common interface to all the variable scopes. These methods are shown in table 6.4.

Table 6.4 Attribute control methods in PageContext

Method	Description
public Object getAttribute(String name, int scope)	Fetches a named attribute from a specific scope. Possible scopes (in all the methods listed in this section) are: PageContext.PAGE_SCOPE, PageContext.REQUEST_SCOPE, PageContext.SESSION_SCOPE, and PageContext.APPLICATION_SCOPE.
public Object getAttribute(String name)	Sets/adds a named attribute in a specific scope.
public void setAttribute(String name, Object attribute, int scope)	Sets/adds attribute in the page scope.
public void removeAttribute(String name, int scope)	Removes a named attribute from a specific scope.
public void removeAttribute(String name)	Removes a named attribute from the page scope.

Table 6.4 Attribute control methods in `PageContext` (continued)

Method	Description
public Object findAttribute(String name)	Fetches a named attribute by searching for it in all scopes; starting with the page scope, continuing with request and session, and ending with application.

PageContext also provides methods to enumerate the names of the attributes in a specific scope and to find the scope of a specific attribute; but these methods are of less importance to us. Also note that all the methods in table 6.4 are actually abstract in the formal `PageContext` class definition. When we manipu-

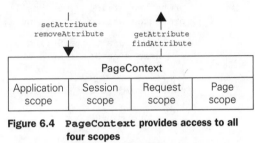

Figure 6.4 `PageContext` provides access to all four scopes

late a `PageContext` instance within our tags (or JSPs), we are referring to a subclass that is implemented by the JSP runtime vendor.

ShowObjectTag example

Since all the needed functionality is easily available through the `PageContext`, there is no longer a reason to use the implicit objects for attribute interaction. Let us now look at an example tag to illustrate the concepts introduced here. We'll build a simple tag to access JSP attributes based on their name and scope which we'll call `ShowObjectTag`.

`ShowObjectTag` prints the value of a named (and optionally scoped) JSP attribute into the response returned to the user. In many ways, it is similar to `ShowFormParamTag`, except that it prints real JSP attribute objects and not simple request parameters. `ShowObjectTag` has two tag attributes that provide it with (1) the name of the JSP attribute to show and (2) an optional scope for this attribute. From these two attributes, the tag will fetch the matching object and present it. The source code for `ShowObjectTag` is displayed in listing 6.12.

Listing 6.12   Source code for ShowObjectTag handler class

```
package book.simpletasks;

import javax.servlet.jsp.JspException;
import javax.servlet.jsp.PageContext;

import book.util.ExTagSupport;
import book.util.LocalStrings;
```

```
public class ShowObjectTag extends ExTagSupport {

    public static final String PAGE_ID = "page";
    public static final String REQUEST_ID = "request";
    public static final String SESSION_ID = "session";
    public static final String APPLICATION_ID = "application";

    static LocalStrings ls =
        LocalStrings.getLocalStrings(ShowObjectTag.class);

    protected String name = null;
    protected String scope = null;

    public void setName(String newName) {
        name = newName;
    }

    public void setScope(String newScope)
    {
        scope = newScope;
    }

    public int doStartTag()
            throws JspException
    {
        Object o = getPointedObject(name, scope);
        try {
            writeHtml(pageContext.getOut(), o.toString());
            return SKIP_BODY;
        } catch(java.io.IOException ioe) {
            // User probably disconnected ...
            // signal that by throwing a JspException
            //
        }
    }

    protected Object getPointedObject(String name,
                                      String scope)
            throws JspException
    {
        Object rc = null;
        if(null != scope) {
            rc = pageContext.getAttribute(name,
                                    translateScope(scope));
        } else {
            rc = pageContext.findAttribute(name);
        }
        if(null == rc) {
            // No such object, this is probably an error
            // signal that by throwing a JspTagException
            ...
        }

        return rc;
    }
```

❶

❷

❷

❸

❹

❺

```
protected int translateScope(String scope)
        throws JspException
{
    if(scope.equalsIgnoreCase(PAGE_ID)) {
        return PageContext.PAGE_SCOPE;
    } else if(scope.equalsIgnoreCase(REQUEST_ID)) {
        return PageContext.REQUEST_SCOPE;
    } else if(scope.equalsIgnoreCase(SESSION_ID)) {
        return PageContext.SESSION_SCOPE;
    } else if(scope.equalsIgnoreCase(APPLICATION_ID)) {
        return PageContext.APPLICATION_SCOPE;
    }

    // No such scope, this is probably an error maybe the
    // TagExtraInfo associated with this tag was not configured
    // signal that by throwing a JspTagException
    //
}
protected void clearProperties()
{
    name = null;
    scope = null;
    super.clearProperties();
}
}
```

❶ **The scope names, page.**

❷ **The tag properties: name and scope.**

❸ **Getting the JSP attribute object pointed by the name and scope and printing it to the result.**

❹ **When both name and atributes are provided, we are using `getAttribute()` to locate the pointed attribute** ❺ **When only the name is provided, `findAttribute()` is the best way to locate an attribute in a consistent way** `getPointedObject()` is where the tag looks for the JSP attribute (and returns it). The method has two parameters: the name of the attribute (mandatory) and the scope (recommended, but optional). When the scope is given, we translate its name to its PageContext identifier (as in `translateScope()`) and call the PageContext method `getAttribute()`. Doing so will cause the PageContext to seek the named attribute in a specified scope. Assuming the parameter can be found in one of the four scopes, findAttribute will return it.

❻ **Translates the scope name to the integer `id` that the `pageContext` understands.**

To ensure proper behavior from our tag, we insist that the user provide a valid scope in our tag's attribute. This is a case in which we apply the tactics we just discussed for validating tag attributes. To do so, we associate a TagExtraInfo derivative (`ShowObjectTagExtraInfo`) that will add a semantic check on the value the JSP author passes to the `scope` attribute. This check will verify that the value is one of the four legal scope names, or null (if not specified at all). `ShowObjectTagEx-traInfo` is displayed in listing 6.13.

Listing 6.13   Source code for the ShowObjectTagExtraInfo class

```
package book.simpletasks;

import javax.servlet.jsp.tagext.TagData;
import javax.servlet.jsp.tagext.TagExtraInfo;

public class ShowObjectTagExtraInfo extends TagExtraInfo {

    public boolean isValid(TagData data)
    {
        String scope = data.getAttributeString("scope");
        if(null == scope) {
            return true;
        }
        if(scope.equals(ShowObjectTag.PAGE_ID) ||
            scope.equals(ShowObjectTag.REQUEST_ID) ||
            scope.equals(ShowObjectTag.SESSION_ID) ||
            scope.equals(ShowObjectTag.APPLICATION_ID)) {
             return true;
        }

        return false;
    }
}
```

Note that `isValid()` does not assume the existence of the `scope` attribute; in fact it is all right for the `scope` to be missing. A problem could arise, however, if the scope name has any value other than those defined, and in such a case the method will notify the JSP runtime by returning `false`.

Now that we have the tag's implementation available, we create a TLD entry for it (listing 6.14) and a driver JSP file (listing 6.15).

Listing 6.14   Tag library descriptor for ShowObjectTag

```
<tag>
    <name>show</name>
    <tagclass>book.simpletasks.ShowObjectTag</tagclass>
    <teiclass>book.simpletasks.ShowObjectTagExtraInfo</teiclass>
    <bodycontent>empty</bodycontent>
    <info>
            Show a certain object by its name.
    </info>
```

```
        <attribute>
                     <name>name</name>
                     <required>true</required>
                     <rtexprvalue>true</rtexprvalue>
        </attribute>
        <attribute>
                     <name>scope</name>
                     <required>false</required>
        </attribute>
</tag>
```

Listing 6.15   JSP file employing ShowObjectTag

```
<%@ page errorPage="error.jsp" %>
<%@ taglib
    uri="http://www.manning.com/jsptagsbook/simple-taglib"
    prefix="simp" %>
<html>
<body>

Here are your application attributes:
<table>                       ❶
<tr><th>Name</th> <th>Value</th> </tr>
<% java.util.Enumeration e = application.getAttributeNames();      ❷
    while(e.hasMoreElements()) {
        String attname = (String)e.nextElement();
%>
    <tr>
        <td> <%= attname %></td>
        <td><simp:show name='<%= attname  %>'               ❸
                       scope="application" /> </td>
    </tr>
<% } %>
</table>
And here they are again (scope not given this time):
<table>
<tr><th>Name</th> <th>Value</th> </tr>
<% e = pageContext.getAttributeNamesInScope(     ❹
                             PageContext.APPLICATION_SCOPE);
    while(e.hasMoreElements()) {
        String attname = (String)e.nextElement();
%>
    <tr>
        <td> <%= attname %></td>
        <td><simp:show name='<%= attname  %>' /> </td>        ❺
    </tr>
<% } %>
</table>
That's all for now.
</body>
</html>
```

❶ **Lists the attributes given the name and the scope.**

❷ **Enumerates the names of the application attributes**   To enumerate, we are using the application object directly. For now we need to use a script to enumerate the attribute names.

❸ **Shows the named attribute using its name and scope (application).**

❹ **Enumerates the names of the application attributes using the `PageContext's getAttri-buteNamesInScope()`**   The results are the same as using the application object directly.

❺ **Shows the named attribute using its name only.**

The JSP driver enumerates the application-scoped attributes in two ways. These techniques are interesting on their own since they demonstrate the manner in which to use the `PageContext` attribute's manipulation methods:

- In the first enumeration, the JSP driver uses the `application` object to enumerate its attributes. Accessing the `application` object makes it possible to call `application.getAttributeNames()`, which retrieves an enumeration of the application-scoped attribute names. Later, the driver will print these attributes to the result returned to the user, using the name and the scope.

- The second shows how to use the `PageContext.getAttributeNamesInScope()` method, instead of directly using the `application` object. In doing so, we gain the use of uniform code when we want to access the different scopes and the end results are the same. This time the driver shows the application attributes only by name (the scope is not provided), yet the results are the same since the attribute names are unique.

The end results of running our JSP driver on Tomcat 3.1 are shown in figure 6.5.

In figure 6.5, the generated page presents two identical tables filled with Tomcat's built-in application attributes (which point to the server's temporary

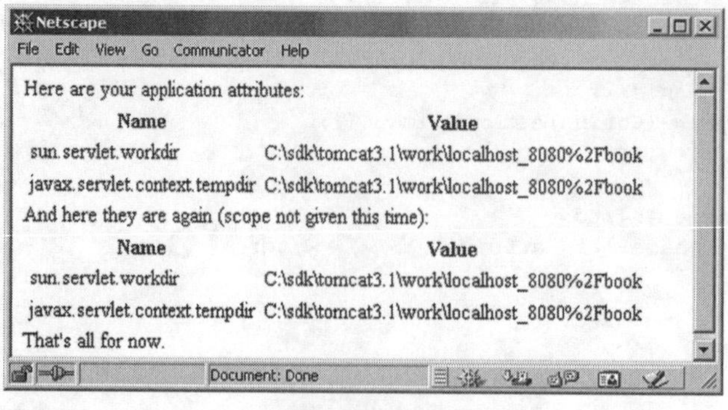

Figure 6.5 Accessing the application attributes

application directory). The attribute `javax.servlet.context.tempdir` is actually part of the Servlet API 2.2 specification, and the `sun.servlet.workdir` is a propriatery implementation attribute used within Tomcat.

In chapter 8 we will show how to use the `TagExtraInfo` class to add scripting variables to the page. Doing so allows you to define and set a variable within a tag and make that variable available to any scriptlets that follow the tag. Adding new variables in this way requires adding new attributes to the environment. We'll discover in chapter 8 that this is done via `setAttribute()` that was neglected in this section.

6.6   *Configuring tags and bundling resources*

Earlier in this chapter, we learned the technique of using tag attributes when passing parameters to our tags. This is a great tool, but tag attributes alone aren't always enough to let us really control tag configuration. Sometimes it's preferable to hide the more complex configuration from the page programmers, instead of burdening them with it. We want to be able to define and modify some applicationwide parameters in a central place and have all of our tags use those parameters. For example, tags sometimes need access to a database. In a data-driven application, it is likely that more than one tag in our library will have to use a single database, in which case it would be beneficial to configure the database properties in a single place (within the application) and have all the tags access this centralized configuration data. It would be an extra burden (not to mention, prone to error) to require JSP page authors to include database configuration in the attributes of every tag on every page.

There are two clear approaches to configuring tags in this way:

- Use the web application built-in configuration. In this way, the tags read configuration items from the `ServletContext` initialization parameters to configure themselves. This approach is very appealing when you need to provide a relatively limited and focused configuration. An example could be a certain application attribute, such as the name of the database connection pool.

- Use homegrown configuration. There are several variants to this approach: (1) Placing the configuration file in the application classpath and using `Class.getResourceAsStream()` to get a reference to the file's contents. (2) Placing the configuration file in the application directories and using `ServletContext.getResourceAsStream()` to get a reference to the file contents. (3) Placing the configuration file somewhere in the file system and informing the tag (using the web application built-in configuration) where this file is. The homegrown configuration is very useful when you need to provide a big chunk of relatively constant information, such as the default behavior of the tags, product license keys, and so forth.

We'll discuss using the web application built-in configuration here. So-called home-grown configurations can offer more control, but vary greatly and are beyond the scope of this book.

6.6.1 Configuring a web application

Since version 2.2 the Servlet API defines two configuration scopes, ServletContext and ServletConfig, as well as an API to access them, in the application scope (accessible via a ServletContext object) you can provide configuration items that all the servlets or JSPs (including tags) can access. In the servlet/JSP scope, accessible via a ServletConfig object, only an individual servlet or JSP file can access the configuration items. The servlet scope holds the most interest for servlet developers. For tags, however, the application scope is much more useful, because it allows a tag to be configured once for the entire application, no matter how many times or on how many pages it is used.

The APIs used by tags to access the configuration parameters (as well as the exact configuration syntax to be used in the web application deployment descriptor) are defined in the Servlet API 2.2 specification. A tag may use the Servlet-Context object to access the broader, application-scoped configuration, and the ServletConfig object for individual JSP file-scoped configuration. In both objects the methods to be used are:

- getInitParameterNames() — Gets an enumeration with the names of the configuration parameters.

- getInitParameter() — Gets the string value of a certain named configuration parameter.

Note that all the parameters are string values. If you want a different type (such as Boolean) in your parameter, you simply need to convert the string value to the desired type.

Accessing the configuration parameters is not available through the PageContext, which makes accessing the various configuration parameters needlessly painful (you need to access the appropriate object and call the needed method). Since accessing configuration parameters is a relatively common practice, we've added a set of initialization parameters handling methods to ExTagSupport and ExBodyTag-Support (our previously defined tag handler base classes) as shown in listing 6.16:

Listing 6.16   Initialization parameter handling in ExTagSupport and ExBodyTagSupport

```
// Some of the class implementation is available above...
protected String getInitParameter(String name)          ❶
{
    return getInitParameter(name,
                          PageContext.APPLICATION_SCOPE);
}

protected Enumeration getInitParameterNames()          ❷
{
    return getInitParameterNamesForScope(
                          PageContext.APPLICATION_SCOPE);
}

protected String getInitParameter(String name,          ❸
                                  int scope)
{
    switch(scope) {
        case PageContext.PAGE_SCOPE:
            return getServletConfig().getInitParameter(name);

        case PageContext.APPLICATION_SCOPE:
            return getServletContext().getInitParameter(name);

        default:
            throw new IllegalArgumentException("Illegal scope");
    }
}

protected Enumeration getInitParameterNamesForScope(int scope)   ❹
{
    switch(scope) {
        case PageContext.PAGE_SCOPE:
            return getServletConfig().getInitParameterNames();

        case PageContext.APPLICATION_SCOPE:
            return getServletContext().getInitParameterNames();

        default:
            throw new IllegalArgumentException("Illegal scope");
    }
}

protected ServletContext getServletContext()
{
    return pageContext.getServletContext();
}

protected ServletConfig getServletConfig()
{
    return pageContext.getServletConfig();
}
// Some of the class implementation continues below...
```

Shortcut method which fetches a named configuration parameter from the default scope (application).

❷ Shortcut method which enumerates the configuration parameter in the default scope (application).

❸ Fetches a configuration parameter based on the parameter name and scope.

❹ Enumerates the configuration parameter in a specified scope.

We've kept to the spirit of `PageContext` by providing scope-based methods to fetch the initialization parameters, as well as shortcut methods for the most common scope (application). This way we can use initialization parameters in our tags while we think in terms of scopes instead of having to remember which object (`Servlet-Config` or `ServletContext`) exposes a certain scope.

ShowConfigTag

To test drive the configuration methods and illustrate how to integrate configuration parameters into your tags, we've written `ShowConfigTag` (listing 6.17). This tag accesses named configuration parameters and prints their values to the result. `ShowConfigTag` has a single tag attribute that allows us to set the name of the configuration property whose value it should display. The tag will look for the value in the page scope first; but, if it is not there, `ShowConfigTag` will look for the value in the application scope.

Listing 6.17   Source code for the ShowConfigTag's handler class

```
package book.simpletasks;

import javax.servlet.jsp.JspException;
import javax.servlet.jsp.PageContext;

import book.util.ExTagSupport;
import book.util.LocalStrings;

public class ShowConfigTag extends ExTagSupport {

    static LocalStrings ls =
        LocalStrings.getLocalStrings(ShowConfigTag.class);

    protected String name = null;

    public void setName(String newName) {
        name = newName;
    }

    public int doStartTag()
            throws JspException
    {
        String conf = getInitParameter(name,
                                    PageContext.PAGE_SCOPE);
```

```
        if(null == conf) {
            conf = getInitParameter(name,
                            PageContext.APPLICATION_SCOPE);
        }

        try {
            writeHtml(pageContext.getOut(), conf);
            return SKIP_BODY;
        } catch(java.io.IOException ioe) {
            // User probably disconnected...
        }
    }

    protected void clearProperties()
    {
        name = null;
        super.clearProperties();
    }
}
```

The next thing to look into is the JSP driver for `ShowConfigTag` (listing 6.18). You should be familiar with the driver's general structure, as it is a modification to the driver used by `ShowObjectTag`. In this case, however, instead of enumerating the JSP attributes in a certain scope, the driver is enumerating the configuration parameters (first in the application scope, then in the page scope).

Listing 6.18 JSP file employing ShowConfigTag

```
<%@ page errorPage="error.jsp" %>
<%@ taglib
    uri="http://www.manning.com/jsptagsbook/simple-taglib"
    prefix="simp" %>
<html>
<body>

Here are your application initialization parameters:
<table>
<tr><th>Name</th> <th>Value</th> </tr>
<% java.util.Enumeration e = application.getInitParameterNames();
    while(e.hasMoreElements()) {
        String name = (String)e.nextElement();       ❶
%>
    <tr>
        <td> <%= name %></td>
        <td> <simp:conf name='<%= name %>' /> </td> </td>
    </tr>
<% } %>
</table>
And here they are again (scope not given this time):
```

```
<table>
<tr><th>Name</th> <th>Value</th> </tr>
<% e = config.getInitParameterNames();
   while(e.hasMoreElements()) {
       String name = (String)e.nextElement();      ❷
%>
   <tr>
        <td> <%= name %></td>
        <td> <simp:conf name='<%= name %>' /> </td>
   </tr>
<% } %>
</table>
That's all for now.
</body>
</html>
```

❶ Enumerates the names and shows the values of the configuration parameter in the application scope.

❷ Enumerates the names and shows the values of the the configuration parameter in the page scope.

The web application descriptor

A more interesting aspect of the JSP driver is the web application deployment descriptor that was generated to provide initialization parameters. Until now we have not provided configuration parameters in any of the samples. This example's web.xml, available in listing 6.19, configures two application-scoped parameters and two page-level parameters.

Listing 6.19   Web application descriptor for the ShowConfigTag JSP driver

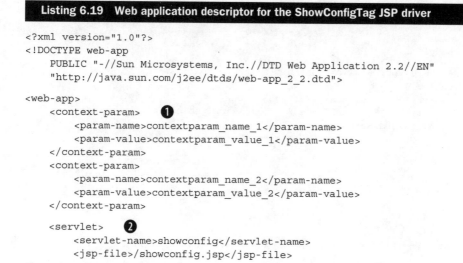

```
<?xml version="1.0"?>
<!DOCTYPE web-app
    PUBLIC "-//Sun Microsystems, Inc.//DTD Web Application 2.2//EN"
    "http://java.sun.com/j2ee/dtds/web-app_2_2.dtd">

<web-app>
    <context-param>      ❶
        <param-name>contextparam_name_1</param-name>
        <param-value>contextparam_value_1</param-value>
    </context-param>
    <context-param>
        <param-name>contextparam_name_2</param-name>
        <param-value>contextparam_value_2</param-value>
    </context-param>

    <servlet>      ❷
        <servlet-name>showconfig</servlet-name>
        <jsp-file>/showconfig.jsp</jsp-file>
```

```
        <init-param>    ❸
            <param-name>pageparam_name_1</param-name>
            <param-value>pageparam_value_1</param-value>
        </init-param>
        <init-param>
            <param-name>pageparam_name_2</param-name>
            <param-value>pageparam_value_2</param-value>
        </init-param>
    </servlet>

    <taglib>
        <taglib-uri>
            http://www.manning.com/jsptagsbook/simple-taglib
        </taglib-uri>
        <taglib-location>
            /WEB-INF/simpletags.tld
        </taglib-location>
    </taglib>
</web-app>
```

❶ **Defines a context (application-scoped) configuration parameter** Each application-scoped configuration parameter is defined in the web deployment descriptor with a `<context-param>` tag. The `<context-param>` wraps two other tags: `<param-name>`, which encloses the name of the configuration parameter name; and `<param-value>`, which encloses the value of the named configuration parameter.

❷ **To provide a configuration parameter for a JSP file, the file needs to be associated with a servlet** ❸ **Defines a servlet (page-scoped) configuration parameter** To associate a JSP file to a servlet name, define a servlet and, in lieu of an implementing class, specify the JSP file as the entity that implements the servlet (later you will be able to bind the JSP-implemented servlet to some arbitrary URLs, instead of the URL that represents the JSP file). When you specify a servlet for the JSP file, add initialization parameters to this servlet by adding an `<init-param>` tag to the servlet definitions. This `<init-param>` will again enclose `<param-name>` and `<param-value>` tags as defined for the application-scoped parameter.

When we are ready[5], we can deploy the JSP driver and the tag. After it has executed, we will have two tables, one with the application-scoped parameters and the other with the page-scoped parameters.

---

[5] We omitted the tag entry in the TLD because we aren't introducing anything new to it here.

NOTE	The example in this section did not use the configuration parameters for configuration, but rather showed you how to access them. Later in this book we will use these techniques for actual configuration purposes.

6.7   *Working with the tag's body*

Until now, our tags paid little attention to their body. In fact, most of the tags we've seen so far simply returned SKIP_BODY from doStartTag(), thereby instructing the JSP environment to disregard their body content altogether. This practice is not, however, always the case. Tags often find body content manipulation to be a very useful tool. Some examples are:

- A tag that displays some data values (like those implemented in this chapter) may need to have its body contain alternative content to be presented in the absence of its intended item.

- A tag that performs the equivalent of an "if-condition" statement needs to have a body that it can execute conditionally.

- A tag that performs looping needs to repeat its body execution until a certain condition is meet.

- A filter/translator type of tag needs to get a reference to its body and replace certain tag occurrences with some specified values, or translate the body into some other format. An example of this is the LowerCaseTag we created in chapter 3.

- A tag that executes a query could have the SQL for its query specified in its body.

These are just a few of the possible instances in which body manipulation in a tag is desirable.

Generally, we can make a clear distinction between:

- Tags that need to enable/disable their entire body evaluation conditionally. Tags that belong in this group either don't include their body, or include it unchanged, after the JSP engine has processed it.

- Tags that need to obtain their body content, either to send a modified version of the body to the user or to use it as an input to another application component.

These two cases differ greatly in the APIs that enable them, and also in the way that the JSP runtime executes the tag. The next few sections are going to tackle these issues, starting with the simple conditional body execution.

6.7.1 *Tag body evaluation*

As explained in chapter 4, enabling and disabling a tag's body evaluation is performed using the doStartTag() return code protocol. As a rule, whenever doStartTag() returns a value of SKIP_BODY, the JSP runtime will ignore the tag's body (if there is one) and neither evaluate it nor include it in the response to the user. Alternatively, a tag can enable its body evaluation by returning a value of EVAL_BODY_INCLUDE (for simple tags) or EVAL_BODY_TAG (for BodyTags, that is, tags that implement the BodyTag interface).

To illustrate this, we'll modify the ShowFormParamTag such that its body can contain text to be shown if the parameter cannot be found (similar to the "alt" attribute for images in the HTML <img> tag). Our goal is to add functionality to the ShowFormParamTag that enables us to specify alternative content like this:

```
<td>
<simp:formparam name="username">  Username was not found
</simp:formparam>
</td>
```

In this JSP fragment, we would expect the tag to send the client the "Username was not found" message when the form parameter username isn't found.

NOTE   You may be asking why you would use the tag's body to specify an alternative content and not some other attribute (e.g., <simp:formparam name="paramname" alt="\"paramname\" was not provided"/>). Using an attribute to specify alternative values is possible, but not as flexible as using the body. The body lets the alternative content be as complex and dynamic as necessary; tag attributes are much more limited. It can also be looked at as a style issue as well, where you can easily wrap your alternative content between start and end tags rather than burying it in an attribute and worrying about quote delimiting and other tedious formatting issues.

To enable this feature in ShowFormParamTag's handler class requires a minimal change (confined to a single method doStartTag()), as illustrated in listing 6.20.

> **Listing 6.20   Modifying ShowFormParamTag's handler class to make it body aware**

```java
public class ShowFormParamBodyTag extends ExTagSupport {

    // Some code was removed

    public int doStartTag()
            throws JspException
    {
```

```
    try {
        HttpServletRequest req =
            (HttpServletRequest)pageContext.getRequest();
        String value = req.getParameter(name);
        if(null != value) {
            writeHtml(pageContext.getOut(), value);
            return SKIP_BODY;                   ❶
        }
    } catch(java.io.IOException ioe) {
        // User probably disconnected ...
        // log an error and throw a JspTagException
        // …
    }
    return EVAL_BODY_INCLUDE;                    ❷
    }
    // Some more code was removed
}
```

❶ **We managed to print, do not show the body.**

❷ **The variable is not available, show the alternative text contained in the body.**

BodyTags and the TLD

When instructing the JSP runtime engine in handling a tag's body, changing the tag handler is only one of the procedures required. Each tag must also provide information regarding its body in the TLD.

Each tag element in the TLD should reflect how its body looks by providing an optional <bodycontent> entry with one of the following three possible values:

- JSP—Specifies that the body of the tag contains JSP. In this case, if the body is not empty, the JSP runtime will process it the same as any other content in a JSP. Choosing this option means that we can include any Java scriptlet or variable references we wish within the tag's body and it will be processed first. The outcome of this processing is passed to the tag as its body or included in the response to the user. If the <bodycontent> entry is missing, the runtime assumes that its value is JSP.

- tagdependent—Specifies that the body of the tag contains tag-dependent data that is not JSP and not to be processed by the JSP runtime.

- empty—The tag body must be empty.

Now it would be advantageous to create a TLD tag entry for ShowFormParam-BodyTag and specify its <bodycontent> type. To allow the body to contain Java scriptlets (if the tag user chooses), we will assign the value JSP to the tag's <bodycontent> entry. A value of JSP is probably the most widely used bodycontent type since it provides the greatest flexibility. Using it, the body can either be empty, contain static content, or contain legal Java scriptlets. The new TLD tag element is provided in listing 6.21.

Listing 6.21   Tag library descriptor for the body aware ShowFormParamTag

```
<tag>
    <name>bformparam</name>
    <tagclass>book.simpletasks.ShowFormParamBodyTag</tagclass>
    <bodycontent>JSP</bodycontent>         ❶
    <info>
        Show a single named form parameter or an alternate content
        taken from the tag's body
    </info>
    <attribute>
        <name>name</name>
        <required>true</required>
        <rtexprvalue>true</rtexprvalue>
    </attribute>
</tag>
```

❶ **Defines the body of the tag to be JSP.**

With our modified tag handler and TLD, we can now develop JSP code such as the one in listing 6.22. In it you see how we take advantage of the fact that alternative values can be used when the required form variable is not available.

Listing 6.22   JSP file employing ShowFormParamBodyTag

```
<%@ page errorPage="error.jsp" %>
<%@ taglib
    uri="http://www.manning.com/jsptagsbook/simple-taglib"
    prefix="simp" %>
<html>
<body>
Checking for a form variable named <tt>"varname"</tt>:<br>

Value of variable "varname" is
<simp:bformparam name="varname"> unspecified </simp:bformparam><br>    ❶

That's all for now.
</body>
</html>
```

❶ **Specifying an alternative content in case the variable "varname" was not sent by the form.**

This section provided a small step toward implementing conditional body evaluation. We will discuss this issue again, in somewhat greater detail, in chapter 9.

6.7.2 *Referencing your tag's body*

The previous section showed an example of conditional body evaluation; that is, letting a tag choose whether or not to include its body based on some logic in the tag. As you noticed, our tag either ignored its body or included it in the response verbatim. There are times when we want to take it one step further and have our tags inspect and modify their body. In chapter 4 we noted that tags with this ability need to implement an interface called BodyTag (which augments the simpler Tag interface). We saw an example of a BodyTag usage in the very simple LowerCaseTag example from chapter 3. Let's take a closer look at this technique as well as some more meaningful examples.

The primary difference between a BodyTag and a simple Tag is that it has access to the content between its opening and closings markups (the tag's body). We covered the BodyTag API and life cycle in chapter 4, but let's recap the important details of the API here.

- BodyTag introduces an additional method called doAfterBody() which is called on a tag handler after the JSP engine reads the tag's body and processes it. This is the method in which the tag handler can inspect and/or change its processed body.

- A tag handler accesses its processed body through its BodyContent object, which can be retrieved simply by calling getBodyContent() as long as the tag handler extends BodyTagSupport.

- Calling getString() on the BodyContent object for a tag returns a String containing the processed body of the tag.

- Calling getEnclosingWriter() on the BodyContent object for a tag returns a JspWriter which can be used to write back to the user. Note that this is different than the pageContext.getOut() method we used in simpler tags. We'll discuss the reason for this difference later in this section.

- doAfterBody() can return EVAL_BODY_TAG to cause the JSP runtime engine to process the body again and call doAfterBody() once more (useful in tags that iterate). It can return SKIP_BODY to inform the JSP engine to proceed to the doEndTag() method.

A discussion of some details of how the runtime engine manages BodyTags will clarify what is happening when a BodyTag is executed, and will also answer the question about why we must use a different JspWriter (accessed via Body-Content.getEnclosingWriter()) to write to the user than we did with standard tags. This section is pretty technical and discusses some of the intricacies of the JSP runtime that you might happily take for granted. Knowing these details will, however, help you truly understand what happens to the tags you are building.

BodyTags and the JSP runtime engine (behind the scenes)

Having gone through an in-depth discussion of the life cycle of `BodyTags` in chapter 4, you might think we know everything possible about JSP engines handling `BodyTags`, right? Although we learned when and why the runtime engine calls the methods of a `BodyTag`, what we didn't cover was how the engine manages the output of `BodyTags`. Since `BodyTags` can modify the contents of their body (which can contain other tags or scriptlets) these modifications must be managed by the engine until the tags are finished changing it. At that point they can be aggregated and sent to the user. This process requires a little juggling by the runtime engine in order to produce the predicted results for pages containing `BodyTags`. Let's take a look at that juggling act.

No matter what the content of a tag's body, whether it be scriptlets, static HTML, or other custom tags, the JSP engine will first process this content (as if it were anywhere else in the JSP) and then pass the results of that processing to the tag as its `BodyContent`. This is not such a simple task. How can all the scriptlets and tags suddenly hand over their results to the `BodyTag`? Redirecting all this output to a new location seems to be a daunting task, but the solution chosen by the JSP specification made it all much simpler than might be imagined.

The JSP specification's solution works on the premise that all output flowing to the user must be written to the implicit `out` object. When the JSP engine begins processing the body of a `BodyTag`, it swaps the implicit `out` with a new `JspWriter` that writes to a temporary holding tank. All the code and/or tags within a `BodyTag`'s body that "think" they are writing to the user, are really writing to some storage managed by the JSP engine. Later, when the body processing is completed, the engine gives the enclosing `BodyTag` access to this storage which now contains all the processed output of the tag's body. Indeed, the JSP specification defines a special `JspWriter` derivative called `BodyContent`, whose role is to serve as this holding tank and to be the implicit `out` variable during the processing of a `BodyTag`'s body. The `BodyContent` provides methods that let its developer access the content written into the `BodyContent`, as well as erase this content when needed. The problem becomes more complex in the face of `BodyTag` recursion—meaning `BodyTag` whose body encloses yet another `BodyTag`, and whose body encloses yet another `BodyTag`, and so forth. All these tags together force the JSP runtime to remember each tag's `BodyContent` and return to it when the enclosed tag is finished. To solve that, the JSP runtime is managing a stack of all the active `JspWriter` instances in the current page. In this way it can always pop the enclosed `BodyContent` out of the stack and return to the previous `JspWriter`.

NOTE   This solution breaks down if one of the page developers breaks the rules and uses the `Writer/OutputStream` exported by the implicit response object. This is one of the reasons you must not use these `Writer/OutputStreams`.

This JSP fragment demonstrates how the JSP runtime uses the writer stack and the `out` implicit variable:

```
<%@ taglib
    uri="http://www.manning.com/jsptagsbook/simple-taglib"
    prefix="simp" %>

<html>
<body>
<simp:BodyTag1>
    Some text
    <simp:BodyTag2>
        Some other text
    </simp:BodyTag2>
</simp:BodyTag1>
</body>
```

Figure 6.6 shows the values taken by `out` and the use of the writer stack at any given moment. In this figure there are five phases in the JSP execution. In the first phase (a) the JSP runtime is passing through the file and approaches the tag named BodyTag1. At this time, the output generated from the JSP execution goes to the original `out` variable (generated by the JSP runtime) and the writer stack is empty.

The next phase (b) occurs when the JSP runtime tackles BodyTag1 and starts to process its body. At this point, the JSP runtime creates a `BodyContent` (out1) to be used inside the body, pushes the original `out` on the writer stack, and sets out1 to be the current implicit `out` variable. From this moment forward, the JSP output goes into out1.

Phase (c) occurs when the JSP runtime tackles BodyTag2 and begins processing its body. The JSP runtime will create yet another `BodyContent`, out2, to be used inside the body, push out1 onto the writer stack (there are now two writers on the stack), and set out2 to be the current implicit `out` variable. Now the JSP output goes into out2.

The finalization of BodyTag2 triggers the next phase (d) and the JSP runtime should return the writer state to the way it was before phase (c). To do that, the JSP runtime pops out1 from the writer stack and sets it to be the implicit `out` variable. The JSP output goes again into out1.

In the final phase (e), when BodyTag1 completes its execution, the JSP runtime should return the output state to its original form in phase (a). To facilitate this, the

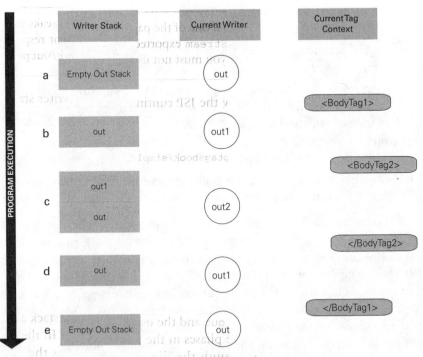

Figure 6.6 Body processing performed by the JSP runtime

JSP runtime pops the original out from the writer stack and sets it into the implicit out variable. The writer stack is empty again and whatever is written by the JSP goes again into the original Writer out.

In general, if the tag decides it wants to process its body, it informs the JSP runtime that it wants its body processed by returning the value BodyTag.EVAL_BODY_TAG. This causes the JSP runtime to do the following:

- The JSP runtime takes the current JspWriter object and pushes it onto the JspWriter stack.
- The JSP runtime takes the new BodyContent and sets it into the out implicit object. This way the new BodyContent will collect all the processed JSP that is written into the out object.
- The JSP runtime sets the new BodyContent object into the BodyTag, allowing the tag to get a reference to its processed body.
- The JSP runtime calls the tag's method doInitBody(). This lets the tag prepare for the body execution. The preparation can be initializing a variable

that is needed through the body processing or introducing new JSP scripting variables (discussed later on in the book).

- The JSP runtime processes the tag's body and writes all the results into the current `JspWriter`.

- When the body evaluation is completed, the JSP runtime needs to know if the tag wants it to repeat the body evaluation one more time. To find out, it will call the tag's method `doEndBody()`. A return code of `BodyTag.EVAL_BODY_TAG` instructs the runtime to repeat the body processing one more time, or a return code of `Tag.SKIP_BODY` instructs the runtime to stop evaluating the body.

- When finished processing the body, the JSP runtime pops the previous `Jsp-Writer` from the stack and assigns its value to the implicit `out` object.

Handling the body obviously involves many steps and is a relatively complex operation that relies on cooperation between the tag and the JSP runtime. Fortunately, most of this complexity is not an issue since it is all handled by the JSP engine.

It should be clear why the `JspWriter` returned by `BodyContent.getEnclosingWriter()` is not always the one returned by `pageContext.getOut()`. In cases in which our tag is enclosed within yet another tag (as BodyTag2 was within BodyTag1) the enclosing writer is the `BodyContent` associated with the enclosing tag; for example, the enclosing writer for out2 in our previous example was out1.

6.7.3 *A BodyTag example–logging messages*

Having covered the low-level details of how `BodyTags` are executed, let's now look at some examples. We can break the usage patterns for `BodyTags` into two logical groups:

1. Tags that inspect and optionally modify their body one time.
   Tags in this group do so by returning `Tag.SKIP_BODY` from `doAfterBody()` the first time it is called.

2. Tags that return `BodyTag.EVAL_BODY_TAG` from `doAfterBody()` until a certain condition is met (at which point it returns `Tag.SKIP_BODY` to mark the end of the processing).
   In this way the tag may repeat its body processing over and over again, possibly while iterating some data source such as an array or a database.

Clearly both of these patterns fulfill two extremely useful cases, and we will deal with both of them at length.

We will now develop a sample tag that uses the first body pattern and offer several examples of the second pattern in chapter 10. This tag will log whatever information is located in its body into the servlet log. With this tag you can log errors in your JSP files as well as improve error handler by logging the thrown exception to the servlet log. Let's first see how a tag can log information to the servlet logger.

Logging in servlets or JSPs

Logging in a servlet or a JSP is quite simple. Tags access the servlet log in the same way servlets do, by using the `ServletContext`. The `ServletContext` has two log methods that accept:

- A message string to be logged
- A message string and a `Throwable` object to be logged

A tag can use the `pageContext` to access the `ServletContext` by calling the method `pageContext.getServletContext()`, after which it can simply call any of the log methods.

Writing the Logging tag

If we want to design a simple tag to log messages we *could* just have it require two tag attributes: a message and a `Throwable` runtime object. The problem with this naïve approach is that it lacks flexibility. For example, there is a limit to what we can put in an attribute; hence, the message is limited and we will not be able to combine scriptlets (or other tags) with constant text. Moreover, you cannot have more than one message line since tag attributes cannot include multiple lines of text.

A preferable solution is to have the log tag take its input from its body. This way we can have any JSP content inside the body (including dynamic entities such as scriptlets and tags) and the log tag will use the processed output without a problem. Based on this argument, we'll build our tag so that it gets its log message from its body, rather than through a tag attribute.

NOTE   Since logging is such a common practice, we implemented log methods in our superclasses `ExBodyTagSupport` and `ExTagSupport`. These log methods simply fetch the `ServletContext` object associated with this page and call the matching log method.

As we approach our log writer implementation, we see that this will not be the last tag we develop that needs to access its body. It will be useful then to have a base class to provide the functionality of body reading so that more specialized tags (such as the log writer) can just inherit from it. To accomplish this, we've built the abstract class `BodyReaderTag` (listing 6.23).

Listing 6.23   Source code for the BodyReaderTag abstract handler

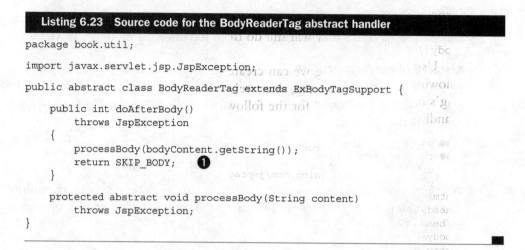

```
package book.util;

import javax.servlet.jsp.JspException;

public abstract class BodyReaderTag extends ExBodyTagSupport {

    public int doAfterBody()
        throws JspException
    {
        processBody(bodyContent.getString());
        return SKIP_BODY;          ❶
    }

    protected abstract void processBody(String content)
        throws JspException;
}
```

❶ **Returning `SKIP_BODY` instructs the JSP runtime not to repeat processing the body**   In essence, the first body pattern is implemented here.

The role of `BodyReaderTag` is to read the body and send it as a string to be processed by the method `processBody()`, implemented by an extending class. With `BodyReaderTag` it is now very easy to implement our log writer tag as presented in llisting 6.24.

Listing 6.24   Source code for the LogWriterTag's tag handler

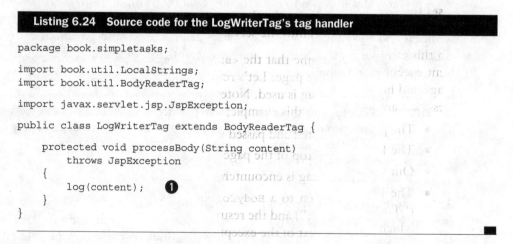

```
package book.simpletasks;

import book.util.LocalStrings;
import book.util.BodyReaderTag;

import javax.servlet.jsp.JspException;

public class LogWriterTag extends BodyReaderTag {

    protected void processBody(String content)
        throws JspException
    {
        log(content);            ❶
    }
}
```

❶ **The method `log()` is implemented by the superclass `ExBodyTagSupport`.**

Listing 6.24 shows how the simple code that is the guts of `LogWriterTag` is dropped nicely into `processBody()`. Other tags may require more complex body processing or initialization before entering the tag's body (through the use of `doInitBody()`), but they will still do the bulk of their processing in our `process-Body()` method.

Using the logger tag we can create a useful error handler page. We'll forgo showing the TLD for this tag, since we've already seen several examples of this. Our tag's name will be "log" for the following example (which implements an error handling page):

```
<%@ page isErrorPage="true" %>
<%@ taglib
    uri="http://www.manning.com/jsptagsbook/simple-taglib"
    prefix="simp" %>
<html>
<head>
</head>
<body>
Sorry but your request was terminated due to errors:
<pre>
<simp:viewError/>
</pre>

<simp:log>
The following exception was thrown: <simp:viewError/>    ❶
</simp:log>
</body>
</html>
```

❶ **Uses the error viewer to print the thrown exeption into the logger's body** This way the exception is reported into the servlet log.

In this example, we assume that the `<simp:viewError>` tag simply writes the current exception out to the page. Let's review what happens during a request to this page and how our new tag is used. Note: we mention only the methods in this process that are important to this example; some life cycle calls have been omitted.

- The page is requested and passed an exception from some other servlet or JSP.
- The HTML at the top of the page is returned to the user.
- Our `<simp:log>` tag is encountered and its body is processed.
- The body is written to a `BodyContent` object, including the static message ("The following …") and the result of the evaluation of `<simp:viewError/>`, which is just the text of the exception.
- `doAfterBody()` is called, which is now handled at our base class. This, in turn, gets the `BodyContent` as a string and invokes `processBody()` on our subclass.
- Our log method is called with the stringified `BodyContent` as its parameter—thereby logging the message and the exception text to the servlet log.

We've now built a useful `BodyTag` and a reusable base class that will be helpful in upcoming examples. Later chapters will build on this section to provide high-level functionality such as conditioning (chapter 9) and iteration (chapter 10) but the fundamental principles we've learned here will not change.

6.8   *Tag cooperation through nesting*

A very powerful technique, though not as widespread as attribute use or even body manipulation, is tag nesting. Until now, none of our tags cooperated directly with any others. Admittedly, sometimes the execution of one tag affected another (such as in the case of the flush and redirect tags, and in our previous logger example), but this was not explicit cooperation. One tag acting alone cannot solve many real-world cases, which brings us to the need for some cooperation between different tags.

One obvious way that tags can cooperate is by using the JSP attributes (not to be confused with tag attributes). In this technique, tags use the JSP attributes as a shared memory space where they can exchange data. However, simple data exchange using the JSP attributes is not always sufficient. For example, what if we have a complex containment relation between two tags such that one tag has meaning only within the body of another? We surely cannot force such relations using the JSP attributes. When JSP attributes are used to coordinate two different tags, the JSP developer is typically required to name the different attributes (usually by providing an ID to the produced attribute) and to link the consumer of the attribute by again providing its name. Sometimes this is unnecessary extra work that can be resolved by another coordination technique. Indeed, JSP custom tags offer an implicit coordination technique by using parent-child relations among tags and the tag's parent attribute. This is known as nesting.

In chapter 4 we said that when a certain tag is contained within the body of another, the containing tag is the parent of the contained one (for instance, in the error handler presented in the previous section, `<simp:log>` was the parent tag of `<simp:viewError>`). Each tag has an attribute named `parent` that holds reference to its parent tag (set by the JSP runtime). This way the tag can traverse its parent list, searching for a specific tag with which it needs to cooperate.

This traversing and searching for a specific class is already implemented by `findAncestorWithClass()` in the class `TagSupport`. This method takes two parameters: a reference to the tag from which it should start to search (in many cases it will be `this`), and a class representing the type of tag handler we are seeking. For example, the following code fragment uses `findAncestorWithClass()` to find a tag in `this` tag parent chain whose class is `WrapperTag`.

```
WrapperTag wrapper =
        (WrapperTag)findAncestorWithClass(this,
                                        WrapperTag.class);
```

The class `TagSupport` provides yet another set of methods to ease tag cooperation through nesting, and these are the methods that deal with value manipulation. In many cases, contained tags will set values into their parents. One way is to have a setter method for each such value. `TagSupport`, however, provides an alternative group of value manipulation methods (including setting, removing, and getting value) that allow tags to exchange values with others without implementing setter methods. (All this value manipulation is implemented by keeping the values in a tag internal hash table and exposing its `set()` and `get()` methods.) So we can now take the wrapped class and set values into it in the following manner:

```
WrapperTag wrapper =
        (WrapperTag)findAncestorWithClass(this,
                                        WrapperTag.class);
wrapper.setValue("valuekey", "some value object");
```

Cooperation through nesting as shown in the previous code fragment is extremely useful when you design a tag family with specific syntactic structure (e.g., tag *x* should be contained within tag *y*), and it provides very easy coordination requiring nothing from the JSP developer. In the next chapter, when we implement a set of email-sending tags, we will see a more concrete example of the benefits and syntax for implementing this powerful feature.

6.9   *Cleaning up*

It's no accident that the final technique to discuss corresponds with the last stage of the tag's life cycle: cleanup. Most nontrivial tags collect state while executing, and these tags must free their state or else resource leaks will happen (Armageddon for an application server). Cleaning resources can be a tricky proposition for components managed by an external environment such as the JSP runtime engine. With tags, however, resource management is not the only motivation for cleanup. Tags are defined as reusable objects and, therefore, any tag is a candidate for pooling and reuse. Not only do tags need to free accumulated state, they also need to recycle themselves so that each reuse starts with all the properties in the exact same states.

To facilitate state cleanup and tag recycling, the JSP specification defines the tag method calls wherein these steps should occur. Cleaning after your tags is not rocket science, but doing it correctly requires a few considerations that we will explore soon. We will begin with a short reminder of the tag's life cycle and then discuss how this life cycle affects your tag design cleanup. We will then see how the tags developed for this book implement cleanup and reuse.

6.9.1 *Review of tag life cycle*

Looking back at the tag's life cycle as explained in chapter 4, we can divide the tag life cycle into five stages:

- A tag is **created**. It should then have some initial state that allows it to be used by the JSP environment as needed.

- The JSP environment **initializes** the tag. At this time, the JSP environment sets various properties into the tag, starting with the `pageContext` and `parent` properties, and ending with other properties as specified by the tag attributes and the TLD.

- The JSP environment puts the tag into **service** by calling `doStartTag()`. The tag is now starting to collect state needed for the current execution.

- The JSP environment informs the tag that the current **service** is done by calling `doEndTag()`. The tag should now free all the resources accumulated for the ended service phase. At the end of `doEndTag()`, the tag should be in a state that allows it to be reused again at the same JSP page.

- The JSP environment puts the tag into **reuse** by calling its `release()` method. The tag should now recycle itself, returning to the same state as when it was **created.**

All this life cycle discussion makes it clear that there are two cleanup points:

1 `doEndTag()`—The tag must free all the state allocated for its current service period.

2 `release()`—The tag must recycle itself. This usually entails clearing the tag's properties (for example `pageContext` and `parent`), since all other state was probably part of the service phase.

6.9.2 *Exceptions and cleanup*

What happens if an exception is thrown somewhere within this life cycle? Most of the tag's methods can throw a `JspException`, but the method may (of course) throw a runtime exception such as `java.lang.NullPointerException`. What then? The answer is rather simple. If `doStartTag()`, `doEndTag()`, or some other tag callback method was called and threw an exception, in JSP1.1 the JSP runtime would immediately call `release()`, not `doEndTag()`. This is not per the specification, but is the common practice and a reasonable solution since the tag should not gather state until the call to `doStartTag()`. For example, look at the following pseudocode fragment that is similar to that generated by Tomcat's JSP1.1 translator.

```
Sometag _t = get Sometag ();
t.setPageContext(pageContext);
t.setParent(null);
t.setSomeProperty(...);

try {
    t.doStartTag();
    // some code was omitted ...
    t.doEndTag();
} finally {
    t.release();
}
```

As you can see, `release()` is executing within a `finally` block, assuring us that it will be called even in the face of exceptions.

JSP1.2 offers an improved and regulated exception handling capability by providing the `TryCatchFinally` interface. Tags that implement `TryCatchFinally` inform the JSP runtime that they want to be notified when exceptions occur during their run. The JSP runtime will assure that the `TryCatchFinally` methods in the tags will be called in the appropriate time.

TryCatchFinally and the JSP runtime

As stated in chapter 4, the `TryCatchFinally` interface exports the following methods:

- `doCatch()` allows the JSP runtime to inform the tag that an exception was thrown while executing it.
  The tag can then respond to the exceptional condition based on the exception parameter and the general state of the tag.
- `doFinally()` is called by the JSP runtime whenever the tag finishes its service phase.
  This way the tag can free the state it accumulated when serving the request.

But how will the JSP runtime assure that?

The answer is elementary. The JSP translator surrounds the tag with code fragments as demonstrated in the following listing;

```
// Execute the tag lifecycle
h = get a Tag();  // get a tag handler

h.setPageContext(pc);  // initialize as desired
h.setParent(null);
h.setFoo("foo");
// Call the lifecycle methods inside a try-catch-finally
// fragment.
```

```
try {
  doStartTag()...
  ....
  doEndTag()...
} catch (Throwable t) {
  // react to exceptional condition
  // assure that doCatch() get called
  h.doCatch(t);
} finally {
  // restore data invariants and release per-invocation resources
  // assure that doFinally() get called
  h.doFinally();
}

... other invocations perhaps with some new setters
...
h.release();  // release long-term resources
```

The code emitted by the JSP runtime makes sure that the tag will be notified of exceptions, no matter what happens in or out of the tag.

Using the `TryCatchFinally` interface, implementing cleanup for our tag is very simple. All we need is to make sure that we use the method `doFinally()` and `doCatch()` to clean up the tag, and the JSP runtime will assure us that these methods are called, even in the face of exceptions.

6.9.3 *Improving our base classes to handle cleanup*

The end result is that a tag should be ready to perform two tasks: cleaning its accumulated state and recycling itself. Although these two tasks will usually occur in different methods, sometimes (when an exception is thrown) both will happen in `release()` (or in `doFinally()`). All this rather complex cleanup logic would fit best in some superclass and the extending classes should just implement their own resource deallocation and recycling. So, in all the samples in this book, most cleanup logic is buried inside `ExTagSupport` and `ExBodyTagSupport`,[6] as seen in listing 6.25.

> **Listing 6.25   Cleanup logic in ExTagSupport and ExBodyTagSupport**

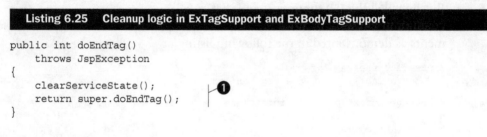

```
public int doEndTag()
    throws JspException
{
    clearServiceState();
    return super.doEndTag();
}
```

---

[6] For JSP1.2 we replace `release()` with `doFinally()` in the `TryCatchFinally` interface.

```
public void release()
{
    clearServiceState();      ②

    clearProperties();        ③
    super.release();
}
protected void clearProperties()   ④
{
}
protected void clearServiceState()   ④
{
}
```

❶ **Implementing service state cleanup, calling `clearServiceState`, and informing that the state is clear.**

❷ **Implementing service state cleanup in the face of exceptions. False value in `isServiceStateClear` means that an exception prevented the execution of `clearServiceState`.**

❸ **Clearing the tag's properties.**

❹ **Placeholder methods for clearing tag's properties and service state.**

The idea behind the presented cleanup logic is to release the developer from thinking in terms of "OK, release is getting called, what should I do?" and instead, think in terms of a specific tag logic ("OK, lets clear these two attributes."). To help, we extend the `ExTagSupport` and `ExBodyTagSupport` classes to expose two methods the tag developer may wish to override. The rules for overriding these methods are the following:

- `clearProperties()`—Overriding this lets the tag clear its specific custom properties.
  If the tag inherits yet another tag with properties of its own, it should add a call to `super.clearProperties()` at the end of its `clearProperties()` method (always do that by default, just to make sure).

- `clearServiceState()`—Overriding this allows the tag to free its service phase state.
  In cases of tag inheritance, the rules for `clearProperties()` are also applicable for `clearServiceState()`. Note that in many cases `clearServiceState()` is being called twice, once in `doEndTag()` and again in `release()`. This is because we need to make sure that `clearServiceState()` will be called in case of an exception.

Using these two methods frees the tag developer to think in terms of the specific tag state, but for the cleanup logic to work, the developer would be wise to follow these rules:

- Tags that override `release()` should call `super.release()` to activate the cleanup logic.
- Tags that override `doEndTag()` should call `super.doEndTag()`.

These rules are not complex or restrictive as most of the tags do not need to override `doEndTag()` and `release()`. For that reason, all the tags developed for this book are going to use this autocleanup mechanism.

JSP1.2 NOTE The ExXXXSupport classes for JSP1.2 implement the cleanup logic using the `TryCatchFinally` interface by putting the call to `clearServiceState()` and `clearProperties()` inside `doFinally()`.

As a final note, you do not have to use this proposed cleanup logic in your own tags (although we recommend it), but it's a good idea to observe the basic cleanup guidelines described in this section.

6.10 *Summary*

We've covered a wealth of useful techniques here, including how to write content to the user, how to use tag attributes, using the servlet API, initializing tags, sharing data in different scopes, `BodyTags`, and cleaning up your tags' resources. The common theme throughout these techniques is providing tags the facilities they need to make them effective. With these skills alone, you can begin building production quality tag libraries for your applications.

There are still several aspects of tag development with which we've only flirted so far. The remainder of the book will focus on strengthening your grasp of the concepts learned here and applying them to real-world examples and scenarios. In the next chapter we apply many of these techniques as we build our first, real-world tag library for sending email.

Building a tag library for sending email

7

195

The concepts we've covered up to now provide the groundwork for building a tag library that supports simple Internet email. Unlike many of the examples we've seen so far, the tags in this chapter will be useful in real-world situations, and will demonstrate appropriate usage of `BodyTags`, tag nesting, tag attributes, and application configuration. We will start with a bare-bones implementation of the library and gradually improve it by adding features and improving usability.

The development goals for the send mail tag library are:

- To implement email functionality in a web application using JSP pages, even without prior knowledge of how email messaging is implemented on the Internet
- To enable tag users with limited development skills to configure their tags in a way that uses application-level configuration (covered in the previous chapter)
- To generate the body of the email dynamically
- To generate the subject of the email dynamically
- To specify senders and receivers of the email dynamically

All of these requirements relate directly to tag development and design. However, since our tags will provide email functionality, a brief discussion of the roles of SMTP (Simple Mail Transfer Protocol) and its Java API is essential.

7.1   Sending email from a Java program

Sending email is by far one of the most common activities on the Web; so it is no surprise that it passed regularization at the protocol as well as API levels. In this section, we will discuss this regularization, starting with the protocol used to send email and ending with the Java API used by a Java program to send email.

7.1.1   The Simple Mail Transfer Protocol

Email transmission was regularized by two standards:

- SMTP, as specified in RFC821, defines how an email client and server should communicate in order to send messages. Briefly, SMTP specifies a client/server architecture (as illustrated in figure 7.1) wherein the SMTP servers listen for incoming SMTP requests on socket port number 25. When a client wishes to send an email it connects to the SMTP server, and then sends the server SMTP commands as defined in RFC821.
- The Internet text messages structure, as specified in RFC822, defines how an email message should appear. Simply put, it begins with a few headers that specify information such as the email sender, the recipients, the subject of the

email, and so forth, followed by an empty line, and then the content of the message body.

Let's look at a scenario in which john@foo.com wishes to send an email to doe@bar.com. To do so, John uses an email client to connect to his mail server. The email client then starts an SMTP session with commands and server return codes similar to those in listing 7.1. Note that return codes sent by the mail server are in bold.

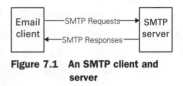

Figure 7.1 An SMTP client and server

Listing 7.1 A sample SMTP session

```
220 mail.foo.com Simple Mail Transfer Service Ready
HELO some-station.foo.com
250 mail.foo.com
MAIL FROM:<john@foo.com>
250 OK
RCPT TO:<doe@bar.com>
250 OK
DATA
354 Start mail input; end with <CRLF>.<CRLF>
From: <john@foo.com>
To: <doe@bar.com>
Subject: Just a test

OK, this is the email's body as defined in RFC822. It is
terminated by a line that contains a single dot.
.
250 OK
QUIT
221 mail.foo.com Connection closed
```

When the SMTP server accepts a request, it begins forwarding it to the recipient user(s). This forwarding may require the help of other SMTP servers that act as a relay, but eventually the message arrives at the mailbox of doe@bar.com.

7.1.2 *Java-based email*

This discussion of SMTP was intended merely to familiarize you with its essence before discussing the sending of email from Java programs. How do we programmatically send email? The most obvious way is to open a socket to the SMTP server and communicate with the syntax in RFC821. Though this works, most seasoned Java developers know that for common functionality there is usually a class (or library) already in existence. Sending email is no exception, so instead of reinventing the wheel, let's work with a readily available option.

Using the SMTPClient class

In searching for ways to send email from a Java program, our first stop is in the class `sun.net.smtp.SmtpClient`, which is provided inside the JDK, though not supported, by Sun. Running `javap` on `sun.net.smtp.SmtpClient` yields the public interface presented in listing 7.2.

Listing 7.2   The public interface of sun.net.smtp.SmtpClient

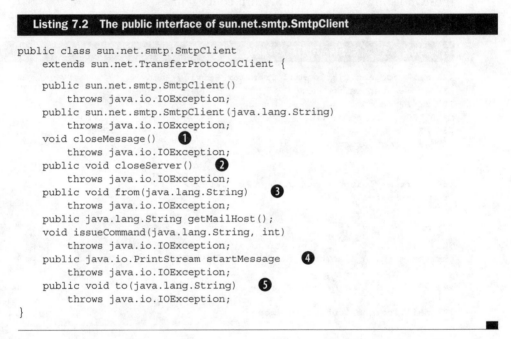

```
public class sun.net.smtp.SmtpClient
    extends sun.net.TransferProtocolClient {

    public sun.net.smtp.SmtpClient()
        throws java.io.IOException;
    public sun.net.smtp.SmtpClient(java.lang.String)
        throws java.io.IOException;
    void closeMessage()                          ❶
        throws java.io.IOException;
    public void closeServer()                    ❷
        throws java.io.IOException;
    public void from(java.lang.String)           ❸
        throws java.io.IOException;
    public java.lang.String getMailHost();
    void issueCommand(java.lang.String, int)
        throws java.io.IOException;
    public java.io.PrintStream startMessage()    ❹
        throws java.io.IOException;
    public void to(java.lang.String)             ❺
        throws java.io.IOException;
}
```

---

❶ Closes the message being sent.
❷ Closes the connection to the SMTP server to which the message is being sent.
❸ This method is passed the email address of the sender.
❹ Connects to the server and starts the message.
❺ This method is passed the email address of the recipient.

Although undocumented, the `SmtpClient` class is well known in the Java community for facilitating email in a way that complies with all Internet mail standards (such as RFC821 and RFC822). Listing 7.3 shows an example of how `sun.net.smtp.Smtp-Client` works in sending email.

Listing 7.3 Sending email with sun.net.smtp.SmtpClient

```
SmtpClient smtp = new SmtpClient("mail.foo.com");
smtp.from("john@foo.com");
smtp.to("doe@bar.com");
java.io.PrintStream msg = smtp.startMessage();

msg.println("From: " + "john@foo.com");
msg.println("To: " + "doe@bar.com");
msg.println("Subject: Just a test");
msg.println();
msg.println("OK, this is the email's body as");
msg.println("defined in RFC822. It is");
msg.println("terminated by a line that contains");
msg.println("a single dot.");
msg.println(".");
smtp.closeServer();
```

❶

---

❶ **Constructing the email message according to RFC822** Headers come first, followed by an empty line, and then the message body.

Working with `sun.net.smtp.SmtpClient` is much easier than writing your own SMTP library, but generating the email's content may be frustrating since you need to write a correct RFC822-compliant message into the `PrintStream` returned from `startMessage()`. To add to this headache, using `sun.net.smtp.SmtpClient` hardcodes us to a specific mail protocol. What if we wish to use Lotus Notes proprietary protocol instead? And what if our message should not be coded as an Internet message? JavaMail package comes to our rescue.

Using the JavaMail API

JavaMail is a standard for Java messaging APIs that defines how a Java application can send, list, and receive email messages in a protocol-neutral manner. The application does not need to know how to structure the message or anything about the internal workings of SMTP. Instead, it can use classes such as `MimeMessage`, `Session`, and `Transport` to send email messages, as demonstrated in listing 7.4. Unlike the somewhat dubious `SmtpClient` class, this API is the standard, Sun-supported method for sending email using Java.

Listing 7.4 Sending email with JavaMail

```
import java.util.Properties;
import javax.mail.*;
import javax.mail.internet.*;

// ... Some code omitted here.
```

```
Properties props = new Properties();

props.put("mail.smtp.host", "mail.foo.com");        ❶

Session session = Session.getInstance(props, null);
MimeMessage message = new MimeMessage(session);
message.setFrom(new InternetAddress("john@foo.com"));
message.addRecipient(Message.RecipientType.TO,
                        new InternetAddress("doe@bar.com"));
message.setSubject("Just a test");
message.setText("OK, this is the email's body as");
message.setText("defined in RFC822. It is");
message.setText("terminated by a line that contains");
message.setText("a line with a single dot.");
Transport.send(message);
```

❶ **Informing the location of the SMTP server via a property**   This approach is much more generic than using a setter.

As shown in listing 7.4, sending email using JavaMail is virtually effortless. Unlike the SmtpClient class, with the JavaMail API we needn't worry about constructing a message to comply with RFC822, as the MimeMessage class handles this for us. We may instead rely on the intuitive setFrom(), addRecipient(), setSubject(), and setText() methods to construct our message properly. Because of its ease of use and feature support, we'll implement our email tag library with JavaMail, instead of SmtpClient or a homegrown solution.

7.2   *Our first email tag*

Revising our requirements for the email tag in light of this knowledge of JavaMail, the tag should have the following information/parameters:

- The mail server (or a Session object that contains it) to send the email
- The address of the sender
- The address of the recipient
- The subject of the email (optional)
- The body of the email

7.2.1   *SimpleJavaMailTag example*

A naïve email tag can be designed as a simple bodyless tag wherein each parameter is set by using tag attributes and property setters. Our email tag's attributes and setter and getter methods are illustrated in table 7.1.

Table 7.1 Attributes and methods in `SimpleJavaMailTag`

Attribute name	Use	Setter/Getter method
`server`	The SMTP server to connect to for sending email	`setServer()`/`getServer()`
`to`	The recipient of the email	`setTo()`/`getTo()`
`from`	The sender of the email	`setFrom()`/`getFrom()`
`subject`	The subject line of the email	`setSubject()`/`getSubject()`
`body`	The body of the email	`setBody()`/`getBody()`

Listing 7.5 SimpleJavaMailTag custom tag

```java
package book.mail;

import book.util.LocalStrings;
import book.util.ExTagSupport;

import java.util.Properties;

import javax.mail.Transport;
import javax.mail.Session;
import javax.mail.Message;
import javax.mail.MessagingException;
import javax.mail.internet.MimeMessage;
import javax.mail.internet.InternetAddress;
import javax.mail.internet.AddressException;
import javax.servlet.jsp.JspException;

public class SimpleJavaMailTag extends ExTagSupport {

    static LocalStrings ls =
        LocalStrings.getLocalStrings(SimpleJavaMailTag.class);

    protected String mailServer = null;      ❶
    protected String from = null;
    protected String to = null;
    protected String body = null;
    protected String subject = null;

    public void setServer(String server)
    {
        this.mailServer = server;
    }

    public void setFrom(String from)
    {
        this.from = from;
    }
```

```
public void setTo(String to)
{
    this.to = to;
}

public void setBody(String body)
{
    this.body = body;
}

public void setSubject(String subject)
{
    this.subject = subject;
}

public int doStartTag()
        throws JspException
{
    try {
        sendMail(mailServer, from, to, body, subject);
        return SKIP_BODY;
    } catch(AddressException ae) {
        // Log the error
    } catch(MessagingException me) {
        // Log the error
    }
    // Throw an exception to inform the error.
}

protected void sendMail(String smtpServer,
                        String sender,
                        String recipient,
                        String content,
                        String subject)
    throws AddressException, MessagingException
{
    Properties props = new Properties();
    props.put("mail.smtp.host", smtpServer);
    Session session = Session.getInstance(props, null);

    MimeMessage message = new MimeMessage(session);
    message.setFrom(new InternetAddress(sender));
    message.addRecipient(Message.RecipientType.TO,
                        new InternetAddress(recipient));
    if(null != subject) {
        message.setSubject(subject);
    } else {
        message.setSubject("");
    }

    if(null == content) { // Empty body
        content = "";
    }
    message.setText(content);
```

2

3

```
        Transport.send(message);
    }
    protected void clearProperties()        ❹
    {
        mailServer = null;
        from = null;
        to = null;
        body = null;
        subject = null;
        super.clearProperties();
    }
}
```

❶ **Tag's properties and their setters.**

❷ **Calls the tag. All we need to do here is send the email based on the parameters that are provided.**

❸ **Sends an email using the specified SMTP server from the sender to the recipient. The email's content and subject are specified parameters.**

❹ **Clears all the properties set into the tag. Called by the cleanup login that is implemented in the superclass.**

SimpleJavaMailTag is aptly named—all it contains are the properties and their setters, in addition to an email sending routine and doStartTag(), that cause the email to be sent.

The TLD for SimpleJavaMailTag
The TLD entry for this tag is provided in listing 7.6.

Listing 7.6   SimpleJavaMailTag entry

```
<tag>
    <name>send</name>
    <tagclass>book.mail.SimpleJavaMailTag</tagclass>
    <teiclass>book.mail.MailTagExtraInfo</teiclass>
    <bodycontent>empty</bodycontent>
    <info>
        Sends an email based on the provided attributes.
    </info>

    <attribute>
        <name>server</name>
        <required>true</required>
        <rtexprvalue>false</rtexprvalue>
    </attribute>
    <attribute>
```

```
        <name>from</name>
        <required>true</required>
        <rtexprvalue>true</rtexprvalue>
    </attribute>
    <attribute>
        <name>to</name>
        <required>true</required>
        <rtexprvalue>true</rtexprvalue>
    </attribute>
    <attribute>
        <name>subject</name>
        <required>false</required>
        <rtexprvalue>true</rtexprvalue>
    </attribute>
    <attribute>
        <name>body</name>
        <required>true</required>
        <rtexprvalue>true</rtexprvalue>
    </attribute>
</tag>
```

As shown in this listing, most of the tag's attributes may have runtime values, only the SMTP server address must, for security reasons, be a constant value. By keeping the SMTP server from accepting runtime expressions, we close a door on the option of tampering with the mail server address. Careful JSP programming can also avoid this danger, but it is not much of a problem to have the server accept only constant strings.

The listing also shows that most attribute values are mandatory. This allows the JSP runtime to verify that all the needed parameters were provided (so it does not have to be done in the tag). Two of the attributes, from and to, may also require a syntax check. Both are supposed to be an email address, so checking them for correctness is possible (e.g., we may want to check that the address looks like userid@domain). Fortunately for us, JavaMail makes a syntactic check for the provided address string when you create an InternetAddress. If the constructor for InternetAddress is passed an invalid email address, an AddressException is thrown.

Adding validation code for email addresses
Recall from chapter 6 that we can specify validation code for tag attributes by defining a subclass of TagExtraInfo to be associated with our tag. In this case, our subclass is called MailTagExtraInfo. In it, we utilize the InternetAddressconstructor to test the validity of the email addresses that are passed as attributes to our tag. Listing 7.7 shows what our MailTagExtraInfo class looks like.

Listing 7.7   MailTagExtraInfo's implementation

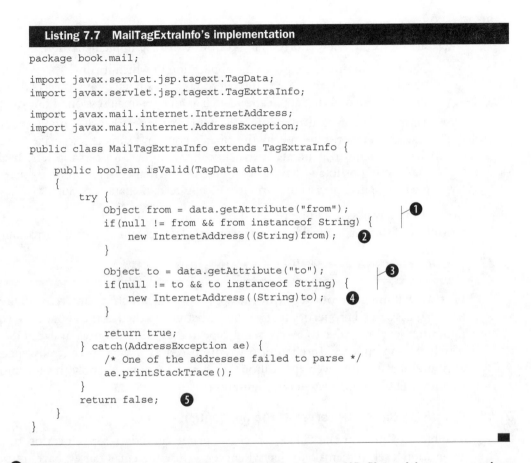

```
package book.mail;

import javax.servlet.jsp.tagext.TagData;
import javax.servlet.jsp.tagext.TagExtraInfo;

import javax.mail.internet.InternetAddress;
import javax.mail.internet.AddressException;

public class MailTagExtraInfo extends TagExtraInfo {

    public boolean isValid(TagData data)
    {
        try {
            Object from = data.getAttribute("from");          ❶
            if(null != from && from instanceof String) {
                new InternetAddress((String)from);    ❷
            }

            Object to = data.getAttribute("to");              ❸
            if(null != to && to instanceof String) {
                new InternetAddress((String)to);    ❹
            }

            return true;
        } catch(AddressException ae) {
            /* One of the addresses failed to parse */
            ae.printStackTrace();
        }
        return false;       ❺
    }
}
```

❶ Checks that the `from` attribute was specified in the JSP file and is not a runtime expression.

❷ Checks that the `from` address is OK by constructing an `InternetAddress`. The construction will throw `AddressException` in case of invalid address.

❸ Checks that the `to` attribute was specified in the JSP file and is not a runtime expression.

❹ Checks that the `to` address is OK by constructing an `InternetAddress`. The construction will throw `AddressException` in case of an invalid address.

❺ We had an exception. This probably means that `InternetAddress` had parsing errors in one of the addresses. We will return `false`.

This tag is a decent start; it provides all required functionality and shields the JSP author from the complexity of Java and SMTP.

Limitations of the SimpleJavaMailTag

There are, however, a few shortcomings of this email tag implementation:

- The tag is not integrated with the application in which it runs.
  We might, for instance, want the tag to take advantage of any objects that are already created in that application (such as an open mail session, if one exists).

- The tag relies on its attributes to collect information, rather than using its body. Having a tag attribute specify the email's body and subject also makes it relatively difficult to generate it dynamically without a lot of scriptlets. It also makes it impossible to have a static email body that contains more than a single line;[1] plus it forces the writer to escape certain characters, such as '"'.

Both of these issues should be resolved to produce a truly useful, reusable tag. The remainder of this chapter will focus on incrementally overcoming these shortcomings.

7.3   Integrating the tag with the application

First we will integrate our tag with the application in which it runs. `SimpleJava-MailTag` has several properties that would be better specified at the application configuration level in order to avoid being repeated as tag attributes in every JSP in which the tag appears. In chapter 6 we discussed how we can centrally specify attributes for an entire web application. We'll now see how to apply this technique to our email tag, improving its configuration.

7.3.1   Specifying the SMTP server at the application level

The tag attribute for the SMTP server is a prime candidate for relocation to the application level. It seems odd that whenever we use the email tag we have to specify the mail server in the JSP file. This intensifies if we imagine what would happen if the name of our SMTP server needed to change. We'd be eternally searching and replacing throughout all the JSP files in our application in order to update them with the new server. It makes sense then to specify the mail server as an application configuration parameter instead (a context initialization parameter) and have the tag conduct the search for it.

7.3.2   Using an existing mail session

Why should the tag get the location of the mail server and repeatedly instantiate a `Session` to it? Assuming that the application is using email extensively, shouldn't the tag be able to use the application's mail session by taking it from the application

---

[1] Tag attributes cannot contain more than one line of text. See chapter 6 for details.

attributes (where it is stored after its first opening)? By allowing the application to hand over an already open mail session, we make it possible for the application to use a non-SMTP server and have our tag operate on this server. This renders our tag much more reusable since it can operate in this way on any valid mail session.

7.3.3 *Specifying the sender's address at the application level*

Another parameter that we may wish to draw from an external configuration is the sender's address. Why? Let's take a look at the following scenario:

- A user wishes to open an account in a web-based service through an HTML interface.
- To ensure that only the logged-in user can access this account, the web application emails an acknowledgement to the user's address with the new username and password.
- The sender of the acknowledgement email has an administrative type of address such as customerservice@ourdotcom.com.

In this scenario, the administrative address may change from time to time and we may also use this address in several different pages. In this case it is logical to place the email address in an application configuration parameter and have the tag implementation read that instead of providing it through a tag attribute.

7.3.4 *An enhanced SimpleJavaMailTag: JavaMailTag*

Given these issues, the following changes should be made to our mailer tag:

- In addition to the tag's attribute properties, the tag must also be capable of searching for alternative configuration parameters in the application configuration. Priority is given to values specified in the tag attributes, but in cases in which no value emanated from the attributes, the tag should search for the value in the application configuration. If no attribute was found, the tag should throw an exception.
- The tag should be able to take mail sessions from the application attributes. The name of the attribute used for this mail session will be hard-coded.

NOTE   These changes make it impossible for the JSP runtime to check that all necessary attributes/parameters are provided by the JSP file developer. That is because some of the configuration values can now come from tag attributes *or* the application (namely, `server` and `from`). When these parameters come from the application layer, the JSP engine won't know whether the parameters are present or absent until runtime, unlike tag attributes that are verifiable at translation time. To provide for this, we should now have the `server` and `from` attributes marked as optional tag attributes, and check for the availability of all the needed information while serving the request (instead of at translation time).

The resulting improved tag is shown in listing 7.8.

Listing 7.8   An improved JavaMailTag implementation

```
package book.mail;

import book.util.LocalStrings;

import java.util.Properties;

import javax.mail.Transport;
import javax.mail.Session;
import javax.mail.Message;
import javax.mail.MessagingException;

import javax.mail.internet.MimeMessage;
import javax.mail.internet.InternetAddress;
import javax.mail.internet.AddressException;

import javax.servlet.jsp.JspException;

public class JavaMailTag extends SimpleJavaMailTag  {       ❶

    public static final String SMTP_SERVER =
                            "smtp_server_host";
    public static final String FROM_ATTRIBUTE =
                            "from_sender";

    static LocalStrings ls =
        LocalStrings.getLocalStrings(JavaMailTag.class);

    protected InternetAddress sender    = null;
    protected InternetAddress recipient = null;
    protected Session session           = null;

    public int doStartTag()
            throws JspException
    {
        try {
            checkParameters();
            sendMail(session, sender, recipient, body, subject);      ❷
            return SKIP_BODY;
        } catch(AddressException ae) {
            log(ls.getStr(Constants.SEND_ADDRESS_ERROR), ae);
        } catch(MessagingException me) {
            log(ls.getStr(Constants.SEND_MESSAGING_ERROR), me);
        } finally {
            sender    = null;
            recipient = null;
```

```
            session    = null;
        }
        // Throw a JspTagException
}
protected void checkParameters()                    ❸
            throws JspException
{
    try {
        if(null == mailServer) {
            session = (Session)
                getServletContext().getAttribute(SMTP_SERVER);
            if(null == session) {
                String configuredSMTP =
                    getInitParameter(SMTP_SERVER);
                if(null == configuredSMTP) {
                    // Throw JspTagException
                }
                Properties props = new Properties();
                props.put("mail.smtp.host", configuredSMTP);
                session = Session.getInstance(props, null);
            }
        } else {
            Properties props = new Properties();
            props.put("mail.smtp.host", mailServer);
            session = Session.getInstance(props, null);
        }

        recipient = new InternetAddress(to);

        if(null == from) {
            String configuredFrom =
                getInitParameter(FROM_ATTRIBUTE);
            if(null == configuredFrom) {
                // Throw JspTagException
            }
            sender = new InternetAddress(configuredFrom);
        } else {
            sender = new InternetAddress(from);
        }
    } catch(MessagingException me) {
        // Throw JspTagException
    }
}

protected void sendMail(Session session,            ❹
                        InternetAddress sender,
                        InternetAddress recipient,
                        String content,
                        String subject)
    throws MessagingException
{
```

```
        MimeMessage message = new MimeMessage(session);
        message.setFrom(sender);
        message.addRecipient(Message.RecipientType.TO,
                            recipient);
        if(null != subject) {
            message.setSubject(subject);
        } else {
            message.setSubject("");
        }

        if(null == content) { // Empty body
            content = "";
        }
        message.setText(content);
        Transport.send(message);
    }
}
```

❶ By extending the `SimpleJavaMailTag` we have all the properties and properties setters.

❷ We separated our service time into two methods, one that checks parameters and creates the email objects, and the one that actually sends the email.

❸ Checks the provided attributes as well as fetching missing properties from the application configuration and attributes   `JavaMailTag` represents a significant change to the simple email sender that we developed in the previous section, not only because we are now reading configuration properties and application attributes, but also because the location wherein we create the JavaMail objects shifted. A new method, `checkParameters()`, was introduced, which is where we find most of our changes. This method has two tasks:

- To make sure that in one way or another we have all the needed mail-sending information. `checkParameters()` will look for the missing properties in the application configuration (sender identity and SMTP server location) as well as in the application attributes (mail session).

- To instantiate some of the JavaMail objects so that the mail-sending method will only need to create the desired message and set the needed parameters into it. Note that instantiating the addresses and the mail session also checks whether the provided configuration parameters are correct (e.g., syntactically correct email addresses).

❹ **Sends the email**   The fact that most of the JavaMail objects are created in `checkParameters()` makes it possible to substantially simplify `sendMail()`. Now it merely sets the already instantiated addresses as well as the subject and body into the JavaMail message object and sends it using the transport object.

The revised TLD entry

Our new TLD entry should now resemble the following (note how "server" and "from" are no longer required attributes):

```
<tag>
    <name>sender</name>
    <tagclass>book.mail.JavaMailTag</tagclass>
    <teiclass>book.mail.MailTagExtraInfo</teiclass>
    <bodycontent>empty</bodycontent>
    <info>
        Sends an email based on the provided attributes
        and application configuration.

        The user can specify the SMTP server address and
        the sender's identity using context parameter. He can
        also provide an already initialized JavaMail session
        object to be used when sending the email.
    </info>

    <attribute>
        <name>server</name>
        <required>false</required>        ❶
        <rtexprvalue>false</rtexprvalue>
    </attribute>
    <attribute>
        <name>from</name>
        <required>false</required>        ❶
        <rtexprvalue>true</rtexprvalue>
    </attribute>
    <attribute>
        <name>to</name>
        <required>true</required>
        <rtexprvalue>true</rtexprvalue>
    </attribute>
    <attribute>
        <name>subject</name>
        <required>false</required>
        <rtexprvalue>true</rtexprvalue>
    </attribute>
    <attribute>
        <name>body</name>
        <required>true</required>
        <rtexprvalue>true</rtexprvalue>
    </attribute>
</tag>
```

❶ **Neither the `from` nor `server` attribute is mandatory.**

7.3.5   The JavaMailTag in action

Armed with our new `JavaMailTag` and TLD, we can now implement improved JSP files that provide increased management over the mail parameters. To demonstrate the working of and advantages associated with the new tag, let's develop a simple registration application. The application's role is to allow users to register themselves at an online resource. Access to the resource requires a user name and password that the registration application emails to the user.

The user first needs to provide standard information such as name, address, email address, desired username, and the like; the site accepts these parameters, comes up with a password, and sends it by email. Since the user may also forget his password or username, the registration application also provides a reminder service whereby the user can provide his email address and the site will again send those to him. It is obvious that the user can access one of two HTML forms:

- Registration form, in which the user provides basic information, thus registering with the service.
- Reminder form, wherein the user can enter his email address so that the site will re-send him his user name and password when necessary.

The system will send one type of email for new accounts and a different type for password reminders, yet these emails share the sender ID and the mail server.

NOTE   In a real-world site, all information should be kept inside a database. Our sample, however, is not yet centered on one, as database access is not our primary concern here and it may move the focus away from email tag usage. Instead, we are using Beans that mimic possible database results by returning random results. This logic is implemented in the class `book.-beans.Registrator`.

The HTML-based registration form

The user registration form is presented in figure 7.2. After the users provide the required information and submit it to the site, the site will then execute the registration JSP file.

The registration JSP file

The registration JSP file is presented in listing 7.9.

Figure 7.2 Sample user registration form

Listing 7.9 The register JSP file, employing the improved mail tag

```
<%@ taglib
    uri="http://www.manning.com/jsptagsbook/email-taglib"
    prefix="mail" %>

<jsp:useBean id="reg" scope="page" class="book.beans.Registrator">      ❶
    <jsp:setProperty name="reg" property="*"/>
</jsp:useBean>
<% reg.register(); %>      ❷

<html>
<body>

<p>
 Dear <jsp:getProperty name="reg" property="name"/>, you were
 registered sucessfuly. <br>
 We are about to email you your user name and password.
</p>

<%
String emailBody = "Dear " + reg.getName();                              ❸
       emailBody += ", you were registered to the";
       emailBody += " service under the username:\n\t";
       emailBody += reg.getUsername();
       emailBody += "\nand the passwrod:\n\t";
       emailBody += reg.getPassword();
       emailBody += ".\n\n";
       emailBody += "Good luck";
```

```
%>
<mail:send
    to='<%= reg.getEmail() %>'                              ❹
    subject="Your new user name and password"
    body='<%= emailBody %>' />
</body>
</html>
```

❶ **Instantiates and initalizes a new Registrator bean, to be used later to register the user.**

❷ **Performs the actual registration work.**

❸ **Creates the email content; we are forced to use a scriptlet.**

❹ **Sends the email itself** Note that the sender's identity and the mail server location are not taken from the JSP file. Instead we specify them in the web application deployment descriptor.

The web application deployment descriptor

The web application deployment descriptor is presented in listing 7.10.

Listing 7.10 A web application descriptor for the registration application

```
<?xml version="1.0" encoding="ISO-8859-1"?>

<!DOCTYPE web-app
    PUBLIC "-//Sun Microsystems, Inc.//DTD Web Application 2.2//EN"
    "http://java.sun.com/j2ee/dtds/web-app_2.2.dtd">

<web-app>

    <context-param>                                          ❶
        <param-name>from_sender</param-name>
        <param-value>sender@foo.com</param-value>
    </context-param>
    <context-param>                                          ❷
        <param-name>smtp_server_host</param-name>
        <param-value>mail.foo.com</param-value>
    </context-param>

    <taglib>
        <taglib-uri>
            http://www.manning.com/jsptagsbook/email-taglib
        </taglib-uri>
        <taglib-location>
            /WEB-INF/mail.tld
        </taglib-location>
    </taglib>
</web-app>
```

❶ Specifies the sender identity.

❷ Specifies the used SMTP server.

By providing the sender and server information as context parameters, we introduce a greater usage flexibility. For example, if we switch mail servers, all we need then is to modify the application configuration in a single location (and probably with some configuration GUI). Had we stayed with our previous `SimpleJavaMailTag`, we would be required to update any and all JSP files that happened to send email. Moreover, the tag users could decide to manage the mail server connectivity themselves and provide a preinitialized mail session object for the tag to use, thus connecting the tag to servers that are not pure SMTP.

Dependence on tag attributes

`JavaMailTag` represents a big step in tag usability and application integration, yet something is still missing. The following code fragment is the mail message body generation code as taken from listing 7.9:

```
<%
String emailBody = "Dear " + reg.getName();
        emailBody += ", you were registered to the";
        emailBody += " service under the username:\n\t";
        emailBody += reg.getUsername();
        emailBody += "\nand the passwrod:\n\t";
        emailBody += reg.getPassword();
        emailBody += ".\n\n";
        emailBody += "Good luck";
%>
```

Notice that we had to generate our message body with a scriptlet. This is undesirable for several reasons:

- The message body is not readable.
- You need to be a programmer to write it (e.g., to escape all the key characters). This defeats the intent that tags be usable by nonprogrammers.
- You can't take advantage of the `jsp:getProperty` tag provided by JSP for fetching bean properties.

Clearly there must be a better solution, and there is. We will introduce that solution in the next section.

7.4 *Collecting attributes from the tag's body*

Had we provided requirements for the mail message body, these would probably be rather complex—and conflicting—requirements. For example, we would like to have a message body that is dynamic, yet easy to specify. We would like it to contain runtime information from the page and request, yet not require that the message author be a scriptlet master. How can we accomplish all that? One way is to use our mail tag's body in place of some of its attributes.

In our tag's current state, both the message subject and body are provided as tag attributes, yet tag attributes pose major restrictions on their structures and content. Instead of a single tag with several attributes, imagine building several tags that could be used cooperatively to facilitate specifying email parameters. Take a look at the following JSP fragment, demonstrating how these cooperative tags might work:

```
<mail:send
    to='<%= reg.getEmail() %>'>

    <mail:subject>
    Your new user name and password
    </mail:subject>
    <mail:body>
Dear <jsp:getProperty name="reg" property="name"/>, you
were registered to the service under the username:
<jsp:getProperty name="reg" property="username"/>
and the password:
<jsp:getProperty name="reg" property="password"/>.

Good luck.

    </mail:body>
</mail:send>
```

Isn't that an improvement? The benefits of this approach are fairly obvious. First, the JSP page author does not need to escape special Java characters. Second, the page author no longer has to know Java, since the message body can now be specified as a simple block of text within the body of the `<mail:body>` tag. Last, the tag author can now use the standard `jsp:getProperty` tag to interact with JavaBeans, eliminating scriptlets from the page entirely.

Rest assured, we don't lose anything with this approach. In fact, we can always return to the old way of sending email by using a JSP fragment similar to the following:

```
<mail:send
    to='<%= reg.getEmail() %>'>
    <mail:subject>
    Your new user name and password
    </mail:subject>
    <mail:body><%= emailBody %></mail:body>
</mail:send>
```

7.4.1 *Implementing body processing*

Of course, implementing our improved solution requires a lot more development effort:

- We will need to implement two new custom tags: one to read the subject and one to read the body.
- The tags will need to verify that they are enclosed within a mail sender tag.
- We will need to convert the mail sender into a body aware tag.
- We will need to modify the TLD entry for the mail sender and add two new entries for the subject and body readers.

But all this effort is worthwhile; creating a more useful email tag will render our users more productive and save them time and money, So, let's proceed.

7.4.2 *Extending the email tag*

We start by extending the email tag one more time and creating a new version (listing 7.11) that allows its body to be processed. This is made possible by returning EVAL_BODY_INCLUDE from doStartTag(), instead of the previously returned SKIP_BODY. Also, some of our mailer tag input is now provided through its body, so we postpone sending the email during execution of doEndTag(). We perform the attribute validation and configuration reading in doStartTag() in order to validate them as soon as possible and throw an exception in case of trouble. We also add a state cleanup routine because we now have state that carries over from doStartTag() to doEndTag(). Note here that the email body and subject are now part of the tag's internal state (instead of the attributes-based properties that they were previously), and so require a cleanup when the tag's execution is complete. Other than that, the mail methods used by the tag have not been radically altered. We use the same body and subject attributes setters, except that now they are called by the enclosed message and subject tags.

Listing 7.11 Source code for BodyJavaMailTag

```
package book.mail;

import book.util.LocalStrings;
import javax.servlet.jsp.JspException;
import javax.mail.MessagingException;

public class BodyJavaMailTag extends JavaMailTag  {

    static LocalStrings ls =
        LocalStrings.getLocalStrings(BodyJavaMailTag.class);
```

```
public int doStartTag()
        throws JspException
{
    checkParameters();         ❶
    return EVAL_BODY_INCLUDE;   ❷
}
public int doEndTag()
        throws JspException
{
    try {
        sendMail(session, sender, recipient, body, subject);    ❸
        return super.doEndTag();
    } catch(MessagingException me) {
        log(ls.getStr(Constants.SEND_MESSAGING_ERROR), me);
    }
    // ...
    // Throw JspTagException
}
protected void clearServiceState()    ❹
{
    sender    = null;
    recipient = null;
    session   = null;
    subject = null;
    body      = null;
    super.clearServiceState();
}
}
```

❶ Input verification is done in `doStartTag()` to abort execution when errors are found.

❷ Lets the JSP runtime into the tag's body.

❸ Sends the email and then calls the superclass's `doEndTag()` to trigger cleanup.

❹ Cleans the tag's state.

Getting the tag to accept body-based parameters did not require much work. We now move to implement the subject and message tags.

7.4.3 Creating tags for subject and message

The subject and message tags are similar to the `BodyReaderTag` presented in the previous chapter, but with a few modifications:

- Both tags should check that they are located within the body of a mail sender.
- The subject tag should trim its body value from unwanted leading and trailing white characters.
- Both tags should set the appropriate values into the mail sender.

Creating a base class

Achieving the first of those bulleted items in a base class that will be verifying the enclosing condition is straightforward. This base class implementation is presented in listing 7.12.

Listing 7.12 Source code for the mail body and subject readers' super class

```
package book.mail;

import book.util.LocalStrings;
import book.util.BodyReaderTag;

import javax.servlet.jsp.JspException;
import javax.servlet.jsp.tagext.Tag;

public abstract class EnclosedMailBodyReaderTag extends
    BodyReaderTag {

    public int doStartTag()
            throws JspException
    {
        checkEnclosedInMailer();              ❶
        return super.doStartTag();
    }

    protected void checkEnclosedInMailer()
            throws JspException
    {
        Tag t = getParent();
        if(null == t) {          ❷
            // Error throw JspTagException
        }
        if(t instanceof BodyJavaMailTag) {    ❸
            return;
        }
        // Error throw JspTagException
    }
}
```

❶ Checks that the tag is enclosed within the wanted parent during `doStartTag()` to abort execution when errors are found. We call the super class's `doStartTag()` to let `BodyReaderTag` do its job.

❷ Checks that there is an enclosing tag.

❸ Checks that the enclosing tag is of the correct type.

Now that the parenthood validation has been performed by a base class, it can be extended by adding the specific actions required by the subject and message-body tags.

Creating the subject tag

Listing 7.13 presents the subject tag.

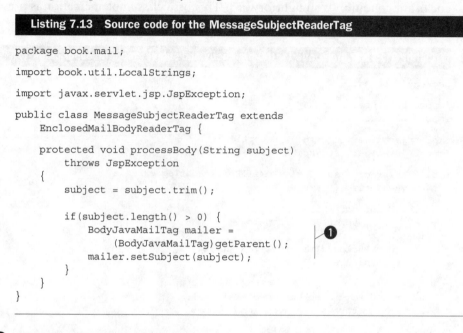

Listing 7.13   Source code for the MessageSubjectReaderTag

```
package book.mail;

import book.util.LocalStrings;

import javax.servlet.jsp.JspException;

public class MessageSubjectReaderTag extends
    EnclosedMailBodyReaderTag {

    protected void processBody(String subject)
        throws JspException
    {
        subject = subject.trim();

        if(subject.length() > 0) {
            BodyJavaMailTag mailer =
                (BodyJavaMailTag)getParent();          ❶
            mailer.setSubject(subject);
        }
    }
}
```

❶ **Sets the subject into the mail sender.**

Listing 7.13 shows how uncomplicated the subject tag is, as almost all the work is performed elsewhere, starting with collecting the body content and ending with syntax/enclosement verification. As a result, when `processBody()` is being called, the tag does not have much to do other than call its parent (which we've verified to be available and of the right type) with the filtered subject. Recall that `process-Body()` was specified in the `BodyReaderTag` base class in the previous chapter.

Creating the message body tag

The message body tag (listing 7.14) is equally simple.

Listing 7.14   Source code for MessageBodyReaderTag

```
package book.mail;

import javax.servlet.jsp.JspException;

public class MessageBodyReaderTag extends
    EnclosedMailBodyReaderTag {

    protected void processBody(String content)
```

```
        throws JspException

    {
        ((BodyJavaMailTag)getParent()).setBody(content);
    }
}
```

Creating the TLD

Now that all relevant tags are in place, we write a TLD (listing 7.15) that describes our new email tag library.

Listing 7.15   Tag library descriptor entries for the mailer tags

```xml
<?xml version="1.0" encoding="ISO-8859-1" ?>
<!DOCTYPE taglib
    PUBLIC "-//Sun Microsystems, Inc.//DTD JSP Tag Library 1.1//EN"
    "http://java.sun.com/j2ee/dtds/web-jsptaglibrary_1_1.dtd">
<taglib>
    <tlibversion>1.0</tlibversion>
    <jspversion>1.1</jspversion>
    <shortname>simplemail</shortname>
    <uri> http://www.manning.com/jsptagsbook/simplemail-taglib </uri>
    <info>
        A tag library that describes the simple mail tag
    </info>

    <tag>
        <name>send</name>
        <tagclass>book.mail.BodyJavaMailTag</tagclass>
        <teiclass>book.mail.MailTagExtraInfo</teiclass>
        <bodycontent>JSP</bodycontent>
        <info>
            Sends an email based on the provided attributes,
            application configuration, and body parameters.

            The user can specify the SMTP server address as well as
            the sender's identity using context parameter. He can
            also provide an already initialized JavaMail session
            object to be used when sending the email.

            The user should specify the email message body through
            the message tag.

            The user can specify the email message subject through
            the subject tag.
        </info>

        <attribute>
            <name>server</name>
            <required>false</required>
```

```
        <rtexprvalue>false</rtexprvalue>
    </attribute>
    <attribute>
        <name>from</name>
        <required>false</required>
        <rtexprvalue>true</rtexprvalue>
    </attribute>
    <attribute>
        <name>to</name>
        <required>true</required>
        <rtexprvalue>true</rtexprvalue>
    </attribute>
</tag>

<tag>
    <name>message</name>
    <tagclass>book.mail.MessageBodyReaderTag</tagclass>
    <bodycontent>JSP</bodycontent>
    <info>
        Provides a place holder for the user to enter the
        contents of the mail's body.
    </info>
</tag>

<tag>
    <name>subject</name>
    <tagclass>book.mail.MessageSubjectReaderTag</tagclass>
    <bodycontent>JSP</bodycontent>
    <info>
        Provides a place holder for the user to enter the
        contents of the mail's message.
    </info>
</tag>
</taglib>
```

Here, our mail tags were redefined to own a body (JSP body) and the body and subject attributes were dropped, as we will use the message and subject tags instead.

Using the tags in a revised registration JSP file

A modified registration handler JSP that uses the new body-based tags is available in listing 7.16 and is much simpler than the one used earlier.

Listing 7.16   The register JSP file, employing the mail, subject, and message tags

```
<%@ taglib
    uri="http://www.manning.com/jsptagsbook/email-taglib"
    prefix="mail" %>

<jsp:useBean id="reg" scope="page" class="book.beans.Registrator">
    <jsp:setProperty name="reg" property="*"/>
```

```
</jsp:useBean>
<% reg.register(); %>

<html>
<body>

<p>
 Dear <jsp:getProperty name="reg" property="name"/>, you were
 registered successfully. <br>
 We are about to email you your user name and password.
</p>

<mail:send to='<%= reg.getEmail() %>'>
    <mail:subject>Your new user name and password</mail:subject>
    <mail:message>
Dear <jsp:getProperty name="reg" property="name"/>, you were
registered to the service under the username:
<jsp:getProperty name="reg" property="username"/>
and the password:
<jsp:getProperty name="reg" property="password"/>.
    Good luck.
    </mail:message>
</mail:send>

</body>
</html>
```

 Composes the message naturally by editing the message tag's body.

With this improvement we've produced a tag library that satisfies all our original goals for functionality and usability. As it stands, our email tag library is a clean, workable solution that satisfies basic email requirements. We improved our tags, not by exposing greater capabilities, but by making them less burdensome to use. Keep in mind that, above all else, using tags must be relatively effortless. It is, in fact, the very nature of tags to offer a simple interface to complex logic. If using them is only slightly less complicated than learning and writing Java, we haven't improved web development for our page authors. Although we've met all our design goals for this library, there is still one more section we can improve: input validation. We will focus on that for the remainder of this chapter.

7.5   *Adding assertions and input validation*

Our registration application certainly functions well enough as it stands, but it could use improvement. Currently, we don't perform any input validation. Our registration JSP assumes that all needed incoming parameters are available and their content is correct; that the user provides a valid email address or name. In the real world, of course, we cannot make such assumptions. The reason is a well-known law of development: "If users can break it, they will."

7.5.1 Performing validation using custom tags

Validating input parameters is by no means limited to a specific registration application. Input validation has a broad range and yet, our application won't be complete without it, so let's check how validation might be implemented with custom tags.

If tags should be declarative, it would then be a design mistake to define a set of tags that lets the user program validation into the page. Instead, we want to look for a declarative and reusable approach that allows a relatively naïve user to specify limitations over the incoming parameters, and an action to take in case said limitation is not met. Fortunately, there is such an approach and it is in widespread use—assertions.

Using assertions

An *assertion* is a programming element with a condition and action which is sometimes implicit. When working with an assertion, the developer can specify its condition and, if this condition is not met, the assertion's action takes place (a failed assertion may trigger a program exit). We might, for example, use an assertion to check whether a particular HTTP form parameter is a number, or to check whether a form field has been left empty by the user. We can use assertions in our page to specify a condition or set of conditions on our parameters, and the action can be to forward the request to an assertion failed handler URI.

Specifying conditions using assertions

A possible syntax is provided in the following JSP fragment:

```
<jspx:assert parameter="paramname"
             handler="path to handler"
             condition1="some condition"
             condition2="some condition"
             ...
             conditionN="some condition"/>
```

The conditions specified in the assertion may range from checking the existence of the parameter to a condition on the parameter value or its type. For example, one could assert on our email address parameter in the following way:

```
<jspx:assert parameter="email"
             handler="/request_parameter_error.jsp"
             exists="true"
             type="emailaddress"/>
```

We can imagine some complex conditions that would not work with this approach to evaluating assertions. Supporting increasingly complex assertions will force us to implement a brand new language for defining conditions, and this is something we'd like to avoid. Luckily, most cases require only a relatively simple condition, such as the one presented in our email assertion sample, so assertions will satisfy our need for declarative parameter checking.

Having chosen a model for parameter verification, we ask ourselves what conditions we might ever pose over incoming parameters:

- Existence conditions
  To check if a certain parameter is available in the input parameters.

- Type conditions
  The parameter may be of type number, alphanumeric string, alpha-only string, email address, and so forth.

- One of condition
  We may want the parameter to be one of the items in a list.

- Interval condition
  We may want the parameter to be in a certain range.

- Equality condition
  We may want the parameter to be of a certain value.

7.5.2 *Creating a tag for the send mail tag library*

There is no end to the conditions we may want to pose; hence, one important characteristic of the assert tag should be its capacity to be extended by adding new assertion conditions. To meet this requirement, the following interface and tag were developed.

The Assertion interface

The cornerstone to `assert` tag is the `Assertion` interface (listing 7.17) that defines what is to be implemented by the developer in adding new assertion logic to our tag.

Listing 7.17   Source code for the Assertion interface

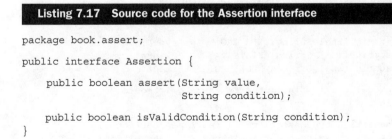

```
package book.assert;

public interface Assertion {

    public boolean assert(String value,
                          String condition);

    public boolean isValidCondition(String condition);
}
```

The assertion developer should implement two methods:

- assert() accepts a value and a condition parameter and performs the assertion logic. It should return true if successful, and false otherwise. For example, a type assertion will get a type specification as the condition parameter and will have to check whether the value is of the given type. AssertTag should use this method while the page is executed.

- isValidCondition() verifies whether its input is a valid assertion parameter. For example, in a type assertion the method should check if the condition parameter is one of the types known to the assertion. This method should be used by the TagExtraInfo to be implemented for AssertTag.

Creating AssertTag

Now that the assertion logic is implemented by different assertion objects, AssertTag (listing 7.18) is more concerned with instantiating the assertion objects, accepting the conditions posed on the assertion, and calling the correct assertion with the correct condition. When the condition fails, the tag takes the failed parameter's name, adds it to the request attributes, and forwards the request to the required handler.

Listing 7.18   Source code for AssertTag

```
package book.assert;

import javax.servlet.RequestDispatcher;
import javax.servlet.ServletRequest;
import javax.servlet.jsp.JspException;
import javax.servlet.jsp.PageContext;

import javax.mail.internet.InternetAddress;

import book.util.LocalStrings;
import book.util.StringUtil;           ❶
import book.util.ExTagSupport;

public class AssertTag extends ExTagSupport {

    public static final String GUILTY_VAR_TAG = "guilty_variable";

    public static final String TYPE_TAG    = "type";
    public static final String EXISTS_TAG  = "exists";
    public static final String ONEOF_TAG   = "oneof";

    // Additional static final objects where omitted for
    // clarity.

    static Assertion typeAssertion   = new TypeAssertion();
    static Assertion existsAssertion = new ExistsAssertion();
    static Assertion oneofAssertion  = new OneOfAssertion();
```

```
protected boolean isAsserted = false;

protected String parameterName  = null;
protected String handlerUri     = null;

protected String type           = null;
protected String exists         = null;
protected String oneof          = null;

public void setParameter(String parameterName)
{
    this.parameterName = parameterName;
}

public void setHandler(String handlerUri)
{
    this.handlerUri = handlerUri;
}

public void setType(String type)
{
    this.type = StringUtil.trimit(type);
}

public void setExists(String exists)
{
    this.exists = StringUtil.trimit(exists);
}

public void setOneof(String oneof)
{
    this.oneof = StringUtil.trimit(oneof);
}

public int doStartTag()
        throws JspException
{
    ServletRequest req = pageContext.getRequest();
    String value = req.getParameter(parameterName);        ❷

    if(null == exists) {
        exists = "true";
    }

    if(!existsAssertion.assert(value, exists)) {           ❸
        isAsserted = true;
    } else if((null != type) &&
            !typeAssertion.assert(value, type)) {
        isAsserted = true;
    } else if((null != oneof) &&
            !oneofAssertion.assert(value, oneof)) {
        isAsserted = true;
    }
    return SKIP_BODY;
}
```

```
public int doEndTag()
        throws JspException
{
    int rc = isAsserted ? SKIP_PAGE : EVAL_PAGE;        ❹

    if(isAsserted) {
        pageContext.setAttribute(GUILTY_VAR_TAG,        ❺
                              parameterName,
                    PageContext.REQUEST_SCOPE);

        ServletRequest req = pageContext.getRequest()   ❻
        RequestDispatcher rd =
            req.getRequestDispatcher(handlerUri);
        try {
            rd.forward(pageContext.getRequest(),
                    pageContext.getResponse());
        } catch(Throwable t) {
            // Log and throw an exception
        }
    }
    super.doEndTag();        ❼
    return rc;
}

protected void clearServiceState()
{
    isAsserted = false;
    super.clearServiceState();
}

protected void clearProperties()
{
    parameterName  = null;
    handlerUri     = null;
    type           = null;
    exists         = null;
    oneof          = null;
    super.clearProperties();
}

static class ExistsAssertion implements Assertion    ❽
{
    public boolean assert(String value,
                        String condition)
    {
        boolean exists =
            new Boolean(condition).booleanValue();

        if(exists && null != value) {
            return true;
        }
        return false;
    }
```

```
        public boolean isValidCondition(String condition)
        {
            return condition.equals("true") ||
                  condition.equals("false");
        }
    }

    static class TypeAssertion implements Assertion
    {
        // Implementation omitted for clarity
    }

    static class OneOfAssertion implements Assertion
    {
        // Implementation omitted for clarity
    }
}
```

❶ `stringUtil` **is a utility class with string-related methods.**

❷ **Gets the named parameter.**

❸ **Runs the assertions** The `exists` assertion is always applied.

❹ **If an assertion fails, we abort the page execution.**

❺ **Adds a request attribute with the name of the failed parameter.**

❻ **Forwards the request to the error handler.**

❼ **Runs the superclass so that the cleanup logic will run.**

❽ **Sample implemenation of an assertion object** All the assertion objects in this listing are implemented as inner classes of the `AssertTag` handler. We did not have to do it this way, but the typical assertion object was small and was used only within the tag handler. The tag handler implements common operations, such as property setters, for all the different conditions that we may pose (and the values are stored internally within the tag). During the later service execution, any non-null condition will trigger an assertion whose failure triggers the execution of the error handler.

One can argue that `AssertTag` implementation is not as generic as it could be. For example, we could instantiate all assertion objects dynamically using `Class.for-Name()`, thereby removing the hard-coded dependency between the tag handler and the different assertions. There is some truth in this claim; however, there is a problem in implementing this approach, namely implementing the property setters and validation for each condition. As you saw in listing 7.17, each assertion object accepts two arguments: the value to assert on and a condition parameter. The handler tag implementation should know in advance all the different assertions, so that it will be able to receive the properties via its property setters when running, and validate them during the translation phase. Chapter 9 discusses implementing such tag-contained action relationships, wherein a tag may validate the properties of some internal condition operation with ease. For now, we will hold off on providing a fully extensible and generic assertion tag and not use `Class.forName()` to instantiate a set of configured assertion objects.

Validating user input

While implementing `AssertTag`, we need to also consider validating the attribute values provided by the user. The user should provide attribute values to be used as condition parameters to the assertions, and it is clear that not all possible values are accepted. Hence, we should validate them during the translation time. To facilitate, `AssertExtraInfo` was created to accompany `AssertTag`; this class validates the conditions posed by the user and ensures that their provided values are correct.

Listing 7.19 Source code for AssertExtraInfo

```
package book.assert;

import javax.servlet.jsp.tagext.TagData;
import javax.servlet.jsp.tagext.TagExtraInfo;

public class AssertExtraInfo extends TagExtraInfo
{
    public boolean isValid(TagData data)
    {
        String cond =
            (String)data.getAttribute(AssertTag.EXISTS_TAG);          ❶
        if((null != cond) &&
            !AssertTag.existsAssertion.isValidCondition(cond)) {
            return false;
        }

        cond = (String)data.getAttribute(AssertTag.TYPE_TAG);
        if((null != cond) &&
            !AssertTag.typeAssertion.isValidCondition(cond)) {
            return false;
        }

        cond = (String)data.getAttribute(AssertTag.ONEOF_TAG);
        if((null != cond) &&
            !AssertTag.oneofAssertion.isValidCondition(cond)) {
            return false;
        }

        return true;
    }
}
```

❶ Gets a condition value and validates it using the appropriate assertion object Note how easy it is to implement `AssertExtraInfo`. All of the actual validation work is performed by `isValidCondition()`, so that all `AssertExtraInfo` needs to do is fetch the condition values from `TagData` and use the appropriate assertion object to validate it.

Creating the TLD

The last item to discuss before using `AssertTag` is its TLD entry (listing 7.20).

Listing 7.20   Tag library descriptor for AssertTag

```xml
<?xml version="1.0" encoding="ISO-8859-1" ?>
<!DOCTYPE taglib
    PUBLIC "-//Sun Microsystems, Inc.//DTD JSP Tag Library 1.1//EN"
    "http://java.sun.com/j2ee/dtds/web-jsptaglibrary_1_1.dtd">
<taglib>
    <tlibversion>1.0</tlibversion>
    <jspversion>1.1</jspversion>
    <shortname>assert</shortname>
    <uri> http://www.manning.com/jsptagsbook/assert-taglib</uri>
    <info>
        A tag library for the assert tag
    </info>

    <tag>
        <name>assert</name>
        <tagclass>book.assert.AssertTag</tagclass>
        <teiclass>book.assert.AssertExtraInfo</teiclass>
        <bodycontent>empty</bodycontent>
        <info>
            Asserts based on a set of conditions
        </info>

        <attribute>
            <name>parameter</name>
            <required>true</required>
            <rtexprvalue>false</rtexprvalue>
        </attribute>
        <attribute>
            <name>handler</name>
            <required>true</required>
            <rtexprvalue>false</rtexprvalue>
        </attribute>
        <attribute>
            <name>type</name>
            <required>false</required>
            <rtexprvalue>false</rtexprvalue>
        </attribute>
        <attribute>
```

```
        <name>exists</name>
        <required>false</required>
        <rtexprvalue>false</rtexprvalue>
    </attribute>
    <attribute>
        <name>oneof</name>
        <required>false</required>
        <rtexprvalue>false</rtexprvalue>
    </attribute>
  </tag>
</taglib>
```

Listing 7.20 shows how all the attributes in `AssertTag` are constant strings. Why did we exclude runtime expressions for this tag? Because translation time validation of runtime attributes is impossible, and incorrectly configured assertions may cause problems ranging from plain embarrassment (this site is throwing exceptions instead of showing a reasonable error page) to profit loss (if the assertion needs to rule out stolen credit card numbers). By preventing assertions from being runtime expressions, we discover any syntax problems in our attributes before the page is requested by a user (at translation time), and well before any damage can occur. It is preferable to be safe than sorry, so we've decided that the assertion tag is one such case.

Using assertion mail tags in the registration JSP file

Having developed the assertions, let's use them in our registration page (listing 7.21). In its current sample state, the registration page accepts three parameters:

- The user's email—Validate with an existence and type (email) assertions.
- The user's name—Validate with an existence and type (alpha) assertions.
- The user's family name—Validate with an existence and type (alpha) assertions.

An error in any one of the three parameters ought to trigger an internal redirection to an error handler that will present the offending parameter.

Listing 7.21   A JSP file employing the assertion email tags

```
<%@ taglib
   uri="http://www.manning.com/jsptagsbook/email-taglib"
   prefix="mail" %>
<%@ taglib
   uri="http://www.manning.com/jsptagsbook/assert-taglib"
   prefix="assert" %>

<assert:assert parameter="email"                    ❶
               handler="/parameter_error.jsp"
```

```
                    type="email"/>
<assert:assert parameter="name"
               handler="/parameter_error.jsp"
               type="alpha"/>
<assert:assert parameter="family"
               handler="/parameter_error.jsp"
               type="alpha"/>

<%-- snip

    Starting with this point we are back to the
    previous JSP file

    snip --%>

</body>
</html>
```

❶ Asserting a single parameter based on its type, the existence assertion is implicit.

Asserting on a named parameter became a very simple matter. We actually reduced many potential scriptlets (to validate parameters) and made our page more robust. Our AssertTag may not be the Holy Grail (we cannot pose really complex questions on the parameters) but it is extensible. However, even with the relatively limited functionality that we have, assertions can solve most problems we confront in our daily work.

7.6 Summary

Tags have clearly facilitated sending emails with dynamically generated content from within a JSP. We have gone from something that usually requires in-depth know-how, such as SMTP and Java mail, and rendered its power in such a pervasive way that any page author comfortable with tags can use it. The key issue was not the underlying email technology, but how to create a simple, robust interface to that technology with custom tags. The role of custom tags is not to develop a new technology, but to enable rapid development and to expose a wanted technology in the most convenient, pervasive way to your JSP developers.

Is there a drawback to the tag approach? Perhaps. A Java developer may look at the tags and believe that they are less easy to use than JavaBeans. He or she may say, "… Hey, I put all that effort into the tag and all I got is functionality that I could have implemented with a couple of scriptlets and a simple email bean…." This may be true, yet that effort freed us from the need to maintain all the scriptlets involved in JavaBeans usage, and helped further separate the duties of Java coders from the JSP page authors.

We also covered how assertions can be implemented. All applications need to check their input parameters, and normally this requires a fair amount of Java code. Yet, as we saw, a great deal of what is needed for parameter checking can be accomplished declaratively, using tags similar to the assertions developed for our tiny application. The key issue here is not that we can cover 100 percent of possible validations, but that we can extend our assertions whenever there is a need and that the code within the assertions can now be reused without any modification.

Ultimately, the goal of this chapter was to apply the previously discussed concepts of tag development to a library with real-world use. A gradual approach was chosen to enforce not only the mechanics of tag development, but also to understand fully the tools at our disposal for producing a well-designed, robust solution.

Using JavaBeans with tags

8

One of the most common tasks in any Java program is to get and set properties of JavaBeans. Web development in Java is no different in that respect. In an object-oriented Java web application, your servlets and JSPs likely contain a good deal of code that interacts with JavaBeans. For servlets, working with JavaBeans is the same as is in any other Java program: beans are instantiated and the proper get or set methods are called. JSPs interact with JavaBeans differently, by using three standard tags that are defined in the JSP specification (`<jsp:usebean>`, `<jsp:setProperty>`, and `<jsp:getProperty>`). These tags, discussed in chapter 2, instantiate beans, introduce them to the page as scripting variables, and set properties in the beans in addition to printing properties back to the user. Unfortunately, the functionality exposed by the JavaBeans-related tags is rather limited. Two of the more troublesome limitations are:

- The tags cannot operate on objects unless they were introduced to the page via a JavaBeans-related JSP tag.
- The tags cannot manipulate indexed properties (properties that have multiple values and are referred to by an index like `getSomeProperty(i)`).

These shortcomings render JavaBeans standard tags useless for solving many practical problems such as iterating over an indexed property of a bean, or printing an attribute value of a bean that we would rather not introduce as a JSP scripting variable. Not surprisingly, developers increasingly find themselves in need of a more versatile set of JavaBeans tags. In this chapter, we address that need.

To this end we'll create a custom tag library that supports interaction with Java-Beans, free from the limitations of today's standard tags. We start with a brief discussion of the Java reflection API, which we'll soon see is crucial to building our JavaBean tags. We then move on to discuss the JavaBean component standard and how reflection assists us in getting and setting properties of Java Beans. We finish by creating our custom tag library which will consist of two tags: one that allows us to expose any JavaBean as a JSP scripting variable, and one that supports printing of the value of any JavaBean property to the user.

8.1   *Java reflection*

If tags are to be useful, they must be created such that they are versatile enough to get and set the properties of any JavaBean. This requires that they be capable of calling a bean's get or set methods, simply by knowing the class name of the Java-Bean and the name of the property to be manipulated. If you've heard of the Java reflection API, you know that it is a set of Java methods and classes that allows us to do just that. Using reflection, we can learn about the attributes of any Java class (including its methods) and even call any method of the class we choose. Before discussing the integration of reflection, JavaBeans, and custom tags, a quick look at the Java reflection API is in order. This will not be an in-depth description of reflection or method invocation by using reflection, but will provide a helpful explanation of the technology, its advantages, and the API that can put it to good use.

8.1.1 *What is reflection?*

Javasoft describes the purpose of the reflection API as "to enable Java code to discover information about the fields, methods, and constructors of loaded classes, and to use reflected fields, methods, and constructors to operate on their underlying counterparts on objects, within security restrictions." Quite a mouthful, so what does all that mean? In brief, the reflection API lets us learn about a particular Java class and then use that knowledge to properly call methods, get and set fields, or call the constructor of any instance of that class. The reflection API is particularly useful for debuggers and development tools that need to browse classes and display certain information from the classes to the user. The API is also useful when parts of your Java program have to interact with any type of Java object and need to learn about it at runtime. The tags we create in this chapter will have this requirement, since they will be designed to work with any and all JavaBeans. This definition can be clarified with a few examples of programs that use Java reflection.

Reflection and development tools

Consider the case of an environment wherein a developer manipulates program components through the GUI of a Java IDE (like JBuilder, Visual Café, etc.). We recognize that the development environment knows nothing about the components in advance, yet it must be able to present the developer with the possible methods that can be used in each component. Spying on the component to discern the interfaces, methods, and properties they expose can be accomplished using the reflection API, and is better known as *Introspection*.

Reflection and scripting engines

Another case is one wherein a user employs a JavaBean-capable scripting engine to create an application. Since a script is not usually precompiled with all its components, it does not know anything in advance about the different JavaBeans components with which it will interact at runtime (not even their type); yet, during runtime it should be able to perform the following:

- Introspect the components to find the method that it should execute.
- Dynamically execute the method on the scripted object.

Both of these functions are available through the reflection API.

By now you have seen how reflection is used to learn about a class at runtime. The tags we build in this chapter, like the standard JavaBean tags, will take as tag attributes the reference to an instance of a JavaBean and, for our printing tag, also the name of the property to print. Since the JSP author may specify any JavaBean instance at all, our tags will need to be able to take that instance at runtime and use reflection to find and call the proper methods. It should be clear that the only way to accomplish this is through the reflection API. Let us look at the syntax of that API in greater detail.

NOTE   Using the reflection API in order to introspect methods and later invoke them follows strict security rules that disallow overriding the Java security model. For example, one may not introspect private and package protected classes.

8.1.2   *The reflection API*

The reflection APIs are contained in the Java package `java.lang.reflect`. Some of the more important classes in this package are shown in table 8.1.

Table 8.1   Classes that are important for reflection

Class	Description
Class	Represents a Java class. Although not part of the `java.lang.reflect` package, this class is very important for reflection.
Method	Represents a method of class (also allows that method to be called).
Array	Supports creation and accessing of Java arrays (without having to know the exact type of the array in advance).
Constructor	Represents a specific class constructor (and allows that constructor to be called).

The Class class

The means to obtain all the constructors, methods, and fields for a particular class (or interface) in Java is through an instance of `java.lang.Class`. We obtain an instance of `Class` that corresponds to a particular Java class in a couple of ways:

- Calling `Class.forName("com.manning.SomeClass")` where "com.manning.SomeClass" is the fully qualified name of the class we want to study.

- Referring to the `class` field of a particular Java class. Code for this looks like:

```
Class c= com.manning.SomeClass.class
```

Once we have a `Class` object for our class, we may use methods such as `getConstructors()`, `getMethods()`, and `getFields()` to retrieve information about this class.

The Method class

For the purpose of this book, the class most important to us is `Method`, mainly because, by obtaining a `Method` object from a certain class, we are able to call that method repeatedly and on any instance of this class. This is the approach we will use to call the `get` and `set` property methods within the custom JavaBean tags we are building. The methods that are part of the `Method` class are presented in table 8.2, along with a brief description of each.

Table 8.2   Methods in the Method class

Method name	Description
`getDeclaringClass()`	Returns a `Class` object that represents the class or interface to which that method belongs. Think of it as the `Class` object that, if you call one of its `getMethod()` methods, will return this as the `Method` object.
`getModifiers()`	Returns an integer representation of Java language modifiers. Later on, the `Modifier` utility class can decode this integer.
`getName()`	Returns the name of the method.
`getParameterTypes()`	Returns an array of `Class` objects that represent the parameter types, in declaration order, of the method.
`getReturnType()`	Returns a `Class` object that represents the return type of the method.
`invoke(Object obj, Object[] args)`	Invokes the underlying method on the specified object with the specified parameters.
`getExceptionTypes()`	Returns an array of `Class` objects representing the types of exceptions declared to be thrown by the method.
`equals(Object obj)`	Compares this `Method` against the specified object.
`hashCode()`	Returns a `hashcode` for this Method.
`toString()`	Returns a string describing this Method.

Some of the methods mentioned in table 8.2, such as `equals()`, `hashCode()`, and `toString()` do not require any real explanation, as anyone familiar with Java programming knows how and when to use these methods. The remainder of the methods, however, require some ground rules:

- All parameters and return codes in `invoke()` are passed wrapped within an object type. If some of the parameters or the return value are of primitive types (such as `char`) they need to be wrapped in an object (such as `java.lang.Character`). Table 8.3 presents the primitive types and their corresponding wrapping objects.

- The object on which `invoke()` will execute the method is passed as the `obj` parameter to `invoke()`.

- Since the number of parameters differs from one method to another, `invoke()` accepts an array of objects in which we place the parameters according to the order of declaration.

- The value returned from the invoked method is returned from `invoke()` (wrapped in an object if necessary).

- Exceptions thrown by the invoked methods are thrown by `invoke()` wrapped inside a `java.lang.reflect.InvocationTargetException` (from which you can then obtain the original exception).

- All methods that return type information, for example `getParameterTypes()`, return `Class` objects that represent this type. Even `void` has a `Class` object of type `java.lang.Void` to represent it.

Table 8.3   The primitive types and their corresponding wrappers

Primitive type	Wrapper class
boolean	java.lang.Boolean
char	java.lang.Character
byte	java.lang.Byte
short	java.lang.Short
int	java.lang.Integer
long	java.lang.Long
float	java.lang.Float
double	java.lang.Double

The `Method` class provides the functionality we need to call any method with whatever arguments are necessary for a given class. This class will be very useful as we build our JavaBean tags.

Array class

The `Array` class offers functionality for manipulating arrays of an unknown type. We'll forgo a deeper discussion of this class since the tags in this chapter won't need to use it.

Constructor class

`Constructor` class represents the constructor of a JavaBean, including any and all parameters to it (much like `Method` class). This class will not be used in our tags either so, once again, we'll forgo discussing it here.

Using reflection: QueryRequestTag

To better understand reflection, let's develop a tag that uses the reflection API. The tag will call some methods (to fetch a request property) of the request (`HttpServletRequest`) object using reflection. The source for the `QueryRequestTag` is in listing 8.1.

Listing 8.1   Source code for the QueryRequestTag handler

```
package book.reflection;

import java.util.Hashtable;
import java.lang.reflect.Method;
import java.lang.reflect.InvocationTargetException;

import book.util.LocalStrings;
import book.util.ExTagSupport;

import javax.servlet.http.HttpServletRequest;
import javax.servlet.jsp.JspException;

public class QueryRequestTag extends ExTagSupport {

    static Object []params = new Object[0];

    static Hashtable methods = new Hashtable();

    static LocalStrings ls =
        LocalStrings.getLocalStrings(QueryRequestTag.class);

    static {
        try {
            Class []p = new Class[0];
            Class reqc = HttpServletRequest.class;
            methods.put("method",
                        reqc.getMethod("getMethod", p));
            methods.put("queryString",
                        reqc.getMethod("getQueryString", p));
            methods.put("requestURI",
                        reqc.getMethod("getRequestURI", p));
```

❶

```
            methods.put("userPrincipal",
                        reqc.getMethod("getUserPrincipal", p));      ❶
            methods.put("remoteUser",
                        reqc.getMethod("getRemoteUser", p));
        } catch(Throwable t) {
        }
    }

    protected String property = null;

    public void setProperty(String property)
    {
        this.property = property;
    }

    public int doStartTag()
            throws JspException
    {
        try {
            Method m = (Method)methods.get(property);         ❷
            if(null != m) {
                writeHtml(pageContext.getOut(),
                        m.invoke(pageContext.getRequest(),      ❸
                                params).toString());
                return SKIP_BODY;
            } else {
                // Log and throw a JspTagException
            }

        } catch(java.io.IOException ioe) {
            // User probably disconnected ...
            // Log and throw a JspTagException
        } catch(InvocationTargetException ite) {           ❹
            // Exception in the called method
            // Log and throw a JspTagException
        } catch(IllegalAccessException iae) {
            // We are not allowed to access this method
            // Log and throw a JspTagException
        }
    }

    protected void clearProperties()
    {
        property = null;
        super.clearProperties();
    }
}
```

❶ **Obtains method objects from the HttpServletRequest class and stores them in a method cache for later use.** First we create an empty array of classes (see note) and procure an instance of HttpServletRequest from which to retrieve the methods.

Instead of the conventional approach, our tag extracts `Method` objects from the `HttpServletRequest` class and stores them in a hashtable. The key to the stored methods is the name of the property the method retrieves.

NOTE Note that we use `Class.getMethod()` to obtain the `Method` objects. `Class.getMethod()` expects two parameters: (1) The name of the method and (2) an array of class objects in which each entry in the array specifies the type of argument. In our case, using this approach was easy since all the needed methods have an empty argument list (array of size zero). This parameter is required since Java supports method overloading; meaning, a class may contain more than one method with the same name as long as the arguments to those methods are different.

---

❷ **Fetches the method object from the method cache; the key to the method cache is the property name** ❸ **Invokes the method using the current request variable; the method parameter list is an empty array of objects (no parameters)** When a request arrives, serving it is a breeze. All we need to do is fetch the method object that is stored in the cache, using the property name as the key. We use the `Method` class's `invoke()` with the current request object as the first parameter, and an empty argument list as the second. We use an empty argument list since none of the methods we are calling takes any arguments.

❹ **Handles the `InvocationTargetException`** If the invoked method throws an exception, we will need to handle it here.

The implementation of `QueryRequestTag` as seen in listing 8.1 is very different from what might have been expected had we worked without reflection. A conventional implementation of this tag would have taken the property name and performed a few `if-else` statements based on its value until it knew the method to use, and then it would call that method. Using reflection completely changes this algorithm.

What did we gain? We could implement this with a simple `if-else` statement. We gained extensibility! Suppose that we want to add new property for the tag to handle—simply add the code to fetch and store the `Method` in the method cache, and we're finished. In the case of this tag, the work to support a new method with reflection isn't much more (if any) than the work it takes to add another condition to an `if-else` statement. To further appreciate reflection, imagine if our tag did not store methods in a hashtable and, instead, simply looked for the methods by name at runtime. This approach would allow our tag to call any get method on the request. If the Servlet API were updated to add new properties to the request object, our tag would still be usable (without changes or even recompilation) since it would always look for a method with the name that was passed as the property attribute. This type of flexibility can only be achieved by using the reflection API. We now see how this flexibility can be applied to JavaBeans.

8.2 JavaBeans and reflection

The topic of JavaBeans has books devoted to the subject, so we needn't delve into its finer points. We will only mention issues that directly affect the tags we develop in this chapter; namely, JavaBean properties, introspection, and what all this has to do with reflection.

What then are JavaBeans? In a nutshell, a JavaBean is merely a Java class. JavaBeans conventions are the de facto development conventions (as introduced by JavaSoft) for Java components. These conventions define how a JavaBean is to expose its properties and events. JavaBeans publish properties and any events they provide through a strict method signature pattern, making these method names predictable so that Java development and debugging tools may easily use the reflection API to learn about the bean and offer a visual interaction with it. When a tool uses reflection to analyze a bean in this way, we call it introspection. The benefit of building Java components that adhere to JavaBeans conventions is that they are guaranteed to work well with any of the multitude of JavaBean supporting software tools available.

8.2.1 Tags and JavaBeans

Most interactions between our tags and beans will revolve around fetching data from the bean and presenting it. Typically, bean interaction will involve a JSP getting the value of some property of a bean and displaying that value to the user. In light of this, we forgo discussing the second role of the JavaBean standard we mentioned, which is defining how events are specified. Primarily, our tags are concerned with two bean-related issues:

- Introspecting the beans to find the properties and get the methods that these tags should call for property retrieval.
- Calling these methods with the correct set of parameters.

The next two sections deal with the properties of JavaBeans and introspecting them.

8.2.2 JavaBeans properties

What makes a JavaBean unique is that it conforms to specific criteria regarding how it exposes its properties and events. What exactly are properties? *Properties* are attributes of the JavaBean, something in its state or functionality that the bean wishes to expose. The code that uses the bean takes advantage of the properties (reads them or modifies them) by calling some of the bean's methods.

Imagine that you want to represent the data you have about a computer user in a bean, so that an administration program will be able to manipulate these users. Table 8.4 lists attributes each user might have.

Table 8.4 Sample User attributes and related properties

User Attribute	Description	JavaBean property
Name	The user's name	name
Family name	The user's family name	family
Password	The password that the user needs to enter when it logs into the computer	pass
Username	The user's login name	username
Groups	An array of user groups in which the user is a member	groups
User state	Specifies whether or not a user is logged in	state

To follow the JavaBean standard, each of the attributes described in table 8.4 will map into a bean property, and the methods that expose these properties in our UserBean would resemble the following code fragment.

```
public class UserBean implements java.io.Serializable {
    public String getName() { ... }
    public void setName(String name) { ... }
    public String getFamily() { ... }
    public void setFamily(String family) { ... }
    public String getPassword() { ... }
    public void setPassword(String pass) { ... }
    public String getUsername() { ... }
    public void setUsername(String name) { ... }
    public String getGroups(int index) { ... }
    public String []getGroups() { ... }
    public void setGroups(int index,
                    String group) { ... }
    public void setGroups(String []groups) { ... }
    public int getState() { ... }
};
```

When we look into these properties we may see differences between them. Some properties such as the user's password are read-write, meaning we can read their value as well as modify them. The user's state, however, is a read-only property; there is no meaning to set the value of this property since it represents something beyond our control (user logged in or logged out). The groups property is an array, since a user may belong to several groups, and we can access the different groups via an index. Our other properties are single values that do not need an index. The JavaBeans specification differentiates between read-only, write-only, and read-write properties, as well as indexed and nonindexed properties.

The differences between read-only, write-only, and read-write properties are manifested in our Java code through the types of methods we use for each. Each property can have a property setter method, getter method, or both. A property with only a getter method is said to be *read-only*, a property with only a setter method is said to be *write-only*, and a property with both methods is *read-write*.

NOTE   The state property has only a getter method. This means that the state is read-only.

Indexed properties are handled by providing getter and setter methods that accept an index parameter. In this way the bean user accesses discrete values of the property by using their index within the property array. The bean may also provide array-based setters and getters to allow the bean user to set the whole property array.

NOTE   The group property implements the indexed access with an integer as an index. One can consider using types other than an integer to index a property (for example, a string) but the JavaBeans specification is vague in the issue of property indexing using noninteger values. We also provide a means for the bean user to get the groups array in a single method call. Both method patterns (array getter/setter and indexed getter/setter) are permitted by the JavaBeans specification.

This clarifies properties and how the user of the JavaBean manipulates the bean's properties using setters and getters. However, how can the bean user find out about the different properties or their methods? As helpful as the beans might be, we cannot use them without knowing what methods to use to access the different properties. We answer this in our next section.

8.2.3 *JavaBeans introspection*

Recall that introspection is the process by which a JavaBean is analyzed, typically by a development tool, through reflection, for the purpose of determining its properties and events. The available properties as well as their `setter` and `getter` methods are discoverable by using introspection as defined in the JavaBeans specification. Introspection requires cooperation between the bean developer, who provides properties information, and the JavaBeans introspector, that reads this information and presents it to the user in a programmatic manner.

8.2.4 *Properties and introspection*

The simplest way for a developer to specify properties and their associated methods is to use the special JavaBean properties method naming conventions and parameter signatures in his or her JavaBeans.

Simple properties (nonindexed)

According to the JavaBean specification, either of the following methods can identify a simple property named `age` of type `int`:

```
public int getAge();
public void setAge(int age);
```

Note that to conform to the JavaBeans standard, we've defined methods whose names are `getProperty()` and `setProperty()` wherein `property` is the name of the property to manipulate; the first character constructing the property name is capitalized (in this case, `age` becomes `Age`). The presence of `getAge()` means that the property called `age` is readable, while the presence of `setAge()` means that `age` is writable. This naming convention applies when the property is of any data type whatsoever, except `boolean`. In such a case, the `setter`/`getter` method looks like the following

```
public boolean isFoo();
public void setFoo(boolean foo);
```

The `getter` method name was changed to reflect the fact that we are making a query on a value that can have only true or false values (by changing `get` to `is`).

Indexed properties

Indexed properties are specifiable in one of two ways. One way is by having an array type as the input and output to the `setter` and `getter`, respectively. This approach is presented in the following code fragment.

```
public Bar[] getFoo();
public void setFoo(Bar[] foo);
```

Another way is by having `setter` and `getter` methods that take an index parameter (e.g., the next code fragment shows a `setter`/`getter` pair with an integer index).

```
public Bar getFoo(int index);
public void setFoo(int index, Bar foo);
```

Either of these index property coding conventions will suffice to inform an introspecting program of the existence of an indexed property of type `Bar[]` and with the name `foo`.

BeanInfo interface

This coding convention approach provides an easy way to inform the system of the existence of properties and their methods. But what happens if we want to provide more explicit property information? In this case, the bean author provides an implementation of the `BeanInfo` interface. A `BeanInfo` object allows the JavaBean author to provide additional information about a bean, ranging from the icon that represents it to the properties and events it exposes. If a JavaBean author opts not to create a `BeanInfo` object for a bean and uses the coding convention approach instead, a `BeanInfo` is automatically created for the class during the introspection and holds on the information that is accessible from the coding conventions. In fact, as we will soon see in code, the `BeanInfo` interface is a crucial component of the introspection process and, therefore, will be used by our custom tags to learn about the Beans with which they are interacting.

How introspection works

The introspection process is provided through a class called `java.beans.Introspector` whose methods provide control over the introspection process as well as methods to obtain `BeanInfo` objects for any JavaBean. The tags in this chapter will be constructed to use an `Introspector` to get a `BeanInfo` object for a particular JavaBean, in order to learn about and manipulate its properties. To reach the crux of this long story, let's look at `getSetPropertyMethod()` (listing 8.2), whose job it is to find the `setter` method of a property in a certain JavaBean (for simplicity, the method does not work on indexed properties).

Listing 8.2   Source code of a method that uses introspection to find a property setter

```
package book.util;

import java.util.Hashtable;

import java.beans.BeanInfo;
import java.beans.Introspector;
import java.beans.PropertyDescriptor;
import java.beans.IndexedPropertyDescriptor;
import java.beans.IntrospectionException;

import java.lang.reflect.Method;

public class BeanUtil {

    // Snipped some of the code...
    /*
     * We are not dealing with indexed properties.
     */
    public static Method
        getSetPropertyMethod(Class claz,
                             String propName)
            throws IntrospectionException,
                   NoSuchMethodException
    {
        Method rc              = null;
        BeanInfo          info = Introspector.getBeanInfo(claz);      ❶
        PropertyDescriptor[] pd = info.getPropertyDescriptors();
        if(null != pd) {
            for(int i = 0; i < pd.length;  i++) {                     ❷
                if(propName.equals(pd[i].getName()) &&
                   !(pd[i] instanceof IndexedPropertyDescriptor)) {
                    Method m = pd[i].getWriteMethod();                ❸
                    if(null == m) {
                        continue;
                    }
                    Class[]params = m.getParameterTypes();
                    if(1 == params.length) {
                        rc = m;
                        break;
                    }
                }
            }
        }
        if(null == rc) {          ❹
            throw new NoSuchMethodException();
        }

        return rc;
    }
}
```

❶ Gets an array of the property descriptors of this class   Listing 8.2 shows an elementary example of bean property introspection that covers all the important introspection issues. The first step in `getSetPropertyMethod()`, as in any method that performs some type of bean introspection, is to get the properties descriptors (or events, depending on what you want to find). To get to properties descriptors we use the built-in bean `Introspector` in two phases; the first one fetches a `BeanInfo` for the class, and later obtains the `PropertyDescriptor` array from `BeanInfo`. The `PropertyDescriptor` interface (as its name implies) provides methods to retrieve logical information about JavaBean properties. The obtained array provides information on all the properties as identified by the `Introspector`, so we can now iterate this array and learn about the bean's properties.

❷ Iterates over all the properties in the class and looks for a property with a nonindexed matching name   A simple `for` statement will suffice; while iterating on the array we can check each of the properties as represented by a `PropertyDescriptor` object.

NOTE   There are two `PropertyDescriptor` types: the one that provides information on nonindexed properties, and `IndexedPropertyDescriptor` that extends `PropertyDescriptor` to provide information on indexed properties. The main difference between them is that `IndexedPropertyDescriptor` also provides a method informing us of the index variable's type.

Since (in this example) we are only looking for a specific named, nonindexed property, we will ignore all other properties and look only at simple properties.

❸ Found a property, performs a sanity check over the mehod. Do we have a method (meaning, is this property writable)? Does the method accept only a single parameter (the value to set)?   When we find a property of the type we want, we need to verify that the method we are seeking exists (maybe the property is read-only?). Thus we get the `setter` method from `PropertyDescriptor` and check it out. (We did not have to check the number of method arguments.)

❹ We could not find a matching property   The method we were looking for does not exist. We should notify the user by throwing an exception.

We have outlined some of the basics of reflection, and more specifically, JavaBean introspection. We'll see more code examples of introspection as we develop our tags in the next section. If, at this point you feel less than entirely comfortable with the topic of introspection and reflection, that's all right. Only the most rudimentary grasp is required to comprehend our custom tags. If you are, however, interested in learning more about reflection, take a look at JavaSoft's tutorial on the subject

which is available online at http://java.sun.com/docs/books/tutorial/reflect/
index.html.

Now, to the main event of this chapter: writing our JavaBean tags.

8.3   *The Show tag*

Our first JavaBeans-related tag is going to improve upon the standard `<jsp:get-`
`property>` tag by providing a JavaBeans property `getter` tag with the following
enhancements:

- No need for previous bean declaration through a `<jsp:useBean>` tag (or any
  other tag).
  This makes it much easier to use the tag.

- Accessibility to all types of properties, including indexed properties with possible index type of string and integer.
  The inability of `<jsp:getproperty>` to access indexed properties cripples
  the use of the property `getters`, and string indices are very important in the
  web arena.

- Bean object specification either through name and scope or using a runtime
  expression.
  We can use this tag with values created within scriptlets.

As we have a rather high level of expectation here, our implementation will be
rather involved. For example, our tag will let JSP authors specify the JavaBean for
the tag to use in two ways:

- By specifying the bean's name and scope explicitly in an attribute
- By specifying the bean as a result of a runtime expression.

Since our tag must confirm that the JSP author properly uses one of these options,
we need to use a `TagExtraInfo` object to verify the tag's attributes (a technique we
saw in chapter 6). We also have the choice of allowing the tag to support indexed
properties, which can become particularly tricky when a method is overloaded with
different indices (such as a `String` index and an `int` index into the same property).
In such a case, we do not want one tag attribute to specify the `String` index and a
different one to specify the `int` index, so we need to design a way to place these two
index value types into a single attribute. We'll soon see how we tackle these ambitious features.

8.3.1 Components of the tag

The implementation of our new property `getter` tag included using four Java classes (table 8.5).

Table 8.5 The classes comprising the bean getter tag

Java class	Description
BeanUtil	A utility class that performs the JavaBeans's introspection.
ReflectionTag	A tag whose role is to collect all our object and properties attributes and fetch the value pointed by them. This way we can reuse the logic in this class (by making it the base class) in other tags that require object property access through reflection.
ShowTag	A tag that takes the value fetched by our basic tag and prints it to the user. This is a relatively simple tag since most of the work is done in `ReflectionTag` from which it inherits.
ReflectionTagExtraInfo	A `TagExtraInfo` class to verify the tag's attributes. Since we want the tag to be very flexible, most of the attributes are not mandatory and some are applicable only in the presence of other attributes (for example, a scope attribute is not applicable without an object name attribute). This `TagExtraInfo` validates this complex attribute syntax.

Let's take a close look at the code for each of these components in order to gain a greater understanding of them.

BeanUtil

The first class we use to compose our `Show` tag is `BeanUtil` which is a utility class that will do the introspection and method caching for a bean. Its source is in listing 8.3.

Listing 8.3 Source code of JavaBeans utility class

```
package book.util;

import java.util.Hashtable;
import java.beans.BeanInfo;
import java.beans.Introspector;
import java.beans.PropertyDescriptor;
import java.beans.IndexedPropertyDescriptor;
import java.beans.IntrospectionException;
import java.lang.reflect.Method;
import java.lang.reflect.InvocationTargetException;

public class BeanUtil {
```

```
static LocalStrings ls =
            LocalStrings.getLocalStrings(BeanUtil.class);

public static final Object []sNoParams = new Object[0];
public static Hashtable sGetPropToMethod = new Hashtable(100);

public static Object
    getObjectPropertyValue(Object obj,
                            String propName,
                            Object index)
        throws InvocationTargetException,
               IllegalAccessException,
               IntrospectionException,
               NoSuchMethodException
{
    Method m = getGetPropertyMethod(obj,      ❶
                                    propName,
                                    null == index ?
                                    null: index.getClass());
    if(null == index) {
        return m.invoke(obj, sNoParams);       ❷
    } else {
        Object []params = new Object[1];       ❸
        params[0] = index;
        return m.invoke(obj, params);
    }
}

public static Method
    getGetPropertyMethod(Object obj,
                         String propName,
                         Class  paramClass)
        throws IntrospectionException,
               NoSuchMethodException
{
    Class    oClass = obj.getClass();
    MethodKey key = new MethodKey(propName,                ❹
                                  oClass,
                                  paramClass);
    Method rc = (Method)sGetPropToMethod.get(key);
    if(rc != null) {
        return rc;
    }
    BeanInfo            info = Introspector.getBeanInfo(oClass);   ❺
    PropertyDescriptor[] pd = info.getPropertyDescriptors();
    if(null != pd) {
        for(int i = 0; i < pd.length;  i++) {
            if(pd[i] instanceof IndexedPropertyDescriptor) {    ❻
                if(null == paramClass ||
                    !propName.equals(pd[i].getName())) {
                    continue;
                }
```

```
                        IndexedPropertyDescriptor ipd =          ➐
                            (IndexedPropertyDescriptor)pd[i];
                        Method m = ipd.getIndexedReadMethod();
                        if(null == m) {
                            continue;
                        }
                        Class[]params = m.getParameterTypes();
                        if((1 == params.length) &&
                            params[0].equals(paramClass)) {
                            rc = m;
                            break;
                        }
                } else {
                        if(null != paramClass ||       ➑
                            !propName.equals(pd[i].getName())) {
                            continue;
                        }
                        rc = pd[i].getReadMethod();
                        break;
                }
            }
        }

        if(null == rc) {
            StringBuffer methodName = new StringBuffer();       ➒
            methodName.append("get");
            methodName.append(propName.substring(0,1).toUpperCase());
            methodName.append(propName.substring(1));
            if(null == paramClass) {
                rc = oClass.getMethod(methodName.toString(),
                                      new Class[0]);
            } else {
                rc = oClass.getMethod(methodName.toString(),
                                      new Class[] {paramClass});
            }
        }
        if(null == rc) {
            // No such method; throw an exception
        }
        sGetPropToMethod.put(key, rc);       ➓
        return rc;
    }
}
```

➊ **Finds the needed method** ➋ **Invokes a nonindexed property** ➌ **Invokes an indexed property** The utility class exports two methods: The first accepts an object, property name, and index, and returns the desired property value from the object by using introspection. The second method introspects the object's class and retrieves the method required to get the property. The first method is not especially interesting; we already know how a method is called using reflection and the only new issue here is that you see how to provide parameters to the invoked method using an array of objects.

④ ⑩ Looks for the method in the introspected methods cache The second method presents several new ideas, starting with the use of a method cache, continuing with introspecting indexed properties, and ending with our own low-level introspection when the default `Introspector` fails us. The method cache was added when we found out how time-consuming introspection is. In fact, in pages loaded with reflection, adding the method cache gave the pages a 33% performance boost. It's important to remember that the key to the cache needs to be a combination of the object's class, property name, and method parameters. This is a rather complex key, so a new method key object was created (when caching methods for indexed `set-ters`, the key is even more involved). If we fail to find a method in the cache, we will introspect it and, when complete, place it in the cache.

⑤ Method not in the cache, start introspecting.

⑥ Skip methods that do not match our needs ⑦ Validate that this method matches our indexed property ⑧ Skip methods that do not match our needs Introspecting the class is different from introspection code in listing 8.2, mainly because we now introspect indexed properties. We iterate over the properties descriptor array and differentiate between indexed (instances of `IndexedPropertyDescriptor`) from non-indexed properties, and then check on the indexed property method. The check includes testing the parameter list of the indexed property, because a certain method in Java may be overloaded. For example, think of the following class:

```
class SuperHero{
    Power getSuperPower(int i);
    Power getSuperPower(String s);
}
```

We may want to inspect `getSuperPower(String)`, yet the `Introspector` will probably give us the descriptor of `getSuperPower(int)`.

We will then need to skip this descriptor and hope our luck is better elsewhere.

⑨ Method was not found using the default introspector; try our own low-level introspection We are finally finished with the property introspection, yet we may not have found the property method. The above example, wherein a specific method has two index types, is a good example of such a case (no, it is not a bug in the default `Introspector`, just our desire to attain more than the simple indexes regulated in JavaBeans). To overcome cases in which the default `Introspector` fails to find the needed method, we employ elementary low-level reflection to look for a method matching our property name and parameter types. If we find such a method, we assume that it is the one we seek.

🔟 **Places the newly introspected method in the cache.**

ReflectionTag

The class presented in listing 8.3 had nothing to do with tags (in fact, you can use it in any program that employs JavaBeans). The next class, ReflectionTag, is an abstract tag handler that integrates the JavaBeans reflection capabilities to the tag's world:

Listing 8.4   Source code for the ReflectionTag base class

```
package book.reflection;

import java.beans.IntrospectionException;
import java.lang.reflect.InvocationTargetException;
import book.util.LocalStrings;
import book.util.ExTagSupport;
import book.util.BeanUtil;
import javax.servlet.jsp.PageContext;
import javax.servlet.jsp.JspException;

public abstract class ReflectionTag extends ExTagSupport {
    public static final String PAGE_ID = "page";
    public static final String REQUEST_ID = "request";
    public static final String SESSION_ID = "session";
    public static final String APPLICATION_ID = "application";

    static LocalStrings ls =
        LocalStrings.getLocalStrings(ReflectionTag.class);

    protected Object obj = null;              ❶
    protected String objName = null;
    protected String objScope = null;

    protected String property = null;         ❷
    protected String index = null;

    public void setObject(Object o)
    {
        this.obj = o;
    }

    public void setName(String name)
    {
        this.objName = name;
    }

    public void setScope(String scope)
    {
        this.objScope = scope;
    }
```

```
public void setProperty(String property)
{
    this.property = property;
}

public void setIndex(String index)
{
    this.index = index;
}

public int doStartTag()
        throws JspException
{
    processObject(getPointed());         ❸
    return SKIP_BODY;
}

protected Object getPointed()
        throws JspException
{
    Object value = (null == obj ?                              ❹
                    getPointedObject(objName, objScope) :
                    obj);
    if(null != property) {
        value = getPointedProperty(value);      ❺
    }
    return value;
}

protected Object getPointedObject(String name,
                                  String scope)
        throws JspException
{
    Object rc = null;
    if(null != scope) {
        rc = pageContext.getAttribute(name,
                                      translateScope(scope));
    } else {
        rc = pageContext.findAttribute(name);
    }
    if(null == rc) {
        // Log and throw a JspTagException
    }

    return rc;
}

protected int translateScope(String scope)
        throws JspException
{
    if(scope.equalsIgnoreCase(PAGE_ID)) {
        return PageContext.PAGE_SCOPE;
    } else if(scope.equalsIgnoreCase(REQUEST_ID)) {
```

```
            return PageContext.REQUEST_SCOPE;
        } else if(scope.equalsIgnoreCase(SESSION_ID)) {
            return PageContext.SESSION_SCOPE;
        } else if(scope.equalsIgnoreCase(APPLICATION_ID)) {
            return PageContext.APPLICATION_SCOPE;
        }

    // Log and throw a JspTagException
    }
    protected Object getPointedProperty(Object v)
            throws JspException
    {
        try {
            Object indexParam = null;
            if(null != index) {
                if(index.startsWith("#")) {            ❻
                    indexParam = new Integer(index.substring(1));
                } else {
                    indexParam = index;
                }
            }
            return BeanUtil.getObjectPropertyValue(v,    ❼
                                                   property,
                                                   indexParam);
        } catch(InvocationTargetException ite) {
            // Log and throw a JspTagException
        } catch(IllegalAccessException iae) {
            // Log and throw a JspTagException
        } catch(IntrospectionException ie) {
            // Log and throw a JspTagException
        } catch(NoSuchMethodException nme) {
            // Log and throw a JspTagException
        }
    }

    protected void processObject(Object v)      ❽
            throws JspException
    {
    }

    protected void clearProperties()
    {
        obj      = null;
        objName  = null;
        objScope = null;
        property = null;
        index    = null;
        super.clearProperties();
    }
}
```

❶ **Points to the object whose property we want to get**   We can have either the object itself or its name and scope (optional). There are two ways to specify the object used by the tag: one way is to set the object as a runtime expression value, the other is to specify the name and the scope. These two object specification methods are mutually exclusive, and our TagExtraInfo implementation should take care of this. But we are getting ahead of ourselves.

❷ ❻ **Refers to the property name and the index (optional) in this property**   The property value is specified by two attributes: the property name and an index into the property. The index is not mandatory and the tag can handle cases in which the index is not specified. The index, you'll recall, may be a string or an integer; but how can we specify two different types using a single attribute? We cheat! We specify the integer within a string, but prefix its value with a '#' so that the tag knows that the value represents an integer. Why are we giving an advantage to the string? Because strings are far more useful as an index when we are creating web pages. In most cases, we will index our properties using a string, as it was felt that string indexing should be easily done.

❸ `doStartTag()` **fetches the property value and lets the tag process it using** `processObject()`.

❹ **Fetches the object**   If the object was configured as a runtime value, either use it, or get a reference to it using the name and the scope.

❺ **As soon as we receive the object, fetches the property value.**

❻ **A '#' prefix denotes an integer**   Translates the string to an integer.

❼ **Gets the propery value using the beans utility class.**

❽ `processObject()` **is a method that an extending class can overide to process the value of our object property**   As previously stated, `ReflectionTag` is an abstract class whose job is to provide access through reflection to properties in the JSP scripting objects. In this spirit, we defined an empty method named `processObject()` that can be overridden by an extending class, whose only goal is to manipulate the property value. Implementing `processObject()` is not mandatory and, for many cases, it may be better to override `doStartTag()` and use the method `getPointed()` directly; however, for the purpose of our new `ShowTag` (listing 8.5), overriding `processObject()` is enough.

ShowTag

The `ShowTag` handler is the handler for the tag to be used by the JSP author, and inherits from `ReflectionTag` to make use of its introspection work. This tag then retrieves the value for a property and prints it to the user.

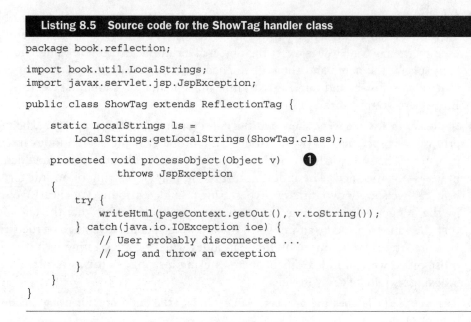

Listing 8.5 Source code for the ShowTag handler class

```
package book.reflection;

import book.util.LocalStrings;
import javax.servlet.jsp.JspException;

public class ShowTag extends ReflectionTag {

    static LocalStrings ls =
        LocalStrings.getLocalStrings(ShowTag.class);

    protected void processObject(Object v)           ❶
            throws JspException
    {
        try {
            writeHtml(pageContext.getOut(), v.toString());
        } catch(java.io.IOException ioe) {
            // User probably disconnected ...
            // Log and throw an exception
        }
    }
}
```

❶ **Overrides `processObject()` to print the property value.**

TagExraInfo for ShowTag

The last portion of code left unseen is the `TagExtraInfo` that we shall attach to the `ShowTag`. In fact, since `ShowTag` does not add any new attribute or syntactic constraints, we can actually take a `TagExtraInfo`, as developed for `ReflectionTag`, and use it for `ShowTag` (listing 8.6).

Listing 8.6 Source code for the ReflectionTagExtraInfo class

```
package book.reflection;

import javax.servlet.jsp.tagext.TagData;
import javax.servlet.jsp.tagext.TagExtraInfo;
import javax.servlet.jsp.tagext.VariableInfo;

public class ReflectionTagExtraInfo
    extends TagExtraInfo {

    public boolean isValid(TagData data)
    {
        Object o = data.getAttribute("object");
        if((o != null) && (o != TagData.REQUEST_TIME_VALUE)) {    ❶
            return false;
        }
```

```
        String name = data.getAttributeString("name");
        String scope = data.getAttributeString("scope");

        if(o != null) {
            if(null != name || null != scope) {
                return false;
            }
        } else {
            if(null == name) {
                return false;
            }

            if(null != scope &&
                !scope.equals(ReflectionTag.PAGE_ID) &&
                !scope.equals(ReflectionTag.REQUEST_ID) &&
                !scope.equals(ReflectionTag.SESSION_ID) &&
                !scope.equals(ReflectionTag.APPLICATION_ID)) {
                return false;
            }
        }

        if((null != data.getAttribute("index")) &&
            (null == data.getAttribute("property"))) {
            return false;
        }
        return true;
    }
}
```

① The object attribute must be the product of a runtime expression.

② If the object was provided through a runtime expression, the name and scope attributes should not be used.

③ If the object is not provided through a runtime expression, we must provide a variable name.

④ The scope value must be one of the four defined scopes.

⑤ We cannot provide an attribute index without specifying a property.

ShowTag's TLD

All that is left for us to do before using ShowTag in a JSP file is to create a TLD (listing 8.7). Note in this listing that not all the attributes are mandatory. This loss of control is required by the flexible functionality that was required from the tag.

Listing 8.7   Tag library descriptor entry for ShowTag

```
<tag>
    <name>show</name>
```

```
<tagclass>book.reflection.ShowTag</tagclass>
<teiclass>book.reflection.ReflectionTagExtraInfo</teiclass>
<bodycontent>empty</bodycontent>
<info>
    Show a certain object property value.
</info>
<attribute>
    <name>object</name>
    <required>false</required>
    <rtexprvalue>true</rtexprvalue>
</attribute>
<attribute>
    <name>name</name>
    <required>false</required>
    <rtexprvalue>false</rtexprvalue>
</attribute>
<attribute>
    <name>scope</name>
    <required>false</required>
    <rtexprvalue>false</rtexprvalue>
</attribute>
<attribute>
    <name>index</name>
    <required>false</required>
    <rtexprvalue>true</rtexprvalue>
</attribute>
<attribute>
    <name>property</name>
    <required>false</required>
    <rtexprvalue>false</rtexprvalue>
</attribute>
</tag>
```

ShowTag in action

We can create a JSP file that uses our new tag to show bean properties; the JSP driver (listing 8.8) uses our tag to explore the values present in the request and response objects (this is possible since both objects are JavaBeans).

Listing 8.8   JSP file that uses ShowTag

```
<%@ page import="java.util.*" %>
<%@ page errorPage="error.jsp" %>
<%@ taglib
    uri="http://www.manning.com/jsptagsbook/beans-taglib"
    prefix="bean" %>
<html>
<body>
<%-- javax.servlet.jsp.jspRequest is the JSP attribute
```

```
      name of the request object
   --%>
<br> <bean:show name="javax.servlet.jsp.jspRequest"          ①
             property="locale"/>

<table>
<tr>
<th> Header </th> <th> Value </th>
</tr>

<% Enumeration e = request.getHeaderNames();          ②
    while(e.hasMoreElements()) {
        String name = (String)e.nextElement();
%>
<tr>

<td> <%= name %> </td>

<td>
    <bean:show object="<%= request %>"               ③
             property="header"
             index="<%= name %>"/>
</td>
</tr>
<%
    }
%>
</table>
<%-- javax.servlet.jsp.jspResponse is the JSP attribute
     name of the response object
    --%>
<br> <bean:show name="javax.servlet.jsp.jspResponse"          ④
             scope="page"
             property="committed"/>

</body>
</html>
```

① **Shows the request locale.**

② **Creates a table of header names and values. Starts by enumerating the header names.**

③ **Prints the header value** We are using runtime expression to define the object we work with and to provide the index into the header property.

④ **Gets the value of the response's committed property** It should be `false`, since writing back to the user has not started.

Throughout the entire JSP file we never defined any of the objects used as a JavaBean; ShowTag will treat any object we give it as a bean, and this lets us take the regular request and response objects and use them without prior definition. This sample JSP file presents different usage patterns for the tag. Sometimes it is employed in an elementary way. For example, we only specify the JSP attribute name associated with the object (optionally the scope) and the name of the property. There might be a case, however, in which the tag is used with runtime expressions and indexed properties; in fact, we produce a fine table with the header names and values by using the tag with the header indexed property.

This section showed how easy it is to print the values of JavaBeans properties back to the response flowing to the user. Now we move on to build the second tag of our library, which allows us to export new JavaBeans from our tags and have them serve as scripting variables in the page.

8.4   *Exporting bean values from tags*

Exporting new scripting variables from a tag is a handy feature. For example, a JDBC connection tag can connect to a database and export a JDBC connection as a scripting variable so that JSP scriptlets further down the page may use the connection object. Though useful, exporting a new scripting variable is more than a minor maneuver for the JSP engine; it first needs to know:

- The Java type of the new scripting variable so that a correct Java scripting variable will be declared for the newly exported object.

- The duration (scope) of the scripting variable. Sometimes you want your Java scripting variable to last until the end of the page; in other cases you may want it to exist within the body of the tag. The JSP environment needs to be informed of that.

- The name of the scripting variable.

This reflective information must arrive at the JSP environment in order to take advantage of it while translating the JSP file to a servlet.

The methods to provide this information were defined in the JSP specification, which we will present now. Next, we take a look at a tag whose job it is to export JavaBean property values as new JSP scripting variables.

8.4.1   *Informing the runtime of exported scripting variables*

The JSP specifications define a simple way to inform the JSP runtime of the exported scripting variables, by overriding yet another method in `TagExtraInfo`. Up until now, the only method we overrode in `TagExtraInfo` was `isValid()`, which we used to validate tag attribute syntax and values. The `TagExtraInfo` class also allows you to indicate any scripting variables your tag will export by overriding `getVariableInfo()`.

The signature for `getVariableInfo()` is presented below:

```
public VariableInfo[] getVariableInfo(TagData data);
```

As you can see, `getVariableInfo()` accepts a `TagData` object which stores the values for the tag's attributes. The method returns an array of objects of type `VariableInfo`, whose methods and static variables are presented in listing 8.9.

Listing 8.9   Methods and static fields in VariableInfo

```
public class VariableInfo {

    public static final int NESTED = 0;
    public static final int AT_BEGIN = 1;
    public static final int AT_END = 2;

    public VariableInfo(String varName,
                        String className,
                        boolean declare,
                        int scope) { ... }

    public String getVarName() { ... }
    public String getClassName() { ... }
    public boolean getDeclare() { ... }
    public int getScope() { ... }
}
```

The job of a `VariableInfo` object is to provide variable information, starting with the variable's name and ending with its scope. A developer wishing to export scripting variables from a tag should first override `getVariableInfo()` and, within the method, use the tag's attributes to decide the exact variables to be exported. Next, for each scripting variable, the JSP author should create a `VariableInfo` instance with the desired variable name, type, and scope, and return an array containing these `VariableInfos`. Based on this information, the JSP page translator will emit Java code to implement the newly exposed scripting variables in a way that scriptlets and other JSP entities can access them.

Constructing a VariableInfo

How de we create a `VariableInfo` object? The parameters to the `VariableInfo`'s constructor have the following semantics:

- The `varName` parameter has two roles. It informs the JSP runtime of the name under which the newly generated JSP attributes (that hold the value of the new scripting variable) are kept; and it tells the JSP runtime the name of the variable it should emit into the generated servlet code. In the second role, the name of the exported scripting variable should match the rules of the scripting language employed in the page; for example, if the language is Java, then the name value may not include the "." character.

- The `className` parameter specifies the type of the exported object. Currently, tags can only export objects, so this is the fully qualified class name. You cannot export primitive types such as `float` values (they should be wrapped in some Java object type such as `java.lang.Float`).

- By default, the JSP engine will declare our variable as a new scripting variable in the JSP. If we want, instead, to assign a value to an existing scripting variable with our tag, we set the `declare` parameter to `false`, informing the JSP runtime that this variable has already been declared and to not declare it as a new variable.

- The `scope` parameter specifies the scope of the scripting variable that the page translator needs to emit into the Java servlet being generated for the JSP file. The `scope` parameter specifies, for example, whether the scripting variable will be known through all of the generated servlet or only within the tag's body (more on this soon).

Scripting variable scope

The last parameter to the `VariableInfo`'s constructor is the variable's scope. The possible values for this parameter (the different scope types as defined in the JSP specification) are listed in table 8.6.

Table 8.6 Possible scope types and their uses

Scope name	Scope in the generated servlet	Use
NESTED	Between the starting and closing marks of the custom tag, as presented in figure 8.1.	The JSP runtime emits a variable declaration in the block of code between the calls to `doStartTag()` and `doEndTag()`. Such NESTED scope variables are very useful in tags that perform iterations and need an iteration index of some sort.
AT_BEGIN	Between the starting mark of the custom tag and the end of the JSP file, as presented in figure 8.1.	The JSP runtime emits a variable declaration so that the variable will live in the block of code between the calls to `doStartTag()` and the end of the JSP file. This way you can define scripting variables whose scope spans the entire JSP file and whose value is specified in `doStartTag()`.
AT_END	Between the ending mark of the custom tag and the end of the JSP file, as presented in figure 8.1.	The JSP runtime emits a variable declaration so that the variable will live in the block of code between the calls to `doEndTag()` and the end of the JSP file. This way you can define scripting variables whose scope spans the entire JSP file and whose value is specified in `doEndTag()`.

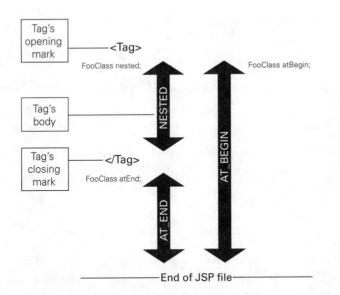

Figure 8.1   Scripting variable scopes illustrated

VariableInfo in action: TestTag example

Let's try to crystallize some of the information presented in this section with an example. We'll look at a simple `BodyTag` example called `TestTag` that exposes three scripting variables:

- sName—A variable of type `java.lang.String` with `ET_BEGIN` scope.
- iName—A variable of type `java.lang.Integer` with `ET_END` scope.
- fName—A variable of type `FooClass` with `NESTED` scope.

Let's look at the `TagExtraInfo` object we need to create for this class in order to export these three variables (listing 8.10).

Listing 8.10   Source code for TestTei

```
import javax.servlet.jsp.tagext.TagData;
import javax.servlet.jsp.tagext.TagExtraInfo;
import javax.servlet.jsp.tagext.VariableInfo;

public class TestTei extends TagExtraInfo {

    public VariableInfo[] getVariableInfo(TagData data)
    {

        VariableInfo[] rc = new VariableInfo[3];
```

```
        rc[0] = new VariableInfo("sName",
                                 "java.lang.String",
                                 true,
                                 VariableInfo.AT_BEGIN);
        rc[1] = new VariableInfo("iName",
                                 "java.lang.Integer",
                                 true,
                                 VariableInfo.AT_END);
        rc[2] = new VariableInfo("fName",
                                 "FooClass",
                                 true,
                                 VariableInfo.NESTED);

        return rc;
    }
}
```

This is an example of how to create and return an array of `VariableInfo` objects, each with its own type name and scope, in order to tell the JSP runtime engine the variables our tag will expose.

NOTE   The JSP specification instructs tag developers to use a special attribute named `id` to let the user name the variable exported by the tag. (Usually a single tag will export only a single object.) The sample provided in this section does not follow this rule; in part because there are several different variables to export, and because we wanted to make it as simple as possible. Do your best to follow this instruction, meaning that if you want your tag `foo` to export a variable, let your user specify this variable name by using an attribute named `id` in the following manner: `<foo id="bar"/>`. The implications of these instructions are that your `TagExtraInfo` implementation should look into the attribute's data, grab the value of the `id` attribute, and use it as the name (first parameter to the `VariableInfo`'s constructor) returned in the `VariableInfo`.

To see how the `TestTag` class affects the servlet code generated at translation time, let's look at the source code generated by Tomcat's JSP translator for `TestTag` when used with our `TestTag` class (listing 8.11).

Listing 8.11   Java that was generated for TestTag

```
TestTag testtag = new TestTag();              ❶
testtag.setPageContext(pageContext);
testtag.setParent(null);
java.lang.String sName = null;      ❷
```

```
try {
    int rc = testtag.doStartTag();
    sName = (java.lang.String) pageContext.getAttribute("sName");    ❸
    if (rc == Tag.EVAL_BODY_INCLUDE)
        // Throw exception. TestTag implements BodyTag so
        // it can't return Tag.EVAL_BODY_INCLUDE
    if (rc != Tag.SKIP_BODY) {
        try {
            if (rc != Tag.EVAL_BODY_INCLUDE) {
                out = pageContext.pushBody();
                testtag.setBodyContent((BodyContent) out);
            }
            testtag.doInitBody();
            do {
                FooClass fName = null;                               ❹
                fName = (FooClass)
                pageContext.getAttribute("fName");

                sName = (java.lang.String)    ❺
                    pageContext.getAttribute("sName");

                // Evaluate body ...

            } while(testtag.doAfterBody() == BodyTag.EVAL_BODY_TAG);
            sName = (java.lang.String)    ❻
                pageContext.getAttribute("sName");
        } finally {
            if (rc != Tag.EVAL_BODY_INCLUDE)
                out = pageContext.popBody();
        }
    }
    if (testtag.doEndTag() == Tag.SKIP_PAGE)
        return;
} finally {
    testtag.release();
}
java.lang.Integer iName = null;                                      ❼
iName = (java.lang.Integer)pageContext.getAttribute("iName");
```

❶ Initializes the `test` tag. Tomcat does not pool its tag handlers, but rather instantiates them.

❷ Declaring `sName` outside of the tag body so that it will be known through the page.

❸ Setting a value into `sName` right after the call to `doStartTag()` to set an initial value.

❹ Declaring and initializing `fName`. Since it is a NESTED variable it will be declared and initialized once per iteration.

❺ Updating `sName`'s value each iteration (so the tag can modify it over and over again).

❻ Updating `sName`'s value one more time when we are bailing out of the body processing loop.

❼ Declaring and initializing `iName`; this is done only once, after the tag processing is done.

Each of the variables is generated within a Java scope that matches the defined variable scope; for example, fName is defined within the curly brackets of the body evaluation loop. The JSP runtime updates the values of the exported variables from the PageContext whenever one of the tag's methods is called so that the tag can modify the value of the scripting variables as often as possible.

Our next step will be to use the information in this section to develop a real-world tag that exports objects into the JSP environment.

8.4.2   *The ExportTag*

ShowTag that we developed earlier in this chapter took the value of the certain bean property and printed it to the response flowing to the user. This capability is handy, but what if the property you want to print is not a primitive value or some type with a reasonable string conversion method that can be easily printed to the user? Or, what if this property is a bean of its own and we only want to echo some of its properties to the user? In these cases, ShowTag falls short of meeting our needs and we require the help of some other tag to export the complex property value into the JSP environment where ShowTag can take this bean property and print it the way we want. For this purpose, ExportTag was developed.

ExportTag acts very much like ShowTag except, instead of printing the property to the response, it exports the property as a JSP scripting variable. This lets us use the variable in scriptlets, just as if we'd defined it in a scriptlet or utilized the <jsp:useBean> standard tag to define it. To facilitate this task, we implemented the two objects presented in table 8.7:

Table 8.7   The ExportTag implementation objects

Java class	Description
ExportTag	Extends ReflectionTag to export the value gathered through reflection. This tag has two additional attributes: id for the user to choose a name for an exported bean, and type for the user to specify a type for the exported object.
ExportTagExtraInfo	Extends ReflectionTagExtraInfo to add an implementation for the method getVariableInfo(), which grabs the value of the id and type attributes and returns a VariableInfo with the desired name and type as well as AT_BEGIN scope.

It may seems as though ExportTag is a waste of time; why not just improve ShowTag such that it will be able to print the property of a property? The answer is twofold: First, this improved ShowTag will be too complex (just how many attributes will it take to print an indexed property of an indexed property)? Second, ExportTag offers clear advantages by being able to export a complex attribute (such as an enumerator) to be used later by our scriptlets. For example, the following JSP fragment:

```
<%
    Enumeration e = request.getHeaderNames();
%>
```

can be replaced by an alternative tag usage that looks similar to:

```
<beans:export id="e" type"enum"
               object="<%= request =>"
               property="headerNames"/>
```

Though this may be a matter of taste, the ability to grab complex properties that will be accessible for other JSP entities to work on (including other custom tags that do not know a thing about reflection) opens a great opportunity for synergy.

ExportTag handler

As a first step, let's look into `ExportTag` handler class (listing 8.12), which is actually the simpler part of the implementation of `ExportTag`.

Listing 8.12 Source code for the ExportTag handler class

```
package book.reflection;

import book.util.LocalStrings;
import javax.servlet.jsp.PageContext;
import javax.servlet.jsp.JspException;

public class ExportTag extends ReflectionTag {

    static LocalStrings ls =
        LocalStrings.getLocalStrings(ExportTag.class);

    public void setType(String type)
    {
        // Unused, needed only for the translation phase
    }

    protected void processObject(Object v)
            throws JspException
    {
        pageContext.setAttribute(id,
                                 v,
                                 PageContext.PAGE_SCOPE);     ❶
    }

    protected void clearProperties()
    {
        id = null;
        super.clearProperties();
    }
}
```

❶ **Exports the object into the JSP runtime by setting its value into the page scope with the `id` serving as the name.**

Listing 8.12 does not show anything new, but the property `setters` in `ExportTag` may seem strange. What happened to the `type` property (we didn't keep it) and why don't we need to implement a property `setter` for the `id` property?

The answer is easy. First, we do not use the `type` property during the service phase (only while translating the page), so keeping its value in the tag handler is not needed. As for the `id` attribute setter, the `TagSupport` base class implements a `setter` method for the property `id` (probably because it was regulated in the JSP specification as the recommended way to name the exported variables).

TagExtraInfo for ExportTag

The second class we implemented for the `ExportTag` is its `TagExtraInfo` implementation shown in listing 8.13. In its base, `ExportTagExtraInfo` should extend `ReflectionTagExtraInfo` to implement `getVariableInfo()`. This implementation is interesting because it shows how you can use the tag's attributes to define your exported variable parameters.

Listing 8.13   Source code for ExportTagExtraInfo

```
package book.reflection;

import java.util.Hashtable;
import javax.servlet.jsp.tagext.TagData;
import javax.servlet.jsp.tagext.TagExtraInfo;
import javax.servlet.jsp.tagext.VariableInfo;

public class ExportTagExtraInfo extends ReflectionTagExtraInfo {

    static Hashtable types = new Hashtable();

    static {
        types.put("iterator", "java.util.Iterator");
        types.put("enum", "java.util.Enumeration");
        types.put("string", "java.lang.String");
        types.put("boolean", "java.lang.Boolean");
        types.put("byte", "java.lang.Byte");
        types.put("char", "java.lang.Character");
        types.put("double", "java.lang.Double");
        types.put("float", "java.lang.Float");
        types.put("int", "java.lang.Integer");
        types.put("long", "java.lang.Long");
        types.put("short", "java.lang.Short");
    }

    public VariableInfo[] getVariableInfo(TagData data)
    {
        VariableInfo[] rc = new VariableInfo[1];
```

❶

```
        rc[0] = new VariableInfo(data.getId(),     ❷
                            guessVariableType(data),     ❸
                            true,
                            VariableInfo.AT_BEGIN);
        return rc;
    }
    protected String guessVariableType(TagData data)
    {
        String type = (String)data.getAttribute("type");
          if(null != type) {
          type = type.trim();
          String rc = (String)types.get(type);     ❹
              if(null != rc) {
                return rc;
              }

              if(type.length() > 0) {
                  return type;
              }
          }
          return "java.lang.Object";
    }
}
```

❶ ❹ **Prepares a translation table for the primitive types as well as a few shortcuts for common types** What is clear from `ExportTagExtraInfo` is that we go a long way to prevent users from specifying primitive types for the exported scripting variable! This is because for now, in JSP1.1 and 1.2, you are not allowed to export primitive types, only objects (less painful than you might think, but something to keep in mind). Other than that, take a look at how we used a `type` attribute to specify the exported bean's `type`. Whenever you export a bean from your tag, you will rarely know the exported type in advance (meaning we export an arbitrary bean) and, since the runtime object that we will reflect is not available during the translation, we will have to convey the type using some attribute (as demonstrated in listing 8.13). The last item to note here is that the `id` property receives special treatment in the `TagData` class which provides a special `getId()` method for easily obtaining the value of the `id` attribute (saving us a call to `data.getAttribute-String("id")`).

❷ **Specifies the value of the `id` property as the name of the exported variable (as specified in the specification).**

❸ **Guesses the exported variable type using the type attribute.**

❹ **Looks for the type in the translation table. If it exists in the translation table, uses the lookup value.**

ExportTag's TLD

The final piece in the implementation of ExportTag is the tag library entry as presented in listing 8.14.

Listing 8.14 Tag library descriptor entry for ExportTag

```
<tag>
    <name>export</name>
    <tagclass>book.reflection.ExportTag</tagclass>
    <teiclass>book.reflection.ExportTagExtraInfo</teiclass>
    <bodycontent>empty</bodycontent>
    <info>
        Exports an object property into the JSP environment
    </info>
    <attribute>
        <name>id</name>
        <required>true</required>
        <rtexprvalue>false</rtexprvalue>
    </attribute>
    <attribute>
        <name>type</name>
        <required>false</required>
        <rtexprvalue>false</rtexprvalue>
    </attribute>
    ... Additional attributes as defined for the ShowTag
</tag>
```

The id and type attributes in listing 8.14 were both defined as nonruntime expression values for a simple reason: we need these values during the translation process. We did not make the type attribute mandatory for the ExportTag, because often the type of the exported variables is not that important; for example, when another reflection-driven tag is processing the exported object. In these cases, Export-TagExtraInfo provides a default type (java.lang.Object), and eases the job of the JSP developer that does not deal with the exact details.

ExportTag in action

The last step of the ExportTag tour is the JSP file that uses it, which is actually a modified version of the JSP file that drove ShowTag.

Listing 8.15 A JSP driver for ExportTag

```
<%@ page errorPage="error.jsp" %>
<%@ taglib
    uri="http://www.manning.com/jsptagsbook/beans-taglib"
    prefix="bean" %>
<html>
```

```
<body>
<table>
<tr>
<th> Header </th> <th> Value </th>
</tr>

<bean:export id="e"
             type="enum"
             object="<%= request %>"
             property="headerNames" />

<% while(e.hasMoreElements()) {
       String name = (String)e.nextElement();
%>
<tr>

<td> <%= name %> </td>

<td>
    <bean:show object="<%= request %>"
               property="header"
               index="<%= name %>"/>
</td>
</tr>
<%
    }
%>
</table>
</body>
</html>
```

The modified portion of the JSP driver is in bold and is relatively straightforward. However, using `ExportTag` is shaded by the fact that we need some (relatively complex) scriptlet to iterate over the exported enumeration. This iteration scriptlet makes the `ExportTag` seem both clumsy (we need to specify a type for the exported value) and useless (if we already have a scriptlet, why add this tag?). We will return to this sample again in chapter 10 when we implement an enumerator that reduces the need for the iteration scriptlet and overcomes this limitation.

8.5 Summary

We have seen how easy it is to integrate beans and tags to produce a winning combination. The tags in this chapter free the JSP developer from the need to use scriptlets such as the following:

```
<%= obj.getPropertyName("index") %>
<% ClassType t = obj.getPropertyName("index"); %>
```

thus reducing the amount of real Java code in our JSPs. By removing Java syntax from JSPs, we further our cause of decoupling presentation logic and business logic; and by making the syntax cleaner and easier, reduce the possibility of writing incorrect or error-prone code. Future chapters show how to perform conditioning and iteration through tags, and how the availability of these bean-property related tags makes it possible to write out JSP files with minimal coding. We will also use bean integration in other future tags (such as conditioning) for which the know-how acquired in this chapter will prove worthwhile.

Part III

Advanced techniques

Now that you are well versed in common tag development techniques, we will show you in chapters 9 through 12 how to apply these techniques to solve some advanced yet common problems. In this section, we examine how to use custom tags for everyday development tasks, such as evaluating conditions in a JSP, iterating over a set of values, accessing a database, and integrating with the many services in the Java 2 Enterprise Edition.

Posing conditions with tags

9

Almost any form of dynamic content generation requires you to evaluate conditions. You may, for example, want to generate different content based on the user's browser (e.g., Internet Explorer does not support some of Navigator's JavaScript, and vice versa), or based on the internal state of server-side objects. If a shopping cart is empty you might not wish to show it to the user, for example. Deciding on what condition-based content to send to the user is a common issue in any web application.

In this chapter, we'll see how JSP authors use conditions to serve their dynamic content without tags, and discuss how this approach could be improved through custom tags. We'll then build a custom tag library that will allow us to evaluate conditions and return dynamic content based on the condition results within our JSPs.

9.1 *Evaluating conditions in JSPs*

For JSPs without custom tags, evaluating such conditions must be done in a scriptlet. The following JSP fragment shows, for instance, how to employ the `User-Agent` header in producing HTML that matches a specific browser:

```
<%
    String userAgent = request.getHeader("User-Agent");
    if((null != userAgent) &&
       (-1 != userAgent.indexOf("MSIE"))) {
%>

You are using Microsoft Internet Explorer

<% } else { %>

I guess that you are using Netscape Navigator

<% } %>
```

The problem with putting conditions inside scriptlets is that the syntax is rather involved. In order to provide conditional HTML using Java, the content developer must be aware of the Java operators, condition syntax, data types, and when and where to put curly brackets and semicolons (all within scriptlets, which are inherently difficult to debug in the first place).

To overcome the problems associated with evaluating conditions in scriptlets, some developers use beans to encapsulate most of the condition logic. For example, the following code fragment produces a browser detection bean and later performs conditions on some of the bean's properties.

```
<jsp:useBean id="browserDetect"
             scope="page"
             class="phony.BrowserDetect">
    <jsp:setProperty name="browserDetect"
                     property="userAgent"
                     value="<%= request.getHeader(\"User-Agent\")%>"/>
```

```
</jsp:useBean>

<%
    if(browserDetect.isMsIE()) {
%>

You are using Microsoft Internet Explorer

<% } else { %>

I guess that you are using Netscape Navigator

<% } %>
```

Using a bean to encapsulate the condition result inside a property yields an improved JSP; yet, if all we are doing here is checking the value of a bean, why should we use a scriptlet? Note also that we are still using the Java `if` statement, which requires that the JSP author know some Java syntax (especially when the bean returns different data types). To clean up this syntax and reduce the likelihood of errors, we can create a custom tag that will perform conditional evaluation. The creation of such a tag is the subject of the rest of this chapter.

We start by exploring a basic custom tag that implements the functionality usually found within a simple `if` condition. Next we'll look at the shortcomings involved with that `if` condition and seek an improved implementation of conditioning using custom JSP tags.

9.2   *IfTag—A simple condition tag*

Let's start by developing a tag that lets the content developer evaluate conditions based on the value of some object or its property within a JSP. We'll want the JSP author to be able to specify an object (either by name and scope or as a runtime expression) and a `boolean` property of that object to evaluate. The tag will then evaluate whether the object's property is `true` or `false`. Before jumping into the code, let's see how it will look in a JSP.

The following JSP fragment shows a possible use of the custom condition tag:

```
<jsp:useBean id="browserDetect"
             scope="page"
             class="phony.BrowserDetect">
    <jsp:setProperty name="browserDetect"
                     property="userAgent"
                     value="<%= request.getHeader(\"User-Agent\")%>"/>
</jsp:useBean>

<cond:if object="<%= browserDetect %>" property="msIE">

You are using Microsoft Internet Explorer

</cond:if>
```

Here the tag poses a condition on the value of the bean property as specified with the tag attributes `object` and `property`. Based on this usage pattern, let's start building our conditional tag.

9.2.1 *Implementing IfTag*

The first issue to note regarding `IfTag` is that we want it to be able to pose conditions on the property values of JavaBeans (as in the previous code snippet). We can inherit most of the necessary functionality for this from `ReflectionTag` that was developed in chapter 8.

`IfTag` will also need to implement some conditional logic inside `doStartTag()` once it gets the JavaBean property. Our `IfTag` will only look at the value of the object or property it received in its attributes, convert the value to a boolean, and, if the boolean value is `true`, evaluate the tag's body into the response. Implementing this logic is no problem if the value on which we base our condition is already boolean; in other cases we just convert the value to a boolean. For `IfTag`, we've chosen an extremely simple conversion logic (since the goal of the tag is to demonstrate conditional execution, not necessarily data-type conversion).

With this in mind, let's take a look at `IfTag`'s implementation.

Listing 9.1   Source code for IfTag handler

```
package book.conditions;

import javax.servlet.jsp.PageContext;
import javax.servlet.jsp.JspException;

import book.util.LocalStrings;
import book.reflection.ReflectionTag;

public class IfTag extends ReflectionTag {

    static LocalStrings ls =
        LocalStrings.getLocalStrings(IfTag.class);

    public int doStartTag()
            throws JspException
    {
        boolean b = evalBoolean(getPointed());        ❶

        if(null != id) {
            pageContext.setAttribute(id,
                                new Boolean(b),
                                PageContext.PAGE_SCOPE);
        }

        if(b) {                                        ❷
            return EVAL_BODY_INCLUDE;
        }
        return SKIP_BODY;
```

```
    }
    protected boolean evalBoolean(Object o)
    {
        if(o instanceof Boolean) {
            return ((Boolean)o).booleanValue();
        }
        if(o instanceof Number) {
            return ((Number)o).intValue() != 0;
        }
        return new Boolean(o.toString()).booleanValue();
    }
}
```

❶ **Sends the pointed variable (our condition) to `boolean` evaluation.**

❷ **Based on the returned value includes the body (if true) or excludes it (false).**

❸ **Evaluates the condition value as `boolean` (the simple way).**

There is nothing too complex in implementing `IfTag`. All the reflection work is implemented by `ReflectionTag` and the rest of the work is actually evaluating the pointed value as a `boolean` and whether to include the tag's body in the response (returning `EVAL_BODY_INCLUDE`) or exclude it (returning `SKIP_BODY`).

What is not obvious about `IfTag` is why it exports a new JSP scripting variable with the result of the condition evaluation. The reason for this is to allow other `IfTag`s and scriptlets to read and possibly react, based on the result of the condition. Because we may not need this capability in all cases, exporting the scripting variable occurs only when the tag's user provides an `id` attribute value.

9.2.2 *The problem with IfTag*

`IfTag` is quite useful for pages in which the content developer is interested in performing very simple conditions on various values. But when trying to develop pages that require the use of complex conditions (such as those provided by the Java's `switch` and `if else`), we run into a problem. At the very least we would like our tag to be able to handle the case wherein the condition fails via an `else` clause. As we will soon see, extending the tag as it currently stands to support an `else` clause proves to be somewhat problematic.

To support an `else` clause, you might expect that we could simply add an `else` tag to our library and proceed with syntax such as the following:

```
<cond:if object="..." property="...">
Some JSP if the condition is true.
<cond:else>
Some JSP if the condition is false.
</cond:if>
```

The problem with the above code fragment is that it does not constitute valid JSP syntax (because JSP tags follow the rules for XML tags). The issue with this fragment is that `<cond:else>` tag must be closed. An alternative is:

```
<cond:if id="someid" object="..." property="...">
Some JSP if the condition is true.
</cond:if>
<cond:else id="someid">
Some JSP if the condition is false.
</cond:else>
```

Another possible alternative is:

```
<cond:if object="..." property="...">
Some JSP if the condition is true.
<cond:else>
Some JSP if the condition is false.
</cond:else>
</cond:if>
```

Though legal JSP, both options have problems that render them undesirable. Namely:

- In the first option, there is no implicit link between `if` and `else`. To rectify this, we had to link `if` and `else` explicitly by supplying an `id` in `<cond:if>` and referencing this `id` in `<cond:else>`. This syntax is somewhat messy and places an unneeded burden on the JSP developer.

- The second option, though possible if we use a `BodyTag` to implement our `<cond:if>` and `<cond:else>` tags, runs the risk of introducing unwanted side effects. Since `<cond:else>` resides within the body of `<cond:if>`, the `<cond:if>` must always evaluate its body to determine whether a `<cond:else>` exists within it. Hence, the body of the `<cond:if>` is evaluated, even if the condition is `false` (in which case, it would be evaluated and ignored). This is a problem, because evaluating the body even when the condition is `false` will cause any scriptlets or tags within the body to be executed, potentially causing side effects like throwing an exception or wasting processing time. It's similar to having a standard Java `if` statement that executes both branches when evaluated, but returns the results of only the proper branch.

- In both cases, the type of condition you impose is bound to be simple since the number of attributes in the tags is becoming unmanageable (we need attributes to point to the property/object, to link the `if` and `else`, and to specify a complex condition).

Based on these complications, it would appear that our initial IfTag is too simplistic to be properly built upon and extended. We can conclude from this that we should implement a new set of tags to cope with complex conditions (including else clauses). Building this more flexible tag library is the subject of the next section.

9.3 *The advanced condition tag family*

Following the discussion in the previous section, an advanced condition tag should:

- Allow the developer to create the equivalent of a chain of Java if-else-if statements that are based on the same object.
- Provide a straightforward syntax for the JSP developer (for example, obviate the entering of needless IDs and object references, even if they want to query a certain object more than once).
- Eliminate the simple and sometime useless conversion of the conditioned object to a boolean, and let the developer specify a more exact condition (such as: the object is a String that contains the sub-string "MSIE").

Considering these requirements, it is clear that what we are looking for is not a single complex tag but a family of tags working together. A single tag, as powerful as it might be, is going to be too complex to develop and use. The library we will develop, which we'll call the advanced condition tags, will have to obtain the Java object on which we want to perform conditions, and evaluate various conditions on the object's values. Also, we want it to have more than one conditional fragment of JSP to be evaluated if its condition is true. For example, we want to have the following ability as demonstrated in this pseudo JSP fragment:

```
<%-- Define the object that we are going to
     query --%>
<withobject name="somevalue"
            property="someproperty">

    <test condition="some true condition on the object">
    <%-- Some JSP is evaluated here--%>
    </test>

    <test condition="some other true condition on the object">
    <%-- Some other JSP is evaluated here--%>
    </test>

</withobject>
```

If both tests are evaluated as true, we want both to run (not exactly an if-else behavior but very useful).

Based on these requirements, we see the need for the following two tags to be developed:

- TestTag
  The role of the TestTag is to pose a condition on the value of a reference object. If this condition is evaluated to be true the body of the TestTag is added to the response that goes to the user.

- WithTag
  The role of WithTag is to wrap one or more of the TestTags and manage them. This includes obtaining and handing over the reference object that the TestTags test (as sketched in figure 9.1), and serving as a repository for information that all the TestTags need to share (e.g., if one of the test tags was evaluated

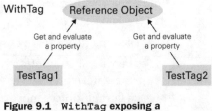

Figure 9.1 WithTag **exposing a** ReferenceObject **for two nested** TestTags **to refer to and evaluate**

to be true). Additionally, WithTag selects one of two test evaluation policies: The first allows only the first TestTag that was evaluated as true to be added to the response; the second allows any TestTag evaluated as true to be added to the response.

To help clarify what these tags do, let's look at an example in which a JSP uses them (listing 9.2):

Listing 9.2   Using our new conditional tags with a Boolean value

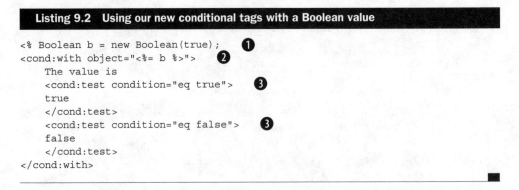

```
<% Boolean b = new Boolean(true);      ❶
<cond:with object="<%= b %>">          ❷
    The value is
    <cond:test condition="eq true">    ❸
    true
    </cond:test>
    <cond:test condition="eq false">   ❸
    false
    </cond:test>
</cond:with>
```

❶ **The object, in this case a Boolean, on which the condition will be evaulated.**

❷ **Usage of the** cond:with **tag, specifying that the object for condition evaluation is b.**

❸ **Usage of the** test **tag, with the condition specified with a special syntax (discussed later).**

We'll look at this syntax in more detail once we've seen the tag handler implementations, but it is helpful at this point to note how the general architecture for these two tags works together. Of specific interest is the way in which the `<cond:with>` tag wraps all the subsequent `<cond:test>` tags and points to the object on which conditions will be evaluated.

Let's now drill down into the implementation of each tag's tag handler class.

9.3.1 *WithTag*

The `WithTag` will manage our `TestTags`, helping glue them together and communicate together. The role of this tag can be greatly clarified by looking at the implementation of its handler (listing 9.3).

Listing 9.3   Source code for the WithTag handler

```
package book.conditions;

import javax.servlet.jsp.PageContext;
import javax.servlet.jsp.JspException;

import book.util.LocalStrings;
import book.reflection.ReflectionTag;

public class WithTag extends ReflectionTag {
    static LocalStrings ls =
        LocalStrings.getLocalStrings(IfTag.class);

    public void setMultichoice(String trueOrFalse)      ❶
    {
        if(trueOrFalse.equals("true")) {
            multiChoice = true;
        }
    }
    protected boolean multiChoice = false;

    public boolean isSelected()      ❷
    {
        return selected;
    }
    public void setSelected(boolean selected)
    {
        this.selected = selected;
    }
    protected boolean selected = false;

    public Object getValueWith()      ❸
    {
        return value;
    }
    protected Object value;
```

```
    public boolean isExecutionPossible()        ❹
    {
        return multiChoice || !isSelected();
    }
    public int doStartTag()
            throws JspException
    {
        selected = false;
        try {
            value = getPointed();              ❺
        } catch(JspException ex) {
            value = null;
        }

        return EVAL_BODY_INCLUDE;
    }
    protected void clearProperties()
    {
        multiChoice = false;
        super.clearProperties();
    }
    protected void clearServiceState()          ❻
    {
        value = null;
        selected = false;
    }
}
```

❶ **A set property method for the multichoice attribute. If this property is on ("true" value), multiple enclosed tags can be evaluated as `true` and enclosed within the output.**

❷ **The selected property is set by the enclosed tags when one is evaluated as `true`.**

❸ **A `getter` for the reference object that the enclosed tags will use.**

❹ **Implements the condition evaluation policy. The enclosed tags will call this method to find out if they are allowed to execute.**

❺ **Gets the pointed object so that the enclosed tags will be able to get a reference to it. If we received an exception, the object is not available (null value).**

❻ **Clears the state that the tag holds while its body is being evaluated.**

The purpose of `WithTag` is to make it possible for the enclosed tags to procure a reference to information and to coordinate with one another. `WithTag` holds the pointed object (the object on which the conditions will be evaluated) for the enclosed tags and hands it over to them, thereby freeing the JSP developer from specifying the referenced object for each `TestTag`. It also coordinates the evaluation of the enclosed `TestTags` by providing `isExecutionPossible()`; each enclosed

TestTag should call this method in order to obtain permission to run (and evaluate its body). In this way we can have different TestTag condition evaluation policies. A final item to note here is the selected property. Each enclosed TestTag should set this property to true if its condition evaluates to true. This information is used inside isExecutionPossible() to produce instruction to the other tags (e.g., if multichoice is off and some tag sets the selected property to true, no other tag is allowed to run). This tag will become clearer shortly, when we see how the TestTags interact with it.

WithTagExtraInfo

WithTag is accompanied by a TagExtraInfo implementation, whose job is to validate its attribute as presented in listing 9.4.

Listing 9.4   Source code for the WithTagExtraInfo class

```
package book.conditions;

import book.reflection.ReflectionTagExtraInfo;

import javax.servlet.jsp.tagext.TagData;

public class WithTagExtraInfo extends ReflectionTagExtraInfo {

    public boolean isValid(TagData data)
    {
        if(!super.isValid(data)) {
            return false;
        }

        String multiChoice =
            data.getAttributeString("multichoice");

        if(null != multiChoice) {
            if(!multiChoice.equals("true") &&
               !multiChoice.equals("false")) {
                return false;
            }
        }

        return true;
    }
}
```

Most of the attribute validation work in WithTagExtraInfo is performed by its superclass ReflectionTagExtraInfo. WithTagExtraInfo is responsible only for the validation of the multichoice attribute (it can only accept true or false).

9.3.2 *TestTag*

Now that you have seen how the WithTag provides access to the reference object and policy for execution of several conditions, we shall move on to examine the implementation of the tag that evaluates conditions and performs branching based on that evaluation: TestTag.

Listing 9.5   Source code for the TestTag handler

```java
package book.conditions;

import java.util.Hashtable;

import javax.servlet.jsp.PageContext;
import javax.servlet.jsp.JspException;

import book.util.LocalStrings;
import book.util.ExTagSupport;
import book.util.StringUtil;

public class TestTag extends ExTagSupport {

    static Hashtable operators = new Hashtable();

    static {
        operators.put("contains",       ❶
                    new ContainsOperator(true));
        operators.put("eq",
                    new EqualsOperator(true));
        operators.put("cleq",
                    new ClequalsOperator(true));
        operators.put("startswith",
                    new StartswithOperator(true));
        operators.put("endswith",
                    new EndswithOperator(true));

        operators.put("ncontains",
                    new ContainsOperator(false));
        operators.put("neq",
                    new EqualsOperator(false));
        operators.put("ncleq",
                    new ClequalsOperator(false));
        operators.put("nstartswith",
                    new StartswithOperator(false));
        operators.put("nendswith",
                    new EndswithOperator(false));
    }

    public static final String OPER_EXISTS = "exists";
    public static final String OPER_NEXISTS = "nexists";

    static LocalStrings ls =
        LocalStrings.getLocalStrings(TestTag.class);

    protected String condition = null;
```

```
public void setCondition(String condition)      ❷
{
    this.condition = condition;
}

public int doStartTag()
          throws JspException
{
    if(evalCondition()) {                         ❸
        return EVAL_BODY_INCLUDE;
    }
    return SKIP_BODY;
}

    protected boolean evalCondition()
          throws JspException
{
    WithTag wrapper =
        (WithTag)findAncestorWithClass(this,      ❹
                                  WithTag.class);
    if(null == wrapper) {
        // Throw a JspTagException
    }
    if(!wrapper.isExecutionPossible()) {          ❺
        return false;
    }

    String []oper = StringUtil.splitArray(condition, " ");
    boolean result = false;

    switch(oper.length) {

        case 1:
        result = unaryOperation(oper[0],
                            wrapper.getValueWith());   ❻
        break;

        case 2:
        result = binaryOperation(oper[0],
                            oper[1],              ❼
                            wrapper.getValueWith());

        break;

        default :
        // Log and throw a JspTagException
    }
    if(result) {
        wrapper.setSelected(true);                ❽
    }
    return result;
}
```

```
protected boolean unaryOperation(String oper,
                                 Object lh)
        throws JspException
{
    if(oper.equals(OPER_EXISTS)) {
        return (null != lh);          ❾
    } else if(oper.equals(OPER_NEXISTS)) {
        return (null == lh);
    } else {
        // Log and throw a JspTagException
    }
}

protected boolean binaryOperation(String oper,
                                  String rh,
                                  Object lh)
        throws JspException
{
    Object oRh = getOperand(rh);
    Operator o = (Operator)operators.get(oper);     ❿
    if(null == o) {
        // Log and throw a JspTagException
    }
    return o.cmp(lh, oRh);
}

protected Object getOperand(String spec)
        throws JspException
{
    Object rc = spec;
    if(spec.charAt(0) == '$') {
        rc = pageContext.findAttribute(spec.substring(1));
    } else if(spec.charAt(0) == '#') {
        rc = new Integer(spec.substring(1));
    }

    if(null == rc) {
        // Log and throw a JspTagException
    }

    return rc;
}

protected void clearProperties()
{
    id = null;
    condition = null;
    super.clearProperties();
}

static interface Operator {                      ⓬
    public boolean cmp(Object lh, Object rh);
}
```

```
static class ContainsOperator implements Operator {
    boolean reference;
    public ContainsOperator(boolean reference) {
        this.reference = reference;
    }
    public boolean cmp(Object lh, Object rh) {
        return ((lh.toString().indexOf(rh.toString()) != -1) ?
                reference :
                !reference);
    }
}
static class EqualsOperator implements Operator {
    boolean reference;
    public EqualsOperator(boolean reference) {
        this.reference = reference;
    }
    public boolean cmp(Object lh, Object rh) {
        return (lh.toString().equals(rh.toString()) ?
                reference :
                !reference);
    }
}

// Other operators were removed for clarity ...
}
```

❶ ❾ ❿ ⓬ Prepares a lookup table with condition operator names as keys and the operator implementation as value TestTag shows (on purpose) two methods to implement multiple condition operators. The unary operators (comparing only one operand) are hard-coded inside TestTag, while the binary operators (comparing two operands) are implemented by a set of classes (each implementing a different operator) and a Hashtable, used as a look-up table for the correct operator. Looking into the two methods, it is obvious that the second is much cleaner and can scale well (i.e., adding many more operators should not pose a problem). By implementing each operator in a different class, it is much easier to extend TestTag to handle new operators. One can modify TestTag to read a resource file with the operator names and implementing classes and avoid the coupling between the tag and its operators.

❷ TestTag has a single attribute which is the condition to test.

❸ If the condition is true, include the body in the response, otherwise ignore it.

❹ Get a reference to the wrapper tag and keep it for later use.

❺ Consult the condition policy logic in the wrapper tag before evaluationg the condition. If we are not allowed to run, this is just like a false condition.

❻ Single operand, send to the unary condition evaluator.

❼ Two operands, send to the binary condition evaluator.

8 If the condition is `true`, notify the policy logic in the wrapping tag using `setSelected()`.

9 The implementation of the unary operators is hard-coded in the tag.

10 Gets the operator object from the operator table. The name of the operator saves as the key.

11 Evaluates the condition operand. Two metachars may prefix the operand value, a # signs for an integer value, a $ informs us that the following string is a JSP scripting attribute name   The condition may have a single operand or two. In both cases the first operand is the one held within the wrapping `WithTag`; the second, however, comes from the condition string. The condition string describes the condition using a syntax we've developed (recall, this string was `eq true` or `eq false` in listing 9.2). In general, the binary condition string looks like: `<condition operator> <condition operand>`, in which the condition operator can be one of the operator names held within the operator tables and the condition operand is the second operand to be used within the condition. We wanted the second operand to be as flexible as possible, but without adding too much of a burden to the JSP developer. The solution was to add some special metacharacters to the operand in the following way:

- If the operand starts with a "#," then following the "#" is an integer value, and the second operand should be an `Integer` object that was created from this value.

- If the operand starts with a "$," then following the "$" is the name of a JSP scripting variable (some Java object) whose value should be used as the second operand.

- If the operand does not start with "$" or "#" it is a plain string value.

These three rules make the second operand very flexible, yet keep things simple for the JSP developer.

12 All our binary operators implement the same `Operator` interface. This way we can handle many different operators the same way.

In a nutshell `TestTag`'s job is to evaluate its condition and, based on the result, to embed (or not) its body content in the response. This is accomplished relatively simply because of the work partition between `WithTag` and `TestTag`.

TestTagExtraInfo

We saw that `TestTag` created a framework where we can plug additional operators as needed. With all these operators, you might expect the `TagExtraInfo` associated with `TestTag` to be huge. Will we have to change it whenever we add a new operator? If so, this entire flexible operator framework does not seem to be worth all that much. The answer to these concerns is in listing 9.6 where you see the implementation of TestTagExtraInfo.

Listing 9.6   Source code for the TestTagExtraInfo class

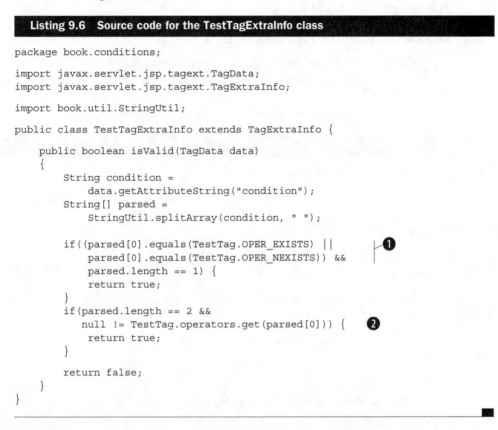

```
package book.conditions;

import javax.servlet.jsp.tagext.TagData;
import javax.servlet.jsp.tagext.TagExtraInfo;

import book.util.StringUtil;

public class TestTagExtraInfo extends TagExtraInfo {

    public boolean isValid(TagData data)
    {
        String condition =
            data.getAttributeString("condition");
        String[] parsed =
            StringUtil.splitArray(condition, " ");

        if((parsed[0].equals(TestTag.OPER_EXISTS) ||      ❶
            parsed[0].equals(TestTag.OPER_NEXISTS)) &&
            parsed.length == 1) {
            return true;
        }
        if(parsed.length == 2 &&
            null != TestTag.operators.get(parsed[0])) {   ❷
            return true;
        }

        return false;
    }
}
```

❶ **Checking the unary operators for correctness, we need to individually check each operator name.**

❷ **Checking the binary operators for correctness, all we need is a single look-up in the operator table.**

TestTagExtraInfo provides one more reason for using an operator table instead of hard-coding the operators in TestTag; just look at the difference between the validation of the unary and binary conditions. Since the implementation of the unary operators is hard-coded in TestTag, TestTagExtraInfo must create an if statement with the specific unary operator, which will force a developer that adds another unary operator to modify both as well as TestTag. On the other hand, since the binary operators are implemented with an operator look-up table, all that is needed to validate the binary operator is to search the look-up table for a valid operator. Happily, this means that a developer will not need to change `TestTagExtraInfo` in order to add new operators.

9.3.3 *TLD for the advanced condition tags*

To complete our discussion of advanced condition tags, we shall also provide the important tag library descriptor, as well as sample JSP code that take advantage of the condition tags.

First, let's look at the tag library descriptor as presented in listing 9.7.

Listing 9.7   Tag library descriptor for the advanced condition tags

```xml
<?xml version="1.0" encoding="ISO-8859-1"?>
<!DOCTYPE taglib
    PUBLIC "-//Sun Microsystems, Inc.//DTD JSP Tag Library 1.1//EN"
    "http://java.sun.com/j2ee/dtds/web-jsptaglibrary_1_1.dtd">

<taglib>
    <tlibversion>1.0</tlibversion>
    <jspversion>1.1</jspversion>
    <shortname>simp</shortname>
    <uri>
    http://www.manning.com/jsptagsbook/condition-taglib
    </uri>
    <info>
        Condition tags library.
    </info>

    <tag>
        <name>with</name>
        <tagclass>book.conditions.WithTag</tagclass>
        <teiclass>book.conditions.WithTagExtraInfo</teiclass>
        <bodycontent>JSP</bodycontent>
        <info>
            Wrap a JSP fragment with test conditions.
        </info>

        <attribute>
            <name>multichoice</name>
            <required>false</required>
            <rtexprvalue>false</rtexprvalue>
        </attribute>
        <attribute>
            <name>object</name>
            <required>false</required>
            <rtexprvalue>true</rtexprvalue>
        </attribute>
        <attribute>
            <name>name</name>
            <required>false</required>
```

```
            <rtexprvalue>false</rtexprvalue>
        </attribute>
        <attribute>
            <name>scope</name>
            <required>false</required>
            <rtexprvalue>false</rtexprvalue>
        </attribute>
        <attribute>
            <name>index</name>
            <required>false</required>
            <rtexprvalue>true</rtexprvalue>
        </attribute>
        <attribute>
            <name>property</name>
            <required>false</required>
            <rtexprvalue>false</rtexprvalue>
        </attribute>
    </tag>

    <tag>
        <name>test</name>
        <tagclass>book.conditions.TestTag</tagclass>
        <teiclass>book.conditions.TestTagExtraInfo</teiclass>
        <bodycontent>JSP</bodycontent>
        <info>
            Pose a condition on the reference object.
        </info>
        <attribute>
            <name>condition</name>
            <required>true</required>
            <rtexprvalue>false</rtexprvalue>
        </attribute>
    </tag>
</taglib>
```

As seen in the TLD, both tags are marked as having JSP contents, which tells the JSP environment to evaluate the body. As for tag attributes, the `WithTag` entry inherits most of its attributes from `ReflectionTag` and adds just a single new `multichoice` attribute, instructing the tag as to the condition evaluation policy that is desired. `TestTag`, on the other hand, is less complex with only a single tag attribute that specifies the condition string.

9.3.4 *Our tag library in action*

We can now take a look at a few JSP fragments that use the tag. You'll recognize the following JSP fragment from earlier in this chapter; and it will prove even more useful based on what we've just learned. This fragment shows how the tag is employed in testing a `boolean` value; the conditions we use are `eq true` and `eq false`, meaning equals true and equals false. We are not doing a simple `if-else` (we actually can't), but instead are asking about two negatives.

Listing 9.8   Using the conditional tags with a boolean value

```
<% Boolean b = new Boolean(true); %>
<cond:with object="<%= b %>">
    The value is
    <cond:test condition="eq true">
    true
    </cond:test>
    <cond:test condition="eq false">
    false
    </cond:test>
</cond:with>
```

You may wonder about the fact that in listing 9.8 we generated our object in a scriptlet (about the easiest way to pass a value to the tag), but don't let it concern you. We could get this value from anywhere in the JSP environment (e.g., we could get this value from a bean) and our tag would work equally well.

Another sample JSP fragment shows a more complex scenario in which the developer grabs the User-Agent header and checks to see what type of client is being served.

Listing 9.9   A complex usage of the conditional tags

```
<cond:with object="<%= request %>"              ❶
    property="header"
    index="User-Agent"
    multichoice="true">            ❷

    Your browser is IE?
    <cond:test condition="contains MSIE">        ❸
    Yes
    </cond:test>
    <cond:test condition="ncontains MSIE">
    No
    </cond:test>
    <br>

    <cond:test condition="contains #98">    ❹
    You are probably using some Windows98 variation.
    </cond:test>
    <br>

    <cond:test condition="nstartswith Mozilla/">    ❺
    What's that? No Mozilla?
    </cond:test>
</cond:with>
```

---

❶ Points to the User-Agent header.

❷ Informs the `wrapper` tag that we are going to allow the execution of multiple successful tests By setting the `multichoice` attribute to `true`, we indicate that all tests wrapped in this `WithTag` should be evaluated. For example, if you try to access this JSP fragment from Internet Explorer running on Win98, both the "MSIE" and "98" containment conditions will come up `true` and you will see the body of these tests in the response. If you wonder why someone would want to have several successful tests in the same JSP fragment, just picture some JSP code in which you want to adapt yourself to the browser as much as possible. In this case you will need to test the browser's capabilities over and over again. Using the `multichoice` option can give you this flexibility.

❸ Execution of an if-else logic—first test if the header contains MSIE and then check that it does not.

❹ Provides an Integer as a second operand.

❺ Checks if the User-Agent header does not start with a Mozilla/ prefix (most browsers do).

Note from these two samples that using our tags is fairly straightforward; the tag attributes make sense and we've kept the syntax to a minimum. It is also easy, using this library, to test the reference object and specify conditions; but aren't these conditions too elementary for many real-world uses? The next section will discuss this concern.

9.4 *Improving our advanced condition tags*

The tags we've built do a fair job of handling condition evaluation, so what's missing? The main shortcoming with our tag library is that many real applications have conditions that use more than two operands, which is the maximum our library can handle. In Java we can have conditions that look like:

```
if(s.trim().equals("somevalue") && someBoolean && otherBoolean) {
 // do something
}
```

Such a condition could not be represented using our current library. Does it mean that we cannot use condition tags in a real-world case? There are a number of possible ways to support these complex conditions within tags. Here are two of them:

- Invent a complex condition language to be used within the tags and extend the tags we developed to use this language.
- Have the user of the tags put all of the complex conditions inside a bean and use the bean's attributes to grab the condition's result inside the tags.

9.4.1 *Supporting complex conditions with a condition language*

Inventing a condition language is a reasonable approach to supporting conditions; in fact, we had a very simple type of condition language in our `TestTag`. Why not improve on it? For example, assume that our condition can look like this:

```
<cond:test condition="Trim($s) = 'somevalue' and
           $someBoolean and $otherBoolean">
Some JSP code ...
</cond:test/>
```

One resounding benefit to creating a new condition language is that you can make it as complex and as powerful as you desire. Since you'll have total control over the language, you can support as many operands, functions, or comparisons as you desire by extending it. At this level, defining our own conditional language seems like a good approach. There are, however, several notable drawbacks.

Drawbacks of complex condition languages

By designing your own condition language you can easily support complicated queries; however, to do so you need first to develop a complex parsing mechanism and then implement all the functionality the language supports, including utility functions (such as `Trim()` in the previous example). This can prove to be a substantial undertaking. Furthermore, once you are finished with new language implementation, you will have to teach it to whomever will be using it. And if that were not enough, you will probably need to provide mechanisms for JSP authors to debug their conditions. Will you provide an IDE to let developers step into your proprietary implementation? After this analysis, it becomes clear that in order to build a debuggable, feature-rich condition language (and the code to support it) you end up building a system similar to commercial products like ColdFusion. Unless you are planning on selling this tag library commercially and for a nifty price, the effort required to support complex conditions this way is not worth it. There must be a better way to solve the problem with a more standard condition language and less effort. One alternative, it turns out, is to use Java.

9.4.2 *Supporting complex conditions with JavaBeans*

JSP already supports Java. To take advantage of this, let's place all our conditions in a JavaBean and query the values of that bean's properties. The JavaBean now contains the complicated Java code that performs the condition, and can leverage all the natural features of the Java language. This approach also makes it very easy to debug the code (since you can simply use your favorite Java IDE), and prevents us from supporting any complex parsing or training JSP authors in our own proprietary language. Though this method requires you to write the beans that contain the conditional logic, this will simply be handled by the business logic developer, freeing the JSP author or content developer from concerns over conditional logic so they may focus on presentation. A solution that bases itself on beans should look something like:

```
<jsp:useBean id="condBean"
             scope="page"
             class="my.condition.Bean">
    <jsp:setProperty name="condBean"
                property="request"
                value="<%= request %>"/>
</jsp:useBean>
<cond:with object="<%= condBean %>"
                property="myQuery">

<cond:test condition="eq true">
<%-- We are here if the query is true --%>
</cond:test>
<cond:test condition="eq false">
<%-- We are here if the query is false --%>
</cond:test>
</cond:with>
```

This approach keeps the JSP syntax clean and straightforward, while enforcing a tidy separation of the business logic and presentation. The advantages of using Java-Beans to evaluate your conditions make it vastly superior to the previous approach, while satisfying all the requirements of supporting complex, real-world use.

9.5   *Summary*

While it is feasible to implement an easy-to-use conditional tag, representing a condition (even a simple one) in a declarative manner is impossible. Therefore, unless you are going to implement your own condition specification language, you will be better off implementing your condition evaluation in a JavaBean, in which you can leverage all the power of the Java language to pre-process and evaluate your conditions. This approach leaves your tags with the sole task of checking the JavaBean's resulting values and including or excluding content based on the bean's exported values.

Once you resolve to never attempt implementing a full-fledged condition specification language, implementing custom conditional tags becomes relatively easy. JSP is well adapted for conditional inclusion (as well as exclusion) of content using the `Tag` method call protocol and JSP will evaluate the conditioned content with no additional effort on your part.

In the next chapter, we will look at how to build tags that support iteration, such as iterating over a list of JavaBean property values. We saw scriptlet code in chapter 8 that performed iteration; now we'll see how to eliminate these scriptlets and replace them with simple to use, flexible custom tags that perform the same functions.

Iterating with tags

10

At the end of chapter 8, we used our newly created JavaBean tags to export an Enu-meration which was then iterated over with a scriptlet. Let's take another look at this JSP fragment.

```
<table>
<tr>
<th> Header </th> <th> Value </th>
</tr>

<bean:export id="e"
             type="enum"
             object="<%= request %>"
             property="headerNames" />

<% while(e.hasMoreElements()) {
        String name = (String)e.nextElement();
%>
<tr>

<td> <%= name %> </td>

<td>
    <bean:show object="<%= request %>"
               property="header"
               index="<%= name %>"/>
</td>
</tr>
<%
    }
%>
</table>
```

As you can see (note the highlighted code), although our JavaBean tags greatly reduce the need for scriptlets, we are still unable to avoid them when working with indexed JavaBean properties that have more than one value. In cases of multivalued properties (Enumerations, arrays, etc.) we typically want to loop through (*iterate*) and perform a function with each value in the property. Without a tag to handle this iteration, we're left using a scriptlet like the one here. This is unfortunate since we want to be able to provide our JSP authors with the ability to perform common functions on JavaBeans without prior knowledge of Java. Ideally, we'd like to offer them a very user-friendly JSP custom tag that would work for iteration.

Iteration, especially enumerating some value, can be very declarative, and, as we've seen, declarative tasks are easily performed with tags. For example, by using iteration tags we can modify the previous JSP fragment:

```
<table>
<tr>
<th> Header </th> <th> Value </th>
</tr>
```

```
<iter:foreach id="name"
               type="String"
               object="<%= request %>"
               property="headerNames" />

<tr>

<td> <%= name %> </td>

<td>
    <bean:show object="<%= request %>"
               property="header"
               index="<%= name %>"/>
</td>
</tr>
<iter:foreach>
</table>
```

This is obviously quite an improvement.

Why should we bother creating special iteration tags when a two-line scriptlet hardly seems demanding for a Java developer? Again, we can't forget that the goal of building custom tag libraries is to make it possible for non-Java developers (presentation/HTML developers) to build complex sites. Though iteration using scriptlets may not be complex for the Java programmer, it does require the JSP developer to:

- Know how to iterate on different Java types—Enumerations, Iterators, arrays, and so forth. To further complicate the situation, iteration methods usually return an Object that the JSP developer will have to cast.

- Position the curly brackets in the correct location. If the JSP developer forgets a curly bracket, the JSP compilation will fail, usually with a relatively obscure error message.

- Maintain and debug yet another portion of Java code.

As a result, iteration tags are necessary to enhance the effectiveness of our JavaBean tags and to keep our JSPs scriptlet-free.

This chapter explores iteration with tags and shows how to build JSP custom tags that perform iteration for us. We'll start with a brief introduction to iterating with custom JSP tags and discuss their design principles; later, we will develop iteration tags to handle cases in which we wish to iterate over Java's common object containers.

NOTE   In this chapter, you will see the word iterator used in two distinct ways. When we use the generic term, we mean any multivalued object (be it an Array, an implementation of the java.util.Enumeration interface or an implementation of the java.util.Iterator interface). When we mention Iterator we are speaking strictly about the Java interface.

10.1 *Iterating with tags 101*

Developing custom JSP tags that iterate over some set of values requires us to work, once again, with the familiar `BodyTag` interface. The `BodyTag` interface provides a method call protocol to control the execution of the tag's body—which we'll need in order to repeat the tag's body for every value in the JavaBean's indexed property.

NOTE	In JSP1.2 a new `IterationTag` interface was defined and we can also create tags using this interface. You can find information regarding the `IterationTag` later in this chapter.

Figure 10.1 shows how a tag can implement iteration using the `BodyTag` method call protocol.

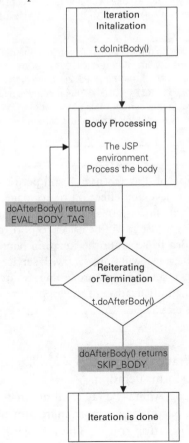

Figure 10.1
Implementing iteration using the `BodyTag` interface

To further illustrate how iteration is accomplished with tags, we've translated the flow chart in figure 10.1 into (roughly) its Java equivalent.

```
t.doInitBody();
do {
    // The JSP runtime execute
    // the tag's body ...
} while(t.doAfterBody() == BodyTag.EVAL_BODY_TAG);
```

As figure 10.1 and the code fragment show, two methods (table 10.1) take part in implementing the iteration:

Table 10.1   Iteration methods

JSP method	Description
doBodyInit()	Used to initialize preiteration JSP scripting variables and the tags' internal values. For example, if your tag exposes some iterator object as a JSP scripting variable, it will probably use doBodyInit() to export its initial value.
doAfterBody()	Controls the iteration with its return codes: To continue the iteration, doAfterBody() returns a value of BodyTag.EVAL_BODY_TAG (or IterationTag.EVAL_BODY_AGAIN in JSP1.2). To break the iteration , it returns a value BodyTag.SKIP_BODY. This method is also where we re-export the iterator value (the current value of the property on which we are iterating), and where we write the result of the current iteration into the response.

> **NOTE**   You can skip the implementation of doBodyInit() and perform its work in doStartTag(). This will not have any effect on performance and may even simplify your tags. Better yet, since doStartTag() is not available in IterationTag, code that does not use it will be easier to port to this new tag. In any case, it is a good idea to separate the iteration handling from doStartTag() so that doStartTag() will only deal with service initialization (e.g., obtaining the object set that we are going to iterate) and doBodyInit() will deal with the initialization of the loop.

10.1.1 *Iteration example: SimpleForeachTag*

Now that you know how to implement iteration in your tags, we will take a look at a sample iterative tag and the code that performs iteration.

Our first iteration tag, SimpleForeachTag, will take a tag attribute that specifies a list of strings, walk over the string list, and, one by one, export an iterator object that contains the current string value for that iteration round. The following JSP fragment shows a sample usage of this tag:

```
<iter:foreach id="item"
    elements="1,2,3,4">
The selected item is <%= item %> <br>
</iter:foreach>
```

Executing the above JSP fragment generates the following content:

```
The selected item is 1 <br>
The selected item is 2 <br>
The selected item is 3 <br>
The selected item is 4 <br>
```

Let's look at the code for the SimpleForeachTag's handler (listing 10.1).

Listing 10.1   Source code for the SimpleForeachTag handler class

```
package book.iteration;

import java.util.StringTokenizer;
import java.util.LinkedList;
import java.util.List;
import java.util.Iterator;
import book.util.LocalStrings;
import book.util.ExBodyTagSupport;
import javax.servlet.jsp.JspException;

public class SimpleForeachTag extends ExBodyTagSupport {

    static LocalStrings ls =
        LocalStrings.getLocalStrings(SimpleForeachTag.class);

    Iterator elementsList = null;

    protected String elements = null;

    public void setElements(String elements)
    {
        this.elements = elements;
    }

    public int doStartTag()
        throws JspException
    {
        parseElements();          ❶

        if(elementsList.hasNext()) {          ❷
            return EVAL_BODY_TAG;
        }
        return SKIP_BODY;
    }

    public void doInitBody()
        throws JspException
    {
        pageContext.setAttribute(id, elementsList.next());          ❸
```

```
    }

    protected void parseElements()
        throws JspException
    {
        List l = new LinkedList();
        StringTokenizer st = new StringTokenizer(elements, ",");     ────●4
        while(st.hasMoreTokens()) {
            l.add(st.nextToken());
        }

        elementsList = l.iterator();
    }

    public int doAfterBody()
        throws JspException
    {
        try {
            getBodyContent().writeOut(getPreviousOut());     ────●5
            getBodyContent().clear();
        } catch(java.io.IOException ioe) {
            // User probably disconnected ...
            log(ls.getStr(Constants.IO_ERROR), ioe);
            throw new
                JspTagException(ls.getStr(Constants.IO_ERROR));
        }
        if(elementsList.hasNext()) {
            pageContext.setAttribute(id, elementsList.next());     ────●6
            return EVAL_BODY_TAG;
        }

        return SKIP_BODY;
    }

    protected void clearProperties()
    {
        id = null;
        elements = null;
        super.clearProperties();
    }

    protected void clearServiceState()
    {
        elementsList = null;
    }
}
```

● **Parses the list of strings into a Java list and creates an enumerator.**

❷ **If we have an element in the list, continues the body evaluation; otherwise skips the body (empty iteration).**

❸ **Sets the iterator variable with the first element in the list.**

❹ Breaks the string list into a Java list.

❺ Writes the results of this iteration back to the user and clears the body buffer.

❻ If we have more elements in the list, exports a new iterator value and repeats evaluating the body.

The work in `SimpleForeachTag` takes place in three designated locations:

- The service phase initialization in `doStartTag()`. The tag initializes the set of objects on which we plan to iterate, and determines if we need to process the body. This is not necessary if the list of objects is empty.
- The loop initialization in `doInitBody()`. The tag exports the needed iterator object by calling `pageContext.setAttribute()` with the name of the object and the object itself. In doing so, we publish the iterator as a scripting variable, so that it ends up in the scope in the JSP (a practice we first came across with JavaBean tags in chapter 8). By exporting the iterator object, other tags and scriptlets can take advantage of it.
- The loop termination/repeating in `doAfterBody()`. The tag writes the results of the last loop into the previous writer (usually the writer that goes to the user) and then clears the body content to prepare it for the next iteration. In the final step, if there are additional items to iterate, the tag exposes a new iterator value and signals the JSP environment to repeat the execution by returning `EVAL_BODY_TAG`.

NOTE   When implementing iterations using tags, you do not have to write the results of each loop separately. You may instead wait for the body execution to finish (no more elements on which to iterate) and then write the complete result. Doing so usually results in improved performance, but it may also cause a delay in the user's receipt of the results. For example, consider reading a substantial amount of data from a database and presenting it to the user with some iteration on the result set. Since we are working with a database, completing the iteration may take a while and writing the response only on completion may cause the user to leave the page. Writing the result of each loop incrementally would (depending on buffer size) cause the results to return to the user incrementally, instead of in a large chunk.

SimpleForeachTag's TagExtraInfo

Following the development of `SimpleForeachTag` we must now create its `TagExtraInfo` counterpart. You may recall from our discussions of the `TagExtraInfo` class in chapters 6 and 8, we need to create a subclass of `TagExtraInfo` whenever we have a tag that exports a scripting variable. Since `SimpleForeachTag` will need to export the values of the iterator, we'll create a `TagExtraInfo` class for it that will inform the runtime of this. We'll call this class `ForeachTagExtraInfo`. Its implementation is in listing 10.2 wherein you see that it merely notifies the JSP runtime that a new scripting variable of type `String` is exported.

Listing 10.2   Source code for the ForeachTagExtraInfo class

```
package book.iteration;

import javax.servlet.jsp.tagext.TagData;
import javax.servlet.jsp.tagext.TagExtraInfo;
import javax.servlet.jsp.tagext.VariableInfo;

public class ForeachTagExtraInfo extends TagExtraInfo {

    public VariableInfo[] getVariableInfo(TagData data)
    {
        VariableInfo[] rc = new VariableInfo[1];
        rc[0] =  new VariableInfo(data.getId(),
                                  "java.lang.String",
                                  true,
                                  VariableInfo.NESTED);
        return rc;
    }
}
```

NOTE   Note that the scope defined for the scripting variable is NESTED, meaning the variable exists and is accessible only within the body of the tag that exported it. This is important since the variable we export is our iterator, and so should exist only within the body of the loop.

SimpleForeachTag in action

Having written `SimpleForeachTag` and its `TagExtraInfo` we can now write JSP code to work with it. Since this is only the beginning of our iteration tags discussion, we will take that same JSP fragment and make it the content of our JSP as seen in listing 10.3.

Listing 10.3   JSP driver for SimpleForeachTag

```
<%@ page errorPage="error.jsp" %>
<%@ taglib
    uri="http://www.manning.com/jsptagsbook/iteration-taglib"
    prefix="iter" %>

<html>
<body>

<iter:foreach id="item"
```

```
                elements="1,2,3,4">
The selected item is <%= item %> <br>
</iter:foreach>

</body>
</html>
```

Now when we execute our JSP, `SimpleForeachTag` will repeat its body four times (one for each string in "elements"); first with 1 as the value of the item (our iterator), and lastly with 4 as its value.

10.2   *Generalized iterating tags*

In perusing the implementation of `SimpleForeachTag` it appears that most of the work done by the tag is not unique to it. In fact, other than the creation of the `Iterator` object in `parseElements()` all the other code was generic. True, some tags will not want to expose an iterator, and others may want to expose more than a single iterator as a scripting variable (for some other tag-specific purpose), but these tags are not representative of the majority. In most cases, tags will differ only in the objects they iterate (some will iterate over an `Enumeration`, others on `Array`, etc.) but the general structure will stay the same; a single iterator scripting variable will be exposed and updated for each element.

Based on this general iterating structure, we'll build:

- A generic iteration interface that lets the tag developer specify how to iterate over some set of objects.
- A basic iterator tag that takes a generic iteration object (`Enumeration`, `Array`, etc.) and iterates on it.

Creating these two, generic components will then streamline the creation of various iteration tags. These specialized iteration tags will be custom-built, based on the type of Java object to be contained in the iterator, and the iterator type in which these objects are to be contained. For example, our `SimpleForeachTag` had an iterator type of `java.util.Iterator`, and contained in that iterator was a list of `Strings`. We are now going to build these two components (the class and interface) and modify `SimpleForeachTag` to use this new, more generic infrastructure.

10.2.1 *A generic iteration interface*

Before looking into the new `ForeachTag`, let's study the generic iteration infrastructure on which it is constructed, starting with the generic iteration interface as seen in listing 10.4.

Listing 10.4   Source code for the generic iteration interface

```
package book.iteration;

import javax.servlet.jsp.JspException;

public interface IterationSupport  {

    public boolean hasNext()
        throws JspException;

    public Object getNext()
        throws JspException;
}
```

Why do we need another iteration/enumeration interface, as Java already offers plenty. You may also wonder, why a `JspException` is thrown from the methods `hasNext()` and `getNext()`. Shouldn't a generic interface remove JSP related ties? We do this because we want to provide better JSP integration. Let's explore our motivation for this integration.

> **NOTE** We could consider the option of defining a new exception type (such as `IterationException`) that the iteration support methods could throw; but why should we? This code is written for the JSP tags, and we are not going to reuse it. In 99 percent of all cases, you are going to throw a `JspException` as a result of the error. Based on this argument, we've rejected the new exception type idea, and continue to use `JspException` as our error-reporting vehicle.

10.2.2 *IterationTagSupport*

Let's look at the basic iteration tag class, `IterationTagSupport`, and how it uses `IterationSupport`. Before taking a look into the implementation of `Iteration-TagSupport` as presented in listing 10.5, let's consider how we would like it to work.

What should IterationTagSupport do?

Most emphatically, the generic iteration tag class should automatically take care of iteration-related issues such as flow control, as well as exporting default iterator variables. In addition, it must be able to:

- Create an `IterationSupport` object out of the elements provided as a tag attribute. This can be accomplished by defining a method that our specialized iteration tags can override and that `IterationTagSupport` will call during its `doStartTag()`. By specialized tag we mean the special version of the tag that is custom built to handle a particular iterator type and a particular type of object in that iterator.

- Export a different set of JSP variables. Whenever `IterationTagSupport` wants to export its iterator value, it should call yet another method that can be overridden by the specialized tag (but the default implementation of the variable exportation method should export only a single iterator).

IterationTagSupport's implementation

`IterationTagSupport` was created with a few methods that may be overridden by specialized iteration tags.

Listing 10.5   Source code for the generic iteration tag handler

```
package book.iteration;

import book.util.LocalStrings;
import book.util.ExBodyTagSupport;
import javax.servlet.jsp.JspException;

public abstract class IterationTagSupport
    extends ExBodyTagSupport {

    static LocalStrings ls =
        LocalStrings.getLocalStrings(IterationTagSupport.class);

    IterationSupport elementsList = null;

    public int doStartTag()
        throws JspException
    {
        fetchIterationSupport();
        if(elementsList.hasNext()) {
            return EVAL_BODY_TAG;
        }
        return SKIP_BODY;
    }

    public void doInitBody()
        throws JspException
    {
        exportVariables();
    }


    public int doAfterBody()
        throws JspException
    {
        try {
            getBodyContent().writeOut(getPreviousOut());
            getBodyContent().clear();
```

```
        } catch(java.io.IOException ioe) {
            // User probably disconnected ...
            // Log and throw a JspTagException
        }

        if(elementsList.hasNext()) {
            exportVariables();
            return EVAL_BODY_TAG;
        }

        return SKIP_BODY;
    }

    protected abstract void fetchIterationSupport()    ❶
        throws JspException;

    protected void exportVariables()    ❷
        throws JspException
    {
        pageContext.setAttribute(id, elementsList.getNext());
    }

    protected void clearProperties()    ❸
    {
        id = null;
        super.clearProperties();
    }

    protected void clearServiceState()    ❹
    {
        elementsList = null;
    }
}
```

❶ **First override point. The specialized tag must implement this method to create and set an IterationSupport object**   The first method that tags can and must override is `fetchIterationSupport()`. This abstract method is the location wherein the overriding tag should implement the creating and setting of the `IterationSupport` object and any specialized iteration tag must provide such objects to make the generic infrastructure work. If problems rise within `fetchIterationSupport()`, it can throw a `JspException` that the generic implementation will pass to the JSP runtime.

❷ **Second override point. The specialized tag may want to export additional objects**   The second method that can be overridden is `exportVariables()`, which is where the generic iteration tag exports the iterator (based in the `id` attribute). An overriding tag may override this method to add more variables. For example, a certain tag iterates a hash table and wants to export both the key to the table and the value itself. In this case you would like to add the exportation of the value variable along with the default iterator.

❸ Override if you have additional attributes in the specialized tag (you probably do).

❹ Override if you have additional service state in the specialized tag.

Listing 10.5 shows that the general structure of IterationTagSupport is very similar to the one presented in SimpleForeachTag. The tag is merely a generic iteration infrastructure with several methods to override as explaned in the annotations. Note also that IterationTagSupport extends our now familiar ExBodyTagSupport, and therefore inherits its functionality.

An improved ForeachTag which uses IterationTagSupport

We've mentioned several times the concept of a specialized tag, by which we infer a tag that uses our generic interface and class for a specific iterator and object type. Let's now look at one such specialized tag, ForeachTag, which uses IterationTag-Support to support an Iterator containing a list of Strings (see listing 10.6).

Listing 10.6   Source code for the ForeachTag handler class

```
package book.iteration;

import java.util.StringTokenizer;
import java.util.LinkedList;
import java.util.Iterator;
import java.util.List;
import book.util.LocalStrings;
import book.util.ExBodyTagSupport;
import javax.servlet.jsp.JspException;

public class ForeachTag extends IterationTagSupport {

    static LocalStrings ls =
        LocalStrings.getLocalStrings(ForeachTag.class);

    protected String elements = null;

    public void setElements(String elements)
    {
        this.elements = elements;
    }

    protected void fetchIterationSupport()
        throws JspException
    {
        List l = new LinkedList();
        StringTokenizer st = new StringTokenizer(elements, ",");      ❶
        while(st.hasMoreTokens()) {
            l.add(st.nextToken());
        }
        elementsList = new IteratorIterationSupport(l.iterator());
    }
}
```

```
    protected void clearProperties()
    {
        elements = null;      ❷
        super.clearProperties();
    }
}

class IteratorIterationSupport implements IterationSupport {      ❸
    Iterator i = null;

    IteratorIterationSupport(Iterator i)
    {
        this.i = i;
    }

    public boolean hasNext()
        throws JspException
    {
        return i.hasNext();
    }

    public Object getNext()
        throws JspException
    {
        return i.next();
    }
}
```

❶ Parsing the list specification string and making an `IterationSupport` out of it.

❷ Clearing the additional tag property.

❸ Implementing an `IterationSupport` class that uses a Java `Iterator` object.

The new `ForeachTag` has most of its code implementing its tag-specific functionality, that is, dealing with an `Iterator` of Strings. Also of note in our implementation is the additional `IteratorIterationSupport` class we created, which is simply an implementation of the generic `IterationSupport` that works on the `java.util.Iterator` interface. We can imagine a similar class that works on `Arrays` and even another for `Enumerations` (or perhaps one that handles all?). The `IteratorIterationSupport` class is not, of course, unique to `ForeachTag` and we will be able to reuse it many times in other specialized tags.

We now have a way to easily create iteration tags that iterate on all sorts of objects. We'll flex the power of this infrastructure in the next section in creating a tag that is capable of iterating on just about anything.

10.3 *IterateTag*

The previous section presented a generic iteration tag infrastructure that we will now use to develop a new iteration tag (named `IterateTag`) which will be able to iterate over the following types of objects:

- `Arrays` of all types
- `Enumerations`—objects of type `java.util.Enumeration`
- `Iterators`—objects of type `java.util.Iterator`.

We're going to put this functionality into a single tag so its users will be able to use one tag for all their iteration chores. They will be able to reference the object they want to iterate in the same way as in chapter 8, using Java reflection. In fact, we'll reuse the reflection code we saw in chapter 8's `ReflectionTag` to accomplish this. In doing so, our tag will be able to take any bean property value and iterate its objects. For example, we will be able to take a shopping cart with a method such as:

```
public Enumeration getProducts();
```

and iterate on the `Enumeration` value returned from it.

10.3.1 *Design considerations for IterateTag*

Given that we have the generic iteration infrastructure, and that we have a previously built basic reflection tag, implementing our tag should be a breeze (almost codeless, you might expect). But this is not quite the case because a Java class cannot inherit two superclasses (no multiple inheritance, if you recall). Also, our `ReflectionTag` did not implement `BodyTag`; instead, it implemented the `Tag` interface, so it cannot serve as a base class for an iteration-related tag. As a result, our iteration tag will have to reimplement the reflection code that we previously developed. There are ways to share the implementation code between the tags, but for simplicity's sake, we will merely copy and paste the needed code.

10.3.2 *Wrapping iterators*

We will use the `ReflectionTag` code from chapter 8 to procure the referenced object from within the iteration tag, but we still need to decide what to do with it; meaning, how are we going to wrap it within an `IterationSupport`? We choose to create an `IterationSupport` implementation for each of the different iterator types (`Iterator`, `Enumeration`, and `Array`), then wrap the object within the matching `IterationSupport` implementation. An `IterationSupport` wrapper for the `Iterator` interface was covered in the previous section, so let's now look at the individual wrappers for `Array` and `Enumeration`.

ArrayIterationSupport

The first `IterationSupport` wrapper class we implement will be for `Arrays`. Implementing `IterationSupport` is not usually too much of a challenge, yet this case is different due to the requirement to be iteratable on any type of `Array` (i.e., an `Array` of `Strings`, an `Array` of `Dates`, etc.). Normally, when the `array` element type is known, indexing the `array` elements is a snap, but how do you do that when the element type is unknown?

The answer, as you might have guessed, is reflection. The reflection package contains an `Array` class with static methods for manipulating `array` elements and querying the `array`'s length. We make use of this reflection class in our implementation of `ArrayIterationSupport`, as seen in listing 10.7.

Listing 10.7   Source code for the ArrayIterationSupport utility class

```java
package book.iteration;

import java.lang.reflect.Array;
import javax.servlet.jsp.JspException;

class ArrayIterationSupport implements IterationSupport {

    protected Object a = null;
    protected int    pos = 0;

    ArrayIterationSupport(Object a)
    {
        this.a = a;
        this.pos = 0;
    }

    public boolean hasNext()
        throws JspException
    {
        return (pos < Array.getLength(a));          ❶
    }

    public Object getNext()
        throws JspException
    {
        if(hasNext()) {
            Object rc = null;
            rc = Array.get(a, pos);          ❷
            pos++;
            return rc;
        }

        // Throw an exception
    }
}
```

① Using `Array`'s static method to find the length of the input `array`.

② Using `Array`'s static method to get an indexed value.

The functionality rendered by the `Array` class is enough for us to be able to have full access to all the `array`'s attributes and elements.

EnumerationIterationSupport

The `IterationSupport` class supporting `Enumerations`, `EnumerationIteration-Support`, is very straightforward, since both the `IterationSupport` and `Enumeration` interfaces are so similar (see listing 10.8)

Listing 10.8   EnumerationIterationSupport

```
package book.iteration;

import java.util.*;

public class EnumerationIterationSupport implements IterationSupport
  {

  Enumeration elements;

  public EnumerationIterationSupport(Enumeration e)
  {
    elements = e;
  }
  public boolean hasNext()
    throws JspException
  {
    return elements.hasMoreElements();      ①
  }
  public Object getNext()
    throws JspException
  {
    return  elements.nextElement();       ②
  }
}
```

---

① Using `Enumeration`'s method to determine if more elements exist.

② Using `Enumeration`'s method to retrieve the current object.

10.3.3 Implementing IterateTag

The next step is the implementation of `IterateTag` (listing 10.9) in which we'll see how all the wrappers, reflection logic, and our generic iteration framework combine in its creation (note that for clarity reasons we snipped the reflection code out of the code listing).

Listing 10.9   Source code for the IterateTag handler class

```java
package book.iteration;

import java.beans.IntrospectionException;
import java.lang.reflect.InvocationTargetException;
import java.util.Enumeration;
import java.util.Iterator;
import book.reflection.ReflectionTag;
import book.util.LocalStrings;
import book.util.BeanUtil;
import javax.servlet.jsp.PageContext;
import javax.servlet.jsp.JspException;

public class IterateTag extends IterationTagSupport {

    static LocalStrings ls =
        LocalStrings.getLocalStrings(IterateTag.class);

    // Reflection related properties and properties setters
    // were removed from this section.

    protected void fetchIterationSupport()
        throws JspException
    {
        Object o = getPointed();          ❶

        if(o instanceof Iterator) {                        ❷
            elementsList =
                new IteratorIterationSupport((Iterator)o);
        } else if(o instanceof Enumeration) {
            elementsList =
                new EnumerationIterationSupport((Enumeration)o);
        } else if(o.getClass().isArray()) {
            elementsList = new ArrayIterationSupport(o);
        } else {
            // Throw an exception to inform that we cannot
            // iterate this object
        }
    }

    // The reflection code below this line
    // was removed from this listing
}
```

❶ `getPointed()` **retrieves the object the tag should iterate on. This method is inherited from** `ExBodyTagSupport`.

❷ **Gets the referenced object and wraps it within the appropriate** `IterationSupport` **implementation.**

Apart from the reflection related code which we've omitted (we've seen how this code works in chapter 8), IterateTag's implementation consists of a single method implementation: fetchIterationSupport(). This method merely checks the object that is passed as the tag attribute and selects an appropriate iterator and IterationSupport wrapper, based on the object's type.

IterateTagExtraInfo

Accompanying the IterateTag is the IterateTagExtraInfo whose implementation is fairly effortless. Once again, we need to create this TagExtraInfo object for our IterateTag because we will be exporting a scripting variable from it. From an attribute and variable exportation point of view, IterateTag and ExportTag (as presented in chapter 8) are quite similar. The only difference is that our current variable is exported as a NESTED variable, meaning its scope only exists within the tag's body. Because they are so similar, all we need to do is inherit ExportTagExtraInfo (again, from chapter 8) and modify the VariableInfo it returns to reflect a NESTED variable. As listing 10.10 shows, this is exactly what we did.

Listing 10.10   Source code for the IterateTagExtraInfo class

```
package book.iteration;

import book.reflection.ExportTagExtraInfo;
import javax.servlet.jsp.tagext.TagData;
import javax.servlet.jsp.tagext.TagExtraInfo;
import javax.servlet.jsp.tagext.VariableInfo;

public class IterateTagExtraInfo extends ExportTagExtraInfo {

    public VariableInfo[] getVariableInfo(TagData data)
    {
        VariableInfo[] rc = new VariableInfo[1];

        rc[0] =  new VariableInfo(data.getId(),
                                  guessVariableType(data),
                                  true,
                                  VariableInfo.NESTED);      ❶
        return rc;
    }
}
```

---

❶ Returns a NESTED variable.

IterateTag's TLD

The last step in our implementation of IterateTag is its tag library descriptor entry as seen in listing 10.11.

Listing 10.11   Tag library descriptor entry for IterateTag

```
<tag>
    <name>iterate</name>
    <tagclass>book.iteration.IterateTag</tagclass>
    <teiclass>book.iteration.IterateTagExtraInfo</teiclass>
    <bodycontent>JSP</bodycontent>
    <info>
        Iterate over an Object. The object can be an array,
        Iterator or Enumeration.
    </info>

    <attribute>
        <name>id</name>
        <required>true</required>
        <rtexprvalue>false</rtexprvalue>
    </attribute>
    <attribute>
        <name>type</name>
        <required>false</required>
        <rtexprvalue>false</rtexprvalue>
    </attribute>
    <attribute>
        <name>object</name>
        <required>false</required>
        <rtexprvalue>true</rtexprvalue>
    </attribute>
    <attribute>
        <name>name</name>
        <required>false</required>
        <rtexprvalue>false</rtexprvalue>
    </attribute>
    <attribute>
        <name>scope</name>
        <required>false</required>
        <rtexprvalue>false</rtexprvalue>
    </attribute>
    <attribute>
        <name>index</name>
        <required>false</required>
        <rtexprvalue>true</rtexprvalue>
    </attribute>
    <attribute>
        <name>property</name>
        <required>false</required>
        <rtexprvalue>false</rtexprvalue>
    </attribute>
</tag>
```

The tag library entry is almost identical to the one we had for `ExportTag`. The only significant difference is that `ExportTag` had an empty body, whereas `IterateTag` has, of course, a JSP body.

10.4 Look, Mom! No scriptlets—IterateTag in action

Armed with `IterateTag` we can now greatly improve our JSP development and even reach the point at which scriptlets are no longer needed. To illustrate, we present a real world example wherein a JSP file shows a user the content of his or her shopping cart. For this example, the shopping cart is kept inside a session variable that the JSP file retrieves to create a table containing the current products in the cart.

The methods provided by the shopping cart and the cart items are available in listing 10.12.

Listing 10.12 The methods exposed by the cart and cart elements

```
public class Cart implements Serializable {

    public int getDollars();
    public int getCents();
    public boolean isEmpty();
    public Enumeration getProducts();
    public Enumeration getProductNames();
    public CartElement getProduct(String key);
    public CartElement []getProductValues();
    public void addProduct(String key, CartElement ince);
    public void removeProduct(String key);
}

public class CartElementImp implements CartElement {

    public int getDollars();
    public void setDollars(int dollars);
    public int getCents();
    public void setCents(int cents);
    public int getQuantity();
    public void setQuantity(int quantity);
    public void setName(String name);
    public String getName();
}
```

10.4.1 Printing the shopping cart with scriptlets

Assuming we have the cart in the session state and we want to display the cart's content in some tabular format (figure 10.2), we *could* create a scriptlet-littered JSP file, such as the one seen in listing 10.13.

Listing 10.13   JSP file that uses scriptlets to present the cart information

```jsp
<%@ page errorPage="error.jsp" %>
<%@ page import="book.util.*,java.util.*" %>        ❶

<html>
<body>

<%
    Cart cart = (Cart)session.getAttribute("cart");   ❷
    if(!cart.isEmpty()) {
%>
Your cart contains the following products:

<table>
<tr><th>Product</th> <th>Quantity</th> <th>Price</th> </tr>
<% java.util.Enumeration e = cart.getProducts();
   while(e.hasMoreElements()) {                       ❸
       CartElementImp p = (CartElementImp)e.nextElement();
%>
    <tr>
       <td> <%= p.getName() %></td>
       <td> <%= p.getQuantity() %> </td>
       <td> <%= p.getDollars() %>.<%= p.getCents() %>$ </td>
    </tr>
<% } %>
    <tr>
       <td> Totals <td>
       <td> <%= cart.getDollars() %>.<%= cart.getCents() %>$<td>  ❹
    <tr>
</table>

<% } else { %>
Your cart is empty.
<% } %>

</body>
</html>
```

❶ **Importing classes to be used in the scriptlets.**

❷ **Gets a reference to the cart.**

❸ **Enumerates the products and presents their properties.**

❹ **Presents the total price (property of the cart).**

Listing 10.13 serves as a basic example for a piece of JSP code that, once introduced to the scriptlets, is no longer manageable by anyone but a Java programmer. The file is replete with the familiar Java curly brackets, Java flow control statements, and casting and import statements—all of which are difficult for a non-Java programmer

Figure 10.2   Cart presentation output

to grasp. Instead of this chaos, we can use the IterateTag we just developed to substantially improve the JSP.

10.4.2 *Printing the shopping cart with IterateTag*

All of the scriptlets in listing 10.13 can be eliminated by making use of our new IterateTag as in listing 10.14. Executing the JSP code on a sample cart content yielded the response presented in figure 10.2.

Listing 10.14   JSP file that uses custom tags to present the cart information

```
<%@ page errorPage="error.jsp" %>
<%@ taglib
    uri="http://www.manning.com/jsptagsbook/iteration-taglib"      ❶
    prefix="iter" %>
<%@ taglib
    uri="http://www.manning.com/jsptagsbook/conditions-taglib"
    prefix="cond" %>
<%@ taglib
    uri="http://www.manning.com/jsptagsbook/beans-taglib"
    prefix="bean" %>

<html>
<body>

<cond:with name="cart" property="empty">
<cond:test condition="eq true">
    Your cart is empty.
</cond:test>
<cond:test condition="eq false">
```

```
    Your cart contains the following products:

    <table>
        <tr><th>Product</th> <th>Quantity</th> <th>Price</th> </tr>

        <iter:iterate name="cart" property="products" id="product">

        <tr>
            <td><bean:show name="product" property="name"/> </td>
            <td><bean:show name="product" property="quantity"/></td>
            <td><bean:show name="product" property="dollars"/>.
                <bean:show name="product" property="cents"/>$</td>
        </tr>
        </iter:iterate>
        <tr>
            <td>Totals<td>
            <td><bean:show name="cart" property="dollars"/>.
                <bean:show name="cart" property="cents"/>$<td>
        <tr>
    </table>

</cond:test>
</cond:with>
</body>
</html>
```

① References all the TLDs we use.

② Enumerates the products (using the enumeration property).

③ Presents the product's properties.

④ Presents the total price (property of the cart).

Comparing listings 10.13 and 10.14 shows the advantages of using custom tags. Listing 10.14 is much simpler: all the curly brackets, type casting, and the like are gone, and it is readable by almost anyone. Moreover, all tag supporting tools can manipulate the file and we feel certain that they will be able to get along with our custom tags. Listing 10.13 is littered with endless scriptlets to the point that developing the page without a programmer's help is very difficult. Which page would you prefer to have your HTML coder maintain?

10.5 *Making it easier on the JSP author*

As convenient as the JSP might be in listing 10.14, there is still something that bothers us from a usability standpoint; namely, the printing of the value of a bean property to the user is too cumbersome. To illustrate, look at the following JSP fragment:

```
<iter:iterate name="cart" property="products" id="product">
```

```
<tr>
    <td><bean:show name="product" property="name"/> </td>
    <td><bean:show name="product" property="quantity"/></td>
    <td><bean:show name="product" property="dollars"/>.
        <bean:show name="product" property="cents"/>$</td>
</tr>
</iter:iterate>
```

Seeing all those `<bean:show>` tags begs the question: why do we need so much overhead associated with using the bean tag and pointing to the property in the product? We know that we are interested in the product object (since we're iterating on it) yet our `<bean:show>` tag forces us to pass it as a `name` attribute for every property we print to the user. Can't we make access to bean-based, nonindexed properties in an iterator less complicated (or friendlier)? We can, but how?

Improving access to nonindexed JavaBean properties

The first thought that comes to mind is to create a tag with a single attribute that points to the property name. When running, this tag will fetch the iterator object from the iteration tag and query its property value. The following JSP fragment shows a revised version of the previous JSP fragment that uses this simplified tag.

```
<iter:iterate name="cart" property="products" id="product">
<tr>
    <td><bean:showp property="name"/> </td>
    <td><bean:showp property="quantity"/></td>
    <td><bean:showp property="dollars"/>.
        <bean:showp property="cents"/>$</td>
</tr>
</iter:iterate>
```

This is an improvement; however, we still are not entirely satisfied with the new JSP fragment, largely because the number of keystrokes we've saved is not especially significant. To make the syntax for retrieving a property extremely terse, we don't want to use a tag at all; we want something that is even more minimal. Syntax such as the following is clearly an improvement for the JSP author, especially if they're building a number of JSPs with property access in iterators.

```
<iter:iterate name="cart" property="products" id="product">
    <tr>
        <td> <$ name $> </td>
        <td> <$ quantity $> </td>
        <td> <$ dollars $>.<$cents$>$ </td>
    </tr>
</iter:iterate>
```

In this JSP fragment we no longer use tags to present the property values of the iterator. Instead, a property value in the current iterator is referenced by using a special directive with field placement syntax `<$property-name$>`. Using this field placement could be a time-saver, but how would we implement it? Up to this point, everything we created was a tag; this new proprietary directive is not. The way to implement this functionality is to modify our iteration tags to perform a pass on their body content and translate these field placement directives into values that should replace them. By processing the body in this way, we can easily swap any special directive we want with some other value; in this case, the value of a JavaBean's nonindexed property.

10.5.1 *Building a better tag*

Remember that the iterator tags implement the `BodyTag` interface; hence, the iteration tags can have direct access to their body *before* they write it to the response stream. All the tag has to do is implement some body parsing in `doAfterBody()`, in which the tag will replace our field placement directives with the actual field values.

Implementing the substitution of field placement directives with their actual values should be done in a generic manner, for several reasons:

- It is not safe to assume that we will always want to use the field placement directives. For example, certain users may not want to use proprietary syntax. In such cases we do not want to take the performance penalty associated with parsing the body. Thus we require the ability to disable/enable substitutions on the fly.

- We can imagine many different objects on which we may iterate, as well as many field types that we may want to show, from JavaBean properties to database columns. We want to build a generic solution such that we do not implement the body parsing differently for each case.

- We may develop many different iteration tags and most of them will need the (extremely nifty) field substitution feature, and we do not want to implement the related substitution logic more than once.

10.5.2 *The design*

To attain these goals, we distribute the implementation of the field substitution into the following units:

- Body parsing—This part of our solution searches for field references and identifies them. We'll implement this functionality in `IterationTagSupport`, our iteration tag superclass. This will make all tags derived from `Iteration-TagSupport` capable of performing field substitution.

- Field fetching—This is the part of our solution that retrieves a field's value when one is found. Whenever `IterationTagSupport` parses and identifies a field reference, it will use an object that implements an interface we'll call `FieldGetter`. This interface will allow us to get the value of the referenced field from the current iterator. Since `FieldGetter` will be an interface, we can create many different implementations of it, such as one that fetches a database column value, or another that gets bean properties. This will become clearer when we see the code.

- Setting the `FieldGetter`—Combining the first two portions of our design, we see that any specialized implementation of `IterationTagSupport` will need a specialized version `FieldGetter`, corresponding to the type of objects the iterator contains. The specialized iteration tag will know the type of objects that it exposes as iterators and will therefore know what type of `FieldGetter` to use. If no `FieldGetter` is used, the tag will not implement any field substitution, hence avoiding the associated performance costs from parsing the body. This accomplishes our previously mentioned goal of making the field substitution optional for performance reasons.

This design should accomplish all our defined goals. Our abstract design will become much more comprehensible as we look at our implementation and an example.

10.5.3 *FieldGetter and ReflectionFieldGetter*

Let's start by looking at the `FieldGetter` interface, which provides one method to set the object whose fields we'll want to retrieve and a second method to get those fields from the object. We present this interface in listing 10.15, along with an implementation of it called `ReflectionFieldGetter` whose job is to implement a `FieldGetter` that gets JavaBeans properties (through reflection).

Listing 10.15   Source code of FieldGetter and ReflectionFieldGetter

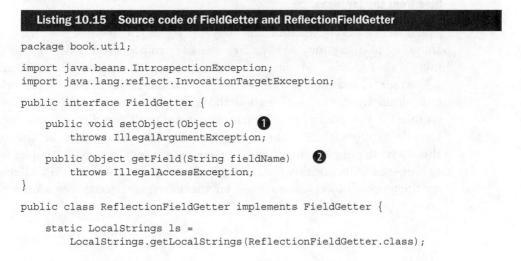

```
package book.util;

import java.beans.IntrospectionException;
import java.lang.reflect.InvocationTargetException;

public interface FieldGetter {

    public void setObject(Object o)          ❶
        throws IllegalArgumentException;

    public Object getField(String fieldName) ❷
        throws IllegalAccessException;
}

public class ReflectionFieldGetter implements FieldGetter {

    static LocalStrings ls =
        LocalStrings.getLocalStrings(ReflectionFieldGetter.class);
```

```
protected Object o;

public void setObject(Object o)        ❸
    throws IllegalArgumentException
{
    this.o = o;
}

public Object getField(String fieldName)        ❹
    throws IllegalAccessException
{
    try {
        return BeanUtil.getObjectPropertyValue(o,
                                               fieldName,
                                               null);        ❹
    } catch(InvocationTargetException ex) {
    } catch(IllegalAccessException ex) {
    } catch(IntrospectionException ex) {
    } catch(NoSuchMethodException ex) {
    }

    // Throw an exception
}
}
```

❶ **Generic method to set the object whose fields we'll later retrieve.**

❷ **Generic method to get an object's field by name.**

❸ **For** `ReflectionFieldGetter`, `setObject` **will be set with a JavaBean.**

❹ **For** `ReflectionFieldGetter`, `getField` **uses reflection (seen in chapter 8) to get a field from the JavaBean.**

`FieldGetter` has two methods: `setObject()` that tells the getter which object we are going to query for a field and `getField()` to procure the field's value. When using a `FieldGetter`, instantiate it, then set an object into the `FieldGetter` using `setObject()`, and then call `getField()` to get the values of the wanted fields. For error notification, `FieldGetter`'s methods can throw exceptions (e.g., if the object set into the `FieldGetter` implementation is not of the right type, say a `ResultSet` for a database-aware `FieldGetter`). To further clarify `FieldGetter`, listing 10.15 also shows the implementation of `ReflectionFieldGetter` which implements the `FieldGetter` functionality for JavaBeans by using the reflection API. Remembering the types of objects `IterateTag` enumerates, it is reasonable to assume that it is going to step over beans in its iterations.

10.5.4 *Integrating FieldGetter with IterationTagSupport*

Having established the nature of the `FieldGetter`, how do we integrate it into the iteration process? The answer is in the updated implementation of `IterationTag-Support` wherein `FieldGetter` was integrated. An updated listing of `Iteration-TagSupport` is in listing 10.16 (for clarity, unmodified code was omitted and whenever new and old code are mixed, the new code is in bold).

Listing 10.16 An updated IterationTagSupport with FieldGetter integration

```
package book.iteration;

import java.io.Reader;
import java.io.IOException;
import book.util.LocalStrings;
import book.util.FieldGetter;
import book.util.ExBodyTagSupport;
import javax.servlet.jsp.JspWriter;
import javax.servlet.jsp.JspException;

public abstract class IterationTagSupport
    extends ExBodyTagSupport {

    static LocalStrings ls =
        LocalStrings.getLocalStrings(IterationTagSupport.class);

    protected IterationSupport elementsList = null;
    protected Object current;                              ❶
    protected FieldGetter fGetter = null;

    // Some unmodified code was removed

    public int doAfterBody()
        throws JspException
    {
        try {
            if(null == fGetter) {                                          ❷
                getBodyContent().writeOut(getPreviousOut());
            } else {
                populateFields();
            }
            getBodyContent().clear();
        } catch(java.io.IOException ioe) {
            // User probably disconnected ...
            // Log and throw a JspTagException
        }

        if(elementsList.hasNext()) {
            exportVariables();
            return EVAL_BODY_TAG;
        }

        return SKIP_BODY;
```

```
    }

    protected void populateFields()
        throws JspException
    {
        String field = null;
        try {
            Reader r = getBodyContent().getReader();
            JspWriter w = getPreviousOut();

            fGetter.setObject(current);                 ❸

            int ch = r.read();                               ❹
            while(-1 != ch) {
                if('<' == ch) {
                    ch = r.read();
                    if('$' == ch) {
                        /* found a field reference */
                        field = readFieldName(r);                  ❺
                        w.print(fGetter.getField(field));
                        ch = r.read();
                    } else {
                        w.write('<');
                    }
                } else {
                    w.write(ch);
                    ch = r.read();
                }
            }
        } catch(IllegalAccessException e) {
            // Throw a JspTagException
        } catch(IOException ioe) {
            // Throw a JspTagException
        }
    }

    protected String readFieldName(Reader r)
        throws JspException, IOException
    {
        StringBuffer sb = new StringBuffer();
        int ch = r.read();
        while(-1 != ch) {                            ❻
            if('$' == ch) {
                ch = r.read();
                if('>' == ch) {
                    /* found a field ending mark */
                    return sb.toString().trim();
                } else {
                    sb.append((char)ch);
                }
            } else {
                sb.append((char)ch);
                ch = r.read();
```

```
            }
        }
        // Throw a JspTagException (parse error, directive
        // was not terminated)
    }

    // Some unmodified code was removed
    protected void exportVariables()
        throws JspException
    {
        current = elementsList.getNext();    ❼
        pageContext.setAttribute(id, current);
    }

    // Some unmodified code was removed

    protected void clearServiceState()
    {
        elementsList = null;
        current = null;
        fGetter = null;
    }
}
```

❶ ❼ **Two new instance variables for the field substitution**   The majority of new code that was added has to do with parsing the body and propagating the current iterator value to the field substitution code. Propagating the value of the current iterator is needed because `doAfterBody()` does not know the value. Implementing the propagation involves adding an instance variable to carry the iterator value as well as initialize this value whenever a new iterator value is exported.

❶ ❷ **If a field getter is available, field substitution is on**   Now that the iterator value is available for all methods, we can use `doAfterBody()` to process the body. Body processing is turned on whenever a value is set to the class `FieldGetter` member, `fGetter`, which informs `IterationTagSupport` that field substitution is required and `populateFields()` is being called.

❸ **Sets the current iterator into the field getter to make it possible to get field values from the iterator   ❹ Searches for a directive starting prefix (<$)   ❺ Reads the field name and prints its value using the getter   ❻ Looks for the directive-terminating sequence ($>)**   `populateFields()` and `readFieldName()` are those that actually implement the field substitution. `populateFields()` parses through the body looking for the substitution directive-starting prefix. Whenever `populateFields()` finds this directive it will ask `readFieldName()` to read the rest of the directive (including its suffix) and return the name of the field referenced therein. Once `populateFields()` holds the referenced field name, it uses the `FieldGetter` to obtain the field's value, print it, and continue parsing the body (looking for other directives).

❼ **Stores the current iterator for later use in** `doEndBody()`.

10.5.5 *Updating IterateTag to perform field substitution*

Now that the modifications to `IterationTagSupport` are complete, the road to field substitution is open. All we need is to modify `IterateTag` and make it set the `ReflectionFieldGetter` into `IterationTagSupport` in order to turn on field substitution. The modifications to `IterateTag` are presented in listing 10.17 (unmodified code was omitted and new code is in bold).

Listing 10.17   An updated IterateTag handler class with field substitution support

```
package book.iteration;

// Some unmodified code was removed

import book.util.LibraryConfig;

// Some unmodified code was removed

public class IterateTag extends IterationTagSupport {

    // Some unmodified code was removed

    protected void fetchIterationSupport()
        throws JspException
    {
        Object o = getPointed();

        if(o instanceof Iterator) {
            elementsList =
                new IteratorIterationSupport((Iterator)o);
        } else if(o instanceof Enumeration) {
            elementsList =
                new EnumerationIterationSupport((Enumeration)o);
        } else if(o.getClass().isArray()) {
            elementsList = new ArrayIterationSupport(o);
        } else {
            // Throw an exception to inform that we cannot
            // iterate this object
        }
        if(LibraryConfig.isFieldPlacementInUse()) {
            fGetter = new ReflectionFieldGetter();
        }
    }

    // Some unmodified code was removed
}
```

Only `fetchIterationSupport()` was modified to add the `ReflectionFieldGetter` into `IterationTagSupport` according to a property in the library configuration.

10.5.6 *Field substitution in action*

Once the tweaking of the iteration code is behind us, we can modify our original JSP (which printed the shopping cart) and adapt it to use field substitution. The end result of this adaptation is shown in listing 10.18 and, as you shall see, the loop that populates the HTML table with cart items has been simplified.

Listing 10.18   A JSP file that uses field substitution

```
<%@ page errorPage="error.jsp" %>
<%@ taglib
    uri="http://www.manning.com/jsptagsbook/iteration-taglib"
    prefix="iter" %>
<%@ taglib
    uri="http://www.manning.com/jsptagsbook/conditions-taglib"
    prefix="cond" %>
<%@ taglib
    uri="http://www.manning.com/jsptagsbook/beans-taglib"
    prefix="bean" %>

<html>

<body>
<cond:with name="cart" property="empty">
<cond:test condition="eq true">
    Your cart is empty.
</cond:test>
<cond:test condition="eq false">
    Your cart contains the following products:

    <table>
        <tr><th>Product</th> <th>Quantity</th> <th>Price</th> </tr>

        <iter:iterate name="cart" property="products" id="product">

        <tr>
            <td> <$ name $> </td>
            <td> <$ quantity $> </td>
            <td> <$ dollars $>.<$cents$>$ </td>
        </tr>
        </iter:iterate>
        <tr>
            <td> Totals <td>
            <td> <bean:show name="cart" property="dollars"/>.
                <bean:show name="cart" property="cents"/>$  <td>
        <tr>
    </table>
</cond:test>
</cond:with>
</body>
</html>
```

This section showed more than a mere ease-of-use enhancement to the iteration task. It showed how to add your own proprietary additions to the JSP syntax. Some developers may reject the idea of working with proprietary JSP additions, since this syntax will not be useful in other settings. However, the additions presented in this chapter are based on custom tags, and since custom tags are a standard JSP feature, the field replacement features developed here will run on all JSP engines. Although our creation's nature is indeed proprietary, our tags and their additions can run anywhere. The simplicity of our field substitution syntax and the time it will save JSP authors who use it are well worth the expense of a bit of proprietary syntax.

10.6 *JSP1.2 and IterationTag*

This chapter created iteration tags using `BodyTag`, but using `BodyTag` for iteration includes within it a hidden performance hazard due to its buffering overhead.

As noted in chapter 6, when using `BodyTag` the JSP runtime places the body into an intermediate buffer (the `BodyContent` object) and leaves it up to the tag to actually do something with the results of the body execution. In our iteration tags, what we did with these results was to copy them into the response flowing to the user, thereby suffering needless buffering overhead. Granted, using the buffer made it possible to develop ease of use techniques such as field placement, but if the JSP file developer decides not to use field placement, why suffer the performance penalty?

10.6.1 *IterationTag*

This performance penalty was solved in JSP1.2 with the introduction of the `IterationTag`, which can repeatedly execute its body for as long as it returns `EVAL_-BODY_AGAIN` from `doAfterBody()`. Hence, all we need do is take the iteration framework that was developed in this chapter and have it work with the JSP1.2 `IterationTag`.

All our iteration-related code was part of a single class, `IterationTagSupport`, which is where we implemented our `doStartTag()`, `doBeforeBody()`, and `doAfterBody()`. All the tags that work with the iteration framework have only to extend `IterationTagSupport` and provide an implementation for a few methods. At this point, we only need to port `IterationTagSupport`, which requires the following steps:

- Remove any code portion related to the field placement (no buffering means no field placement).

- Return `EVAL_BODY_INCLUDE` from `doStartTag()` so that the JSP runtime includes the body's results into the stream flowing to the client.

- Export variables in doStartTag() instead of doBeforeBody(), since IterationTag does not have a doBeforeBody() method.

- Return EVAL_BODY_AGAIN from doAfterBody() as per the JSP1.2 specification.

When we have finished, our iteration tags can take advantage of the IterationTag interface and its improved performance. Listing 10.19 presents such an adaptation of IterationTagSupport to the JSP1.2 IterationTag interface.

Listing 10.19   IterationTagSupport adapted to the JSP1.2 IterationTag

```
package book.iteration;

import book.util.LocalStrings;
import book.util.ExTagSupport;
import book.util.StringUtil;
import javax.servlet.jsp.JspWriter;
import javax.servlet.jsp.JspException;

public abstract class IncludedIterationTagSupport
    extends ExTagSupport {

    static LocalStrings ls =
        LocalStrings.getLocalStrings(IncludedIterationTagSupport.class);

    protected IterationSupport elementsList = null;
    protected Object current;

    public int doStartTag()
        throws JspException
    {
        fetchIterationSupport();
        if(elementsList.hasNext()) {
            exportVariables();
            return EVAL_BODY_INCLUDE;
        }
        return SKIP_BODY;
    }

    public int doAfterBody()
        throws JspException
    {
        if(elementsList.hasNext()) {
            exportVariables();
            return EVAL_BODY_AGAIN;
        }

        return SKIP_BODY;
    }

    protected abstract void fetchIterationSupport()
        throws JspException;
```

```
    protected void exportVariables()
        throws JspException
    {
        current = elementsList.getNext();
        pageContext.setAttribute(id, current);
    }

    protected void clearProperties()
    {
        id = null;
        super.clearProperties();
    }

    protected void clearServiceState()
    {
        elementsList = null;
        current = null;
    }
}
```

`IncludedIterationTagSupport` presented in Listing 10.19 is much less compli-cated than `IterationTagSupport`. This simplicity comes partially from the removal of the field placement code, and partially from the fact that we no longer need to handle the `BodyContent` buffer and write its content back to the user.

To summarize, all tags developed in this chapter should be able to run unmodi-fied in JSP1.2 (as `BodyTag` is supported there). However, tags wishing to take advan-tage of the new `IterationTag` interface should abandon the field placement as a means of populating the iterator's fields, since the tags can then extend our new `IncludedIterationTagSupport` and gain performance improvements.

10.7 Summary

Iteration is a crucial task in almost any web application, yet until the arrival of cus-tom JSP tags, it could only be accomplished using scriptlets. As we stated, iteration scriptlets render the JSP code difficult to read and maintain, and even worse, place a premium on the content developer's knowledge of Java. Custom tags fix these problems at a reasonably low price.

We also presented a generic way to develop iteration tags. In fact, the code developed for this chapter can be used in your own daily work (e.g., iteration on something that is not an `Array`, `Enumeration`, or `Iterator`) with a relatively small time investment. Simply extend `IterateTag` or `IterationTagSupport`, override a method, and gain full access to the custom tag iteration functionality.

As a last phase in enhancing the quality and ease-of-use of our iteration tags, body content processing was added to the iteration tags to make using the iterator properties easier. This body content processing is by no means unique to iteration tags. In fact, you can implement it in any tags that extend the `BodyTag` interface and have complete control over their body. Body content processing in this way can speed up the work of the JSP developer, by allowing you to introduce simple, proprietary syntax in your JSPs. It should be considered an appealing alternative to using smaller custom tags, such as the show tags that we developed, especially in cases in which the size of the parsed content is small compared to the size of the entire page.

Next we'll see how we can integrate custom tags with a database to provide simple tag-based access to a database server.

Database access with tags

The vast majority of web applications communicate with a database—for reasons which vary from one application to another; but, as a general statement, a large portion of the important information on the web is located somewhere in a database. Databases will store *any* important information your site needs.

Because database access is a cornerstone of interactive web sites, having a custom tag library provide that access allows content developers to handle the task without the help of a Java guru, resulting in faster development time. In this chapter we will build a library which uses Java's standard database access API, Java Database Connectivity (JDBC), to implement database access.

11.1 *Choosing how to present database information*

There are a number of approaches for handling database presentation and storage in a Java web application. Chapter 2 presented two such approaches, Model-1 and Model-2.

Model-2 uses the popular Model-View-Controller (MVC) pattern for integrating servlets/JSPs with a database. In a purist's implementation of Model-2, JSP files are only supposed to present data that was obtained by a servlet. These servlets give and receive data to and from JSPs which in turn display and collect the data, and do not get involved with its storage or retrieval.

Under Model-2, the servlet can grab the dynamic data, place it in the JSP scripting environment as a request, session, or application attribute, and ask a JSP page to render a response based on the dynamic content. The servlet that places the data in the JSP scripting environment can either wrap the data in a set of beans (hiding the data complexity from the JSP page) or leave the data in its raw format, as a JDBC ResultSet object, and let the JSP pull data from rows and columns of the ResultSet as needed.

For cases in which the data is wrapped inside a set of beans, we can use the custom JavaBeans tags we developed in chapter 8 to get and set the bean properties (and ultimately, records in the database). The second case, wherein data is kept in a raw format instead of in beans, requires that our JSP file use scriptlets to process JDBC access itself; yet, there must be a better way than using scriptlets— which is in fact handling JDBC with tags.

Under Model-1 the JSP file is also supposed to access the dynamic data through JavaBeans. However, if we need only to present raw data from a database and do not wish to use beans for each query, we will probably want to access the database with some database tags. Right?

11.1.1 Why not just wrap everything in a JavaBean?

Why would we have our JSPs perform database access directly through tags, instead of using a Model-2 approach, wherein a servlet hits the database and wraps everything in an object. We can also use Model-1 (if it fits our development style) and again, only see JavaBeans. So, why access the database directly?

It is largely a matter of taste and requirements, but we might decide to use raw database results from within JSP, in an attempt to provide the rationale for this choice. To start with, not all data requests require that an object be associated with them for enforcing or implementing business rules. Sometimes all we want is to present the results of a complex query in a table, and nothing more.

Consider a case in which the user wants to produce a tabular report from an SQL database. In a common design approach, a controller servlet can submit an SQL query (specified by the user) to the database, then retrieve and pass the results to a JSP. The JSP takes those results and uses them to populate an HTML table that is returned to the user. Since the user could specify one of any number of different queries, we would need many different beans to represent the different result sets, yet these beans would not be mandatory for the report generation and could even be considered overkill. We can easily imagine presenting the user with a UI flexible enough to produce any one of thousands of possible data result combinations, from any number of database tables. We certainly wouldn't want to create a JavaBean for every possible query permutation, and creating a generic bean to support any result would essentially force us to rewrite the JDBC `ResultSet` class (and some of its helper classes). In a case such as this, a tag library that could effortlessly iterate over any JDBC `ResultSet` and present the results to the user would clearly be more efficient than wrapping everything in a JavaBean.

This type of ad hoc querying and reporting is common for web applications, but using direct database access (without an intermediate Java object layer) is also desirable for prototyping and testing, and small tasks that do not warrant building an object model. In cases such as these, or any others in which modeling query results with JavaBeans is undesirable, direct database access can reduce both your development time and your runtime overhead. Having a set of tags that makes this database access easy and overcomes the need for scriptlets proves to be a big help. In this chapter, we'll create tags that allow direct database access and address this need.

11.2 Designing our database presentation tag library

Before discussing the presentation of database data using tags, we need to frame our approach by addressing a couple of design questions:

- Where will the code that opens and closes the database connections live?

- How do we pass database results from that code to the JSP?

Answering these two questions will provide a necessary prerequisite in implementing our database presentation tag.

11.2.1 *Handling database connectivity and passing results*

The answers to our two design questions are a matter of personal choice. We've chosen to proceed with a design that borrows from the Model-2 architecture; but instead of using JavaBeans (for reasons already discussed), the controller servlet passes the database results directly to the JSP. The object the servlet passes in this scenario is an instance of `java.sql.ResultSet` (the standard JDBC object for representing a query response) which the servlet retrieves from the JDBC query. Figure 11.1 shows, using this design, what happens when a user request arrives:

- A servlet will be executed to serve the request. The servlet will open a connection to the database, query its values, and store the `ResultSet` object returned from the database in the request attributes. This answers our question regarding where the database code will go.

- The servlet will hand the request, with the `ResultSet` stored inside, to the JSP so it can generate the response content. This answers our second design question of how the JSP would get the database results.

- The JSP file now executes. At a certain point in the JSP file's execution, it will find (and execute) one or more database-aware tags, which will take the `ResultSet` object from the request attributes and use it to populate the response returned to the client with the values stored in the database.

- As the response is finished, the request handling returns to the servlet which closes the database connection.

We now have a clear design pattern, the servlet code is our site to create the connection, obtain data from the database, and dispose the connection. The JSP will only present the data obtained from the database in the response. One benefit of this design is that we can implement resource-leaking protection (ensuring that all database connections are closed) in a central location in the servlet. This tactic avoids the possibility that JSP authors could accidentally create resource leaks within their own code.

11.2.2 *Additional design considerations*

In addition to simply passing data from the controller servlet to the JSP, and ultimately, our new tag we need to consider how the data is presented. We should note,

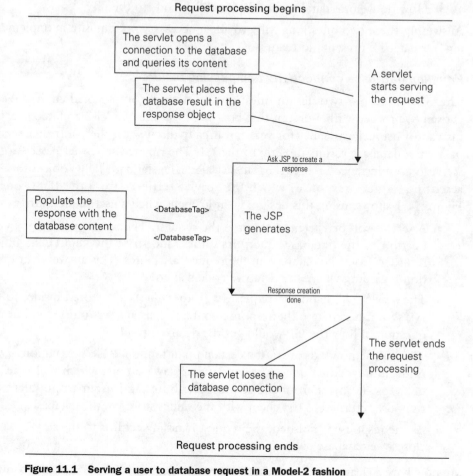

Figure 11.1 Serving a user to database request in a Model-2 fashion

of course, the likelihood of the database results spanning multiple rows and columns, and that we will sometimes want to specify the order by which we present the columns. At other times we might instead want to preserve the order of the rows that the query returns, such as when the database sorts the rows based on the SQL query. With this in mind, our design will need to be able to:

- Iterate over the database results. At a code level this means that we will be iterating over the JDBC `ResultSet` object.

- Present column values by their name or index. We may reference the columns as the first column, second column, and so forth, or as a named column based on the column name in the database table.

11.2.3 *Implementation conclusions*

Keeping these requirements in mind, we at last contemplate writing our library. Even given all our features, creating a database presentation tag library will not prove to be too daunting as we have some useful base tags (from previous chapters) from which we can borrow valuable functionality.

Two of the requirements for our library, iteration and field presentation, will be handled by a tag we'll call the `IterateResultTag`. This tag can reuse much of the infrastructure we developed in chapter 10, such as the `IterationSupport` and `FieldGetter` interfaces. Recall that we defined a generic interface, `IterationSupport`, that could be extended to iterate over any type of Java object. For our database tags, all we need to do is create an `IterationSupport` that will iterate over a `ResultSet` (which, again, our tag gets from the controller servlet) and a `FieldGetter` that gets fields out of that `ResultSet`.

11.3   *IterateResultSetTag*

`IterateResultTag` will be used to iterate on the `ResultSet` that the JSP receives from the controller servlet. This iteration tag extends the one developed in the previous chapter, which lets us use the reflection infrastructure in `IterateTag` to fetch `ResultSet`. All that is left to do is to modify `fetchIterationSupport()` so that it will set an `IterationSupport` object. This in turn iterates a `ResultSet` and a `FieldGetter` that can read columns out of that `ResultSet`. All this reuse, in fact, means that the whole implementation of `IterateResultSetTag` (listing 11.1) consists of only one short method.

> **Listing 11.1   implementation of the IterateResultSetTag handler class**

```
package book database;

import java.sql.ResultSet;

import book.iteration.IterateTag;
import book.util.LocalStrings;
import book.util.LibraryConfig;

import javax.servlet.jsp.PageContext;
import javax.servlet.jsp.JspException;

public class IterateResultSetTag extends IterateTag {

    static LocalStrings ls =
        LocalStrings.getLocalStrings(IterateResultSetTag.class);

    protected void fetchIterationSupport()
        throws JspException
    {
```

```
        Object o = getPointed();

        elementsList = new ResultSetIterationSupport((ResultSet)o);    ❶

        if(LibraryConfig.isJDBCFieldPlacementInUse()) {    ❷
            fGetter = new JDBCFieldGetter();
        }
    }
}
```

❶ Uses the `ResultSetIterationSupport` class to wrap a `ResultSet`.

❷ If we are using JDBC Field placement, we create a `JDBCFileGetter` to get `ResultSet` fields.

`IterateResultSetTag` by itself isn't especially interesting. The action in this tag resides in the `ResultSetIterationSupport` and `JDBCFieldGetter` classes it uses, which we present in the next code listings.

11.3.1 ResultSetIterationSupport class

First let's look at `ResultSetIterationSupport`, a class which takes a `ResultSet` object and wraps it so that it can be iterated by the framework developed in chapter 10.

```
package book.database;

import java.sql.ResultSet;
import java.sql.SQLException;

import book.util.LocalStrings;
import book.iteration.IterationSupport;

import javax.servlet.jsp.JspException;

class ResultSetIterationSupport implements IterationSupport {
    static LocalStrings ls =
        LocalStrings.getLocalStrings(ResultSetIterationSupport.class);

    protected ResultSet rs = null;
    protected boolean nextAvailable = false;
    protected boolean nextAvailableValid = false;

    ResultSetIterationSupport(ResultSet rs)
    {
        this.rs = rs;
    }

    public boolean hasNext()
        throws JspException
    {
        if(nextAvailableValid) {
            return nextAvailable;
```

```
        }
        try {
            nextAvailable = rs.next();
            nextAvailableValid = true;
            return nextAvailable;
        } catch(SQLException sqe) {
            throw new JspException(ls.getStr(Constants.SQL_EXCEPTION));
        }
    }

    public Object getNext()
        throws JspException
    {
        if(hasNext()) {
            nextAvailableValid = false;
            return rs;
        }
        throw new JspException(ls.getStr(Constants.NO_MORE_ROWS));
    }
}
```

The most interesting part of `ResultSetIterationSupport` is `hasNext()` which wraps `next()`, provided by `ResultSet`, and adapts it to the needs of the iteration framework. `next()` returns `true` if there is a next row to read in `ResultSet`, but it also has the side effect of moving to this next row. If we call `next()` twice we may get two different results, and skip one of the rows. This row skipping behavior is not acceptable for our iteration tags, so `hasNext()` and `getNext()` cooperate to eliminate row skipping by keeping track of what the user does in `ResultSet`, thus avoiding needless calls to `next()`.

11.3.2 *JDBCFieldGetter class*

The success of `IterateResultSetTag` is then made possible by `JDBCFieldGetter`, which also builds on the iteration framework from chapter 10. It accomplishes this by implementing the `FieldGetter` interface which, you may recall, provides some basic methods for getting field values out of a Java object. In this case, the Java object is simply a `ResultSet`. All `JDBCFieldGetter` does is fetch named column values by calling JDBC methods over the `ResultSet` object.

```
package book.database;

import java.sql.ResultSet;
import java.sql.SQLException;

import book.util.FieldGetter;
import book.util.LocalStrings;

public class JDBCFieldGetter implements FieldGetter {

    static LocalStrings ls =
```

```
        LocalStrings.getLocalStrings(JDBCFieldGetter.class);

    protected ResultSet rs;

    public void setObject(Object o)        ❶
        throws IllegalArgumentException
    {
        if(!(o instanceof ResultSet)) {        ❶
            throw new IllegalArgumentException(ls.getStr(Constants.NOT_AN_RS));
        }
        this.rs = (ResultSet)o;        ❶
    }

    public Object getField(String fieldName)
        throws IllegalAccessException
    {
        try {
            return rs.getObject(fieldName);        ❷
        } catch(SQLException ex) {
        }

        throw new IllegalAccessException(ls.getStr(Constants.SQL_EXCEPTION));
    }
}
```

❶ Sets the object, in this case, a `ResultSet`.

❷ Retrieves the field value for a given field name from the `ResultSet`.

11.3.3 *IterateResultSetTag in action*

Combining `IterateResultSetTag`, `ResultSetIterationSupport`, and `JDB-CFieldGetter`, we now have a tag that can be used to iterate over an SQL query result and present it to the user. Note again that, since we rely heavily on the iteration tag framework, the amount of coding needed was relatively minor, leaving us to concentrate on the unique portion of our problem: the iterating and presenting of a `ResultSet`.

A sample JSP file that uses `IterateResultSetTag` can be seen in listing 11.2 (note that the name chosen for `IterateResultSetTag` is dbenum).

Listing 11.2   A sample JSP file that uses IterateResultSetTag

```
<%@ page errorPage="error.jsp" %>
<%@ taglib
    uri="http://www.manning.com/jsptagsbook/database-taglib"
    prefix="db" %>
<html>
<head>
<title> Database query results </title>
</head>
<body>
```

```
    <h1> Database query results </h1>
    <table border="1"  bgcolor="#c0c0c0">
<tr>
    <th bgcolor="#a0a0a0">id</th>
    <th bgcolor="#a0a0a0">First name</th>
    <th bgcolor="#a0a0a0">Last name</th>
    <th bgcolor="#a0a0a0">Street</th>
    <th bgcolor="#a0a0a0">City</th>

</tr>
    <db:dbenum name="result" id="i">     ❶
        <tr>
            <td> <$ ID $> </td>              ❷
            <td> <$ FIRSTNAME $> </td>
            <td> <$ LASTNAME $> </td>
            <td> <$ STREET $> </td>
            <td> <$ CITY $> </td>
        </tr>

    </db:dbenum>
    </table>
</body>
</html>
```

❶ **Starts the iteration over the `ResultSet` in the JSP attribute named result.**

❷ **Presents the various columns in the `ResultSet`.**

As listing 11.2 shows, presenting the database results in the JSP became fairly easy. What previously required a number of complex scriptlets is now a simple use of a custom tag. A sample response created with the JSP file in listing 11.2 is presented in figure 11.2; the data populated in the table is from the sample content provided by the (free and open-source) hypersonic database.

This tag does some impressive work with a database, but on its own is not yet a fully functional database presentation tag library. In the next section we discuss some of the shortcomings of this tag, and some of the features we would like to see in our library.

11.4 *Full JDBC connectivity through tags*

In the previous section we built a tag displaying the result of an SQL query in a JSP. This tag may be useful, but much more can be done with databases that we'd like to support and, unfortunately, being able to show the results of a query is not always enough.

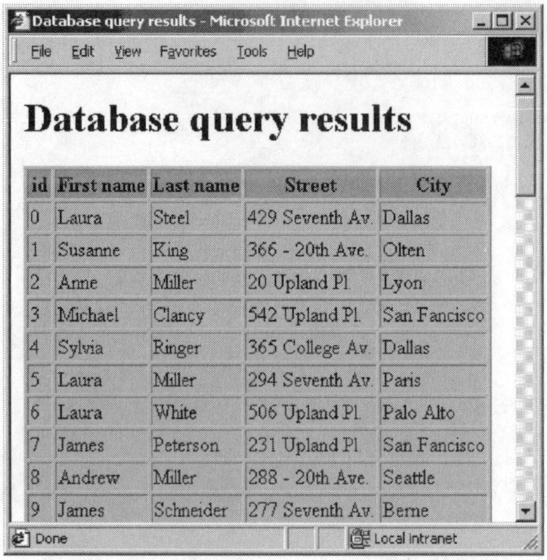

Figure 11.2   The output of the Model-2 user to database
access with `IterateResultSetTag`

11.4.1 *Improving our one-tag approach*

`IterateResultTag` served its design purpose well, but as we consider broader JSP to database needs, we can identify areas for improvement.

Making database access available to JSP authors

The previous section was based on the assumption that there is a controller servlet which opens a connection to the database, executes the query, and finally closes the results and connection. Though this approach does an adequate job of protecting the database access code, its shortcoming is that we are forced to keep a Java programmer on hand to modify query code whenever database tables and/or columns are added, removed, or changed. This restriction is especially problematic when you want only to create a simple, department-level online reporting page, or if your site provides searchable access to tables that are added on a regular basis. Under such circumstances, we'd ideally like to offer our content developers some tags that could perform database tasks without the controller servlet. We will solve this problem by providing a stronger database access tag library.

Improving resource utilization

Another problem with our `IterateResultSetTag` is that the database connection and the accompanying query results are kept open during the entire time of the JSP file's execution. This ties our precious database resources up for a longer period than necessary. In a basic JSP file, the execution will not take long; but complex, database-driven JSPs will probably be more time consuming (e.g., because portions of the page need to be written to the user). In these pages, the allocated database connection will be occupied for a relatively lengthy period, yet it will be idle most of the time. Any connection to the database causes a substantial penalty in terms of memory usage, file handles, sockets, and other resources allocated for the connection. Moreover, since connecting to the database also takes time, most server applications use database connection pool techniques. This allows a few connections, used later by the server's threads, to be allocated in advance. Thus, if we keep a connection for too extended a period, the pool will reach its maximum number of open connections and start to block service threads, which leads to yet another performance failure. It is clear then, that keeping the open connection's idle time to a minimum will ensure that we use fewer resources to satisfy our database needs.

Improvement conclusions

Taking into account all of these areas for improvement, it is clear that having only a single, simple data presentation tag like IterateResultTag is not enough to satisfy many common database needs. To address this, we create tags that can obtain a database connection, execute a query, and free the connection. This will address both improvement areas, as it will also allow us to:

- Use tags in our JSP file to manipulate the database, rather than coding in Java in some controller servlet.
- Have fine-grained control over the duration of the connection to the database, including just-in-time (JIT) opening/closing of the connection.

These are some genuine benefits, but we must be ever mindful of at least one possible gotcha: resource leaking. Resource-leaking is well-known by all who work with databases and can be summarized in one sentence: If you do not close each of the connections you opened, given enough requests, the system will crash. You could say that the solution is obvious: just close all the connections; yet closing the connections is not so trivial in the face of exceptions. With IterateResultSetTag, we didn't have to worry about this contingency, because our servlet handled all connection use. By making our tags more flexible, and putting connection creation in the hands of the JSP author, we surrender this control in exchange for versatility. We need to be aware of this danger as we construct our tags, and take precautions to minimize the likelihood of a resource leak as much as possible, since its effects can be crippling.

The next sections in this chapter will deal with the design and implementation of a database manipulation custom tag library. First we'll explore the requirements for the library and its design, then take a look at its implementation.

11.5 *Database tag library design*

In order to build a truly useful custom tag solution, we need to create a tag library that addresses the shortcomings of our `IterateResultSetTag` and takes into consideration additional requirements, to be covered shortly. Our ultimate goal is to build a library that JSP authors can use to easily create dynamic pages that will display data from a database in a flexible way (and with minimal effort). To reach this goal, we need to first look at a definitive list of all the requirements we want our library to meet. Following this assessment, we will decide how we may build our library to implement those requirements; in short, we must decide how many tags the library requires and what each tag should do.

11.5.1 *Requirements*

As always, the design flows from our requirements, so let's now look at each in detail. The prerequisites we cited for `IterateResultTag` were fairly modest, this list raises the bar for a tag library that is much more useful for everyday development.

Database query support

First, we want our tag library to include at least one tag that defines:

- A connection to a database, including all the necessary parameters such as connecting user name and password.

- A query on some table, such that we can actually provide an SQL query that will later run on a defined connection. The user should be able to construct the SQL query dynamically from within JSP.

- A way to present the query results to the user while taking into account that the response could span multiple rows we subsequently must iterate over.

NOTE   We are very thin here in the area of result manipulation, especially if we do not define any data-related conditions that allow the creation of conditional HTML based on database results. We could require a tag to pose an `if` condition on the database response and, based on the result of this `if`, create a different table entry; for example, color table rows differently based on the state of some column. However, while these tags add functionality, they will not provide anything new.

The required functionality will necessitate the development of three tags. We will discuss how these tags look and communicate later in this chapter.

Resource allocation and deallocation

The next requirement is to support fine-grained control over the allocation of database connections and then free the connections without leaking them. This is actually a behavioral requirement implying that our tags should allocate resources in a JIT fashion. We will not allocate a connection and execute a query until we actually need to present it and we will free the connection as soon as the presentation is done. In the face of exceptions of all types and shapes, we will free allocated connections. This leads to the following needs:

- The presentation tag should allocate and free the connections (this is the JIT presentation requirement)
- The presentation tag should have a fail-safe mechanism to free database resources, probably in its `doEndTag()`/`release()` or some other method called from them.

This requirement places a burden on the presentation tag, but more important is the possibility that, since the presentation tag needs to handle information retrieved in other tags, it will need to know about the internal implementation. The design of the library should handle that.

Integration with application architectures

Integration with application architectures such as Model-2 is also an important requirement. Just because we give more responsibility to the JSP author does not mean that the controller servlet is no longer in the picture. We want to be able to define connections and queries in controller servlets and send them to the JSP for JIT execution and presentation.

Connection extensibility

Another requirement is the ability to add new connection and query tags to the library, even those not developed by the original library developer, and seamlessly integrate them with the current tags. This flexibility is crucial because different applications and application servers may have several ways of obtaining JDBC connection objects. For example, you may want to use a proprietary connection pool or a J2EE-compliant pool, and you will need to modify the connection tags to match your needs.

Configuration support

Finally, there is the need for integration with configuration mechanisms such as the web application deployment descriptor (in order to facilitate the user configuring your tags).

11.5.2 *Choosing our tags*

With these requirements in mind, the first design step is to think of tags that the library should contain and what each should do, in terms of functionality and attributes. When reviewing the types of operations we want to perform with our tag library, we have a number of options (table 11.1).

Table 11.1   Database tag library design options

Design option	Description
A single tag approach	Uses one tag that has all the needed functionality in it, such as opening a connection, defining a database query, and presenting the results.
A tag for each task approach	Uses one tag for opening a connection, one for defining a database query, and another for presenting the results. In this scenario, the tags would communicate by exporting objects which obey a predefined set of interfaces to the JSP environment.
A tag for each task approach (with tag nesting)	Similar to #2, except that the tags will communicate using a nested, parent tag model, accomplished by enclosing all the tags in a single wrapper parent tag.

Clearly the first option is the easiest to implement, but it does not answer some of our requirements. When using a single monolithic tag it is difficult to extend the library with new tags representing different types of connections, queries, and presentations. A single monolithic tag is also somewhat harder to use because it will include an excessive number of attributes to handle the different tasks. As a result, a divide-and-conquer approach that uses several tags to implement our different tasks is more effective.

Now that the first approach is eliminated, which of the other two tag options should we use? Both suggest the use of several tags and the communication between tags is accomplished through exporting and exchanging objects. There is, however, a big difference in how this communication takes place.

Generally speaking, the third option, wherein the tags use parenthood relations to exchange information, is easiest to use by the JSP programmer because all coordination between tags is implemented internally by the tag family. On the other hand, using the JSP environment to communicate between tags makes it possible for Model-2 style controller servlets to export objects into the JSP environment and communicate with the database tags. This capability makes the second option much more suitable for Model-2 applications.

Moreover, by exporting variables, other JSP entities such as scriptlets and Java-Beans can access the database resources. Both the second and third methods have their merits (integration versus ease of use); however, due to the extended integration available when the tags communicate using the JSP environment, we've decided to develop the tag library using the second approach.

The tags that make up our library

Having settled on our design approach, let's consider the tags we need to achieve this. There are at least four tags to implement. We list each tag function and the name of the corresponding tag used to implement it in table 11.2:

Table 11.2 Our tag library's functions and the tags that will perform them

Tag function	Description	Tag name
Connection definition	Defines the connection to be used for the query and how to use it. This tag has attributes that let the user define parameters such as the JDBC URL for the connection and the username and password for the current connection. In doStartTag(), the connection tag will read the connection parameters, merge them with the application configuration, and export a new connection object.	DBConnectionTag
Query definition	Defines the SQL query that we should show. This should be a BodyTag and the SQL query should be provided in its body; this way the users of the query tag can specify complex queries with dynamic content. The query tag should also obtain (in its attributes or via parenthood relations if the third approach is in use) a reference to the connection object that it would use in order to make the query to the database. The query tag exports result objects that other JSP entities can use in order to handle (and free) the query's results.	SQLQueryTag
Result iteration	Iterates over the result of the SQL query and makes sure that the query is closed when the iteration is done. This tag gets the identity of a result object as a parameter and then iterates over the result. When the iteration is complete, it will make sure that the result object is closed.	EnumRsTag
Database column presentation	Takes the current row and shows the value of a named column in it. The input to this tag is the name of the column and a reference to the query result object.	ViewRsTag

Sharing information between our tags

Now that our library's main cornerstone (the identity of the tags) is in place, we need to decide what objects should be exported by the tags in order to allow cooperation between them. The tags in our library will communicate among themselves using interfaces that wrap the actual database objects which are handed over to the result presentation layer when needed. For our design there will be two such wrapper interfaces:

- DbConnectionWrapper
  Wraps a database connection. A database connection tag exports a DbConnectionWrapper object to allow other entities (such as other tags and scriptlets) inside the JSP file reference and free database connections.

- DbResultWrapper
  Wraps the result of a database query. A database query tag exports a DbResultWrapper object to let other entities (such as other tags and scriptlets) inside the JSP file reference the results of a database query.

The way we'll share these objects between the tags (and the JSP) is to have the tags export the wrapper objects to the page scope of the JSP attribute table (a practice we first saw in chapter 8). Using this mechanism we achieve a loose and flexible integration:

- Since the integration is based on interfaces and not actual objects, anyone can provide other implementation to the interfaces and in this way extend the library.

- Since the wrapper interfaces are referenced from the JSP attribute table there is a very loose coupling between the producer of the wrapper and its consumer.

In fact, it is this loose integration that allows the users of the tag library to extend it by adding new tags, because the new tags have only to export/reference objects that obey the DbConnectionWrapper and DbResultWrapper interfaces.

Another important aspect of using wrapper interfaces and the JSP attribute table-based communication method is that they make it relatively easy to integrate controller servlets and JSP database tags. If a controller servlet wants to use the JSP database tags to present an SQL result, it has only to export objects of type DbResultWrapper and, perhaps, DbConnectionWrapper into the JSP environment and the database tag in the JSP file will use them as if they were created by a tag.

DBConnectionWrapper and DBResultWrapper interfaces

After this lengthy introduction, let's take a look into the DbConnectionWrapper and DbResultWrapper interfaces presented in listing 11.3.

Listing 11.3 The DbConnectionWrapper and DbResultWrapper interfaces

```
package book.database;

import java.sql.Connection;
import java.sql.SQLException;
import java.sql.ResultSet;

public interface DbConnectionWrapper {

    public Connection getConnection()
        throws SQLException;

    public void freeConnection();
}
public interface DbResultWrapper {

    public ResultSet getResultSet()
        throws SQLException;

    public void freeResult();
}
```

Each interface has a method to get the database-related resource as well as a method to free it. You may find it alarming that these interfaces do not specify when the resource was created or what parameters were used in its creation (e.g., there is no method to get the SQL query that caused the generation of the DbResultWrapper object). However, such information is of no interest to the users of these objects; the presentation layers do not care what usernames and passwords were used to connect to the database.

Since the resources are fetched using getter methods (getConnection() and getResultSet()), these methods can create the wanted resource at the time it is asked for. This is consistent with our desire to use database resources during presentation, thus reducing the amount of time these resources are tied up to an absolute minimum.

With this, we have finished our design which should produce both a solid and flexible implementation of our original requirements. We know which tags we are going to implement and roughly how they will be implemented, so let's begin the implementation of our database presentation custom tag library.

11.6 *Implementing the library*

This section presents the implementation of the tag library design that we developed in the previous section, using the JSP attribute table to integrate between the different tags. Our design becomes clearer now as we look at how each of these tags will cooperate (namely, which objects they will use and export) in order to

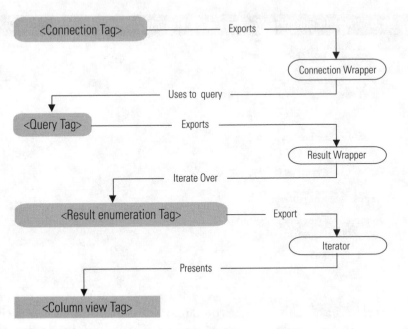

Figure 11.3 Dependencies among the database library tags

accomplish their allotted tasks. Figure 11.3 illustrates this cooperation, which can be summed up in the following steps:

- The connection tag (`DBConnectionTag`) exports a `DbConnectionWrapper` that the query tag uses to produce the result.
- The query tag (`SQLQueryTag`) uses the `DbConnectionWrapper` and exports a `DbResultWrapper` that the database result enumerator iterates on.
- The database result enumerator tag (`EnumRsTag`) exports an iterator that the column viewer presents in the generated content.

We'll discuss each of these tags in the order in which they appear in this workflow. You will first see how the connection and query tags were implemented, followed by the database result enumeration tag, and lastly, the column viewer tag.

11.6.1 *DBConnectionTag*

The goal of `DBConnectionTag` is to gather information that will be used to connect to a database. When the information gathering phase is complete, the tag will export a `DbConnectionWrapper` scripting variable that other JSP entities may use to connect to the database. Using JDBC, the information needed by the connection tag includes:

1   The JDBC driver class—used to connect to a database of a specific type.

2   The database URL—used to locate a connection to the specified database.

3   The connecting user name.

4   The connecting user's password.

The tag should be able to figure out these parameters, either through tag attributes or other configurations. For a robust approach, we'll build the tag so that it first looks for the JDBC parameters as tag attributes. If the JSP file does not specify a certain parameter through an attribute, the tag will attempt to grab it from the page/application initialization parameters (as defined in the application deployment descriptor). When the tag completes its parameter gathering, it exports a `DbConnectionWrapper` implementation that reflects the tag's obtained configuration and finishes its execution. This implementation is presented in listing 11.4.

Listing 11.4   Source code for the DbConnectionTag handler class

```
package book.database;

import javax.servlet.jsp.JspException;
import javax.servlet.jsp.PageContext;
import book.util.LocalStrings;
import book.util.ExTagSupport;

public class DbConnectionTag extends ExTagSupport {
    public static final String DBUSER  = "db_user";
    public static final String DBPASS  = "db_pass";
    public static final String DBURL   = "db_url";
    public static final String DBDRIVER = "db_driver";

    static LocalStrings ls =
        LocalStrings.getLocalStrings(DbConnectionTag.class);
    protected String dbuser   = null;
    protected String dbpass   = null;
    protected String dburl    = null;
    protected String dbdriver = null;

    public void setUser(String user)
    {
        this.dbuser = user;
    }

    public void setPass(String pass)
    {
        this.dbpass = pass;
    }
    public void setUrl(String url)
    {
        this.dburl = url;
```

```
    }
    public void setDriver(String driver)
    {
        this.dbdriver = driver;
    }

    public int doStartTag()
        throws JspException
    {
        checkParameters();                              ❶
        exportWrapper(createDbConnectionWrapper());      ❷
        return SKIP_BODY;
    }

    protected void clearProperties()
    {
        id       = null;
        dbuser   = null;
        dbpass   = null;
        dburl    = null;
        dbdriver = null;
        super.clearProperties();
    }

    protected void checkParameters()
        throws JspException
    {
        if(null == dbuser) {
            dbuser = findInitParameter(id+"."+DBUSER);
        }
        if(null == dbpass) {
            dbpass = findInitParameter(id+"."+DBPASS);       ❸
        }
        if(null == dburl) {
            dburl = findInitParameter(id+"."+DBURL);
        }
        if(null == dbdriver) {
            dbdriver = findInitParameter(id+"."+DBDRIVER);
        }

        if(null == dburl) {
            // Throw an exception, we must have a url
        }
        if(null == dbdriver) {
            // Throw an exception, we must have a driver class
        }
    }

    protected void exportWrapper(DbConnectionWrapper con)
        throws JspException
    {
        pageContext.setAttribute(id,            ❹
                                    con,
```

```
                              PageContext.PAGE_SCOPE);
    }

    protected DbConnectionWrapper createDbConnectionWrapper()
        throws JspException
    {
        try {
            Class.forName(dbdriver).newInstance();      ❺
            return new DbConnection(id,      ❻
                              getServletContext(),
                              dburl, dbuser, dbpass);
        } catch(ClassNotFoundException cnfe) {
            // Throw an exception
        } catch(InstantiationException ie) {
            // Throw an exception
        } catch(IllegalAccessException eae) {
            // Throw an exception
        }
    }
}
```

❶ **Checks and merges the JDBC parameters.**

❷ **Exports a connection wrapper that represents the connection parameters.**

❸ **Merges the application and page initialization properties and the tag's attribute values** Merging the initialization parameters and the tag attributes value is one of the more interesting tasks that we face in DbConnectionTag. As discussed previously, if the tag's attributes provide a valid value, we use it; but, absent a value, we look for it in the page and application initialization parameters. So that these parameters might serve more than a single database connection tag, we are using the tag's id attribute (the only mandatory attribute for this tag) as the prefix to all initialization parameters. For example, if the tag's id is con and we want to configure it with a URL, the initialization parameter should be named con.db_url. By taking advantage of the standard configuration parameters we make it possible for the users of our tags to bundle them with their applications preconfigured, without having to add nonstandard property files that may require special handling. The only possible reason for concern over the merging of initialization parameters is that the default TLD entry for DbConnectionTag (listing 11.5) must have all JDBC-related attributes optional. This is a drawback since there is no way for us to ensure that the parameter is either a tag attribute or application parameter. It is therefore possible that the JSP author could fail to specify it in either place and discover it only when the servlet (the one created from the JSP translation) receives a request, rather than at compile/translation time.

❹ **Exports the wrapper variable into the JSP environment.**

❺ **Loads the database driver**   Before exporting the DbConnection, DbConnectionTag guarantees that the database driver class is loaded by creating an instance of the class; in this way DbConnectionTag knows that at least the supplied driver parameter is valid. Testing the rest of the parameters is impossible without allocating a database connection, so no actual testing is done on them.

❻ **Creates a connection wrapper with the configured parameters**   As you have probably noticed, listing 11.4 does not contain any real JDBC code. In fact, it does not even import any of the java.sql classes. Instead, it creates and exports an implementation to the DbConnectionWrapper interface that is going to use JDBC APIs to access the database. This wrapper implementation class, DbConnection, implements the DBConnectionWrapper interface and handles all the JDBC code for us. We will see the implementation of DBConnection in the next section.

Let's now look at the TLD for DBConnectionTag:

Listing 11.5   TLD for DBConnectionTag

```
<tag>
    <name>connection</name>
    <tagclass>book.database.DbConnectionTag</tagclass>
    <teiclass>book.database.DbConnectionExtraInfo</teiclass>
    <bodycontent>empty</bodycontent>
    <info>
            Defines a database connection. The JDBC parameters may
        come from the attributes or from the web application's
        initialization parameters.
    </info>

    <attribute>
    <name>id</name>
    <required>true</required>
    <rtexprvalue>false</rtexprvalue>
</attribute>
<attribute>
    <name>user</name>
    <required>false</required>
    <rtexprvalue>true</rtexprvalue>
</attribute>
<attribute>
    <name>pass</name>
    <required>false</required>
    <rtexprvalue>true</rtexprvalue>
</attribute>
<attribute>
    <name>url</name>
    <required>false</required>
    <rtexprvalue>false</rtexprvalue>
</attribute>
```

```
        <attribute>
            <name>driver</name>
            <required>false</required>
            <rtexprvalue>false</rtexprvalue>
        </attribute>
    </tag>
```

You'll notice that none of the attributes are specified as required in this TLD. Once again, we allow the information regarding the JDBC parameters to be specified as tag attributes *or* in the environment.

DbConnection class

DbConnection is the implementation of one of our two interfaces used for sharing among the tags—DbConnectionWrapper. As previously pointed out, DbConnection-Tag does not perform any JDBC-related work itself; it exports an instance of type DbConnection instead. DbConnection source code is presented in listing 11.6.

Listing 11.6 Source code for DbConnection

```
package book.database;

import java.sql.Connection;
import java.sql.SQLException;
import java.sql.DriverManager;

import javax.servlet.ServletContext;

import book.util.LocalStrings;

public class DbConnection implements DbConnectionWrapper {

    static LocalStrings ls =
        LocalStrings.getLocalStrings(DbConnection.class);

    protected String id;
    protected ServletContext app;
    protected String dburl;
    protected String dbuser;
    protected String dbpass;
    protected Connection con;

    public DbConnection(String id,
                        ServletContext app,
                        String dburl,
                        String dbuser,
                        String dbpass)
    {
        this.id = id;
        this.app = app;
        this.dburl = dburl;
```

```
        this.dbuser = dbuser;
        this.dbpass = dbpass;
        this.con = null;
    }

    public Connection getConnection()
        throws SQLException
    {
        if(con == null) {
            con = DriverManager.getConnection(dburl,          ❶
                                              dbuser,
                                              dbpass);
        }

        return con;
    }

    public void freeConnection()
    {
        try {
            if(null != con) {          ❷
                con.close();
            }
        } catch(Throwable t) {
            app.log(ls.getStr(Constants.SQL_EXCEPTION), t);
        }
    }

    protected void finalize()
        throws Throwable
    {
        freeConnection();          ❸
    }
}
```

❶ **Creates the connection once and returns it thereafter** ❷ **Closes the connection (avoids database resource leak)** ❸ **When garbage-collected, makes sure connections are closed** In essence, DbConnection keeps the JDBC parameters that were handed over to the tag and later creates a JDBC connection to a database as specified in the parameters. It also ensures that the connection is closed by:

- Providing a method named freeConnection() that allows a user class to free the encapsulated connection (created on the first call to getConnection())
- Implementing finalize(), ensuring that even if the using class (or JSP) does not call freeConnection(), it will be called when the object is garbage-collected. Relying on the garbage collector to free the connection is not always a great idea; it may execute after we lose interest in the connection, and relying on it could cause us to waste the connection resource for this duration.

A class that wishes to use the database connection encapsulated within DbConnection should first call getConnection(), thereby triggering the connection's creation and getting a reference to it. Later, the connection should be used and, when the user is through with it, the user should release it by calling freeConnection().

NOTE   The JIT capabilities that we wanted to inject into our database library are coming to life with the implementation of DbConnectionTag and DbConnection. These two classes cooperate to ensure that the connection is created only when getConnection() is called. A different implementation, for example one in which the tag creates the connection and simply lets DbConnection close it, would jeopardize the JIT goal, as it would create the connection before using it.

11.6.2 *SQLQueryTag*

SQLQueryTag is, of course, the tag that actually performs the SQL query and shares the results of this query with the JSP. Recall from our discussion of tags' information sharing, that SQLQueryTag engages in a great deal of sharing in performing its job. First, it gets the DbConnectionWrapper that DBConnectionTag has put into scope for it, and uses that connection to create a DbQueryResult which implements the DbResultWrapper interface. It then shares the results of the query by placing the DbQueryResult in the JSP environment. We present SQLQueryTag in listing 11.7.

Listing 11.7   Source code for the SQLQueryTag handler class

```
package book.database;

import javax.servlet.jsp.PageContext;
import javax.servlet.jsp.JspException;

import book.util.LocalStrings;
import book.util.BodyReaderTag;

public class SQLQueryTag extends BodyReaderTag {

    static LocalStrings ls =
        LocalStrings.getLocalStrings(SQLQueryTag.class);

    protected String connection = null;

    public void setConnection(String connection)
    {
        this.connection = connection;
    }

    protected void processBody(String content)
        throws JspException
```

```
    {
            exportWrapper(getDbConnectionWrapper(), content);        ❶
    }

    protected void exportWrapper(DbConnectionWrapper c,
                                    String query)
        throws JspException
    {
        pageContext.setAttribute(id,          ❷
                        new DBQueryResult(id,
                                            query,
                                            getServletContext(),
                                            c),
                        PageContext.PAGE_SCOPE);
    }

    protected DbConnectionWrapper getDbConnectionWrapper()
        throws JspException
    {
        return
        (DbConnectionWrapper)pageContext.findAttribute(connection);        ❸
    }

    protected void clearProperties()
    {
        connection = null;
        super.clearProperties();
    }
}
```

❶ **Exports a wrapper with the related connection and query string.**

❷ **Exports the result wrapper variable into the JSP environment.**

❸ **Finds the connection wrapper in the JSP environment.**

SQLQueryTag is unique in that not all of its parameters come from its attributes. In fact, the single most important parameter, the SQL query, is provided within the tag's body (which is why SQLQueryTag is a BodyTag). The reasons for making the SQL query provided within the body are elementary: the query is a relatively complex parameter that may span several lines and we may want to embed dynamic content within it. Consider the following query:

```
select * from product
where cost > <%= request.getParameter("mincost") %>
order by name
```

This is a valid SQL query with dynamic content in the where clause, but it cannot be specified in a mere tag attribute. It is, however, completely reasonable to encapsulate it within the JSP body of the query tag.

SQLQueryTag provides the first incidence within this library wherein two tags communicate using the JSP environment. In getDbConnectionWrapper() we are looking for the DbConnectionWrapper object that was previously exported to the JSP environment, and whose name is within a mandatory query tag attribute to be provided by the user. This shows us how the two tag handlers are not programmed to work with each other, and yet manage to cooperate by exchanging objects using the JSP environment table.

The next code fragment shows the TLD entry for SQLQueryTag. SQLQueryTag is an easy to use single attribute and body-based input tag but, as we will later see, the need to point with the attribute to a specific DbConnectionWrapper is not especially convenient.

```
<tag>
    <name>query</name>
    <tagclass>book.database.SQLQueryTag</tagclass>
    <teiclass>book.database.DbResultExtraInfo</teiclass>
    <bodycontent>JSP</bodycontent>
    <info>
        Defines a database query. The SQL query should be enclosed
        within the body of the tag. The connection attribute should
        point to a valid connection tag id.
    </info>
    <attribute>
        <name>id</name>
        <required>true</required>
        <rtexprvalue>false</rtexprvalue>
    </attribute>
    <attribute>
        <name>connection</name>
        <required>true</required>
        <rtexprvalue>false</rtexprvalue>
    </attribute>
</tag>
```

DBQueryResult

In much the same way as DbConnection implemented the generic DbConnection-Wrapper interface, DbQueryResult implements the DbQueryResultWrapper interface, which we wrote as a wrapper to provide access to a JDBC ResultSet. DBQueryResult is the merging point between the connection and query information, and is also where the actual SQL query is executed. In a nutshell, it uses DbConnectionWrapper and the SQL query string defined by SQLQueryTag to perform an SQL query over the connection contained in DbConnectionWrapper. From a timing perspective, DBQueryResult performs the query only when the query's

ResultSet is called upon. Database resources such as connections and results are therefore allocated on demand and only upon explicit request.

Listing 11.8   Source code for DBQueryResult

```java
package book.database;

import java.sql.Connection;
import java.sql.SQLException;
import java.sql.Statement;
import java.sql.ResultSet;

import javax.servlet.ServletContext;

import book.util.LocalStrings;

public class DBQueryResult implements DbResultWrapper {

    static LocalStrings ls =
        LocalStrings.getLocalStrings(DBQueryResult.class);

    protected String id;
    protected String querySql;
    protected ServletContext app;
    protected DbConnectionWrapper c;
    protected Connection con;
    protected Statement st;
    protected ResultSet rs;

    public DBQueryResult(String id,
                         String querySql,
                         ServletContext app,
                         DbConnectionWrapper c)
    {
        this.id = id;
        this.querySql = querySql;
        this.app = app;
        this.c = c;
        this.con = null;
        this.st = null;
        this.rs = null;
    }

    public ResultSet getResultSet()
        throws SQLException
    {
        if(null == rs) {                    ❶
            boolean finished = false;
            try {
                con = c.getConnection();
                st = con.createStatement();       ❷
                rs = st.executeQuery(querySql);
                finished = true;
            } catch(SQLException sqe) {
```

```
                    app.log(ls.getStr(Constants.SQL_EXCEPTION), sqe);
                    throw sqe;
                } finally {
                    if(!finished && null != con) {
                        freeResult();
                    }
                }
            }

        return rs;
    }

    public void freeResult()
    {
        closeJdbcObjects();
        id = null;
        querySql = null;
        app = null;
        c = null;
        con = null;
        st = null;
        rs = null;
    }

    protected void closeJdbcObjects()
    {
        if(null != rs) {
            try { rs.close(); } catch (Throwable t) {}
        }
        if(null != st) {
            try { st.close(); } catch (Throwable t) {}
        }
        if(null != con) {
            try { c.freeConnection(); } catch (Throwable t) {}
        }
    }

    protected void finalize()
        throws Throwable
    {
        freeResult();
    }
}
```

❸ at `if(!finished && null != con) {`

❹ at `closeJdbcObjects();`

❺ at `try { rs.close(); } catch (Throwable t) {}`

❻ at `freeResult();`

❶ **Makes the query the first time only.**

❷ **Performs the query on the connection enclosed within the connection wrapper.**

❸ **Makes sure that all resources are freed upon errors** DBQueryResult exerts a considerable effort to ensure that nothing will cause database resource leaking, and its first concern is in the method that allocates these resources. When opening the connection, DBQueryResult traces the resource allocation and, if there are errors, will make sure that all the resources are freed.

❹ Frees all database resources and nulls the internal state (to mark closure)   ❺ Closes all database resources, ignores exceptions   ❻ When garbage-collected, makes sure database resources are freed DBQueryResult also prevents resource leaking in the location in which freeResult(), closeJdbcObjects(), and finalize() are implemented. A class using DBQueryResult should make sure that it calls freeResult() to free all the database resources. freeResult() will call closeJdbcObjects() forcing closure on all database resources, even if exceptions are thrown (exceptions are ignored). On a final note, if freeResult() is not called, DBQueryResult implements finalize() to make sure that resources are freed upon garbage collection.

From the previous code listings, DBQueryResult and DbConnection clearly cooperate to provide database results to anyone wishing to use them. It is time now to present this using a class, which happens to be the database results enumerator tag—EnumRsTag.

11.6.3 *EnumRsTag*

It is EnumRsTag that brings the work of DBConnectionTag and SQLQueryTag to fruition, by permitting access to the values of an SQL query. It uses the DBQueryResult that SQLQueryTag puts into scope to obtain the wrapped ResultSet and to iterate on the ResultSet rows. EnumRsTag is a descendant of IterationTagSupport, from which it inherits iteration (and iterator export) capabilities. Using these capabilities means that EnumRsTag should implement the method fetchIteration-Support() and use it to set an IterationSupport object and (optionally) a Field-Getter in cases in which we want field placement.

Listing 11.9   Source code for the EnumRsTag handler class

```
package book.database;

import java.sql.SQLException;

import book.util.LocalStrings;
import book.util.LibraryConfig;

import book.iteration.IterationTagSupport;

import javax.servlet.jsp.JspException;

public class EnumRsTag extends IterationTagSupport   {

    static LocalStrings ls =
        LocalStrings.getLocalStrings(EnumRsTag.class);

    protected String query = null;
    protected DbResultWrapper rs = null;
```

```
public void setQuery(String query)
{
    this.query = query;
}

protected void fetchIterationSupport()
    throws JspException
{
    rs = (DbResultWrapper)pageContext.findAttribute(query);    ❶

    if(null == rs) {
        // Throw an exception
    }

    try {                                                      ❷
        elementsList =
            new ResultSetIterationSupport(rs.getResultSet());
    } catch(SQLException sqe) {
        // Throw an exception
    }
    if(LibraryConfig.isJDBCFieldPlacementInUse()) {
        fGetter = new JDBCFieldGetter();
    }
}

protected void clearProperties()
{
    query = null;
    super.clearProperties();
}

protected void clearServiceState()
{
    if(null != rs) {          ❸
        rs.freeResult();
    }
    rs = null;
    super.clearServiceState();
}
}
```

❶ **Fetches the result wrapper from the JSP environment**   ❷ **Sets the support objects into the iteration infrastructure**   fetchIterationSupport() starts by referencing the DbResultWrapper from the JSP environment. We assume nothing about this DbResultWrapper, and we especially do not assume that it is an instance of DBQueryResult, is exactly what it is. We simply call its getResultSet() method to obtain the wrapped ResultSet. Having this ResultSet, we need to provide an IterationSupport for it. Fortunately, we have implemented the requisite support objects for our previous (and plain) result set iteration tag, and can reuse them now.

❸ **Frees the database resources** After setting the support objects, the generic iteration code developed in chapter 10 will perform all the iteration-related work we need in EnumRsTag, so our next implementation stop is to clean up the tag's state. EnumRsTag has a very important state associated with it, the database result wrapper. Failing to free the result wrapper will result in severe resource leaks, which we must avoid. Happily, freeing the wrapper state is an easy chore since we already have a state clearing callback designed for this type of work, clearServiceState(), and now we only need to use it to free our wrapper.

Handling exceptions (and preventing resource leaks) in EnumRsTag

You may wonder what might result if an exception is thrown somewhere in the body of EnumRsTag, the likely locus of our resource leaking if we fail to catch the exception and properly close the database resources. In order to answer this, let's take a look at the following code fragment taken from our ExBodyTagSupport base class.

```
public int doEndTag()
    throws JspException
{
    clearServiceState();
    return super.doEndTag();
}

public void release()
{
    clearServiceState();
    clearProperties();
    super.release();
}
```

You probably recognize this as the JSP1.1 clean-up code used by all our tags for cleaning up their resources after use. clearServiceState() is called twice: in doEndTag() (if no exception is thrown), and in release(), which is more central to the current discussion, because in JSP1.1 release() always executes, even in the face of exceptions. In JSP1.2 we can use the TryFinally interface, making our work easier. Our implementation is safe, because the servlet generated from the JSP file places the call to release() in a finally clause. Look at the following code fragment that was generated by Tomcat's JSP1.1 translator.

```
book.database.EnumRsTag _jspx_th_db_enum_0 = new book.database.EnumRsTag();
jspx_th_db_enum_0.setPageContext(pageContext);
jspx_th_db_enum_0.setParent(null);
JspRuntimeLibrary.introspecthelper(_jspx_th_db_enum_0, "id","i",null,null,
    false);
JspRuntimeLibrary.introspecthelper(_jspx_th_db_enum_0,
    "query","above12",null,null, false);
try {
    int _jspx_eval_db_enum_0 = _jspx_th_db_enum_0.doStartTag();
```

```
    // some code was omitted …
    if (_jspx_th_db_enum_0.doEndTag() == Tag.SKIP_PAGE)
        return;
} finally {
    jspx_th_db_enum_0.release();
}
```

Tomcat placed the `release()` call in the `finally` section; hence, `release()` will execute even if an exception happens inside `EnumRsTag`'s body. Calling `release()` will, of course, result in a call to `clearServiceState()` which will ultimately free the database result. This confirms the safety of our design, since we can now be assured that, *no matter what*, our database resources are cleared.

EnumRsTag's TLD

With `EnumRsTag` complete, we are only one TLD entry away from being able to use it with the query and connection tags. `EnumRsTag`'s TLD entry is presented in the next code fragment. Note that it has only two attributes: `id` to define the iterator identifier, and `query` to define the result that we are about to present.

```
<tag>
    <name>enum</name>
    <tagclass>book.database.EnumRsTag</tagclass>
    <teiclass>book.database.EnumRsTagExtraInfo</teiclass>
    <bodycontent>JSP</bodycontent>
    <info>
        Presents a database result set.
    </info>

    <attribute>
        <name>id</name>
        <required>true</required>
        <rtexprvalue>false</rtexprvalue>
    </attribute>

    <attribute>
        <name>query</name>
        <required>true</required>
        <rtexprvalue>false</rtexprvalue>
    </attribute>
</tag>
```

11.6.4 Using our library for the first time

We can now create the first JSP file that uses our new database tag library. We won't start with anything fancy, just a JSP file that accesses a database and presents the query results in a table. The uniqueness of this file (listing 11.10) however, is that we manage to query a database table from it without using even a single scriptlet or importing any Java class into our JSP. For the purpose of this as well as other samples that use database through this book, we are using an open-source, pure Java database called Hypersonic SQL which we've populated with some autogenerated data.

Listing 11.10 A JSP file that uses the database library

```
<%@ page errorPage="error.jsp" %>
<%@ taglib
    uri="http://www.manning.com/jsptagsbook/database-taglib"
    prefix="db" %>
<html>
<head>
<title> Database query results </title>
</head>
<body>
    <h1> Database manipulation  </h1>
    Creating a connection, query a database and presenting the
    results. All from within JSP tags. <br>
    <db:connection id="con"
                   user="sa"
                   url="jdbc:HypersonicSQL:http://localhost:8090/"
                   driver="org.hsql.jdbcDriver" />


    <db:query connection="con" id="above12">
    select * from product where cost > 12
    </db:query>

    <table border="1"  bgcolor="#c0c0c0">
        <tr>
            <th bgcolor="#a0a0a0">id</th>
            <th bgcolor="#a0a0a0">Name</th>
            <th bgcolor="#a0a0a0">Cost</th>
        </tr>
        <db:enum query="above12" id="i">
        <tr>
            <td> <$ ID $> </td>
            <td> <$ NAME $> </td>
            <td> <$ COST $> </td>
        </tr>
        </db:enum>
    </table>
</body>
</html>
```

❶ **Defines a connection to the database** The first tag encountered here is the connection tag. We define a JDBC connection named con to the Hypersonic SQL database and provide almost all of the JDBC connection properties, except for the user's password (a null password works fine for this database connection).

❷ **Defines the query that we'll be making** Immediately after defining the connection, we define the query that we are going to execute over the database. Note how the SQL query is defined. Later, we will see how to construct an SQL query with values taken from dynamic data; but for the purpose of this sample, a static SQL query will suffice. The query tag references the connection using its connection attribute; this is why we must define the connection before approaching the query.

❸ **Enumerates the results** This is where we enumerate the result and present it to the user. Up to now we did not implement a special tag to present the result's rows, and we have to work with the field getter supplied by the iteration tag.

❹ **Presents the results with our field getter** `<db:enum>` comes with a long list of responsibilities:

- Coordinating the database access by using the result object.
- Iterating on the results.
- Reading and presenting the results.

Yet, since `EnumRsTag` was built out of several layers (each with its own responsibility), programming it to perform all these tasks was relatively easy (and actually didn't require special JSP or web knowledge).

When we test the JSP file in listing 11.10, it produces the results in figure 11.4. Voila! We can now access a database, issue a query, and present the response by writing a JSP with absolutely *no* Java scriptlets required.

11.6.5 *ViewRsTag*

Our current library supports almost all of our original requirements; however, one thing is still missing—a tag to present the value of a particular field (column) in a query's result. Why might we need such a tag, since we seemed to be doing just fine with the field placement extension? Is a code segment that looks like:

```
<td> <db:view query="i" field="ID"/> </td>
```

preferable to:

```
<td> <$ ID $> </td> ?
```

In fact, you might even say that the `<db:view/>` tag is clumsy compared to the elegant (and short) field placement. Why then do we need a presentation tag?

For several reasons:

- Our field placement extension added a nonstandard feature to the library that some users may reject. Tags are the standard way of doing things on the Web and purist web developers may not like using other syntax.

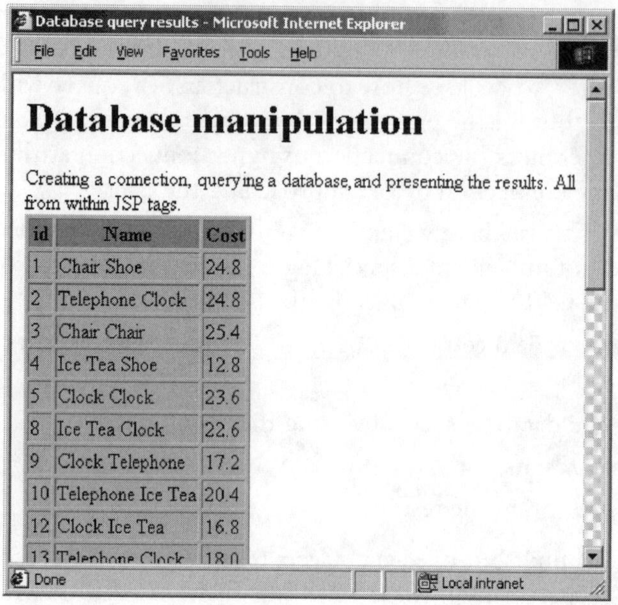

Figure 11.4 Accessing a database with the database tag library

- There is overhead associated with the parsing of the iteration tag body, especially when the body is relatively long.

- It is very easy for tools to integrate with tags. JSP development tools can use the TLD to find out about tags and their attributes, but the field placement is a proprietary feature hidden in our tags.

- In JSP1.2 the `IterationTag` interface works well to implement bufferless iteration. Our field placement mechanism will not work with the `Iteration-Tag` interface, yet the `<db:view/>` tag will.

For these reasons we've decided to develop the `ViewRsTag`, which is the `ResultSet` column viewer tag in listing 11.11. `ViewRsTag` accepts two parameters through its attributes: the name of the JSP environment attribute under which the `ResultSet` is stored (the iterator as exported by `EnumRsTag`) and the name of the column the tag should present. We can then use `ViewRsTag` to present the columns in the iterator object that `EnumRsTag` exports.

Listing 11.11   Source code for the ViewRsTag handler class

```java
package book.database;

import java.sql.ResultSet;
import java.sql.SQLException;

import javax.servlet.jsp.JspException;

import book.util.LocalStrings;
import book.util.ExTagSupport;

public class ViewRsTag extends ExTagSupport {

    static LocalStrings ls =
        LocalStrings.getLocalStrings(ViewRsTag.class);

    protected String query = null;
    protected String field = null;

    public void setQuery(String query)
    {
        this.query = query;
    }

    public void setField(String field)
    {
        this.field = field;
    }

    public int doStartTag()
            throws JspException
    {
        ResultSet rs = null;
        try {
            rs = (ResultSet)pageContext.findAttribute(query);        ❶
            if(null != rs) {
                writeHtml(pageContext.getOut(),                      ❷
                        rs.getString(field));
            }
            return SKIP_BODY;
        } catch(java.io.IOException ioe) {
            // Throw an exception
        } catch(SQLException sqe) {
            // Throw an exception
        }
    }

    protected void clearProperties()
    {
        query = null;
        field = null;
        super.clearProperties();
    }
}
```

❶ Fetches the ResultSet **from the JSP environment.**

❷ Writes the wanted column value to the response.

ViewRsTag in action

Armed with our new presentation tag, we can now develop database presentation
JSPs without using field placement. One such JSP file is presented in listing 11.12.

Listing 11.12   A JSP file that uses the view tag to present column values

```
<%@ page errorPage="error.jsp" %>
<%@ taglib
    uri="http://www.manning.com/jsptagsbook/database-taglib"
    prefix="db" %>
<html>
<head>
<title> Database query results </title>
</head>
<body>
    <h1> Database manipulation  </h1>
    Creating a connection, query a database and presenting the
    results. All from within JSP tags. <br>
    <db:connection id="con"
                user="sa"
                url="jdbc:HypersonicSQL:http://localhost:8090/"
                driver="org.hsql.jdbcDriver" />

    <db:query connection="con" id="above12">                  ❶
    select * from product
    where cost > <%= request.getParameter("mincost") %>
    order by name
    </db:query>

    <table border="1"  bgcolor="#c0c0c0">
        <tr>
            <th bgcolor="#a0a0a0">id</th>
            <th bgcolor="#a0a0a0">Name</th>
            <th bgcolor="#a0a0a0">Cost</th>
        </tr>
        <db:enum query="above12" id="i">
        <tr>
            <td> <db:view field="ID" query="i"/> </td>        ❷
            <td> <db:view field="NAME" query="i"/> </td>
            <td> <db:view field="COST" query="i"/> </td>
        </tr>
        </db:enum>
    </table>
</body>
</html>
```

Figure 11.5   Tag-only database access results with constraint
on one of the columns`

❶ **Defines a query with dynamic parameters**   The query incorporates a request parameter into itself and uses it to select the type of rows to be presented. In our case, we are looking for a request parameter named `mincost` and using it as a condition in our SQL query. Because the SQL query is defined within the JSP body of the query tag, it is very easy to construct dynamic SQL queries using the known JSP syntax. The query tag then takes this query and uses it to select information from the database. Note that the SQL query spans a couple of lines, something that would not have been doable if the SQL query had been a tag attribute (due to an inherent rule for tag attributes that they be contained in a single line).

❷ **Presents the columns using tags**   The database results view tag frees us from the need to use the proprietary syntax associated with the field placement.

A sample result created by an execution of this listing is available in figure 11.5. In this execution, the `mincost` parameter has the value of `20`, which is reflected in the fact that all of the products we see in the table cost more then 20 dollars.

11.7 *Integrating a controller servlet with our new library*

To round out our implementation discussion, let's look at a basic integration between a controller servlet and a JSP that uses our database tags. This will not be anything extraordinary, just a servlet that integrates our wrapper objects with the database presentation tags (namely, the `EnumRsTag` and the `ViewRsTag`).

The first step in integrating the controller servlet and the JSP tags is to decide on the objects that the servlet will expose in the JSP runtime, allowing the tags to cooperate with the servlet. Generally speaking, the servlet may expose either a `DbConnectionWrapper` or a `DbResultWrapper`. In the first case, the JSP tags must define a query that uses the `DbConnectionWrapper` that would be exposed by the controller servlet. In the second case, the JSP tags will use the servlet-generated `DbResultWrapper` directly, and we will not have to define either of these through tags. In listing 11.12 is an example in which the servlet exposes a `DbResultWrapper`. Note that in one sense it reduces the flexibility associated with having the SQL defined in the JSP (because the query and database parameters are hard-coded in the servlet); however, it adds the ability to employ complex Java logic in constructing `DbConnectionWrapper` and `DbResultWrapper`. Such logic may verify the query parameters and gracefully check that the database is working.

11.7.1 *The controller servlet*

Listing 11.13 shows the core of the controller servlet. Interesting to note is how the servlet passes the created `DbResultWrapper` to the JSP file and the tags within it. (The logic that was used to create this is not of particular interest and depends on your actual case.)

Listing 11.13   Source code for the controller servlet

```
package book.util;

import java.io.IOException;
import book.database.*;
import javax.servlet.*;
import javax.servlet.http.*;

public class DbTagIntegrationControllerServlet extends HttpServlet {

    public void init(ServletConfig config)
        throws ServletException
    {
        super.init(config);

        try {
            Class.forName("org.hsql.jdbcDriver").newInstance();
```
❶

```
        } catch(Exception e) {
            // Log and throw an exception
        }
    }

    public void doGet(HttpServletRequest request,
                    HttpServletResponse response)
                    throws ServletException, IOException
    {
        RequestDispatcher rd =
            getServletContext().getRequestDispatcher("/dbexplorservlet.jsp");

        DbConnectionWrapper con =
            new DbConnection("servlet-creation-con",
                getServletContext(),
                "jdbc:HypersonicSQL:http://localhost:8090/",
                "sa",
                null);
        DbResultWrapper res =        ❷
            new DBQueryResult("servlet-creation-res",
                "select * from product where cost > 12",
                getServletContext(),
                con);
        request.setAttribute("above12", res);        ❸
        rd.include(request, response);
    }
}
```

❶ **Loads the JDBC driver** ❷ **Creates a `DbResultWrapper` to be presented in the JSP** One task faced by the controller servlet is to prepare the `DbResultWrapper` for use within the JSP tags. This portion of the code was oversimplified in listing 11.13. A real-world controller implementation would, of course, do much more than has been done here, such as create `DbConnectionWrapper` that uses some application's internal database connection pool, or construct a complex SQL query, and so forth. These are, however, application-specific details that vary from one application to another, but the method by which we expose `DbResultWrapper` stays the same.

❸ **Adds the `DbResultWrapper` to the request attributes and executes the JSP** As stated previously, our main event in the controller servlet is the method that we used to export a servlet-created object into the JSP attributes table. Exporting the attribute is not a daunting undertaking. It involves adding the object into the `ServletRequest` attributes along with a name for the attribute. Remember though, the exported attribute will never be a `page`-scoped attribute. The fact that the exported attributes do not arrive to the `page` scope is the reason why we used `findAttribute()` in our tags. You may recall from chapter 6, findAttribute() walks over all the available scopes and looks for the named attribute. Even if our attribute is request-scoped (which is the case with our controller servlet) or even session- or application-scoped, it will be found and returned to the tag.

11.7.2 *The JSP*

The second part of our servlet-JSP combination is, of course, the JSP file itself. Do we really need to change anything that we currently have in the JSP file? Yes, we need to remove all the tags that defined the database connection and the query since we no longer need them (the servlet will now be providing this functionality). Therefore, the JSP file can be slightly stripped down. Look at listing 11.14, which presents the JSP file that cooperates with the controller servlet.

Listing 11.14   A JSP file that uses the object exported from the servlet

```
<%@ page errorPage="error.jsp" %>
<%@ taglib
    uri="http://www.manning.com/jsptagsbook/database-taglib"
    prefix="db" %>
<html>
<head>
<title> Database query results </title>
</head>
<body>
    <h1> Database manipulation  </h1>
    Presenting a query that was defined in a controller servlet. <br>

    <table border="1"  bgcolor="#c0c0c0">
        <tr>
            <th bgcolor="#a0a0a0">id</th>
            <th bgcolor="#a0a0a0">Name</th>
            <th bgcolor="#a0a0a0">Cost</th>
        </tr>
        <db:enum query="above12" id="i">         ❶
        <tr>
            <td> <db:view field="ID" query="i"/> </td>
            <td> <db:view field="NAME" query="i"/> </td>
            <td> <db:view field="COST" query="i"/> </td>
        </tr>
        </db:enum>
    </table>
</body>
</html>
```

---

❶ **References the object that was exported from the servlet using its name**   The actual integration between the controller servlet and the JSP tags is accomplished via the

JSP attributes table, which is why we could drop the tag-generated wrappers and replace them with the servlet-generated objects. The JSP developer links the `<db:enum>` tag to the JSP attribute exported by the servlet using the attribute's name, which in our case is `above12`.

Listings 11.14 and 11.12 are very similar except that listing 11.14 omits the `<db:connection>` and `<db:query>` tags in listing 11.12. This is because the work that the tags did for us in listing 11.12 is now part of the controller servlet. The end result of the entire system is similar to that achieved with the JSP file in listing 11.12.

11.8 *Summary*

The main lesson we learned in this chapter was related to the tag library's functionality, but we were increasingly concerned with good database—and even general—tag design:

- Database resources conservation—By using JIT activation, we only allocate resources when we really need to.
- Prevention of resource leakage—By checking, double checking, and checking again, we can determine that all allocated database resources are freed, even if an exception occurs.
- Extensibility—By using interfaces to communicate between the different tags in the library we can switch a tag's implementation and still use the library.
- Integration with the Model-2 architecture—By using the JSP environment to exchange information, we make is possible for controller servlets to start the database access and hand the presentation task to the tags in the JSP file. All that these database presentation tags are required to do is to work with JSP environment entries created by servlets, and fetch the wrapper objects from them.

Although the library created in this chapter is quite versatile, there are plenty of enhancements from which it could benefit. It could, for instance, be improved by using the `ResultSet`'s metadata to print the data in a more content-oriented manner. From the metadata we could find the exact SQL type of a certain column and print its values accordingly; for example, we could format a date or currency column in a number of different ways.

Also missing from this library are tags for performing operations on the results (other than merely presenting them). It would be quite useful to have tags:

- Export column values as JSP variables so that scriptlets and other tags are able to use their value.

- Perform conditions on the values of certain columns. This functionality could be achieved by using the column value export tag previously described and the condition library implemented in chapter 9, but exporting the values and then posing a condition is not as slick as a single integrated tag.

- Perform updates on the database. Our library concentrates primarily on presenting data as it becomes available in the database; but one may also want to update the database directly from the JSP file.

This list could continue indefinitely, but, the purpose of this chapter not so much to create an exhaustive database tag library, as to encourage you to think like a tag developer and introduce the underlying design principles of the tag library.

In the next chapter, we examine how to use custom tags in accessing resources defined by the (J2EE) specification—such as email services, directory services, and Enterprise JavaBeans.

Custom tags and J2EE

In this chapter

- Introducing J2EE
- Introducing EJB
- Developing tags that work with J2EE resources
- Developing tags that work with EJB

Java 2 Enterprise Edition (J2EE) is a popular and very important standard that defines a Java environment for the development and deployment of enterprise applications. Among the standards included in J2EE are Enterprise Java Beans (EJBs) which is Java's enterprise component architecture, the Servlet API, Java Naming and Directory services (JNDI), Java Messaging Services (JMS), an email API (JavaMail) and Java Transaction Services (JTS). This significant feature list and the success of the Java language itself have contributed to a widespread adoption of the J2EE standard by software vendors. In fact, Sun Microsystems estimates that close to 90 percent of the application server market is already occupied by J2EE-compliant products.

By writing servlets, JSPs, and custom JSP tags, we've already dabbled in the realm of J2EE. However, the Servlet API only scratches the surface of the many programming standards set forth by J2EE. With all that this standard has to offer, the benefits that many web applications will derive come quickly to mind. We can easily imagine cases wherein our JSPs need to interact with J2EE's email API, or use its directory services to gain access to database or user information, or to interact with an EJB. As in most of our JSP tasks, building tags that facilitate interaction with J2EE can assist us in decoupling our presentation logic and business logic, and provide us with basic building blocks for code reuse.

We'll begin this chapter with an introduction to J2EE, zeroing in on EJBs. EJB is the standard for Java's enterprise component and is, therefore, a central part of many J2EE applications. Next we'll look at the environment J2EE services run in; namely, how services are defined and configured, and how one J2EE component shares information with another. Finally, we'll see how to begin leveraging all the great features of J2EE within our custom tags.

If you're sufficiently familiar with J2EE, you can jump ahead to section 12.4, in which we discuss building a custom tag that gets a database connection using J2EE. If this topic is new to you, read on to equip yourself with the tools you'll need for the subject matter to be covered later in this chapter.

12.1   *What is J2EE?*

J2EE is a platform definition for enterprise applications in Java: a set of several standards that Java developers can follow in building large-scale applications. Its goal is to streamline the building of distributed, enterprise-level applications in Java by giving developers a common set of services to use, a standard approach to, and a unified platform for application configuration. Since J2EE is no more than a collection of standards with integration semantics, we will look briefly at what those standards are and why they are a part of J2EE. Table 12.1 lists the standards included in the 1.3 version of the J2EE specification with a brief description of each:.

Table 12.1 The J2EE standards

Standard	Description
Enterprise Java Beans (EJB)	A standard component model for enterprise development in Java. This model serves the same purpose the JavaBean standard serves for ordinary Java applications.
Java Database Connectivity (JDBC)	A standard API for accessing databases.
Java Servlet API (includes JSP and custom JSP tags)	A standard for defining dynamic web components in Java.
Java Transaction API (JTA)	Defines an interface for J2EE application components to use for handling transactions.
JavaIDL	An API that allows Java components to communicate with objects defined in CORBA (Common Object Request Broker Architecture).
Java Message Service (JMS)	A standard API for messaging in Java, ultimately facilitating J2EE components to send point-to-point messages to one another, or to use a publish-subscribe approach.
Java Naming and Directory Interface (JNDI)	A standard API for listing and offering directory access to J2EE resources (such as a phone book for J2EE services).
JavaMail	A standard API for sending email.
Java API for XML Parsing (JAXP)	A standard API for parsing XML documents.
J2EE Connector Architecture	A standard interface that facilitates connectivity to existing legacy and other non-Java enterprise systems and services.
Java Authentication and Authorization Service (JAAS)	A standard API for authentication and enforcement of access control on users of a J2EE application.

We've already seen a couple of these standards in this book, namely JDBC (in chapter 11) and the Servlet API (which we've worked with since chapter 2). Of the other standards, a few (EJBs and JNDI) are used in many J2EE applications, while others (the connector architecture or JavaIDL) address needs that are not found in most applications. Though all of the standards in J2EE provide useful functions, we'll focus our attention on EJB, JNDI, JDBC, and JavaMail.

Before we delve too deeply into any one standard, let's look at J2EE application architecture (server components and their Java and non-Java clients), general deployment in J2EE, and why all of this fits so comfortably into custom JSP tags.

12.1.1 *J2EE server components and client access*

One axiom that can be promulgated of any J2EE application component is that it needs a place to run. When writing a J2EE component such as an EJB or a Servlet, we develop our Java code and compile the class, but then what? The components must be deployed to a site that actually runs them for our use. Part of the J2EE standard is the definition of server-side containers in which enterprise applications run. As seen in figure 12.1, the server-side components hosted in these containers are:

- Servlets and JSPs running inside a web container.

- EJBs running inside an EJB container.

These server components can be used by a number of clients (including Java components) that connect to the server entities:

- Stand-alone Java clients that can use JNDI to find EJBs (and other services) and then access them via a remote method invocation protocol such as RMI/IIOP.[1]

- Java applets running inside a user's browser can access either EJBs or servlets and JSP files using HTTP.

- HTML browsers can access servlets and JSP files using HTTP.

NOTE   Note that even though servlets and EJBs are server components, they are not excluded from acting as clients of other J2EE components. It is, in fact, quite common for a servlet or JSP or tag to interact with EJBs to get and set data within a web application. The same is true of EJBs that use other EJBs.

The server-side containers in J2EE not only run components like EJBs and JSPs, but provide them with lifecycle management and accessibility to other enterprise Java facilities such as JNDI, JDBC, JMS, JavaMail, as well as to other EJB and servlet/JSP components deployed in the same J2EE server. These containers create the playground in which all J2EE components and services operate, and are typically wrapped into a single product most commonly known as a J2EE application server. IBM WebSphere, BEA WebLogic, and Borland Application Server are just a few examples of J2EE application servers on the market.

---

[1] RMI is a remote method invocation infrastructure that allows a Java program to seamlessly call methods on objects located in remote Java virtual machines (JVMs). IIOP is the communication protocol that was selected for the J2EE RMI method calls.

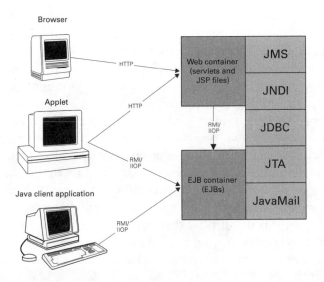

Figure 12.1   Clients and servers in J2EE

12.1.2 Deployment in J2EE

In addition to writing J2EE components, parts of the J2EE specification are standards for deploying and configuring applications. In J2EE, each application (or in the case of EJB, even a component) has a unique deployment descriptor containing metadata that instructs the container in deploying it, and includes a standard jar file structure (similar to the deployment descriptor and WAR format discussed in chapter 2). The deployment descriptors are XML documents with syntax as defined in the J2EE specification. These standards-based deployment descriptors and the jar file structure are essential when it comes to deploying an application, since the deployment tools can take the standard jar file and automatically import it into the application server's configuration repository. This standard, easy deployment is one of the strengths of the J2EE architecture, ensuring that any J2EE-compliant component is deployable on any J2EE-compliant product (no matter which vendor actually makes the product). As a J2EE developer you can take the EJBs and JSPs written for your WebLogic server and run them on a WebSphere server with no fear of incompatibility.

12.1.3 Why custom tags and J2EE are a good fit

Now that you know what J2EE is, why is it so important to you, the JSP custom tag developer? Knowing how much J2EE offers—from a rich email API to a scaleable, enterprise-level component model—it isn't difficult to imagine how your applications might benefit from it. Since JSP files may execute within J2EE-compliant application servers, with all those services available, you are likely to want or even need one or more of these standards in many of your web applications. For example, common tasks such as fetching a database connection or sending an email within your tags will require you to use J2EE standard interfaces. This chapter will demonstrate how to use many of these J2EE facilities from within your custom JSP tags.

The first J2EE member we'll study, in anticipation of integrating it into our custom tags, is EJBs. In many applications, one common task for your custom tag will be to interact with EJBs. EJBs can be used to encapsulate business logic and database access at a very high level, letting the EJB container (the software in which the EJBs run) take care of low-level details such as generating proper SQL statements and handling transactions. These benefits render EJBs a popular choice for building software components; thus, it is no surprise that you will often need to let your dynamic web site (and namely, your custom tags) communicate with these server-side beans. Before we discuss how this interaction works, let's take a moment to further specify what EJBs are.

12.2   What are EJBs, and why learn of them?

You can't go anywhere in the Java world without seeing or hearing about EJBs. There are currently some twenty-seven EJB container implementations available on the market, and there have been dozens of white papers written about creating dynamic web sites using EJBs. What is all the fuss? We answer this question and provide an overview of EJB in the following sections. After this introduction we will look at a sample EJB to clarify the concepts introduced in the coming sections.

12.2.1 EJBs—What are they?

The EJB specification is a distributed, secure, scalable, and transaction-aware component architecture for Java. In one sense, EJBs are the industrial-strength version of the JavaBean component standard. Both standards define a way of packaging Java code in objects to make them usable by other Java code. The similarities end there, however, since EJBs offer much more functionality and control than simple JavaBeans.

Its specification defines how an EJB container (the software that hosts and runs EJBs) instantiates and manages EJBs, how clients locate these components and/or call methods on them, and how Java developers can write an EJB.

One of the greatest attributes of this technology is that it defines a framework that makes it easy to develop distributed and transactional business logic components without having to consider the painstaking details of coding transaction and distribution logic. Such magic is possible because the EJB container and

J2EE-compliant deployment tools create the necessary code to handle functionality such as distribution, load balancing, fault tolerance, and transactions.

The anatomy of an EJB

To produce a component that benefits from the services offered by an EJB container, the developer has only to follow the EJB guidelines for creating one. These guidelines specify a number of classes and interfaces that need to be created for each EJB, with each class and interface filling a specific role for the component. Table 12.2 lists the pieces of an EJB:

Table 12.2   The parts of an EJB

Class/Interface	Description
EJB Home interface	Offers methods for finding, creating, and removing a particular EJB.
EJB Remote interface	Offers the business methods that your EJB will expose.
EJB Implementation class	The actual Java class that implements the methods in the Remote Interface.
EJB Primary Key class (optional)	A class that represents the data that makes a particular entity EJB unique (such as a primary key in a relational database table).

If you follow the EJB specification of first creating these classes and interfaces, then deploying them properly to an EJB container, the container will run the bean and make it available to other Java code that requires access to it.

EJB container

The EJB container as sketched in figure 12.2 is where EJB components live. The container manages the EJB components' lifecycles and exposes the components by listing each EJB within a JNDI directory (which acts like a phone book for EJBs). Clients use the JNDI API to look up a particular EJB by name, then receive a reference to the home interface of that EJB.

Using the home interface, the client can obtain a reference to the specific EJB by creating it or by finding an existing instance of it that is already running in the container. After obtaining the reference to the needed EJB, the client can invoke methods on it.

These method invocations appear to the client code as if they are taking place in the same way they would on any other Java object within the local VM. However, behind the scenes, calling a method uses RMI over IIOP to communicate with an

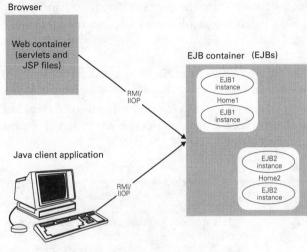

Figure 12.2   The EJB container, homes, and EJBs

EJB which is typically running on a different machine. This seamless support for distributed computing is one of the benefits of the J2EE standard.

What do we mean when we say that an EJB container manages the EJB's lifecycle? The EJB specification defines a certain set of states, state transition rules, and a method calling protocol for EJB components. The container is responsible for the state of a particular EJB and that state is unknown to any client. When a client wants to access a particular bean, the container may already have it in memory, may create a new instance of it, or may activate an instance that was previously in memory and has been "passivated" (a process that persists the current contents of the bean to disk or some other persistent storage). As a result, the container freely moves its EJBs between the allowed states to conserve scarce resources and to sustain transaction integrity.

For example, if a certain EJB instance is no longer in use, the container will passivate the bean and return it to the bean instance pool for reuse. In fact, some EJBs can be reused after any method call. Though this management by the container helps control transactions and maintain valuable server resources, it does present some development considerations; such as, at no point can the EJB developer assume that an EJB is in memory, since the container may have chosen to passivate it for memory conservation.

12.2.2 *Types of EJB components*

There are two main flavors of EJB components, *session EJBs* and *entity EJBs*.

Session EJBs

Session EJBs can be used to control complex transactional operations and to model business processes. In plainer terms, session beans are components that typically perform any logic or calculations that are useful for your application. You might use a session EJB to control online order processing using a credit card. The bean would need to verify the credit card, place the order inside the order database, and actually charge the credit card. A session EJB is used in performing simple distributed services such as sending an email. It can be used by a single client application, and may be seen as the application's remote hand on the server side. Typically, a session bean only exists for the duration of the client's session, and only one client will access any single instance of a session bean.

There are two subtypes of session EJBs differentiated by their state preservation policy: *stateless* and *stateful*. Stateless session EJBs do not keep state between method calls. Stateful beans, on the other hand, accumulate state information that carries from method call to method call, but this does not override server shutdown or crash. When a stateful session bean is destroyed, so is the state information it contains.

Entity EJBs

Entity EJBs are persistent, domain-specific objects that model a record located in some persistent storage (usually in a database). An entity EJB can represent a credit card, saving account, catalogue item, user account or any other real-world object that has persistent data. Unlike the typical session bean model, entity beans may be used by multiple clients and persist indefinitely, even in the face of server shutdown and crash. Each entity EJB has a *primary key*, its identity, which makes sense when you consider that an entity bean almost always represents a record of data in a database. User applications search for entity beans based on their primary key, and occasionally based on other EJB attributes.

There are two subtypes of entity EJBs differentiated by their state persistency mechanism, *Bean Managed Persistency* (BMP) and *Container Managed Persistency* (CMP). BMP entity EJBs implement persistency on their own; the container manages the transactions for them, but the code that persists them (such as JDBC code for storing the bean's data in a database) needs to be written by the EJB developer. By contrast, CMP entity EJBs let the container implement their persistency, which typically includes the container automatically generating JDBC and SQL related code and storing the bean's data using this generated code. The CMP capabilities available in EJB are very important for several reasons, but the three most important are:

1   We eliminate coding the persistency (saves lots of development time).

2   Since the persistency code is gone, the EJBs are now database agnostic. You can switch databases and still use the same EJBs.

3   The container can perform persistency optimizations in the container level (opens the door to major performance improvements).

On the other hand, CMP EJBs are notorious for their poor performance and limited persistency capabilities. More complicated entity beans, such as those that pull their data from multiple tables, often have nontrivial persistence rules that the container cannot know. For these nontrivial cases, the EJB developer must write the persistence code that stores the bean's properties back into the database.

It is also important to know that the EJB container supports automatic transaction management. It is possible to write an EJB without any transaction aware code; however, during the deployment the administrator may assign transaction properties to the EJB method so that this method will take part in a transaction. This capability greatly simplifies any transaction related job, and eliminates a lot of hard work and complex transaction management code.

The differences between session and entity beans

Entity and session EJBs are quite different in a number of ways:

- Session EJBs are transient; entity EJBs persist forever.
- A single session EJB's instance can be used by a single client; an entity EJB can be used by many clients.
- An entity EJB may be looked up by using a primary key that identifies it; there is no real identity for a session EJB.
- Session EJBs are used to model a certain process and logic; entity EJBs are used to model a persistent real-world object.

To clarify the differences, imagine we need to develop a set of EJBs for an airline application. The EJBs should offer functionality that lets the airline system book and cancel reservations, as well as keep track of open seats for each flight. It should be clear that flights, seats, and orders will need to be persistent objects, to be stored as records in our database, thus, we should make these items entity EJBs. In addition to these persistent objects, our system also needs to support several operations:

- List all free seats for a particular flight.
- List all reserved seats for a particular flight.
- Reserve a seat.
- Cancel a seat reservation.
- List all flights from city *x* to city *y*.

These are logical operations in our system; we therefore package them as session EJBs, with methods implementing each operation. As there is no need for us to keep track of any state (each of these operations is autonomous and independent) we use the stateless variety of session beans. Our example also needs some transactional support. For instance, the method that reserves a seat should modify the state of a certain seat by using its entity EJB, and then creating a new EJB to represent the reservation. To maintain the system in its correct state, both operations must be performed under the same distributed transaction, which the container manages for us automatically (provided we indicate the transactional methods at deployment time).

Let's now see what EJBs can do for us.

12.2.3 *EJBs and their functions*

We mentioned that J2EE has two different container types, the web container (that manages servlet and JSP files) and the EJB container (that manages EJBs), but we did not discuss the differences between EJBs and servlet/JSPs. Though their differences might seem quite stark, EJBs and servlets do have a few attributes in common:

- Both are server-side components managed by a container.
- Both are distributed.
- In both, the containers can provide scalability and fault tolerance.

What then is the real difference? The answer sheds light on using EJBs inside web applications.

EJBs vs servlets

The major difference between these two specifications is the type of solution each offers. Servlets are stream-oriented services, designed from the start with one goal in mind: serving stream-based clients such as web browsers. The HTTP servlets in web applications were designed for one purpose only: to serve web clients. EJBs, on the other hand, were designed to provide *generic*, secure, transactional, and distributed components—pure overkill when it comes to serving HTML, but exactly what you need to build scalable distributed data based models.

EJBs cannot accept HTTP requests (at least not in a natural way), so they cannot serve requests emanating from a browser. An EJB cannot then implement the presentation and control layers for a web application. On the other hand, servlets and servlet-derived technologies such as JSP are great when implementing web presentation and control, but have no built-in provisions to handle distributed transactions. Where do the EJBs shine? They shine in implementing transaction and database oriented application models. Moreover, EJBs, unlike servers, can be easily called from any Java-based client.

We'll borrow from the Model-2 approach to summarize: in a web application, servlets and JSPs construct the controllers and the views. The model (where the data is stored) that is manipulated by the controller servlet and presented by the JSP (the view) can be implemented in any number of ways. We've seen examples in which the model is a set of JavaBeans representing business data for our application, or where it is a set of JDBC calls that get and set data directly from and to a database—without even a JavaBean object wrapper. These models work well for many different applications; however, under certain conditions, the model is best implemented using EJBs.

When to use EJBs

What are the conditions under which EJBs are a good fit for the model in our Model-2 (MVC) web application? The answer is in the benefits of EJBs:

- EJB gives you easy-to-use transactions. If your application needs distributed transactions, you should use EJBs.

- EJB lets you distribute the work among different computers with ease. For example, you may decide that for management/performance reasons you should place the entire database access code on a limited set of nodes and provide access to the information located in the database via entity EJBs.

- You can improve the scalability of your model by adding a tier between the servlets and the databases (sometimes at the expense of response time). This tier is probably going to be an EJB tier as EJB components and their containers are the perfect fit for this task. Better scalability is achieved because the EJB container provides smart resource pooling as well as queuing of incoming requests. In addition, the container may also provide smart data caching (depending on the vendor). You can probably develop these capabilities yourself, but it would take a great deal of time to do so, and life is too short. Use EJBs.

- If your application model needs to be accessible to many types of clients, EJBs can help. Imagine that the model we are using must serve clients arriving from the web (with the help of servlets, JSP, and custom tags), nontraditional web clients (such as those using WAP and VoiceXML browsers), and corporate employees using a full Java application to access the model information. By storing most of the model inside a set of EJBs you make it possible to use the same model with all clients. Additionally, such design can also solve the scalability/performance problems that often occur when multiple clients access a database directly.

- Though the EJB market is young, many foresee a strong market for EJB components in the future. In such a market you will be able to buy (perhaps pick up for free) existing components for your applications. EJB technology makes incorporating these third-party EJB products a cinch.

Despite all their benefits, EJBs are not the Holy Grail. Developing simple models with EJBs is not as effortless as developing a standard JavaBean model utility class. Adding needless EJBs to your application is likely to increase development effort and may even reduce performance. Like any new technology, sometimes a developer's desire to use something cool and cutting-edge can overshadow smart design decisions. There is a cost associated to use this technology. For many applications, these costs are minute compared to the benefits of gaining a scalable, transactional platform to which you may deploy large applications. For other systems, the benefits of using EJBs do not outweigh the costs. In short, if your application cannot realize a clear benefit from using EJBs, you are best off avoiding them.

12.2.4 *Example: catalogue entry EJB*

Let's solve a problem using an EJB. We shall only take on a very small problem and in the process develop a fairly elementary EJB, but this exercise will demonstrate how EJBs are written and hosted by the container. All the interfaces and objects we create in this example will adhere to the EJB1.1 specification which instructs us as to which types of exceptions should be thrown, valid method call return types, and the like.

For this example, imagine that we have a catalogue of products which we keep in a database. The catalogue is a collection of many entries with each entry keyed off the product's serial number. Each entry also has fields such as the product's name, price, description, and so on. We want to provide easy access to the information in these catalogue entries so that user applications won't have to deal with database connections and JDBC calls, but can instead use a simple object-based interface.

Given these parameters, we have two options for our implementation:

1 Write a set of utility classes (which we could write as standard JavaBeans) and isolate the database code in them.

2 Create an EJB to represent the catalogue entries.

Although the relative simplicity of our application may not warrant EJB use, we'll try them anyway, for purposes of illustration. To minimize our work, our catalogue entry EJB will use container-managed persistence—the container will be the one responsible for persisting the various catalogue entries to the database, freeing us to concentrate on the details of the application itself and the interfaces that the EJB should support.

Let's now look at each of the interfaces and objects we need to create in building our EJB. Recall from table 12.2 that each EJB will need:

- A Remote interface that exposes the methods the EJB will support.
- A Home interface that provides life cycle (creation, finding, etc.) methods for the EJB.
- An Implementation class that is the guts of the EJB, including any business rules and logic it needs. This would also be the site to place any code for retrieving and setting the EJB's properties (from/to the database); but since we are using container managed persistence, we don't have to write this code; the container does it for us.

The remote interface

The first action to take with our new EJB is to define its functionality through its remote interface, which specifies the methods available for its users. If we were writing a plain JavaBean, the public methods of our JavaBean would be the business methods we expose to other Java classes. The methods in an EJB's remote interface are analogous, in this way, to the public methods in a JavaBean. The operations we want to conduct over the catalogue entries include reading the values stored in the entry and updating them. Supporting these operations yields the remote interface presented in listing 12.1.

Listing 12.1   The remote interface of the CatalogueEntry EJB

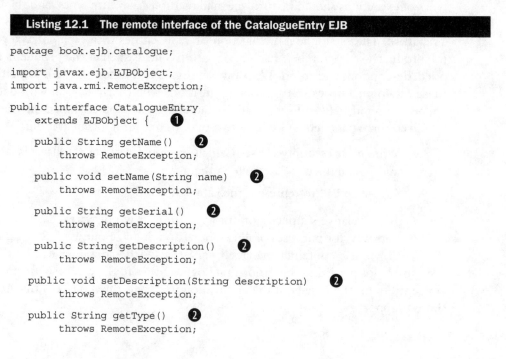

```
package book.ejb.catalogue;

import javax.ejb.EJBObject;
import java.rmi.RemoteException;

public interface CatalogueEntry
    extends EJBObject {        ❶

    public String getName()        ❷
        throws RemoteException;

    public void setName(String name)        ❷
        throws RemoteException;

    public String getSerial()        ❷
        throws RemoteException;

    public String getDescription()        ❷
        throws RemoteException;

    public void setDescription(String description)        ❷
        throws RemoteException;

    public String getType()        ❷
        throws RemoteException;
```

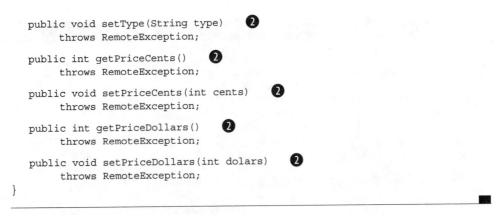

```
    public void setType(String type)     ❷
        throws RemoteException;

    public int getPriceCents()     ❷
        throws RemoteException;

    public void setPriceCents(int cents)     ❷
        throws RemoteException;

    public int getPriceDollars()     ❷
        throws RemoteException;

    public void setPriceDollars(int dolars)     ❷
        throws RemoteException;
}
```

❶ **Declaration of the CatalogueEntry interface** Two things are obvious about this remote interface (both required by the EJB specification):

1 The remote interface does not extend the interface `java.rmi.Remote` in the same way that the usual RMI remote interfaces do; instead, it extends `javax.ejb.EJBObject`. The methods in `javax.ejb.EJBObject` (that are implemented by the container) let their caller perform operations such as removing the EJB from the container

2 All the methods in the interface throw a `RemoteException` because EJBs are subject to distribution and, in most cases, a method call on an EJB is actually a remote method call. In these cases we need the `RemoteException` to signal us that some error has occurred.

Other than these two findings, the methods seem obvious. We have methods to set and get most of the catalogue entry's properties, with the sole exception being that the serial number has only a getter, since it is the key to the catalogue entry and cannot be changed.

❷ **Business methods we want to expose to users of this EJB.**

The home interface

Looking at listing 12.1, we see no methods that help us create or get a reference to an instance of the `CatalogueEntry` EJB. This inability will be a problem for us since we want to, of course, create catalogue entries and search for products. You do not see these services in the EJB's remote interface because these are not services that the EJB itself provides, but are services provided by its home interface. An EJB's home interface is implemented by the EJB container and, using the container, this home implementation will support creation and searching for our `CatalogueEntry` EJB. To make this possible, all we need to do is define a home interface as seen in listing 12.2.

Listing 12.2 The home interface of the CatalogueEntry EJB

```
package book.ejb.catalogue;

import java.util.Collection;
import java.rmi.RemoteException;
import javax.ejb.EJBHome;
import javax.ejb.CreateException;
import javax.ejb.FinderException;

public interface CatalogueEntryHome
    extends EJBHome {

    public CatalogueEntry create(String serial,
                                 String type,
                                 String name,
                                 String description,
                                 int dollars,
                                 int cents)
        throws RemoteException, CreateException;

    public CatalogueEntry findByPrimaryKey(String serial)
        throws FinderException, RemoteException;

    public Collection findByType(String type)
        throws FinderException, RemoteException;
}
```

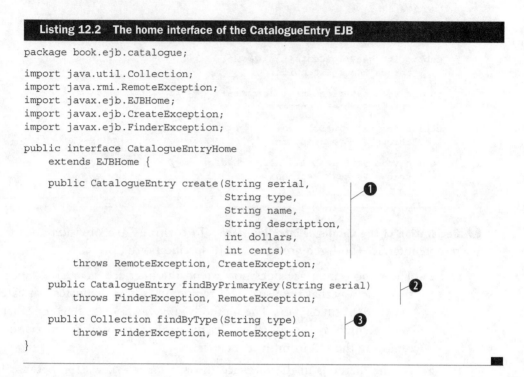

❶ **Creates a method used to create an instance of** `CatalogueEntry` **EJB** ❷ **Finds a** `CatalogueEntry` **EJB by its serial number** ❸ **Finds a** `CatalogueEntry` **EJB by its type** The home interface defines a creation method as well as numerous `find-XXX()` methods. Using these methods, one can create EJB instances and then search for them by serial number or type. We should also note here that all the home interface's methods throw some type of exception: (1) The creation methods throw a `CreateException`, which signals that the creation failed. (2) The `findXXX()` methods can throw a `FinderException` which indicates that there was some error while looking for the appropriate EJBs. (3) All methods throw a `RemoteException` to signal a possible communication error with the remote server. In using these exceptions one gains a good idea of its method call status.

❷ ❸ The find methods that are looking for a set of catalogue entries return a `Collection` object. This collection will contain references to all EJBs that match the find criteria. For example if we are looking for all the books in our catalogue, the returned `Collection` will let us reference all the `CatalogueEntry` EJBs that represent books.

The EJB implementation class

By now we have some idea of what functionality will be exposed by the EJB and how we can create or look for a catalogue entry. Now we must implement the `CatalogueEntryEJB` itself. The code we include in this class is the code that executes any time a remote method is invoked on the `CatalogueEntry` interface by a client (listing 12.3).

Listing 12.3   The implementation of the CatalogueEntry EJB

```
package book.ejb.catalogue;

import javax.ejb.EntityBean;
import javax.ejb.EntityContext;
import javax.ejb.CreateException;

public class CatalogueEntryEJB
    implements EntityBean {

    public String serial;
    public String type;
    public String name;
    public String description;
    public int dollars;
    public int cents;

    private EntityContext context;

    public String getName()          ❶
    {
        return name;
    }

    public void setName(String name)   ❶
    {
        this.name = name;
    }

    public String getSerial()         ❶
    {
        return serial;
    }

    public String getDescription()    ❶
    {
        return description;
    }

    public void setDescription(String description)   ❶
    {
        this.description = description;
    }
```

```java
public String getType()                    ❶
{
    return type;
}

public void setType(String type)           ❶
{
    this.type = type;
}

public int getPriceCents()                 ❶
{
    return cents;
}

public void setPriceCents(int cents)       ❶
{
    this.cents = cents;
}

public int getPriceDollars()               ❶
{
    return dollars;
}

public void setPriceDollars(int dollars)   ❶
{
    this.dollars = dollars;
}

public String ejbCreate(String serial,     ❷
                        String type,
                        String name,
                        String description,
                        int dollars,
                        int cents)
    throws CreateException
{
    if(null == serial        ||
       null == type          ||
       null == name          ||
       null == description   ||
       0 > dollars || 0 > cents) {
         throw new CreateException("The productId is required.");
    }

    this.serial      = serial;
    this.type        = type;
    this.name        = name;
    this.description = description;
    this.dollars     = dollars;
    this.cents       = cents;

    return serial;
```

```
        }
        public void ejbPostCreate(String serial,    ❸
                                  String type,
                                  String name,
                                  String description,
                                  int dollars,
                                  int cents) { }
        public void ejbActivate()    ❹
        {
            serial = (String)context.getPrimaryKey();
        }
        public void ejbPassivate()    ❺
        {
            serial      = null;
            name        = null;
            type        = null;
            description = null;
            cents       = 0;
            dollars     = 0;
        }
        public void ejbRemove() { }         ❻
        public void ejbLoad() { }
        public void ejbStore() { }
        public void setEntityContext(EntityContext context)
        {
            this.context = context;
        }
        public void unsetEntityContext()
        {
            context = null;
        }
}
```

❶ **Implementaion of the business methods exposed by this EJB in the remote interface.**

❷ **Called by the container to construct our EJB** Note how the create() methods in the EJB's home and the actual EJB implementation match in terms of parameters. For every create() in the home interface, the EJB should implement an ejbCreate() with the same argument list. When executing create() on the home interface the call will be proxy to the matching ejbCreate() in the EJB implementation.

❸ For this EJB, nothing is needed here **❹ Called by the container to activate the EJB. Reloads the serial number** **❺ Called by the container to passivate the EJB. Resets all private variables** **❻ Lifecylce methods that we don't need to implement for our EJB** The EJB implementation is flooded with methods that use the naming convention ejbXXX(). The ejbXXX() methods are actually part of the EJB specification and are callbacks to be used by the EJB container. Some of these callbacks are called when the EJB is created, others are called when the EJB is to be stored in a database, and so on. These methods facilitate the container's ability to control the life cycle of our bean.

The amazing thing about listing 12.3 is that we do not see a single line of database access code because CatalogueEntryEJB uses container-managed persistence. CatalogueEntryEJB has six container-managed fields (serial, type, name, description, dollars, and cents), and there is no JDBC/SQL code to store/load them or to perform the find operations on the EJBs. The container implements all this distasteful database code. This is a victory because we wrote a relatively simple piece of code, and we end up with something that uses database connection pooling and SQL. Our only responsibility is specifying the exact SQL queries to be used by the find methods, and the table structure for the container managed fields. The container does the rest.

You may ask why CatalogueEntryEJB doesn't implement the remote interface CatalogueEntry? After all, this is the interface that CatalogueEntryEJB should implement, isn't it? The answer is that CatalogueEntryEJB does not have to implement the remote interfaces (CatalogueEntry and CataloogEntryHome) because the container takes care of them instead. The container wraps CatalogueEntryEJB with the implementation of its home and with an implementation of the remote and home interfaces (which is what the user sees), and this container-created remote interface implementation references CatalogueEntryEJB and calls its methods.

The fact that the container implements the remote interface and calls the methods on CatalogueEntryEJB gives rise to method call interception. Interception occurs when the container implements the remote interface in a way that places specific logic before calling the actual EJB implementation. This logic intercepts remote method calls and acts upon them. In these interception points, the container may implement security and transaction propagation (as defined in the EJB specification) before actually calling CatalogueEntryEJB's methods.

The CatalogueEntryEJB client
The last step in our EJB coding sample is to write the client application, as in listing 12.4.

Listing 12.4   The implementation of the CatalogueEntry EJB

```
package book.ejb.catalogue;

import java.util.Collection;
import java.util.Iterator;

import javax.naming.Context;
import javax.naming.InitialContext;
import javax.rmi.PortableRemoteObject;

public class ProductClient {
    public static void main(String[] args)
    {
        String regLocation = args[0];
        String serial = args[1];

        try {
            Context initial = new InitialContext();              ❶
            Object objref = initial.lookup(regLocation);

            CatalogueEntryHome home = (CatalogueEntryHome)       ❷
                PortableRemoteObject.narrow(objref,
                                CatalogueEntryHome.class);

            CatalogueEntry entry = home.findByPrimaryKey(serial);  ❸
            print(entry);

            System.out.println("Print all books");
            Collection c = home.findByType("books");              ❹
            Iterator i = c.iterator();
            while (i.hasNext()) {
                entry = (CatalogueEntry) PortableRemoteObject.
                        narrow(i.next(),CatalogueEntry.class);
            }
        } catch(Exception ex) {
            System.err.println("Caught an exception." );
            ex.printStackTrace();
        }
    }

    public static void print(CatalogueEntry ce) throws Exception
    {
        System.out.println("Informaton on   : " +
            ce.getName());
        System.out.println("Description is   : " +
            ce.getDescription());
        System.out.println("Serial number is: " +
            ce.getSerial());
        System.out.println("Type is          : " +
            ce.getType());
        System.out.println("Price is         : " +
            ce.getPriceDollars() + "." + ce.getPriceCents());
    }
}
```

❶ **References the EJB using the JNDI registry** Obtains a reference to the home object through the JNDI registry. The container signs up the EJB home (container-generated) implementation in the JNDI registry. The EJB's user references this home by resolving its name from the JNDI registry.

❷ **Narrows the returned home to the actual class** Casts the home reference into the correct home class. The process of casting the home from a remote reference as retrieved from the JNDI registry to a real object may differ from one remote method call implementation to another, so the client uses the class `javax.rmi.Por-tableRemoteObject` to perform the protocol and platform-specific casting.

❸ **Uses a single EJB by its primary key** ❹ **Lists all the books by finding based on the type attribute** Uses one of the finder (or create) methods to reference an EJB instance and then calls any desired instance methods. Note that when the finder method returns more than a single result, it will return all these results within a `Collection` object that the client iterates through to fetch returned EJBs.

Overall, and considering what we managed to achieve (locating a remote object and calling methods that actually go to a database), the complexity price is not that high. In the code samples in this section, we created a program that accesses a database and searches for specific table entries within that database with very little fuss. This showcases some of the advantages of EJB technology.

12.2.5 *Points to keep in mind*

The goal of this EJB tutorial was not to turn you into an EJB wizard, but to acquaint you with EJB terminology and the programming model. The key points here are that EJBs are distributed objects, that you access them by connecting to their home interface (retrieved through JNDI), and that you create or find the EJB you want through their home. Once you reference an EJB, you can call its methods as if the EJB were running locally inside your client process.

The information will be important when we implement custom tags that provide access to an EJB.

12.3 *Using and configuring J2EE services*

As a JSP tag developer you will likely find yourself working with a J2EE-compliant application server. That is, again, because the servlet and JSP specification is a subset of the larger J2EE specification. This has prompted many vendors to release application server products that adhere to *all* the J2EE standards, not only those portions detailing servlets and JSP. How will you take advantage of the services rendered by the container? How will you reference database connections and EJBs in your tags?

A component running inside a J2EE-enabled container can take advantage of many container-provided and managed services. These services include:

- Distributed transactions and persistency, using EJB and JTA.
- Database pooling, employing the JDBC2.0 standard extensions.
- Naming services, with JNDI.
- Message queuing services, with JMS.
- Mailing services, using JavaMail.

12.3.1 *Getting services*

These services are all helpful, but obtaining them would be a nightmare if the containers did not provide access in a simple, standard way. To avoid the nightmare, the J2EE specification defines a means of referencing the service by looking them up according to a unique name in a directory, the equivalent of a Yellow Pages for J2EE components. The API that supports this directory functionality is called JNDI. This system works by having each J2EE-compliant system provide a JNDI service called an *environment*, which contains environment variables (values to be shared across the application), EJB references, and resource factory references (references to objects that create common J2EE resources). Each J2EE application can have a description of the environment variables, EJBs, and resources that it uses. The J2EE server looks at the descriptor and then binds the values described in the descriptor into the JNDI name space, thereby making them available for the application. Before we see how to enter and retrieve services with JNDI, let's look at what these environment variables, EJBs, and resources actually do for us:

- Environment variables allow application customization by providing initial parameter values. The environment duplicates some of the functionality provided by the web application-scoped initialization parameters. The JNDI URLs for these values start with java:comp/env.
- EJBs' references allow applications to refer to EJB homes using logical names instead of JNDI registry values. EJB references are part of the environment name space provided by J2EE but have a unique focus on EJB. Using these references, an application can easily access EJBs, and in a customized manner. The JNDI URLs for EJB values should start with java:comp/env/ejb.
- Resource references allow applications to refer to resource factories (objects that create desired resources) by using a logical name. These resources can be JDBC connections, JMS connections, mail connections, and so forth. The JNDI URLs for resource values starts with java:comp/env/jdbc, java:comp/env/jms, java:comp/env/mail.

An example of accessing the environment

To help understand how environment entities are registered and accessed, let's assume that a certain web application needs an environment variable named `intValue` with the value 1. In this case, the deployment descriptor of the application should include an entry of type `<env-entry>` that looks like:

```
<env-entry>
    <env-entry-name>intValue</env-entry-name>
    <env-entry-type>java.lang.Integer</env-entry-type>
    <env-entry-value>1</env-entry-value>
</env-entry>
```

To access the value of `intValue` we use JNDI in our application in a manner similar to the following fragment:

```
Context initContext = new InitialContext();
Context envContext = initContext.lookup("java:comp/env");

Integer intValue = (Integer)envContext.lookup("intValue");
// use intValue …
```

Accessing the environment is easy, but managing it seems to require a considerable amount of work by the J2EE runtime and the administrators. In that light, you may ask yourself why we need all of this when you could just hand-code most of the functionality provided here. The answer is threefold:

1 The infrastructure exposed here provides a tight integration to the container services in a container-neutral manner.

2 Having a standard configuration infrastructure allows tool vendors to create tools that help the administrator. This also makes it possible for all those involved in developing and deploying an application to master only a single configuration method.

3 Though you could code and manage this entire configuration process on your own and in a proprietary way, you probably do not want to. It is much easier to defer to the container for these types of configuration features.

The next section explains what we as custom tag developers must know in order to integrate with J2EE environments.

12.3.2 Tag and servlet API integration

Knowing that custom JSP tags are one aspect of a larger whole, the J2EE specification, you may wonder how the two specifications interact. Are we supposed to use any new APIs to employ this integration? What about the web application deployment descriptor? J2EE integration is not solely a set of APIs, but is also a way to allow the use of current APIs available in the standard version of Java, Java Standard Edition (JSE), in a more integrated fashion. If you have already used JNDI, which is itself part of JSE, you needn't learn any new APIs in order to gain access to J2EE services within your tags. All that is required is that these environment variables, EJB references, and resource factory references be listed as entries inside the web application deployment descriptor for your web application. Doing so impels the servlet container to publish those services in the JNDI directory that we access within our tags. The following sections explain the process of configuring a web application deployment descriptor in this way, for the purpose of exposing and gaining access to J2EE services.

12.3.3 *Setting environment entries*

First we look at J2EE service's configuration for environment variables. To do this, we need to modify the web application deployment descriptor (web.xml, which we first saw in chapter 2) by making an entry for each variable. Specifically, in the deployment descriptor, we encapsulate an environment variable within an `<env-entry>` tag. Like most entries in the deployment descriptor, you can assign it an optional description in addition to several mandatory values (table 12.3).

Table 12.3 **Important environment variable information**

Elements of the `<env-entry>` tag	Description
<env-entry-name>	Specifies the environment name to which the value is bound.
<env-entry-type>	Specifies the environment variable type as one of the following: java.lang.Boolean java.lang.Byte java.lang.Double java.lang.Float java.lang.Integer java.lang.Long java.lang.String
<env-entry-value>	Specifies an optional property value that must match the type supplied within the `<env-entry-type>`. If the value is not specified within the deployment descriptor, one must be specified during the deployment.

Next is a fragment taken from a descriptor that creates a string environment variable with a predefined value:

```
<env-entry>
   <description> Sample environment value</description>
   <env-entry-name>sampleValue</env-entry-name>
```

```
    <env-entry-type>java.lang.String</env-entry-type>
    <env-entry-value>This is a sample String</env-entry-value>
</env-entry>
```

With the above entry in our web.xml file, let's see how the code for gaining access to sampleValue looks:

```
// Getting a naming initial context.
javax.naming.Context initContext = new javax.naming.InitialContext();
// Printing the environment value.
System.out.println(initContext.lookup("java:comp/env/sampleValue"));
```

Getting the value requires using some of the JNDI APIs. First you need to obtain the default naming context by instantiating a new Java naming context, which provides a handle into the directory in which the services and environment variables are listed. With the directory context in hand, you simply look up the environment value by its JNDI URL, in this case, "java:comp/env/sampleValue".

12.3.4 *Setting EJB reference entries*

The second J2EE service we will gain access to is an EJB. Once again, we can create an entry in the environment Yellow Pages for our EJB by putting an entry in the web application deployment descriptor. Within the file, an EJB reference is encapsulated within an <ejb-ref> tag, which has an optional description as well as the EJB-referencing related information shown in (table 12.4).

Table 12.4 Properties for EJB references

Elements of the `<ejb-ref>` tag	Description
`<ejb-ref-name>`	The unique, environment entry name for the EJB. This is the JNDI name by which it can be retrieved.
`<ejb-ref-type>`	The EJB's type, either `Session` or `Entity`.
`<home>`	The fully qualified class name of the EJB's home interface.
`<remote>`	The fully qualified class name of the EJB's remote interface.

As an example of using EJBs within a J2EE container let's take our catalogue entry EJB and see how it will look like in the J2EE environment.

As a first step, we put the EJB reference into the deployment descriptor:

```
<ejb-ref>
    <description> Reference to the Catalogue EJB </description>
    <ejb-ref-name>ejb/catalogue</ejb-ref-name>
    <ejb-ref-type>Entity</ejb-ref-type>
    <home>book.app.ejb.CatalogueEntryHome</home>
    <remote>book.app.ejb.CatalogueEntry</remote>
```

```
</ejb-ref>
```

Now look at how we would access the EJB that this deployment descriptor entry makes available:

```
try {
    Context initial = new InitialContext();
    Object home = initial.lookup("java:comp/env/ejb/catalogue");


} catch(Exception e) {
    // Handle errors
}
```

Clearly, specifying and getting access to an EJB using the environment is a simple task.

12.3.5 *Setting resource factory reference entries*

The way we specify and access some J2EE resources such as database connection in our custom tags is through the use of a resource factory reference. Earlier we said a resource factory reference represents a handle to a factory class that can produce some J2EE resource, such as a database connection, a JMS object, a JavaMail connection, and so forth. A resource reference is specified in the deployment descriptor within a `<resource-ref>` tag. As with other entries, it may include an optional description as well as the resource referencing information shown in table 12.5.

Table 12.5 Properties for resource references

Elements of the `<resource-ref>` tag	Description
`<res-ref-name>`	The environment name for the resource (its JNDI name).
`<res-ref-type>`	The type of resource factory used. The J2EE specification contains several standard resource factories: `javax.sql.DataSource` for JDBC connection factories, `javax.jms.QueueConnectionFactory` or `javax.jms.TopicConnectionFactory` for JMS connection factories, `javax.mail.Session` for JavaMail connection factories and `java.net.URL` for general URL connection factories.
`<res-auth>`	Resource authentication type. Specifies the way to perform authentication with this resource. Possible authentication values can be `Container` or `Bean`. `Container` instructs the container to authenticate using properties configured during the deployment. `Bean` instructs the container to let the application authenticate programmatically.

For an example of using resources within a J2EE container, let's look at the following resource entry, which specifies a database resource.

```
<resource-ref>
    <description> Some JDBC reference</description>
    <res-ref-name>jdbc/somedatabase</res-ref-name>
    <res-type>javax.sql.DataSource</res-type>
    <res-auth>Container</res-auth>
</resource-ref>
```

Getting a JDBC resource factory from this reference can be done easily with code such as the following:

```
    // Construct the database source
    try {
        Context ctxt = new InitialContext();

        // Get the JDBC factory from the JNDI registry.
        DataSource mDs = (DataSource)
            ctxt.lookup("java:comp/env/jdbc/somedatabase");
        …
    } catch(NamingException ne) {
        // Handle errors
    }
```

Instead of using the JDBC `DriverManager`, we are using the `DataSource` object (which is standard practice in J2EE applications). `DataSource` is a standard extension of JDBC2.0 that facilitates the application server's control over allocation of database connections. To obtain a JDBC connection out of a `DataSource` all you need to do is call one of its `getConnection()` methods. When you are done with the JDBC connection, close it. Some `DataSource` variants also provide built-in database connection pooling (using the class `PooledConnection`). In such a case, calling `close()` on the database connection will not really close the connection, but will inform the application server that the user is finished with the connection and that it can be reused.

12.3.6 *Wrap it up*

We now know that the J2EE environment provides a standardized means of defining and referencing resources and we have seen several examples of how this is accomplished. The next few sections will demonstrate the integration of tags with these J2EE services, starting with a J2EE capable version of the previously defined database tags, and finishing with the newly encountered EJBs.

12.4 *J2EE database connection tags*

Working with databases from within J2EE is somewhat different from the simple database access demonstrated in chapter 11. Most notably, the allocation of the database connection changes considerably:

- With standard JDBC, we used the `DriverManager` class to attain new connections. The input to `DriverManager` was complex and included several configuration items such as user name, password, driver class, and a URL specifying the exact location to which we want to connect.
- In the brave new world of J2EE, we no longer use the `DriverManager`. In its place we use JNDI to obtain a reference to a `DataSource` object, from which we can get a connection. All the configuration information specified to the `DriverManager` is now specified in one place, the web application deployment descriptor.

The `DataSource` object requires some explanation, and now would be a good time to start that.

12.4.1 *DataSource*

`DataSource` is a factory class whose job is to create new database connections. It is part of the JDBC2.0 standard and was designed especially for application servers to provide database access to components running within them. The methods in `DataSource` are presented in listing 12.5 and, as you can see, most of them deal with some connection retrieving aspect.

Listing 12.5   The methods in DataSource

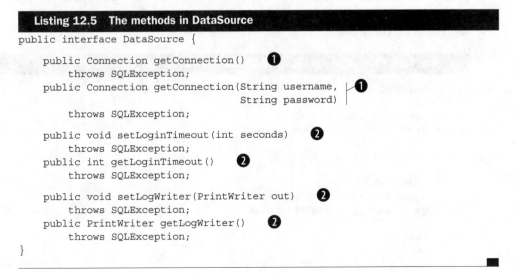

```
public interface DataSource {

    public Connection getConnection()                       ❶
        throws SQLException;
    public Connection getConnection(String username,        ❶
                                    String password)
        throws SQLException;

    public void setLoginTimeout(int seconds)                ❷
        throws SQLException;
    public int getLoginTimeout()                            ❷
        throws SQLException;

    public void setLogWriter(PrintWriter out)               ❷
        throws SQLException;
    public PrintWriter getLogWriter()                       ❷
        throws SQLException;

}
```

❶ **Returns a JDBC Connection object**   The first two methods in `DataSource` basically
return a JDBC database connection that we can use for our queries, closing after
use. The difference between the two `getConnection()` methods is that the param-
eterless `getConnection()` method uses the applications server's configuration to
authenticate to the database (known as `Container`-typed authentication), while the
second one accepts a username and password parameters that were in some way
obtained by the using classes (known as `Bean`-typed authentication).

❷ **Helper methods that let us set parameters**   The four remaining methods are help-
ers that let us set up login timeout (so that we do not block forever on a `getCon-`
`nection()` method call) and logging destination. Messages from the `DataSource`
and `DataSource`-generated object will be directed to this destination.

12.4.2 *Updating database tags to use J2EE conventions*

Other than using the `DataSource` object to create JDBC connections, nothing
changes in the way JDBC is used within J2EE. When considering the effects on the
database tag library we built in chapter 11, we need only modify the database connection tag and the `DbConnectionWrapper` object exported by it. We'll do that now
by rewriting `DbConnectionTag` and `DbConnection` in order to adapt them to J2EE.

J2EEDbConnectionTag

The first class we are going to implement is `J2EEDbConnectionTag`, the handler
class for the J2EE aware database connection tag. The implementation of this tag is
in listing 12.6 and, as you shall see, things have changed considerably since the
plain JDBC connection tag we developed in chapter 11. The greatest change is that
`J2EEDbConnectionTag`'s role shifts to finding the `DataSource` that will later be
used to get a connection.

Listing 12.6   The implementation of J2EEDbConnectionTag

```
package book.j2ee;

import javax.servlet.jsp.JspException;
import javax.servlet.jsp.PageContext;

import javax.sql.DataSource;

import javax.naming.Context;
import javax.naming.InitialContext;
import javax.naming.NamingException;

import book.util.LocalStrings;
import book.util.ExTagSupport;
import book.database.DbConnectionWrapper;
```

```
public class J2EEDbConnectionTag extends ExTagSupport {

    public static final String DBURL = "db_url";

    static LocalStrings ls =
        LocalStrings.getLocalStrings(J2EEDbConnectionTag.class);

    protected String dburl = null;

    public void setUrl(String url)
    {
        this.dburl = url;
    }

    public int doStartTag()
        throws JspException
    {
        check parameters;
        exportWrapper(createDbConnectionWrapper());
        return SKIP_BODY;
    }

    protected void clearProperties()
    {
        id      = null;
        dburl   = null;
        super.clearProperties();
    }

    protected void checkParameters()
        throws JspException
    {
        if(null == dburl) {
            dburl = findInitParameter(id+"."+DBURL);
        }

        if(null == dburl) {
            // Log and throw an Exception.
        }
    }

    protected void exportWrapper(DbConnectionWrapper con)
        throws JspException
    {
        pageContext.setAttribute(id,
                                 con,
                                 PageContext.PAGE_SCOPE);
    }

    protected DbConnectionWrapper createDbConnectionWrapper()
```

```
        throws JspException
    {
        try {
            Context initial = new InitialContext();
            DataSource ds = (DataSource)initial.lookup(dburl);
            initial.close();

            return new J2EEDbConnection(getServletContext(),
                                        ds);
        } catch(NamingException ne) {
            // Log and throw an Exception.
        }
    }
}
```

❶ **Fetches the DataSource from the configured JNDI URL** Once we have our single configuration parameter, we need only to fetch the DataSource from JNDI. There is nothing especially unique in this step since the JNDI method call sequence should be well known by now. Note only that we close the JNDI Context object once we are through with it. Doing so is very important since different application servers are using the context differently and, in some, keeping the Context open may lead to a resource leak.

❷ **Creates a J2EE aware wrapper object** The last notable action taken by J2EEDbConnectionTag is the creation of a new J2EE-aware DbConnectionWrapper to wrap the DataSource in such a way that the rest of the database tag library will understand.

J2EEDbConnectionTag shown in listing 12.6 was greatly simplified by the move to J2EE. In the past, the connection tag had many input parameters (username, password, driver class, JDBC database URL). We can now accomplish all this with one parameter, the JNDI URL wherein we placed the reference to the DataSource (e.g., java:comp/env/jdbc/BookDataSource). The reason, again, for the decrease in the number of input parameters is that the application server itself will hold the configuration for each of the configured DataSources. When we retrieve a DataSource in this way, it comes preconfigured with all the JDBC parameters specified at the application server level. With fewer input parameters, we need fewer attribute setter methods in our tag handler, and our checkParameters() method is much smaller and simpler. Fewer input parameters also mean an easier to use tag.

J2EEDbConnection

The J2EE aware connection object, J2EEDbConnection, is presented in listing 12.7. As can be seen, the only method in DataSource essential to us is the plain and parameter-free getConnection().

This method grabs all the information it needs from the application server's configuration. One could argue that not letting the programmer who is using the tag provide username and password dynamically makes our connection tag less attractive in certain cases; yet, these cases in which the database user and its password are determined dynamically are generally rare in the web environment, so we forgo handling them in our tag.

Listing 12.7   The implementation of J2EEDbConnection

```java
package book.j2ee;

import java.sql.Connection;
import java.sql.SQLException;
import javax.sql.DataSource;

import javax.servlet.ServletContext;

import book.util.LocalStrings;
import book.database.DbConnectionWrapper;

public class J2EEDbConnection implements DbConnectionWrapper {

    static LocalStrings ls =
        LocalStrings.getLocalStrings(J2EEDbConnection.class);

    protected ServletContext app;
    protected DataSource ds;
    protected Connection con;

    public J2EEDbConnection(ServletContext app,
                            DataSource ds)
    {
        this.app = app;
        this.ds = ds;
        this.con = null;
    }

    public Connection getConnection()
        throws SQLException
    {
        if(con == null) {                            ❶
            con = ds.getConnection();
        }

        return con;
    }

    public void freeConnection()
    {
```

```
        try {
            if(null != con) {
                con.close();
                con = null;
            }
        } catch(Throwable t) {
            // Log the exception.
        }
    }

    protected void finalize()
        throws Throwable
    {
        freeConnection();
    }
}
```

❶ **Gets a JDBC connection from the DataSource** Moving to J2EE made our database connection wrapper easier to implement. J2EEDbConnection is smaller in size (than DbConnection) and is much simpler due to the omission of security-related parameters. In general the omission of JDBC parameters from our tag also makes it possible for the administrator to manage the connection's attributes from the application server's management console (or other configuration tool used by the server). This capability makes it a breeze to perform a variety of operations, such as switching between databases, connection pooling policies, and changing security attribute, among others.

Adding a JDBC resource reference for use with our new tag

Once the connection tag is available, we need only add a JDBC resource reference in the web-application deployment descriptor, and we can execute our JSP files using the J2EE managed database connection. Adding a resource reference to the deployment descriptor may seem tricky the first time, so let's look at listing 12.8 wherein we see a stripped down web-application deployment descriptor used for testing J2EEDbConnectionTag.

Listing 12.8   A working web deployment descriptor with JDBC resource reference

```
<?xml version="1.0" encoding="ISO-8859-1"?>

<!DOCTYPE web-app
    PUBLIC "-//Sun Microsystems, Inc.//DTD Web Application 2.2//EN"
    "http://java.sun.com/j2ee/dtds/web-app_2.2.dtd">

<web-app>
    <taglib>
        <taglib-uri>
```

```
        http://www.manning.com/jsptagsbook/j2eedatabase-taglib
        </taglib-uri>
        <taglib-location>
          /WEB-INF/j2eedatabase.tld
        </taglib-location>
    </taglib>

    <resource-ref>
        <description>A sample database connection for
                     J2EEDbConnectionTag </description>
        <res-ref-name>jdbc/BookDataSource</res-ref-name>
        <res-type>javax.sql.DataSource</res-type>
        <res-auth>Container</res-auth>
    </resource-ref>
</web-app>
```

❶ **Declares a JDBC connection resource** The `<resource-ref>` entry indicates that a JDBC connection named `java:comp/env/jdbc/BookDataSource` should be offered by the container and that the authentication to the database is to be based on the container's configuration parameters. Note that the `java:comp/env/` part of the name is omitted from the `<res-ref-name>` value for all J2EE environment entries.

If you wonder where the promised linking between the resource reference and the actual database connection configuration is, the answer is that this part is server specific. You will not find it in the deployment descriptor, and will have to use the application server configuration tools provided by your particular application server vendor to link the application's URL (`java:comp/env/jdbc/BookDataSource`) with the actual connection configuration.

> **NOTE** Developers are often confused about JNDI entries and their scopes. This is usually due to the environment entries starting with `java:comp/env/`. All such entries are actually JNDI URLs, so, can one URL (say `java:comp/env/foo`) serve a variety of web applications? Can these same URLs point to different values? Couldn't these URLs become mixed up? The answer is that the environment space is private to the application, such that you may have different web applications come from different vendors that use the same environment entries, and the application server will know to differentiate between them. Thus, each application will always receive whatever was specified for it.

Our new J2EEDBConnectionTag in action

Using the deployment descriptor as specified earlier, we can write a new version of our database-driven JSP files (listing 12.9).

Listing 12.9 Sample JSP file that uses our J2EE database connections

```
<%@ page errorPage="error.jsp" %>
<%@ taglib
    uri="http://www.manning.com/jsptagsbook/j2eedatabase-taglib"    ❶
    prefix="db" %>
<html>
<head>
<title> Database query results </title>
</head>
<body>
    <h1> Database manipulation  </h1>
    Creating a connection, query a database and presenting the
    results. All from within JSP tags. <br>
    <db:connection id="con"
                   url="java:comp/env/jdbc/BookDataSource"/>      ❷

    <db:query connection="con" id="above12">
    select * from product where cost > 12
    </db:query>

    <table border="1"  bgcolor="#c0c0c0">
        <tr>
            <th bgcolor="#a0a0a0">id</th>
            <th bgcolor="#a0a0a0">Name</th>
            <th bgcolor="#a0a0a0">Cost</th>
        </tr>
        <db:enum query="above12" id="i">
        <tr>
            <td> <$ ID $> </td>
            <td> <$ NAME $> </td>
            <td> <$ COST $> </td>
        </tr>
        </db:enum>
    </table>
</body>
</html>
```

❶ **References the J2EE tag library** The `taglib` reference now points to a different tag library entry (the J2EE database library).

❷ **Fetches the JDBC connection from the specified URL** The connection tag accepts only a single attribute, which is the JNDI pointer URL.

Listing 12.9 is merely one of the JSP files developed for chapter 11, modified to use our new `J2EEDBConnectionTag`. We made changes to two locations (shown in bold):

12.5 *J2EE email tag*

Recalling that we talked at length about the JavaMail API in chapter 7, let us now look at how we can modify the `<send>` tag from that chapter to use J2EE. The modified version of the `<send>` tag will ask the environment for a `javax.mail.Session`, rather than using `ServletContext` parameters, as in the previous implementation of the tag (and instantiating the `Session` ourselves). Of course, we must first define a mail `Session` in the application server configuration, so that the environment can pass it to the `<send>` tag. Let's look at how we define our mail service first, then see how our tag will access this `Session`.

12.5.1 *Defining a mail service*

The J2EE specification does not define how a certain resource is configured in the application server. This means that the J2EE specification does not specify how a mail service should be defined. It only tells us that we should assign a JNDI URL to the configured `Session` so that it can be referenced from inside our applications. The actual URL to use and configuration practice differ from vendor to vendor. It may be of benefit to look at such vendor-specific configurations. Listing 12.10 shows how to define a mail service in Orion. Your application server will probably vary, so consult the documentation for the exact syntax it uses.

Listing 12.10 Defining a mail service in the Orion application server

```
<mail-session location="mail/mailSession"
             smtp-host="mail.smtp.host">
  <property name="mail.from"
           value="your.name@email.address"/>
  <property name="mail.transport.protocol"
           value="smtp"/>
  <property name="mail.smtp.from"
           value="your.name@email.address"/>
</mail-session>
```

In the case of Orion, this listing would be written into a file called server.xml, the server configuration file. Again, since the J2EE specification leaves the details of this task up to the application server vendor, this approach might not translate precisely to your particular vendor.

For the Orion application server, adding this entry to server.xml will add an environment entry to the application that can be retrieved with the JNDI URL `java:comp/env/mail/mailSession`. The value of this resource will, of course, be a `javax.mail.Session` resource factory. By following this practice you can define a number of different mail services, usable from one or more applications.

12.5.2 Referencing the mail service

Although the mail service's configurations may differ across vendors, the J2EE specification is clear on how our applications should reference such external resources to render them accessible by the components inside the application. Listing 12.11 is an example of how a `Session` resource factory is referenced from within a web application.

Listing 12.11   Referencing the mail Session from a web-application

```
<resource-ref>
    <description>Mailing Service</description>
    <res-ref-name>mail/mailSession</res-ref-name>
    <res-type>javax.mail.Session</res-type>
    <res-auth>Container</res-auth>
</resource-ref>
```

In the listing we make sure that a mail `Session` will be available for use by the various parts of the application by looking up the JNDI URL `java:comp/env/mail/mailSession`, in the same way we've seen throughout the chapter (most recently in listing 12.6).

Sending a simple email

Let's look at how we could use this session in the code snippet that appears in listing 12.12.

Listing 12.12   Sending an email

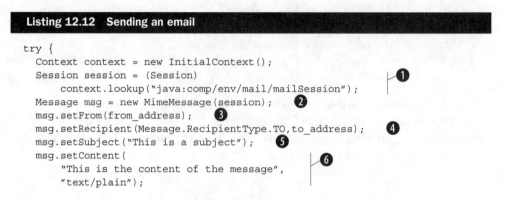

```
try {
  Context context = new InitialContext();
  Session session = (Session)                                      ①
    context.lookup("java:comp/env/mail/mailSession");
  Message msg = new MimeMessage(session);          ②
  msg.setFrom(from_address);        ③
  msg.setRecipient(Message.RecipientType.TO,to_address);     ④
  msg.setSubject("This is a subject");       ⑤
  msg.setContent(                                ⑥
      "This is the content of the message",
      "text/plain");
```

```
    Transport.send(msg);        ❼
} catch(NamingException ne) {
    // Handle errors
} catch(MessagingException me) {
    // Handle errors
}
```

❶ Retrieves the `Session` instance.

❷ Creates a new `Message`.

❸ Sets the sender's `InternetAddress`.

❹ Sets the `InternetAddress` of the recipient of the `Message`.

❺ Sets the subject of the `Message`.

❻ Sets the content and specifies the MIME type for this content.

❼ Sends the message to the recipient.

In this example, we use the `Session` to send a single-part message to a single recipient.

Sending attachments with email

At times, however, you may wish to send attachments along with your messages. This is also simple to do, as described in listing 12.13.

Listing 12.13 Sending a multipart email

```
try {
    Context context = new InitialContext();
    Session session = (Session)
        context.lookup("java:comp/env/mail/mailSession");
    Message msg = new MimeMessage(session);
    msg.setFrom(from_address);
    msg.setRecipient(Message.RecipientType.TO,to_address);
    msg.setSubject("This is a subject");
    Multipart multipart=new MimeMultipart();        ❶
    MimeBodyPart part1=new MimeBodyPart();          ❷
    part1.setContent(                                       ❸
        "This is the content of the message",
        "text/plain");
    MimeBodyPart part2= new MimeBodyPart();         ❷
    part2.setContent(                                           ❸
        "<HR>This is an attachment to the message<HR>",
        "text/html");
    part2.setFileName("attachment.html");           ❹
    multipart.addBodyPart(part1);       ❺
    multipart.addBodyPart(part2);
    msg.setContent(multipart);          ❻
    Transport.send(msg);
```

```
} catch(NamingException ne) {
  // Handle errors
} catch(MessagingException me) {
  // Handle errors
}
```

❶ Creates a **MimeMultipart** instance.

❷ Creates a **MimeBodyPart**   First we create two different MimeBodyPart instances.

❸ Sets the content and speciies the MIME type for this content for this **MimeBodyPart**.

❹ Sets the filename for this **MimeBodyPart**   The second MimeBodyPart was given a filename, so that when the recipient views this email, he will see this as the name of the HTML file attached to the message.

❺ Adds the **MimeBodyParts** to the **MimeMultipart** instance   We add these instances to a MimeMultipart instance.

❻ Sets the content to be the **MimeMultiPart**   We add this instance as content to the MimeMessage.

Notice that we add the text message first, as email readers often open the first part of a multi-part email for viewing by default. If, for some reason, we want to add the attachment before the default part, we can specify the precedence that the added part should have by adding an int value at the time of adding the MimeBodyPart to the MimeMultiPart instance. The signature of this method should then look like multipart.addBodyPart(part1,0). Notice that the numbering of the parts starts at zero, which is normal in Java.

12.5.3 J2EE send tag

Although J2EE greatly reduces the amount of code required in order to send an email, we still want to wrap this up in some neat tags that will make this attainable from our JSP pages. We will do this by extending the <send> tag from chapter 7, in a manner described in listing 12.14.

Listing 12.14   Implementation of the J2EE Send tag

```
package book.j2ee;

import book.util.LocalStrings;

import java.util.Properties;

import javax.mail.Transport;
import javax.mail.Session;
import javax.mail.Message;
import javax.mail.MessagingException;
```

```
import javax.mail.internet.MimeMessage;
import javax.mail.internet.InternetAddress;
import javax.mail.internet.AddressException;

import javax.servlet.jsp.JspException;
import javax.servlet.jsp.JspTagException;

import book.mail.BodyJavaMailTag;
import javax.naming.*;

public class J2EEMailTag extends BodyJavaMailTag  {

  protected String sessionName;

  static LocalStrings ls =
  LocalStrings.getLocalStrings(J2EEMailTag.class);

  public void setSessionName(String sessionName){
    this.sessionName=sessionName;
  }
  protected void checkParameters() throws JspException
  {
    try {
      if(null == sessionName){
        session=Session.getDefaultInstance(new Properties(),null);      ❶
      }else{
        InitialContext context=new InitialContext();
        session=(Session)context.lookup(                                ❷
              "java:comp/env/mail"+sessionName);
      }
      recipient = new InternetAddress(to);
      if(from!=null){
        sender=new InternetAddress(from);      ❸
      }
    } catch(NamingException ne) {
      throw new JspTagException(
              ls.getStr(Constants.SEND_SESSION_ERROR));
    } catch(AddressException ae){
      throw new JspTagException(
              ls.getStr(Constants.SEND_ADDRESS_ERROR));
    } catch(MessagingException me){
      throw new JspTagException(
              ls.getStr(Constants.SEND_MESSAGING_ERROR));
    }
  }

  protected void sendMail(Session session,
                          InternetAddress sender,
                          InternetAddress recipient,
                          String content,
                          String subject)
                          throws MessagingException
  {
```

```
MimeMessage message = new MimeMessage(session);
if(null!=sender){
  message.setFrom(sender);                                    ❹
}
message.addRecipient(Message.RecipientType.TO, recipient);
if(null != subject) {
  message.setSubject(subject);
} else {
  message.setSubject("");
}
if(null == content) { // Empty body
  content = "";
}
message.setText(content);
Transport.send(message);
}


protected void clearServiceState()
{
  sessionName    = null;
  super.clearServiceState();
}
}
```

❶ Gets the default `Session` instance.

❷ Looks up the specified `Session` instance.

❸ Creates an `InternetAddress` for a specified sender if one is given.

❹ Adds the sender's `InternetAddress` if one is given.

In listing 12.14, we do more or less the same as with the `<send>` tag in chapter 7. We override the `checkParameters()` method in order to look up a mail `Session` or defined default if a mail `Session` name is not given. As the `from` parameter is optional, we create a sender `InternetAddress` only if the `from` parameter is given; otherwise we will assume that the tag user wants us to use the default sender address as configured in the application server. There is no way to verify whether a default sender is specified in the configuration of the mail `Session` *before* the message is given to the `Transport`. Thus we also have to override the `sendMail()` method to ensure that a `sender` is only added to the message if so specified.

The J2EE send tag TLD

In order to use our new tag, we need to write a new tag library descriptor. This should look like listing 12.15.

Listing 12.15   Tag library descriptor for the Send tag

```xml
<?xml version="1.0" encoding="ISO-8859-1" ?>
<!DOCTYPE taglib
        PUBLIC "-//Sun Microsystems, Inc.//DTD JSP Tag Library 1.1//EN"
        "http://java.sun.com/j2ee/dtds/web-jsptaglibrary_1_1.dtd">

<!-- A tag library descriptor for the J2EE mail tags  -->

<taglib>
    <tlibversion>1.0</tlibversion>
    <jspversion>1.1</jspversion>
    <shortname>j2eemail</shortname>
    <uri> http://www.manning.com/jsptagsbook/j2ee-mail-taglib</uri>
    <info>
        A tag library that describes the j2ee mail tags
    </info>
    <tag>
        <name>send</name>
        <tagclass>book.j2ee.J2EEMailTag</tagclass>
        <teiclass>book.mail.MailTagExtraInfo</teiclass>
        <bodycontent>JSP</bodycontent>
        <info>
            Sends an email based on the provided attributes
            and mail Session configuration.
        </info>
        <attribute>
            <name>sssionName</name>
            <required>false</required>
            <rtexprvalue>false</rtexprvalue>
        </attribute>
        <attribute>
            <name>from</name>
            <required>false</required>
            <rtexprvalue>true</rtexprvalue>
        </attribute>
        <attribute>
            <name>to</name>
            <required>true</required>
            <rtexprvalue>true</rtexprvalue>
        </attribute>
    </tag>
    <tag>
        <name>message</name>
        <tagclass>book.mail.MessageBodyReaderTag</tagclass>
        <bodycontent>JSP</bodycontent>
        <info>
            Provides a place holder for the user to enter the
            contents of the mail's body.
        </info>
    </tag>
```

```
    <tag>
        <name>subject</name>
        <tagclass>book.mail.MessageSubjectReaderTag</tagclass>
        <bodycontent>JSP</bodycontent>
        <info>
            Provides a place holder for the user to enter the
            contents of the mail's message.
        </info>
    </tag>
</taglib>
```

As you can see, the tag library descriptor is basically a modification of our previous mail tag library.

J2EE send tag in action

Now, with the tag library descriptor in place and our web application configured with a `mailSession` service, we can use our new tag as in listing 12.16.

Listing 12.16   Sample JSP file that uses our J2EE mail tag

```
<%@ taglib
    uri="http://www.manning.com/jsptagsbook/j2eemail-taglib"
    prefix="mail" %>
<HTML>
<HEAD>
  <TITLE>Sending mail </TITLE>
</HEAD>
<BODY BGCOLOR="#FFFFFF">
  <HR>
  <H1>Sending email..</H1>
  <mail:send to="your.name@email.address">        ❶
    <mail:subject>a J2EE mail</mail:subject>       ❷
    <mail:message>   ❸
Hi there!
This mail was sent to you by the use of the <send> tag.
    </mail:message>   ❹
  </mail:send>   ❺
  <H1>Email sent</H1>
  <HR>
</BODY>
</HTML>
```

❶ Start of message where receiver is defined.

❷ Sets the subject of the message.

❸ Start of the body of the message.

❹ **End of message body.**

❺ **End of message, points where mail gets sent.**

Executing the JSP in listing 12.16 will send a short email to the recipients stated. Note that since we are not specifying a JNDI URL for the mail `Session`, the tag will use the default. All line breaks and blank characters inside the body of the `<message>` tag will be included in the sent content, so be careful with source code styling. In the example, we do not state a sender of the message; therefore, the sender defined in the mail session will be used. If no such sender is defined, a `MessagingException` will be thrown.

12.6 *Using EJBs from within JSP*

The advantages of J2EE for accessing powerful resources are becoming apparent, and fussing over the intricate details of how those resources are shared and implemented is left to the application server vendor. One of these powerful resources is the EJB layer. As explained earlier, EJBs are commonly used as a controller layer (a place to deposit business logic and processes) and as a way of persisting objects. The server vendor is responsible for ensuring that the objects are stored correctly, and that simultaneous access is handled properly. With EJBs, it is possible to write the entities that represent our system without having to design the underlying data structure for storage. We can use session beans to control access to these entities and offer utility operations that the client developers may utilize without having to be versed in their implementation.

12.6.1 *Writing custom tags for EJB access*

It should come as no surprise that our preferred method of accessing EJBs in JSP is through custom tags. To facilitate utilization of the EJB layer, we will create tags that assist us in accessing them. We do so by writing a tag library that will contain two tags:

- `<home>` allows instantiation of a home interface of a specific EJB.
- `<use>` grants the capacity to use the home interface to find existing entities or create new session or entity EJBs.

After an EJB has been retrieved, we treat it as any other bean with our tags. You can use any of the JavaBean tags we've developed in the book so far, such as `<show>`, to display EJB entity fields in a JSP page, and so forth.

As RMI over IIOP is used behind the scenes whenever an EJB method is called, all returned home or remote interfaces must be narrowed before being used. Both the `<home>` and `<use>` tags will therefore narrow the instances before adding them to the given scope. We also need to extend our tags for iteration so that all remote interfaces in a collection are narrowed before usage.[2] We therefore develop a third EJB tag that will be an `<iterator>` for collections of remote interfaces.

12.6.2 *Retrieving the EJB home interface*

The `<home>` tag retrieves home interfaces for EJBs that are defined as EJB references in our web applications deployment descriptor. The tag then narrows and adds the home interface to the JSP page scope so that it can be used to our heart's desire. In listing 12.17, you can see the implementation of this tag.

Listing 12.17   The implementation of the home tag

```
package book.j2ee;

import javax.ejb.*;
import javax.naming.*;
import javax.servlet.http.*;
import javax.servlet.jsp.*;
import javax.servlet.jsp.tagext.*;
import book.util.ExTagSupport;

public class HomeTag extends ExTagSupport
{
  protected String name;
  protected String type;

  public void setName(String name)
  {
    this.name = name;
  }

  public void setType(String type)
  {
    this.type = type;
  }

  public int doStartTag() throws JspException
  {
    try{
      InitialContext context = new InitialContext();          ❶
      ClassLoader classLoader=
            pageContext.getPage().getClass().getClassLoader();  ❷
      EJBHome home =                                            ❸
        (EJBHome)javax.rmi.PortableRemoteObject.narrow(
            context.lookup("java:comp/env/"+name),
            Class.forName(type, true, classLoader));
```

---

[2] The narrow method is used to check whether a certain remote or abstract interface can be cast to a given type.

```
      pageContext.setAttribute(this.getId(), home);
      return SKIP_BODY;
    }
    catch(NamingException e)
    {
      throw new JspTagException(
             "NamingException: " + e.getMessage());
    }
    catch(ClassNotFoundException e){
      throw new JspTagException(
             "ClassNotFoundException: " + e.getMessage());
    }
  }

  protected void clearServiceState()
  {
    name = null;
    type = null;
  }
}
```

❶ Creates an `InitialContext` The tag creates an `InitialContext` which it will use to look up the EJB.

❷ Retrieves the page's `ClassLoader` The tag retrieves the current page's `Class-Loader`, which will be used to instantiate a class of the type specified by the user.

❸ Narrows the returned home to the specified class type The tag uses the `Initial-Context` to look up a JNDI path consisting of the root string `java:comp/env/` plus the JNDI name given by the user (such as `ejb/MyHome`). The returned class is then narrowed to the specific home type specified by the user. Finally, we add the home interface to the `page` scope.

HomeTEI

We must now define how this home interface is available throughout the page, which requires us to make it available as a scripting variable. As we have seen several times in this book, the way to specify a tag published scripting variable is to define a `TagExtraInfo` object for the tag. We do this in listing 12.18.

Listing 12.18   The implementation of HomeTEI

```
package book.j2ee;

import javax.ejb.*;
import javax.naming.*;
import javax.servlet.jsp.*;
import javax.servlet.jsp.tagext.*;
```

```java
public class HomeTEI extends TagExtraInfo
{
  public VariableInfo[] getVariableInfo(TagData data)
  {
    return new VariableInfo[]
    {
      new VariableInfo(
        data.getId(),
        data.getAttributeString("type"),
        true,
        VariableInfo.AT_BEGIN
      ),
    };
  }
}
```

Here we specify that a variable with the given ID and the given type will be added to the page scope from the start of this tag to the end of the page.

The HomeTag TLD

Now we need to write a tag library descriptor and the HomeTag will be complete. Listing 12.19 is the descriptor we will need.

Listing 12.19   The HomeTag TLD

```xml
<?xml version="1.0" encoding="ISO-8859-1" ?>
<!DOCTYPE taglib PUBLIC "-//Sun Microsystems, Inc.//DTD JSP Tag Library 1.1//
  EN" "http://java.sun.com/j2ee/dtds/web-jsptaglibrary_1_1.dtd">
<taglib>
  <tlibversion>1.0</tlibversion>
  <jspversion>1.1</jspversion>
  <shortname>ejb-tags</shortname>
  <uri>http://www.manning.com/jsptagsbook/ejb-taglib</uri>
  <info>EJB Taglib</info>
  <tag>
    <name>home</name>
    <tagclass>book.j2ee.HomeTag</tagclass>
    <teiclass>book.j2ee.HomeTEI</teiclass>
    <bodycontent>empty</bodycontent>
    <info>Adds a EJB Home interface to the page scope</info>
    <attribute>
      <name>id</name>
      <required>true</required>
      <rtexprvalue>false</rtexprvalue>
    </attribute>
    <attribute>
      <name>name</name>
      <required>true</required>
```

```
      <rtexprvalue>false</rtexprvalue>
    </attribute>
    <attribute>
      <name>type</name>
      <required>true</required>
      <rtexprvalue>false</rtexprvalue>
    </attribute>
  </tag>
</taglib>
```

In the tag library descriptor, we state that the tag library will contain a `<home>` tag that requires an ID, a name, and a type, which cannot be a runtime expression (so that it will be available in the translation phase).

HomeTag in action

Since the `CatalogueEntry` EJB has been given an EJB reference in an applications deployment configuration, we may access its home interface from JSP in the way described in listing 12.20.

Listing 12.20   Accessing the CatalogueEntry home interface from JSP

```
<%@ taglib uri="http://www.manning.com/jsptagsbook/ejb-taglib"
           prefix="ejb" %>
<HTML>
<HEAD>
  <TITLE>Accessing an EJB home interface</TITLE>
</HEAD>
<BODY BGCOLOR="#FFFFFF">
  <H1>Accessing an EJB home interface</H1>
  <HR>
  Retrieving the EJB home interface..<BR>
  <ejb:home id="home"                                            ❶
            type="book.ejb.catalogue.CatalogueEntryHome"
            name="ejb/catalogueEntry"/>
  The EJB home interface is retrieved.<BR>
  <HR>
</BODY>
</HTML>
```

❶ **Adds the home interface to the page scope.**

In the page, the `<home>` tag is passed the ID to use when adding our home interface to the `page` scope. We also ascribe the tag with the type of class that we want returned when we look up our EJB home with the given name.

12.6.3 *Using the EJB home interface*

Now that the home interface of an EJB is retrievable, we may access its methods with the use of tags from earlier in the book. For example, we could use the `<iterate>` tag in a fashion as described in listing 12.21.

Listing 12.21 Using the EJB home interface

```
...
<ejb:home id="home"
          name="ejb/catalogueEntry"
          type="book.ejb.catalogue.CatalogueEntryHome"/>
<iter:iterate id="entry"
              type="book.ejb.catalogue.CatalogueEntry"
              object="<%=home.findByType(\"pda\").iterator()%>">
  <bean:show name="entry"
             property="serial"/><BR>
</iter:iterate>
...
```

In this listing, we let the `<iterate>` tag iterate over the collection of entries as returned from the finder method, introduce the entries using their remote interface, and display the serial number property for each `CatalogueEntry` of the type `pda`. As previously stated, executing this JSP on an application server that uses RMI over IIOP could throw an exception, as the remote interfaces that the `<iterate>` tag returns to the page have not been narrowed. Later we will solve this by extending the `<iterate>` tag further. Yet, the narrowing problem is not unique for the `<iterate>` tag and is going to appear for any remote interface returned by an EJB, so we need a tag that allows us to use the home interface by retrieving and narrowing a remote interface. We'll now build the `UseTag`, which will do just that.

UseTag

Our `UseTag` is somewhat analogous to the standard JSP `<jsp:useBean>` tag, but differs in that it lets us use and put into scope an EJB, instead of a standard JavaBean (listing 12.22).

Listing 12.22 The implementation of UseTag

```
package book.j2ee;

import javax.ejb.*;
import javax.naming.*;
import javax.servlet.http.*;
import javax.servlet.jsp.*;
import javax.servlet.jsp.tagext.*;
import book.util.ExTagSupport;
```

```
public class UseTag extends ExTagSupport
{
  protected String type;
  protected EJBObject instance;

  public void setType(String type)
  {
    this.type = type;
  }

  public void setInstance(EJBObject instance)
  {
    this.instance = instance;
  }

  public int doStartTag() throws JspException
  {
    EJBObject object=null;
    try{
      ClassLoader classLoader=
            pageContext.getPage().getClass().getClassLoader();      ❶
      object = (EJBObject)javax.rmi.PortableRemoteObject.narrow(     ❷
            instance, Class.forName(type, true, classLoader));
    }
    catch(ClassNotFoundException e){
      throw new JspTagException(
            "ClassNotFoundException: " + e.getMessage());
    }
    pageContext.setAttribute(this.getId(),object);
    return SKIP_BODY;
  }

  protected void clearServiceState()
  {
    type = null;
    instance = null;
  }
}
```

❶ Retrieves the page's `ClassLoader`.

❷ Narrows the instance to the specified class type.

UseTag is given an EJB instance as a parameter through the `instance` attribute. It then adds the instance given to the `page` scope after narrowing it into an `EJBObject` that matches the type that was provided as attribute. The code is very similar to the code used to retrieve the home interface, the only major difference being that we needn't use lookup since the instance was given to us as a parameter to the tag. Next let's look at the TEI given in listing 12.23.

UseTEI

`UseTag` will put an instance of any EJB it is used with into `page` scope. Here's a look at how this is accomplished.

Listing 12.23   The implementation of UseTEI

```
package book.j2ee;

import javax.ejb.*;
import javax.naming.*;
import javax.servlet.jsp.*;
import javax.servlet.jsp.tagext.*;

public class UseTEI extends TagExtraInfo
{
  public VariableInfo[] getVariableInfo(TagData data)
  {
    return new VariableInfo[]
    {
      new VariableInfo(
        data.getId(),           ❶
        (String)data.getAttribute("type"),    ❷
        true,
        VariableInfo.AT_BEGIN
      ),
    };
  }
}
```

❶ **Publishes the scripting variable with the `id` that is specified by tag attribute.**
❷ **Publishes a variable of a type that is also specified by a tag attribute.**

In listing 12.23, we specify that a variable named with the given ID and the given type will be added to the `page` scope from the start of this tag to the end of the page, just as in `HomeTEI`.

Updating the TLD to include UseTag

We should now update the EJB tag library descriptor by adding the tag descriptor as in listing 12.24.

Listing 12.24   Adding the tag to the descriptor

```
...
<tag>
    <name>use</name>
    <tagclass>book.j2ee.UseTag</tagclass>
    <teiclass>book.j2ee.UseTEI</teiclass>
```

```
<bodycontent>empty</bodycontent>
<info>Adds a EJB Remote Interface to the page scope</info>
<attribute>
  <name>id</name>
  <required>true</required>
  <rtexprvalue>false</rtexprvalue>
</attribute>
<attribute>
  <name>instance</name>
  <required>true</required>
  <rtexprvalue>true</rtexprvalue>
</attribute>
<attribute>
  <name>type</name>
  <required>true</required>
  <rtexprvalue>false</rtexprvalue>
</attribute>
</tag>
...
```

In the addition to the tag library descriptor, we state that the library will also contain the `<use>` tag, which requires an ID, an instance, and a type as parameters. Of these parameters, only instance can be a runtime expression.

UseTag in action

Because the `CatalogueEntry` EJB described in the beginning of this chapter has received an EJB reference in an application's deployment configuration, we may use the EJB's home interface from JSP in the way described in listing 12.25.

Listing 12.25   Using the CatalogueEntry home interface in JSP

```
<%@ taglib uri="http://www.manning.com/jsptagsbook/ejb-taglib"
           prefix="ejb" %>
<HTML>
<HEAD>
  <TITLE>Accessing an EJB home interface</TITLE>
</HEAD>
<BODY BGCOLOR="#FFFFFF">
  <H1>Accessing an EJB home interface</H1>
  <HR>
  Retrieving the EJB home interface..<BR>
  <ejb:home id="home"
            type="book.ejb.catalogue.CatalogueEntryHome"
            name="ejb/catalogueEntry"/>
  The EJB home interface is retrieved.<BR>
  Finding the Entry with serial ABC123..<BR>
```
❶

```
<ejb:use id="entry"
         type="book.ejb.catalogue.CatalogueEntry"
         instance="<%=home.findByPrimaryKey(\"ABC123\")%>"/>
The entry was found.<BR>
<HR>
</BODY>
</HTML>
```
❷

❶ **Defines an instance of `CatalogueEntryHome` into the JSP scope**   Walking through the JSP, you'll see that we add the home interface for the `CatalogueEntry` EJB to the page scope with an ID of `home`.

❷ **Uses the home interface to find a `CatalogueEntry` and to return its remote interface**   Next, we use the `<use>` tag to narrow and add the remote interface of `CatalogueEntry` EJB to the `page` scope, by asking the home interface to find the `CatalogueEntry` that has a serial of `"ABC123"`. If such an entry is found, we can refer to `"entry"` as a scripting variable through the remainder of the JSP, calling methods of the EJB as desired.

IterateEJBTag

In order to iterate through collections of remote interfaces returned by methods called on the EJB home interfaces, we need a tag that works similarly to the `<iterate>` tag of chapter 10. The only difference will be that this tag will try to narrow the remote interface to the specified type before adding it to the given scope (see listing 12.26). Note that there is an alternative to the updated `<iterate>` tag. We could use the `<use>` tag to narrow the iterator exported from the `<iterate>` tag prior to using it. However this forces the JSP coder to develop insight into the intrinsics of EJB, something we chose to avoid.

Listing 12.26   The implementation of IterateEJBTag

```
package book.j2ee;

import java.util.Enumeration;
import java.util.Iterator;
import javax.ejb.*;
import javax.servlet.jsp.JspException;
import book.iteration.*;

public class IterateEJBTag extends IterateTag
{

  protected String type;

  public void setType(String type)           ❶
```

```
{
  this.type=type;
}

public String getType()
{
  return type;
}

protected void exportVariables() throws JspException
{
  try{
    current = elementsList.getNext();
    ClassLoader classLoader=
          pageContext.getPage().getClass().getClassLoader();
    EJBObject object =
      (EJBObject)javax.rmi.PortableRemoteObject.narrow(
      current,Class.forName(getType(),
      true, classLoader));
    pageContext.setAttribute(id, object);
  }catch(ClassNotFoundException cnfe){
    throw new JspException(cnfe.getMessage());
  }
}
}
```

 Overriding setType() to save the type The tag overrides setType() of the Iter-ateTag class and adds a method for reading this value. We will need the type's value in order to narrow the iterator object into a concrete type in exportVariables().

❷ **Retrieves the page's ClassLoader** ❸ **Narrows the next remote interface to the specified class type** The tag overrides exportVariables() of the IterationTag-Support class. In that method, the tag first retrieves the current page's ClassLoader. The tag then narrows the next item in the collection into the remote interface type specified by the user. Finally, we add the remote interface to the page scope.

As the new tag can use the same TEI as the original <iterate>, we needn't create a TEI for this tag.

The IterateEJBTag TLD
We now need to update the EJB TLD by adding the tag descriptor as in listing 12.27.

Listing 12.27   Adding the tag to the descriptor

```
...
<tag>
  <name>iterate</name>
  <tagclass>book.j2ee.IterateEJBTag</tagclass>
  <teiclass>book.iteration.IterateTagExtraInfo</teiclass>
  <bodycontent>JSP</bodycontent>
  <info>
    Iterate over an Object. The object can be an array, an Iterator
    or an Enumeration of Remote interfaces.
  </info>
  <attribute>
    <name>id</name>
    <required>true</required>
    <rtexprvalue>false</rtexprvalue>
  </attribute>
  <attribute>
    <name>type</name>
    <required>true</required>
    <rtexprvalue>false</rtexprvalue>
  </attribute>
  <attribute>
    <name>object</name>
    <required>false</required>
    <rtexprvalue>true</rtexprvalue>
  </attribute>
  <attribute>
    <name>name</name>
    <required>false</required>
    <rtexprvalue>false</rtexprvalue>
  </attribute>
  <attribute>
    <name>scope</name>
    <required>false</required>
    <rtexprvalue>false</rtexprvalue>
  </attribute>
  <attribute>
    <name>index</name>
    <required>false</required>
    <rtexprvalue>true</rtexprvalue>
  </attribute>
  <attribute>
    <name>property</name>
    <required>false</required>
    <rtexprvalue>false</rtexprvalue>
  </attribute>
</tag>
...
```

In this addition to the tag library descriptor, we state that the library will also contain the `<iterate>` tag, which requires the same parameters as the original `<iterate>` tag, with the difference that the attribute `type` is now required.

IterateEJBTag in action

Let's change the example given in listing 12.21 so that it takes advantage of our new tag as described in listing 12.28.

Listing 12.28   Using the EJB home interface with the EJB iterate tag

```
...
<ejb:home id="home"
          name="ejb/catalogueEntry"
          type="book.ejb.catalogue.CatalogueEntryHome"/>
<ejb:iterate id="entry"
             type="book.ejb.catalogue.CatalogueEntry"
             object="<%=home.findByType(\"pda\").iterator()%>">
  <bean:show name="entry"
             property="serial"/><BR>
</ejb:iterate>
...
```

Here, we first use the `<home>` tag to retrieve a home interface. We then use the new `<iterate>` tag from the EJB tag library to iterate through the collection returned by the home interface's `findByType()` method. Every remote interface iterated, will be narrowed before it is added to the `page` scope.

Final thoughts

From the listings it is clear that using tags to access the EJB layer is easily done and allows us to write less code than if we were to use a servlet, or, if we were unconcerned with using scriptlets. The complexity of the EJB as seen in this chapter is virtually the tip of the EJB iceberg. If you are looking for a pervasive way to incorporate EJBs into your JSP, tags are probably your only alternative.

A common practice with EJBs is to write session EJBs that provide access methods to the various entities (and entity EJBs) that comprise your applications. This approach makes it easy to add or change the sanctioned methods of retrieving these entities. Such session EJBs usually include utility methods that perform functions, such as returning all entities as a `Collection`, making it even easier for the developers to divide the application into separate layers and pare down still more of the code required for the presentation.

Note that the EJB tags we present could be even further optimized. For instance, there are utility methods in the EJB home interface that find out the type of the named EJB's home and remote interfaces. With a little knowledge of EJB, these tags can be enhanced so that the user has only to specify the name of the EJB, and the tags will themselves find out what types to use for them. We have not taken on this topic, as it would divert attention from tags to advanced EJB usage, which is not the scope of this book.

12.7 Summary

EJBs are well poised to have a huge impact (beyond their already stunning acceptance) in coming years. In light of this, designing your tags from the ground up with J2EE integration in mind will give your tag library a head start.

As we illustrated, using resources such as database connections and JavaMail sessions from within a J2EE-compliant container is easier and provides a much greater flexibility than using them from within a plain-Jane servlet container. When using J2EE managed resources, a major part of the extra code that we usually devote to integration and configuration is handled by the container. Moreover, most (if not all) J2EE capable application servers add additional, sometimes proprietary, capabilities such as database connection pooling to their `DataSources`—another problem that we, the component developers, are more than willing to pass to the middleware vendor.

We looked at EJBs in this chapter and developed tags that facilitate the use of EJBs within a JSP. The EJB standard is a great addition to the enterprise Java arsenal and more and more JSP files will directly access them. Yet, as we've seen, the EJB programming model and APIs are somewhat complex. Hiding the gory details of this complexity within custom tags helps lower the bar of using EJBs within your JSP files.

When dealing with a topic as daunting as J2EE, it is impossible to cover everything without devoting an entire book to the subject. We did not cover the usage of one of the more significant subtopics in J2EE, the JMS. With JMS, one can use a message queue to bridge the gap between systems and build message-oriented Middleware (MOM)-based applications. J2EE-related issues associated with using JMS are similar to the principles covered in other sections of this chapter, such as the discussion of J2EE JDBC.

This concludes part III of the book. In the next two chapters, we showcase all of the concepts introduced so far in two real-world applications that use custom tags.

Part IV

Case studies

We depart from the academic discussion of tag development of the preceding chapters to look at real-world tag libraries in detail. The two chapters in part IV build on the concepts covered thus far, illustrating them in two tag library case studies: a JDBC-driven web store and an EJB-driven WAP store.

JDBC-driven WebStore

13

445

13.1 *Introduction*

In the hypothetical case study presented in this chapter we take a deeper look at tag usage within a web application. We go through the requirements of a web store, design it, and then look at the implementation of the solution. Throughout this study, we make intense use of the tags developed in earlier chapters, so it is crucial that you feel confident with them before beginning this adventure.

The application is built as a Model-2 or MVC (model view controller) layered solution, with emphasis on the view layer. The system is divided into the three layers described in table 13.1. For more information about Model-2, see chapter 2.

Table 13.1　The three layers of Model-2.

Layer	Description
Model	Data storage, and any entities that represent data found in that storage. Entities will be implemented as beans. These beans are normally initiated in the control layer, and then used in the presentation layer.
View	The user interfaces. These user interfaces are normally implemented as JSP pages, called by the control layer, using beans representing the model to produce dynamic output.
Controller	All processing functions that our system will need. Controllers are normally implemented as servlets. When a user requests information, a controller is called, performs control-related actions (such as validating user, retrieving data from model, initializing beans, etc.), and then calls an appropriate view to display the information.

The application we study throughout this chapter commits to the J2EE 1.2 standard and should run on any application server that follows this standard. On the companion web site (http://www.manning.com/shachor) you will find the full application and two application servers that can be used to test it. Read appendix C for more information about deploying the application.

13.1.1 *Custom tags used*

Throughout the application, we utilize the custom tags provided in table 13.2. In the table, you will find the name of the tag, the tag library to which it belongs, and a short description of its usage. The table also references the chapter wherein you can brush up on a particular tag. The tags are ordered by the tag library to which they belong.

We will create two new tags in this chapter: <currency> and <nocache>.

Table 13.2 The custom tags used in the WebStore application

Tag	Tag library	Usage	Chapter
`<command>`	Bean-taglib	Executes methods on objects	15
`<show>`	Bean-taglib	Shows bean properties	8
`<with>`	Conditional-taglib	Creates conditions that can be tested	9
`<test>`	Conditional-taglib	Tests conditions	9
`<connection>`	Database-taglib	Retrieves a database connection	11
`<enum>`	Database-taglib	Enumerates through the query results	11
`<query>`	Database-taglib	Defines an SQL query	11
`<iterate>`	Iteration-taglib	Iterates through collections	10
`<currency>`	Locale-taglib	Displays currency formatted with a certain locale	13
`<message>`	Mail-taglib	Defines messages for emails	7
`<send>`	Mail-taglib	Defines start, recipients, and senders for emails	7
`<subject>`	Mail-taglib	Defines subjects for emails	7
`<nocache>`	Simple-taglib	Prevents client-side caching of the page	13
`<redirect>`	Simple-taglib	Redirects the request to a given location	6

13.2 *Overview*

Cosmetics, a small firm supplying retail chains with ecological beauty cosmetics, has experienced an increased demand for its products. The company has three full-time employees and is based in a garage owned by one of the founders. Accompanying the increased demand for the products is a huge increase in paperwork. Cosmetics must either hire a full-time employee for order handling, or find a solution that makes order handling more efficient.

Management decides it would be best to set up a small site wherein customers can order online. If this is successful, Cosmetics employees can focus on filling orders more quickly, rather than using time writing them down as customers call in, then filling the order.

Once the company is in better financial shape, management will probably want to establish a full-scale online system. The delay may have a positive effect: management can evaluate customers' reactions before overinvesting in a new service.

Cosmetics contacted us to set up the service as our prices are fair and we have a good reputation in business. We agreed to analyze, design, and implement a solution that matches the company's requirements.

After an initial chat, in which we attempted to persuade them to accept a J2EE-compliant EJB-based solution, we agreed that as a first step, the store would be based upon JDBC.

13.3 *Requirements*

Cosmetics management listed fifteen development requirements for the system. Based on the requirements, all of which will be discussed in this section, we will design a solution and study its implementation.

General

The initial system will feature basic layout and design. Cosmetics will improve this in-house over time. The presentation layer must be easy to manipulate by nontechnical people with limited knowledge of Java programming.

Orders that are not confirmed by the user need not be committed to memory.

Users

The system must handle two different types of users—regular (those who are logged on) and anonymous (those who are not logged on to the system). Unless otherwise specified, user refers to those who are logged on, not anonymous users.

All users should, at any time, be able to browse the products and reach the welcome page. A user should be able to, on demand, see a brief description of the current order and be able to view all the order's details, update the stored profile, add products to the current order, and log off the system, becoming anonymous.

The anonymous user must always be able to register a profile with the system. A valid registration must be stored in the customer database. The anonymous user should also be able to log on and, when doing so, the user's profile should be loaded from the storage, making them a regular user.

Existing data sources

Cosmetics has an existing customer database in a DBMS called hSQL in which the company has stored product and category information. The new system may reuse this data, although the tables will want to be expandable and editable as needed.

The existing customer database (table 13.3) is currently primarily used for:

- Printing package delivery labels
- Call-backs to identify customers when taking orders
- Faxing receipts of orders

Table 13.3 Existing customer data

Attribute name	Data type	Description
Id	Integer	The unique identifier of a customer.
Company	Varchar	The customer's company name.
Name	Varchar	The customer's name.
Address	Varchar	The customer's address.
Phone	Varchar	The customer 's phone number.
Fax	Varchar	The customer's fax number.

To place an order, a user must have an existing profile in the customer database. This provides Cosmetics an index of the number of its customers. Currently, no record is kept on the number of orders a customer logs. Keeping track of this will be part of the solution, but at the moment, only the total number of orders, not the number of orders per customer, is of interest.

The existing category data (table 13.4) is primarily used for grouping the products into their various lines. As understood by the table definition, Cosmetics' current system allows categories only in single-depth. No category tree is needed or asked for in the new system.

Table 13.4 The existing category data

Attribute name	Data type	Description
Id	Integer	The unique identifier of the category.
Name	Varchar	The name of the category.

The existing product information (table 13.5) is used with the product line information for printing flyers and other merchandising.

Table 13.5 The existing product data

Attribute name	Data type	Description
SKU	Varchar	Stock keeping unit, the unique identifier of the product.
Name	Varchar	The name of the product.
Price	Decimal	The product price.
CategoryId	Integer	The ID of the category to which the product belongs.

As understood by the definition in table 13.4, every product belongs to only one category. A category can be empty.

Welcome

Each user will be greeted with a welcome message which displays information about Cosmetics and contact information. All information should be easy to redo without editing the actual view.

Category list

Whenever a user chooses to list available product categories, the result will be displayed in a two-colored list containing the categories' names. If a user chooses to view a certain category, it will be displayed according to the requirements given in the Product list. Cosmetics would like to introduce category images, so the presentation of the category list must be prepared for that.

Product list

The company would like a list of products displayed whenever a user selects a certain category. Cosmetics wants this list to be two-colored, displaying product's:

- SKU
- Name
- Price

No product description is needed because Cosmetics' products are well known and need no further presentation among the primary targeted customers.

The price will be formatted for American dollars initially, although Cosmetics requests that it be easy to change to any other currency without updating the actual view.

If the product list is presented to a customer, the user should be able to add a given amount of a certain product to the current order.

Short order

A short list of items in the current order must be displayed at all times and contain the SKU, name, and ordered quantity.

Full order

All details about the current order need to be accessible. The information to be displayed will be the SKU, name, price, quantity, and row total for every item in the order, together with a total price.

The user should be able to send the order to Cosmetics for processing from this view.

Order summary

When a user elects to send the current order to Cosmetics for processing, an order summary view will be displayed. This view will display the order total price and the user's shipping address and give the user a chance to cancel before the order is sent to Cosmetics for processing.

If the user confirms the order, it should be processed and a confirmation displayed. If the user cancels the order, the full order view is to be displayed.

Order processing

Order processing involves storing the order in Cosmetics' database then displaying an order confirmation. As product descriptions and prices might change before an order is delivered, all relevant information about the order is stored in the database. For the same reasons, the customer's name, company, and address at the time of ordering must also be stored.

Order confirmation

After the system has processed an order, a confirmation message, containing an order reference number, should be displayed and a receipt based on the processed order is sent to the user.

The user may continue to use the system, but the confirmed order should not be accessible for further processing. Any items added to the current order need to go into a new order.

Logon

When a user wants to log on, the system must ask for the username and password. When the user submits the required information, a greeting should be displayed if a matching profile is found. If no matching profile is found, the user is asked again for the username and password.

Logoff

When a user wants to log off, a message will be displayed, welcoming the user back at another time.

Any current order not confirmed by the user needn't be stored for future visits.

Update profile

A user ought to be able to update his profile at any time. If the changed data is valid it should be committed to the database, and a confirmation message should be displayed to the user. Otherwise, no changes need be committed, and the user is prompted to retry.

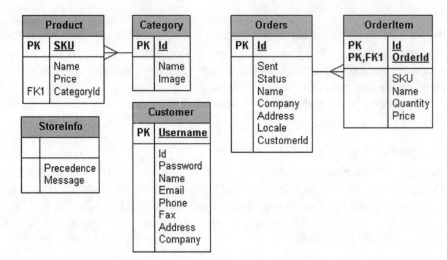

Figure 13.1 Overview of tables

Registration

A user who is not logged on ought to be able to register his profile with the system. If the supplied information is valid, the user information should be stored in a new profile and a message displayed welcoming the user to the community. The user would be considered logged on at this stage. If the supplied information is not valid, the user is prompted to enter the requested information anew.

13.4 Design

We are now ready to design a solution to meet Cosmetics' requirements. We will keep to the MVC approach and focus on the views of the solution and how to implement the requirements.

13.4.1 Model

Here is a summary of the data sources we will use and their representations as beans. Figure 13.1 is an overview of the tables we will need.

StoreInfo

The StoreInfo (table 13.6) holds a number of messages to be displayed on the welcome page in the order described by a precedence value given to every message. To make it easy for Cosmetics to insert new messages in the middle of existing ones, we will define the precedence as a decimal number.

Table 13.6   The StoreInfo data table

Attribute name	Data type	Description
Precedence	Decimal	The sequence order for messages.
Message	Varchar	The message to display.

As the StoreInfo message does not need additional control or filtering, we will not give it any bean representation. Instead, the page displaying the messages will fetch them directly from the data source.

Customer

The Customer table will be extended to look like table 13.7. We have added an email address for sending receipts, and a username and password so that users may identify themselves to the system and retrieve their profiles. We will (with an agreement from Cosmetics) switch the primary key from the ID to the username, in order to make sure that no two users have the same username in the system. Of course, this means that we take the full responsibility that the customer's ID remains unique.

Table 13.7   The extended customer data

Attribute name	Data type	Description
Id	Integer	A unique ID for a customer.
Username	Varchar	The unique identifier of a customer.
Password	Varchar	The password to the customer's profile.
Company	Varchar	The customer company name.
Name	Varchar	The customer's name.
Address	Varchar	The customer's address.
Email	Varchar	The customer's email address.
Phone	Varchar	The customer's phone number.
Fax	Varchar	The customer's fax number.

The bean representation of the customer will have get/set methods for these values and a utility method, isValid(), that tells us that information given during registration is considered valid. At this time, we will only check that the obligatory values are not null or empty. We will also add a utility method, named `isLoggedOn()`, to check whether or not the current customer is logged on.

The bean will be held in the `session` scope throughout the user's visit to the system.

Category

We will extend the existing category data with a field that can hold an image URL, so that the category data appears as in table 13.8.

Table 13.8   The extended category data

Attribute name	Data type	Description
Id	Integer	The unique identifier of the category.
Name	Varchar	The name of the category.
Image	Varchar	An optional image URL.

Because we need only one presentation of the category list, and all categories should be displayed in that view (no processing), and we have a nice set of database-related tags, we need not make a bean representation of the categories. Instead we will let the views retrieve and display the category information straight from the tables.

Product

We will not extend the existing product data in any way, but let it remain as is (table 13.9). In the future, Cosmetics will likely want a separate presentation of each product, and at that time we should probably have to add descriptions to the product data. But that is not what we are doing now.

Table 13.9   The existing product data

Attribute name	Data type	Description
SKU	Varchar	Stock keeping unit, the unique identifier of the product.
Name	Varchar	The name of the product.
Price	Decimal	The product price.
CategoryId	Integer	The ID of the category to which the product belongs.

As with the category data, we will not provide it with a bean representation, but will fetch the data directly from the data source.

Order

We create a table to store completed orders (table 13.10). Notice that an order will have an ID reference to the customer placing the order, but will store a copy of the customer's address information at the time of ordering.

Table 13.10   The new Orders data

Attribute name	Data type	Description
ID	Integer	The unique identifier of the order and also the order reference number.
Sent	Timestamp	The time the order was sent in.
Status	Char	'S' for sent.
CustomerID	Integer	The ID of the customer.
Name	Varchar	The name of the customer.
Company	Varchar	The customer's company.
Address	Varchar	The address of the customer.
Locale	Varchar	The locale used for currency when the order was sent.

This is something you would probably not want to try at home. Having the order reference number as an incrementing number provides any ordering customer the exact number of orders received by the company so far. But Cosmetics management was unconcerned as they could always add a dummy order with a very high number into the table to obscure the real number of orders sent up to then. We let it stay an incrementing number, knowing that we can always change it when our customer has gained experience of online ordering. At that time, we can easily create a unique hash key for the customer as a reference order ID.

The order data will have a bean representation with get/set methods for id. It will also hold a number of OrderItems in a collection that can be retrieved by get-Entries(). In order to add and remove OrderItems from this collection, addEntry() and removeEntry() will be available.

The bean will also hold a utility method that allows us to check if the order is empty, called isEmpty(). getTotalPrice() will return the order's total price.

OrderItem

We will add a table to hold the items that comprise the order, consisting of the data displayed in table 13.11. The table needs its own unique ID, as well as a reference to the order of which it is a part. These two IDs will be used to identify a unique row in this table.

Table 13.11 The new OrderItem data

Attribute name	Data type	Description
ID	Integer	The unique identifier of the OrderItem row, part of unique key.
OrderId	Timestamp	The order ID, part of unique key.
SKU	Varchar	The item's SKU.
Name	Varchar	The name of the item at the time of ordering.
Quantity	Integer	The ordered quantity.
Price	Decimal	The item price at the time of ordering.

We will store the name of the product so that we do not lose this information if the product description is changed or the product is removed. We will store the price of the product at the time of ordering, so that future changes upon the product won't affect the stored order.

The OrderItem data will have a bean representation with get/set methods for SKU, name, quantity, and price. At this time, neither the ID nor the OrderId need be available, since this information is only of interest after the order has been sent. In the future, we might want to include get/set methods for this data, too.

We will add a utility method called getTotalPrice() that will return the Order-Items' total price. The order bean will use this method to calculate the order total price.

13.4.2 View

We will implement a number of views and let some act also as controllers, in the sense that they both retrieve and present data.

General

As most views will display a short list of the user's current order and the available options, this will be implemented as two separate views that will be included in others by the use of the standard JSP tag <include>.

In order to ensure that pages holding user-specific dynamic content will not be cached by the user's browser, we need to create a <nocache> tag.

We will configure the database access settings in context parameters described in the web.xml file, so that we only have to change settings at one place. All <connection>

tags will then be used without giving these parameters, so that the tag will instead look in the Context for them. Likewise, we will configure our mail settings in the same location for the same reason.

Welcome

This view welcomes the user by displaying a number of messages from the Store-Info table. This page will also serve as the first displayed page of the system.

We will use the <connection> tag for creating a connection to the data source, and then use the <query> tag for creating and running a query that should give us all messages from the StoreInfo table ordered by precedence. We will output the result with the use of the <enum> tag .

Menu

The menu view displays options available to the current user, as well as ensuring that there are Customer and Order objects available for manipulation at all times.

We will use the <with> and <test> tags to display menu choices for all users, as well as for checking whether or not the user has a current order.

We use the <show> tag to get the application's ContextPath from the Request object to ensure that we have an absolute path to our image directory, wherein Cosmetics' logotype shall be stored.

Short order

The short order view displays a short list of all items in a user's current order.

We will use the <with> and <test> tags to check whether the user has a current order. If a current order exists, the <iterate> tag will display all of the rows currently in the user's order. The <show> tag will be used to retrieve the SKU, name, and quantity of each item in the order.

Category list

The category list view displays a selectable list of all available categories to the user.

Normally, there would be a controller collecting the data from the data source, turning it into a bean representation of this data, and sending these beans to a JSP page that would represent the category list. But as Cosmetics has only a single category depth, and no processing of the data is needed before it is displayed, we decided to let the view handle the data retrieval, thereby eliminating the need for beans to represent the data. If the information requires further processing before it is displayed, we can insert a controller to handle this.

We use the <connection> tag for creating a connection to the data source. We will then use the <query> tag for creating and running a query that should give us all categories currently in the category table. We output the result with the use of the <enum> tag.

We use the `<with>` and `<test>` tags for checking whether or not a category image should be displayed, as well as switching between background colors to achieve aa two-color list.

Product list

The product list view displays a list of all available products in a given category. As with the category list, the view will retrieve and display the information needed.

The `<connection>` tag will serve for creating a connection to the data source and a `<query>` tag for creating and running a query that tells us all products currently available in the selected category. The result will be output with the use of the `<enum>` tag of the database tag library. We will use the same tags to receive the name of the currently selected category.

The `<with>` and `<test>` tags shall check whether or not a category image is to be displayed. These tags are also used to switch between background colors to achieve a two-color list. These tags will also serve to decide whether or not the current user should be able to order the listed products, depending upon whether the user is logged on.

A `<currency>` tag will need to be created for displaying the product prices with the local currency. The tag should be able to fetch the currency in the form of a string representing a locale from the servlet `Context`, so that we don't have to specify the locale in each view needing currency formatting.

Registration

This is the view wherein a user may supply information needed for registering a profile with the system. Upon submitting this page, `RegistrationHandler` is called.

We will use `<with>` and `<test>` tags to check whether the user is logged on. If so, we will redirect them, using the `<redirect>` tag, to the profile view.

The `<show>` tag will be used to display the data currently held in the customer bean.

Registration successful

The registration successful view displays a message welcoming the user to the Cosmetics community. The page is displayed after a user has successfully registered.

The `<with>` and `<test>` tags will check whether the user is logged on. If the user is not logged on, we will redirect him, using the `<redirect>` tag, to the logon form.

The `<show>` tag will display the user's name.

Logon

The logon view displays a form wherein the user identifies himself to the system with a username and password. The form will be submitted to the logon handler for processing.

Logon successful

The logon successful view displays a message that welcomes the user back.

We will use the `<show>` tag to display the user's name.

Full order

The full order view displays all items in a user's current order together with price information and the option to remove items from the order. The user should also be able to submit an order from this view (see order summary view).

First, we will check whether the current user is logged on with our `<with>` and `<test>` tags. If the current user is not logged on, we use the `<redirect>` tag to redirect the user to the logon view.

We then need to check if the user's order holds any items. For this, we will use the conditional tags with the order bean's `isEmpty()` method. If the order is empty, we display a message saying so; otherwise, we display the full order.

To format the order's total price with the local currency, we use the `<currency>` tag with the locale specified in the servlet `Context`. This will also be used to format all order item prices.

We will use the `<iterate>` tag to pass through the order items to display all of them.

For every order item, we will use the `<show>` tag to display its details, and also to get the key (SKU) for removing the item from the order (by calling the remove item handler).

Order summary

This view displays the order's total price and the address to which the order will be shipped. The user can then confirm the order, which calls the confirmation handler, or cancel the action, which displays the full order view.

We use the `<with>` and `<test>` tags to verify that the user is logged on. We then verify that the user's order is not empty. If so, we redirect the user to the full order view. To format the order's total price with the local currency, we use the `<currency>` tag with the locale specified in the servlet `Context`.

Order confirmation

The order confirmation view displays an order reference number for a successfully received order, and sends the user a receipt with the order details. The order will be removed from the `session` scope by the confirmation handler, but a copy will be available in the `request` scope.

We use the `<show>` tag to display the order reference number and the `<email>` tags to send a receipt to the customer. The `<to>` tag is set to the value of the email address in the user's profile. We then use the `<subject>` tag to set an appropriate subject for the mail, and the `<message>` tag to set the body of the mail.

The `<iterate>` tag passes through the order and fills the mail body with information about the order rows. For each row, we use the `<currency>` tag to display the currency of the locale specified in the servlet `Context`.

Order confirmation error

This view displays a message urging the user to try again if we are unable to successfully store the user's sent order.

Profile

The profile view displays a form where a logged-on user might review and update his stored profile. The user can submit any changes, which will go to the profile update.

With the help of `<with>` and `<test>` tags, we verify whether the current user is logged on and, if not, we use the `<redirect>` tag to redirect the user to the Logon form.

After that, we display a form that includes the data from the user's profile. This data is retrieved with the `<show>` tag.

Profile updated successfully

This view displays a message to the user telling him that his profile was successfully updated. This view will be called by the profile update handler.

We use `<with>` and `<test>` tags to check if the current user is logged on, and then display the message telling the user that the profile was updated.

Logoff

This view logs off the current user and makes sure that the session is invalidated. We also display a message telling the user that we hope to see him or her again soon.

We use the `<command>` tag to invalidate the current user's session, and then display a message welcoming the user back at another time.

Generic error

This view catches `JSPTagExceptions` that might be thrown, and displays a friendly message to the user instead of a stack trace.

Mail error

This view catches any mail-related exceptions that might be thrown while sending receipts to the customer, and displays a friendly message ensuring the user that the order was received but that no receipt could be sent.

To display the order reference number, we use the `<show>` tag.

Number error

Sooner or later some user will try to add invalid amounts when ordering products. We will use this view to display a message telling the user to use valid numeric data when entering quantities.

13.4.3 Control

To carry this out, we will implement six controllers as servlets (table 13.12).

Table 13.12 The servlets making up the Control layer

Servlet name	Description
RegistrationHandler	Stores the user's profile with the system.
LogonHandler	Logs in the user, thereby adding the user's stored profile as a customer bean in the session scope.
AddItemHandler	Adds a product to the user's current order.
RemoveItemHandler	Removes an item from the user's current order.
OrderConfirmationHandler	Stores the user's current order in the database, then removes this order from the session scope, so that it cannot be further manipulated.
ProfileUpdateHandler	Updates the user's profile.

13.4.4 Utilities

Commonly used methods will be generalized into a database handler holding generic methods for executing queries and updates against stored data, as well as a method to set the properties of a given bean with the parameter values passed in by the request.

13.5 Implementation

Now we look at the implementation of the different views of the system and how these views utilize tags; and implement two new tags needed by our application.

We will not look deeper at the model or control layers as this information is available in the form of source code and table definitions at http://www.manning.com/shachor. In appendix C, there is information on deploying the application.

13.5.1 *Tags*

The application will need to display local currency amounts and prevent dynamic pages from being cached (table 13.13). As we have no tags with the necessary functionality in our existing tag libraries, we need to implement them now.

Table 13.13   The new tags that we need to implement

Name	Description
<nocache>	Prevents dynamic pages from being cached.
<currency>	Displays currency amounts formatted for a specified locale.

DisableCacheTag

The goal of `DisableCacheTag` will be to prevent dynamic pages from being cached. The user requires the option to decide whether this should be accomplished with the use of header fields or with metatags. We have already looked at header fields in chapter 1, so you are probably comfortable with these by now. Metatags are normally inserted into the head part of an HTML page, and are treated in the same way as header fields by most browsers. Depending on the usage of the tags, metatags or header fields are preferred. Our new tag will accept the attributes listed in table 13.14.

Table 13.14   The attributes for DisableCacheTag

Attribute name	Use	Setter/Getter Method
useHeaders	Tells the tag to use header fields to prevent pages from being cached.	setUseHeaders()
useMetaTags	Tells the tag to use meta tags to prevent pages from being cached.	SetUseMetaTags()

Listing 13.1 shows the implementation of the tag, which will be part of the simple tag library that we built in chapter 6.

Listing 13.1   The DisableCacheTag

```
package book.simpletasks;

import book.util.ExTagSupport;
import javax.servlet.http.HttpServletResponse;
import javax.servlet.jsp.JspWriter;
import javax.servlet.jsp.JspException;
import javax.servlet.jsp.JspTagException;

public class DisableCacheTag extends ExTagSupport
{
```

```
protected boolean useHeaders = true;
protected boolean useMetaTags = true;

public void setUseHeaders(String useHeaders)          ❶
{
  this.useHeaders = new Boolean(useHeaders).booleanValue();
}

public void setUseMetaTags(String useMetaTags)        ❷
{
  this.useMetaTags = new Boolean(useMetaTags).booleanValue();
}

public int doStartTag() throws JspException
{
  try {
    if(useHeaders) {
      HttpServletResponse res =
      (HttpServletResponse)pageContext.getResponse();
      if(res.isCommitted()) {                         ❸
        throw new JspTagException("RES_COMMITTED_ERROR");
      }
      res.setHeader("Cache-Control", "no-cache");            ❹
      res.setHeader("Pragma", "no-cache");
      res.setDateHeader("Expires", 0);
    }
    if(useMetaTags) {
      JspWriter w = pageContext.getOut();                    ❺
      w.print("<META HTTP-EQUIV=\"Cache-Control\"");
      w.print(" CONTENT=\"no-cache\">");
      w.newLine();
      w.print("<META HTTP-EQUIV=\"Pragma\"");
      w.print(" CONTENT=\"no-cache\">");
      w.newLine();
      w.print("<META HTTP-EQUIV=\"Expires\"");
      w.print(" CONTENT=\"-1\">");
      w.newLine();
    }
  }catch(java.io.IOException ioe) {
    throw new JspTagException("IO_ERROR");
  }
  return SKIP_BODY;
}

protected void clearProperties()
{
  useHeaders = true;
  useMetaTags = true;
  super.clearProperties();
}
}
```

Parameter to decide if header fields should be used   If the user passes `true` to `set-UseHeaders()`, the tag should output the necessary headers to prevent caching.

❷ **Parameter to decide if metatags should be used**   If the user passes `true` to `set-UseMetaTags()`, the tag should output the necessary metatags to prevent caching.

The default value for both parameters is `true`, so if no parameter is passed to the tag, both headers and metatags will be used.

❸ **Checks if response is committed**   `doStartTag()` checks whether header fields should be used. If so, it makes sure that the response has not already been committed, as this would prevent it from writing the header fields.

❹ **Sets cache preventing header fields**   As long as the response has not been committed, the tag sets the headers of the response to prevent the page from being cached.

❺ **Outputs cache preventing meta tags**   The tag checks whether metatags should be used. If so, the tag writes the needed metatags to the page.

In listing 13.1, we let the user specify if a new tag extends the `ExTagSupport` class. The tag can receive two parameters, one for each cache-disabling technique that it can handle.

The TLD for DisableCacheTag
The TLD for this tag is given in listing 13.2, and should be added to the tag library descriptor we created for the simple tags in chapter 6.

Listing 13.2   DisableCacheTag entry

```
...
<tag>
  <name>nocache</name>
  <tagclass>book.simpletasks.DisableCacheTag</tagclass>
  <bodycontent>empty</bodycontent>
  <info>
    Disable the browser cache
  </info>
  <attribute>
    <name>useMetaTags</name>
    <required>false</required>
  </attribute>
  <attribute>
    <name>useHeaders</name>
    <required>false</required>
  </attribute>
</tag>
...
```

As shown in listing 13.2, neither of the attributes is required; there is no obvious reason to let the attribute allow runtime values.

Example usage of DisableCacheTag

Usage of `DisableCacheTag` would look something like in listing 13.3.

Listing 13.3   DisableCacheTag usage

```
<%@ page contentType="text/html;charset=UTF-8"%>
<%@ taglib
    uri="http://www.manning.com/jsptagsbook/simple-taglib"
    prefix="simple" %>
<HTML>
  <HEAD>
    <TITLE>A cache disabled page</TITLE>
    <simple:nocache useMetaTags="true"/>
  </HEAD>
  <BODY BGCOLOR="#FFFFFF">
    <P>This page should not be cached!</P>
  </BODY>
</HTML>
```

In listing 13.3, we put the `<nocache>` tag in the head of the HTML page, as we want to use metatags to prevent the page from being cached. If we are about to use header fields instead, the placement of the tag is of less importance, although it is a good rule to place them as early on in the page as possible.

LocaleTag

In order to implement the `LocaleCurrencyTag` that formats a given amount as currency using a specified `Locale`, we first need a way of looking up the `Locale` we want. Other tags could take advantage of this ability to implement functionality for formatting numbers, dates, and percentages. Considering this, it makes sense to implement a basic tag that will then extend to format currencies.

`LocaleTag` accepts the attribute listed in table 13.15.

Table 13.15   The attribute for LocaleTag

Attribute name	Use	Setter/Getter Method
locale	The locale to use for further formatting	`setLocale/getLocale()`

The abstract `LocaleTag` that we will use as a base is listing 13.4.

Listing 13.4   The LocaleTag

```
package book.locale;

import java.util.Hashtable;
import java.util.Locale;
import java.util.StringTokenizer;
import book.util.ExTagSupport;
import javax.servlet.jsp.PageContext;
import javax.servlet.jsp.JspException;

public abstract class LocaleTag extends ExTagSupport {
  static final Hashtable localesCache = new Hashtable();
  public static final String LOCAL_INIT_PARAM = "locale";
  protected Locale locale = null;

  public void setLocale(Object l)
  {
    if(l instanceof Locale) {          ❶
      locale = (Locale)l;
    } else {
      locale = localeFromString(l.toString());
    }
  }

  protected Locale getLocale()
  {
    if(null != locale) {
      return locale;
    }
    Locale l = null;
    String localId = findInitParameter(LOCAL_INIT_PARAM);    ❷
    if(null != localId) {
      l = localeFromString(localId);
    }
    if(null == l) {
      l = pageContext.getRequest().getLocale();     ❸
    }
    return l;
  }

  protected Locale localeFromString(String spec)
  {
    Locale rc = (Locale)localesCache.get(spec);    ❹
    if(null != rc) {
      return rc;
    }
    StringTokenizer st = new StringTokenizer(spec.toString().trim(),
                                             "-_");
    String language = st.nextToken();
    String country = st.nextToken();
    rc = new Locale(language, country);
    if(null == rc) {
```

```
      rc = Locale.getDefault();
    }
    localesCache.put(spec, rc);     ⑤
    return rc;
  }
  protected void clearProperties()
  {
    locale = null;
    super.clearProperties();
  }
}
```

❶ **Checks if the object passed in is a `Locale`** The first thing we do in listing 13.4 is to check if the object passed in is a `Locale`. If it is not, we parse the string representing a `Locale` with `localeFromString()`.

❷ **Gets the string representing a `Locale` from initialization parameters** In `getLocale()` we check if a `Locale` has been specified. If not, we load an initialization parameter specifying a string representation of a `Locale` that we then pass in to `localeFromString()`.

❸ **Gets user's current `Locale`** If no `Locale` was specified as an initialization parameter, we will use the user's current `Locale` from the `Request`.

❹ **Gets the `Locale` from cache** In `localeFromString()` used to parse a string and find the `Locale` it represents, we first check if the string representation has already been parsed and put into our cache. If it hasn't, we use a `Stringtokenizer` to get the country and language from the given string. We then use these values and try to create a `Locale` from them. If this does not succeed, we use the system default `Locale` instead. If that works, we store the `Locale` in the cache with the string representation as key and return the `Locale` to the caller of the method.

❺ **Stores `Locale` in cache.**

Notice that this tag needs to be extended with some specific behavior before it will be usable.

LocaleTagExtraInfo

We will now create a `TagExtraInfo` class that is primarily used to verify that any specified string representation of a `Locale` passed in as a parameter to the `LocaleTag` is in the correct format. A correct string representation of a `Locale` is either in the form "en_US", where "en" is the language used and "US" is the country; or in the form "en-US," the form in which most browsers represent locales.

Other tags that will extend the `LocaleTag` to implement specialized behavior can also take advantage of the `LocaleTagExtraInfo` in listing 13.5.

Listing 13.5   The LocaleTagExtraInfo

```
package book.locale;

import javax.servlet.jsp.tagext.TagData;
import javax.servlet.jsp.tagext.TagExtraInfo;

public class LocaleTagExtraInfo extends TagExtraInfo {
  public boolean isValid(TagData data)
  {
    Object o = data.getAttribute("locale");
    if((o != null) && (o != TagData.REQUEST_TIME_VALUE)) {
      String localSpec = (String)o;
      if(localSpec.length() != 5) {
        return false;
      }
      if(localSpec.charAt(2) != '-' && localSpec.charAt(2) != '_') {
        return false;
      }
    }
    return true;
  }
}
```

`LocaleTagExtraInfo` overrides the `isValid()` method of the `TagExtraInfo` class which this TEI extends. In this method, it is verified that any string representation of a `Locale` consists of a five-character string, with either an underline or a hyphen symbol.

LocaleNumberTag

We now have `LocaleTag` that retrieves a `Locale` and need a tag that uses that `Locale` to format a given amount. As a third step, our `LocaleCurrencyTag` will extend this tag to format the given amount as currency. `LocaleNumberTag` will accept the attributes listed in table 13.16.

Table 13.16   The attributes for LocaleNumberTag

Attribute name	Use	Setter/Getter Method
locale	The locale to use for further formatting. Inherited from `LocaleTag`.	`setLocale/getLocale()`
amount	The amount to format into a localized number presentation.	`SetAmount()`

Listing 13.6 shows the implementation of `LocaleNumberTag`.

Listing 13.6 LocaleNumberTag

```java
package book.locale;

import java.util.Hashtable;
import java.util.Locale;
import java.text.NumberFormat;
import book.util.ExTagSupport;
import javax.servlet.jsp.PageContext;
import javax.servlet.jsp.JspException;
import javax.servlet.jsp.JspTagException;

public class LocaleCurrencyTag
    extends LocaleNumberTag {

    static LocalStrings ls =
        LocalStrings.getLocalStrings(LocaleCurrencyTag.class);
  protected double amount = 0.0;

  public void setAmount(double amount)         ❶
  {
    this.amount = amount;
  }

  public int doStartTag() throws javax.servlet.jsp.JspException
  {
    try {
      writeHtml(pageContext.getOut(),             ❷
      getNumberInstance().format(amount));
    } catch(java.io.IOException ioe) {
      throw new JspTagException(ls.getStr(Constants.IO_ERROR));
    }
    return SKIP_BODY;
  }

  protected NumberFormat getNumberInstance()
  {
    return NumberFormat.getInstance(getLocale());    ❸
  }

  protected void clearProperties()
  {
    amount = 0.0;
    super.clearProperties();
  }
}
```

❶ **Sets the `amount` property** The tag handles an amount property that will be sent in as a parameter by the user.

Writes out the formatted number In `doStartTag()`, the tag writes out the formatted amount with the `Locale` inherited from the `LocaleTag`. To do so, the method uses the `NumberFormat` class returned by `getNumberInstance()`. The `NumberFormat` utility class will format the amount with the specified `Locale`.

❸ **Gets a `NumberFormat` handler** `getNumberInstance()` uses the `Locale` to get a suitable `NumberFormat` instance. The `Locale` to use is handled by the `LocaleTag` and can be either specified by the user (as `Locale` or string), read from initialization parameters, resolved from the user's request or specified as the system default `Locale`.

The `java.text.NumberFormat` class provides three convenient methods for formatting numbers (table 13.17). For this tag, we used `getInstance()` to retrieve a `NumberFormat` instance for formatting numbers for the given `Locale`.

Table 13.17 The three convenient NumberFormat methods

Method	Description
`getInstance(Locale)`	Returns a number format for the specified locale.
`getCurrencyInstance(Locale)`	Returns a currency format for the specified locale.
`getPercentInstance(Locale)`	Returns a percentage format for the specified locale.

These three methods can also be used without specifying a `Locale`. The returned format will then be for the system default `Locale`.

The TLD for LocaleNumberTag

The TLD for `LocaleNumberTag` (listing 13.7) is the start of a new tag library descriptor that we will use to hold our `Locale` formatting tags. We will call this file localetags.tld.

Listing 13.7 LocaleNumberTag entry

```xml
<?xml version="1.0" encoding="ISO-8859-1" ?>
<!DOCTYPE taglib
    PUBLIC "-//Sun Microsystems, Inc.//DTD JSP Tag Library 1.1//EN"
    "http://java.sun.com/j2ee/dtds/web-jsptaglibrary_1_1.dtd">

<taglib>
  <tlibversion>1.0</tlibversion>
  <jspversion>1.1</jspversion>
  <shortname>locale</shortname>
  <uri> http://www.maning.com/jsptagsbook/locale-taglib </uri>
  <info>
    Locale tags library.
  </info>
```

```
<tag>
  <name>number</name>
  <tagclass>book.locale.LocaleNumberTag</tagclass>
  <teiclass>book.locale.LocaleTagExtraInfo</teiclass>
  <bodycontent>empty</bodycontent>
  <info>
    Prints a certain amount based on a specified locale
  </info>
  <attribute>
    <name>amount</name>
    <required>true</required>
    <rtexprvalue>true</rtexprvalue>
  </attribute>
  <attribute>
    <name>locale</name>
    <required>false</required>
    <rtexprvalue>true</rtexprvalue>
  </attribute>
</tag>
</taglib>
```

The `<number>` tag uses `LocaleTagExtraInfo` to verify any string representation of a `Locale`. The tag accepts two values, `amount` and `locale`, of which both can be runtime expressions, but only `locale` is optional.

Example usage of LocaleNumberTag
In listing 13.8, `LocaleNumberTag` is used to format an amount expressed as a runtime expression.

Listing 13.8   LocaleNumberTag usage

```
<%@ page contentType="text/html;charset=UTF-8"%>
<%@ taglib
    uri="http://www.manning.com/jsptagsbook/locale-taglib"
    prefix="locale" %>
<HTML>
  <HEAD>
    <TITLE>Displaying a formatted number</TITLE>
  </HEAD>
  <BODY BGCOLOR="#FFFFFF">
    <P>Below we format the amount 13.547 for the system default Locale</P>
    <P><locale:number amount="13.547"/></P>
  </BODY>
</HTML>
```

We used the `<number>` tag without specifying any `Locale`. As long as no application default value is specified, the tag would use the system default `Locale` to format the number. For example, if the system default `Locale` were "sv_SE" (Swedish), the output of the `<number>` tag usage would be "13,547".

LocaleCurrencyTag

With `LocaleTag` and `LocaleNumberTag` in place, it is now time to write `LocaleCurrencyTag` that will serve to format a given amount into a representation of a local currency. This tag will accept the same attributes (table 13.18) as `LocaleNumberTag`.

Table 13.18 The attributes for LocaleCurrencyTag

Attribute name	Use	Setter/Getter Method
locale	The locale to use for further formatting. Inherited from `LocaleTag`.	`setLocale/getLocale()`
Amount	The amount to format into a localized currency presentation. Inherited from `LocaleNumberTag`.	`SetAmount()`

Listing 13.9 shows the implementation of `LocaleCurrencyTag`.

Listing 13.9 LocaleCurrencyTag

```
package book.locale;

import java.util.Hashtable;
import java.util.Locale;
import java.text.NumberFormat;
import book.util.ExTagSupport;
import javax.servlet.jsp.PageContext;
import javax.servlet.jsp.JspException;

public class LocaleCurrencyTag extends LocaleNumberTag {
  static final Hashtable currencyFormatCache = new Hashtable();

  protected NumberFormat getNumberInstance()
  {
    Locale l = getLocale();
    NumberFormat rc = (NumberFormat)currencyFormatCache.get(l);
    if(null == rc) {
      rc = NumberFormat.getCurrencyInstance(l);
      currencyFormatCache.put(l, rc);
    }
    return rc;
  }
}
```

In listing 13.9, we define a `HashTable` that acts as a cache of local currency format-ted amounts. We then override `getNumberInstance()` of `LocaleNumberTag`. In this method, we first query the cache for any preprocessed instances of `NumberFormat` used for the given `Locale`. If no instance is found, we create one and add it to the cache before returning it to the caller of this method.

The TLD for LocaleCurrencyTag

The TLD for `LocaleCurrencyTag` (listing 13.10) should be added to `locale-taglib`.

Listing 13.10   The LocaleCurrencyTag entry

```
<tag>
        <name>currency</name>
        <tagclass>book.locale.LocaleCurrencyTag</tagclass>
        <teiclass>book.locale.LocaleTagExtraInfo</teiclass>
        <bodycontent>empty</bodycontent>
        <info>
            Prints a certain amount based on a specified locale
        </info>
        <attribute>
            <name>amount</name>
            <required>true</required>
            <rtexprvalue>true</rtexprvalue>
        </attribute>
        <attribute>
            <name>locale</name>
            <required>false</required>
            <rtexprvalue>true</rtexprvalue>
        </attribute>
    </tag>
```

The `<currency>` tag uses the same TEI class as the `<number>` tag. The tag accepts the two values' `amount`s and `locale`s, both of which can be runtime expressions. The `locale` attribute is optional, while both values can be runtime expressions.

Example usage of LocaleCurrencyTag

Listing 13.11 shows an example usage of `LocaleCurrencyTag`, wherein a given amount is formatted into a local currency.

Listing 13.11   LocaleCurrencyTag usage

```
<%@ page contentType="text/html;charset=UTF-8"%>
<%@ taglib
    uri="http://www.manning.com/jsptagsbook/locale-taglib"
    prefix="locale" %>
<HTML>
  <HEAD>
    <TITLE>Displaying a number as currency</TITLE>
  </HEAD>
  <BODY BGCOLOR="#FFFFFF">
    <P>Below we format the amount 23.512 as currency using
       the system default Locale</P>
     <P><locale:currency amount="23.512"/></P>
  </BODY>
</HTML>
```

In listing 13.11 we use the `<currency>` tag to format an amount using the system default `Locale`. If the system default `Locale` were Swedish ("sv_SE"), the output of the tag would be "23,51 kr". If the system default `Locale` were American ("en_US"), the output of the tag would instead be "$23.51".

New tags summary

The `<currency>` and the previous `<number>` tags are extremely useful for localizing content for an international market. But even if you wish only to display amounts for a single given `Locale`, the tags could be useful as they handle the formatting very skillfully.

There are, of course, other tags that could be helpful in an international application. For instance, a `<date>` tag would come in handy. At this stage it should be no problem to extend the `LocaleTag` and produce a `<date>` tag if needed. If nothing else, it could be good practice to produce such a tag.

We have now created the last of the tags that our application will need, and can thus continue with their usage. The next section describes how we take advantage of the various tags in the implementation of the different views that we will need.

13.5.2 Views

Nineteen views make up the system. We will study them one by one, going through all the details. The files found within the application are named in the listing titles.

Welcome

Listing 13.12 shows the source for the welcome view. This file is index.jsp.
Figure 13.2 is the Welcome page.

[HOME | CATALOGUE | LOGON | REGISTER]

Welcome!

We at Cosmetics are proud to be the number one supplier of
ecological cosmetic products on the American market.

If you are one of our customers, please log on in order to be able
to order our products.

If you are just interested in our products, feel free to browse our
ever increasing line of ecological products for all occations.

Questions or suggestions can be sent to info@cosmetics.com.

Figure 13.2
Welcome view

Listing 13.12   index.jsp

```jsp
<%@ page contentType="text/html;charset=UTF-8"%>
<%@ taglib
    uri="http://www.manning.com/jsptagsbook/database-taglib"
    prefix="db" %>
<%@ taglib
    uri="http://www.manning.com/jsptagsbook/simple-taglib"
    prefix="simple" %>
<db:connection id="con"/>          ❶
<db:query connection="con"                         ❷
          id="store">
select message from storeinfo order by precedence
</db:query>
<simple:nocache useHeaders="true"/>      ❸
<HTML>
<HEAD>
<TITLE>Cosmetics</TITLE>
</HEAD>
<BODY BGCOLOR="#FFFFFF">
<CENTER>
  <TABLE CELLSPACING="0"
         CELLPADDING="0"
         BORDER="0">
    <TR>
      <TD>
        <jsp:include page="userMenu.jsp"      ❹
                     flush="true"/>
```

```
      </TD>
    </TR>
    <TR>
      <TD ALIGN="center">
        <FONT SIZE="+2"><B>Welcome!</B></FONT>
      </TD>
    </TR>
    <TR>
      <TD WIDTH="400">
<db:enum query="store" id="i">        ❺
        <P ALIGN="justify">             ❻
          <$ MESSAGE $>
        </P>
</db:enum>        ❼
        <P ALIGN="justify">
        Questions or suggestions can be sent to <A HREF="mailto:info@cosmet-
  ics.com">info@cosmetics.com</A>.
        </P>
      </TD>
    </TR>
    <TR>
      <TD ALIGN="center">
        <BR>
        <jsp:include page="shortOrder.jsp" flush="true"/>        ❽
      </TD>
    </TR>
  </TABLE>
</CENTER>
</BODY>
</HTML>
```

❶ **Creates a connection to the database**   By not passing in any parameters other than the ID that we will use to refer to the connection, we force the <connection> tag to look for the needed parameters in the servlet Context, in which they should be defined as context parameters. In listing 13.13, which is a cutout from the web.xml file of our web application, you can see what this configuration looks like.

❷ **Creates a query using the previously defined connection**   After that, we define the query that we want to run. This query will gather all the message fields from the store-info table.

❸ **Makes sure that this page won't get cached** · In order to make sure that the client's browser does not cache the page locally, we use the <nocache> tag with the option to use headers.

❹ **Includes the user menu view**   We use the <enum> tag to iterate through the message fields returned by the previously defined query, and display these messages.

❺ **Start of the enumeration of the result.**

6 **Displayed for every row in the result.**
7 **End of the enumeration of the result.**
8 **Includes the short order view** We end the page by including the short order view.

In the JSP, we first tell the container that we will be using the database and Simple Tag libraries. We then create a connection to our database.

Listing 13.13   The configuration of the DB Connection in the web.xml file

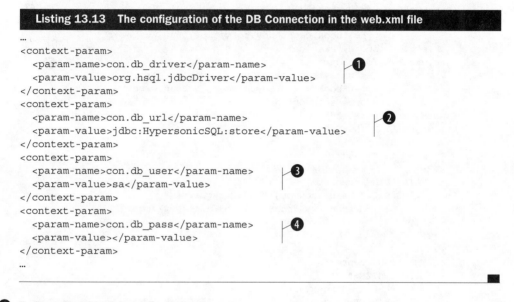

```
...
<context-param>
  <param-name>con.db_driver</param-name>
  <param-value>org.hsql.jdbcDriver</param-value>
</context-param>
<context-param>
  <param-name>con.db_url</param-name>
  <param-value>jdbc:HypersonicSQL:store</param-value>
</context-param>
<context-param>
  <param-name>con.db_user</param-name>
  <param-value>sa</param-value>
</context-param>
<context-param>
  <param-name>con.db_pass</param-name>
  <param-value></param-value>
</context-param>
...
```

1 **Defines the database driver class to use.**
2 **Defines the URL to the database.**
3 **Defines the username to use when accessing the database.**
4 **Defines the password to use when accessing the database.**

The configuration in listing 13.13 tells the container the names and values of a number of `Context` parameters that the `<connection>` tag will look for when these values are not given as parameters.

Menu

Listing 13.14 provides the source code for the implementation of our menu view, which most other views will include in order to display options available to the user. The file is userMenu.jsp.

Listing 13.14   userMenu.jsp

```jsp
<%@ taglib
    uri="http://www.manning.com/jsptagsbook/conditions-taglib"
    prefix="cond" %>
<%@ taglib
    uri="http://www.manning.com/jsptagsbook/beans-taglib"
    prefix="bean" %>
<jsp:useBean id="customer"                                              ❶
             beanName="book.casestudy.cosmetics.bean.Customer"
             type="book.casestudy.cosmetics.bean.Customer"
             scope="session"/>
<jsp:useBean id="order"                                                 ❷
             beanName="book.casestudy.cosmetics.bean.Order"
             type="book.casestudy.cosmetics.bean.Order"
             scope="session"/>
<TABLE CELLSPACING="0"
       CELLPADDING="0"
       BORDER="0"
       WIDTH="100%">
  <TR>
     <TD ALIGN="center">
     <IMG SRC="<bean:show object="<%=request%>"                         ❸
                property="contextPath"/>/images/logo.gif">
    </TD>
  </TR>
  <TR>
    <TD ALIGN="center">
      <FONT SIZE="-2">
        [ <A HREF="index.jsp">HOME</A>
        | <A HREF="categoryList.jsp">CATALOGUE</A>
        |
<cond:with name="customer"                                             ❹
           property="loggedOn"
           scope="session">
  <cond:test condition="eq true">                                      ❺
    <cond:with name="order"                                            ❻
               property="empty"
               scope="session">
      <cond:test condition="neq true">                                 ❼
         <A HREF="fullOrder.jsp">ORDER</A> |
      </cond:test>                                                     ❽
    </cond:with>                                                       ❾
         <A HREF="profileUpdateForm.jsp">PROFILE</A>
       | <A HREF="logoffHandler.jsp">LOGOFF</A>
  </cond:test>                                                         ❿
  <cond:test condition="neq true">                                     ⓫
         <A HREF="logonForm.jsp">LOGON</A>
       | <a href="registrationForm.jsp">REGISTER</a>
  </cond:test>                                                         ⓬
</cond:with>                                                           ⓭
      ]
```

```
        </FONT>
        <BR><BR>
      </TD>
    </TR>
  </TABLE>
```

❶ **Adds Customer bean to session if not already there.**

❷ **Adds Order bean to session if not already there.**

❸ **Displays the full image URL**   We make sure that we get the full image URL whenever we display an image because we can't be sure of the current document root when the page is used. This might differ when the page is called from a servlet and when locally referenced.

❹ **Creates condition on Customer bean.**

❺ **Tests if user is logged in.**

❻ **Creates condition on Order bean.**

❼ **Tests if Order bean is not empty.**

❽ **Ends the testing of Order bean containing items.**

❾ **End of the condition on Order bean.**

❿ **Ends the testing of user being logged in.**

⓫ **Tests if user is not logged in.**

⓬ **Ends the testing of user not being logged in.**

⓭ **End of the condition on Customer bean.**

In the JSP, we first make sure that there are a Customer and an Order bean in the session. We then check if the user is logged in. If so, we check whether his order is empty. We do this in order to display certain options to users, and others to customers with a current order.

We needn't worry about caching, as this page will always be included in a page that handles that for us.

Short order

Listing 13.15 is the source code for the implementation of our short order view, which most other views will include in order to display the user's current order. The file is shortOrder.jsp.

Listing 13.15   shortOrder.jsp

```jsp
<%@ taglib
    uri="http://www.manning.com/jsptagsbook/iteration-taglib"
    prefix="iter" %>
<%@ taglib
    uri="http://www.manning.com/jsptagsbook/conditions-taglib"
    prefix="cond" %>
<%@ taglib
    uri="http://www.manning.com/jsptagsbook/beans-taglib"
    prefix="bean" %>
<cond:with name="order"
           property="empty"                  ❶
           scope="session">
  <cond:test condition="neq true">           ❷
<BR>
<TABLE CELLSPACING="0"
       CELLPADDING="0"
       BORDER="1">
  <TR>
    <TD>
      <FONT SIZE="-1">
        <B>Your current order</B>
      </FONT>
    </TD>
  </TR>
  <TR>
    <TD>
      <TABLE CELLSPACING="0"
             CELLPADDING="2"
             BORDER="0"
             WIDTH="100%">
        <TR>
          <TH ALIGN="LEFT">
            <FONT SIZE="-1">SKU</FONT>
          </TH>
          <TH ALIGN="LEFT">
            <FONT SIZE="-1">Name</FONT>
          </TH>
          <TH ALIGN="RIGHT">
            <FONT SIZE="-1">Quantity</FONT>
          </TH>
        </TR>
    <iter:iterate id="item"                   ❸
type="book.casestudy.cosmetics.bean.OrderItem"
                  name="order"
                  property="entries"
                  scope="session">
        <TR>
          <TD>
            <FONT SIZE="-1">
```

```
                      <bean:show name="item"                    ❹
                                 property="SKU"/>
                </FONT>
              </TD>
              <TD>
                <FONT SIZE="-1">
                  <bean:show name="item"                         ❺
                             property="name"/>
                </FONT>
              </TD>
              <TD ALIGN="RIGHT">
                <FONT SIZE="-1">
                  <bean:show name="item"
                             property="quantity"/>              ❻
                </FONT>
              </TD>
            </TR>
        </iter:iterate>          ❼
          </TABLE>
        </TD>
      </TR>
  </TABLE>
    </cond:test>          ❽
  </cond:with>          ❾
```

❶ Creates a condition on Order.

❷ Tests if order is empty.

❸ Start of the iteration of the Order items.

❹ Displays the item's SKU.

❺ Displays the item's name.

❻ Displays the ordered quantity.

❼ End of the iteration of the Order items.

❽ End the testing of order being empty.

❾ End of the condition on Order.

In this JSP, we tell the container that we are going to use the Iteration, Conditions, and Beans tag libraries, then test whether the user has a current order. If so, we create an iteration of all the items in that order. For every item found, we display the SKU, name, and quantity ordered with the help of the <show> tag. We then end the iteration block and close the <test> and <with> tags. If we had wanted to display a message to the user saying that he does not have a current order, we would have done so before closing the <with> tag.

We needn't worry about caching, as this page will always be included in another page, and we'll make sure that any page that includes this view will disable caching.

Category list

The category list view is implemented as displayed in listing 13.16. The file is categoryList.jsp in our application. Figure 13.3 shows the results line by line.

Figure 13.3
Category list view

Listing 13.16   categoryList.jsp

```
<%@ page contentType="text/html;charset=UTF-8"%>
<%@ taglib
    uri="http://www.manning.com/jsptagsbook/database-taglib"
    prefix="db" %>
<%@ taglib
    uri="http://www.manning.com/jsptagsbook/simple-taglib"
    prefix="simple" %>
<%@ taglib
    uri="http://www.manning.com/jsptagsbook/conditions-taglib"
    prefix="cond" %>
<%@ taglib
    uri="http://www.manning.com/jsptagsbook/beans-taglib"
    prefix="bean" %>

<db:connection id="con"/>               ❶
<db:query connection="con"             ❷
          id="categories">
select id,name,image from category      ❸
</db:query>      ❹
<simple:nocache useHeaders="true"/>     ❺
<HTML>
<HEAD>
<TITLE>Cosmetics</TITLE>
</HEAD>
<BODY BGCOLOR="#FFFFFF">
```

```
<CENTER>
  <TABLE CELLSPACING="0"
         CELLPADDING="0"
         BORDER="0">
    <TR>
      <TD>
        <jsp:include page="userMenu.jsp"              6
                     flush="true"/>
      </TD>
    </TR>
    <TR>
      <TD><B>Catalogue</B><BR>
        <BR>
      </TD>
    </TR>
    <TR>
      <TD>
        <TABLE CELLSPACING="0"
               CELLPADDING="0"
               BORDER="0"
               WIDTH="100%">
          <TR BGCOLOR="#FF3900">
            <TH COLSPAN="2"
                ALIGN="LEFT">
              Line of products:
            </TH>
          </TR>
          <db:enum query="categories"           7
                   id="i">
          <cond:with object="<%=(i.getRow()%2>0)%>">       8
            <cond:test condition="eq true">      9
          <TR BGCOLOR="#FFFFFF">
            </cond:test>      10
            <cond:test condition="neq true">      11
          <TR BGCOLOR="#F9F05E">
            </cond:test>      12
          </cond:with>      13
          <TD>
        <cond:with object="<%=(i.getString(\"IMAGE\")!=null)%>">      14
            <cond:test condition="eq true">      15
          <A HREF="productList.jsp?id=<$ ID $>">
            <IMG SRC="<bean:show object="<%=request%>"      16
property="contextPath"/>/images/<$ IMAGE $>"
                 BORDER="0">
          </A>
            </cond:test>      17
          </cond:with></TD>      18
          <TD>
            <A HREF="productList.jsp?id=<$ ID $>">
              <$ NAME $>
            </A>
```

```
              </TD>
            </TR>
            </db:enum>      ⓙ
          </TABLE>
        </TD>
      </TR>
      <TR>
        <TD ALIGN="center">
          <BR>
          <jsp:include page="shortOrder.jsp"        ⓴
                      flush="true"/>
        </TD>
      </TR>
    </TABLE>
  </CENTER>
</BODY>
</HTML>
```

❶ **Creates a connection to the database.**

❷ **Creates a query using the previously defined connection.**

❸ **The query to perform.**

❹ **The end of the query.**

❺ **Makes sure that this page won't get cached.**

❻ **Includes the user menu view.**

❼ **Start of the enumeration of the result.**

❽ **Creates a condition on the row number.**

❾ **Tests if the row number is even** For every line, we use the row number of the `ResultSet` to decide what background color to use. For even row numbers we will set the background to white; for odd row numbers we will set the background to yellow.

❿ **The end of the testing for an even row number.**

⓫ **Tests if the row number is odd.**

⓬ **Ends the testing of an odd row number.**

⓭ **Ends the row number condition.**

⓮ **Creates a condition on the category image.**

⓯ **Tests if the image is not null** We test if the current category has an image. If so, we display it.

⓰ **Displays the full image URL.**

⓱ **Ends the test if image is not null.**

⓲ **Ends the condition on the category image.**

⓳ **Ends the enumeration of the result.**

⓴ **Includes the user menu view** At the end of the page, we include the short order view, so that any items currently in the user's order are displayed.

In the JSP, we first create a connection to our database. As before, the needed parameters will be looked up in the `Context`. We then create a query for looking up all available categories.

After that, we include the user menu view to display the navigation for the user.

With that, we iterate through the `ResultSet` from our query and display all categories, line by line as was shown in figure 13.3.

Product list

Listing 13.17 is the source code for the implementation of our product list view. The file is productList.jsp (see figure 13.4).

COSMETICS

[HOME | CATALOGUE | ORDER | PROFILE | LOGOFF]

Catalogue: Eco Eye Line

SKU	Name	Price		
cosm-102.2	Panda Eyeliner	$75.50	1	Order
cosm-107.1	Eyedrops	$50.50	1	Order
cosm-222.1	Eagle Eyeliner	$100.00	1	Order

Your current order

SKU	Name	Quantity
cosm-102.2	Panda Eyeliner	2
cosm-222.1	Eagle Eyeliner	5
cosm-107.1	Eyedrops	3

Figure 13.4
Product list view, including the short order view

Listing 13.17 productList.jsp

```
<%@ page contentType="text/html;charset=UTF-8"%>
<%@ page errorPage="categoryList.jsp" %>        ❶
<%@ taglib
    uri="http://www.manning.com/jsptagsbook/iteration-taglib"
    prefix="iter" %>
<%@ taglib
    uri="http://www.manning.com/jsptagsbook/conditions-taglib"
    prefix="cond" %>
<%@ taglib
    uri="http://www.manning.com/jsptagsbook/simple-taglib"
    prefix="simple" %>
<%@ taglib
    uri="http://www.manning.com/jsptagsbook/database-taglib"
```

```
    prefix="db" %>
<%@ taglib
    uri="http://www.manning.com/jsptagsbook/beans-taglib"
    prefix="bean" %>
<%@ taglib
    uri="http://www.manning.com/jsptagsbook/locale-taglib"
    prefix="local" %>
<db:connection id="con"/>                    2
<db:query connection="con"                    3
          id="category">
select name from category
where id=<bean:show object="<%=request%>"              4
                     property="parameter"
                     index="id"/>
</db:query>          5
<simple:nocache useHeaders="true"/>          6
<HTML>
<HEAD>
<TITLE>Cosmetics</TITLE>
</HEAD>
<BODY BGCOLOR="#FFFFFF">
<CENTER>
    <TABLE CELLSPACING="0"
           CELLPADDING="0"
           BORDER="0">
      <TR>
        <TD>
          <jsp:include page="userMenu.jsp"          7
                       flush="true"/>
        </TD>
      </TR>
      <TR>
        <TD><B>Catalogue:
<db:enum query="category"          8
         id="i">
          <$ NAME $>
</db:enum>          9
<db:query connection="con"          10
          id="products">
select sku,name,price,categoryid from product
where categoryId=<bean:show object="<%=request%>"
                            property="parameter"
                            index="id"/>
</db:query>          11

          </B><BR>
          <BR>
        </TD>
      </TR>
      <TR>
        <TD>
          <TABLE CELLSPACING="0"
```

```
                    CELLPADDING="0"
                    BORDER="0"
                    WIDTH="100%">
              <TR BGCOLOR="#FF3900">
                <TH ALIGN="LEFT">
                  SKU
                </TH>
                <TD>
                   
                </TD>
                <TH ALIGN="LEFT">
                  Name
                </TH>
                <TD>
                   
                </TD>
                <TH ALIGN="RIGHT">
                  Price
                </TH>
                <TD>
                   
                </TD>
                <TD>
                   
                </TD>
              </TR>
<db:enum query="products"
         id="i">
  <cond:with object="<%=(i.getRow()%2>0)%>">
    <cond:test condition="eq true">
          <TR BGCOLOR="#FFFFFF">
    </cond:test>
    <cond:test condition="neq true">
          <TR BGCOLOR="#F9F05E">
    </cond:test>
  </cond:with>
              <TD>
                <code>
                  <$ SKU $>
                </code>
              </TD>
              <TD>
                 
              </TD>
              <TD>
                <$ NAME $>
              </TD>
              <TD>
                 
              </TD>
              <TD ALIGN="RIGHT">
```

⑫ ⑬ ⑭ ⑮ ⑯ ⑰ ⑱

```
        <local:currency amount="<%=i.getDouble(\"PRICE\")%>"/>    ⑲
          </TD>
          <TD>
             
          </TD>
  <cond:with name="customer"                    ⑳
           property="loggedOn"
           scope="session">
    <cond:test condition="eq true">             ㉑
          <FORM ACTION="addProduct">
            <TD ALIGN="RIGHT">
               
              <INPUT TYPE="hidden"
                     NAME="id"
                     VALUE="<$ CATEGORYID $>">
              <INPUT TYPE="hidden"
                     NAME="sku"
                     VALUE="<$ SKU $>">
              <INPUT TYPE="text"
                     NAME="quantity"
                     SIZE="2"
                     MAXLENGTH="2"
                     VALUE="1">
              <INPUT TYPE="image"
                     SRC="<bean:show object="<%=request%>"    ㉒
property="contextPath"/>/images/order.gif"
                     BORDER="0">
            </TD>
          </form>
          <TD>
             
          </TD>
    </cond:test>    ㉓
  </cond:with>    ㉔
          </TR>
</db:enum>    ㉕
      </TABLE>
    </TD>
  </TR>
  <TR>
    <TD ALIGN="center">
      <BR>
      <jsp:include page="shortOrder.jsp"    ㉖
                   flush="true"/>
    </TD>
  </TR>
  </TABLE>
</CENTER>
</BODY>
</HTML>
```

① **Defines `categoryList` as error page**   We define that the page will use the category list view as an error page, so if any exception is thrown, the category list view will be displayed.

② **Creates a connection to the database.**

③ **Creates a query using the previously defined connection.**

④ **The query to perform.**

⑤ **The end of the query.**

⑥ **Makes sure that this page won't get cached.**

⑦ **Includes the user menu view.**

⑧ **Start of the enumeration of the result.**

⑨ **End of the enumeration of the result**   The second query retrieves all products in the currently selected category.

⑩ **Creates a query using the previously defined connection.**

⑪ **The end of the new query.**

⑫ **Start of the enumeration of the result.**

⑬ **Creates a condition on the row number.**

⑭ **Tests if the row number is even**   For every product returned in the `ResultSet`, we use the row number to decide what background color to use. For even row numbers we will set the background to white, and for odd row numbers we will set the background to yellow, just as we did in the category list view.

⑮ **The end of the testing for an even row number.**

⑯ **Tests if the row number is odd.**

⑰ **Ends the testing of an odd row number.**

⑱ **Ends the row number condition.**

⑲ **Displays the locally formatted price**   For every product we show, we also display its price. The tag will look for the locale in the `Context`, where we store the current one. In listing 13.17 you can see how the `Locale` is configured inside the web application for the `<currency>` tag to find it.

⑳ **Creates condition on Customer.**

㉑ **Tests if user is logged on**   For every product displayed, we check whether the current user is logged on. If so, we display an order button and a form where the user can specify the quantity to order.

㉒ **Displays the full image URL.**

㉓ **Ends the test of whether user is logged on.**

㉔ **Ends the condition on Customer.**

㉕ **Ends the enumeration of the result.**

㉖ **Includes the User menu view.**

In this JSP page, we make two queries against the database. The first is to get and display the name of the currently selected category. If no category ID was passed to the page, an exception will be thrown.

Listing 13.18   An applicationwide Locale setting in the web.xml file

```
...
<context-param>
  <param-name>locale</param-name>          ❶
  <param-value>en_US</param-value>         ❷
</context-param>
...
```

❶ **Defines the name of the** `Context` **parameter.**

❷ **Defines the value of the** `Context` **parameter.**

In listing 13.18 we define the name of the `Context` parameter to be `locale`, which is the parameter name that the `<currency>` tag will look for in the `Context`. We set the value of the parameter to be a string representing the locale, which the tag will then use to construct a `Locale`.

As you can see in the code, we will call the add item handler with the SKU and the quantity specified whenever a user wants to put a product into an order.

Registration

Listing 13.19 is the source code for the implementation of our registration view. The file name is registrationForm.jsp.

Listing 13.19   registrationForm.jsp

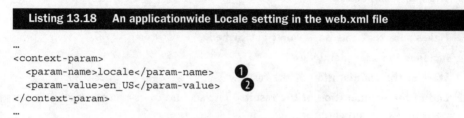

```
<%@ taglib
    uri="http://www.manning.com/jsptagsbook/conditions-taglib"
    prefix="cond" %>
<%@ taglib
    uri="http://www.manning.com/jsptagsbook/beans-taglib"
    prefix="bean" %>
<%@ taglib
    uri="http://www.manning.com/jsptagsbook/simple-taglib"
    prefix="simple" %>
<cond:with name="customer"                          ❶
          property="loggedOn">
  <cond:test condition="eq true">                   ❷
    <simple:redirect location="profileUpdateForm.jsp"/>   ❸
```

```
    </cond:test>          ④
    <cond:test condition="neq true">          ⑤
      <simple:nocache useHeaders="true"/>          ⑥
<HTML>
<HEAD>
<TITLE>Cosmetics</TITLE>
</HEAD>
<BODY BGCOLOR="#FFFFFF">
<CENTER>
  <form action="registrationHandler" method="post">
  <TABLE CELLSPACING="0"
         CELLPADDING="0"
         BORDER="0">
    <TR>
      <TD>
        <jsp:include page="userMenu.jsp"          ⑦
                     flush="true"/>
      </TD>
    </TR>
    <TR>
      <TD>
        <P><B>Registration</B></P>
        <P>Fill in the form below to register.</P>
      </TD>
    </TR>
    <TR>
      <TD ALIGN="center">
        <BR>
        <TABLE CELLSPACING="0"
               CELLPADDING="0"
               BORDER="0"
               WIDTH="100%">
          <TR>
            <TH ALIGN="LEFT">
              Username:
            </TH>
            <TD>
              <input type="text"
                     name="username"
                     value="<bean:show name="customer"          ⑧
                                       property="username"/>">
            </TD>
          </TR>
          <TR>
            <TH ALIGN="LEFT">
              Password:
            </TH>
            <TD>
              <input type="password"
                     name="password"
```

```
                              value="<bean:show name="customer"                        9
                                            property="password"/>">
          </TD>
        </TR>
        <TR>
          <TH ALIGN="LEFT">
            Company:
          </TH>
          <TD>
            <input type="text"
                   name="company"
                   value="<bean:show name="customer"                          10
                                 property="company"/>">
          </TD>
        </TR>
        <TR>
          <TH ALIGN="LEFT">
            Name:
          </TH>
          <TD>
            <input type="text"
                   name="name"
                   value="<bean:show name="customer"                          11
                                 property="name"/>">
          </TD>
        </TR>
        <TR>
          <TH ALIGN="LEFT"
              VALIGN="top">
            Address:
          </TH>
          <TD>
            <textarea name="address"
                      rows="4"
                      cols="40"><bean:show name="customer"                     12
property="address"/></textarea>
          </TD>
        </TR>
        <TR>
          <TH ALIGN="LEFT">
            Email:
          </TH>
          <TD>
            <input type="text"
                   name="email"
                   value="<bean:show name="customer"                          13
                                 property="email"/>">
          </TD>
        </TR>
        <TR>
          <TH ALIGN="LEFT">
```

```
                    Phone:
                  </TH>
                  <TD>
                    <input type="text"
                           name="phone"
                           value="<bean:show name="customer"
                                             property="phone"/>">
                  </TD>
                </TR>
                <TR>
                  <TH ALIGN="LEFT">
                    Fax:
                  </TH>
                  <TD>
                    <input type="text"
                           name="fax"
                           value="<bean:show name="customer"
                                             property="fax"/>">
                  </TD>
                </TR>
              </TABLE>
              <BR>
              If you don't want to register at this time, press Cancel below.<BR>
              <BR>
              <INPUT TYPE="image"
                     SRC="<bean:show object="<%=request%>"
property="contextPath"/>/images/confirm.gif"
                     BORDER="0"
                     ALIGN="LEFT">
              </A>
              <A HREF="index.jsp">
                <IMG SRC="<bean:show object="<%=request%>"
property="contextPath"/>/images/cancel.gif"
                     BORDER="0"
                     ALIGN="RIGHT">
              </A>
              <BR>

          </TD>
        </TR>
      </TABLE>
      </form>
  </CENTER>
  </BODY>
</HTML>
  </cond:test>
</cond:with>
```

🄐🄐 14

🄐🄐 15

🄐🄐 16

🄐🄐 16

🄐🄐 17

🄐🄐 18

❶ Creates a condition on the Customer.

❷ Tests if the user is not logged on.

❸ Redirects to the profile view.

❹ Ends the test if the user is not logged on.

❺ Tests if the user is logged on.

❻ Makes sure that this page won't get cached.

❼ Includes the user menu view.

❽ Displays the username for editing.

❾ Displays the password for editing.

❿ Displays the company name for editing.

⓫ Displays the name for editing.

⓬ Displays the address for editing.

⓭ Displays the email address for editing.

⓮ Displays the phone number for editing.

⓯ Displays the fax number for editing.

⓰ Displays the full image URL.

⓱ Ends the test of whether the user is logged on.

⓲ Ends the condition on the Customer.

In this JSP we display a form for the user to fill out with profile information. We fill the form with the data currently held by the user's Customer bean and use the <show> tag to fill in the form fields.

Registration successful

Listing 13.20 is the source code for the implementation of our registration successful view. The file name is registrationConfirmation.jsp.

Listing 13.20   registrationConfirmation.jsp

```
<%@ page contentType="text/html;charset=UTF-8"%>
<%@ taglib
    uri="http://www.manning.com/jsptagsbook/beans-taglib"
    prefix="bean" %>
<%@ taglib
    uri="http://www.manning.com/jsptagsbook/conditions-taglib"
    prefix="cond" %>
<%@ taglib
    uri="http://www.manning.com/jsptagsbook/simple-taglib"
    prefix="simple" %>
    <cond:with name="customer"
               property="loggedOn"          ❶
               scope="session">
```

```
   <cond:test condition="neq true">         ❷
     <simple:redirect location="logonForm.jsp"/>        ❸
   </cond:test>         ❹
   <cond:test condition="eq true">          ❺
<simple:nocache useHeaders="true"/>          ❻
<HTML>
<HEAD>
<TITLE>Cosmetics</TITLE>
</HEAD>
<BODY BGCOLOR="#FFFFFF">
<CENTER>
   <TABLE CELLSPACING="0"
          CELLPADDING="0"
          BORDER="0">
     <TR>
       <TD>
         <jsp:include page="userMenu.jsp"         ❼
                      flush="true"/>
       </TD>
     </TR>
     <TR>
       <TD>
         <P>
           <B>
             Welcome to our community <bean:show name="customer"          ❽
                                       property="name"
                                       scope="session"/>
             !
           </B>
         </P>
         <P>
           We hope that you will find many interesting
           products in our catalog.
         </P>
       <TD>
     </TR>
   </cond:test>         ❾
</cond:with>         ❿
     <TR>
       <TD ALIGN="center">
         <BR>
         <jsp:include page="shortOrder.jsp"         ⓫
                      flush="true"/>
       </TD>
     </TR>
   </TABLE>
</CENTER>
</BODY>
</HTML>
```

❶ Creates a condition on the Customer.

❷ Tests if the user is not logged on.

❸ Redirects to the logon view.

❹ Ends the test if the user is not logged on.

❺ Tests if the user is logged on.

❻ Makes sure that this page won't get cached.

❼ Includes the user menu view.

❽ Displays the user's name.

❾ Ends the test whether the user is logged on.

❿ Ends the condition on the Customer.

⓫ Includes the short order view.

We will use this JSP to display a message telling the user that his profile has been successfully stored. Apart from checking that the user is logged on, all we do is display the message incorporating the user's name.

Logon

Listing 13.21 is the source code for the implementation of our logon view. The file name is logonForm.jsp. The logon view is illustrated in figure 13.5.

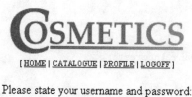

COSMETICS

[HOME | CATALOGUE | PROFILE | LOGOFF]

Please state your username and password:

Username: abc

Password: ****

Logon

Figure 13.5
Logon view

Listing 13.21   logonForm.jsp

```
<%@ page contentType="text/html;charset=UTF-8"%>
<%@ taglib
    uri="http://www.manning.com/jsptagsbook/simple-taglib"
    prefix="simple" %>
<%@ taglib
    uri="http://www.manning.com/jsptagsbook/beans-taglib"
    prefix="bean" %>
```

```
<simple:nocache useHeaders="true"/>
<HTML>
<HEAD>
<TITLE>Cosmetics</TITLE>
</HEAD>
<BODY BGCOLOR="#FFFFFF">
<CENTER>
  <TABLE CELLSPACING="0"
         CELLPADDING="0"
         BORDER="0">
    <TR>
      <TD>
        <jsp:include page="userMenu.jsp"
                     flush="true"/>
      </TD>
    </TR>
    <TR>
      <TD>
        <P>
        Please state your username and password:
        </P>
      </TD>
    </TR>
    <TR>
      <TD>
        <TABLE WIDTH="100%">
          <FORM ACTION="logonHandler"
                METHOD="post">
          <TR>
            <TD>
              Username:
            </TD>
            <TD>
              <INPUT TYPE="text"
                     name="username">
            </TD>
          </TR>
          <TR>
            <TD>
              Password.
            </TD>
            <TD>
              <INPUT TYPE="password"
                     name="password">
            </TD>
          </TR>
          <TR>
            <TD COLSPAN="2">
              <INPUT TYPE="image"
                     SRC="<bean:show object="<%=request%>"
property="contextPath"/>/images/logon.gif"
```

❶

❷

❸

```
                            BORDER="0"
                            ALIGN="RIGHT">
              </TD>
            </TR>
          </TABLE>
        </TD>
      </TR>
      <TR>
        <TD ALIGN="center">
          <BR>
          <jsp:include page="shortOrder.jsp"          ❹
                    flush="true"/>
        </TD>
      </TR>
    </TABLE>
  </CENTER>
</BODY>
</HTML>
```

❶ Makes sure that this page won't get cached.

❷ Includes the user menu view.

❸ Displays the full image URL.

❹ Includes the user menu view.

The JSP displays a form in which the user can specify the username and password, which is sent to the logon handler. Apart from that, there is not much action going on in that page, so we leave it at that, and continue with the next one.

Logon successful

Listing 13.22 is the source code for the implementation of our logon successful view. The file name is logonConfirmation.jsp.

Listing 13.22   logonConfirmation.jsp

```
<%@ page contentType="text/html;charset=UTF-8"%>
<%@ taglib
   uri="http://www.manning.com/jsptagsbook/beans-taglib"
   prefix="bean" %>
<%@ taglib
   uri="http://www.manning.com/jsptagsbook/conditions-taglib"
   prefix="cond" %>
<%@ taglib
   uri="http://www.manning.com/jsptagsbook/simple-taglib"
   prefix="simple" %>
<cond:with name="customer"
        property="loggedOn"          ❶
        scope="session">
  <cond:test condition="neq true">          ❷
```

```
      <simple:redirect location="logonForm.jsp"/>    ❸
   </cond:test>    ❹
   <cond:test condition="eq true">    ❺
<simple:nocache useHeaders="true"/>    ❻
<HTML>
<HEAD>
<TITLE>Cosmetics</TITLE>
</HEAD>
<BODY BGCOLOR="#FFFFFF">
<CENTER>
   <TABLE CELLSPACING="0"
          CELLPADDING="0"
          BORDER="0">
     <TR>
       <TD>
         <jsp:include page="userMenu.jsp"    ❼
                      flush="true"/>
       </TD>
     </TR>
     <TR>
       <TD>
         <P>
           <B>
             Welcome back <bean:show name="customer"    ❽
                                     property="name"
                                     scope="session"/>
             !
           </B>
         </P>
         <P>
           We hope that you will find many interesting
           products in our catalog.
         </P>
       <TD>
     </TR>
   </cond:test>    ❾
</cond:with>    ❿
     <TR>
       <TD ALIGN="center">
         <BR>
         <jsp:include page="shortOrder.jsp"    ⓫
                      flush="true"/>
       </TD>
     </TR>
   </TABLE>
</CENTER>
</BODY>
</HTML>
```

❶ **Creates a condition on the Customer bean.**

❷ **Tests if the user is not logged on.**

❸ **Redirects to the logon view.**

❹ **Ends the test if the user is not logged on.**

❺ **Tests if the user is logged on.**

❻ **Makes sure that this page won't get cached.**

❼ **Includes the user menu view.**

❽ **Displays the user's name.**

❾ **Ends the test of whether the user is logged on.**

❿ **Ends the condition on the Customer bean.**

⓫ **Includes the short order view.**

In the JSP page we check whether the user is indeed logged on, and thereafter we display a message, including the user's name, with a welcome back.

Full order

Listing 13.23 is the source code for the implementation of our full order view. The file name is fullOrder.jsp. The order view is illustrated in figure 13.6.

[HOME | CATALOGUE | ORDER | PROFILE | LOGOFF]

Your current order

Below you find the details about your current order.

SKU	Name	Price	Quantity	Total	
cosm-102.2	Panda Eyeliner	$75.50	2	$151.00	✕
cosm-222.1	Eagle Eyeliner	$100.00	5	$500.00	✕
cosm-107.1	Eyedrops	$50.50	3	$151.50	✕
Total:				**$802.50**	

Send

Figure 13.6
Full order view

Listing 13.23 The fullOrder.jsp

```
<%@ page contentType="text/html;charset=UTF-8"%>
<%@ taglib
    uri="http://www.manning.com/jsptagsbook/iteration-taglib"
    prefix="iter" %>
<%@ taglib
    uri="http://www.manning.com/jsptagsbook/conditions-taglib"
    prefix="cond" %>
<%@ taglib
    uri="http://www.manning.com/jsptagsbook/simple-taglib"
    prefix="simple" %>
<%@ taglib
    uri="http://www.manning.com/jsptagsbook/locale-taglib"
    prefix="local" %>
<%@ taglib
    uri="http://www.manning.com/jsptagsbook/beans-taglib"
    prefix="bean" %>
<jsp:useBean id="order"
             beanName="book.casestudy.cosmetics.bean.Order"      ❶
             type="book.casestudy.cosmetics.bean.Order"
             scope="session"/>
<cond:with name="customer"                      ❷
           property="loggedOn"
           scope="session">
  <cond:test condition="neq true">              ❸
    <simple:redirect location="logonForm.jsp"/>      ❹
  </cond:test>  ❺
  <cond:test condition="eq true">               ❻
<simple:nocache useHeaders="true"/>             ❼
<HTML>
<HEAD>
<TITLE>Cosmetics</TITLE>
</HEAD>
<BODY BGCOLOR="#FFFFFF">
<CENTER>
  <TABLE CELLSPACING="0"
         CELLPADDING="0"
         BORDER="0">
    <TR>
      <TD>
        <jsp:include page="userMenu.jsp"        ❽
                     flush="true"/>
      </TD>
    </TR>
    <TR>
      <TD>
        <P><B>Your current order</B></P>
    <cond:with name="order"                     ❾
               property="empty"
               scope="session">
```

```
        <cond:test condition="neq true">          ⑩
          <P>Below you find the details about your current order.</P>
        </TD>
      </TR>
      <TR>
        <TD>
          <TABLE CELLSPACING="0"
                 CELLPADDING="5"
                 BORDER="0"
                 WIDTH="100%">
            <TR>
              <TH ALIGN="LEFT">
                SKU
              </TH>
              <TH ALIGN="LEFT">
                Name
              </TH>
              <TH ALIGN="RIGHT">
                Price
              </TH>
              <TH ALIGN="center">
                Quantity
              </TH>
              <TH ALIGN="RIGHT">
                Total
              </TH>
            </TR>
            <TR>
              <TD COLSPAN="5">
                <HR SIZE="1">
              </TD>
            </TR>
          <iter:iterate id="item"
                type="book.casestudy.cosmetics.bean.OrderItem"     ⑪
                     name="order"
                     property="entries"
                     scope="session">
          <TR>
            <TD>
              <bean:show name="item"          ⑫
                         property="SKU"/>
            </TD>
            <TD>
              <bean:show name="item"          ⑬
                         property="name"/>
            </TD>
            <TD ALIGN="RIGHT">
                <local:currency amount="<%=item.getPrice()%>" />     ⑭
            </TD>
            <TD ALIGN="center">
              <bean:show name="item"          ⑮
```

```
                             property="quantity"/>
            </TD>
            <TD ALIGN="RIGHT">
              <local:currency amount="<%=item.getTotalPrice()%>"/>          ⑯
            </TD>
            <TD>
              <A HREF="removeProduct?sku=<bean:show name="item"            ⑰
                                    property="SKU"/>">
                <IMG SRC="<bean:show object="<%=request%>"                 ⑱
property="contextPath"/>/images/remove.gif"
                       BORDER="0"
                       ALT="Remove">
              </A>
            </TD>
          </TR>
        </iter:iterate>       ⑲
          <TR>
            <TD COLSPAN="5">
              <HR SIZE="1">
            </TD>
          </TR>
          <TR>
            <TH COLSPAN="4"
                ALIGN="LEFT">
             Total:
            </TH>
            <TH ALIGN="RIGHT">
             <local:currency amount="<%=order.getTotalPrice()%>"/>         ⑳
            </TH>
          </TR>
          <TR>
            <TD COLSPAN="5">
              <HR SIZE="1">
            </TD>
          </TR>
        </TABLE>
      </TD>
    </TR>
    <TR>
      <TD>
        <A HREF="sendOrder.jsp">
          <IMG SRC="<bean:show object="<%=request%>"                      ㉑
                     property="contextPath"/>/images/send.gif"
              BORDER="0">
        </A>
      </TD>
    </TR>
    </cond:test>        ㉒
    <cond:test condition="eq true">        ㉓
  <P>
  Your current order is empty
```

```
    </P>
      </cond:test>     ㉔
    </cond:with>      ㉕
  </cond:test>        ㉖
</cond:with>          ㉗
  </TABLE>
</CENTER>
</BODY>
</HTML>
```

❶ Adds the order to the `page` scope   In the page, we first add the Order bean from the `session` scope to the `page` scope, so that we can reference it easily from within other tags. We need to do this so that we may pass the order total to the `<currency>` tag for formatting.

❷ Creates a condition on Customer.

❸ Tests if user is not logged on   If the user is not logged on, he should be redirected to the logon view, as only logged on customers can order.

❹ Redirects to the logon view.

❺ Ends test of whether user is not logged on.

❻ Tests if user is logged on.

❼ Makes sure that this page won't get cached.

❽ Includes the user menu view.

❾ Creates a new condition on order.

❿ Tests if order is not empty.

⓫ Iterates through the order items   We iterate through all the items in the order. For every item, we display its information, including its price at the time it was added to the order.

⓬ Displays the item's SKU.

⓭ Displays the item's name.

⓮ ⓰ Displays the locally formatted item price   We format the price using the `<currency>` tag, with the `Context` parameter `Locale` as the one to use for formatting.

⓯ Displays the ordered quantity of the item.

⓰ Displays the locally formatted row total price.

⓱ Builds a link using the the item's SKU.

⓲ Display the full URL of the image.

⓳ Ends the order item iteration.

⓴ Displays the locally formatted order total price   As the `<currency>` tag takes an amount as parameter and cannot look up any values from the `session` scope, we were forced to add the order to the page scope to allow passing in the total price as the amount parameter to the tag.

㉑ **Retrieves the application's deployment path and uses it to display URL to image.**

㉒ **Ends the test of whether the order is not empty.**

㉓ **Tests if the order is empty.**

㉔ **Ends the test if order is empty.**

㉕ **Ends the condition on Order.**

㉖ **Ends the test of whether user is logged on.**

㉗ **Ends the condition on Customer.**

Order summary

Listing 13.24 is the source code for the implementation of our order summary view. The file name is sendOrder.jsp. The order summary is illustrated in figure 13.7.

[HOME | CATALOGUE | ORDER | PROFILE | LOGOFF]

Order Confirmation

Your order with a total sum of $802.50 will be sent to the following address:

Acme
Foo Bar
Big Street Big City Big State Big Country

By confirming this order, the order will be sent to Cosmetics for further processing. You will receive an order receipt at your email address (magnus.rydin@cypoint.se) as a confirmation.

If you don't want to confirm the order at this time, press Cancel below.

Confirm   Cancel

Figure 13.7
Order summary view

Listing 13.24   sendOrder.jsp

```
<%@ page contentType="text/html;charset=UTF-8"%>
<%@ taglib
    uri="http://www.manning.com/jsptagsbook/beans-taglib"
    prefix="bean" %>
<%@ taglib
    uri="http://www.manning.com/jsptagsbook/conditions-taglib"
    prefix="cond" %>
<%@ taglib
    uri="http://www.manning.com/jsptagsbook/simple-taglib"
```

```
    prefix="simple" %>
<%@ taglib
    uri="http://www.manning.com/jsptagsbook/locale-taglib"
    prefix="local" %>
<jsp:useBean id="order"                                                          ❶
             beanName="book.casestudy.cosmetics.bean.Order"
             type="book.casestudy.cosmetics.bean.Order"
             scope="session"/>
<cond:with name="customer"                              ❷
           property="loggedOn"
           scope="session">
  <cond:test condition="neq true">          ❸
    <simple:redirect location="logonUser.jsp"/>              ❹
  </cond:test>  ❺
</cond:with>  ❻
<cond:with name="order"                     ❼
           property="empty"
           scope="session">
  <cond:test condition="eq true">         ❽
    <simple:redirect location="fullOrder.jsp"/>          ❾
  </cond:test>  ❿
</cond:with>  ⓫
<simple:nocache useHeaders="true"/>           ⓬
<HTML>
<HEAD>
<TITLE>Cosmetics</TITLE>
</HEAD>
<BODY BGCOLOR="#FFFFFF">
<CENTER>
  <TABLE CELLSPACING="0"
         CELLPADDING="0"
         BORDER="0">
    <TR>
      <TD>
        <jsp:include page="userMenu.jsp"        ⓭
                     flush="true"/>
      </TD>
    </TR>
    <TR>
      <TD>
        <P><B>Order Confirmation</B></P>
        <P>
        Your order with a total sum of
        <local:currency amount="<%=order.getTotalPrice()%>" />         ⓮
        will be sent to the following address:
        </P>
        <TABLE BORDER="1"
               CELLSPACING="0"
               CELLPADDING="0">
          <TR>
            <TD>
```

```
        <B>
          <bean:show name="customer"
                     property="company"
                     scope="session"/>
        </B>
        <BR>
        <bean:show name="customer"
                   property="name"
                   scope="session"/>
        <BR>
        <bean:show name="customer"
                   property="address"
                   scope="session"/>
      </TD>
    </TR>
  </TABLE>
  <BR>
  By confirming this order, the order will be sent to
  Cosmetics<BR>for further processing. You will receive
  an order receipt at your<BR> email address
  ( <bean:show name="customer"
               property="email"
               scope="session"/>
  ) as a confirmation.<BR>
  <BR>
  If you don't want to confirm the order at this time, press
  Cancel below.<BR>
  <BR>
  <A HREF="confirmationHandler">
    <IMG SRC="<bean:show object="<%=request%>"
               property="contextPath"/>/images/confirm.gif"
         BORDER="0"
         ALIGN="LEFT">
  </A>
  <A HREF="fullOrder.jsp">
    <IMG SRC="<bean:show object="<%=request%>"
               property="contextPath"/>/images/cancel.gif"
         BORDER="0"
         ALIGN="RIGHT">
  </A>
  <BR>
      </TD>
    </TR>
  </TABLE>
</CENTER>
</BODY>
</HTML>
```

❶ Adds the order to the page scope.

❷ Creates a condition on Customer.

❸ Tests if user is not logged on.

❹ Redirects to the logon view.

❺ End of test if user is not logged on.

❻ Ends condition on customer.

❼ Creates a condition on order.

❽ Tests if order is empty.

❾ Redirects to the full order view.

❿ End of test of whether order is empty.

⓫ Ends condition on order.

⓬ Makes sure that this page won't get cached.

⓭ Includes the user menu view.

⓮ Displays the locally formated order total price   As the `<currency>` tag takes an amount as parameter and cannot look up any values from the `session` scope, we were forced to add the Order to the `page` scope to pass in the total price as the amount parameter to the tag.

⓯ Displays the user's company name.

⓰ Displays the user's name.

⓱ Displays the user's address.

⓲ Displays the user's email.

⓳ Display the full image URL.

In the JSP file, we add the Order bean currently in the user's session to the `page` scope, so that we can use it inside other tags in this page. After that, we make sure that the customer is logged on and that there are items in the order. We then display the total order price, using the currently defined currency. After that, we display the user's address and email information to which we will send the receipt.

Order confirmation

Listing 13.25 is the source code for the implementation of our order confirmation view. The file name is orderConfirmation.jsp. The order confirmation is illustrated in figure 13.8.

[HOME | CATALOGUE | ORDER | PROFILE | LOGOFF]

Order Confirmation

Your order with a total sum of $802.50 will be sent to the following address:

> **Acme**
> Foo Bar
> Big Street Big City Big State Big Country

By confirming this order, the order will be sent to Cosmetics for further processing. You will receive an order receipt at your email address (magnus.rydin@cypoint.se) as a confirmation.

If you don't want to confirm the order at this time, press Cancel below.

Confirm   Cancel

Figure 13.8
Order confirmation view

Listing 13.25   orderConfirmation.jsp

```jsp
<%@ page contentType="text/html;charset=UTF-8"%>
<%@ page errorPage="mailException.jsp" %>
<%@ taglib
    uri="http://www.manning.com/jsptagsbook/simple-taglib"
    prefix="simple" %>
<%@ taglib
    uri="http://www.manning.com/jsptagsbook/email-taglib"
    prefix="mail" %>
<%@ taglib
    uri="http://www.manning.com/jsptagsbook/beans-taglib"
    prefix="bean" %>
<%@ taglib
    uri="http://www.manning.com/jsptagsbook/iteration-taglib"
    prefix="iter" %>
<%@ taglib
    uri="http://www.manning.com/jsptagsbook/locale-taglib"
    prefix="local" %>
<jsp:useBean id="customer"
            type="book.casestudy.cosmetics.bean.Customer"
            scope="session"/>
<jsp:useBean id="order"
            type="book.casestudy.cosmetics.bean.Order"
            scope="request"/>
<simple:nocache useHeaders="true"/>
<HTML>
```

1

2

3

```
<HEAD>
<TITLE>Cosmetics</TITLE>
</HEAD>
<BODY BGCOLOR="#FFFFFF">
<CENTER>
  <TABLE CELLSPACING="0"
         CELLPADDING="0"
         BORDER="0">
    <TR>
      <TD>
        <jsp:include page="userMenu.jsp"                  ❹
                     flush="true"/>
      </TD>
    </TR>
    <TR>
      <TD ALIGN="center">
        <FONT SIZE="+2">
          <B>Order Received</B>
        </FONT>
      </TD>
    </TR>
    <TR>
      <TD>
        <P ALIGN="justify">
        Your order has been received by Cosmetics.
        </P>
        <P ALIGN="justify">
        Your order reference number is
        <B>
          <bean:show name="order"                         ❺
                     property="id"
                     scope="request"/>
        </B>.
        </P>
<mail:send to="<%=customer.getEmail()%>">                 ❻
  <mail:subject>Order <bean:show name="order"             ❼
                                  property="id"
                                  scope="request"/></mail:subject>
      <mail:message>          ❽
ORDER CONFIRMATION
This email confirms that we have received your order
(reference number <bean:show name="order"                ❺
                              property="id"
                              scope="request"/>).
Consisting of the following items:
  ----------------------------------------------------------------
<iter:iterate id="item"                                   ❾
              type="book.casestudy.cosmetics.bean.OrderItem"
              name="order"
              property="entries"
              scope="request">
```

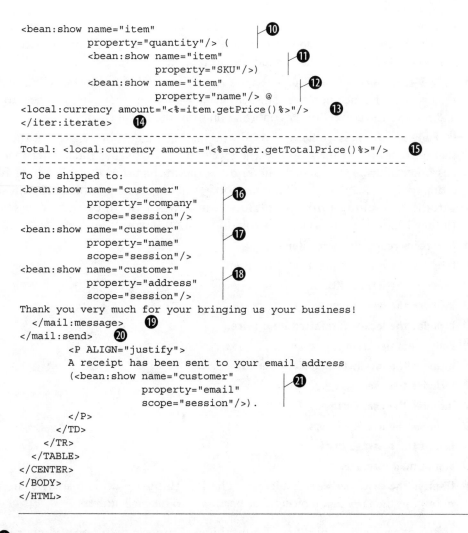

```
<bean:show name="item"
           property="quantity"/> (         ⓾
           <bean:show name="item"
                      property="SKU"/>)      ⓫
           <bean:show name="item"
                      property="name"/> @    ⓬
<local:currency amount="<%=item.getPrice()%>"/>   ⓭
</iter:iterate>    ⓮
----------------------------------------------------------------
Total: <local:currency amount="<%=order.getTotalPrice()%>"/>    ⓯
----------------------------------------------------------------
To be shipped to:
<bean:show name="customer"
           property="company"        ⓰
           scope="session"/>
<bean:show name="customer"
           property="name"           ⓱
           scope="session"/>
<bean:show name="customer"
           property="address"        ⓲
           scope="session"/>
Thank you very much for your bringing us your business!
   </mail:message>    ⓳
</mail:send>    ⓴
           <P ALIGN="justify">
           A receipt has been sent to your email address
           (<bean:show name="customer"
                       property="email"        ㉑
                       scope="session"/>).
           </P>
         </TD>
      </TR>
   </TABLE>
</CENTER>
</BODY>
</HTML>
```

❶ **Adds the customer to the page scope.**

❷ **Adds the order to the page scope.**

❸ **Makes sure that this page won't get cached.**

❹ **Includes the user menu view.**

❺ **Displays the order reference number.**

❻ **Defines the receiver of the mail message**   We define a mail message that we will send to the user's email address. As you can see in the code, we don't give the <send> tag any parameters such as which mail server to use, or the sender's address. The <send> tag will look for these in the Context, wherein they are defined for our application. We have defined these parameters in listing 13.26 below. As we must supply the `<send>` tag with an email address, and that email address is held by the customer object located in the `session` scope, we had to add the customer to the page `scope`.

⑦ Defines the subject of the mail message As subject of the mail message, we include the order's reference number. This will make it easy for frequent customers to find and retrieve the correct order confirmation from their mail clients.

⑧–⑲ Body of mail message body We fill the mail message's body with all the rows that make up the order as well as the locally formatted order total. After that, the customer address is added to the body of the message. Any blank row or blank character included in the mail message body will be included in the mail sent, so be careful to include only the blanks you want in the message. The source (listing 13.25) has line wraps that you do not want in your actual source code.

⑨ Iterates through the order items.

⑩ Includes the ordered quantity of the item.

⑪ Includes the item's SKU.

⑫ Includes the item's name.

⑬ Includes the locally formatted item price.

⑭ Ends the order item iteration.

⑮ Includes the locally formatted order total price.

⑯ Includes the user's company name.

⑰ Includes the user's name.

⑱ Includes the user's address.

⑲ End of the message body.

⑳ End of mail message.

㉑ Displays the customer's email address The last thing we do is display a message informing the user that a receipt has been sent to his mail address.

In the page, we do a number of nifty things. First, we define that if any runtime exception is thrown in this page, the file mailException.jsp is to be displayed. After that, we verify that we have an Order bean in the request scope (placed there by the confirmation handler) and add it to the page scope (to use as part of parameter in tags). We also add the Customer bean from the session scope to the page scope.

We then display the order reference number to the user.

Listing 13.26   The configuration of the mail service in the web.xml file

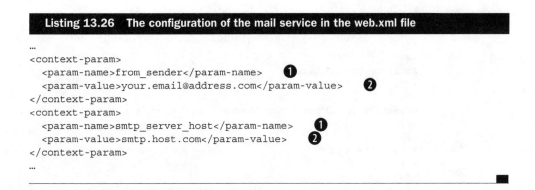

```
...
<context-param>
  <param-name>from_sender</param-name>        ❶
  <param-value>your.email@address.com</param-value>        ❷
</context-param>
<context-param>
  <param-name>smtp_server_host</param-name>        ❶
  <param-value>smtp.host.com</param-value>        ❷
</context-param>
...
```

❶ **Defines the name of the** `Context` **parameter.**

❷ **Defines the value of the** `Context` **parameter.**

In listing 13.26 we define the names of the two `Context` parameters where our `<send>` tag will look for the sender address and the SMTP server host to use for sending the email.

Order confirmation error

Listing 13.27 is the source code for the implementation of our order confirmation error view. The file name is confirmationError.jsp.

Listing 13.27   confirmationError.jsp

```
<%@ page contentType="text/html;charset=UTF-8"%>
<%@ taglib
    uri="http://www.manning.com/jsptagsbook/beans-taglib"
    prefix="bean" %>
<HTML>
<HEAD>
<TITLE>Cosmetics</TITLE>
</HEAD>
<BODY BGCOLOR="#FFFFFF">
<CENTER>
  <TABLE CELLSPACING="0"
         CELLPADDING="0"
         BORDER="0">
    <TR>
      <TD>
        <jsp:include page="userMenu.jsp"        ❶
                     flush="true"/>
      </TD>
    </TR>
    <TR>
      <TD>
```

```
        <P>
        <B>Comfirmation Error</B>
        </P>
        <P>
        An error has occurred.
        </P>
        <P>
        Cosmetics could not process your order at this time.
        </P>
        <P>
        Please try again.
        </P>
        <P>
        If the problem persists, please contact the administrator.
        </P>
        <A HREF="javascript:history.go(-1);">
          <IMG SRC="<bean:show object="<%=request%>"            ❷
                    property="contextPath"/>/images/back.gif"
              BORDER="0"
              ALIGN="RIGHT">
        </A>
      </TD>
    </TR>
    <TR>
      <TD ALIGN="center">
        <BR>
        <jsp:include page="shortOrder.jsp"                      ❸
                    flush="true"/>
      </TD>
    </TR>
  </TABLE>
</CENTER>
</BODY>
</HTML>
```

❶ **Includes the user menu view.**

❷ **Displays the full image URL.**

❸ **Includes the short order view.**

The page informs the user that an error prevents the order from being processed at this time, and that another attempt should be made or the user should contact the administrator.

Profile

Listing 13.28 is the source code for the implementation of our profile view. The file name is profileUpdateForm.jsp.

Listing 13.28   profileUpdateForm.jsp

```
<%@ taglib
    uri="http://www.manning.com/jsptagsbook/conditions-taglib"
    prefix="cond" %>
<%@ taglib
    uri="http://www.manning.com/jsptagsbook/beans-taglib"
    prefix="bean" %>
<%@ taglib
    uri="http://www.manning.com/jsptagsbook/simple-taglib"
    prefix="simple" %>
<cond:with name="customer"                              ❶
            property="loggedOn">
  <cond:test condition="neq true">                      ❷
    <simple:redirect location="logonForm.jsp"/>         ❸
  </cond:test>                                          ❹
  <cond:test condition="eq true">                       ❺
<simple:nocache useHeaders="true"/>                     ❻
<HTML>
<HEAD>
<TITLE>Cosmetics</TITLE>
</HEAD>
<BODY BGCOLOR="#FFFFFF">
<CENTER>
  <form action="profileHandler" method="post">
  <TABLE CELLSPACING="0"
         CELLPADDING="0"
         BORDER="0">
    <TR>
      <TD>
        <jsp:include page="userMenu.jsp"                ❼
                     flush="true"/>
      </TD>
    </TR>
    <TR>
      <TD>
        <P><B>Profile</B></P>
        <P>Below is your profile in our system.</P>
        <P>To change the profile, make the changes and press 'Commit'.</P>
      </TD>
    </TR>
    <TR>
      <TD ALIGN="center">
        <BR>
        <TABLE CELLSPACING="0"
               CELLPADDING="0"
               BORDER="0"
               WIDTH="100%">
          <TR>
            <TH ALIGN="LEFT">
              Username:
```

```
      </TH>
      <TD>
        <bean:show name="customer"                    8
                   property="username"/>
      </TD>
    </TR>
    <TR>
      <TH ALIGN="LEFT">
        Company:
      </TH>
      <TD>
        <input type="text"
               name="company"
               value="<bean:show name="customer"     9
                                 property="company"/>">
      </TD>
    </TR>
    <TR>
      <TH ALIGN="LEFT">
        Name:
      </TH>
      <TD>
        <input type="text"
               name="name"
               value="<bean:show name="customer"      10
                                 property="name"/>">
      </TD>
    </TR>
    <TR>
      <TH ALIGN="LEFT"
          VALIGN="top">
        Address:
      </TH>
      <TD>
        <textarea name="address"
                  rows="4"
                  cols="40"><bean:show name="customer"   11
                             property="address"/></textarea>
      </TD>
    </TR>
    <TR>
      <TH ALIGN="LEFT">
        Email:
      </TH>
      <TD>
        <input type="text"
               name="email"
               value="<bean:show name="customer"      12
                                 property="email"/>">
      </TD>
    </TR>
```

```
      <TR>
        <TH ALIGN="LEFT">
          Phone:
        </TH>
        <TD>
          <input type="text"
                 name="phone"
                 value="<bean:show name="customer"                    ⑬
                                   property="phone"/>">
        </TD>
      </TR>
      <TR>
        <TH ALIGN="LEFT">
          Fax:
        </TH>
        <TD>
          <input type="text"
                 name="fax"
                 value="<bean:show name="customer"                    ⑭
                                   property="fax"/>">
        </TD>
      </TR>
    </TABLE>
    <BR>
    If you don't want to update your profile at this time, press Cancel
below.<BR>
    <BR>
    <INPUT TYPE="image"
           SRC="<bean:show object="<%=request%>"                      ⑮
                property="contextPath"/>/images/confirm.gif"
           BORDER="0"
           ALIGN="LEFT">
    </A>
    <A HREF="index.jsp">
      <IMG SRC="<bean:show object="<%=request%>"                      ⑮
                property="contextPath"/>/images/cancel.gif"
           BORDER="0"
           ALIGN="RIGHT">
    </A>
    <BR>

  </TD>
  </TR>
  <TR>
  <TD ALIGN="center">
    <BR>
    <jsp:include page="shortOrder.jsp"            ⑯
                flush="true"/>
  </TD>
  </TR>
</TABLE>
</form>
```

```
</CENTER>
</BODY>
</HTML>
  </cond:test>    ⑰
</cond:with>      ⑱
```

❶ Creates a condition on the customer.

❷ Tests if the user is not logged on.

❸ Redirects to the logon view.

❹ Ends the test of whether the user is not logged on.

❺ Tests if the user is logged on.

❻ Makes sure that this page won't get cached.

❼ Includes the user menu view.

❽ Displays the user's username.

❾ Displays the user's company name for editing.

❿ Displays the user's name for editing.

⑪ Displays the user's address for editing.

⑫ Displays the user's email address for editing.

⑬ Displays the user's phone number for editing.

⑭ Displays the user's fax number for editing.

⑮ Displays the full image URL.

⑯ Includes the short order view.

⑰ Ends the test on whether the user is logged on.

⑱ Ends the condition on the customer.

In the JSP file, we verify whether the user is logged on. If not, we redirect him to the Logon view. After that, we show a number of input fields that we will fill out with the data from the user's profile.

Profile updated successfully

Listing 13.29 is the source code for the implementation of our profile updated successfully view. The file name is profileUpdateConfirmation.jsp.

Listing 13.29   profileUpdateConfirmation.jsp

```
<%@ page contentType="text/html;charset=UTF-8"%>
<%@ taglib
    uri="http://www.manning.com/jsptagsbook/conditions-taglib"
    prefix="cond" %>
<%@ taglib
```

```
        uri="http://www.manning.com/jsptagsbook/simple-taglib"
        prefix="simple" %>
<cond:with name="customer"                          ❶
            property="loggedOn"
            scope="session">
  <cond:test condition="neq true">                  ❷
    <simple:redirect location="logonForm.jsp"/>     ❸
  </cond:test>                   ❹
  <cond:test condition="eq true">            ❺
<simple:nocache useHeaders="true"/>              ❻
<HTML>
<HEAD>
<TITLE>Cosmetics</TITLE>
</HEAD>
<BODY BGCOLOR="#FFFFFF">
<CENTER>
  <TABLE CELLSPACING="0"
         CELLPADDING="0"
         BORDER="0">
    <TR>
      <TD>
        <jsp:include page="userMenu.jsp"         ❼
                     flush="true"/>
      </TD>
    </TR>
    <TR>
      <TD>
        <P>
          <B>
            Profile updated
          </B>
        </P>
        <P>
        Your profile has been updated according to the information given by you.
        </P>
      <TD>
    </TR>
  </cond:test>          ❽
</cond:with>         ❾
    <TR>
      <TD ALIGN="center">
        <BR>
        <jsp:include page="shortOrder.jsp"          ❿
                     flush="true"/>
      </TD>
    </TR>
  </TABLE>
</CENTER>
</BODY>
</HTML>
```

❶ Creates a condition on the customer.

❷ Tests if the user is not logged on.

❸ Redirects to the logon view.

❹ Ends the test of whether the user is not logged on.

❺ Tests if the user is logged on.

❻ Makes sure that this page won't get cached.

❼ Includes the user menu view.

❽ Ends the test of whether the user is logged on.

❾ Ends the condition on the customer.

❿ Includes the short order view.

We make sure that the user is logged on, and display a message saying that the requested changes to the user's profile has been carried out.

Logoff

Listing 13.30 is the source code for the implementation of our logoff view. The file name is logoffHandler.jsp.

Listing 13.30   logoffHandler.jsp

```
<%@ page contentType="text/html;charset=UTF-8"%>
<%@ taglib
    uri="http://www.manning.com/jsptagsbook/simple-taglib"
    prefix="simple" %>
<%@ taglib
    uri="http://www.manning.com/jsptagsbook/beans-taglib"
    prefix="bean" %>
<simple:nocache useHeaders="true"/>            ❶
<bean:command object="<%=session%>"            ❷
              command="invalidate"/>
<HTML>
<HEAD>
<TITLE>Cosmetics</TITLE>
</HEAD>
<BODY BGCOLOR="#FFFFFF">
<CENTER>
  <TABLE CELLSPACING="0"
         CELLPADDING="0"
         BORDER="0">
    <TR>
      <TD>
        <jsp:include page="userMenu.jsp"       ❸
                   flush="true"/>
      </TD>
    </TR>
```

```
      <TR>
        <TD ALIGN="center">
          <P>
          <B>Welcome back later!</B>
          </P>
          <P>
          We at Cosmetics hope that you will soon return.
          </P>
        </TD>
      </TR>
    </TABLE>
  </CENTER>
</BODY>
</HTML>
```

1 **Makes sure that this page won't get cached.**

2 **Invalidates the user's session.**

3 **Includes the user menu view.**

In the rather small JSP page, we use the generic <command> tag to execute invalidate() on the user's current session object. By doing so, we ensure that the user's Customer and Order beans are removed. If any other page is requested, the user will be given a fresh session and new beans.

Generic error

Listing 13.31 is the source code for the implementation of our generic error view. The file name is jspException.jsp.

Listing 13.31   jspException.jsp

```
<%@ page isErrorPage="true"      1
     contentType="text/html;charset=UTF-8"%>
<%@ taglib
    uri="http://www.manning.com/jsptagsbook/beans-taglib"
    prefix="bean" %>
<HTML>
<HEAD>
<TITLE>Cosmetics</TITLE>
</HEAD>
<BODY BGCOLOR="#FFFFFF">
<CENTER>
  <TABLE CELLSPACING="0"
         CELLPADDING="0"
         BORDER="0">
    <TR>
      <TD>
```

```
            <jsp:include page="userMenu.jsp"
                         flush="true"/>
      </TD>
    </TR>
    <TR>
      <TD>
        <P><B>Error</B></P>
        <P>An error has occurred.</P>
        <P>
          <CODE>
            Message: <bean:show object="<%=exception%>"
                             property="message"/>
          </CODE>
        </P>
        <P>If the problem persists, please contact the administrator.</P>
        <A HREF="javascript:history.go(-1);">
          <IMG SRC="<bean:show object="<%=request%>"
                    property="contextPath"/>/images/back.gif"
              BORDER="0"
              ALIGN="RIGHT">
        </A>
      </TD>
    </TR>
    <TR>
      <TD ALIGN="center">
        <BR>
        <jsp:include page="shortOrder.jsp"
                     flush="true"/>
      </TD>
    </TR>
  </TABLE>
</CENTER>
</BODY>
</HTML>
```

❶ Defines this page as an error page.
❷ Includes the user menu view.
❸ Displays the exception message.
❹ Displays the full image URL.
❺ Includes the short order view.

We tell the container that this is an error page, and that it should be given any exception thrown. We use <show> tag to display the exception message to the user.

Notice that this view is defined as an error page in the web-applications configuration file (web.xml) and does not need to be defined in any page that could throw a generic runtime exception. This configuration looks like listing 13.32, which is cut out from the web.xml file of our web application.

Listing 13.32   The configuration of the JspException handler in the web.xml file.

```
...
<error-page>
  <exception-type>javax.servlet.jsp.JspException</exception-type>
  <location>jspException.jsp</location>
</error-page>
...
```

The configuration tells the container that whenever an uncaught `JspException` is thrown, the file jspException.jsp should be invoked. Notice that any error page defined for use within a page overrides the applicationwide setting.

Mail error

Listing 13.33 is the source code for the implementation of our mail error view. The file name is mailException.jsp.

Listing 13.33   mailException.jsp

```
<%@ page isErrorPage="true"       ❶
         contentType="text/html;charset=UTF-8"%>
<%@ taglib
    uri="http://www.manning.com/jsptagsbook/beans-taglib"
    prefix="bean" %>
<simple:nocache useHeaders="true"/>     ❷
<HTML>
<HEAD>
<TITLE>Cosmetics</TITLE>
</HEAD>
<BODY BGCOLOR="#FFFFFF">
<CENTER>
  <TABLE CELLSPACING="0"
         CELLPADDING="0"
         BORDER="0">
    <TR>
      <TD>
        <jsp:include page="userMenu.jsp"      ❸
                     flush="true"/>
      </TD>
    </TR>
    <TR>
      <TD ALIGN="center">
        <FONT SIZE="+2">
          <B>Order Received</B>
        </FONT>
```

```
          </TD>
      </TR>
      <TR>
        <TD>
          <P ALIGN="justify">
          Your order has been received by Cosmetics.
          </P>
          <P ALIGN="justify">
          Your order reference number is
          <B>
            <bean:show name="order"
                       property="id"                    ④
                       scope="request"/>
          </B>.
          </P>
          <P ALIGN="justify">
          A receipt could not be sent to your email address
          (<bean:show name="customer"
                       property="email"                 ⑤
                       scope="session"/>),<br>
          due to an internal error.</P>
          </P>
        </TD>
      </TR>
    </TABLE>
  </CENTER>
</BODY>
</HTML>
```

❶ Defines this page as an error page.

❷ Makes sure that this page won't get cached.

❸ Includes the user menu view.

❹ Displays the order reference number.

❺ Displays the user's email address.

In this page, we inform the container that this is an error page, and that it should be given the exception thrown. Notice that we never show this exception to the user. Instead we assure the user by saying that the receipt could not be sent, but that the order is received.

Number error view

Listing 13.34 is the source code for the implementation of our number error view. The file name is numberformatException.jsp.

Listing 13.34 numberFormatException.jsp

```jsp
<%@ page isErrorPage="true"                    ❶
         contentType="text/html;charset=UTF-8"%>
<%@ taglib
    uri="http://www.manning.com/jsptagsbook/beans-taglib"
    prefix="bean" %>
<HTML>
<HEAD>
<TITLE>Cosmetics</TITLE>
</HEAD>
<BODY BGCOLOR="#FFFFFF">
<CENTER>
  <TABLE CELLSPACING="0"
         CELLPADDING="0"
         BORDER="0">
    <TR>
      <TD>
        <jsp:include page="userMenu.jsp"          ❷
                     flush="true"/>
      </TD>
    </TR>
    <TR>
      <TD>
        <P><B>Illegal value</B></P>
        <P>Please specify a valid numeric value.</P>
        <P>
          <CODE>
            Message:
            <bean:show object="<%=exception%>"          ❸
                       property="message"/>
          </CODE>
        </P>
        <A HREF="javascript:history.go(-1);">
        <IMG SRC="<bean:show object="<%=request%>"          ❹
property="contextPath"/>/images/back.gif"
              BORDER="0"
              ALIGN="RIGHT">
        </A>
      </TD>
    </TR>
    <TR>
      <TD ALIGN="center">
        <BR>
        <jsp:include page="shortOrder.jsp"          ❺
                     flush="true"/>
      </TD>
    </TR>
  </TABLE>
</CENTER>
</BODY>
</HTML>
```

❶ **Defines this page as an error page.**

❷ **Includes the user menu view.**

❸ **Displays the exception message.**

❹ **Displays the full image URL.**

❺ **Includes the short order view.**

In the page, we tell the container that this is an error page, and that it should be given the exception thrown. We then include the user menu view. After that, we display the message for the exception thrown. Finally, we include the short order view.

As with the generic error view, this page is configured to act as an error page in our web application's configuration file.

Table 13.19 Suggestions for expansion

Area	Description
Product descriptions	Adds product descriptions and product views.
Order history	Adds views to display order history and details about historical orders.
Administration	Adds a web application for administration of the shop.
Category tree	Changes the flat category structure into a category tree.
Optimize tag usage	Tag usage in this application is not near optimal. See if you can enhance it.
Shopping list	Adds shopping lists/favorite product views.
One-click buying	Adds banners with one-click buying.
Validation of profile	Extends the validation of profile information.

13.6 *Summary*

After this in-depth look at tag usage within the scope of an application, you should feel more comfortable with tags' use in simplifying your development of web applications and how tag libraries can help you cut the time needed for development.

Although we have tried to describe every tag throughout this application, we are sure there is much that could bear further explanation. We recommend that you deploy the application as described in appendix C so that you can step through the application and gain a deeper understanding of how the tags are being used.

A good way to gain a still deeper understanding of tags is to customize and expand the application further. Table 13.19 lists examples of possible directions.

EJB-driven WAPStore

14

14.1 *Introduction*

This case study will illustrate tag usage in an EJB-driven WAP application. We will start by reviewing what WAP and EJB are, and then walk through the application with our focus on tag usage. For information about the EJBs used, how to retrieve the full source code from this book's web site, and how to deploy the full application, see appendix C.

The application described in this chapter is tested on Orion (http://www.orion-server.com), but should work just as well on any application server that commits to the J2EE standard and supports the public draft of the EJB 2.0 specification. As a client, the r320s browser that comes with the Ericsson's WAP IDE 2.1 was used.

There should be a number of application servers supporting EJB 2.0 from which to choose.

14.1.1 *Custom tags used*

Throughout the application, we will utilize the custom tags given in table 14.1. The table lists the chapter where you may get more information. The tags are ordered by the tag library to which they belong.

Table 14.1   Custom tags used throughout this application

Tag	Tag library	Usage	Chapter
`<command>`	Bean-taglib	Executes methods on objects.	15
`<show>`	Bean-taglib	Shows bean properties.	8
`<with>`	Conditional-taglib	Creates conditions that can be tested.	9
`<test>`	Conditional-taglib	Tests conditions.	9
`<home>`	EJB-taglib	Retrieves the home interface of an EJB.	12
`<iterate>`	EJB-taglib	Iterates through a collection of EJB remote interfaces.	12
`<use>`	EJB-taglib	Retrieves the remote interface of an EJB.	12
`<message>`	J2EEMail-taglib	Defines messages for emails.	12
`<send>`	J2EEMail-taglib	Defines start, recipients, and senders for emails.	12
`<subject>`	J2EEMail-taglib	Defines subjects for emails.	12
`<currency>`	Locale-taglib	Displays currency formatted with a certain `Locale`.	13
`<nocache>`	Simple-taglib	Prevents client-side caching of the page.	13
`<redirect>`	Simple-taglib	Redirects the request to a given location.	6

14.1.2 *WAP*

WAP, as you recall from chapter 1, is used to interact with online services from wireless devices such as cellular phones and PDAs. This chapter will present an application for generating WAP content.

Since some WAP devices do not support cookies, WML content must use URL encoding techniques in order to maintain a session state. Adding the current Session ID to any URL reference does this. In most cases our application server handles this for us; the few occasions in which we have to do so manually are illustrated in the JSP pages in this chapter.

In the application for this case study, we have tried to minimize the number of interactions between the client and the server, while still maintaining control of the flow of events. The application features a rather rude interface in order to support as many devices as possible. We have elected to develop the application for WML 1.1, as this is commonly supported by a large number of devices.

14.1.3 *EJB*

Throughout this case study, we will use EJBs as a control layer and as the model layer. Session beans will control the interaction between the user's request and the entities, and we will implement the entities as Entity beans. For more information about EJB and J2EE, see chapter 12.

14.2 *Overview*

One month after we delivered the (hypothetical) online ordering system to Cosmetics (see chapter 13), the company contacted us to reengineer its way of doing business. Cosmetics, now known as Cosmetix, is selling its products door-to-door. The salesmen are free agents, hence Cosmetix will deliver to the salesmen and charge them for the product. The salesmen will deliver the goods and charge the buyers, making a profit on the difference.

As the salesmen are on the road most of the time, Cosmetix wants them to be able to place their orders via cellular phones, making WAP the primary solution to their problems.

Cosmetix does not want to keep its old web solution, because too many orders from phantom customers were placed. Instead, it wants us to view that solution as a prototype for building a new one, a WAP-enabled solution.

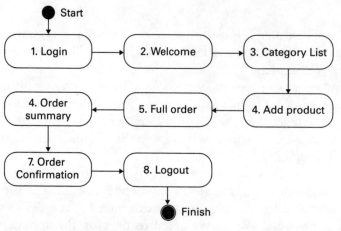

Figure 14.1   The normal flow of events

14.3 *Implementation*

In this section, we will cover the implementation of the WAP system built for Cosmetix. As our focus is on the tag usage in this application, we will only briefly describe the EJB Sessions and Entities our application utilizes. You'll likely recognize the names used for the parts of the application from the case study in chapter 13.

14.3.1 *Normal flow of events*

The normal flow of events describes the most common interaction between a user and the application. Figure 14.1 describes the normal flow of events for this application in the form of an activity diagram.

1 The logon view is displayed, asking the user to identify himself. The user does so.

2 The welcome view is displayed with a number of options. The user selects to view the catalogue.

3 The category list is displayed. The user browses this and adds a number of products to his order.

4 The products are added to the order. The user elects to view his current order.

5 The full order view is displayed. The user elects to send his order.

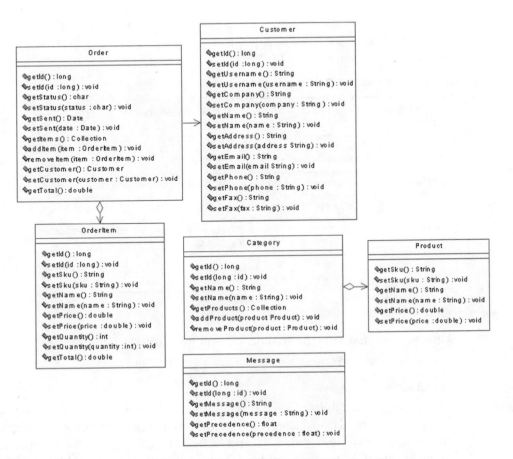

Figure 14.2   The remote interfaces for the EJB Entities and their internal relations

6   The order summary view is displayed. The user elects to confirm his order.

7   The order confirmation is displayed. The user selects to end his session by logging out.

8   The user is logged out and the logon view is displayed anew.

Remember that what we describe is the *normal* flow of events. There are other options that are not considered normal, which are listed among the others below.

14.3.2 *Model*

The model is implemented as a number of EJB Entities, as described in figure 14.2.

For more information about these entities' actual implementation, download the application as described in appendix C. There you will find the source code for all the entities given in table 14.2.

Table 14.2   The Entity EJBs acting as model

EJB	Description
Customer	Represents the stored profile of a customer.
Category	Represents a line of products. It has a name and contains a number of products.
Product	Represents a product on sale. It has a stock keeping unit (SKU), name, and price.
Message	Represents a line of text that should be displayed to the user on the welcome view.
Order	Represents an order created by a user. It has a total price and contains a number of OrderItems. It belongs to a customer.
OrderItem	Represents a single row in an order. It holds the SKU, name, price, and ordered quantity of a certain product.

14.3.3 View

Fifteen views make up the system. We will go through each in order to describe their intended usage.

Logon view

The logon view is displayed each time a user tries to access the application without being logged on. This is achieved by setting the access rights for the pages that should allow only registered users, and by defining this page as the login form. All of this is defined in the web.xml file. The view is made up of two different cards, in which the first card loads the second card.

Listing 14.1 is the source for the logon view. This file is called login.jsp inside the application.

Listing 14.1   login.jsp

```
<%@ page contentType="text/vnd.wap.wml;charset=UTF-8" %>     ❶
<%@ taglib
    uri="http://www.manning.com/jsptagsbook/simple-taglib"
    prefix="simple" %>
<simple:nocache useHeaders="true"                            ❷
                useMetaTags="false"/>
<?xml version="1.0"?>
<!DOCTYPE wml PUBLIC "-//WAPFORUM//DTD WML 1.1//EN"
"http://www.wapforum.org/DTD/wml_1.1.xml">
<wml>
```

```
  <card id="image"
        ontimer="#login"
        title="Cosmetix">
    <timer value="100"/>
    <p>
       <img src="images/logo.wbmp"
            alt="Cosmetix"/>
    </p>
  </card>
  <card id="login"
        title="Cosmetix">
    <do type="options" label="Login">
<go href=
"j_security_check?j_username=$username&amp;j_password=$passwd"/>
    </do>
     <p align="left">
     <input type="text"
            name="username"
            format="32A"
            title="Username:"/>
      <input maxlength="32"
            type="password"
            size="7"
            name="passwd"
            title="Password"/>
    </p>
  </card>
</wml>
```

❶ Sets the content type to WML   We set the headers to show the client that the content returned is in WML.

❷ Makes sure that this page won't get cached   We use the <nocache> tag to set the headers that tell the client that this page should not be cached locally. Notice that we use headers and not <META> tags for this, as some WML clients do not recognize cache-preventing <META> tags.

We then tell the client that this content is for XML version 1.0, and where to find the DTD that defines it. After that, we state that this WML file contains a Cosmetix card that will display an image for ten seconds and then call the second card. This will look like figure 14.3.

The second card, the one called by the previous one, is also titled Cosmetix. This card will prompt the user for username and password.

Figure 14.3   The Cosmetix card.

❸ **Calls the authentication handler** The card will also hold an option called Login, that calls the application's authentication handler with the username and password that identify the user to the system. This card will look like figure 14.4.

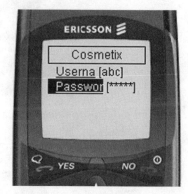

When the user selects the login option, the authentication handler will check the request for a username and password, and try to match these against the users in its principal file. A principal file holds the name and password for users, as well as the user's role in the system. If the user is found, he will be authen-

Figure 14.4   The login card

ticated by the application server and can then access the protected pages.

The security configuration of our web application looks like listing 14.2, which is part of the web.xml file of our web application.

Listing 14.2   The application's security configuration as defined in the web.xml file

```
...
<security-constraint>
  <web-resource-collection>
    <web-resource-name>Cosmetix</web-resource-name>
    <url-pattern>/index.jsp</url-pattern>         ❶
    ...
    <url-pattern>/userMenu.jsp</url-pattern>       ❶
    <http-method>*</http-method>                   ❷
  </web-resource-collection>
  <auth-constraint>
    <role-name>users</role-name>                   ❸
  </auth-constraint>
</security-constraint>
<login-config>
  <auth-method>FORM</auth-method>                  ❹
  <form-login-config>
    <form-login-page>/login.jsp</form-login-page>   ❺
    <form-error-page>/login.jsp</form-error-page>   ❻
  </form-login-config>
</login-config>
<security-role>
  <description>Cosmetix users</description>
  <role-name>users</role-name>
</security-role>
...
```

❶ The pages to protect   We tell the container what pages to protect, in this case most of the pages that makes up our application, except for the login view and the login error view.

❷ The HTTP methods to protect (in this case all). We define the methods to protect, which will be both POST and GET in this case.

❸ The role any user must have to access the protected pages. After that we define the roles users must belong to in order to access the protected pages. In this case, we tell the container that only users of the role "users" should have access to the protected pages.

❹ The authentication method to use (in this case a FORM). The authentication method must also be defined. We define it as FORM authentication.

❺ The name of the page holding the FORM for authentication. As we are using FORM-based authentication, we must tell the container what view will hold the form where the user can specify his username and password.

❻ The name of the page holding the authentication error FORM. We must also tell the container the view that should be used to handle any authentication errors.

For more information about the available authentication methods or the settings for these, look at the servlet specification.

14.3.4 *Welcome view*

The welcome view (listing 14.3) will display a number of messages inside a single card to the user. This file is called index.jsp inside our application.

Listing 14.3   index.jsp

```
<%@ page contentType="text/vnd.wap.wml;charset=UTF-8" %>      ❶
<%@ taglib
    uri="http://www.manning.com/jsptagsbook/simple-taglib"
    prefix="simple" %>
<%@ taglib
    uri="http://www.manning.com/jsptagsbook/beans-taglib"
    prefix="bean" %>
<%@ taglib
    uri="http://www.manning.com/jsptagsbook/ejb-taglib"
    prefix="ejb" %>
<simple:nocache useHeaders="true"
                useMetaTags="false"/>        ❷
<?xml version="1.0"?>
<!DOCTYPE wml PUBLIC "-//WAPFORUM//DTD WML 1.1//EN"
"http://www.wapforum.org/DTD/wml_1.1.xml">
<wml>
```

```
        <card id="welcome"
               title="Welcome!">
    <jsp:include page="userMenu.jsp"
                 flush="true"/>
    <ejb:home id="home"
              type="book.casestudy.cosmetix.ejb.MessageHome"
              name="ejb/message"/>
    <ejb:iterate id="msg"
                 type="book.casestudy.cosmetix.ejb.Message"
                 object="<%=home.findAll().iterator()%>">
      <p align="left">
    <bean:show name="msg"
               property="message"/>
      </p>
    </ejb:iterate>
    </card>
    </wml>
```

❶ **Sets the content type to WML** We set the headers so that the client will understand that the content returned is in WML.

❷ **Makes sure that this page won't get cached** We use the `<nocache>` tag to set the headers telling the client that this page should not be cached locally.

We then define that this WML file contains a card with the title "Welcome!" (normally displayed in the client display).

❸ **Includes the user menu view** The user menu view will set up a number of options for the user.

❹ **Gets the message EJB's home interface** With the help of the `<home>` tag, we procure the home interface of the `Message` EJB by telling the tag the reference name of the EJB and the interface that should be returned.

❺ **Starts iterating through the message EJBs** We use the `<iterate>` tag to go through the remote interfaces of the `Message` EJB that we receive by calling `findAll()` on the `Message` EJB's home interface. The card will look like figure 14.5.

❻ **Displays the message.**

❼ **Ends the iteration.**

In order for any page inside a web application to be able to access an EJB directly, an EJB reference must be defined in the web application's configuration (listing 14.4).

Figure 14.5 Welcome card

Listing 14.4   An EJB reference defined in the web.xml file

```
...
<ejb-ref>
  <description>Messages</description>
  <ejb-ref-name>ejb/message</ejb-ref-name>
  <ejb-ref-type>Entity</ejb-ref-type>
  <home>book.casestudy.cosmetix.ejb.MessageHome</home>
  <remote>book.casestudy.cosmetix.ejb.Message</remote>
</ejb-ref>
...
```

We tell the container that our web application should be able to access the remote and home interfaces of the Message EJB by using the name ejb/message.

User menu view

Most other pages will include the user menu view to define the options available. This view will contain no card of its own. Listing 14.5 is the source for the user menu view.

Listing 14.5   userMenu.jsp

```
<%@ taglib
    uri="http://www.manning.com/jsptagsbook/conditions-taglib"
    prefix="cond" %>
<%@ taglib
    uri="http://www.manning.com/jsptagsbook/ejb-taglib"
    prefix="ejb" %>
<jsp:useBean id="customer"                                          ❶
             type="book.casestudy.cosmetix.ejb.Customer"
             scope="session"/>
<ejb:home id="home"                                                 ❷
          type="book.casestudy.cosmetix.ejb.OrderManagerHome"
          name="ejb/orderManager"/>
<ejb:use id="orderManager"                                          ❸
         type="book.casestudy.cosmetix.ejb.OrderManager"
         instance="<%=home.create(customer)%>"/>
<ejb:use id="order"                                                 ❹
         type="book.casestudy.cosmetix.ejb.Order"
         instance="<%=orderManager.getOrder()%>"/>
<do type="options" label="Catalogue" name="catalogue">
  <go href="categoryList.jsp"/>
</do>
<cond:with object="<%=(order.getItems().size()>0)%>">              ❺
  <cond:test condition="eq true">           ❻
<do type="options" label="Short Order" name="shortOrder">
  <go href="shortOrder.jsp"/>
```

```
</do>
<do type="options" label="Full Order" name="fullOrder">
  <go href="fullOrder.jsp"/>
</do>
<do type="options" label="Send Order" name="sendOrder">
  <go href="sendOrder.jsp"/>
</do>
  </cond:test>      ❼
</cond:with>      ❽
<do type="options" label="Your Profile" name="yourProfile">
  <go href="profile.jsp"/>
</do>
<do type="options" label="Logoff" name="logoff">
  <go href="logoffHandler.jsp"/>
</do>
<do type="options" label="Home" name="home">
  <go href="index.jsp"/>
</do>
```

❶ **Gets the remote interface of the `Customer` EJB** We first try to retrieve the remote interface of the `Customer` EJB from the `session` scope. If this is not found, an exception will be thrown and caught by the instantiation error view.

❷ **Gets the home interface for the `OrderManager` EJB.**

❸ **Creates a remote interface for the `OrderManager` EJB** We try to use the home interface to create a remote interface to `OrderManager`. To do so we need to pass in the `Customer` EJB as parameter.

❹ **Retrieves the user's current `Order` EJB** We then use the remote interface of the `OrderManager` to retrieve a remote interface for the user's current `Order` EJB. After that, we display options that all users should have.

❺ **Creates a condition on the number of items in the order** ❻ **Tests if the number of items in the order is more than 0** We use the `<with>` and `<test>` tags to test whether the user's current `Order` contains any items. If so, we display options that should only be available to users with a nonempty `Order`. We end the test clause and display additional options that should be available to all users. The result will look like figure 14.6.

❼ **Ends the test.**

❽ **Ends the condition.**

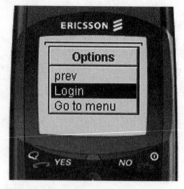

Figure 14.6   Selecting options

Short order view

The short order view displays a short list of the user's current order in a single card. This file is called shortOrder.jsp (listing 14.5).

Listing 14.6   shortOrder.jsp

```
<%@ page contentType="text/vnd.wap.wml;charset=UTF-8" %>
<%@ taglib
    uri="http://www.manning.com/jsptagsbook/conditions-taglib"
    prefix="cond" %>
<%@ taglib
    uri="http://www.manning.com/jsptagsbook/beans-taglib"
    prefix="bean" %>
<%@ taglib uri="http://www.manning.com/jsptagsbook/ejb-taglib"
    prefix="ejb" %>
<%@ taglib
    uri="http://www.manning.com/jsptagsbook/simple-taglib"
    prefix="simple" %>
<jsp:useBean id="customer"
             type="book.casestudy.cosmetix.ejb.Customer"
             scope="session"/>                                      ❶
<simple:nocache useHeaders="true"
                useMetaTags="false"/>          ❷
<?xml version="1.0"?>
<!DOCTYPE wml PUBLIC "-//WAPFORUM//DTD WML 1.1//EN"
"http://www.wapforum.org/DTD/wml_1.1.xml">
<wml>
<ejb:home id="home"
          type="book.casestudy.cosmetix.ejb.OrderManagerHome"
          name="ejb/orderManager"/>                                ❸
<ejb:use id="orderManager"
         type="book.casestudy.cosmetix.ejb.OrderManager"
         instance="<%=home.create(customer)%>"/>                   ❹
<ejb:use id="order"
         type="book.casestudy.cosmetix.ejb.Order"
         instance="<%=orderManager.getOrder()%>"/>              ❺
  <card id="shortOrder"
        title="Your Order">                  ❻
<jsp:include page="userMenu.jsp"
             flush="true"/>
<cond:with object="<%=(order.getItems().size()>0)%>">          ❼
  <cond:test condition="eq true">            ❽
    <ejb:iterate id="item"
                 type="book.casestudy.cosmetix.ejb.OrderItem"      ❾
                 object="<%=order.getItems().iterator()%>">
      <p align="left">
        <bean:show name="item"               ❿
                   property="quantity"/>
        <bean:show name="item"            ⓫
                   property="sku"/>
```

```
    </p>
    </ejb:iterate>      ⑫
  </cond:test>      ⑬
  <cond:test condition="neq true">      ⑭
    <p align="left">
      Is empty
    </p>
  </cond:test>      ⑮
</cond:with>      ⑯
  </card>
</wml>
```

----

① **Retrieves the remote interface of the** `Customer` **EJB** We try to retrieve the `Customer` EJB from the `session` scope.

② **Makes sure that this page won't get cached** We make sure that the client will not cache this page locally.

③ **Adds a home interface for the** `OrderManager` **EJB** We add an `OrderManager` home interface to the `page` scope.

④ **Creates an remote interface for the** `OrderManager` **EJB** We use the `OrderManager` home interface to create an `OrderManager` remote interface with the `Customer` EJB as parameter.

⑤ **Retrieves the user's current** `Order` **EJB** We use the remote interface of the `Order-Manager` to retrieve the user's current `Order` EJB. If it contains any `OrderItems`, we iterate through this `Order`, displaying the ordered quantity and the SKU for all `Order-Items`. If it does not hold any `OrderItems`, we display a message saying that the order is empty. Either way, all content goes into a single card.

⑥ **Includes the user menu view.**

⑦ **Creates a condition on the number of items in the current order.**

⑧ **Tests if the number of items in the current order are more than none.**

⑨ **Iterates through the order's** `OrderItems`**.**

⑩ **Displays the ordered quantity of the** `OrderItem`**.**

⑪ **Displays the SKU of the** `OrderItem`**.**

⑫ **Ends the Iteration.**

⑬ **Ends the test.**

⑭ **Tests if the number of items in the current order are none.**

⑮ **Ends the test.**

⑯ **Ends the condition.**

Category list view

The category list view displays Cosmetix's product lines. To limit the number of interactions a user has to perform to find the desired products, this view is used to display both the categories and the products the categories contain. There will be one card for showing the list of categories. These categories will each have separate cards whereon their products are displayed. For every product, there will be a separate card with the option to order. All cards except for the category list will be created dynamically, in an amount that matches the actual number of currently existing categories and products. This file is called categoryList.jsp, (listing 14.7).

Listing 14.7   categoryList.jsp

```jsp
<%@ page contentType="text/vnd.wap.wml;charset=UTF-8" %>
<%@ taglib
    uri="http://www.manning.com/jsptagsbook/simple-taglib"
    prefix="simple" %>
<%@ taglib
    uri="http://www.manning.com/jsptagsbook/conditions-taglib"
    prefix="cond" %>
<%@ taglib
    uri="http://www.manning.com/jsptagsbook/beans-taglib"
    prefix="bean" %>
<%@ taglib
    uri="http://www.manning.com/jsptagsbook/ejb-taglib"
    prefix="ejb" %>
<%@ taglib
    uri="http://www.manning.com/jsptagsbook/locale-taglib"
    prefix="local" %>
<simple:nocache useHeaders="true"                    ❶
                useMetaTags="false"/>
<?xml version="1.0"?>
<!DOCTYPE wml PUBLIC "-//WAPFORUM//DTD WML 1.1//EN"
"http://www.wapforum.org/DTD/wml_1.1.xml">
<wml>
  <template>
    <do type="prev">
      <go href="#listCategories"/>
    </do>
<jsp:include page="userMenu.jsp"                     ❷
             flush="true"/>
  </template>
  <card id="listCategories"
        title="Product Lines">
<ejb:home id="home"                                                    ❸
          type="book.casestudy.cosmetix.ejb.CatalogueManagerHome"
          name="ejb/catalogueManager"/>
```

```
<ejb:use id="catalogueManager"                                              ❹
        type="book.casestudy.cosmetix.ejb.CatalogueManager"
        instance="<%=home.create()%>"/>
<ejb:iterate id="category"                                                  ❺
        type="book.casestudy.cosmetix.ejb.Category"
        object="<%=catalogueManager.getCategories().iterator()%>">
   <p align="left">
     <a href="#cat<bean:show name="category"                               ❻
                             property="id"/>">
        <bean:show name="category"                                         ❼
                 property="name"/>
     </a>
   </p>
</ejb:iterate>                                                              ❽
  </card>
<ejb:iterate id="category"                                                  ❾
        type="book.casestudy.cosmetix.ejb.Category"
        object="<%=catalogueManager.getCategories().iterator()%>">
   <card id="cat<bean:show name="category"                                 ❿
                           property="id"/>"
       title="<bean:show name="category"                                   ⓫
                         property="name"/>">
       <ejb:iterate id="product"                                           ⓬
                 type="book.casestudy.cosmetix.ejb.Product"
              object="<%=category.getProducts().iterator()%>">
    <p align="left">
      <a href="#prod<bean:show name="product"                             ⓭
                              property="sku"/>">
        <bean:show name="product"                                         ⓮
                              property="name"/>
      </a>
    </p>
       </ejb:iterate>                                                       ⓯
   </card>
   </ejb:iterate>                                                          ⓰
<ejb:iterate id="product"                                                   ⓱
        type="book.casestudy.cosmetix.ejb.Product"
        object="<%=catalogueManager.getProducts().iterator()%>">
   <card id="prod<bean:show name="product"                                ⓲
                            property="sku"/>"
       title="<bean:show name="product"                                    ⓳
                         property="name"/>">
    <do type="options" label="Add to order" name="addToOrder">
      <go href="itemAdder.jsp">
        <postfield name="sku"
                  value="<bean:show name="product"                         ⓴
                                   property="sku"/>"/>
        <postfield name="quantity"
                  value="$(quantity)"/>
      </go>
    </do>
```

```
    <p align="left">
      SKU: <bean:show name="product"
                      property="sku"/>
    </p>
    <p align="left">
      Price: <![CDATA[<local:currency
                      amount="<%=product.getPrice()%>" />]]>
    </p>
    <p align="left">
      <input maxlength="3"
             format="*N"
             size="2"
             name="quantity"
             title="Quantity:"/>
    </p>
  </card>
  </ejb:iterate>
</wml>
```

❷①

❷②

❷③

① **Makes sure that this page won't get cached.**

② **Includes the user menu view in a template** We include the user menu view in a template card. By doing so, the user menu will be inherited by all cards of this deck, making any options available in the template also appear in all cards.

③ **Add the home interface of the CatalogueManager.**

④ **Creates a remote interface for the CatalogueManager** We use the home interface of the CatalogueManager to retrieve a remote interface for the same EJB.

⑤ **Iterates through the categories** We use the <iterate> tag of the EJB taglib to iterate through all available Category EJBs. For each Category we show a link that will go to a card defined in this deck. The link will contain the keyword cat followed by the current Category's ID. For the visible part of the link, we use the name of the Category. The resulting card will look like figure 14.7

⑥ **Creates a link to a dynamically created card.**

⑦ **Displays the link name using the category name.**

⑧ **Ends the Iteration of categories.**

⑨ **Iterates through the categories** We iterate through all Category EJBs again, and create one card per Category, using the keyword cat and the Category's ID as card ID.

⑩ **For each category, adds a card.**

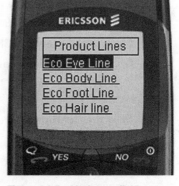

Figure 14.7 Listing available categories

⑪ Sets the card's name using the category name.

⑫ Iterates through the products   Inside each card, we iterate through the current Category's Product EJBs and display a link built up of the keyword prod. This we add the Product SKU to as a target of the link, with the Product name as the name of the link. Each such card will appear as in figure 14.8 when selected.

⑬ Creates a link to a dynamically created card.

⑭ Displays the link name using the product name.

⑮ Ends the iteration of products.

⑯ Ends the iteration of categories.

⑰ Iterates through the products.   For every Product, a card is created with its ID made up of the keyword prod and the Product's SKU. In each card an option to add the Product to the user's current Order is available. Inside the card, the Product's SKU and price are listed together with an input field wherein the user can specify the amount they wish to order. The price is formatted for the currently used locale. The result will look like in figure 14.9.

⑱ Adds a card for each product.

⑲ For each card, uses the product name as title.

⑳ Adds an option to add the product to the current order.

㉑ Displays the product's SKU.

㉒ Displays the product's price.   As the <currency> tag is used without any specified locale, the tag will look in the context for it. Listing 14.8 shows a Locale setting in the web.xml file.

㉓ Ends the iteration of products.

Figure 14.8   Viewing a category card

Figure 14.9   Viewing a product card

Listing 14.8   An applicationwide available Locale setting in the web.xml file.

```
...
<context-param>

   <param-name>locale</param-name>      ❶
   <param-value>en_US</param-value>     ❷
</context-param>
...
```

❶ Defines the name of the `Context` **parameter.**

❷ Defines the value of the `Context` **parameter.**

In the listing we define the name of the `Context` parameter to be `locale`, which is the parameter name that the `<currency>` tag will look for. We set the value of the parameter to be a string representing the locale, which the tag will then use to construct a `Locale`. As the dollar sign is used to define a variable in WML, we must be sure that we will not run into problems when displaying prices such as $100 (which could be interpreted as referencing the variable defined with a name of `100`). In Listing 14.7 and other listings where we use the `<currency>` tag, we display all prices inside the CDATA block, which tells the client that the information inside is character data and should not be parsed.

Full order view

The full order view displays full information about the user's current order, together with an option to remove unwanted items. The name of this file is fullOrder.jsp. The source of the page is in listing 14.9.

Listing 14.9   fullOrder.jsp

```
<%@ page contentType="text/vnd.wap.wml;charset=UTF-8" %>
<%@ taglib
    uri="http://www.manning.com/jsptagsbook/conditions-taglib"
    prefix="cond" %>
<%@ taglib
    uri="http://www.manning.com/jsptagsbook/simple-taglib"
    prefix="simple" %>
<%@ taglib
    uri="http://www.manning.com/jsptagsbook/locale-taglib"
    prefix="local" %>
<%@ taglib
    uri="http://www.manning.com/jsptagsbook/beans-taglib"
    prefix="bean" %>
<%@ taglib
    uri="http://www.manning.com/jsptagsbook/ejb-taglib"
    prefix="ejb" %>
<jsp:useBean id="customer"                                           ❶
            type="book.casestudy.cosmetix.ejb.Customer"
            scope="session"/>
<ejb:home id="home"                                                  ❷
        type="book.casestudy.cosmetix.ejb.OrderManagerHome"
        name="ejb/orderManager"/>
<ejb:use id="orderManager"                                           ❸
        type="book.casestudy.cosmetix.ejb.OrderManager"
        instance="<%=home.create(customer)%>"/>
<ejb:use id="order"
```

```
            type="book.casestudy.cosmetix.ejb.Order"          ❹
            instance="<%=orderManager.getOrder()%>"/>
<simple:nocache useHeaders="true"            ❺
               useMetaTags="false"/>
<?xml version="1.0"?>
<!DOCTYPE wml PUBLIC "-//WAPFORUM//DTD WML 1.1//EN"
"http://www.wapforum.org/DTD/wml_1.1.xml">
<wml>
  <card id="fullOrder"
        title="Your Order">
<jsp:include page="userMenu.jsp"          ❻
             flush="true"/>
<cond:with object="<%=(order.getItems().size()>0)%>">          ❼
  <cond:test condition="eq true">          ❽
    <ejb:iterate id="item"          ❾
                 type="book.casestudy.cosmetix.ejb.OrderItem"
                 object="<%=order.getItems().iterator()%>">
    <p align="left">
      SKU: <bean:show name="item"          ❿
                 property="sku"/>
    </p>
    <p align="left">
      NAME: <bean:show name="item"          ⓫
                 property="name"/>
    </p>
    <p align="left">
      PRICE: <![CDATA[<local:currency          ⓬
                     amount="<%=item.getPrice()%>" />]]>
    </p>
    <p align="left">
      QUANTITY: <bean:show name="item"          ⓭
                       property="quantity"/>
    </p>
    <p align="left">
      SUM: <![CDATA[<local:currency          ⓮
                  amount="<%=item.getTotal()%>" />
    </p>
    <p align="left">
      <%
        HttpServletResponse res=(HttpServletResponse)response;          ⓯
      %>
      <a href="<%=res.encodeURL(          ⓰
"itemRemover.jsp?sku="+item.getSku())%>">REMOVE</a>
    </p>
    <p align="center">--</p>
    </ejb:iterate>          ⓱
    <p align="left">
      <strong>
        TOTAL: <![CDATA[<local:currency          ⓲
                       amount="<%=order.getTotal()%>" />]]>
      </strong>
```

```
    </p>
  </cond:test>        ⑲
  <cond:test condition="neq true">        ⑳
    <p>
      Is empty
    </p>
  </cond:test>        ㉑
</cond:with>        ㉒
  </card>
</wml>
```

_____ ■

❶ **Gets the remote interface of the** `Customer` **EJB**   We add the remote interface of the `Customer` EJB to the page scope.

❷ **Adds the home interface of the** `OrderManager` **EJB**   We add the home interface of the `OrderManager` to the page scope.

❸ **Creates an** `OrderManager` **EJB**   We use the `Customer` EJB to retrieve a remote interface of an `OrderManager` EJB from the home interface of the same EJB.

❹ **Retrieves the user's current** `Order` **EJB**   From the `OrderManager` EJB, we get the user's current `Order` EJB.

❺ **Makes sure that this page won't get cached.**

❻ **Includes the user menu view**   We define a card that displays the order within. Inside the card, we include the options from the user menu view.

❼ **Creates a condition on the number of items in the current order**   We check whether the `Order` contains any `OrderItems`.

❽ **Tests if the number of items in the current order is more than none.**

❾ **Iterates through the** `OrderItems`   If the order contains the remote interfaces of the `OrderItem`, EJBs are iterated. For every `OrderItem`, the SKU, name, and price are displayed, together with the ordered quantity and the row sum.

❿ **Displays the SKU of the** `OrderItem`.

⓫ **Displays the name of the** `OrderItem`.

⓬ **Displays the price for the** `OrderItem`.

⓭ **Displays the ordered quantity of the** `OrderItem`.

⓮ **Displays the sum for the** `OrderItem`.

⓯ **Casts the** `ServletResponse` **into an** `HttpServletResponse`   We have to perform a little trick to make sure that the application server will encode the URL that we display as a link to remove an item from the `Order`. The application thinks that we are taking full responsibility for the URL as we are building it up with dynamic content. Our trick is to cast the existing `ServletResponse` into an `HttpServletResponse` and manually use the `HttpServletResponse encodeURL()` method to encode the URL.

⑯ **Encodes the URL using the `HttpServletResponse`.**

⑰ **Ends the iteration.**

⑱ **Displays the order total price** As with all other prices displayed, we use the currently defined locale to display it in a correct way. As before, the `<cur-rency>` tag looks for—and finds—a `Locale` in the `Context`. The result will look figure 14.10.

⑲ **Ends the test.**

⑳ **Tests if the number of items in the current order are less than none** If the `Order` EJB doesn't contain any `OrderItem` EJBs, we display a message telling the user that the order is empty.

㉑ **Ends the test.**

㉒ **Ends the condition.**

Figure 14.10   Full order card

Order summary view

The order summary view displays a single card holding a summary of the user's current order and the address to which the order will be sent. This view is used primarily to solicit a confirmation from the user that the order and registered address are correct, and that we are to ship the ordered items. This page is called sendOrder.jsp inside our application, and looks like listing 14.10.

Listing 14.10   sendOrder.jsp

```
<%@ page contentType="text/vnd.wap.wml;charset=UTF-8" %>
<%@ taglib
    uri="http://www.manning.com/jsptagsbook/conditions-taglib"
    prefix="cond" %>
<%@ taglib
    uri="http://www.manning.com/jsptagsbook/simple-taglib"
    prefix="simple" %>
<%@ taglib
    uri="http://www.manning.com/jsptagsbook/locale-taglib"
    prefix="local" %>
<%@ taglib
    uri="http://www.manning.com/jsptagsbook/beans-taglib"
    prefix="bean" %>
<%@ taglib
    uri="http://www.manning.com/jsptagsbook/ejb-taglib"
    prefix="ejb" %>
<jsp:useBean id="customer"
```

```
                  type="book.casestudy.cosmetix.ejb.Customer"          ❶
                  scope="session"/>
<ejb:home id="home"
          type="book.casestudy.cosmetix.ejb.OrderManagerHome"          ❷
          name="ejb/orderManager"/>
<ejb:use id="orderManager"                                              ❸
          type="book.casestudy.cosmetix.ejb.OrderManager"
          instance="<%=home.create(customer)%>"/>
<ejb:use id="order"                                                     ❹
          type="book.casestudy.cosmetix.ejb.Order"
          instance="<%=orderManager.getOrder()%>"/>
<cond:with object="<%=(order.getItems().size()>0)%>">                   ❺
  <cond:test condition="neq true">                   ❻
    <simple:redirect location="fullOrder.jsp"/>              ❼
  </cond:test>          ❽
</cond:with>          ❾
<simple:nocache useHeaders="true"          ❿
                useMetaTags="false"/>
<?xml version="1.0"?>
<!DOCTYPE wml PUBLIC "-//WAPFORUM//DTD WML 1.1//EN"
"http://www.wapforum.org/DTD/wml_1.1.xml">
<wml>
  <card id="sendOrder"
        title="Send Order">
    <do type="options" label="Confirm Order" name="confirmOrder">
      <go href="orderConfirmation.jsp"/>
    </do>
    <jsp:include page="userMenu.jsp"          ⓫
                 flush="true"/>
    <p align="left">
        Your order with a total sum of
        <![CDATA[<local:currency
                  amount="<%=order.getTotal()%>" />]]>          ⓬
        will be sent to the following address:
    </p>
    <p align="left">
      <bean:show name="customer"          ⓭
                 property="company"/>
    </p>
    <p align="left">
      <bean:show name="customer"          ⓮
                 property="name"/>
    </p>
    <p align="left">
      <bean:show name="customer"          ⓯
                 property="address"/>
    </p>
    <p align="left">
      By confirming this order, the order will be sent to
      Cosmetix for further processing. You will receive
      a order receipt at your email address
```

```
      ( <bean:show name="customer"
                 property="email"/>)
        as a confirmation.
      </p>
      <p align="left">
        To confirm the sending of the order,
        select 'Confirm Order' from the option list.
      </p>
    </card>
</wml>
```

① **Gets the remote interface of the `Customer` EJB** After retrieving the remote interface of the `Customer` EJB from the `session` scope we add it to the `page` scope.

② **Adds the home interface of the `OrderManager` EJB.**

③ **Creates a remote interface of the `OrderManager` EJB** We use the `OrderManager` EJB's home interface to get a remote interface for the `OrderManager` EJB, using the `Customer` EJB as parameter.

④ **Retrieves the user's current `Order` EJB** We use the remote interface of the `OrderManager` to retrieve the remote interface of the user's current `Order` EJB.

⑤ **Creates a condition on the number of items in the current `Order`.**

⑥ **Tests whether the number of items in the current `Order` is less than 1.**

⑦ **Redirects the user to the full order view** If the user's current `Order` does not contain any `OrderItem` EJBs, we redirect the user to the full order view. Otherwise, we start building the card.

⑧ **Ends the test.**

⑨ **Ends the condition.**

⑩ **Makes sure that this page will not be cached.**

⑪ **Includes the user menu view** We include the user menu view and add an additional option to confirm the order.

Figure 14.11   The order summary card

⑫ **Displays the order's total price** We display the total price of the `Order`, using the `<currency>` tag without specifying a locale, which will cause the tag to look in the `Context` for any specified locale. There it will find the locale we have specified, and use it to format the total price.

⓭ Displays the customer's company name   ⓮ Displays the customer's name   ⓯ Displays the customer's address   ⓰ Displays the customer's email address   Finally, we display the address to which the order will be sent, and end the card. The resulting card is illustrated in figure 14.11.

Order confirmation view

The order confirmation view is used to display an order confirmation to the user in a single card, including the order reference number. The page is also used to send a receipt to the user. This page is called orderConfirmation.jsp inside our application, and looks like listing 14.11.

Listing 14.11   orderConfirmation.jsp

```
<%@ page contentType="text/vnd.wap.wml;charset=UTF-8"
        errorPage="mailException.jsp"%>                                ❶
<%@ taglib
    uri="http://www.manning.com/jsptagsbook/simple-taglib"
    prefix="simple" %>
<%@ taglib
    uri="http://www.manning.com/jsptagsbook/ejb-taglib"
    prefix="ejb" %>
<%@ taglib
    uri="http://www.manning.com/jsptagsbook/conditions-taglib"
    prefix="cond" %>
<%@ taglib
    uri="http://www.manning.com/jsptagsbook/locale-taglib"
    prefix="local" %>
<%@ taglib
    uri="http://www.manning.com/jsptagsbook/j2eemail-taglib"
    prefix="mail" %>
<%@ taglib
    uri="http://www.manning.com/jsptagsbook/beans-taglib"
    prefix="bean" %>
<jsp:useBean id="customer"                                             ❷
            type="book.casestudy.cosmetix.ejb.Customer"
            scope="session"/>
<ejb:home id="home"                                                    ❸
         type="book.casestudy.cosmetix.ejb.OrderManagerHome"
         name="ejb/orderManager"/>
<ejb:use id="orderManager"                                             ❹
        type="book.casestudy.cosmetix.ejb.OrderManager"
        instance="<%=home.create(customer)%>"/>
<ejb:use id="order"                                                    ❺
        type="book.casestudy.cosmetix.ejb.Order"
        instance="<%=orderManager.confirmOrder()%>"/>
<cond:with object="<%=(order.getStatus()=='S')%>">          ❻
  <cond:test condition="neq true">          ❼
    <simple:redirect location="fullOrder.jsp"/>          ❽
```

```
    </cond:test>        9
</cond:with>            10
<simple:nocache useHeaders="true"
                useMetaTags="false"/>              11
<?xml version="1.0"?>
<!DOCTYPE wml PUBLIC "-//WAPFORUM//DTD WML 1.1//EN"
"http://www.wapforum.org/DTD/wml_1.1.xml">
<wml>
  <card id="orderConfirmation"
        title="Confirmation">
      <jsp:include page="userMenu.jsp"
                   flush="true"/>              12
    <p align="left">
      <strong>
        Order Received
      </strong>
    </p>
    <p align="left">
      Your order reference number is
      <strong>
        <bean:show name="order"
                   property="id"/>              13
      </strong>.
    </p>
    <% request.setAttribute("orderId",new Long(order.getId()));%>   14
      <mail:send to="<%=customer.getEmail()%>">          15
        <mail:subject>Order <bean:show name="order"           16
                          property="id"/></mail:subject>
          <mail:message>          17
ORDER CONFIRMATION
This email confirms that we have received your order
          (reference number <bean:show name="order"           18
                                        property="id"/>).
Attached to this mail are your receipt and the delivery address.
Thank you very much for your bringing us your business!


-----------------------------------------------------------------
ORDER <bean:show name="order"           18
                 property="id"/>
-----------------------------------------------------------------
<ejb:iterate id="item"                                         19
             type="book.casestudy.cosmetix.ejb.OrderItem"
             object="<%=order.getItems().iterator()%>">
<bean:show name="item"                                         20
           property="quantity"/>
(<bean:show name="item"                                        21
            property="sku"/>)
<bean:show name="item"                                         22
           property="name"/> @
<local:currency amount="<%=item.getPrice()%>" />        23
</ejb:iterate>     24
```

```
--------------------------------------------------------------
Total: <local:currency amount="<%=order.getTotal()%>" />    25
--------------------------------------------------------------
DELIVERY ADDDRESS FOR ORDER <bean:show name="order"         18
                                        property="id"/>

<bean:show name="customer"                                  26
            property="company"/>
<bean:show name="customer"                                  27
            property="name"/>
<bean:show name="customer"                                  28
            property="address"/>
--------------------------------------------------------------
</mail:message>    29
    </mail:send>    30
  <p align="left">
    A receipt has been sent to your email address
    (<bean:show name="customer"                             31
                property="email"/>).
  </p>
 </card>
</wml>
```

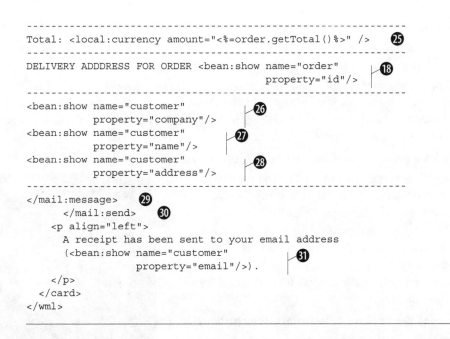

❶ **Defines the mail error view as error page**   We first declare that the mail exception view should be used to handle any runtime exceptions thrown when this page is accessed.

❷ **Gets the remote interface of the** `Customer` **EJB**   We retrieve the remote interface of the `Customer` EJB from the `session` scope and add it to the `page` scope.

❸ **Gets the home interface for the** `OrderManager` **EJB**   We add the `OrderManager` EJB's home interface to the `page` scope.

❹ **Creates a remote interface for the** `OrderManager` **EJB**   We use the home interface of the `OrderManager` EJB to create a remote interface of the `OrderManager` EJB using the `Customer` EJB as parameter.

❺ **Confirms the order**   We ask the `OrderManager` EJB to confirm the user's current `Order`. The `OrderManager` will then return the user's current `Order` EJB.

❻ **Creates a condition on the order's status**   ❼ **Tests whether the status of the order is not 's'**   ❽ **Redirects the user to the full order view**   If the `Order` is not returned with a status of `'S'` (for sent), we redirect the user to the full order view.

❾ **Ends the test.**

❿ **Ends the condition.**

⓫ **Makes sure that this page will not be cached.**

⓬ **Includes the user menu view**   Inside the card, we display the `Order`'s reference number

⑬ **Displays the** `Order ID`.

⑭ **Stores the** `Order ID` **in the request** This way we can access the reference number from within an error page if anything goes wrong when sending the receipt.

⑮ **Defines a new mail** Defines a mail message with the `Customer`'s email address as recipient, as we don't specify any `mail Session` name in the `<send>` tag. The result will be that the default mail `Session` will be used. (For more on configuring the mail `Session`, see chapter 12.)

⑯ **Defines a subject containing the** `Order ID`.

⑰ **Start of message** As content of the mail, we display a message containing the `Order`'s reference number and all the `OrderItem` EJBs of the `Order`, as well as the total price. All prices are formatted using the `Context`-defined locale. This is done by not telling the `<currency>` tag what locale to use, which will make it look for a defined locale in the `Context`.

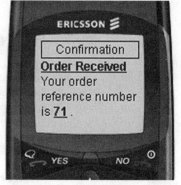

Figure 14.12 The order confirmation card

⑱ **Includes the** `Order ID` **in the attachment body.**

⑲ **Iterates through the** `OrderItems` **in the order.**

⑳ **Includes the ordered quantity of the** `OrderItem`.

㉑ **Includes the SKU of the** `OrderItem`.

㉒ **Includes the name of the** `OrderItem`.

㉓ **Includes the price of the** `OrderItem`.

㉔ **Ends the iteration.**

㉕ **Includes the order's total price.**

㉖ **Includes the customer's company name** ㉗**Includes the cusomer's name** ㉘**Includes the customer's address** We include the delivery address of the `Order`. This information is gathered from the user's online profile stored in the `Customer` EJB.

㉙ **End of message.**

㉚ **Ends the mail.**

㉛ **Displays the customer's email address** We display a message telling the user that a receipt has been sent to his email address, and that's the end of the card, which is available in figure 14.12.

Profile view

The profile view displays the information contained in the online profile of the user. This information is available from the `Customer Entity` EJB. This page contains a single card and is called profile.jsp inside our application, and looks listing 14.12.

Listing 14.12   profile.jsp

```
<%@ page contentType="text/vnd.wap.wml;charset=UTF-8" %>
<%@ taglib
    uri="http://www.manning.com/jsptagsbook/beans-taglib"
    prefix="bean" %>
<jsp:useBean id="customer"                                          ❶
             type="book.casestudy.cosmetix.ejb.Customer"
             scope="session"/>
<?xml version="1.0"?>
<!DOCTYPE wml PUBLIC "-//WAPFORUM//DTD WML 1.1//EN"
"http://www.wapforum.org/DTD/wml_1.1.xml">
<wml>
  <card id="profile"
        title="Your Profile">
<jsp:include page="userMenu.jsp"           ❷
             flush="true"/>
    <p align="left">
      <bean:show name="customer"                    ❸
                 property="username"/>
    </p>
    <p align="left">
      <bean:show name="customer"                       ❹
                 property="company"/>
    </p>
    <p align="left">
      <bean:show name="customer"              ❺
                 property="name"/>
    </p>
    <p align="left">
      <bean:show name="customer"                    ❻
                 property="address"/>
    </p>
    <p align="left">
      <bean:show name="customer"            ❼
                 property="email"/>
    </p>
    <p align="left">
      <bean:show name="customer"            ❽
                 property="phone"/>
    </p>
    <p align="left">
      <bean:show name="customer"          ❾
                 property="fax"/>
    </p>
  </card>
</wml>
```

❶ Gets the remote interface of the `Customer` **EJB.**

❷ Includes the user menu view

❸ Displays the user's username

❹ Displays the user's company name

❺ Displays the user's name

❻ Displays the user's address

❼ Displays the user's email address

❽ Displays the user's phone number

❾ Displays the user's fax number

We first retrieve the remote interface of the `Customer` EJB from the `session` scope and add it to the `page` scope, after which we define a card that will display the data found in the user's profile (the `Customer` EJB). Notice that we do not disable caching of this page, as the information presented is less liable to change over time.

Logoff view

The logoff view ends the user's session with the system. This page is called logoff-Handler.jsp inside our application, as in listing 14.13.

Listing 14.13   logoffHandler.jsp

```
<%@ page contentType="text/vnd.wap.wml;charset=UTF-8" %>
<%@ taglib
    uri="http://www.manning.com/jsptagsbook/simple-taglib"
    prefix="simple" %>
<%@ taglib
    uri="http://www.manning.com/jsptagsbook/beans-taglib"
    prefix="bean" %>
<bean:command object="<%=session%>"                 ❶
             command="invalidate"/>
<simple:redirect location="index.jsp"/>     ❷
```

❶ Asks for the user's session to be invalidated.

❷ Redirects to the welcome view   The user can select to log on anew.

Add item view

The add item view is used to add `OrderItems` to the user's current `Order`. The page is called itemAdder.jsp in our application and looks like listing 14.14.

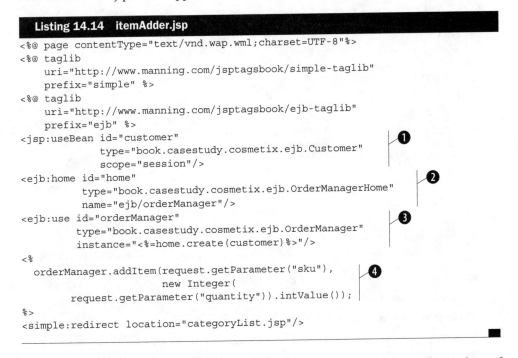

```
Listing 14.14  itemAdder.jsp
<%@ page contentType="text/vnd.wap.wml;charset=UTF-8"%>
<%@ taglib
    uri="http://www.manning.com/jsptagsbook/simple-taglib"
    prefix="simple" %>
<%@ taglib
    uri="http://www.manning.com/jsptagsbook/ejb-taglib"
    prefix="ejb" %>
<jsp:useBean id="customer"                                         ❶
             type="book.casestudy.cosmetix.ejb.Customer"
             scope="session"/>
<ejb:home id="home"                                                ❷
          type="book.casestudy.cosmetix.ejb.OrderManagerHome"
          name="ejb/orderManager"/>
<ejb:use id="orderManager"                                         ❸
         type="book.casestudy.cosmetix.ejb.OrderManager"
         instance="<%=home.create(customer)%>"/>
<%
  orderManager.addItem(request.getParameter("sku"),                ❹
                  new Integer(
      request.getParameter("quantity")).intValue());
%>
<simple:redirect location="categoryList.jsp"/>
```

❶ **Gets the remote interface of the `Customer` EJB** We retrieve the remote interface of the `Customer` EJB from the `session` scope and add it to the `page` scope.

❷ **Gets the home interface for the `OrderManager` EJB.**

❸ **Creates an `OrderManager` Session EJB** We use the `OrderManager` EJB's home interface to create an `OrderManager` remote interface using the `Customer` EJB as parameter.

❹ **Adds the specified quantity of the specified product to the order** We use the remote interface of the `OrderManager` to add a specified quantity of a certain product as an `OrderItem` to the users' current `Order`. Then we redirect the user back to the category list view.

Remove item view

The remove item view is used to add `OrderItems` to the user's current order. The page is called itemRemover.jsp in our application, and looks like listing 14.15.

Listing 14.15   itemRemover.jsp

```
<%@ page contentType="text/vnd.wap.wml;charset=UTF-8"%>
<%@ taglib
    uri="http://www.manning.com/jsptagsbook/simple-taglib"
    prefix="simple" %>
<%@ taglib
    uri="http://www.manning.com/jsptagsbook/ejb-taglib"
    prefix="ejb" %>
<jsp:useBean id="customer"
            type="book.casestudy.cosmetix.ejb.Customer"
            scope="session"/>
<ejb:home id="home"
          type="book.casestudy.cosmetix.ejb.OrderManagerHome"
          name="ejb/orderManager"/>
<ejb:use id="orderManager"
         type="book.casestudy.cosmetix.ejb.OrderManager"
         instance="<%=home.create(customer)%>"/>
<%
  orderManager.removeItem(request.getParameter("sku"));
%>
<simple:redirect location="fullOrder.jsp"/>
```
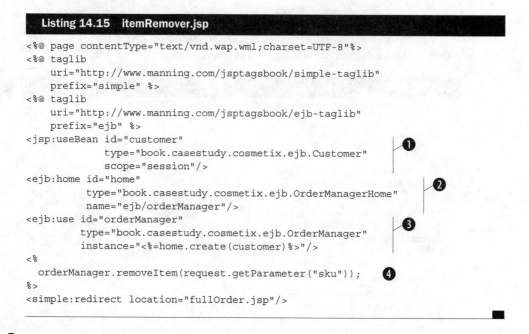

❶ Gets the remote interface of the `Customer` EJB   We retrieve the remote interface of the `Customer` EJB from the `session` scope and add it to the `page` scope.

❷ Gets the home interface for the `OrderManager` EJB.

❸ Creates an `OrderManager` EJB   Uses the `Customer` EJB as parameter.

❹ Removes the `OrderItem` with the specified SKU from the order.

Generic error view

The generic error view is a single card view used to catch any error thrown by any of our JSP pages that does not explicitly name another error page. This page is called jspException.jsp inside our application, as displayed in listing 14.16.

Listing 14.16   jspException.jsp

```
<%@ page contentType="text/vnd.wap.wml;charset=UTF-8"
        isErrorPage="true" %>
<%@ taglib
    uri="http://www.manning.com/jsptagsbook/beans-taglib"
    prefix="bean" %>
<?xml version="1.0"?>
<!DOCTYPE wml PUBLIC "-//WAPFORUM//DTD WML 1.1//EN"
"http://www.wapforum.org/DTD/wml_1.1.xml">
<wml>
  <card id="welcome"
```
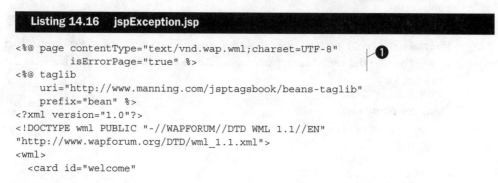

```
        title="Cosmetix">
    <jsp:include page="userMenu.jsp"
                 flush="true"/>
    <p align="left">
       <bean:show object="<%=exception%>"
                  property="message"/>
    </p>
  </card>
</wml>
```

1 Defines this page as an error page.

2 Includes the user menu view.

3 Displays the exceptions message.

This view is defined as an error page in the web application's configuration file (web.xml) and does not therefore need to be defined in any page that could throw a generic runtime exception. This configuration looks like listing 14.17, which is cut out from the web.xml file of our web-application.

Listing 14.17 The configuration of the JspException handler in the web.xml file

```
...
<error-page>
  <exception-type>javax.servlet.jsp.JspException</exception-type>
  <location>jspException.jsp</location>
</error-page>
...
```

The configuration tells the container that whenever an uncaught JspException is thrown, jspException.jsp should be invoked. Any error page defined within a page overrides the applicationwide setting.

Instantiation error view

The instantiation error view is called when we try to access the Customer EJB from the session scope but no such object exists. The page is called instantiationException.jsp in our application and looks like listing 14.18.

Listing 14.18 instantiationException.jsp

```
<%@ page contentType="text/vnd.wap.wml;charset=UTF-8"
         isErrorPage="true" %>
<%@ taglib
    uri="http://www.manning.com/jsptagsbook/ejb-taglib"
    prefix="ejb" %>
```

1

```
<ejb:home id="home"
          type="book.casestudy.cosmetix.ejb.CustomerManagerHome"        ❷
          name="ejb/customerManager"/>
<ejb:use id="customerManager"
         type="book.casestudy.cosmetix.ejb.CustomerManager"             ❸
         instance="<%=home.create()%>"/>
<ejb:use id="customer"
         type="book.casestudy.cosmetix.ejb.Customer"                    ❹
         instance="<%=customerManager.getCustomer(
request.getUserPrincipal().getName())%>"/>
<%
  session.setAttribute("customer",customer);                            ❺
%>
<jsp:include page="userMenu.jsp"                                        ❻
                flush="true"/>
```

❶ **Defines this page as an error page.**

❷ **Gets the home interface for the** `CustomerManager` **EJB.**

❸ **Creates a remote interface for the** `CustomerManager` **EJB.**

❹ **Retrieves the** `Customer` **EJB with the username of the user currently logged in**   The User's name is found in the request.

❺ **Adds the** `Customer` **EJB to the** `session` **scope.**

❻ **Includes the user menu view**   This is normally the first page to request the existence of the `Customer` EJB in the `session` scope.

Mail error view

The mail error view is an error page invoked if any exception is thrown from the order confirmation view. It displays a single card alerting the user that the order has been received, although no receipt could be sent. The page is called mailException.jsp in our application and looks like listing 14.19.

Listing 14.19   mailException.jsp

```
<%@ page contentType="text/vnd.wap.wml;charset=UTF-8"                    ❶
         isErrorPage="true" %>
<%@ taglib
    uri="http://www.manning.com/jsptagsbook/simple-taglib"
    prefix="simple" %>
<%@ taglib
    uri="http://www.manning.com/jsptagsbook/conditions-taglib"
    prefix="cond" %>
<%@ taglib
    uri="http://www.manning.com/jsptagsbook/beans-taglib"
    prefix="bean" %>
<?xml version="1.0"?>
```

```
<!DOCTYPE wml PUBLIC "-//WAPFORUM//DTD WML 1.1//EN"
"http://www.wapforum.org/DTD/wml_1.1.xml">
<wml>
  <card id="orderConfirmation"
        title="Confirmation">
    <jsp:include page="userMenu.jsp"              ❷
                 flush="true"/>
    <p align="left">
      <strong>
        Order Received
      </strong>
    </p>
    <p align="left">
      Your order reference number is
      <strong>
        <%=request.getAttribute("orderId")%>      ❸
      </strong>.
    </p>
    <p align="left">
      A receipt has not been sent to your email address
      (<bean:show name="customer"                 ❹
                  property="email"/>)
      , as we encountered delivery problems.
    </p>
  </card>
</wml>
```

❶ **Defines this page as an error page.**

❷ **Includes the user menu view.**

❸ **Displays the value of the parameter 'orderId' in the** `request` **scope.**

❹ **Displays the user's email address as stored in the** `Customer` **EJB in the** `session` **scope**
We tell the user that the order has been received, but that we were unable to mail a receipt to the user's email address as it appears in the user's profile (`Customer` EJB). We don't need to use the `Customer` EJB for anything but displaying its information, so we never add it to the `page` scope.

14.3.5 *Controller*

The controllers are implemented as a number of Session EJBs. Figure 14.13 illustrates their remote interfaces and their relations to the entity EJBs described earlier.

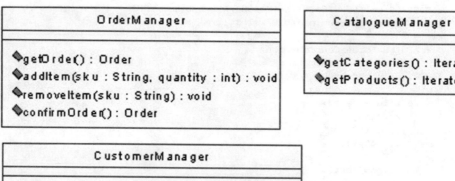

Figure 14.13   The Session EJBs acting as controllers in the application

There are three `Session` EJBs. For more information about their implementation, download the application as described in appendix C. Inside the application, you will find the source code for all the EJBs listed in table 14.3.

Table 14.3   The Session EJBs acting as Controllers

EJB	Description
CatalogueMan-ager	Used to retrieve collections of remote interfaces for the `Category` and `Product Entity` EJB in the form of Collections.
CustomerManager	Used to retrieve the remote interface of the `Customer Entity` EJB. A username must be passed as a string to the `getCustomer()` method of the `CustomerManager`.
OrderManager	To create an `OrderManager` remote interface, a `Customer Entity` EJB has to be passed in to the home interface of the `OrderManager`. The `CustomerManager Session` EJB is used to retrieve the user's current order by calling the `getOrder()` method. If there is no current order, a new order will be returned instead. The `OrderManager` is used to add or remove items from the current order and to confirm the user's current order.

Table 14.4   Ideas for improvements

Area	Description
Scriptlets	Some scriptlets have been left in the source code. Try to find tags that can substitute the scriptlets or write new tags to handle these operations.
WML Scripting	Implement WML script that will let the user add a number of products from the catalogue to his order all in one go.
Error pages	Implement error pages that will handle `FinderExceptions` and `CreateExceptions` in order to catch errors that could occur when trying to add or find users.
Administration	Add an administration web application that will let an administrator add and remove products, categories, and customers, in addition to processing orders received.

14.4   *Summary*

It is a good idea to download the entire application from this book's website, as described in appendix C, so that you may go through the configuration files and source code not covered in this chapter. If you feel as we do, that the best way to learn the basics about a new technology is to incorporate your own changes to an existing application, we've listed a number of ideas in table 14.4. You can use them to extend the application or to try out your own knowledge of the tags in this book and of WML.

Part V

Design

Chapter 15 rounds out the book by emphasizing the dos and don'ts of tag development and design. These should help you to avoid common pitfalls while taking advantage of all the benefits of custom tag development.

JSP tag libraries— tips and tricks

Like most complex component models, a complete book on JSP custom tags can offer a thorough understanding of the subject without ever addressing all the possible pitfalls you might encounter. While developing a tag library, you'll find it easy to fall into one of the less obvious traps. For example, you might develop your library on Tomcat only to find out that you could not find a tag-pooling and reuse-related bug. Since Tomcat does not currently reuse tags, you'd be in trouble. In this chapter, we'll troubleshoot, suggesting techniques to avoid some common mistakes:

- Developing tags that can only run on a single web container
- Developing tags with the wrong functionality
- Developing tags that are not usable

We'll also explore the necessity to know your tags' intended user and the user's needs. While we won't concentrate on actual design methodologies or patterns, we will provide general hints regarding the development of tag libraries, and we'll make recommendations based on experience gained while developing tags.

15.1 The case for custom tags

Understanding the need for custom tags is crucial. To benefit from tag usage and gain awareness of implicit design goals, you need to comprehend the reasons why using custom tags is better than using the scriptlets and beans combination. For example, if you know that tags should be part of the nonprogrammer's arsenal, you are more likely to do your best to improve the ease-of-use of your tags.

Let's look at a few primary reasons to use custom tags.

15.1.1 Tags and nonprogrammers

We are often confronted by Java developers who do not understand why they need concern themselves with custom tags. The main arguments in their case against tags are:

- Java is a comfortable, easy-to-use language. We already know its syntax, and we can use it freely.
- We can place most of our application logic and data in a JavaBean component and access it through scriptlets. In doing so, we minimize the number of scriptlets in our applications.
- Custom tags will force us to learn a new proprietary syntax to achieve the same development goals; so why should we use them?

Our answer is usually: *If only your first argument were correct, you might, indeed, have a case. However, Java is not an easy language, especially not for nonprogrammers.*

Java, like all programming languages, assumes that its user knows how to program. It is full of strange syntactic elements such as: ;, ||, &&, ==, (), {, and so forth. For example:

What is the difference between `<% if(x && y) { %>` and `<% if(x & y) { %>`? One is a Boolean "and" operator, and the other is a binary "and" operator. Would you care to explain that to your nonprogrammer friend?

We realize that some people will never understand how to program scriptlets in any language although they can become productive when using the simpler custom JSP tags.

As we'll see later in this chapter, a custom tag ideally provides documentation geared toward the nonprogrammer user. Such documentation should explain how and when to use the tag. Instead of learning a new general purpose programming language, tag users can, instead, read a short document that illustrates how to use the tag, and then develop their pages. In this way, nonprogrammers often gain a productivity boost when using tags. Suddenly, they can send an email from a JSP page with live database-driven data! And, given that tags are only tags, not Java scripts, the nonprogrammer's set of "normal" everyday editing tools can understand the tags—or at least ignore them gracefully.

This productivity improvement makes it possible for a relatively naïve developer to accomplish complex tasks—tasks that he or she could never hope to achieve without using tags. Letting the non-Java programmer perform complex operations in JSP is one of the bigger selling points of tags. The overall lesson here is that custom tags often appeal more to the HTML developer than to the Java developer.

15.1.2 *Reusing tags*

Can you reuse your scriptlets? Doubtful. Can you reuse ten lines of JSP-embedded Java that

- Set attributes into a send-mail bean
- Instruct the bean to send an email
- Catch exceptions
- Redirect the page (in some cases) to an error handler?

Copy-and paste is probably not going to serve you well on this one, as fixing a bug in the original scriptlet is not going to update all its copies. Tags, however, are reusable components by definition. The lines of code and testing efforts that you invest into developing a send-mail set of tags are ten times more useful than the ten-line, send-mail scriptlet. This also means that when developing new projects, you can take advantage of tested assets developed for past projects.

This reusability provides huge savings in development and testing time: one more reason to use tags and one more consideration when developing tags. Always develop your tags with reusability in mind.

15.1.3 *Maintaining tags*

Once you have finished developing your application, you need to maintain it. Roughly speaking, application maintenance includes fixing business logic bugs and fixing/updating the presentation. (The latter will be your major maintenance activity.)

As long as you are not using scriptlets, fixing the presentation does not require any Java skills. If you use scriptlets, however, any change to the presentation may require a review by a Java programmer and maybe even a testing session. Using tags frees you from this burden.

On the business logic front, when you use tags instead of scriptlets, you needn't check out the JSP files. Fixing a bug becomes an issue of stepping through the Java code; all JSP files can be left untouched.

Clearly, in addition to reusability and improved productivity for the nonprogrammer, using tags also reduces your maintenance costs.

15.1.4 *Tags and application performance*

Many die-hard scriptlet coders complain to us that tags are slower than scriptlets and using them renders JSP performance unacceptable. These are the same people who insist, "Real programmers code in assembly." In reality, the performance impact (if any) of using tags is overshadowed by the savings in development time and by pared down maintenance.

Using tags may have a negative effect on performance. After all, we are creating additional objects (the tag handler) and making more method calls (for attribute setting and tag execution). Nonetheless, most new Java virtual machines (JVMs), such as Hotspot, can handle small and short-lived objects as well as in-lining method calls. This performance problem is thus diminished every day. Also, the JSP container can employ object pooling on the tag handlers, thereby reducing the burden on the garbage collector. Finally, the performance impact related to the custom tags is negligible when compared to the impact of the work they perform. For example, what is the impact of tag creation versus an SQL query to a database? Negligible.

The effect that custom tags have on performance is not that much of an issue. More crucial than performance and which methods perform better is the discussion of the trade-offs between scriptlets and custom tags and a consideration of the long-term costs of each development method. Yes, tags may cause some performance degradation, but if this is critical, you can solve it by throwing money at the hardware. In the end, this will be much cheaper than having to deal with scriptlets during the development and maintenance phase.

15.2 Development considerations

When developing tags, you need to consider a few important dos and don'ts.

15.2.1 Tag development dos

If it is declarative it is probably a tag

If you're wondering whether a particular action should become a tag, check to see if the action is declarative, or can become declarative. If the answer is yes, making a tag out of the action should be a breeze, and using the new tag should be easy.

Remember, even if the action is not always declarative, you can check to see if an interesting, simple instance of that action does exist that can become declarative. For example, iterating arbitrarily over an array is not declarative, but moving on the array one cell at a time can be.

A tag represents a single operation

Do not try to put too much into a single custom tag. A tag should implement a basic, well-defined action; hopefully something that can be described in a single sentence. Imagine an instance in which the tag `foo` sends email/queries a database iterates on a database result—each of these alternative activities represents a reasonable tag. If a description for your tag looks like "… the tag queries a database and uses the data from the database to send an email …" then something will go wrong with it. Perhaps you'll find the tag is difficult to use (you need to specify both email and database parameters in the same tag), or maybe the tag will not be as reusable as two separate tags would be, or some other issue may arise. The point is, a tag that performs both actions is not going to be as useful as the combination of two simpler tags.

Generally, when a tag does more than a single operation, four issues arise:

1 It is more difficult to explain the tags to the users, and, therefore, harder for the users to use them.

2 Since the tags requires more input, understanding all the different input parameters is a daunting task. Again, the tag is harder to use.

3 Integrating the tag along with other tags is more of a burden because it already does some of their job.

4 It is harder to mix and match tags based on their quality.

Having said that, life is stronger than any rule of thumb, and sometimes you will want to forget the rule of one-tag single operation. For example,

- The iteration tags we developed in chapter 10 can also present the values of certain fields in the iterator. This means that the tag implements two operations (iterating and printing), yet the ability to use the iteration tags to also print the iterator values is so useful that we gave up.

- Suppose you need tags to connect two different tag libraries or families. For example, you may wish to have a tag that reads a field out of a JDBC `Result-Set` and sets it into a bean. Such a tag (like that presented in listing 15.1) seems to perform two operations: reading the database field and setting the bean value. Yet, performing these two operations is what lets the tag bind the two tag libraries together, so we forget our rule of thumb.

Listing 15.1   Source code for the BeanSetterTag handler class

```
package book.database;

import java.sql.ResultSet;
import java.sql.SQLException;
import java.lang.reflect.Method;

import javax.servlet.jsp.JspException;
import javax.servlet.jsp.JspTagException;

import book.util.LocalStrings;
import book.util.ExTagSupport;
import book.util.BeanUtil;

public class BeanSetterTag
  extends ExTagSupport {
    static LocalStrings ls =
    LocalStrings.getLocalStrings(BeanSetterTag.class);
  protected String query = null;
  protected String field = null;
  protected String bean = null;
  protected String property = null;
  protected Object o = null;

  public void setQuery(String query)
  {
    this.query = query;
  }

  public void setField(String field)
  {
    this.field = field;
  }
```

```
public void setObject(Object o)
{
  this.o = o;
}

public void setBean(String bean)
{
  this.bean = bean;
}

public int doStartTag()
    throws JspException
{
  checkAttributes();
  ResultSet rs = null;
  try {

    rs = (ResultSet)pageContext.findAttribute(query);          ❶
    if(null != rs) {
      Object []p = new Object[]{rs.getString(field)};
      Method m =
        BeanUtil.getSetPropertyMethod(o, property);            ❷
      m.invoke(o, p);
    } else {
      throw new NullPointerException();
    }
    return SKIP_BODY;
  } catch(SQLException sqe) {
    // Throw a JspTagException
  } catch(java.lang.IllegalAccessException iae) {
    // Throw a JspTagException
  } catch(java.lang.NoSuchMethodException nme) {
    // Throw a JspTagException
  } catch(java.lang.reflect.InvocationTargetException ite) {
    // Throw a JspTagException
  } catch(java.beans.IntrospectionException ie) {
    // Throw a JspTagException
  }
}

protected void checkAttributes()
  throws JspException
{
  if(null == field) {
    field = property;
  }
  if(null == o) {
    o = pageContext.findAttribute(bean);
    if(null == o) {
      throw new NullPointerException();
    }
  }
}
```

```
    }
    protected void clearProperties()
    {
      query = null;
      field = null;
      property = null;
      bean = null;
      o = null;
      super.clearProperties();
    }
}
```

❶ Takes a column value out of the `ResultSet`. This is the first action performed by the tag.

❷ Sets the column value into a bean. This is the second action performed by the tag.

While it is important that a single tag perform one operation, this often isn't the most efficient approach. As with many rules in real life, we can sometimes ignore this one (though we may sacrifice some advantages associated with obeying it).

Use TagExtraInfo

Supplying a `TagExtraInfo` implementation is not mandatory (unless you export variables); but neglecting its implementation is not good, not good at all.

If your tags have a complex set of attributes, with limits on the attribute values and the relations between them (as we saw in the reflection case), you must provide a `TagExtraInfo` implementation along with your tags. Even for tags with only attribute values constraints, you will want to implement `TagExtraInfo`.

The reason is, even if you have great tag documentation, errors will be associated with the tag attribute usage, due to copy-paste operations performed by the tag's user or, perhaps, innocent confusion. If `TagExtraInfo` implementation is not provided, two problems will arise:

1 The JSP file will compile, but will throw runtime exceptions that the creator of the JSP file does not follow. If I am the developer of the JSP file and I get a `NullPointerException` from a tag (a missing attribute, actually), I will immediately consider it a bug in the tag handler. The tag developer will consider it a usage error.

2 Once the JSP file compiles and serves a request, the developer of the JSP file assumes that tag usage in this file is correct, because the JSP file managed to compile and serve a request. Yet, as we know, tags may stand inside fragments of conditional JSP that your tests did not cover. Thus, you have usage errors in JSP files that compile and run, and which you assume to be okay.

The only way to avoid these problems is to provide `TagExtraInfo` to validate the attribute syntax. This solves the first problem since the JSP translator will generate error messages while translating the file, and the messages will say, in effect, "There is an error in the attributes values for tag `foo`", which leaves no ambiguity in the nature of the error. The second problem is resolved since the JSP translator covers the entire JSP file without paying attention to conditional HTML (so the entire JSP file is checked for errors).

To summarize, as your tag will not be complete without a validating `TagExtraInfo`, create one.

Document your tags' usage

Tag documentation is not composed of Javadocs. The users of your tags are not intended to be Java programmers, and the Javadocs are not going to make any sense for them.

The tag's documentation should be more akin to a reference manual, wherein you explain the tag in terms of its functionality, usage, and attributes. For each tag attribute you want to specify the attribute's functionality—whether it is a required attribute, whether it can accept runtime values, what the expected values are, and so forth. Also specify other parameters affecting the tag, such as the application and page-based configuration parameters and the J2EE environment values, and provide a few tag usage samples.

By reading this documentation, the HTML developer (remember, little or no Java background) will know how to use your tag. Documentation that describes advanced features that can only be understood by a fellow Java programmer should be kept in a different document or labeled "advanced topics."

We are not professing that you should never Javadoc your tags, nor are we warning you to stay away from Javadoc, the tool. In fact, by developing a few custom *doclets* (Javadoc extension components), you should be able to draw the user level documentation you need using Javadoc.

Design your tags with usability in mind

The user of your tag is probably a veteran HTML coder who will feel comfortable using tags; nevertheless, most users don't like tags with too many attributes and overly complex functionality. Imagine what would happen if you created a tag with six or seven attributes and complex relationships between attributes. Most users cannot overcome that many possible attribute value combinations. This means:

- Always consult the users of the tags (i.e., the HTML developers) to achieve a high degree of usability.

- When a certain action requires a number of input parameters, try to break the action into several reasonable tags.

- Before adding an attribute to the tag, ask yourself if the attribute is absolutely necessary.

By following these guidelines, the tags that you create are more likely to be usable.

15.2.2 *Tag development don'ts*

Tags are great at taking data from the business logic, embedding it into the page, and replacing scriptlets; however, we want to avoid certain pitfalls when implementing tags.

Do not mimic HTML tags with JSP custom tags

Many Java developers have a tendency to mimic HTML functionality with custom JSP tags. We met a developer who said he is considering developing a set of tags to provide "style" for the JSP files. He explained that he would hold a single style file for the entire site and inject specific HTML tags using his custom JSP tags. We pointed out that the Cascading Style Sheets (CSS) specification does exactly this, only on the client side.

This anecdote exposes an important issue, which is that you should not duplicate HTML functionality using customs tags for several reasons:

- With advances in CSS, HTML4, and XHTML, it is a waste of time and CPU power to mimic certain HTML tag configurations with JSP tags. You can achieve better results by using standards-based techniques and placing the burden on the client (instead on the server).

- Unless you are developing an editing tool that uses your tags, the page designers will have a difficult time adding these tags to the content. For example, since a simple browser or editor will not be able to show your JSP, the editing will not be in a "what you see is what you get" (WYSIWYG) fashion.

- Tags that mimic HTML or any other markup language functionality will not be useful for other presentation languages such as WML. All your document developers' know-how regarding these custom tags will be irrelevant as soon as you are not working with the certain markup language, which means that important knowledge is lost.

Our recommendation is to leave content formation to the document and have the tags perform business logic and complex operations such as sending email and querying a database.

NOTE A tendency exists to duplicate the functionality of the HTML form tag and the HTML controls with a set of custom tags. In this case, the custom tags can be responsible for the following actions: injecting the form-related tags, injecting JavaScript code to run on the client's machine and verify the form's content before submitting it, and putting default values in the control fields based on a bean value. This last case is "different" since the JSP custom tags not only create the form tags but perform logic to set default values and create automatic verification. Here you will have to judge for yourself if the results justify the considerable effort related to creating all the necessary custom tags.

Do not generate tagged content with JSP custom tags

Sometimes developers try to place markup in the result of the tag. For example, the author of an exception writer tag may decide that surrounding the exception's stack trace with a pair of HTML `<pre> </pre>` tags will make a lot of sense.

Putting even the smallest markup inside your tag's output greatly limits the tag usage. All the disadvantages discussed in the previous section apply in these cases but, more than that, you are limiting the tag usage. What if you want to email the stack trace to the system administrator using the JavaMail tag developed in chapter 7 and the exception writer tag? The `<pre> </pre>` markup is not going to help us in a plain text email. Our recommendation, again, is to keep markup and presentation issues out of your tags. Tags should perform logic, not create presentation.

Do not invent a programming language

Many developers make a nonobvious mistake and try to develop custom tags that will allow their users to program explicitly in the JSP file. Look at the following JSP fragment, which employs the tags `<for>` and `<arrayaccess>`:

```
<for low="1" high="10" step="1" indexname="i">
  The value is <arrayaccess array="myarrayname" index="i"/> <br>
</for>
```

This code fragment example is a piece of explicit programming. The tag developer wants to write the first ten entries in the array into the response sent to the user. Using the supplied tags, the developer needs to explicitly program everything, starting with the `for` loop that walks over the array and ending with fetching the array elements. This is not the declarative programming we discussed. To achieve something with this type of tags, a complete, tag-based programming language must be defined—not something we want to do.

Inventing a tag-based programming language is going to be a colossal effort. In addition, inventing such a programming language would force the learning of a new programming language and miss the audience of custom tags—meaning the HTML developers. We already have a programming language for JSP: Java (or another language specified in the JSP `language` attribute). If you feel the urge to use explicit programming, use Java.

15.3 *Further development and testing*

Tags are no cinch to develop and test. A normal code-compile-test-debug cycle for a Java component can be done within a single integrated development environment. When developing a tag library, you need a servlet container to test your tags, a JSP file to drive the tags, and a coding and debugging environment.

Let's look at a few key development and testing issues that may arise while developing tags.

15.3.1 *Debugging tags*

Debugging tags is a relatively complex operation: You need to create a JSP file and deploy the tag library in a container, then make an HTTP request to this JSP file. With all this trouble, many developers forget that all they need to debug is the tag handler class and, although the test environment is strange, they can use a debugger to step through their handler class code.

Tag handlers are merely a piece of Java code. Run the servlet container inside your favorite IDE and place breakpoints within the handler's code. Some tags presented in this book were debugged using Tomcat inside an IDE. In fact, when using an open source container such as Tomcat, one can even step in and out of the container's implementation source.

The alternative to using a debugger is placing trace statements within the code. While it is true that tracing has its virtues,[1] it cannot fully replace a debugger.

15.3.2 *Testing tags on more than one JSP container*

JSP is a standard. Servers should pass the compatibility kit test, but nobody prohibits the containers from implementing value-added features into the container. This phenomena implies that, when you develop your tags on a specific container, you may find yourself relying (unconsciously) on a specific added value feature available only in this specific container.

---

[1] See *The Practice of Programming* by Brian W. Kernigan and Rob Pike.

Consider an example of such an added value feature and see what can result. Let's say that, while developing a tag, we needed it to take a `Boolean` runtime expression attribute. This was okay, and we had our tag taking such attributes in no time. This tag was used on the Orion application server with success. Life seems good. The tag even managed to accept `boolean` runtime values (yes, `boolean`, the primitive type; not `Boolean`, the object). Then we took the library and discovered that it cannot accept `boolean` values on Tomcat because Tomcat blindly followed the JSP specification and did not provide the needed translation from `boolean` to `Boolean`. Guess what? We had to add yet another setter method.

Let that be a lesson learned: Never test on a single JSP container.

When developing tags it is predictable to conclude that tags are strange beasts requiring a special development environment. This assumption is why many developers fail to use a debugger to test their code. It is even easier to decide that just because a tag executes within a certain container it will execute on all containers. Never assume. Test with several different containers.

15.4 Design recommendations

When developing a tag library (as opposed to developing a single tag), you may want to invest extra effort into designing the library so that it better fits your target users. Some of the more useful value-add options are presented in this section.

15.4.1 Opening library internals

Crosby, Stills, Nash, & Young sang, "…If you can't be with the one you love, love the one you're with." The problem with applying this attitude to the JSP world is that loving the tag library you are with is not going to work if you cannot adapt it to your needs.

Even if you believe that your tag library is complete, it's important to allow users to extend its functionality and document the extension methods. For instance, we can extend our iteration tags by supplying helper objects for the iteration and getting the field values. By documenting this feature, we ensure that whoever purchases our tags will be able to extend them to handle any new requirements that come up.

The same thing applies, of course, to the database library developed in this book. In fact, one fault in our database library is that we execute only queries and do not support updates. The solution to this shortcoming is easy if we open the library interfaces. In this case, a third-party developer could take a database connection created by a connection tag and use it inside an update tag to modify the database.

It is clear that opening the library for third-party changes may require a special license. It may also require a change in the library price model. However, if you are planning to sell the tags or use them in-house, the ability to modify the library will provide users with a substantial advantage in the long run.

15.4.2 *Generalizing your tags*

There is good reason to assume that if you need a specific action, then, most likely, that action is a specific case of a more generalized need. In chapter 6 we developed a tag whose role is to flush the output stream that is connected to the user; but we can generalize that. Flushing the output stream was a method call, but it was also a command that we gave to the `JspWriter` object. Command objects are a known design pattern[2] that can be useful within the JSP programming environment.

Command is a behavioral design pattern whose intent is to encapsulate a request as an object—in everyday cases, this means a method call on an object. By encapsulating a request as an object, you can bridge the differences between systems and hide complex operations within an easy-to-use interface. (Additional uses for the Command pattern exist, but we will not go into them here.)

A simple command pattern example

To make the Command pattern concrete, let's take a look at a basic example. We have a command class named `SendMail` whose job is to send email. `SendMail` has three command parameters:

- `to`—the email's receiving end
- `subject`—the email's subject
- `body`—the email's body

and has an `execute` method to send the email.

Using the `SendMail` command from within a Java program looks like:

```
SendMail cmd = new SendMail();
cmd.setTo("some@address");
cmd.setSubject("some subject");
cmd.setBody("Some body ...");
cmd.execute();
```

It is possible to implement the first four lines using the standard JSP `<jsp:useBean>` and `<jsp:setProperty/>` tags presented in chapter 2. We can also instantiate the command and set its parameters within a servlet and send the command to

---

[2] For more information on design patterns, see *Design Patterns Elements of Reusable Object-Oriented Software* by Erich Gamma, et. al.

be executed within the JSP, but something is missing. Calling `execute()` is not possible from within any of the tags we have discussed thus far. If we want to use the Command pattern from within our JSP files without using some scriptlet, we need to remedy this problem.

A generalized tag: CommandTag

Forget for a moment that we are dealing with a design pattern and, instead, concentrate on what is keeping us from using the design pattern. Our problem is that we cannot trigger the execution of the command object. We can't trigger the command object because triggering involves calling a method, something that the standard bean tags (available as part of JSP) are not doing. Thus, we need a tag that implements the logic to execute methods with a void parameter list. This solves this issue, and, indeed, such a tag is available in listing 15.2.

As you can see, `CommandTag` accepts three attributes:

- the name of the `command` method
- the `command` object instance (optional information, can be replaced by the `command` object name)
- the `command` object name (optional information, can be replaced by the `command` object instance)

After collecting these attributes, `CommandTag` uses reflection to invoke the `command` execution method on the `command` object.

Listing 15.2   Source code for the CommandTag handler class

```
package book.reflection;

import java.lang.reflect.InvocationTargetException;
import java.lang.reflect.Method;

import book.util.LocalStrings;
import book.util.ExTagSupport;

import javax.servlet.jsp.PageContext;
import javax.servlet.jsp.JspException;
import javax.servlet.jsp.JspTagException;

public class CommandTag
  extends ExTagSupport {

  static final Class []emptyParamsType = new Class[0];
  static final Object []emptyParamsValue = new Object[0];

  static LocalStrings ls =
    LocalStrings.getLocalStrings(CommandTag.class);
```

```
    protected Object obj = null;
    protected String objName = null;
    protected String cmd = null;

    public void setObject(Object o)
    {
      this.obj = o;
    }

    public void setName(String name)
    {
      this.objName = name;
    }

    public void setCommand(String cmd)
    {
      this.cmd = cmd;
    }

    public int doStartTag()
          throws JspException
    {
      obj = getPointed();
      fireCommand();
      return SKIP_BODY;
    }

    protected Object getPointed()
          throws JspException
    {
      return (null == obj ?
          pageContext.findAttribute(objName) :
          obj);
    }

    protected void fireCommand()
          throws JspException
    {
      try {
        Method m = obj.getClass().getMethod(cmd, emptyParamsType);    ❶
        m.invoke(obj, emptyParamsValue);    ❷
      } catch(InvocationTargetException ite) {
        //Throw a JspTagException
      } catch(IllegalAccessException iae) {
        //Throw a JspTagException
      } catch(NoSuchMethodException nme) {
        //Throw a JspTagException
      }
    }

    protected void clearProperties()
    {
      obj     = null;
      objName = null;
```

```
        cmd    = null;
        super.clearProperties();
    }
}
```
■

❶ **Locates the command method to be invoked.**

❷ **Invokes the command method with an empty argument list.**

Generalizing the problem here yielded an extremely useful tag, one we can utilize in many other cases. For example, the following JSP fragment can send an email using our new command tag:

```
<jsp:useBean id="mailer" scope="page" class="SendMail">
  <jsp:setProperty name="mailer" property="to" value="john@doe.com" />
  <jsp:setProperty name="mailer" property="subject" value="your email subject"
  />
  <jsp:setProperty name="mailer" property="body" value="your email body" />
</jsp:useBean>
<jspx:cmd command="execute" name="mailer"/>
```

Sometimes, simple tags are only an indication of a more generalized problem waiting to be solved. Don't be shy about the generalized problem. Solving it will benefit you.

15.4.3 *Integration and the surrounding environment*

Integration has been a key theme throughout this book. We have seen numerous examples:

- We started with the application context parameters used by our tags (and this way, those tags were integrated into the web application).
- We continued with the usage of the J2EE environment (the tags were integrated into J2EE).
- We ended with opening the libraries to objects set by the application's servlets (the tags were tightly tied into the servlet's implementation).

We see two advantages for integration:

1 Ease of use: It is much easier to configure tags if they are integrated into your application's configuration infrastructure.

2 Usefulness: The ability to set objects from the application to the tags, and vice-versa, increases the code's usefulness.

It is true that integrating your tags with the application requires coding that may not be obvious. Why, you may wonder, do you need to place the database URL inside the application deployment descriptor when you can hard-code it in the JSP? Because the results help create a flexible and easy-to-use application. Switching from one database to another, for example, will require a change to a single place.

15.4.4 *Tags and general purpose libraries*

Although the tag libraries developed throughout this book are general purpose, not all tag libraries must be so. By general purpose, we mean that the libraries are not part of a bigger program, but may stand alone as a set of components usable in any application.

Some tag libraries have meaning only within the context of a greater whole. Say you are developing an online catalogue product, and you want to open it up for JSP. One way to do so is to make the catalogue accessible through JavaBeans. This is an acceptable option, but, as you might guess, we have a better idea: access the catalogue through JSP tags. That way, you can take advantage of all the custom tag advantages described in this book.

The tags developed in this book can contribute to almost any web application because they perform common activities that virtually all web applications require. A tag library that serves as a gateway to a specific catalogue contributes only to applications that use the catalogue. This means fewer applications.

To summarize, adding a tag interface to some proprietary product will improve its usability and provide added value not possible before custom tags. Even an application server vendor should consider adding tags to its server distribution to facilitate the creation of online server status reports.

15.5 *Additional points to remember*

This section lists bits of information, not easily categorized, that we feel are important enough to review.

15.5.1 *The tag life cycle*

When the JSP runtime creates a tag, you cannot assume anything about its life cycle other than what is specified by the tag API. More specifically, you cannot pass the tag instance and store it anywhere once `doEndTag()` or `release()` are called. It is easy to forget that tags can be recycled. Recently, the Duke Pet Store from Sun was known to use tags after `doEndTag()` and `release()` were called, which made the applications behave strangely, at best, for application server vendors that reused the tags.

The exact error that existed in Duke Pet Store can be explained using the following code fragment:

```
<sometag>
  <someothertag id="a">
  <someothertag id="b">
</sometag>
```

As you can see in this code fragment, we have the tag named `sometag` enclosing two tags of type `someothertag`. In this instance, the JSP environment can employ reuse techniques and use the tag instance created for `someothertag-a`, also in `someothertag-b`. The bug in Duke Pet Store was that the implementation of `someothertag-a` and `someothertag-b` added a reference to itself into `sometag`. This reference broke down when the JSP environment recycled `someothertag-a` and reused it to execute `someothertag-b`.

Lesson learned. Remember the tag life cycle and follow it without regard to the portion of the life cycle that the JSP environment implements. Do not pass around a reference to the tag. Instead, use objects created in the tag just as we did in our database library.

15.5.2 *The case for scriptlets*

Sometimes you do not have to get into the overhead of developing tags. If the action performed by the scriptlet is short, does not repeat itself, and is not significant to you, then there's not much need to wrap the action with a tag.

Note, however, that if the action repeats itself (even if slightly differently) in several places, it should be wrapped (or a generalization of it) in a tag, even if the action is small in size (say, `<%= request.getAttribute("somename") %>`).

15.5.3 *Freeing allocated resources*

The tags developed through this book use an automatic resource deallocation technique. All that is needed is to implement (`clearServiceState()` and `clearProperties()` and your state is clean.

In reality, many tags are developed without paying attention to resource deallocation. Why? That's a good question. Usually, the tags were not designed from the ground up with resource management in mind but evolved into tags that allocated a good deal of resources.

When developing your tags, keep in mind that you will have to clean up both your tag's state and property values. Make sure that you are doing so. Failing to clear your properties will yield bugs, and failing to free resources will bring the web application down, due to resource leaking.

15.5.4 *Caching expensive results*

Cache results of intermediate computations. An example of caching results is available in our `BeanUtil` class. `BeanUtil` introspects the classes of our beans and looks for specific `Method` objects, which can take a lot of time. To improve performance, we keep the results of our intermediate computations (`Method` objects) in a hashtable, thus providing a considerable performance boost.

15.5.5 *Supporting JSP1.1 and JSP1.2*

JSP1.2 has been released in the form of a proposed final draft. It took more than a year from the time of the JSP1.1 public draft until the majority of the application servers and servlet containers implemented it in a supported release version. This means that you will have to deal with a mixture of two JSP versions for a long time to come.

Luckily, the difference between your JSP1.1 and JSP1.2 tags should not be that big. As we've shown throughout the book, you'll find it easy to support the modified tag life cycle in your tag's base class. A problem arises only when you want to use the new `IterationTag` to implement efficient, copy-free iteration (as explained in chapter 10). This feature is supported solely by JSP1.2, thus any tag that relies on the `IterationTag` limits you to using JSP1.2-only containers.

Our recommendation is to implement both versions of the iteration related tag, one based on `BodyTag`, and the other based on `IterationTag`. This way your library can work in both JSP versions (and, using the iteration framework presented in chapter 10, you can easily implement the two tag versions).

15.6 *Summary*

Tags carry the promise of improved productivity for the nonprogrammer, simpler code maintenance, and improved reusability. This is why you should consider using them in the first place. Do your best to achieve all of the above with your tags (otherwise, you'll miss out on some benefits).

Remember, ease of use is one of your main goals. Make your tags as uncomplicated as possible (if a tag is getting too involved, break it into two cooperating tags), document their usage and provide, as many usage samples as possible. Always keep in mind that the user of the tags may not be a programmer; so, do not assume too many programming skills.

You will want to make your tags as reusable as possible. For example, an iteration tag that knows how to iterate over arrays, containers, enumerations, and the like is going to be much more useful than several different iteration tags (one for array, another for some container type, and so on).

The reusability and ease of use offered by tags may cause small performance degradation. Nonetheless, performance is not a silver bullet. As important as it is, performance is just one more factor that affects the cost of deploying a software-based solution. If achieving good performance renders your tags too complex (or interferes with reusability), make a clear decision regarding which factor is going to cost more—performance or lack of usability.

Tags should not attempt to overachieve. A tag implementing a single, declarative action and accompanied by a `TagExtraInfo` to validate its attribute input will be easiest to use. Tags also should not format their output. Putting markup and other formation decisions inside the tag locks them outside of the page designer's reach, and locks your tags to the specific markup—not really something you want to have happen.

Try not implement low-level, programming languagelike functionality using tags (unless absolutely necessary). Creating such tags is a colossal effort and is always going to fall short of a task (and require programming know-how or a steep learning curve). If you require a programming language for your JSP files, use scriptlets.

Finally, many ways exist to improve your library; some more useful ones are the integration options with the JSP environment, the generalization of the tags contained in the library, and the ability to extend the library to support new requirements. You do not have to apply all these tools, yet each will greatly improve the usefulness of your library.

Having said all this, remember that a tag library does not have to be a general-purpose library that can be used as a stand-alone product. A tag library can be part of a greater product and used only to expose its capabilities in an easy and pervasive manner and, so, provide added value to the product.

What is XML?

A

Extensible Markup Language (XML) is a metalanguage used to describe documents containing structured data. Because this generic definition can seem confusing, let's define our terms. A metalanguage is a higher-level language that describes lower-level languages. As we'll soon see, XML defines a basic syntax to use in creating your own language for sharing data in documents. We often think of a document as a file containing information. In XML, a document is not geared typically toward presentation (as is an HTML document). On the contrary, an XML document is used for data description, namely, holding structured data. This concept of structured data is something that can be best explained through an example. Imagine that you want to create a text file to save information about a new computer you're buying. You may decide to keep the information in an unorganized paragraph in which you list all the features the computer will have. This paragraph is an example of unstructured data. Another option for describing your new computer might be to create a table and place the features and specifications logically into columns within the table. Now, the data is structured. XML provides a way to define markup languages that describe such structured data.

How do XML and its structured data apply to JSP custom tags? The TLDs that we developed, as well as the web application deployment descriptor, are XML documents. In fact, any J2EE deployment descriptors are also XML documents, as are the configuration files for many popular application servers. Because XML is so widely used in the arena of custom tags, understanding XML can help you avoid simple problems.

Let us then begin with our XML tutorial.

A.1 *XML vs HTML*

XML is a markup language like HTML, meaning that you use tags to annotate your data. The main differences between HTML and XML are:

- In HTML, both the syntax and semantics of the document are defined by the HTML specification. You can use HTML alone to create a visible interface to the user. XML, on the other hand, only allows you to define document syntax.

- In HTML, documents are not well-formed (i.e., they don't adhere to strict rules). Not all tags are closed with a matching tag, and occasionally users may omit matching closing tags without creating a problem for most web browsers. XML documents, on the other hand, are well-formed, easing parsing and extending the content and syntax of the documents.

A.2 *XML syntax*

Let's look at a sample XML document to get a feel for the syntax:

```
<?xml version="1.0"?>    ❶

<!-- define a batch command with two parameters and a single
     processing point -->    ❷
<batchoperation>         ❸
<parameter>
    <type>integer</type>
    <value>1</value>
    <name>copies</name>
</parameter>

<parameter>
    <type>string</type>
    <value>print</value>
    <name>command</name>
</parameter>

<process priority="high"/>    ❹

</batchoperation>
```

The sample XML document contains the following document parts:

❶ **Declaring tht this is an XML file** In the first line, a processing instruction `<?xml ver-sion="1.0"?>` identifies the document as an XML document. The general structure of an XML processing instruction (PI) is `<?pi-name pi-value?>`. The XML parser should treat PIs as information passed from the XML author to the parser. In processing the `<?xml version="1.0?">` tag, for example, the PI informs the parser of the XML version. In the absence of this PI, the parser would have to guess the version.

❷ **An XML comment** A developer can place comments inside the XML document. XML comments have a prefix of `<--` and a suffix of `-->`. Everything in between (other than `-->` or `--`) is considered part of the comment.

❸ **A tag with a body** Several XML elements (tags) form the majority of the markup in the file. Most elements define something about their content. For example, the data enclosed within a `<parameter>` element represents a parameter. Some elements have content (such as the `<parameter>` tag). Each element with content has a start-tag *as well as* an end-tag. Empty elements (e.g., the `<process/>` tag) have only a start-tag, which must be terminated with a trailing "`/>`" sign as in the example. These two conditions on elements' markup are a crucial part of the "well formed-ness" associated with XML.

❹ **A bodyless tag** Each XML start-tag can have a list of attributes. Each attribute in that list is a name value pair that looks like `name="value"`.

Because our sample XML fragment is well-formed, any standard XML parser can parse it without a problem, even if we did not provide syntax information. This ease of parsing is possible because our document obeys strict rules regarding its formation, and the parser relies on this adherence.

A.2.1 *DTDs*

Occasionally, you may wish to have the XML parser validate your file based on a syntax definition supplied by you. To accomplish that, those syntax definitions must be specified in a file called a document type declaration (DTD). Keep in mind that a program may output or input XML without using a DTD. However, for situations in which your program needs to validate the incoming XML to ensure its adherence to a particular format, you need a DTD. A DTD tells the XML parser which syntax rules to use while parsing an XML document. For example, a DTD can describe the tag names for entities; the attributes that can be associated with each tag; the tags that can have content (and what type of content); and so forth. Following this, either embed the DTD directly in the document or–and this is more common–store the DTD in another location and point to it by providing the parser with a reference to the type declaration. Since the XML descriptors in use within J2EE simply reference the DTD as defined by the J2EE committees, we will only discuss referencing a DTD from the document.

Referencing a DTD

You can refer the XML parser to an external DTD by using the `<!DOCTYPE>` directive as we do in the following XML fragment:

```
<?xml version="1.0"?>
<!DOCTYPE taglib
    PUBLIC "-//Sun Microsystems, Inc.//DTD JSP Tag Library 1.1//EN"
    "http://java.sun.com/j2ee/dtds/web-jsptaglibrary_1_1.dtd">
```

The general structure of a `<!DOCTYPE>` directive is rather complex . A version that you will see frequently in J2EE descriptors is `<!DOCTYPE Name ExternalID>`, wherein the `Name` represents the DTD (`taglib` in the example) and the `ExternalID` references a DTD located outside the document (often on another server). In the sample `<!DOCTYPE>` declaration above, the `ExternalID` has two parts:

1 `PUBLIC "-//Sun Microsystems,Inc.//DTD JSP Tag Library 1.1//EN"` identified the document type as a public document with a public identifier. The parser can look for a DTD based on only the public identifier. In our case, the parser will look for a type declaration, or DTD, for `"-//Sun Microsystems, Inc.//DTD JSP Tag Library 1.1//EN"`.

2 `"http://java.sun.com/j2ee/dtds/web-jsptaglibrary_1_1.dtd"` operates as a system identifier. The system identifier identifies a URI that points

to the location from which you can take the type definition (in our case the URI points to a location in Sun's website).

The `<!DOCTYPE>` directive must be the first thing the parser sees in the document (or just after the initial `<?xml?>` PI) so that the parser is able to read it before processing, and thus validating, the XML file.

Using a DTD

Now that we know how to refer the parser to a DTD, let's get back to our batch processing XML sample and add a DTD reference to it. We will not define a DTD (that is a bit out of the scope of this tutorial). Instead, we will simply add a fictional DTD reference to the batch processing example as in the next XML fragment:

```
<?xml version="1.0"?>
<!DOCTYPE bogus
    PUBLIC "-//Bogus batch processing//EN"
    "http://bogus.acme.com/bogus_batch.dtd">

<!-- define a batch command with two parameters and a single
     processing point -->
<batchoperation>
<parameter>
    <type>integer</type>
    <value>1</value>
    <name>copies</name>
</parameter>

<parameter>
    <type>string</type>
    <value>print</value>
    <name>command</name>
</parameter>

<process priority="high"/>

</batchoperation>
```

Here we have added a DTD reference (boldface) to a bogus DTD that uses a public identifier. With this DTD reference in place, an XML parser will now go beyond reading and parsing the document; the parser will fetch the DTD from bogus.acme.com, and use it to validate the XML document.

A.3   XML pitfalls

Most developers found out about XML after previous experiences with markup languages such as HTML and SGML. Yet, when we try to apply our previous markup experience to XML, we find ourselves making errors. Why? Simply because of the different (and stronger) syntax associated with XML.

Unlike HTML, case *does* matter in XML. For example, `<SOMETAG>`, `<sometag>`, and `<SOMETAg>` are three different markups in XML! When you add something to a TLD file or a web application deployment descriptor, you will want to watch your caps-lock key. The same rule applies, of course, to attribute names.

Another problem occurs with nonempty entities and their start- and end-tags. In XML, you must mark an element's content with a start- and end-tag. No other option exists. So, in XML, the following fragment

```
<parameter>
    <type>string
    <value>print
    <name>command
</parameter>
```

is not valid. And the fragment

```
<parameter>
    <type/>string
    <value/>print
    <name/>command
</parameter>
```

has a completely different meaning from this fragment:

```
<parameter>
    <type>string</type>
    <value>print</value>
    <name>command</name>
</parameter>
```

Another common error is typos in empty elements. A trailing "`/>`" should terminate an empty element. However, a background in HTML (wherein `<br>` does not create a problem), coupled with an approaching deadline, can make us forget the necessity for precision in XML. Typos are, of course, errors and, unfortunately, not always easy to locate.

A.4   Why XML?

Now that we've explored basic XML, we need to consider why and for what, in particular, we might want to use XML. XML typically is used to share data in heterogeneous environments, from one system type to another.

To illustrate this point, let's imagine a fictional company, BuyAWreck.com, which offers information about used cars for sale on its website. It wouldn't make sense for BuyAWreck's internal systems, such as payroll, email, sales, and so forth, to use XML to share data since the company has total control over what systems (hardware and software) are being used. Software packages, such as Lotus Notes, are designed to share information and data between multiple clients and servers with common databases, and communication protocols and file formats. Changing this data sharing so that it's accomplished via XML would hardly be beneficial, because XML parsing and transmission inflicts an unnecessary performance penalty. This performance hit isn't worth absorbing when your software client and server are both under your control and can be configured to share data in the manner intended by the software vendor. Car dealerships, however, which supply BuyAWreck with information about vehicles, are outside the company's control. For them, it makes sense to define an XML language, using a DTD, that all the dealerships must speak if they wish to provide data to BuyAWreck. With this approach, Bob's Junk Heap can create a compliant XML file from its Paradox database, while Old Joe's Lemons can properly format its Oracle data, and Tim's Jalopies can write the file by hand (if so desired). When any of these XML files arrives at BuyAWreck, it is validated against the pre-defined DTD and easily imported, despite the fact that each file came from a different source.

Data sharing such as this is the most tangible benefit of XML. This same logic applies to why J2EE-compliant servers use XML, since each vendor may build their application server in a slightly different way. By adhering to a DTD for TLDs, deployment descriptors, and the like, one file can work in any vendor's application server environment.

A.5   Summary

Despite the hype and relative mystique surrounding it, XML is, in reality, no mystery. It is basically a set of constructs that can be used to describe your own data language. Already, thousands of DTDs are available for sharing XML data in every industry imaginable—from medical to entertainment. By remembering that XML is not HTML (especially when it comes to syntactic rules), you should be able to wriggle out of any XML-related errors with no real difficulty.

A.6   Additional reading

XML is documented in many books as well as different locations throughout the web. However, if you are an XML rookie, your first step would be the great tutorial written by Norman Walsh. This tutorial is available at http://www.xml.com/pub/98/10/guide1.html. When you have finished with the tutorial, you may want to refer to the resources section at http://www.xml.com/pub/resourceguide/

index.html. Also, *XSLT Quickly* by Robert DuCharme (Manning Publications, 2001) provides an excellent guide for exploring Extensible Stylesheet Language Transformation (XSLT), a language that allows the conversion of XML documents into other XML documents, into HTML documents, or nearly any other type of document you wish.

The Tag Library Descriptor

B

597

TLD is an XML file that provides tag library-based information to the JSP parser and various JSP editing tools. In general, the TLD is an XML file whose elements provide two types of information:

- Basic information listing the version of the library and the JSP version on which the library depends.
- A list of tags included in the library, as well as a list of implementing classes, names, attributes, and so on.

The TLD needs to comply with basic XML guidelines (as seen in appendix A), yet also needs to comply with a specific syntax defined for type library descriptor elements.

This appendix will present the elements used within the TLD, their syntax, their semantics, and so forth. We will also offer a few examples of TLDs.

B.1   TLD elements

Let's look first at the elements in a TLD, starting with the topmost (`taglib`).

B.1.1   The taglib element

The root element of the TLD is the `taglib` element. Its purpose is only to sign the tag library description portion and to enclose all the other TLD elements. Within the `taglib` element, you can find a set of subelements, as presented in table B.1.

Table B.1   The top TLD elements and their meanings

Element	Description	Mandatory
tlibversion	Specifies the version of the tag library. Development tools can read this value and present it to the developer.	Yes
jspversion	Specifies the JSP version that this tag library needs to work. If not specified, the default value is 1.1.	No
shortname	Provides a sample short name (prefixes the tags in the JSP) that the developer can use.	Yes
uri	Specifies a public URI that uniquely identifies this version of the tag library. It is recommended that the URI be a URL to a public location where people can find this TLD.	No
info	Descriptive information about the tag library.	No
tag	Each tag library can contain one or more tags, and for each you should have a TLD `tag` element. This element encloses a definition of some tag.	Yes

The order of appearance of the `taglib` elements in the TLD matches the order of appearance in table B.1 (i.e., the element `tlibversion` will precede the element `info`, which precedes the `tag` elements). As noted in table B.1, the `info` and `jsp-version` elements are optional, although we always recommend providing information on your library through the `info` tag.

Some elements in table B.1 have an obvious use. It is clear why we need elements of type `tag` and `info`, but why do we need the other elements? Why, for instance, do we need an element such as `shortname`? A human reader of a TLD should be able to come up with a reasonable `shortname` for the tags. Elements such as `shortname`, `uri`, `tlibversion`, and the like are geared toward development and component management tools. A component repository will find the `uri` element extremely helpful—it provides an obvious repository key for the library—and an authoring tool can use `shortname` to automatically generate `<%@ taglib %>` directives and let its user utilize the tags in the library.

The TLD is more general than what many of us (tag developers) tend to think is necessary. It holds many elements that we may never need, but those elements will be used by other pieces in the development puzzle when the tags are finished.

B.1.2 *The tag element*

Now that we have seen all the top tags in the TLD, we may delve into the most important element (for us), the `tag` element. The `tag` element is used to describe a specific tag in the tag library. It has to provide information on issues such as the classes implementing the tag, the tag's attributes, and the tag's body behavior. The elements used within the `tag` element are presented in table B.2.

Table B.2 The elements used to define a tag's element and meaning

Element	Description	Mandatory
name	Specifies the tag name. Together with the tag's prefix, it will form the tag name within the JSP file.	Yes
tagclass	Specifies the class implementing the tag's handler. This is the class that the JSP runtime will instantiate to execute the tag.	Yes
teiclass	Specifies the class implementing the tag's TagExtraInfo object. This is the class that the JSP runtime will instantiate to validate the tag's usage while transforming the page.	No

Table B.2   **The elements used to define a tag's element and meaning (continued)**

Element	Description	Mandatory
bodycontent	Specifies how the tag uses its body. The JSP environment will use this value to understand how the tag wants the runtime to handle its body. The values that a bodycontent can have are: empty (denotes that the tag should have an empty body), JSP (denotes that the body includes JSP content), and tagdependent (denotes that the body includes content the tag should interpret). If the bodycontent element is not available, the default value should be JSP.	No
info	Descriptive information about the tag.	No
attribute	Each custom tag can have several attributes that the JSP developer can use to set parameters into the tag. Each attribute is described by a TLD attribute element (that encloses more elements that provide attribute information).	No

The elements presented in table B.2 are comprehensible once you know something about tag development. Most of the tag information is used by the JSP runtime to properly work with a tag. For example, the runtime will need the tagclass element in order to instantiate the tag handler. Likewise, the teiclass element is used (optimally) to instantiate the TagExtraInfo implementation class.

The attribute element

One element in table B.2 that differs from the others is attribute. The attribute element describes, as you might guess, a tag attribute acceptable by the tag handler. All the information about a particular tag attribute is made available to the JSP runtime right from this attribute element. This information includes the attribute's name, whether or not that name is mandatory, and whether or not it can accept values taken from runtime expressions.

To represent all this information, the attribute element encloses the elements described in table B.3.

Table B.3 The elements used to define an attribute and its meaning

Element	Description	Mandatory
name	Specifies the attribute's name. The user will use this name to specify values to this attribute. The JSP runtime will use this name to introspect the tag handler and to locate the setter method for this attribute.	Yes
required	Specifies whether the attribute is mandatory. The user must assign values to mandatory attributes when he uses the tag. Can accept the values true, false, yes, and no. If not available, the default is false.	No
rtexprvalue	Specifies whether the attribute can accept values extracted from a runtime expression as specified in the JSP file. Can accept the values true, false, yes, and no. If not available, the default is false.	No

Each attribute information piece is delivered in a different element wherein some of the elements actually provide a boolean value of true/false.

B.1.3 *Element Recap*

Let's summarize this section by reviewing the elements that can be found in a TLD:

- The root taglib element encloses all the tag library information.
- Within the root taglib element we can find tag library-related information described by elements presented in table B.1. These elements provide general tag library-related information as well as a list of tags as implemented in this library.
- Each library tag is defined using the elements presented in table B.2. These elements provide tag-related information such as the tag's name and implementing classes, as well as a list of attributes.
- Each specific tag's attributes are defined using the elements presented in table B.3. These elements provide attribute related information, such as the attribute's name.

Now that we have presented the TLD elements, let's sharpen our knowledge with a sample.

B.2 A sample TLD

Before you construct a TLD, the first thing to remember is that a TLD is also an XML file. As an XML file the TLD requires XML information, such as a DTD reference to be specified, before we define any of our tags. Any JSP-compliant TLD that you create should start with the following XML fragment:

```
<?xml version="1.0"?>
<!DOCTYPE taglib
    PUBLIC "-//Sun Microsystems, Inc.//DTD JSP Tag Library 1.1//EN"
    "http://java.sun.com/j2ee/dtds/web-jsptaglibrary_1_1.dtd">
```

After putting this DTD reference into the new TLD file, you can start writing your library description:

Here is a sample library description file :

```
<?xml version="1.0" encoding="ISO-8859-1" ?>
<!DOCTYPE taglib
    PUBLIC "-//Sun Microsystems, Inc.//DTD JSP Tag Library 1.1//EN"
    "http://java.sun.com/j2ee/dtds/web-jsptaglibrary_1_1.dtd">

<!-- An XML comment in the tag library descriptor.
     Since the TLD is an XML file we can freely use XML comments
  -->

<taglib>
    <tlibversion>1.0</tlibversion>
    <jspversion>1.1</jspversion>
    <shortname>assert</shortname>
    <uri> http://www.maning.com/jsptagsbook/assert-taglib</uri>
    <info>
        This library contains tags to assert on various conditions.
    </info>

    <!-- This library has only a single tag in it -->
    <tag>
        <name>assert</name>
        <tagclass>book.assert.AssertTag</tagclass>
        <teiclass>book.assert.AssertExtraInfo</teiclass>
        <bodycontent>empty</bodycontent>
        <info>
            Asserts based on a configured condition
        </info>

        <!-- And the tag's attributes. -->
        <attribute>
            <name>parameter</name>
            <required>true</required>
            <rtexprvalue>false</rtexprvalue>
        </attribute>
        <attribute>
            <name>handler</name>
```

```
                <required>true</required>
                <rtexprvalue>false</rtexprvalue>
            </attribute>
            <attribute>
                <name>type</name>
                <required>false</required>
                <rtexprvalue>false</rtexprvalue>
            </attribute>
            <attribute>
                <name>exists</name>
                <required>false</required>
                <rtexprvalue>false</rtexprvalue>
            </attribute>
            <attribute>
                <name>oneof</name>
                <required>false</required>
                <rtexprvalue>false</rtexprvalue>
            </attribute>
        </tag>
</taglib>
```

The sample shows the TLD developed for the assert tag library from chapter 7. The first part of the tag library descriptor is the XML header, which includes the `<?xml?>` processing instruction and a public reference to the `taglib` DTD. After this header comes the main event, which is the definition of the library. A `<taglib>` set of tags encloses the definition of the library. (The `taglib`, remember, is the root element of the tag library description.) Within the `taglib` element for this TLD, we can find

- A `tlibversion` element that informs the version of the library (1.0)
- A `jspversion` element telling us that this library requires JSP1.1
- A `shortname` element that recommends the name assert as the library's prefix
- A `uri` element providing a unique URI to serve as a key to the library
- An info section that provides general information on the library
- A single tag description section describing the assert tag, the only tag in this library.

Constructing the TLD above (or virtually any other TLD) is not difficult. All you need to do is to follow the instructions in the previous section and fill in the values that match your library needs.

NOTE   Throughout the TLD you can use an XML comment (i.e., `<!--this is a comment-->`) to explain your steps. The XML parser employed by the JSP runtime (as well as most editing tools) will ignore the values of these elements, so you can also comment out unwanted portions of the TLD.

B.3   JSP1.2 and the new TLD entries

One of the additions to JSP1.2 is an extended TLD structure that includes the JSP1.1 elements and adds new elements to serve three goals:

- improved support for development and management tools
- support for new features in the servlet API2.3
- support for the extended verification phase added to JSP1.2.

Let's look now at additions to the TLD structure, starting again with the root `taglib` element and ending with the `attribute` element.

B.3.1   New taglib elements

The elements added beneath the `taglib` element are presented in table B.4.

Table B.4   New elements used beneath the `taglib` element.

Element	Description	Mandatory
display-name	Short descriptive name to be used by tools to represent the library.	No
small-icon	Icon to be used by tools to represent the library.	No
large-icon	Icon to be used by tools to represent the library.	No
validatorclass	Tag library validator class that may walk over and check the XML representation of the JSP file.	No
listener	Event listener that can listen to events associated with the application or the users sessions.	No. A tag library can have zero or more event listeners associated with the application events.

As you can see in table B.4, three main additions to the global tags enclosed by the `taglib` element exist:

1   The `display-name`, `small-icon`, and `large-icon` elements provide a better way to present the library in development and documentation tools

(think of `display-name`, `small-icon`, and `large-icon` as what you will probably see in a toolbar representing the library).

2 The `validatorclass` lets you specify a JSP file validator able to work on an XML representation of the JSP file and check whether the usage of the tags contained by the library is correct.

3 The `listener` element allows you to specify listeners for events that happen within the application, and therefore provide improved application integration.

B.3.2 New tag elements

The next modification to the TLD is in the content of the `tag` element. The added elements are presented in table B.5:

Table B.5 New elements used beneath the tag element.

Element	Description	Mandatory
display-name	Short descriptive name used by tools to represent the tag.	No
small-icon	Icon used by tools to represent the tag.	No
large-icon	Icon used by tools to represent the tag.	No
variable	Provides static scripting variable information.	No. A tag can have one or more.

Most of the new elements added to the `tag` element are for aesthetics, like the `display-name`, the `small-icon`, and the `large-icon` elements. Again, these elements will typically serve development tools and the like. However, the `tag` element has a new arrival—`variable`—whose job is radically new. It defines exported variables. In JSP1.1, the only way to define variables was through the `TagExtraInfo` class, allowing for a flexible and dynamic variable definition that was relatively difficult to use because of the need to code the class.

The variable element

The `variable` elements describe exported variables, using the elements presented in table B.6.

Table B.6 Elements used in the new variable element.

Element	Description	Mandatory
`name-given`	Assigns a name to the variable.	No[a]
`name-from-attribute`	Assigns a name to the variable, based on the translation time value of the named attribute.	No[a]
`class`	Provides the name of the class for the exported scripting variable. The default class value is `String`.	No
`declare`	Informs the JSP runtime whether or not to declare the exported variable. The default is `true`.	No
`scope`	Defines the scope of the scripting variable (`NESTED` by default).	No

[a] One of the `name-given` and `name-from-attribute` elements must be provided in order to name the variable.

The variable we can define offers a great deal of flexibility. In many tags developed for this book, we could use this variable definition and not develop a `TagExtraInfo`. For example, our database connection tag could use a variable definition as we do in the following fragment:

```
<variable>
    <name-from-attribute>
        id
    </name-from-attribute>
    <class>
        book.database.DbConnectionWrapper
    <class>
    <scope>
        AT_BEGIN
    </scope>
</variable>
```

In JSP1.2 we need to declare a variable through a `TagExtraInfo` when we need to perform proprietary logic to decide

- The number of exported variables
- The type of the variable (e.g., the `ExportTagExtraInfo` class developed in chapter 8)
- The name of the variable (especially when a tag exports more than a single variable)
- The scope of the variable.

Most of the cases described above are rare. In the majority of instances, using the variable tag will suffice.

B.3.3 *New attribute elements*

The last addition to the TLD is in the `attribute` element. In attributes that take the value of a runtime expression, you can now specify a type for the value of the runtime expression.

Table B.7   New element used beneath the attribute element.

Element	Description	Mandatory
type	Specifies the type of a runtime expression attribute.	No

Note that, for attributes that do not take their value out of a runtime expression, the new `type` element does not change anything (since their type must be a Java string).

B.4   *Summary*

The TLD is nothing more than an XML file with a specific DTD defined in the JSP specification. When creating a TLD, think of the values that identify your library and the tags that construct it, then use TLD elements to write them down in the TLD file. If you think that you should document what you are doing in the TLD, use an XML comment.

Using the code examples

Each chapter in this book contains several example tags, and two case studies were developed in chapters 13 and 14. In this appendix we explain how to use these examples or compile them when necessary.

C.1   *Using the example tags*

As you will see, using example tags is relatively easy. Compiling the tags, however, will require effort on your part.

C.1.1   *Obtaining example tags*

To obtain the example tags, you need only access the book's website located at http://www.manning.com/shachor and download the example's .zip file. This file contains the following directories:

Table C.1   Structure of the source distribution archive

Directory	Description
src	Contains full listing of all the example tags
WEB-INF/classes	Contains the compiled samples
WEB-INF	Contains the tag library descriptors for the tag libraries developed in the book as well as the application deployment descriptors used
build	Contains build scripts
jsp	Contains the JSP files used through the chapters. Most files are in the form listingXXX.jsp where XXX corresponds to the actual listing in the book (e.g., listing10.1.jsp corresponds to listing 10.1).

When you have finished downloading, unzip the file into some directory (say, jsp_tags). You can now start using the samples.

C.1.2   *Using the example tags*

The downloaded .zip file contains the compiled tags in the WEB-INF/classes directory. To use them, complete the following steps:

1   Add the contents of the WEB-INF/classes directory to the web application where you want to use the tags. For Tomcat and Orion, copy the contents of the classes directory into the classes directory of your web application.

2   Put the tag library descriptors (.tld files) under the WEB-INF directory of your web application. For example, copy the tld files from the WEB-INF

directory in the downloadable .zip file to the WEB-INF directory of your web application.

3 Add a reference to the tag library descriptor from within the application's deployment descriptor. You can use the sample web application deployment descriptors available in the .zip file as a starting point.

Now, just reference the tag libraries from the JSP files and use the tags.

C.1.3 *Compiling the example tags*

Building the examples is a complex operation and is usually not recommended (since you already have a compiled version of the tags). Nevertheless, you may want to compile the tags with minor additions of your own (e.g., additional tracing logs to assist you in tracing the execution of the tag).

NOTE An obvious prerequisite for the compilation process is that you must have installed a JDK (at least 1.2.2) in your environment, added the Java executable into the path, and defined the environment variable JAVA_HOME to point to the JDK's root directory.

The samples' .zip file contains a directory named build wherein you will find the following files:

Table C.2   Required files for tag compilation

File Name	Description
build.bat	A script file that can be used to build the samples under the Windows operating systems
build.sh	A script file that can be used to build the samples under the UNIX operating systems
build.xml	An XML file that instructs our build program (ant) how to build the samples

You will also need to download the packages in table C.3:

Table C.3   Required packages for tag compilation

Package Name	Description
Ant	This is a freely available Java-based build tool. You can download it from http://jakarta.apache.org. After downloading ant's binary version, unpack it into a directory, and declare an environment variable named ANT_HOME to point to ant's root directory.
Orion	The build process requires many jar files that are part of J2EE. The easiest way to get them all is to download and install a J2EE server. Since we already use Orion as our case studies server, we also use it to build the samples (and then you can compile the samples and use them in the same server with no need for double downloads). Just download the latest stable version of Orion from http://www.orionserver.com, unpack it, and declare an environment variable named ORION_HOME to point to Orion's root directory.
Xerces	Ant requires an XML parser, so download xerces (at least version 1.2) from http://xml.apache.org , unpack it, and copy the file xerces.jar (located in the lib directory) into our build directory.

When you finish downloading all packages:

1 Open a command shell

2 Change your location to the build directory

3 Make sure that all the needed environment variables are defined (JAVA_HOME, ORION_HOME, ANT_HOME)

4 Execute the build script

When the build process is completed, you will see the file jsp_tags.jar in the build directory. This contains the compiled tag libraries.

C.2   *Using the case studies*

Let's look at how we can obtain, configure, and deploy the case studies presented in this book.

C.2.1   *The WebStore application*

Here you will find instructions for obtaining, configuring, and deploying the case study presented in chapter 13.

Obtaining the WebStore application

Getting the application is easy, all you need to do is to access the book's web site located at http://www.manning.com/shachor/ and download the cosmetics .zip file. This file contains the following directories:

1 `cosmetics-web` contains the web application.
2 `database` contains the hSQL database files.

Setting up the application

Copy the directory `cosmetics-web` into your applications directory. For the Orion application server, use the `/orion/applications/` directory. For the Tomcat web container, your applications directory will be the `/TOMCAT_HOME/webapps/` directory.

Edit the file `cosmetics-web/WEB-INF/web.xml` and change the mail settings to reflect your environment regarding the SMTP host and the sender email address. Look for the lines displayed below:

```
<context-param>
    <param-name>from_sender</param-name>
    <param-value>your.email@address.se</param-value>
</context-param>
<context-param>
    <param-name>smtp_server_host</param-name>
    <param-value>your.smtp.server</param-value>
</context-param>
```

Change the value of `from_sender` and `smtp_server_host` to reflect your environment.

Copy the files `store.properties` and `store.script` to the root directory of your application server. If using Orion, the files should be copied to the `/orion/` directory.

Deploying the application

Ways to deploy a web-application vary between different vendors. Tomcat auto-deploys any web applications found in the `TOMCAT_HOME/webapps/` directory. For the Orion, you would:

1 Edit the file `/orion/config/application.xml` and add the line given below:

```
<web-module id="cosmetics-web" path="../applications/cosmetics-web" />
```

2 Edit the file `/orion/config/default-web-site.xml` and add the line given below:

```
<web-app application="default" name="cosmetics-web" root="/cosmetics" />
```

If it's running, the application server should now deploy the web application.

Testing the application

In a web browser, enter the URL http://localhost/cosmetics/. You should now receive the Welcome page of the Cosmetics application. A default user has been set up with the username "abc" and the password "123". You can use these if you don't feel like registering your own username. Remember to update the default user's email address to your own in order to be able to receive receipts on any orders.

C.2.2 The WAPStore application

Below you will find instructions for obtaining, configuring, and deploying the case study presented in chapter 14. The application is written for Orion and might need some customization before it can be used in another application server, as some features used are based on the public draft of the EJB 2.0 specification. The application is set up to work on a default installation of the Orion application server. If you have customized your Orion setup, you might have to reconfigure the application to make it deploy and behave correctly.

Obtaining the WAPStore application

Getting the application is easy. Access the book's website at http://www.manning.com/shachor and download the cosmetix .zip file. This file contains a directory named `cosmetix` that holds the entire application.

Setting up the application

1. Copy the `cosmetix` directory into your `/orion/applications/`directory.

2. Set up a mail session in the file `/orion/config/server.xml` so that it looks like:

```
<mail-session location="mail/mailSession" smtp-host="your.smtp.host">
    <property name="mail.transport.protocol" value="smtp" />
    <property name="mail.smtp.from" value="your.email@address.se" />
    <property name="mail.from" value="your.name" />
</mail-session>
```

   Replace the values of `smtp-host`, `mail.smtp.from`, and `mail.from` to reflect your environment.

3. To receive receipts on your orders, edit the file `/cosmetix/cosmetix-ejb/META-INF/ejb-jar.xml`. Look for the part listed below:

```
<env-entry>
    <description>The email address for the default user</description>
    <env-entry-name>default_user_email</env-entry-name>
    <env-entry-type>java.lang.String</env-entry-type>
    <env-entry-value>your.email@address.se</env-entry-value>
</env-entry>
```

Replace the value of the `default_user_email` entry with your own email address.

Deploying the application

In order to deploy the application on Orion:

1   Edit the file `/orion/config/server.xml` and add the following line:

```
<application name="cosmetix" path="../applications/cosmetix" />
```

2   Edit the file `/orion/config/default-web-site.xml` and add the following line:

```
<web-app application="cosmetix" name="cosmetix-web" root="/cosmetix" />
```

If the application server is running, it should now deploy the application.

Populating the application

Using a web browser, enter the URL http://localhost/cosmetix/admin/. You should receive an HTML page with a button labeled "Populate." Click it and the application will be populated.

Testing the application

Using a WAP browser, enter the URL http://localhost/cosmetix/. You should receive the login card of the Cosmetix application. A default user has been set up with the username "abc" and the password "123", enabling you to gain access to the application.

references

Allaire Corporation. Quick Reference to CFML.
http://www.allaire.com.

DuCharme, Bob. *XSLT Quickly*. Greenwich, CT: Manning Publications, 2001.

Fields, Duane K., Mark A. Kolb. *Web Development with JavaServer Pages*. Greenwich, CT: Manning Publications, 2000.

Enterprise Java Beans specification.
http://www.javasoft.com/products/ejb/index.html.

Enterprise Java Beans tutorial.
http://www.javasoft.com/products/ejb/.

eXtensible Markup Language (XML) 1.0 2nd Ed.
http://www.w3.org/TR/2000/REC-xml-20001006.

eXtensible StyleSheet Language Transformations (XSLT) 1.0.
http://www.w3.org/TR/xslt.html.

Gamma, Erich, Richard Helm, Ralph Johnson, John Vlissides. *Design Patterns: Elements of Reusable Object-Oriented Software*. Reading, MA: Addison-Wesley, 1995.

HTTP (RFC2616). http://www.w3.org/Protocols/rfc2616/rfc2616.html.

Internet Mail Message Format (RFC822).
http://www.cis.ohio-state.edu/htbin/rfc/rfc822.html.

Internic. RFC 831 (the SMTP Standard). ftp://ds.internic.net/rfc/rfc822.txt

JavaBeans Activation Framework Specification.
java.sun.com/products/javabeans/glasgow/jaf.html.

JavaBeans Specification. http://www.javasoft.com/products/javabeans/.

Java Database Connectivity Specification.
http://www.javasoft.com/products/jdbc/index.html.

JavaMail API Specification.
http://www.javasoft.com/products/javamail/index.html.

Java Naming and Directory Interface API Specification.
www.javasoft.com/products/jndi/index.html.

JavaServer Pages Specification. http://java.sun.com/products/jsp/.

Java Servlet API. http://www.javasoft.com.

JGuru. JavaMail FAQ.
http://www.jguru.com/jguru/faq/faqpage.jsp?name=JavaMail.

Orion application server. http://www.orionserver.com.

Reflection (tutorial).
http://java.sun.com/docs/books/tutorial/reflect/index.html.

Reflection overview.
http://java.sun.com/j2se/1.3/docs/guide/reflection/index.html.

SMTP (RFC821). http://www.cis.ohio-state.edu/htbin/rfc/rfc821.html.

Tomcat. http://jakarta.apache.org.

WAP Forum. Technical Specifications. http://www.wapforum.org.

WAP Forum. WAP-190, Wireless Application Environment Specification.
http://www.wapforum.org/what/technical.htm.

WAP Forum. WAP-191, Wireless Markup Language Specification.
http://www.wapforum.org/what/technical.htm.

XML from the inside out. http://www.xml.com.

index

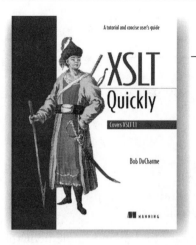

XSLT Quickly

Bob DuCharme
Softbound, 325 pages, $29.95
ISBN: 1-93011-11-1

Ebook edition
PDF files, $13.50
Available from publisher's site:
www.manning.com/ducharme

As XML continues to win converts, demand for XSLT con-tinues to grow. This W3C standard and the range of free software springing up around it make it possible to convert an XML document into other XML documents or even to non-XML formats such as HTML, RTF, and flat text.

XSLT Quickly has two parts: Part 1 is a tutorial that gets the reader up to speed in XSLT. It is short, deliberate, and covers all the basic concepts you need for the most common XSLT tasks. Part 2 is a task-oriented user's guide to more advanced techniques for XML document manipulation. It is not organized by keywords and XSLT syntax, but by the XSLT tasks themselves—for example, converting elements to attributes or reading in multiple documents at once. This makes it easy to find the help you need quickly. The book also includes a glossary, a quick reference to XSLT syntax, and a thorough index to help you find the information you need as easily as possible.

XSLT Quickly is designed for people who want to hit the ground running with XSLT development: web designers, Java developers, and anyone interested in the latest XML technology.

3D User Iterfaces with Java 3D

Jon Barrilleaux
Softbound, 528 pages, $49.95, August 2000
ISBN 1-884777-90-2

Ebook Edition
PDF files 14 MB, $13.50
Ebook edition only available from publisher's site:
www.manning.com/barrilleaux

A practical guide on how to design and implement the next generation of sophisticated 3D user interfaces on present-day PCs without exotic devices like head-mounted displays and data gloves.

Written for user-interface designers and programmers, the book systematically discusses the problems and techniques of letting users view and manipulate rich, multidimensional information. It teaches how to tackle the design challenges of 3D user interfaces which support such tasks as e-commerce, product configuration, system monitoring, and data visualization.

"Jon Barrilleaux should be given a standing ovation for producing such an excellent piece of work for a topic (Java 3D) that desperately needs more documentation."

—j3d.org

Web Development with JavaServer Pages

Duane K. Fields and Mark A. Kolb
Softbound, 584 pages, $44.95, April, 2000
ISBN 1-884777-99-6

Ebook edition
PDF files, 14 MB, $13.50
Ebook edition only available from publisher's site:
www.manning.com/fields

This best-selling book will teach you how to create dynamic content—personalized, customized, and up-to-the minute—a key ingredient of site development on the World Wide Web today. It covers all aspects of JSP development, as well as comparisons to similar dynamic content systems such as CGI, Active Server Pages, Cold Fusion, and PHP. It clearly demonstrates the advantages offered by JSP as a full-featured, cross-platform, vendor-neutral technology for dynamic content generation.

Full coverage of JSP 1.1 syntax teaches beginners the basics. More advanced readers can jump straight into techniques for mixing databases and web pages, how to make an elegant and scalable architecture, and even subtleties such as how JSP helps to better divide the labor between page designer and programmer. Detailed code and good design techniques are included, as well as complete reference materials on JSP tags and the JSP API.

"...the best offering, head and shoulders above the rest for both the Web designer and the Java developer interested in picking up JSP skills. None of the other JSP books offer the same depth of coverage on the different JSP topics."

—JavaWorld